The First Writing

Over 5,000 years ago the first writing began to appear in Egypt and Mesopotamia. Later still, ancient scripts flourished in China and Mesoamerica, with secondary developments in places such as Scandinavia. Drawing on top scholars, *The First Writing* offers the most up-to-date information on these systems of recording language and meaning. Unlike other treatments, this volume focuses on the origins of writing less as a mechanistic process than as a set of communicative practices rooted in history, culture, and semiotic logic. An important conclusion is that episodes of script development are more complex than previously thought, with some changes taking place over generations, and others, such as the creation of syllabaries and alphabets, occurring with great speed. Linguists will find much of interest in matters of phonic and semiotic representation; archaeologists and art historians will discover a rich source on administration, display, and social evolution within early political systems.

STEPHEN HOUSTON is Professor of Anthropology, Brown University. He has written extensively on anthropological topics and was co-editor of *Royal Courts of the Ancient Maya*, Volumes I and II (Westview Press, 2001). He is a recipient of fellowships from, among others, the School of American Research and the John Simon Guggenheim Memorial Foundation.

The First Writing

Script Invention as History and Process

STEPHEN D. HOUSTON
Brown University

CAMBRIDGE UNIVERSITY PRESS
Cambridge, New York, Melbourne, Madrid, Cape Town,
Singapore, São Paulo, Delhi, Tokyo, Mexico City

Cambridge University Press
32 Avenue of the Americas, New York, NY 10013-2473, USA

www.cambridge.org
Information on this title: www.cambridge.org/9780521728263

© Cambridge University Press 2004

This publication is in copyright. Subject to statutory exception
and to the provisions of relevant collective licensing agreements,
no reproduction of any part may take place without the written
permission of Cambridge University Press.

First published 2008
Reprinted 2005
First paperback edition 2008
Reprinted 2010 (twice), 2011

A catalog record for this publication is available from the British Library.

ISBN 978-0-521-83861-0 Hardback
ISBN 978-0-521-72862-3 Paperback

Cambridge University Press has no responsibility for the persistence or accuracy of URLs for external or third-party Internet Web sites referred to in this publication and does not guarantee that any content on such Web sites is, or will remain, accurate or appropriate.

To Anders Bliss Houston and Hannah McCrea Houston
First in all things, and in my heart

Contents

List of figures and tables   [page ix]
List of contributors   [xviii]

PART I ORIENTATION AND THEORY

1 Overture to *The First Writing*   *Stephen D. Houston*   [3]

2 The possibility and actuality of writing   *John S. Robertson*   [16]

3 Writing systems: a case study in cultural evolution   *Bruce G. Trigger*   [39]

PART II CASE STUDIES OF PRIMARY AND SECONDARY SCRIPT FORMATION

4 Babylonian beginnings: the origin of the cuneiform writing system in comparative perspective   *Jerrold S. Cooper*   [71]

5 The state of decipherment of proto-Elamite   *Robert K. Englund*   [100]

6 The earliest Egyptian writing: development, context, purpose   *John Baines*   [150]

7 Anyang writing and the origin of the Chinese writing system   *Robert W. Bagley*   [190]

8 Writing on shell and bone in Shang China   *Françoise Bottéro*   [250]

9 Reasons for runes   *Henrik Williams*   [262]

10 Writing in early Mesoamerica   *Stephen D. Houston*   [274]

PART III EPILOGUE

11 Beyond writing *Elizabeth Hill Boone* [313]

12 Final thoughts on first writing *Stephen D. Houston* [349]

References [354]
Index [395]

Figures and tables

Fig. 2.1 Holistic, immediate perception. [*page* 17]
Fig. 2.2 Mediated, temporal perception. [18]
Fig. 2.3 Intersection between visual and auditory perception. [19]
Fig. 2.4 Direct and indirect access to the spoken sign. [21]
Fig. 2.5 Visual connection to the auditory object. [22]
Fig. 2.6 Indirect reference to homonymous forms. [22]
Fig. 2.7 Potential ambiguity in strictly visual reference to the spoken sign. [23]
Fig. 2.8 Deixis of orientation (Gardiner 1957:25). [26]
Fig. 2.9 The relationships between the object of the spoken sign and its spoken and written counterparts. [27]
Fig. 2.10 The relationships between (a) the spoken sign and the object of the spoken sign; (b) the written sign and the object of the spoken sign; and (c) the written sign and the spoken sign. [29]
Fig. 2.11 Acrophonic derivations of certain members of the Classic Mayan syllabary [30]
Fig. 2.12 The iconic nature of certain acrophonically derived members of the Classic Mayan syllabary [31]
Fig. 3.1 Some historical relations among script types [62]
Fig. 4.1 The Near East in the Uruk period. Important Uruk Expansion sites include Abu Salabikh (1), Ur (27), Susa (25), Godin (6), Nineveh (19), Jebel Aruda (2), and Habuba Kabira (9) (Stein 1999:95, fig. 6.4). [73]
Fig. 4.2 A cylinder seal and a modern impression of it (courtesy Musée du Louvre). [74]
Fig. 4.3 Sealed hollow clay bulla from Susa. Inside it were four spherical clay tokens and one cylindrical token, corresponding to the impressions on its surface (Le Brun and Vallat 1978:45, fig. 3:3). [75]
Fig. 4.4 Numerical tablets from Jebel Aruda in Syria (left) and Uruk (Englund 1998:51f., figs. 13 and 15). [75]

x List of figures and tables

Fig. 4.5 "Numerico-ideographic" tablets from Uruk (left), Susa, and Godin (Englund 1998:54, fig. 16). [76]
Fig. 4.6 Uruk IV cattle receipts (Englund 1998:154 and 156, figs. 52 and 53). [77]
Fig. 4.7 Archaic list of offices and professions (Englund 1998:104, fig. 32). Each entry is preceded by the numeral 1, signifying "item." [79]
Fig. 4.8 Uruk III tablets with complex column formats. Top: account of male and female workers from Uruk (Englund 1998:177, fig. 65). Bottom: grain account over eight-year period from Uqair (Englund 1996:no. 1). [81]
Fig. 4.9 Archaic Ur (c. 2800 BC) land account with uniform column format (Burrows 1935:no. 87). [82]
Fig. 4.10 The construction and evolution of cuneiform signs. [85]
Fig. 4.11 Proto-cuneiform pictographs based on vessels and animal heads, and the sign AK (from Englund 1998:fig. 22; Green and Nissen 1987:no. 2). [86]
Fig. 4.12 From the Stela of the Vultures, Eanatum of Lagash (25th-century BC). The inscription runs along the top above the soldiers' heads, along the band dividing the upper from the lower register, and in the space beneath Eanatum's spear on the lower right (courtesy Musée du Louvre). [87]
Fig. 4.13 Ashurnasirpal II of Assyria (9th-century BC), flanked by attendants, on wall of palace at Nimrud (ancient Kalkhu). The lengthy cuneiform inscription forms an indistinct band beginning below the attendants' waists and below the king's knee (courtesy British Museum). [88]
Fig. 5.1 Map of western Asia. [102]
Fig. 5.2 Major sites of Late Uruk and proto-Elamite inscriptions in Persia. [103]
Fig. 5.3a Semantic structure of the proto-Elamite accounts. [105]
Fig. 5.3b Correspondence of proto-Elamite and proto-cuneiform accounts. [106]
Fig. 5.4 Numerical systems attested in proto-Elamite accounts. [107]
Fig. 5.5 Attestations of the sexagesimal system. [109]
Fig. 5.6a Attestations of the decimal system. [111]
Fig. 5.6b Attestations of the decimal system. [112]
Fig. 5.7 Attestations of the bisexagesimal system. [114]
Fig. 5.8a Attestations of the grain capacity system. [115]

Fig. 5.8b   PLOW = $2N_{39b}$, YOKE = $2\frac{1}{2}N_{39b}$ ($\frac{1}{2}N_1$). [116]
Fig. 5.9   Attestations of the area system. [118]
Fig. 5.10   Examples of simple (left) and complex (right) "tokens" from Uruk (digital images courtesy of CDLI [Cuneiform Digital Library Initiative]). [119]
Fig. 5.11   Examples of sealed (top), sealed and impressed (middle) bullae, and a "numerical" tablet (all from Susa – top: Sb 1932; middle: Sb 1940; bottom: Sb 2313; digital images courtesy of CDLI). [120]
Fig. 5.12   Development of cuneiform, after Schmandt-Besserat (1992). [121]
Fig. 5.13   Complex tablet rotation among proto-Elamite tablets (Scheil 1905:no. 4997). [123]
Fig. 5.14   Semantic and graphic correspondences between proto-cuneiform and proto-Elamite ideograms. [125]
Fig. 5.15   Scheil (1923:no.45), an account of 7 labor gangs, totaling 591 workmen. [126]
Fig. 5.16   Stylus shank case dividers on a numerical tablet from Uruk (digital image of original courtesy of CDLI). [127]
Fig. 5.17   Uruk "numero-ideographic" texts. [128]
Fig. 5.18   Persian "numero-ideographic" texts. [129]
Fig. 5.19   A comparison of "numero-ideograms" in Mesopotamia and Persia. [130]
Fig. 6.1   Selection of bone tags from tomb U-j at Abydos. Naqada IIIa period. Average height c. 1.5 cm (courtesy Deutsches Archäologisches Institut). [155]
Fig. 6.2   Samples of four tag designs from tomb U-j at Abydos. After Dreyer et al. (1998b:nos. 67–69, 103–105, 134–135, 142–143). Nos. 67–69 and 103–105 are, respectively, examples of the same design. The back of no. 69 shows a scoring line that derives from the production process (see text). Dreyer proposes that the design of nos. 134–135 signifies "east" and that of nos. 142–143 "west" (see text, courtesy Deutsches Archäologisches Institut). [156]
Fig. 6.3   Two sample wavy-handled pots with inscriptions from tomb U-j at Abydos. The sign on the left pot (height of vessel 25.7 cm) represents a scorpion and that on the right pot (height of vessel 33.5 cm) a bucranium on a pole with a palm frond or similar ornament; for drawings of the signs, see Fig. 6.4 (courtesy Deutsches Archäologisches Institut). [159]

Fig. 6.4 Three inscription types from pottery in tomb U-j; all fragmentary and completed from parallel examples in the tomb: (a) scorpion and tree (?); (b) seashell and vertical stroke; and (c) bucranium in two variants, with and without added frond (?; see Fig. 6.3). Drawings after Dreyer *et al.* (1998b:figs. 33a, 40, 45, courtesy Deutsches Archäologisches Institut). [160]

Fig. 6.5 (a) The Hunters' Palette, probably from Abydos (either temple or necropolis). Naqada IIIa period (?). Height *c.* 64 cm. Siltstone. British Museum EA 20790, 20792, Louvre E 11254. Drawing after W. Smith (1949:111, fig. 25). (b) Detail of the design of building and double bull at the top of the Hunters' Palette. Drawing by Christine Barratt; after Baines (1995:112 and 151, fig. 5). [168]

Fig. 6.6 The Scorpion Macehead, main decorated area, from Hierakonpolis Main Deposit. The only writing preserved is the pair of signs in front of the central figure of the king, but no more than a third of the decorated area is preserved. Dynasty 0. Height *c.* 30 cm. Limestone (Oxford, Ashmolean Museum E 3632; drawing by Marion Cox, courtesy Ashmolean Museum). [169]

Fig. 6.7 Tag of Narmer from Umm el-Qaʻab Cemetery at Abydos (uncontexted find). Mixed writing and emblematic representation. The upper register shows a catfish, which writes the Nar- ($nʻr$-) element in the king's name, smiting a northern foe, while the full form of the name is written on the extreme right. The lower register probably specifies a quantity of oil. Late dynasty 0. Height 3.65 cm, width 4 cm. Material not stated, probably bone. Drawing after Dreyer *et al.* (1998a:139, fig. 29, with photograph pl. 5c). [173]

Fig. 6.8 Wooden tag of Aha from Cemetery B at Abydos, tomb complex of Aha. Mixed writing and pictorial representation. The lowest register specifies oil and probably other products. The principal events of the top register seem to be the manufacture of a cult image together with a visit to the temple of Neith at Sais in the Nile Delta. 1st dynasty. Height not given. Present location not known. After Petrie (1901:pl. X:2). [174]

Fig. 6.9 Sample cylinder seals of the 1st–2nd dynasties with unintelligible pseudo-writing. All but one are organized partly as scenes, with a seated figure at the right, and thus are semi-pictorial. British Museum EA 65853, 66812, 65872 (all black steatite, height 1.9, 1.6, 1.5 cm, respectively), 36462 (wood, height 2.8 cm). All unprovenanced. Drawings by Richard Parkinson, copyright British Museum. Publication with different drawings: Spencer (1980:nos. 423, 446, 432, 414).   [183]

Table 6.1 Chronological table: Predynastic and Early Dynastic Egypt, periods and rough dates.   [153]

Fig. 7.1 Rubbing of a turtle plastron. Reign of Wu Ding, *c.* 1200 BC. After Zhang (1962:no. 247).   [192]

Fig. 7.2 Turtle plastron (*Yibian* 3380) with brush-written inscription. Reign of Wu Ding, *c.* 1200 BC. (Photograph courtesy of Institute of History and Philology, Academia Sinica.) On brush-written oracle inscriptions, see *Kaogu* (1991[6]:546–554, 572).   [193]

Fig. 7.3 Rubbing of a turtle plastron. Reign of Wu Ding, *c.* 1200 BC. After Zhang (1962:no. 207).   [194]

Fig. 7.4 Huayuanzhuang Dongdi H3, a pit containing divination shells and bones excavated at Anyang in 1991 (shown crated for removal in a mass). The deposit dates from Wu Ding's reign and includes both royal and non-royal divinations. It also mixes inscribed and uninscribed pieces: of 755 complete turtle shells, fewer than 300 are inscribed. (The total count of 1,558 shells and shell fragments includes 574 with writing. Of 25 pieces of bone, 5 have writing.) See preliminary excavation report (*Kaogu* 1993[6]:488–499). Illustration after *Yinxu* (2001:pl. 24).   [195]

Fig. 7.5 Inscriptions of bronze vessels from the tomb of Lady Hao, Anyang, *c.* 1200 BC. After *Yinxu Fu Hao Mu* (1980:figs. 29.2, 27.8, 35.3, 35.8).   [201]

Fig. 7.6 Inscriptions of bronze vessels from Xiaotun M18, a tomb near Lady Hao's, Anyang, *c.* 1200 BC. After *Kaogu xuebao* (1981[4]:496).   [203]

Fig. 7.7 Oracle-bone characters, after Shima (1971): (a) *bu* ("divination"); (b, c) *yu* (proper name; "to fish"); (d) *zheng* (proper name; "to attack, subdue"); (e) *wei* (proper name; "to guard"?); (f) *yu* ("writing brush"); (g) *ce* ("document"); (h) *dian* ("document, record"); (i) *xiang* (name of a ritual feast); (j) *Fu Ding* ("Father Ding"); (k, l) *mu* ("dusk"); (m) *quan* ("dog"); and (n) *ya* (a rank).   [204]

Fig. 7.8 Bronze axe. Probably thirteenth or twelfth century BC. Height 32.7 cm. (Courtesy of the Freer Gallery of Art, Smithsonian Institution, Washington, DC; accession no. F1946.5.)   [205]

Fig. 7.9	Inscription of a bronze vessel, twelfth century BC, in the Musée Cernuschi, Paris. After Luo (1937:12.57.1). [206]
Fig. 7.10	Inscription of a bronze vessel from the tomb of Lady Hao, Anyang, *c.* 1200 BC. After *Yinxu Fu Hao Mu* (1980:fig. 25.2). [207]
Fig. 7.11	Inscription of a bronze vessel, eleventh-century BC. Avery Brundage Collection, Asian Art Museum of San Francisco (accession no. B60B1046). (Courtesy Asian Art Museum.) [208]
Fig. 7.12	Inscription of a bronze vessel, eleventh-century BC. Gugong Bowuyuan, Beijing. After Yu (1957:no. 274). [209]
Fig. 7.13	Inscription of a bronze vessel, twelfth- or eleventh-century BC. After *Shanghai Bowuguan Cang Qingtongqi* (1964:no. 13). [210]
Fig. 7.14	Inscription of the *Zuoce Zhizi you*. Eleventh-century BC. Gugong Bowuyuan, Beijing. After Yu (1957:no. 273). [212]
Fig. 7.15	Jade *ge* blade with brush-written inscription from Xiaotun M18, a tomb near Lady Hao's, Anyang, *c.* 1200 BC. Length 20.5 cm. After *Kaogu xuebao* (1981[4]:504). [215]
Fig. 7.16	Potsherd from Anyang with inscription brush-written in ink. After Li Ji (1956:pl. 22). [217]
Fig. 7.17	Potsherd from Anyang with inscription brush-written in vermilion. Length of top edge about 15 cm. After *Kaogu* (1989[10]:900). [218]
Fig. 7.18	Bamboo *ce* from Mawangdui tomb no. 1, Changsha, Hunan province, *c.* 168 BC. The document is an inventory of the contents of the tomb in which it was found. After *Changsha Mawangdui Yihao Han Mu* (1973, II:pl. 270). [219]
Fig. 7.19	Emblems from Dawenkou pottery (top) and Liangzhu jades (bottom). Neolithic, third millennium BC. After *Wenwu* (1987[12]:75); Li Xueqin (1985:157). [229]
Fig. 9.1	Bone comb from Vimose, Denmark. The inscription reads **harja**, a personal name. (Picture: Nationalmuseet, Copenhagen.) [264]
Fig. 9.2	Woman's fibula (brooch) from Himlingøje, Denmark. The inscription reads **hariso**, a personal name. (Picture: Nationalmuseet, Copenhagen.) [269]
Table 9.1	The oldest runic letters (*c.* AD 150–800). Number, shape, order, and the division into three groups are evidenced by

	fifth-century inscriptions of the rune-row (the futhark). The names (designations), their meaning, and the sound value of the individual runes are derived from ninth-century and later manuscripts. The derivations from Roman letters (third column) are found in H. Williams (1996). [263]
Fig. 10.1	Early linear texts: (a) Monte Albán Danzante, MA-D-55 (Urcid Serrano 2001:fig. 4.47); (b) La Venta Monument 13 (Coe 1968:148, drawing by Miguel Covarrubias). [277]
Fig. 10.2	Linear Teotihuacan script (Taube 2000b:20, 34–35, fig. 27). [278]
Fig. 10.3	Kaminaljuyu "Stela" 10 texts (after rubbing supplied by Albert Davletshin). [281]
Fig. 10.4	Olmec icons: (a) toponym (Tate and Reilly 1995:pl. 127); (b) another toponym (Tate and Reilly 1995:pl. 131); (c) cloud icon, Chalcatzingo Monument 31 (Taube 1995:fig. 24c); and (d) emergence cleft (Taube 2000a:fig. 2f). [285]
Fig. 10.5	Nominal elements in headdress, San Lorenzo Monument 2 (Coe and Diehl 1980:fig. 425). [289]
Fig. 10.6	Danzante from Monte Albán (J. F. Scott 1978:D-59). [295]
Fig. 10.7	Tuxtla Statuette (Winfield Capitaine 1988:23, corrected against original by Houston). [297]
Fig. 10.8	Dismembered captive, possibly from Tikal, on unprovenanced altar, Petén, Guatemala (after photograph by Houston). [302]
Fig. 10.9	Peabody Museum statuette (Coe 1973:pl. 1). [307]
Fig. 11.1	The Codex Féjerváry-Mayer, a religious and divinatory codex from Aztec Mexico. [316]
Fig. 11.2	Algebraic notation for "the momentum (or energy) imparted by the gravitational field to the matter per unit," from Albert Einstein's general theory of relativity (Einstein 1996:163). [319]
Fig. 11.3	The opening of stanza 2 of the Dumbarton Oaks Concerto by Igor Stravinski, 1938 (photograph courtesy of Dumbarton Oaks). [321]
Fig. 11.4	Dance notation recording profiles of motion for four dancers, reading left to right, accompanied by the score (Tufte 1990:117). [321]
Fig. 11.5	The Feuillet system of dance notation recording the early eighteenth-century dance "The Pastorall." It concentrates on the footwork, knowing the torso and arms will follow conventionally (Guest 1984:fig. 10.1). [322]

Fig. 11.6   Labanotation: notation for five dancers, reading bottom to top. On either side of the central vertical line representing the body's center, the defined areas identify fields of the body (support, leg, torso, arm, head), and geometric forms indicate the actions (Guest 1984:fig. 12.10). [323]

Fig. 11.7   Venn Circles used to express relationships such as "no S is M" (Gardner 1982:40). [324]

Fig. 11.8   Molecular formula for benzene, which is composed of six carbon atoms and six hydrogen atoms. [325]

Fig. 11.9   Structural diagram of benzene molecule (Pauling 1967:117). [325]

Fig. 11.10   Structural diagram of benzene showing the carbon bonds but omitting the hydrogen atoms (Pauling 1967:121). [325]

Fig. 11.11   Ball-and-stick model of collagen, composed of three left-handed single-chain helixes that wrap around each other with a right-handed twist (Dickerson and Geis 1969:42). [326]

Fig. 11.12   Space-filling model of collagen (Schulz and Schirmer 1979:72). [327]

Fig. 11.13   Cord model of hemoglobin concentrates on its quaternary structure and the shapes and intertwining spatial relationships of the four subunits (drawing by Irving Geis [Armstrong 1989:100]). [328]

Fig. 11.14   James Watson and Francis Crick with their three-dimensional stick model of DNA, 1953 (McClelland and Dorn 1999: fig. 15b). [329]

Fig. 11.15   A partial list of deceased veterans named "Smith," from the Directory of Names at the Vietnam Veterans Memorial. Given are the name, rank, service, birthdate, deathdate, home town, and panel and line number locating the name on the memorial (Tufte 1990:43). [330]

Fig. 11.16   Table organizing verbal, mathematical, and graphic language into the steps that lead from basic parts to conceptual exposition (Owen 1986:171, fig. 8.17). [331]

Fig. 11.17   Timeline diagram of New York City's weather in 1980 effectively summarizes 2,220 numbers (Tufte 1983:30). [332]

Fig. 11.18   James Elkins' (1999:80) trilobed model of the graphic catalogue. [335]

Fig. 11.19   Section of the annals history in the Codex Mexicanus (72), which records natural and climactic phenomena for the years

List of figures and tables   xvii

	10 House (left) to 13 Flint (right). An earthquake rocked the land in 10 House, in 11 Rabbit there was a hailstorm so severe that the fish in the lake died, a plague of grasshoppers descended to devour the corn in 12 Reed, and 13 Flint was parched by drought (courtesy of the Bibliothèque Nationale, Paris). [336]
Fig. 11.20	Almanac listing the twenty day signs and their patrons or mantic influences, Codex Borgia 22b–24 (reconfigured from 1993 edition). [338]
Fig. 11.21	Almanac grouping the twenty day signs with six travelers, Codex Borgia 55 (1993 edition). [339]
Fig. 11.22	Diagram of the *in extenso* almanac presenting the 260 days of the cycle in 5 registers that span 8 pages, reading right to left, Codex Borgia 1–8 (1993). [340]
Fig. 11.23	Page 1 of the *in extenso* almanac in Fig. 11.22 (Codex Borgia 1993). [341]
Fig. 11.24	Codex Féjerváry-Mayer 1 (1971 edition). [343]
Fig. 11.25	Diagram of the 260-day almanac on Féjerváry-Mayer 1 (1971). [344]
Fig. 11.26	Byrhtferth's diagram of the Christian world (Kauffmann 1975:pl. 21). [345]

Contributors

ROBERT W. BAGLEY is Professor of Art and Archaeology at the Department of Art and Archaeology, Princeton University.

JOHN BAINES is Professor of Egyptology at the Oriental Insitute, Oxford University.

ELIZABETH HILL BOONE holds the Martha and Donald Robertson Chair in Latin American Art at Newcomb Art Department, Tulane University, New Orleans.

FRANÇOISE BOTTÉRO is Chargée de Recherches, Centre de Recherches Linguistiques sur l'Asie Orientale, L'Ecole des Hautes Etudes en Sciences Sociales, Paris.

JERROLD S. COOPER is Professor of Assyriology at the Department of Near Eastern Studies, The Johns Hopkins University.

ROBERT K. ENGLUND is Professor of Assyriology and Sumerology at the Department of Near Eastern Languages and Cultures, University of California.

STEPHEN D. HOUSTON is Professor of Anthropology, Brown University.

JOHN S. ROBERTSON is Professor of Linguistics at Brigham Young University.

BRUCE G. TRIGGER is James McGill Professor at the Department of Anthropology, McGill University, Montreal.

HENRIK WILLIAMS is Professor i Nordiska Språk, Institutionen för Nordiska Språk, Uppsala Universitet.

PART I

Orientation and Theory

1 | Overture to *The First Writing*

STEPHEN D. HOUSTON

The theme of this book is the first writing systems – early cuneiform, proto-Elamite, Egyptian (all prior to 3000 BC, by some centuries), Chinese (prior to 1000 BC), and Maya and its Mesoamerican precursors (beginning ca. 500 BC). These are the scripts that first represented units of sound and meaning in systematic fashion, if in contexts that often elude full study because of deficient evidence and opaque coatings from antiquity. The first writing is involved with so many different processes – administrative development, sacred display, the establishment of consultable precedent, statements of being, even the hermeneutic probing and decipherment of such writing systems – that it deserves repeated attention, more than once in any one generation of scholars. The present book also looks more briefly at what might be called "secondary inventions," including late ones like Scandinavian runic. Such systems allow us to understand how the processes of primary and secondary creation differ fundamentally or conform to similar patterns.

This book came into existence for several reasons. The earliest writing records voices of antiquity with an immediacy to the past that lies beyond potsherds and lithics. Those voices come to us through momentous steps in representation that implicate, in structured fashion, sound, meaning, and sight. Many specialists have noted patterns of convergence and divergence around the world, with the understanding that universals, if present or detectable, involve similar conditions and strategies rather than pat laws of script invention and use. The moments of decisive, singular change (the "history" in the title) and general trends ("process") require judicious acts of weighing and evaluation. The good news is that the topic of the first writing remains a productive mine of insight. There is still much to do.

Earlier works managed to plumb the subject in part yet not always in ways that are fully satisfactory. An otherwise excellent work edited by Wayne Senner (1989) came from a lecture series that arose, it seems, from little to no communication between the authors. By scanning the book, a reader benefits from comparisons that, because of the volume's manner of preparation, would have escaped its many contributors. By the same token – I use the term advisedly, with an apology to cuneiformists – general works on writing systems enrich our debates (Coulmas 1989, 1996; Roy Harris 1986; Sampson 1985), but several of them place too much emphasis on narrow issues, such as rectifying in acerbic fashion what are felt to be misconceptions about Chinese (DeFrancis 1984:133–220, 1989:89–121).

More recently, Peter Daniels and William Bright (1996) have produced a massive, edited review of the world's writing systems, including handy introductions to the study of writing systems, origins, and decipherment. The parallel format throughout the volume promotes a high degree of comparability and facilitates the detection of specific parallels, very much on display in Bruce Trigger's contribution to the present volume; John Robertson, too, benefitted from this magisterial source. The Daniels and Bright volume highlights the need to focus on the behavior of units in script, such as syllables and morphophonemic particles. As such, it fuels a comparative approach to the study of writing systems, although there remains a strong measure of disagreement about the nature of such comparisons. Are they best left vague and general, with a sensitivity to historical and cultural setting, or should they commit to something along the lines of Joseph Greenberg's enthusiasm for linguistic universals, with which such studies potentially have much in common (e.g., Justeson and Stephens 1994)? More than likely, both approaches need attention. At its least effective, depending on the chapter, the Daniels and Bright volume reduces writing systems to skeletal checklists of attributes and sample texts. As in all such books, the chapters on Mesoamerican systems are, to a specialist's eye, out-of-date because of the rapid pace of work in that region. One wonders if similar problems impair other chapters.

The need for conversation

In my view, a strong edited volume should be neither a set of chapters fashioned at different times and places nor a vision imposed by any single editor, whatever his or her sagacity or level of energy. There must be a conversation between different kinds of experts, possibly conducted via email or other media of communication but done best of all in a seminar format, in the heat and negotiation of direct conversation. This is what took place at Sundance, Utah, over a three-day period in the Spring of 2000. The editor assembled a group of scholars to present papers before an audience of, at most, other contributors and selected scholars invited from Brigham Young University and a few other universities. The emphasis was less on polished presentation than discussion. Houston sent briefing papers to each participant, including sets of questions worth posing and, perhaps, answering. After the seminar, Houston distributed a set of summary perspectives and specific guidance for each chapter. This book results from that interaction, some comments from anonymous reviewers, and further thinking on the part of the editor and his gracious, ever-patient authors.

It is important to frame the mentality that created the seminar, the needs and expectations that urged it into existence. In the first place, it was clear to me that most scholars of early scripts are fascinated by writing in general. The series on writing produced by the British Museum has only enhanced that interest by presenting specialist knowledge in brief, readable treatments (e.g. Moore 2000). With that interest, however, has come a growing understanding that comparison is best done, not by a single person, often misconstruing data and debates in areas far from their speciality, but within an interactive setting that convenes authorities from diverse fields. From this will emerge, it is hoped, a shared vocabulary and a sharpened sense of problems and prospects relating to each system. Dialogue cannot exist unless scholars tune to the same wavelength.

At times it seemed probable during our gathering that more meetings would be needed before such a wavelength could be found and clear signals discerned. Disciplinary boundaries and preoccupations die hard, and anthropological regard for cross-cultural comparison can seem, to some, over-generalizing and distorting. As an editor, I struggled with a desire to get others to frame questions as I do. Eventually I understood that this might not be a good thing: other voices and approaches need to be heard. By scholarly predisposition, anthropologists tend also to be suspicious of "presentism," the idea that past mentalities are easily accessed by acts of empathy or that present-day terms and categories correspond to those in the past. For example, several participants felt that "utilitarian" was a non-problematic concept, while others considered "magic" or apotropaic functions to be as "utilitarian" as any accounting of emmer harvests (cf. Postgate, Wang, and Wilkinson 1995:475). By similar predisposition, humanists and philologists are inclined to question an enterprise that casually poaches evidence from classical disciplines going into their second or third century of existence. Yet, as this book shows, the encounter is worthwhile. The conversation must proceed.

The "ideological model" of writing

There were other potent motivations for this book. As became clear at Sundance, there is increasing discomfort with, and outright rejection of, the gradualistic and unievolutionary models of script development championed by Ignace Gelb and others (1963; see also Damerow 1999b:4–5; Schmandt-Besserat 1992; cf. Michalowski 1993b). Instead, much evidence indicates that script developed step-wise, in rapid bursts – at our scale of analysis, we can see this in terms of a single human lifetime, albeit with subsequent modifications that extend over centuries. Depending on region, some of these developments were independent of other scripts, with each traveling along distinctive trajectories. This process loosely resembles Niles Eldredge and Stephen Jay Gould's model of "punctuated equilibrium," in which rapid speciation interrupts long periods of stasis. Gould himself has developed the notion of "punctuational change" to describe the sudden effects of historically unique moments – *contingency* or, in his words, "wondrous and unrepeatable particulars" – that radically alter the world (Gould 1999:xxii).

As a result of these changes, there is now a deepening influence of what has been called the "ideological model of literacy." It sees writing as both a concrete object and the product of social practices within particular cultural settings and power structures (Street 1993:7). From this vantage-point, writing can be understood principally as a system of communication with subtle, seldom-understood relations to orality, as in the performance or "recitation literacy" attested in Mesoamerica (Houston 1994a:29–31). Naturally, this would also have an impact on the pace of script creation, for the logical reason that systems of communication require rapidly coalescing *systems* of graphs to encode such messages: what good is a lone syllabic sign when many are needed to record a language, or one logograph when the totality of lexemes in ancient languages compels, even in the most limited register, a far broader range of symbols? In no known case does a logograph exist without other, contrastive ones. What comes to the fore in considering the ideological model are indigenous concepts of what writing was and what writing does, who was entitled to read and write (implying gender relations as well as those of social status), and the predicaments of cross-generational transmission. Ensuring that a script endures must involve the strategies of pedagogy and apprenticeship.

The backdrop that this perspective replaces, the "autonomous model of literacy," sees writing as a technology with consequences that erupt independently of social setting (Street 1993:5). Invariable cognitive effects are thought to occur when writing, especially alphabetic writing, appears (e.g. Goody and Watt 1963), a conclusion that has met with massive disapproval from some quarters (cf. Halverson 1992; Houston 1994a) and continued defense from others (Goody 2000:5–9). Elsewhere, David Noble has underscored the deep-seated amour in occidental thinking for the perfectability and uniform results of technology (Noble 1999; see also R. McC. Adams

1996). Writing would not appear to lie outside those notions. A subset of mechanistic views of writing is the theory that the properties of certain languages, especially those emphasizing single-syllable morphemes, lent themselves to script invention (Daniels 1996b:585). William Boltz, a valued participant in our seminar, has extended this theory by suggesting that principally monosyllabic languages, such as Mayan, Chinese, and Sumerian, were more likely to possess homophones and were thus further inclined to explore the graphic possibilities of rebus (Boltz 2000:4, 15). From this process came writing. Daniels' and Boltz's proposition stands in acute contrast to the ideological or cultural model by situating the origins of graphic communication in features of language, leaving to the side other motivations that would seem more applicable. Moreover, Mayanists would find two propositions in Daniels' and Boltz's theory difficult to accept: that Maya writing was the first in its general region (it is not, deferring to Zapotec, later Olmec developments, and, probably, Isthmian); and that Mayan languages are structured like Chinese (they are not, requiring a large number of prefixes and suffixes; see Houston, ch. 10, this volume).

A key suggestion here is that the use of certain metaphors constrains and channels interpretation. If regarded much like McCormick's reaper or Edison's light bulb, writing becomes a transportable technology like any other, a series of mechanical parts detached from their fundamental communicative function. To put this a different way, the medium has come to dominate the message, along with the dialogue that prompted that message. Most volumes on the origins of writing also use the metaphorical conceit of genealogy and descent lines, as though systems of writing consisted of self-contained packages of DNA that bear multiple offspring (e.g. DeFrancis 1989:figs. 10–13). This biological conceit is an unwelcome visitor from linguistics, prompting the reflection: why are there references to "daughter languages" when no historian or anthropologist would allude to "daughter polities?" However, the ideological model is not without flaws. Its emphasis on power relations subordinates cultural values and communicative strategies to blunt mechanisms of inequality. This makes some discussions of writing seem rather like moral parables of cunning that triumphs over virtue (e.g. Larsen 1988:177). It populates the world of early writing with self-conscious actors among elites and slack-jawed dupes among non-elites. Or, in another twist, Marxists of various stripes replace the slack-jawed caricature with another, that of the passive–aggressive peasant in sullen resistance and intermittent rebellion (e.g., J. C. Scott 1976:188–189). These views do have the benefit of recognizing that literacy comprises two processes, writing and reading, and two sets of people, the communicator and the receiver, roughly paralleled by the principal features of the hermeneutic literature on intention and reception (Machor and Goldstein 2000). In addition, writing itself can be seen as a fetishizing and vitalizing act that imparted properties to an inscribed object beyond its physical existence as a textual medium, a subject that has been explored by David Stuart in unpublished work: at stake in particular are the associations between names and personal identities on the one hand and possessions or gifts on the other.

Nonetheless, a heightened accent on cultural setting runs the risk of overlooking transcendent human solutions to common challenges: that is, how are sound and meaning noted graphically, and how do such marks relate to an external world? Hieroglyphic systems preserve those existential links, although it now appears that most primary scripts followed or began in tandem with representational systems that adhered to fairly rigid canonical conventions (see chapter by Robertson). The relation of script to image needs further discussion by scholars working in places where ancient peoples favored hieroglyphs. What, for example, is the connection of emblematic aids and their capacity for showing action to any changes that might be detected in writing? Here, as everywhere, scholars must weigh a search for general patterns against the need to respect the presence of real human diversity.

Writing and the "state"

The First Writing also responds to a long-standing argument about the inception of early scripts. In the New World, Joyce Marcus is the purest advocate of the "statist" or "political" view of writing, which treats script as a correlate of the "competition for prestige and leadership" and, even more controversially, equates complexity of writing with complexity of "state" control, an assertion belied by Mixtec data from Postclassic Mexico (Marcus 1992:435). In Mesoamerica, for example, the probable existence of "recitation literacy," which interweaves reading with acts of verbal performance, complicates the public reach of texts to a great degree, since even a small text could extend to a wide audience by means of recitation. Conversely, some ostentatious texts, as in the Maya area, may well have been covered by now-perished textiles, making their concealment and selective but intentional *failure* to transmit part of the overall message (D. Stuart 1996). Here, writing is firmly distinct from reading, or, as I have stated elsewhere, "textual production" – the painting, incision, and sculpting of written signs – must be separated analytically from responses to them (Houston 1994a:28–29). Some texts may not even have been intended for human or living "readers" but simply to curse or to indicate that certain acts had been performed (Gager 1992; Bodel 2001:19–24). The important point is that writing-in-use and writing-in-context – what might be called the "pragmatics" of writing (Brown and Yule 1983:27, 35) – are complex matters that necessitate a comparable depth of interpretation.

Still, a cybernetic focus on information storage needs to be acknowledged. The density of encoding surely increases with writing as does the importance of writing as a mechanism for the cultural homogenization of elites, who, the more they compete, the more they look the same (Wheatley 1971:377). Norman Yoffee puts this well, suggesting, after James Scott, that complex polities aim, through script and, I would say, iconography, to regularize themselves by ensuring "legibility," the joint understanding, perception, and, ultimately, control of social arrangements (Yoffee 2001:768). To use a variety of metaphors, complexity unravels unless everyone follows the same "play book," the same system of measurement, the same naming patterns, the same legal codes and modes of taxation, and, of course, the same rationalizations of difference and social hierarchy. The shared play book does not complicate life – it simplifies it, leading to a regularity of code that has now, in the twenty-first century, reached its ultimate expression in digital communication. By itemizing the products of human effort, scribes allowed such goods and services to be identified and managed. There is, however, a more subtle point as well: with these systematic expectations and joint views, people transcended purely local knowledge or any direct familiarity with interlocutors. The collective understandings transformed those who were unknown into, at least, those who were understood. In turn, the breach of those expectations – obviously idealized in part – became more evident to the supervisory polity, which could then move to censure and rectify infractions of the play book.

James Scott makes it clear that the penetrative oversight of such polities often fails (1998), and it may be that the controlling traditions of premodern states worked more effectively. These traditions did not, as Yoffee indicates, come from the top or from outside but grew out of preexisting "commonalities" (Yoffee 2001:769). If so, one wonders why the invention of script would dramatically change that which seemed already to exist. How did it shape those commonalities in such a way as to make them more cogent or more penetrative? A perplexing counter-example comes from ancient Mesoamerica. How did the vast constructions of the first millennium BC in the Mirador Basin of Guatemala grow out of societies that were apparently preliterate yet displayed an astonishing homogeneity of material culture (Forsyth 1993)? Arguably, the buildings themselves, as bulky as hills, provided unavoidable daily reminders of social covenants, of how people ought to fit into larger communities, in much the same way that medieval cathedrals embodied community and covenants beyond any one person or any one generation. On present evidence, Maya script developed at about the time the Basin societies began to disintegrate (Houston, ch. 10, this volume). In no way can writing be seen to shape the societies of this area. Rather, strangely enough, its first appearance marks their time of decay. It may not be a coincidence that the development of linear script in Mesoamerica took place at the *end* of the Olmec civilization (Houston, ch. 10, this volume).

Episodes of script development

Archaeologists have long observed that journalists – and those scholars supplying juicy copy – forever stress the earliest and the biggest. These attributes make for clear stories, without any need for tiresome academic hedging and exposition. Two recent stories in a prominent newspaper zero in on earlier dates for supposed Chinese script in central Asia (*c.* 2300 BC), long before its appearance in China itself, and another set of alphabetic texts in Egypt that occur well before their emergence in the Sinai peninsula and the Levant (Wilford 1999, 2001). The underlying point of the reports is that monogeneticism applies in both cases, Egyptian writing engendering the alphabet, an unspecified central Asian script leading to the later florescence of Chinese. Although stated less explicitly in these articles, it appears that some scripts came into existence in places of cultural contact, less as blatant copying than as counter-markings pertaining to opposing ethnic or linguistic groups. Most "biscripts" of pivotal importance to decipherment, including the Rosetta Stone, Diego de Landa's Maya *abecedario*, the Pyrgi tablets, and late Ogam and Latin texts in Wales, come from collisions between, and accommodations among, dominant and subordinate groups. At such membranes of contact the newly devised script often displayed radically different principles of organization from its parent or stimulus, as in the early alphabet, Sequoyah's syllabary, Ogam or Naxi. That is, such scripts differ for reasons other than the low intelligence and phonetic obtuseness of copyists – in this, Peter Daniels' distinction between "sophisticated" and "unsophisticated" origins of script is unhelpful (Daniels 1996b:579). "Ideological" or, in less loaded terms, "cultural" models of script invention find such matters of far greater interest than the very notions of "monogenesis" or "multiple-genesis." In key cases, stimulus diffusion – the practice of copying or imitation at a very general level – can be impossible to prove or disprove, resting as it does on arguments about dates and relative physical proximity. More to the point, if writing is socially and culturally rooted, why are such broad, pan-millennial, and pan-continental formulations of any interest? Is their sole purpose to show that humans are imaginatively impoverished and that the proverbial mouse-trap could only be invented once? The monogenetic view can be exhilarating in its broad scope. However, in my opinion, it devalues the details of human experience by its sheer grandiosity, a scriptural equivalent to Arnold Toynbee's lofty and somewhat discredited utterances about civilization (McNeill 1989:177).

What journalists do miss, however, is writing as a sequence of step-like inventions, a point alluded to before. For example, Mayanists have long made the mistake of seeing Maya script according to a "synoptic fallacy" by which all developments are conflated into a single writing system (Houston on Mesoamerica, ch. 10, this volume). In fact, there is abundant evidence that the Maya changed their views about the iconic motivation of certain signs ("reinterpretation principle"), begat glyphs from other glyphs ("extension principle"), and employed rebus to engender consonant + vowel syllables ("syllabification principle"). Quotative expressions, which recognize an encapsulated speech world reflected indirectly in script, come late as well (Houston and D. Stuart 1993; Grube 1998). Peter Damerow labels the earliest, linguistically incomplete notations "proto-writing" (1999b:2), a species of record that requires heavy doses of oral contextualization and background information. In this volume, John Baines makes the point that early writing systems may not principally have had "language-notating" in mind, a point underscored by their extreme abbreviation and isolated occurrence, neither of which accords with the linear sequencing of language. At the time of their invention, Egyptian hieroglyphs were not thought teleologically to be "proto-anything" (see also Bagley, this volume). They fulfilled a contemporary need admirably, although their variance from some later forms suggests a stage antecedent to the codifications of dynasties 0 and 1. Codifications elevate an idiosyncratic marking device to the level of a broadly used system, so the finds from the U-j tomb described by Baines may, if correctly dated, hint at scribal practices of highly limited dissemination, used within a tiny script community, a group of habitual writers, readers, and teachers of the same writing system.

To an extent, then, what Damerow says is true, although his detachment of proto-writing from language should not discount the widely accepted presence of logographs or "word signs" in early cuneiform (Englund, this volume). Seen another way, however, the lack of explicit phonic clues cannot be taken as evidence that lexemes were exclusively semantic in their referents, only that the lexemes and their graphic equivalents had no further specifications of phonic value. To a striking degree, most primary scripts display under-grammaticalization and phonic opacity in their earliest examples. Later steps in script development augment those frameworks with ever greater specifications of sound and meaning, and these changes are in many respects as intriguing as the first signs. In secondary inventions, under-specification can also take place, as in runes (H. Williams, this volume), whose earliest examples eschew explanatory glosses and fully grammaticalized phrases, or they may leap quickly to fulfill several functions at once. Indeed, such variety of function may prompt this second step of grammaticalization and the increasing appearance of strict conventions in signaries. Yet, in another sense Damerow does not acknowledge, as Mesoamericanists must do now, that oral contextualization and the necessity of extrinsic background information remain a part of many traditions of writing and reading.

To say that the earliest script assigns lesser importance to "language-notating" is not the same as claiming that it exists apart from a linguistic setting. In most instances we simply do not know how the first writing was read or what reading meant as a form of social practice. Moreover, a general suspicion grows that most early script did not expand to fulfill every conceivable function – an anachronistic fallacy – but served, at least initially, very limited needs. A common problem in viewing ancient writing systems is a modern inclination to see them as logically extending to all possible uses, from king list to laundry list, much as our own use of writing ranges over a wide variety of functions. However, there is no inherent reason why this should be so, despite the fact that such reasoning may be found in some treatments of the origins of writing (e.g. Postgate *et al.* 1995). Supposedly, if accounting could be done with writing, then it must have been, the absence of evidence being ascribed to "sampling problems," to documents that have, for various reasons, disappeared systematically. There is little question that early cuneiform and proto-Elamite were chiefly concerned with such matters of accounting, but those working with other traditions tend to feel a sense of disquiet when features of that, perhaps the earliest, system are assumed to represent a template for other scripts.

Mesoamerica and the New World

There is much new evidence from Mesoamerica and the Maya in particular, much of it unpublished or, from the generalist's viewpoint, obscurely circulated. The gathering that led to this book was partly based on the premise that this evidence should not be treated as an afterthought. The single most influential book on writing systems, by Gelb (1963), fails to accept that true script existed in the New World, thus preserving the parental role of cuneiform and his monogenetic theory of writing. A year before the Sundance gathering, a conference took place on the origins of writing at the Center for Ancient Studies, University of Pennsylvania. Out of seventeen presentations, one dealt with Mesoamerica. In point of fact, any discussion of origins must take the Mesoamerican evidence seriously, as, even more than China, this region offers the least controversial support for the multiple origins of writing. At Sundance, it also became clear from a presentation by Gary Urton on khipu that this system too achieved a high level of complexity and semantic encoding. The purpose of the Sundance meeting was in part to engage the Old World and the New, and to spice unleavened bread with chile pepper. Those goals were amply met at the seminar itself. However, for various reasons, principally because of scheduling conflicts and alternative commitments, Mesoamerica is, in all candor, not adequately reflected in this volume. Houston and, to some extent, Boone and Robertson, alone report on Mesoamerican evidence. The editor rues the gap. Also, the volume leaves to the side undeciphered scripts such as Isthmian of southern Mexico and, elsewhere in the world, Indus and Rongorongo. Their undetermined content means that they cannot, as yet, contribute much of substance to debates about the first writing. Because of serious difficulties in decipherment, many scholars are skeptical that they will ever reach that requisite stage of understanding.

We have also decided not to scrutinize so-called "ethnographic" inventions, the cultural circumstances of creativity, the conditions for acceptance of such imaginative discoveries, and the acquisition of writing and accomplished literacy by any one person. Why leave such matters to the side? Ethnographic situations are germane in one sense, for they point to the revelatory origin of many writing systems and their narrow function at the time of invention (Senner 1989:10–21). Seers rather than technocrats may have been the more likely creators of scripts, with innovations coming not from efficiency studies but, as ethnographic cases suggest, from dreams and visions: it is in this context that innovation may be accepted in traditional societies that do not prize novelty for its own sake. Such scripts, however, may not be relevant in other cases, or at least only with respect in our gathering to the case of Scandinavian runes, which can be seen now to derive directly from Latin characters, under indirect influence from an aggressive Roman empire. The creators of runes both emulated the script of that empire and chose deliberately to depart from it in significant ways (H. Williams, this volume), rather in the same way that British and Irish Ogam developed in response to, and reaction against, Roman letters (Sims-Williams 1993). Ethnographic evidence offers rich detail about the creation and use of scripts. However, in using these writing systems as models for the remote past, we risk the anthropological fallacy of searching the world for "contemporary ancestors," when, in fact, most such scripts derive from particular historical moments of the colonial and post-colonial periods. As such, they are shaped by the processes of ethnic revivalism and revitalization. The first writing requires close study in its own terms, as does, in a separate context, the last writing – the "death" of particular scripts (Houston, Baines, and Cooper 2003).

The Sundance Seminar and this book

At Sundance, the following participants gave their best: Robert Bagley (early Chinese, Princeton University), John Baines (Egyptian, Oxford University), William Boltz (early Chinese, University of Washington), Elizabeth Boone (Aztec, Tulane University), Françoise Bottéro (early Chinese, Ecole des Hautes Etudes en Sciences Sociales), Michael Coe (Mesoamerica and decipherment, Yale University), Jerrold Cooper (early cuneiform, Johns Hopkins University), Robert Englund (proto-Elamite, University of California, Los Angeles), Byron Hamman (Mixtec, Ph.D. student, University of Chicago), Stephen Houston (Mesoamerica, Brigham Young University), Simon Martin (Maya script, Institute of Archaeology, University of London), John Robertson (linguistics, Brigham Young University), Gary Urton (khipu, Colgate University), Mark van Stone (calligraphy, University of Texas, Austin), and Henrik Williams (runes, Uppsala University). Generous funding came from Houston's Jesse Knight University Professorship, which defrayed most of the costs, along with support from the Department of Anthropology (Joel Janetski, chair), and Clayne Pope, former dean of the College of Family, Home, and Social Sciences at Brigham Young University. Evie Forsythe assisted with accounting and scheduling, and Alan Ashton opened his home in Sundance for the final day of the seminar. His contribution, which included catering, was facilitated by Noel Reynolds of Brigham Young University. Allen Christenson, John Gee, and Jack Welch also attended when their time permitted. Jerry Cooper and David Webster improved this introduction with their comments, and to Jerry and John Baines the editor expresses his admiration and gratitude for their moral support throughout the project. The *Norwegian Archaeological Review* gave kind permission to reprint a revised version of Bruce Trigger's piece, "Writing Systems: A Case Study in Cultural Evolution" (1998[31, 1]: 39–59). To these and other friends, but especially to the contributors of *The First Writing* and Simon Whitmore of Cambridge University Press, the editor and organizer gives his warm thanks. It is to his children, Anders Bliss and Hannah McCrea, that he dedicates his editorial efforts with love and affection. May their lives flourish with as much success as did the first writing.

2 | The possibility and actuality of writing

JOHN S. ROBERTSON

The question of how writing systems emerge is related to, but different from, the question of how writing is possible. Possibility precedes actuality; the kinetic is not possible without the potential. The evolution of writing systems raises many issues, including: what is the relationship between speech and writing; among pictographs, ideographs, and logographs; among rebus, syllabaries, and alphabets; between logographic and phonographic signs; between acrophony and phoneticism? All of these are vital to understanding the nature of writing, and they will occupy a good portion of this chapter. What has received little attention, however, is the question of how writing systems are possible in the first place. It is knowledge of the parameters of the *possibility* of writing that allows for a more thorough understanding of its inception and later evolution. In short, what makes writing possible precedes any explanation of the emergence and development of writing. This chapter treats the possibility of writing as it bears on its emergence and later extension.

In two discussions that are short if rich in implications, Roman Jakobson (1971a, 1971b) provides the theoretical foundation for understanding how writing is possible. Although the articles do not focus on writing *per se*, his observations about the nature of visual and auditory signs provide valuable insight into the possibility of writing. The essence of Jakobson's observations is that visual signs are prototypically atemporal, imitative, and immediate, whereas auditory signs are essentially temporal, imputed and mediate. Visual signs are atemporal because they persist as long as the medium that preserves them lasts, while auditory signs vanish with the airwaves that carry them. Visual signs are prototypically imitative in the sense that our visual images are depictions of their objects. By contrast, auditory perceptions take on meaning when a signal is assigned to its object. Finally, visual perception is holistic and immediate, whereas auditory perception is processed piecemeal through time, achieving holism by systematic, hierarchical mediation.

In comparing painting (imitative and visual) and music (non-imitative and auditory), Jakobson (1971b:334) observes that "nonobjective,

Fig. 2.1 Holistic, immediate perception.

nonrepresentational, abstract painting or sculpture meets with violent attacks, contempt, jeers, vituperation, bewilderment, whereas calls for imitations of external reality are rare exceptions in the perennial history of music . . ." In other words, of the four possibilities, (1) representational art, (2) non-representational art, (3) representational music, and (4) non-representational music, both (1) and (4) are uncontrived and unmarked, whereas (2) and (3) seem more fabricated and aberrant.

Furthermore, Jakobson (1971b:335–336) points to a "widespread tendency to interpret various spots, blotches or broken roots and twigs as effigies of animate nature, or still life, in short, as imitative art." With vision there is an irresistible tendency to make mimetic, iconic interpretations even out of naturally occurring objects that otherwise have no significative function. By contrast, acoustic signs do not emphasize the iconic relationship between sign and object. For example, when anyone hears actual recordings of "railroad stations and trains, streets, harbors, sea, wind, [or] rain," it is almost impossible to identify the objects that such recordings represent (Jakobson 1971b:334). The natural course in interpreting acoustic signs does not call for similarity-to-object but requires a mediated intellectual processing.

Perception of visual signs is, by their essential nature, holistic and therefore immediate, whereas coherent cognition of any auditory sign comes piece by piece through time, requiring a mediated assembling of parts on a timeline to achieve a congruous, cognitive whole. Consider Fig. 2.1. Although it is possible to spend time looking at any drawing, there is an immediacy to visual content that is impossible with signs that are interpretable through time. Now consider the content of Fig. 2.2. This illustration consists only of three words. The content is heard aurally but that process (a) takes time,

Nits make lice.

Fig. 2.2 Mediated, temporal perception.

and (b) requires mediated processing – a notably different process from the interpretation of Fig. 2.1.

Jakobson (1971a:343) makes the point that, in the fifth century, the Indian scholar Bhartrhari proposed three stages to speech. The first is conceptualization, where the speaker has the idea of what is to be said. This stage is atemporal, since no time is involved. Second is the actual performance and interpretation, which takes place in and through time. Bhartrhari sees this second stage in terms of what we might call encoding and decoding, both of which are temporal in nature. The third stage results in comprehension, where the sequence of the utterance is transformed into a holistic idea, whose parts are all simultaneously present. Clearly, visual interpretation of signs is more immediate than acoustic interpretation, since "a complex visual sign involves a series of simultaneous constituents, while a complex auditory sign consists, as a rule, of serial successive constituents" (Jakobson 1971b:336).

A Peircean perspective

In the Peircean trichotomy *icon*, *index*, and *symbol* we find a fundamental correlation between *icon* and *symbol* on the one hand, and *visual* and *acoustic* on the other. Bear in mind the following description of *icon*, *index*, and *symbol*:

First is the icon, which exhibits a similarity or analogy to the subject of discourse; the second is the index, which like a pronoun demonstrative or relative, forces the attention to the particular object intended without describing it; the third [or symbol] is the general name or description which signifies its object by means of an association of ideas or habitual connection between the name and the character signified. (1.369)[1]

Peirce's description of "icon" suggests a notable correspondence to Jakobson's discussion of visual perception. Prototypically representational, art is iconic since it "exhibits a similarity or analogy" between the sign and its object. Even naturally occurring objects, when taken as signs that exhibit a similarity to an imagined object, are iconic by Peirce's definition. Furthermore, both visual perception and icons are atemporal, given their inherent

Fig. 2.3 Intersection between visual and auditory perception.

qualities of simultaneity and continuance. In short, visual perception is prototypically iconic.

Peirce's "symbol" and Jakobson's description of auditory perception suggest a further correlation. A symbol is a habitual (and therefore an arbitrary) connection between sign and object. More particularly, a linguistic symbol – be it a spoken word, or phrase, or proposition, or even a whole discourse – is in the end a patterned synthesis of parts-to-whole through time. Such synthesis depends on mediated, habitual behavior. In short, spoken language is predominantly symbolic behavior. Iconism is certainly a part of spoken language, but carries relatively less weight than symbolism. The term *cock-a-doodle-doo* is strongly iconic, since *similarity* is the means of identifying the object, which is the actual crowing of the rooster. Onomatopoeia is exceptional in the lexicon, but even lexical icons still have a significant element of symbolism. Language is mainly symbolic, where its terms call up their object by mediated habit.[2] For example, the word *rooster* is a symbol since the means by which its object is identified is "an association of ideas or habitual connection." Unlike *cock-a-doodle-doo*, there is nothing in the sign itself that draws attention to the rooster.

The possibility of writing

The intersection of these two highly developed avenues of human perception – visual (iconic) and auditory (symbolic) perception – allows for the possibility of writing. Consider, for example, the Venn diagram shown in Fig. 2.3. As will be shown below, the potential for writing results in writing systems that have all the properties of visual/iconic and auditory perception / symbolic systems discussed above. Writing includes both the holistic characteristics of visual perception, and at the same time, without contradiction, the sequential character of auditory perception. It is at once atemporal and temporal, iconic and symbolic. In short, the potential for writing is at the nexus linking the visual and the auditory channels of perception.

The purpose of writing

If visual properties combined with aural attributes of human perception constitute the possibility of writing, then those selfsame visual properties also give writing certain advantages over speech. A simple explanation is that its visual nature makes writing preservative, against the transient nature of speech. A more detailed account is that the speech act is transient, semelfactive (once-occurring), and temporary. By contrast, visual perception allows language to overcome its original, transient temporal nature by making writing as enduring as the medium upon which it appears. The advantage of endowing spoken language with permanence through writing allows for the preservation of feelings, facts, and ideas through time and space. This power to conserve – the ramifications of which extend far beyond the scope of this chapter – has changed the face of the world. It is small wonder that such an advantage would prompt the potential of writing to instantiate itself as an omnipresent reality.

The relationship of writing to speech

An expression such as "it is written *in* English or *in* Mayan," and so on, bespeaks the most basic relationship between speech and writing: *writing is truly writing when it systematically represents speech.*[3] Of course, it would be naïve or even wrong to discount the fact that writing always takes on a life of its own – that other important graphic and notational systems grow out of writing systems of the type discussed in this volume. Nevertheless, it would also be wrong to confuse the unique nature of writing with its true relationship to speech, which is this: the purpose of a given written sign is to represent a corresponding spoken sign. Writing is truly writing when the written sign attempts to represent *the spoken sign*. Technically, such representation can be either direct or indirect. Direct representation is when the written symbols correspond to syllables, or phonemes of the spoken sign; indirect representation is when a written sign first represents an object of the spoken sign, which in turn references the spoken sign (Fig. 2.4).

The fact that writing aims to represent spoken language is essential to the correct understanding of the nature of writing. Sampson (1985:149) makes this point about Chinese writing, which is strongly logographic but still with an undeniably important phonographic component. Even logographs, however, are not mere representations of ideas without regard for Chinese words: "The truth is, however, that Chinese writing comes no closer than English or any other to 'signifying thoughts directly,' or to expressing 'things'

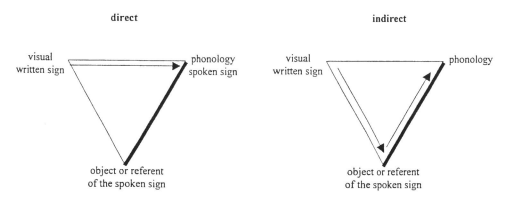

Fig. 2.4 Direct and indirect access to the spoken sign.

rather than 'words.' Chinese script... symbolizes units of a particular spoken language, namely the Chinese language, with all its quirks and illogicalities."[4] Finally, it is important to recognize that the dark lines of Fig. 2.4 predate writing, which is the connection between the spoken word and its object. The light lines of the triangles show the relationships between (a) the written sign and the object of the spoken word, and (b) the written sign and the spoken word itself.[5]

First writing

The preservation of speech in a written medium is not straightforward in light of the seemingly contradictory properties of visual and aural perception outlined above. These are two opposing forces that always bring tension in true writing. First, because visual perception is essentially iconic, it is natural that a first writer would draw a picture of the object of the spoken sign, as shown in Fig. 2.5. Second, spoken language is chiefly symbolic, representing the object through units of sound. Therefore, the most efficient means of representing any spoken sign – especially foreign words, grammatical signs, and names – is by spelling.

Given this opposition of iconic naturalness to symbolic efficiency, what seems to happen first in writing needs elaboration. The first path a hypothetical first writer appears to take in connecting a visual representation to a corresponding spoken sign is by indirection: drawing a picture of the object in question – which is connected to its spoken sign – as shown in Fig. 2.6. This singular, pictographic approach, however, brings two impossible difficulties. The first is that the majority of objects of the spoken sign have no possible iconic representation, given the symbolic nature of language.

22 John S. Robertson

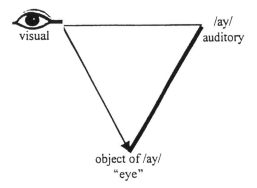

Fig. 2.5 Visual connection to the auditory object.

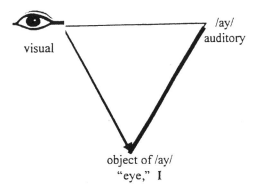

Fig. 2.6 Indirect reference to homonymous forms.

As pointed out by scholars on innumerable occasions, linguistic concepts – beyond those of the most concrete objects – do not lend themselves to such simplistic iconography. It is not easy to draw unambiguously a picture of the preposition *for*. The second difficulty is that, even where iconic representation is possible, the possibility of ambiguity is infinite. The pictograph of the eye of Fig. 2.7, for example, could conceivably not only have reference to the noun "eye," or even "vision," but also to verbs like "to see," or "to eyeball," "to look at," "to watch," "to scan," "to visualize," and so on.

In the context of the indirect means of representing the spoken sign (see Fig. 2.4), first writers typically used any of several measures to specify *which* spoken sign the written sign was to reference. The first measure relies on similarity and has two parts, one based on the universal notion of homonymy (rebus principle), and the other on synonymy (polyphonic principle).[6] The second method exploits the opposition of visual versus auditory perception. Specifically, a first writer often used determiners to

The possibility and actuality of writing

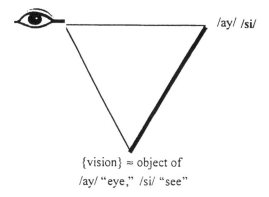

Fig. 2.7 Potential ambiguity in strictly visual reference to the spoken sign.

designate the appropriate spoken sign. The determiners were either semantic or phonological in nature. The final method was to devise symbolic logographs. Each of these methods is treated below.

Homonymy and synonymy

The rebus principle

A homonym is a word that has more than one referential meaning. The rebus principle makes use of this notion. The so-called "rebus principle," defined as a logograph that stands for two objects, the first an iconically similar object, the second an unrelated object, whose spoken sign sounds like the first sign. Fig. 2.6 diagrams the rebus principle, where the object "I" is a possible referent of the pictograph because of the homophonous nature of the spoken sign /ay/.

Rebus played an important role in the early evolution of first writing. Jerrold Cooper (1996:42) claims that writers of cuneiform script took measures to augment iconic script by the rebus principle because of the restrictive nature of pictographs. In Mayan the logograph for "one," pronounced /huun/, was substitutable in late contexts for "paper," also pronounced /huun/. The principle can extend beyond strict homonymy. In Sumerian the glyph for "/ti/ 'arrow' was extended to stand also for the near-homophone /til/ 'life'" (Sampson 1985:54). Jerrold Cooper (1996:43) makes the point that when Sumerian cuneiform came to express adequately "natural language in a broad range of contexts – letters, commemorative inscriptions, legal documents, literary texts, technical literature – [it was facilitated by] the increasing use of rebus phoneticism to write grammatical affixes." The point is that rebus appeals to the spoken sign not only to help delimit ambiguity, but also as a means of going beyond pictographic representation.

The polyphonic principle

While the rebus principle relies on homonymy, its complement – the polyphonic principle – draws on synonymy. A given written sign could have a general semantic sense, made specific by two (or more) different words, as shown in Fig. 2.7. William Boltz (1996:193) gives an example of this from Chinese: "There is a written sign, which presumably depicted an orifice of some kind, and which represented the word [for] 'mouth.' The words *míng* 'call out' and *kou* 'mouth' clearly have nothing in common in pronunciation; but just as clearly they are linked semantically." These two complementary ways of representing the spoken sign and its object – the rebus principle and the polyphonic principle – are owing to the notion of resemblance. Rebus results from a similarity between the spoken sign and two (or more) objects, and polyphony is an effect of a similarity of meanings between two (or more) spoken signs.

Semantic and phonological determiners

Synonymy and homonymy in the spoken sign are the bases of the rebus and polyphonic principles. Semantic and phonological determiners, on the other hand, find their starting place in the visual and auditory mechanisms of perception discussed earlier. Boltz (1996:194) says that "to solve the problem of ambiguity, the [early] Chinese scribes appended secondary graphic components, called *determinatives*, to ambiguous primary graphs; such components specify either the intended meaning or the pronunciation." In Sumerian cuneiform, beginning in the archaic period, the texts "employ a series of semantic classifiers called *determinatives* that had no phonological realization and were probably developed to help disambiguate polyvalent signs" (Cooper 1996:43). Ritner (1996a:76) makes it clear that "determinatives are often the only distinguishing features among homonyms. Thus, the concluding 'book-role' determinative characterizes the word ... 'writing' in contrast to 'scribe,' determined with a seated man."

Up to this point, we have shown that the indirect selection of the spoken sign (see Fig. 2.4) is ultimately impossible because the vast majority of objects of spoken signs are not depictable. Even those that *can* be pictured are unacceptably ambiguous. These problems find at least a partial, but incomplete, solution with (a) rebus and polyphony as well as (b) semantic and phonological determiners. The fact that so many early writing systems, apparently independently from each other, developed these strategies at the earliest recorded stages suggests certain universal tendencies: the tendency to exploit the iconicity of visual perception and then for further disambiguation to exploit homonymy and synonymy as well as determinatives of an iconic and symbolic nature. Such stretching only goes so far, however. Writing systems naturally and universally used another technique allowing for the referencing of the appropriate spoken sign: the ideograph.

From icon to symbol

The terms *icon*, *index*, and *symbol* nicely classify the relationship between the spoken or written sign and the object of the spoken sign. By way of reminder, the term *cock-a-doodle-doo* establishes an iconic relationship of similarity between the spoken sign and the actuality of what the rooster "says." The word *this* of *this rooster* determines an indexical relationship of contiguity between speaker and rooster in the here-and-now of space and time. The term *rooster* produces a connection based on habit between the sign itself and its referent or object.

Similar relationships describe the path connecting the written sign to the object of the spoken sign. An iconic relationship is one that shows a similarity between the object and the written sign. The term *pictograph* describes that relationship. A symbolic relationship indicates an association of habit between the written sign and the object of the spoken sign. The term I use here in describing such a symbolic relationship is *ideograph*.[7] A term I use indifferently to describe either an iconic (pictographic) or symbolic (ideographic) relationship between the written sign and the object of the spoken sign is *logograph*. Finally, some written signs are best described as strongly iconic or strongly symbolic, but it would be fruitless to try to classify all written signs exclusively as one or the other, since all feasible blends of symbol and icon are possible. The term *logograph* is useful, because it defines any connection between the written sign and the object of the spoken sign, be that connection strongly iconic or symbolic, or anywhere in between.

Yet, it is important to note that the indexical sign is somewhat different in use and scope in writing than it is in speech. The reason is not far to seek. Since spoken language is rooted in and through time, some words like *I*, *you*, *here*, *there*, *left*, *right*, and so on refer to the temporal and spatial immediacy of the speech act. However, since written language by its very nature transcends time (relative to spoken language), it follows that such temporally and spatially dependent language would have distinctive use

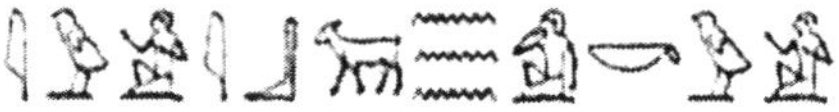

Fig. 2.8 Deixis of orientation (Gardiner 1957:25).

in writing. Indeed, writing typically requires much more contextualization than one would find in speech. For example, in conversation one could walk into a room and say "I don't know what you are doing here right now," and the referent of every word would be perfectly clear. The objects of the spoken deictics *I, you, here, right now* would all be transparent in the spatio-temporal setting of the speech act. On the other hand, an identical sentence found on an unprovenanced piece of paper would be referentially opaque, since the spatio-temporal context is nonexistent.

It is nonetheless possible for a deictic to refer to the media of writing, as, for example, "this spear point belongs to Ralph," or "this monument commemorates Ralph's victory over Rudolph," or even, "this letter is to inform Ralph to beware of Rudolph." Even with these particular examples, however, the object is the referent of the deictic words, so that these deictics *ipso facto* cannot overcome the immediacy of their objects.

Another kind of index specific to writing, however, is the deixis of orientation. A good example occurs in Egyptian writing (Gardiner 1957: 25): "The signs that represent persons, animals, and birds, as well as other signs that have fronts and backs, almost always face the beginning of the inscription in which they occur, so that the direction in which this is to be read is but rarely in doubt." Fig. 2.8, with birds, men, kid, and basket with handle, "must be read from left to right" since they all face toward the left. There is no term comparable to *pictograph* and *ideograph*. Fig. 2.9 summarizes these relationships.

As shown below, there seems to be a process of change in writing systems that approaches law: if a logograph changes form, it goes from icon to symbol and not the reverse.[8] One does not have to look far in the literature to find many instances of pictographs in the earliest attestations of writing which have become ideographs at later stages in that system. Boltz (1996:192) explicitly shows that at least some of the earliest Chinese logographs were "realistic pictures of easily depictable things" which stood "for the name of the thing in question."[9] Later, these same logographs changed from imagistic icons (pictographs) to evolved symbols (ideographs), where the association became habitual, no longer based on similarity. Despite the somewhat richer iconism in attestations of the earliest writing, however, it is nonetheless true that symbolic logographs are always present even at the earliest attested

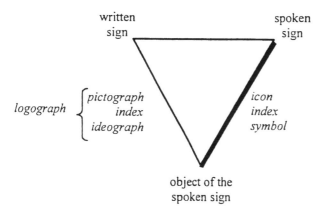

Fig. 2.9 The relationships between the object of the spoken sign and its spoken and written counterparts.

dates. Pictographs in emergent written systems are only natural since visual perception is by nature iconic, but the intellectual objects of spoken language not subject to imaging are so numerous that it is not surprising to find symbolic logographs even in the first attestations of writing.

However, no known writing system is based on logographs alone. While rebus/polyphony, determiners, and ideographs could theoretically expand the limits of pictographic representation infinitely, there are some practical limitations to purely logographic representation. Several come to mind. First, the sheer number of morphemes in a language makes it difficult for any writer to remember all the logographs contrived to represent those morphemes. Second is the necessity to transcribe words borrowed from another language, especially proper nouns. It is impossible to invent logographs that could appropriately represent the phonology (or approximate phonology) of another language. Third is the linguistic fact that morphemes/words that signal grammatical relationships seem to require special treatment. It appears that the words susceptible to logographic representation are those whose objects lend themselves most readily to ready paraphrase or cross-linguistic definition. That is, if someone asked, "what is a *nit*?" the definition might be "a louse egg." Conversely, if someone were to ask for a definition of the word *for*, it would be difficult indeed. Grammatical items like *a* and *the*, *plural* and *singular*, and so on, seem not to be susceptible to logographic representation.[10] Finally, and most importantly, since writing represents spoken language, it is only natural that the indirection of the originally logographic text would soon come to represent the spoken sign.[11]

Relationships between the written sign and the spoken sign

Just as *icon, index,* and *symbol* describe the relationships between the spoken sign and its object, and just as *pictograph, index,* and *ideograph* describe the relationship between the written signs and the objects of the spoken sign, so the terms *orthography, punctuation,* and a new term, *heterography,* define a corresponding set of relationships between the written sign and the spoken sign, as shown in Fig. 2.10. The terms *icon, index,* and *symbol* correspond to *orthography, punctuation,* and *heterography,* as explained below. Peirce's (2.277) description of iconic images and iconic diagrams also underscores the notions of pictograph and orthography: "Those which partake of simple qualities . . . are images; those which represent the relations . . . of the parts of one thing by analogous relations in their own parts, are diagrams; those which represent the representative character of a representamen by representing a parallelism in something else, are metaphors." It seems clear enough that pictographic signs are imagistic icons, since they "partake of simple qualities" of the object of the spoken sign. In contrast, orthographic signs correspond to Peirce's description of diagrammatic icons. The meaning of the term *orthography* – the way written signs correspond to their phonetic counterparts – speaks to the diagrammatic icon. This is another way of saying that orthographic writing is an iconic type "which represent[s] . . . the parts of one thing" (for example, the phonemes/syllable of a spoken sign) "by analogous relations in their own parts" (for example, the written letters/syllables). Thus, the letters of the spelling *mat* correspond to their phonemic counterparts /mæt/.

Just as there is a difference between pictographic (imagistic) and orthographic (diagrammatic) icons, there is also a corresponding difference between ideographic (symbolic) indices and what we here term *heterographic* symbols. An example might be the written signs *right, write, wright,* where the relationship to the spoken sign /rayt/ is not wholly iconic (ortho+graphic); rather, it is symbolic (hetero + graphic). Thus, a diagrammatic icon would be, for instance, *not,* but a more symbolic spelling would be *knot,* where the letters would not have an orthogonal, point-to-point relationship with the phonemes of the spoken word. Some authors have extended the term *logographic* to include what is here termed *heterographic* (symbolic) relationships of the type *rite, right, write, wright.* Sampson (1985:207), for example, goes so far as to say that "modern English spelling has as much title to be called logographic and phonographic."[12] For purposes of technical clarity, however, it is useful to reserve the term *logograph* to the relationship between the written sign and the object of the

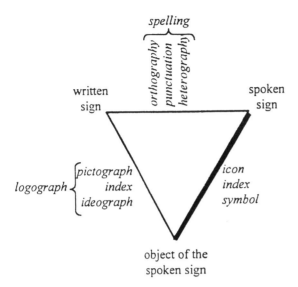

Fig. 2.10 The relationships between (a) the spoken sign and the object of the spoken sign; (b) the written sign and the object of the spoken sign; and (c) the written sign and the spoken sign.

spoken sign. Just as we use the term *logograph* to include the iconic notion *pictographic* and the symbolic *ideographic* writing, so we use the term *spelling* to refer to both *orthographic* and *heterographic* writing.

Just as there are logographic indices so there are also spelling (or phonographic) indices or punctuation marks that reference the phonological content of written signs themselves. Although typically in Luwian "texts are written continuously without word breaks, [t]here is a word divider,)|, but it is not employed consistently" (Melchert 1996:121). Furthermore, "there is a sign)) ((... which explicitly marks logographic use, but it appears only sporadically" (Melchert 1996:123). Spacing among phonological or syllabic signs to mark boundaries seems to be something that emerges as writing systems mature.

Acrophony: the possible source of diagrammatic icons, or orthographic signs

Acrophony is apparently the means of moving iconic logographs squarely into the notion of diagrammatic icon. Consider, for example, the Luwian hieroglyphs, where "the syllabic values are derived by acrophony, i.e. by taking the first syllable(s) of the word represented by a logogram. For

		Reconstruction	Meaning
ba	CM	*baah	"pocket gopher"
hu	CCh	*huj	"iguana"
ka	CM	*kar	"fish"
ko	LL	*kok	"small turtle"
k'u	CM	*q'uu'	"nest"
ch'o	CM	*ch'o'	"mouse, rat"
lu	CM	*luk	"hook," to fish
mo	LL	*mo'	"macaw"
na	CCh	*na'	"mother"
ne	CCh	*neh	"tail"
no	CM	*nooq'	"cloth"?
pu	CWC	*puj	"cattail"
to	CCh	*tyooq	"mist, cloud"
tzu	CWC	*tzu'	"gourd"
wi	CM	*wi'	"root"
we?	LL	*we'	"eat"?

Fig. 2.11 Acrophonic derivations of certain members of the Classic Mayan syllabary. (CM means "Common Mayam," CCh is "Common Ch'olan," LL is "Lowland," and CWC is "Common Wastek-Ch'olan.")

example, the sign tara/i is derived from [tarri-] 'three,' that for the ta from [targasna-] 'ass, donkey,' and so on. Our knowledge of the Luwian lexicon is quite limited, and it is likely that nearly all syllabic values are derived in this manner" (Melchert 1996:12). The development of the Mayan hieroglyphic syllabary seems to have had similar origins. The examples in Fig. 2.11 are illustrative (Houston, Robertson, and Stuart 2000:328). Without knowing details of the ancient language, we do not have some of the lexical sources for elements of the Mayan syllabary. Yet, it is plausible that all members of the syllabary were acrophonically derived. Furthermore, the words from which the syllabary came are in many cases iconic logographs, as shown in Fig. 2.12.[13] This selection from the Mayan syllabary once again has its roots in the iconicity of visual perception, for the written sign is a logographic icon. Sampson (1985:81) makes a strong case for the original Semitic script having developed acrophonically from pictographs – which was also the case for Egyptian. Unlike Luwian and Mayan, however, the Egyptian and Semitic scripts were consonantal and not syllabic. It is difficult to tell the extent to which languages of the Old World influenced each other in their development, but the fact that Mayan, detached from the Old World, developed a spelling system acrophonically along the same

Fig. 2.12 The iconic nature of certain acrophonically derived members of the Classic Mayan syllabary.

lines suggests that acrophony is a highly valued approach in developing phonography.

Types of heterographic spelling

Lexical items of the type *rite, write, wright* are one kind of heterographic spelling. This first type is lexigraphic. There are other kinds of heterography that play an important role in some spelling systems, and which may have even played a role in the development of Mayan writing. The first is phonological in nature, and the second is morphophonemic.

Indirect indication of phonemic distinctions

Phonological heterography has to do with "silent" letters that affect the way a word is pronounced when read. Swedish distinguishes tense and lax vowels by using a single consonant to signal tense vowels, and two consonants to signal lax vowels, as *dam* ("lady"), *damm* ("dust"), *glas* ("glass"), *glass* ("ice cream"), and so on. In Mayan, there is a phenomenon akin to the process in English where the so-called "silent" [e] indicates a so-called "long" (tense) vowel, as, for example, "writ/write," "met/mete," "mat/mate," "rot/rote," and "cut/cute." The appearance of the silent vowel effects a change in the way the reader interprets the root vowel. Thus, without the final "silent" [e], the vowels in the above examples are simple: /i, e, æ, a/, and /ə/ respectively. With the final [e], the vowels are complex and pronounced with the off-glide /y/ or /w/: /ay, iy, ey/, and /yuw/ respectively.

Just as a silent [e] in English prompts a different reading of the root vowel, so an unpronounced final vowel in the Mayan hieroglyphs similarly provokes a different reading of the root vowel (Houston, Stuart, and Robertson 1998). Since the Classic Mayan script was a syllabary, the canonical spoken form CVC had to be written CV-CV, the second vowel being a so-called "silent vowel." Specifically, if the Mayan silent vowel was different from the root vowel, it signaled a "complex" vowel. A complex vowel – never a short vowel – takes one of the following constructions, all followed by a consonant: long vowel (VVC); vowel h (VhC); or vowel glottal stop (V'C). For example, the written form CHAK-*ki* would have been pronounced either /*chaak*/, /*chahk*/, or /*cha'k*/ but never /*chak*/, since the root vowel (*a*) and the "silent vowel" (*i*) are disharmonic. We know, however, by comparison with modern languages, that /*chahk*/ was the likely spoken form.

Another significant attribute is this: if the silent vowel is the same as the root vowel – if the vowels are synharmonic – then the root vowel is typically short, but may also be complex. Consider, for example, the following synharmonic words:

Written	Pronounced	Meaning	Reconstruction
ta-ja	taj	"pitch pine"	*t^{y}aj
wi-tzi	witz	"hill"	*witz
chu-ku	chuk	"seize"	*chuk
K'IN-ni	k'iin	"day"	*kii~
ta-na	tahn	"chest"	*tahn
yu-mu	yuum	"owner"	*yuum

It is significant that the synharmonic words can take either long or short vowels, whereas with one exception the disharmonic constructions *always* express complex vowels. Thus, we conclude that the synharmonic construction is unmarked and therefore liable to wider referential variation, whereas the disharmonic constructions are marked and therefore subject to a narrower variation.

Under-representation of morphemic variation

One of the most important facts of writing is that in many ways the written sign under-represents the spoken sign. It is quite common in languages of the world for morphemes to display some variation in form. For example, the English past tense / participial ending, invariantly written as -*ed*, has three different spoken forms that are conditioned by the shape of the preceding phoneme: -əd occurs after t and d; t occurs after all other voiceless consonants; d occurs after voiced consonants and vowels – start-əd "started," bət-əd "butted," bæk-t "backed," bæg-d "bagged." When English speakers read words like *started, butted, backed, bagged*, they automatically produce the appropriate form of the morpheme. Without special training, however, they are unaware that the morpheme seen as *-ed* is pronounced three different ways, depending on the form of the previous speech sounds. The spelling system nicely avoids spoken morphophonemic variation simply with the invariant past tense morpheme, *-ed*.

Such heterographic forms have a strong presence in the Mayan script. These are called morphosyllables (Houston, Robertson, and Stuart 2001) and function much like the English *-ed* past tense marker. For example, by comparative linguistic means, we know that the marker for a class of transitive verbs is vowel-harmonic with the root vowel. The written syllabic form is [wa] for this verb class, but there is strong evidence to suggest that the form would have been variously pronounced, for example *-chok-ow* ("scatter"), *-jul-uw* ("spear"), and *-mak-aw* ("cover"). Like the English *-ed*, the [wa] under-represents the variety of phonologically conditioned forms. A similar vowel-harmonic variation occurs with a class of mediopassive verbs. The written syllabic form is [yi], but it is certain that these verbs correspond with the attested sixteenth-century Ch'olti'an verbs of the type *-putzui [puȼ'-uy]* ("escape"), *-locoi [lok'-oy]* ("to drip out") *-tabai [t'ab'-ay]* ("ascend"), *-emei [em-ey]* ("descend"). Again, the vowel-harmonic pronunciation is under-represented by a single morphme [yi]. The relationship between the root vowels and the spoken morphemes is iconic, since the suffixed form and the root vowel "harmonize." There is also, however, a symbolic relationship, where the suffix and the root vowel are not predictably related; rather, the vowel of the suffix is arbitrarily (habitually) related to the stem. Whereas [wa] and [yi] were vowel-harmonic (the vowel of the root determined the vowel of the suffix), the morpheme [-il] was not. The variants include *-il, -el, -al, -ol, -ul* (written simply [-il]) and cannot be predictably linked to the root vowel. The *-il* form occurs most frequently, but which form will appear with which root is unpredictable. The meaning roughly corresponds to the English *-ness*, as in *goodness*.

There are other languages that do similar things: in Arabic the letter for *a* marks the accusative ending *an*. The silent letter *a* – which has no phonetic value – is also added to third person plural and the imperative plural which end in *w* (T. Bauer 1996:562). Also, "The history of Korean is characterized by a tug-of-war between phonemicists and morphophonemicists. Phonemicists wrote Korean as it was pronounced taking into account its many automatic sound changes, while morphophonemicists strove to write verb and noun bases in one constant shape, ignoring automatic sound changes" (King 1996:223).

The direction of change in writing systems

There seems to be a regular direction that writing systems follow as they emerge from the potential of writing to their first realization to their more developed states. A look at Chinese or Egyptian suggests that there is a relatively rapid initial development with an ultimate homeostasis, where change is much less abrupt with a high degree of conventionalized stability. Nevertheless, if there are changes they seem to be either from icon to symbol, or from icon to phoneticism or both. Mayan writing maintained a strong iconic component, but with time become more phonographic. Egyptian remained strongly iconic, but also, over time, developed more phoneticism. Chinese, on the other hand, never did develop a robust phoneticism, but the logographs became more symbolic.

There is also the widely accepted observation that when a writing system serves as the stimulus for a new writing system for another language, there is the tendency for the adaptation to include a strong component of phoneticism, as evidenced by the stimulus of Chinese for Japanese or Korean; or Egyptian for Semitic; or Semitic for Greek. The conclusion seems to be this: because visual perception is representationally iconic and speech symbolic, writing starts more iconic and less symbolic, but ends up more symbolic and less iconic. Even the diagrammatic iconism of orthography is a step removed from the imagistic logographs found in, say, Egyptian. In other words, the written sign tends to represent with greater precision the spoken sign.

Laws of the spoken sign compared to laws of the written sign

It should not be surprising to find some of the same laws that work in spoken language also apply to written language. This is not only because, like spoken language, writing is a semiotic system, but also because the written sign tends to become ever more directly reflective of the phonological units of the spoken sign. Three examples will illustrate. We have already seen an example of markedness, where in Mayan the disharmonic construction signals a complex root vowel, but where a synharmonic construction is indifferent to the simplicity or complexity of the root vowel. Similarly, whereas in English the spelling sequence *oa* in a CVC sequence invariantly signals the phoneme /o/, the unmarked grapheme *o* can signal either /o/ (for example, *host*) or

/a/ (for example, *cost*). These are good examples of markedness, where the unmarked member of the set has a much wider range of reference than the marked member. The word *lions* can refer to male lions, female lions, or any combination of the two. The word *lioness*, on the other hand, can only refer to the female of the species.

The Hebrew *matres lectionis* is another example of a markedness hierarchy. Sampson (1985:87) lists several rules, which gradually developed to include vowels in Hebrew writing. Given a five-vowel system, it is well known that *a* is the unmarked vowel, with *i* and *u* being second most marked, while the mid vowels *e* and *o* are the most marked (see Jakobson and Waugh 1990:289). Interestingly, the forms [y] and [w] were used obligatorily to signal the long vowels /i:/ and /u:/, while those same semivowels *optionally* signaled the more marked vowels /e:/ and /o:/. It cannot be accidental that exactly these same oppositions are at play when the Nordic futhark (alphabet) was reduced from 24 runes (letters) to 16. The rune that originally referenced the phoneme /i/ came to be used for the phoneme /e/ and the semivowel /y/ as well, while the rune that signaled /u/ came to signal /o/ and /u/ in a parallel fashion. The runes for /e/ and /o/ were lost (Elliott 1989:26). Furthermore, given the original runic opposition *t* and *d*, the unmarked (voiceless) *t* took over the more marked (voiced) *d*, and the unmarked (voiceless) *k* took over the voiced *g*. Interestingly, however, in the labials, the voiced *b* took over the unvoiced *p* – the exact opposite of what happened with the alveolars and velars. This is consistent with phonology, however, since specialists have found that with labials, the *b* is often the unmarked member of the pair. In Old English, for example, there are more instances of *b* than *p*. In the Parker MS (A), which records that language, there are 1,092 instances of *b*, while there are only 568 instances of *p* (jebbo.home.texas.net/asc/a/a.html, Manuscript A: Parker MS; CCCC 173ff. 1–32).

In general, we find that written language is subject to those same kinds of markedness constraints that are a recognized part of spoken language. Even though certain distinctions are made in the spoken language, those distinctions can be (and often are) *systematically* ignored in writing, based on the kinds of markedness hierarchies pointed out above. Genuine writing is, after all, a semiotic system inextricably linked to speech, and subject to similar laws of organization and change.

Summary

The thesis of this chapter is simple: the possibility of writing is a consequence of the two most significant capacities of human perception: the visual and the auditory. Because visual capacity seems to be iconic and auditory symbolic, many of the initiatory and developmental characteristics of writing find their explanation in the Peircean notions of icon and index.

(1) The nature of writing builds upon the fact that the medium of vision (photons bouncing off existing objects) tends toward permanency and later inspection, whereas the nature of the medium of auditory perception (the movement of molecules of air) is transitory, temporal, and memory-dependent. Recorded on a medium that endures, language finds a new usefulness. It is sufficient to say that complex human institutions would be impossible without bringing permanency to the spoken word.

(2) Pictographic symbols (iconic logographs) are more plentiful in the initial burst of development in writing systems; these symbols subsequently develop into ideographs (symbolic logographs). This occurs because (a) visual perception is fundamentally iconic, and (b) spoken language is at its base symbolic. Accordingly, writing should start out more iconic and become more symbolic, since writing is a representation of spoken language.

(3) The development of phonography is acrophonic in nature. The most obvious reason for this is that the written symbol will initially emphasize the visually iconic; phonography must come later. Given such beginnings, iconic symbols indirectly representing the spoken word (Fig. 2.4) become the phonetic stuff of syllabaries and alphabets (Fig. 2.12).

(4) From the nature of visual and auditory perception, it follows that even that small portion of writing systems that does not directly represent speech *per se* – the so-called classifiers – also have a visual and auditory mode of being. The classifiers reference words that either look like or sound like related words.

(5) The direct and indirect connections (Fig. 2.4) between the written sign and the spoken word both have analogues in the Peircean triad of icon, index, and symbol. In the original connection between the spoken sign and its object, the triad mentioned above is clearly apparent. In the connection between the written sign and the object of the spoken sign there are logographs, either the iconic pictograph or the symbolic ideograph. There is also the notion of index, which has to do with indications of direction of reading in script. The connection between the written sign and the spoken sign also has analogues: the diagrammatical icon is orthography, where there is a point-to-point relationship between the written and spoken sign. The phonographic symbol is the heterograph, where spelling does not match the phonemic nature of the sign. There are purely lexical instances, as English *one, knight*, and the like, but there are also lexical indices, such as the silent vowels in English and Mayan, or consonantal doubling as in Swedish. There is also morphophonemic writing, where the written sign is invariant but stands for morphophonemic variation in spoken language. The index is

punctuation, which signals word boundaries, sentence boundaries, or even mood, including interrogative, imperative, and declarative.

(6) The written sign is an attempt to represent spoken language. Those same features of markedness, so characteristic of spoken language, manifest themselves in the related but distinct realm of written language. Markedness is as important to the written word as to the spoken. If writing exists, it is because it had a prior, potential mode of being long before it took its various visual shapes found in the languages with a written tradition.

Notes

1. In citing Peirce, I will use the standard means of citation; since his *Collected Papers* (1931–1966) comprise eight volumes, and since each paragraph is numbered, 5.35 would mean "volume 5, paragraph 35."
2. Here I am speaking of onomatopoeia in the lexicon. There is a high degree of diagrammatic iconicity in grammatical systems.
3. Boone (this volume) makes the point that there are many highly systematic, graphic codes (mathematical, dance, musical, chemical) which clearly do not represent the spoken word. The issue is whether such systems constitute writing. The answer seems to be definitional. Whether one requires the graphic symbol to represent spoken language to earn the label "writing," as I do in this chapter, or whether the requirement is Boone's more expansive conventional, permanent, visual marks to communicate relatively specific ideas, it is important to recognize that the discussion is more definitional than substantial. No one denies that graphic systems representing writing are real; no one denies that the highly significant, non-linguistic graphic systems reported by Boone are an integral part of the human condition. The systems Boone insightfully studies deserve our most careful attention. Nonetheless, it would be imprudent to ignore those written symbols intimately and inextricably connected to the spoken word: above all, the connection has a profound effect on such signs. The development of syllabaries and alphabets, the special nature of logographs in written systems, the emergence of morphophonemic writing, and markedness relationships deserve thoughtful study and explanation. Furthermore, careful comparison and contrast of written language along with other graphic systems can only help refine our understanding of all permanently recorded systems.
4. Boltz (1996) says essentially the same thing: "No character ever stood for an 'idea' independently of a word. Chinese characters stood, and continue to stand, for words, and only by extension for the ideas those words convey." Although Boltz says "the word 'ideogram' (or 'ideograph') is thus inapplicable to Chinese characters," I am using the term *ideograph* here to suggest the relationship that the written sign has with the object of *the spoken sign*, so that, in principle, Boltz and I agree. I am simply giving a different technical definition to the term *ideograph*. See below for further discussion.

5. There is a stage, not treated in this chapter, that Sampson (1985:28) calls "semasiography." Boone (this volume) describes a rich Mesoamerican tradition of such writing. The ideas contained in the semasiograph, however, are prelinguistic since they have no one-to-one correlation with any particular linguistic sign. The triangles given in Fig. 2.4, however, are proposed to be the prototype for writing, since they represent the visual connection to the linguistic sign – the linguistic name and object.
6. I became acquainted with this term in Boltz (1996:193).
7. I use the terms *pictograph* and *ideograph* in a technical sense to specify how the written term refers to the object of a spoken term. These terms are sometimes used to mean "reference to an idea independent of language," but for the purposes of this chapter I mean them to refer to language itself.
8. This is not to underestimate the iconic nature of logographs. Egyptian and Mayan, for example, retain a strongly iconic nature. It is still the case that when logographs change, it is almost inevitably in the direction: icon > symbol.
9. For a similar change from icon to symbol for Sumerian, see Sampson (1985:52). In this case, the change was largely owing to the medium of cuneiform, where the stylus in soft clay made the written sign less imagistic. Nonetheless, because language is essentially symbolic, it is quite natural that written signs should move from icon to symbol, whatever other ancillary causes might precipitate such changes.
10. Another possible limitation on logographs might be proper nouns. Proper nouns differ from common nouns in this: each person is unique and therefore requires a unique name, so it stands to reason that the object of a proper noun cannot be generalized. Conversely, all the possible referents of a given common noun are considered to be the same. Thus, the object of *John Smith* is ideally seen as a unique person, even if there is more than one person with that name, whereas the objects of the term *rooster* cannot be numbered. Therefore, a pictograph of a single object would have to be a portrait, which is obviously impractical; the restriction of one ideograph to a single object would be equally inefficient.
11. DeFrancis (1989) strongly makes the point that writing is not writing without a phonetic component, which I believe is true. On the other hand, he claims that depictive writing "is not protowriting nor a forerunner of full writing" (DeFrancis 1989:47). The place of acrophony in Mayan writing (from clearly iconic depictions), in Semitic writing, and apparently other newly developing written systems (see below for further discussion) seems to contradict this rather extreme assertion. Furthermore, the movement from icon to symbol (pictograph to ideograph – see note 7) suggests that pictography was an important genesis of first writing.
12. The term *phonographic* here refers to all referencing of the spoken sound, including rebus and phonological classifiers.
13. I thank Stephen Houston for this information.

3 | Writing systems: a case study in cultural evolution

BRUCE G. TRIGGER

Today the concept of sociocultural evolution is widely condemned as erroneous and unethical. It is asserted that, among its many shortcomings, it minimizes the extent of variability in human behavior, encourages acceptance of a mechanistic, ecological determinism, denies human agency, and ignores the symbolically mediated nature of cultures. It is also objected that it privileges change at the expense of stasis instead of treating both equally. Finally, sociocultural evolution is condemned for allegedly supporting a variety of right-wing political agendas, including economic exploitation, colonialism, disempowerment of ethnic minorities, and trying to naturalize patriarchy (Diamond 1974; Freidel, Schele, and Parker 1993; Giddens 1984; Johnson 1996; Mann 1986; McGaw 1996; Rowlands 1989; Shanks and Tilley 1987; for more on sociocultural evolution, Trigger 1998).

Since the decline of culture-historical archaeology in the 1960s, little attention has been paid to the study of innovation and diffusion (an exception is Barnett and Hoopes 1995). Neoevolutionism viewed cultural change as a response to external, ecological factors and assumed that people were able to use their powers of observation and reason to adapt in a relatively straightforward and unproblematical fashion to new conditions (Binford 1962; P. Watson, LeBlanc, and Redman 1971). Postprocessualism often focuses on traditions and cultural constraints and hence tends to emphasize stasis (Hodder 1991). As a result, neither approach has encouraged the empirical investigation of cultural innovation and the nature of cultural change, the study of which has become retarded by comparison with many other subjects of archaeological concern.

Grammatology, the study of writing systems, offers a useful way to evaluate evolutionary approaches to understanding change in cultural phenomena. Because of writing's role as a recording device, its development is historically better documented than is that of many forms of material culture. Writing, like languages and symbolic systems generally, requires an inner ordering to be effective. In a fully developed writing system, a finite, and hence learnable, set of symbols must be capable of recording an unlimited variety of utterances. Yet, as a form of technology, scripts are also subject to some degree of material constraint. Some systems may be more easily learned, written, or read than others and, as demands for the use of such systems grow and technologies for handling print communication diversify and change, such developments should favor the creation of more efficient writing systems (DeFrancis 1989:262–269; Rogers 1995; Sampson 1985:18–19).

Evolutionary grammatology

Writing has been associated with evolutionary theorizing since the eighteenth century. It has long been posited as the primary innovation distinguishing civilization from barbarism (Childe 1950; Gelb 1963:221; Goody 1986; Morgan 1907:12; Sjoberg 1960:32–34, 38). Yet writing, as distinguished from various other mnemonic devices of varying degrees of sophistication, such as knotted ropes (Ascher and Ascher 1981; Quilter and Urton 2002) and collections of tokens (Schmandt-Besserat 1992), was not present in the indigenous civilizations of Peru and West Africa. Nor was a system capable of recording connected speech present in the central highlands of Mexico at the time of the Spanish conquest. Yet it is impossible to maintain that the Inkas were not civilized while the Old Kingdom Egyptians were, or that the lowland Mayas, who possessed a fully developed writing system, were more advanced than the Aztecs, who did not. In ancient Egypt, Mesopotamia, China, and among the Mayas, writing was used variously to record economic transactions, convey messages, record ritual texts, celebrate the deeds of rulers, and preserve medical, calendrical, and divinatory knowledge (Postgate, Wang, and Wilkinson 1995). Yet, in these societies, even specialized knowledge remained closely linked to oral traditions, and distinctive literary forms and devices for organizing and conveying knowledge did not develop to any considerable degree until a much later period. For that reason writing's impact on thought in the early civilizations was much more limited than Jack Goody (1986, 1987:300) and others have proposed.

In a formal, organizational sense, writing has long been thought to develop through a unilinear evolutionary sequence. In the late nineteenth century, Isaac Taylor (1883, I:5–6) proposed that writing progressed from pictorial and then pictographic (semasiographic) communication, both of which used visible marks to express meaning without systematic reference to linguistic elements, through verbal (logographic) and syllabic forms of writing, to a final and supremely efficient alphabetic system. Taylor's scheme was systematized by Ignace Gelb (1963:205, 252), who linked it with his "Principle of Unidirectional Development" which postulated that all writing systems had to develop through these successive stages and that it was not possible for any system to reach a more advanced stage without having passed through all the preceding ones.

The logic underlying this scheme was the observation that phrases, morphemes (minimal meaningful semantic units: words or parts of words), syllables (speech segments consisting of consonants and accompanying vowels), and phonemes (minimal culturally meaningful units of sound) represent increasingly basic and esoteric levels of analysis but at the same time offer ever more efficient means by which to record speech. Linguists agree that it would be impossible to learn to read or write a script that had a separate sign for each sentence or phrase (Unger and DeFrancis 1995). On the other hand, it is believed that morphemes, or words, are more obvious units for recording speech than are sounds and that it is easier to invent symbols to represent many morphemes than it is to devise ways to represent either syllables or phonemes (Sampson 1985:36). Nevertheless, it is also recognized that, given the nature of language, it is impossible to represent speech without employing some purely phonetic elements (DeFrancis 1989). Therefore it is believed that scripts evolved from largely logographic beginnings in the direction of increasing reliance on writing sounds. It has also been assumed that, because it is easier for linguistically unsophisticated speakers to distinguish among syllables than among individual sounds, phonography moves through a syllabic phase to an alphabetic one. David Diringer (1962:17) has encoded the development of scripts in a Darwinian framework by arguing that the "struggle for survival" is the principal condition for the existence of a particular script and that, barring the "severe interference" of religious, cultural, or political factors, scripts will evolve in the direction of simplicity and utility. It is widely assumed that the basic principles of alphabetic writing, which have not changed for the last 2,500 years, represent the ultimate development of writing systems and that the adoption of this kind of script is necessary for civilization to enjoy "its full potentialities of progress" (Huxley 1960:30). In the nineteenth century, it was widely assumed that the Chinese and Japanese scripts, with their large numbers of logograms, made low levels of literacy inevitable and that their survival reflected the general inertia and backwardness of East Asian societies. It was frequently asserted that these societies would have to adopt alphabetic scripts as a precondition for modernization and industrialization. This argument has become increasingly hard to sustain as a result of the vast economic and social progress that has transformed China, and even more dramatically Japan, in the course of the twentieth century, but not induced them to abandon their traditional writing systems.

Yet unilinear evolutionary studies of scripts also displayed significant non-evolutionary tendencies. As late as the 1960s, it was widely assumed that all early scripts probably were derived from the Sumerian writing system that had developed in southern Iraq beginning in the late fourth millennium BC. The fact that this script appeared to have taken longer to develop than any other was interpreted as evidence that it had evolved locally (Gelb 1963:219; cf. Gaur 1987, 1995; Kroeber 1948:514; Pope 1966:23). It was argued that knowledge of writing had diffused along with various other cultural traits from Sumer to Elam, Egypt, the Indus Valley, and eventually Northern China, giving rise to the oldest scripts in each of those regions. The geographically remote Maya script, which was then undeciphered, was debarred from consideration by alleging that it was merely an example of semasiography, not writing (Gelb 1963:51–59). Often study was restricted to those scripts that clearly were related to ones that had originated in the Middle East (Pope 1966, 1975).

The Middle East also was lauded as the region where older and more cumbersome writing systems had evolved into the consonantary script that the Greeks in turn had transformed into a true alphabet by adding vowels. It was further suggested that, just as the idea of writing had been invented only once, so the alphabet had a single origin (Kroeber 1948:509). This diffusionist scenario corresponded with more general Eurocentric beliefs that, while Western civilization had begun in the Middle East, it had been perfected in Europe (Childe 1925; Montelius 1899). It also accorded with a long-standing idealization of Greece as a font of cultural perfection and the equating of major cultural achievements with Aryan, or Indo-European, peoples (M. Bernal 1987).

Various arguments, in addition to the claim that logographic scripts and alphabets each had a single origin, contradicted the evolutionary notion of gradual, parallel development in different parts of the world. It was also maintained that, because the effectiveness of a writing system depends on its systemic properties, writing would have had to develop rapidly and that the transformation from one type of script to another would have had to occur quickly (Boltz 1994:38; Michalowski 1996:35–36). Kurt Sethe (1939) argued that there was no evidence that a syllabary had ever evolved into an alphabet, as these are traditionally defined, and maintained that syllabic writing was an evolutionary blind alley. To counter this claim, Gelb maintained that the West Semitic consonantal scripts, from which the Greek alphabet was derived, were really syllabaries in which a consonant could be followed by any vowel. Thus, on the basis of a single example and a novel definition,

Gelb (1963:211) argued that "an alphabet could not develop from anything else but a syllabary."

Finally, much attention was paid to how scripts diffused from one culture to another. Most often an existing script was adapted to write another language. This might result in varying degrees of remodeling, but even when the changes were extensive the historical relations between the two scripts remained obvious. In other instances a new script might be devised by individuals who were familiar with an existing writing system but created one that either was based on different principles or at least did not visually resemble the original. In these cases some combinations of signs and meanings or sound values still tended to be shared, even if in general the scripts were functionally or formally dissimilar. Finally, there were examples of scripts devised by people who knew about writing but were themselves non-literate. These scripts, which constitute examples of what Alfred Kroeber (1940) called "stimulus diffusion," might copy signs from existing writing systems but without knowledge of their semantic meaning or phonetic values. The basic organizing principles of such scripts were also likely to bear little resemblance to those of the one being emulated. Gelb (1963:210–211) maintained that all such scripts had to be created at the semasiographic level but quickly evolved into syllabaries, which he regarded as the form of script ideally suited for "primitive societies."

A unilinear evolutionary approach to studying the development of writing uncritically incorporated many Eurocentric prejudices into untested deductive schemes concerning how this development ought to have occurred. These schemes were modified by concepts that were unrelated or antithetical to an evolutionary perspective, but seemed necessary to account for obvious discrepancies between evolutionary deductions and factual evidence. Other anti-evolutionary concepts represented agenda-driven efforts to impose still more Eurocentric prejudices on the study of writing. This mixture was typical of the uncritical approach that characterized most forms of what passed for sociocultural evolutionary thinking in past times (Trigger 1998).

Definitions and general concepts

There has been a long-standing disagreement about the definition of writing. A broad definition maintains that it is "a system of intercommunication by means of conventional visible marks" (Gelb 1963:253; Haas 1976; F. Salomon 2001; Sampson 1985), while a narrower one restricts writing to being "a system of more or less permanent marks used to represent an utterance in such a way that it can be recovered more or less exactly without the intervention of the utterer" (Daniels 1996c:3). Those who define writing as the recording of speech refuse to recognize semasiography as writing (Bloomfield 1933:283; Coe 1992:13; DeFrancis 1989:20–64; Lounsbury 1989:203; Unger and DeFrancis 1995). It also has been denied that semasiography can develop into more complex writing systems (Daniels 1996c:3; DeFrancis 1989). This debate has grown more heated in recent years as a result of some Mesoamericanists seeking to have highland Mexican record-keeping accepted as writing (Boone and Mignolo 1994; Marcus 1992; M. Smith 1973). Next to whether or not speech is recorded, the most important difference between semasiography and glottography (speech recording) is that a particular semasiographic system can only record information about a specific domain, such as economic accounts or group histories, each of which employs its own conventions, while a system that represents language can record information of any kind (DeFrancis 1989). Hence many maintain that semasiography lacks the generality required to qualify as a writing system.

A broad definition of writing is not inherently objectionable, provided that its use does not obscure important differences between various categories of writing. It would be counterproductive, for example, to ignore the differences between Aztec record-keeping, which did not record speech (although it recorded individual names), and the Maya writing system, which did so. In the seventeenth century, the Huron Indians of Canada left pictographic messages along trails reporting how many people were traveling, by what means, from what villages (identified by their symbols), and some of the problems they might be encountering (Wrong 1939:251–252). Yet they regarded the ability of the French to transmit precise verbal messages over long distances by means of writing as being wholly different from anything they themselves could do (Thwaites 1896–1901, XVII:135). The Peruvians reacted similarly to Spanish writing (Classen 1993:125–128). It therefore might be more informative to refer to semasiography as *recording* and reserve the term *writing* for systems that represent language.

No writing system (thus defined) records all the linguistic structure of speech. Few have developed means for systematically noting the tone, stress, pitch, speed, or loudness of specific utterances. Logographic writing omits the phonemic structure of speech, and phonographic writing may omit vowels and fail to distinguish various classes of consonants. Phonographies also represent morphemes with varying degrees of conventionality (Daniels 1996c:11–12). In general, linguistic detail is sacrificed in order to enhance the efficacy with which writing achieves its primary goal, which is to record morphemes, or words, in the order in which they are strung together to form phrases and sentences.

A writing system must be capable of being learned, written, and read with reasonable efficiency. Success in achieving one of these goals does not necessarily imply success in achieving the other two. A limited number of signs must be able to record with minimum ambiguity a limitless number of utterances. Speech can be represented at the morphemic, syllabic, or phonetic level (Rogers 1995:36). The impossibility of using a writing system that would employ a different sign for every different thought ties developed writing systems to the spoken word. Even a logographic script, however, could not handle a different sign for each word, or even morpheme, without a considerable amount of cipherability that relates signs to the spoken language (Unger and DeFrancis 1995:53). This requires incorporating a phonographic element into the script. Hence logographic scripts must always be logophonic, or more precisely morphophonic (morphemic + phonetic signs), ones (DeFrancis 1989:58; A. Hill 1967).

With purely phonographic scripts, representing the phonemic rather than the more extensive phonetic properties of language reduces the number of signs that are required without sacrificing intelligibility. On the other hand, having fewer signs than are needed to approximate the phonemic structure of a language creates problems. The use of single letters to represent more than one consonant in the early modern Arabic script, which resulted from the Arabic language having more consonants than did the Aramaic language from which its script was derived, eventually required adding dots to distinguish various consonants (Bauer 1996:559). Likewise, the reduction of some versions of the Scandinavian futhark, or runic alphabet, from twenty-four to sixteen letters, beginning in the eighth century AD, led to the development of "pointed" or "dotted" runes to restore clarity (Elliott 1996:336). While it is assumed that alphabetic scripts generally seek to represent the spoken language as closely as possible, the desire to promote easier reading, accommodate dialect variation, and preserve access to records of earlier periods encourages logographic tendencies in such scripts. In English the shared morpheme in *photograph/er* and *photograph/ic* is written but not pronounced in the same manner. Contrariwise, the words *blew* and *blue* or *right* and *rite* are pronounced the same but their semantic difference is emphasized by their being spelled differently. Noam Chomsky and M. Halle (1968) maintain that such deviations from a purely phonemic representation of spoken English enhance the intelligibility of written English. In phonographic systems there is an enduring tension between pure phonemicism and stressing morphemes.

There are also few, if any, pure scripts. Terms such as *logophonic*, *syllabic*, and *alphabetic* refer to a script's predominant organizing principles. They do not exclude the presence of other forms of recording information. Semasiography abounds in modern Western societies alongside alphabetic writing. As a result of growing multilingualism in cosmopolitan centers, signs that regulate traffic, indicate how to assemble and use equipment, zone smoking, and denote gendered washrooms have become increasingly semasiographic in form (Sampson 1985:30–32). Numerals also constitute an internally highly ordered semasiographic system that can be read in any language. Logograms are used to write words such as *and* (&) or *dollar/dollars* ($). Many of the problems encountered in classifying scripts result from the deductive manner in which such classifications have been conceptualized in accordance with evolutionary preconceptions. As a consequence, stages in the development of scripts have been distinguished in too absolute a fashion and different types of scripts have been merged to form convenient but deceptive evolutionary types: the latter process being most evident in the omnibus use of the term *alphabet* (Diringer 1962; Kroeber 1948). As a result of both tendencies significant variation has been overlooked. On the other hand, cross-cultural regularities have been detected in writing systems that are too specific to be considered in this general survey (Justeson 1976).

Historical survey

This section traces the development of writing systems, paying particular attention to their specific organizing principles and historical relations. By moving forward in time following actual lines of development, we seek to avoid imposing a theory-derived deductive structure on this presentation.

Semasiography

Whether or not it is classified as writing, semasiography (Gelb's descriptive-representational and identifying-mnemonic devices) has been practised in many parts of the world and in societies at many levels of development. Its principal feature is the use of pictograms or ideograms to represent ideas. A pictogram has a specific meaning but this meaning can be expressed verbally in many ways (Doblhofer 1973:15–29; Gelb 1963:11–12; Sampson 1985:28–30). Plains Indian year lists represented the year 1876 by depicting the death of a long-haired American cavalry officer. This could be read as "The year Long-hair was killed by the Sioux," "The year we defeated

General Custer," or "When we won the battle of the Little Bighorn" (Nabokov 1996:39–41). Plains Indians also used pictograms to write personal names, such as Red Cloud, Big Bear, and Red-Horn Bull. Thus a logographic element was present even in some of the most rudimentary forms of recording. This supports Gelb's (1963:66) suggestion that the need to represent proper names encouraged the development of logography.

More advanced forms of what might be called "semasiologography" (Gelb's limited system) are found in highland Mesoamerican cultures and in Iraq and Egypt at the dawn of civilization. The Aztecs had professional scribes who produced elaborate barkcloth codices. In some of these books they used standardized symbols to record the migrations of families and ethnic groups and the births, marriages, and deaths of leading individuals. Other books recorded the tribute owing from various parts of the empire as well as divinatory information. The Aztecs also had a well-developed system for representing calendar dates. Nevertheless, their codices recorded ideas, not actual sequences of words. Verbal accounts had to be conveyed orally, while the pictograms served to refresh the transmittor's memory. Some pictograms were used as rebuses to suggest the names of people and places, but it is unclear how far the process of phoneticization had developed prior to the Spanish conquest. On the Tizoc Stone, which dates from the 1480s, the town of Tochpan was identified by a rabbit (*tochtli*) and Matlatzinco by a mat (*matatl*), but few phonetic sounds were added to specify even common secondary elements such as locatives and diminutives. Phoneticism may have increased in the late prehispanic Aztec recording of proper names and been more common in some neighboring regions of highland Mexico. There is, however, no evidence of standardization in the writing of abstract concepts (Nicholson 1973:5–6).

An analogous situation is found with proto-cuneiform texts, which begin to appear in southern Iraq about 3400 BC. These texts used signs to itemize goods, names, and quantities but phonetic complementation was rare and for several centuries no attempt was made to record speech or even to present information in a specific (grammatical) order (DeFrancis 1989:214–216; Nissen 1986; Cooper, Englund, this volume). It was only around 2900 BC that homophony began to play a significant role in extending the range of concepts that could be recorded and not until *c.* 2400 BC that the Sumerians wrote extended texts with spoken language determining the order of signs. Even then vital grammatical elements that native speakers of Sumerian could supply from context were often omitted (J. Bottéro 1992:80; Cooper 1996:37, 43, and this volume; Nissen, Damerow, and Englund 1993:123; Sampson 1985:50).

In southern Egypt, probably around 3300 BC, royal officials attached to at least the most powerful ruler in that region began to use signs to keep records of goods. Small bone and ivory tags from tomb U-j at Abydos, which is dated *c.* 3250 BC, appear to employ phonetic (rebus) signs as well as logograms (Baines, this volume; Davies and Friedman 1998:35–38). Thus, when it is first attested, the Egyptian recording system seems to have been more advanced in the devices that it employed than was the Mesopotamian one. Semasiologography continued to be used by Egyptian royal officials to record personal names, toponyms, the contents of containers, and, in an increasingly mnemonic fashion, the events of particular years. John Baines has concluded that continuous speech began to be recorded in the late Second and the early Third Dynasties, *c.* 2700 BC. Around that time signs were also standardized and their number greatly reduced. While Egyptians may have begun to use semasiologography later than the Sumerians, they appear to have developed an effective writing system about the same time as, or even ahead of, their Iraqi neighbors (Baines 1983:574–577, and this volume; Ray 1986).

The Maya script appears to have evolved from the same Olmec(oid) recording system (1140–400 BC) that gave rise to Isthmian writing and the semasiographic systems of highland Mexico. Maya texts, consisting of glyphs with minimal syntactical transparency and syllabic context appear in the archaeological record between 100 BC and AD 150. Shortly thereafter pronouns began to be represented, making it clear that a Maya language was being recorded. Syllabograms appeared by the beginning of the Early Classic period (*c.* AD 250, Houston, ch. 10, this volume).

There is no evidence that, at the time of the Spanish conquest, highland Mesoamerican semasiologographic recording, which had been employed for a long time, was evolving in the direction of a logophonic system. Only for noting proper names was there sometimes a tie between signs and specific languages (Houston, ch. 10, this volume). On the other hand, in Iraq and Egypt analogous recording systems evolved into true writing systems over the course of 1,000 and 600 years respectively. It is salutary to remember that the early stages of Sumerian and Egyptian recording were basically similar in type to that of highland Mexico, with no effort being made to write phrases or sentences. Yet, for Iraq and Egypt, this early recording has habitually been referred to as writing, while for highland Mesoamerica until recently the term *writing* was generally avoided. This has given the impression that the recording of speech developed earlier in Iraq and Egypt than it actually did and has diverted attention from two examples of semasiologographic recording systems evolving into true writing. While Sampson (1985:49) has argued that Archaic Sumerian was logophonic because its signs appear to have stood for elements of a spoken language, he concedes that in the absence of full sentences or significant rebusing "the distinction between semasiography and logographic writing tends to dissolve." The Sumerian and Egyptian examples indicate not only that logophonic writing systems can develop from semasiographic recording but also that this development need not be rapid. The theory of the rapid origin of writing erred in assuming that, to be useful, recording systems had from the beginning to be able to record everything (Boltz 1986:432; Michalowski 1996:35–36). The latter was an emergent property of systems that at first had recorded information about highly delimited subject matters.

Logophonic scripts

Four early scripts that represented the spoken word are understood well enough to be compared. These are the writing systems of the Sumerians, Egypt, Shang China, and the Mayas of Mexico and Central America. All of them were based on generally similar principles. Signs represented both words or morphemes (logograms) and sounds (syllabograms or phonograms), while in all but the Maya script taxograms that had no sound values were used to classify words. In these scripts only the taxograms stood for "ideas" independently of language. Chinese has four characters each of which signifies a different word meaning *red*. Since these terms do not refer to different varieties of red, a recording system that was semasiographic rather than logophonic would have needed only one character (Sampson 1985:149). Logograms that stood for words that could be represented easily (sometimes called "zodiographs" [Boltz 1994:33, 54]) were extended semantically to represent more abstract concepts. In ancient Egyptian a circle representing *r'* ("sun") was also used to write "day" ("hrw"). Such signs were also expanded phonetically, or in rebus fashion, to indicate homonyms or near-homonyms: Egyptian *nb* ("basket") was also used to write *nb* ("lord"). To reduce the resulting uncertainty about which reading was intended, semantic extensions were often supplied with phonetic complements that provided clues to their pronunciation, while homonyms were distinguished by determinatives that indicated a general meaning class with which the word was associated (in Egyptian *nb* ["lord"] could be followed by the taxogram for "king") (Boltz 1994:12–13).

Despite these highly significant similarities, the four writing systems varied considerably from one another. The Sumerian script was a logosyllabic one. In general, signs were used logographically to write unbound morphemes, such as nouns, verbs, and adjectives, and syllabically to write bound morphemes, including grammatical particles and affixes, as well as to provide phonetic complements to clarify the readings of logograms. Sumerian syllables took the forms CV (consonant–vowel), V, VC, and CVC (which often was represented as CV + VC). By 2500 BC, Sumerian employed an informal syllabary of 100 to 150 signs as well as several hundred logograms and taxograms (Cooper 1996:37–45).

Ancient Egyptian, by contrast, was a logoconsonantal script. In its phonographic notation vowels were omitted. This was facilitated by ancient Egyptian being an Afroasiatic language in which semantic meaning was expressed largely through consonants and grammatical meaning by means of vowels; hence native speakers normally could supply vowels from context. Most Egyptian words contained one to three consonants and a consonantary was developed consisting of 26 signs representing single consonants (uniliterals), about 80 signs representing two successive consonants (biliterals), and approximately 70 signs representing three successive consonants (triliterals; Ritner 1996a). In the Middle and New Kingdoms special forms of full or group writing, which sought to represent vowels as well as consonants, were used to transcribe foreign names. In both periods a few consonant signs were routinely employed to represent essential vowels in Egyptian that were difficult to predict from context (Allen 2000:220–221; Gelb 1963:168–171). The ancient Egyptians made extensive use of their consonantary to provide phonetic complements for logograms. Throughout most of Egyptian history about 700 signs were used at any one time.

The Chinese script first appears in the late Shang period, around 1200 BC, and is assumed to have been created about that time. Li Chi (1977:170) suggested that the absence of evidence of earlier Shang writing results from the failure of inked (as opposed to engraved) inscriptions to survive on oracle bones. Nevertheless, the absence of earlier inscriptions on bronze vessels supports Boltz's (1999:108) view that the Chinese script probably began to be used not long before its earliest archaeological attestation. While there is no evidence of semasiography in the immediately preceding Erligong and Erlitou periods, it has been suggested that series of graphs etched onto the sides of pottery vessels from the Dawenkou culture of Shandong province, dating from c. 2500–2000 BC, may mark an early stage in the development of the Chinese writing system. Most scholars do not accept marks found incised or painted on pottery vessels of the Yangshao culture, as early as the fifth millennium BC, or even earlier signs engraved on shell and bone, as parts of a true recording system (Hsu and Linduff 1988:6–7; Li Xueqin *et al.* 2003).

Chinese writing is often described as purely logographic because it provides a separate character for each morpheme. Thus every homonym is represented by a different sign. When the script is first attested, the vast majority of translated characters, numbering about 1,000, represented single morphemes, often in recognizable pictorial form. Yet, as a result of the use of both phonetic and semantic extensions to represent more abstract words, it was necessary to supply clues to pronunciation and meaning in order to maintain the intelligibility of characters. This was done by combining simple characters to create compound ones, one part of which provided a clue to pronunciation, the other an indication of meaning. Gradually the semantic classifying element (or radical) came to be written on the left side of the character and the phonetic indicator on the right (Boltz 1999; F. Bottéro, this volume).

The fact that most words in Early Chinese were monosyllabic meant that there were no syllables and hence no characters without semantic meaning. In the Han period, however, scribes began to use alternative homophonous signs to write the same word, thus moving in the direction of syllabic writing. This trend was arrested by imposing semantic classifiers on all characters to ensure that they remained logographic. Thereafter, a limited subset of characters (many otherwise obsolete) were used phonetically only to transliterate foreign words (Sampson 1985:166–167). The practical reasons for opposing phoneticization are said to have been the increasing homophony of spoken Chinese and the growth of dialects in the Han period. It also has been argued that phoneticization was opposed because it was viewed as threatening a highly valued cultural order in which writing and speech were symbolically dichotomized (Boltz 1994:170–177). Despite the triumph of logography, 66 percent of the characters used to write modern Mandarin are described as "functionally syllabograms" and 99 percent offer some phonetic specification for their reading (Unger and DeFrancis 1995:52). Because of that, the Chinese writing system has been described not inappropriately as a huge, but imprecise, syllabary as well as a logography. Although about 50,000 characters are listed in dictionaries, 2,400 suffice to write 99 percent of all words (Boltz 1986, 1994).

The Maya script was logosyllabic. It used a large number of logograms to write nouns, verbs, and other unbound morphemes, and a relatively compact CV syllabary to write affixes, to clarify the reading of multivocal logograms, and sometimes to replace logograms. While the Maya script had approximately 800 signs, some 150 of which had a syllabic function, only 200 to 300 of these signs were actively employed at any one time (Coe 1992:262; Justeson 1989).

Each of these early writing systems systematized the use of signs to record speech. To do this, it was necessary to devise ways to represent sound patterns as well as morphemes. Yet these four scripts exhibit radical variations in the way this was accomplished. The two most functionally similar are Sumerian and Maya, both of which are logosyllabic. Yet they are the most widely separated in time and space and differ radically in their formal properties. While it has been suggested that there is some evidence of Sumerian influence on the formation of a few Egyptian signs (Baumgartel 1955:48; Diringer 1962:47; A. Spencer 1993:61–62), it is now evident that Egyptian recording began while Sumerian was still at a semasiologographic stage. Moreover, the overall organization of Egyptian as a logoconsonantal script is very different from that of Sumerian. At most, influences from Iraq might have had a minor effect on the development of Egyptian writing, although it is not clear how or when this would have occurred. The Chinese script is unique in its enduring adherence to the principle that each character must have semantic value. Despite its appearance of formidable complexity, the structure of Maya writing was more economical than that of the other three. These differences not only suggest the separate construction of these scripts but caution against following Gelb (1963) and Daniels (1996b:585) in labeling all of them "logosyllabic."

There are a number of other logophonic scripts that could have been original inventions or derived by stimulus diffusion from Sumerian or Egyptian prototypes. These include proto-Elamite (Englund 1996, this volume; Vallat 1986), the Indus script (Parpola 1986, 1996), Cretan Hieroglyphic (Bennett 1996; Olivier 1986) and Hittite Hieroglyphs, which were used to write Luwian (Hawkins 1986; Melchert 1996). The last two scripts may be historically connected. Other logophonic scripts in Western Asia were directly or indirectly derived from Sumerian writing, as it was adapted to write other languages. In general, these scripts exhibit fewer logographs and a greater reliance on syllabic writing.

The first of these adaptations was the Old Akkadian script, which recorded the Semitic language of Iraq beginning in the third millennium BC and developed into the cuneiform systems that later were used to write Babylonian and Assyrian. Old Akkadian developed about the same time that proto-cuneiform was being perfected for writing Sumerian. While Sumerian cuneiform remained heavily logographic and made limited use of phonography, in Akkadian almost any word could be written phonographically or logographically, as individual scribes preferred. In discursive texts of all kinds logography rarely exceeded 15 percent (Cooper 1996:52). Moreover, relations between sounds and graphs grew more complex as Sumerian logographs and even words written syllabically in Sumerian were used logographically to write Akkadian equivalents. The values of syllabograms also became increasingly multivalent as Akkadian-derived sound values were added to existing Sumerian ones. This made taxograms more important for specifying correct readings. Yet, at most periods Akkadian scribes used only 200 to 300 signs, while a scholar at the Assyrian court might have had to know the syllabic and/or logographic values of approximately 600 signs (Cooper 1996:45–57; Nissen *et al.* 1993:117–118; Sampson 1985:56–57). Still later, cuneiform scripts derived from Old Akkadian or Neo-Assyrian, such as Elamite, Hurrian, and Urartian, used a reduced number of logograms and far more limited and systematically organized syllabaries. However, Hittite cuneiform, which recorded an Indo-European language, maintained many of the complexities of Akkadian (Gragg 1996).

Chinese was used as a written language by various neighboring peoples who did not speak Chinese. Some of these groups created logographic, Siniform scripts, resembling Chinese but employing distinctive characters, to write their own languages. The Tangut script, introduced in AD 1036 to write a Tibeto-Burman language of present northwestern China, had approximately 6,600 characters (Kychanov 1996) and the Yi script of southwestern China is estimated to have used 8,000 to 10,000 (Shi 1996). The Kitan and Jurchin of Manchuria made use of syllabograms and phonemic symbols in addition to logograms to write their languages (Kara 1996b).

As the Chinese script was adapted to write Japanese words and then the structurally very different Japanese language, characters (*kanji*) derived from Chinese writing were given both *on*-readings, based on their pronunciation in numerous Chinese loan-words, and *kun*-readings, representing the corresponding morpheme in Japanese. In the ninth century, two stylistically different syllabaries (*kana*), which eventually were standardized at forty-nine signs each, were derived from the *kanji*. Each syllabary would have been sufficient by itself to write Japanese. Since then *kanji* have been used to write nouns, verbs, and adjectives, as well as some adverbs, while *kana* are used to write particles, auxiliary verbs, and grammatical elements and to annotate *kanji*. At present about 2,000 *kanji* are being used regularly (Sampson 1985:172–193; J. Smith 1996). The Koreans added specifically Korean meanings and readings to Chinese characters and invented new Siniform ones to render native Korean words but Chinese writing continued to dominate Korean high culture into the twentieth century (King 1996; Sampson 1985:120–144).

In Iraq, Egypt, China, and Mesoamerica, logophonic systems, once established, tended to persist unchanged in their general principles over long periods. None of these scripts showed signs of evolving into a purely phonographic one. Nor did the Maya script have any significant impact on neighboring recording systems. On the other hand, in both Western Asia and East Asia, most scripts derived from, or modeled on, the Sumerian and Chinese ones made greater use of phonographic techniques for representing speech and less use of logographic ones than did the parent writing systems. Gelb (1963:196) maintains that "in all cases it was the foreigners who were not afraid to break away from sacred traditions and were thus able to introduce reforms which led to new and revolutionary developments." Likewise Kroeber (1948:517) has argued that, even if the ancient Egyptians had realized that they could have written their language using only uniliterals, they would have been unwilling to discard 96 percent of their writing system. East Asian secondary scripts have adhered to Chinese cultural values by continuing to place far more emphasis on logography than is the case in western Asia and Europe. While Japan has had a potentially self-sufficient syllabic script for over 1,000 years, *kanji* have not been abandoned and in recent decades the use of such signs has been increasing.

Phonographic scripts

Historical evidence indicates that scripts that relied almost wholly upon the representation of sounds to record speech appeared later than logophonic ones. Gelb (1963) assumed that the elimination of the logographic element in scripts produced syllabaries and these in turn gave rise to the alphabet. Yet, in addition to the historical problems with this position, the conventional dichotomy between syllabaries and alphabets tends to exaggerate the differences among phonographic scripts. From Roman times into the nineteenth century reading and spelling were taught syllabically rather than alphabetically; hence it could be argued that alphabets were regarded merely as an economical way of writing syllables (Justeson and Stephens 1993:4–6). On the other hand, the classification of phonographic scripts now recognizes at least four different types: (1) syllabaries, in which signs denote particular syllables and there are no systematic graphic resemblances among characters representing phonetically similar syllables; (2) consonantaries, or *abjads*, in which the signs indicate individual consonants only; (3) alphabets, in which the signs denote individual, usually phonemically significant, vowels and consonants; and (4) alphasyllabaries, or *abugidas*, where each sign denotes a consonant accompanied by a specific vowel (usually *a*) and other vowels are denoted by systematic modifications of the signs (Daniels 1996c:4).

There are no clear examples of a functioning syllabic script, as defined above, developing directly from a logophonic one. Mycenaean Greek Linear B was a syllabic script and the earlier Minoan Linear A appears to have been also, although Linear A texts have not been deciphered. Linear A may have developed from Cretan Hieroglyphic but there is no proof of this (Olivier 1986). Neither Linear B nor the related Cypriot syllabary that was used to write Greek between 800 and 200 BC gave rise to any later scripts (Bennett 1996). Japanese writing provides an example of a potentially self-sufficient syllabary being derived from a logophonic script but this did not result in the elimination of logograms. While Japanese writing is often called a "mixed system" (Sampson 1985), it can be classified more economically as a logosyllabic one with a highly regular and comprehensive syllabary (Coe 1992:264).

On the other hand, when scripts are devised by non-literate groups who have come into contact with peoples who use alphabets or consonantaries, these new writing systems often take the form of syllabaries. A number of scripts of this sort were devised by aboriginal North Americans during the nineteenth century, most notably the Cherokee syllabary invented by Sequoah, a non-literate Indian silversmith, in 1824. Syllabaries inspired by the Roman alphabet were also produced to write the Woleaian language of the Caroline Islands beginning in 1905 and the Ndjuka creole language of Surinam before 1916. Several syllabaries were invented in the nineteenth and twentieth centuries by West Africans who had been in contact with people using the Arabic consonantary (Daniels 1996a; Justeson and Stephens 1993:7–9, 10–21; Scancarelli 1996; Shingler 1996; Walker 1996). While some of these scripts went through brief periods of experimentation with semasiography and logography before developing into syllabaries, not all did. This disproves Gelb's (1963:206–211) assertion that scripts that arise as a result of stimulus diffusion must pass successively through all the stages through which scripts originally developed before they become syllabaries. It is now being argued that these syllabaries arose as a result of non-literate individuals misconstruing the recitation of the names of letters of alphabets or consonantaries as indicating that these letters stood for syllables (Justeson and Stephens 1993). An early example of this appears to be the syllabic portion of the Iberian scripts that developed in the seventh century BC following Phoenician contact with Spain (Justeson and Stephens 1993:21–30; Swiggers 1996a). Yet, while syllabaries appear to have been devised among numerous groups who were superficially exposed to alphabets or consonantaries but did not understand their basic principles, there is no evidence that syllabic scripts constitute an intermediate stage in the development of writing between logographic systems and purely phonemic ones.

Consonantaries were invented among the Semitic-speaking peoples of the Middle East beginning in the Middle Bronze Age (2000–1525 BC) and were increasingly used in the Late Bronze (1525–1200 BC) and Iron Ages (after 1200 BC). The earliest well-documented example of this type of writing is a cuneiform script consisting of 30 freely invented letters that were used to record the West Semitic language spoken at Ugarit, Syria, in the fifteenth and fourteenth centuries BC. By the beginning of the Iron Age, various poorly attested linear consonantaries dating from as early as 1700 BC had given rise to a cluster of Northern Linear consonantaries of approximately 22 letters that were used to write Phoenician, Old Hebrew, and other West Semitic languages, and to a very different 28-letter south linear consonantary that was used to write North and South Arabic and eventually Ge'ez, a Semitic language spoken in Ethiopia. In these systems each sign represented a single consonant. While the southern linear consonantaries retained a purely consonantal structure, between the ninth and fifth centuries BC the northern scripts began to use the consonants `aleph, `ayin, waw, and yodh to indicate the presence of long vowels. The majority of vowels continued, however, to be omitted. Because so many vowels are not specified, a reader must be familiar with words in advance in order to read them correctly (O'Connor 1996).

It is unknown precisely where in the Levant this form of writing developed, and whether it was invented once or several times. Its creators were almost certainly West Semitic speakers. A consonantal script was suitable for a language in which, as in ancient Egyptian, consonants indicated most of the semantic meaning, while vowels expressed grammar and to a large degree could be inferred from context by native speakers. These consonantal scripts structurally resemble the uniliterals that were employed to indicate single consonants in ancient Egyptian writing, although the shape–sound combinations of the individual letters are totally different. It is possible that one or more individuals with a limited knowledge of ancient Egyptian used the idea of uniliterals to create a simple but comprehensive system for writing West Semitic languages. If so, they effected a radical simplification that seems never to have been contemplated by the ancient Egyptians (Millard 1986).

The Phoenician script gave rise to a distinctive Aramaic consonantary and by 700 BC this Semitic language and its writing system were established as the primary media of communication in the Middle East. Eventually both the Hebrew and North Arabic languages, which were already recorded using the Phoenician and South Linear consonantaries respectively, came to be written in their own versions of Aramaic script. Between AD 600 and 1000, Aramaic, Hebrew, and Arabic developed the use of specialized points or diacritics that could be written above or below consonants to indicate the correct pronunciation of all vowels that were not already indicated by consonants. Pointing was used mainly to resolve ambiguities and ensure the correct reading of religious texts. In secular contexts Arabic and Hebrew continue to be written as unpointed consonantaries (T. Bauer 1996; Daniels 1996a).

In due course Aramaic scripts were adapted for writing various non-Semitic languages of central Asia: Persian, Parthian, Sogdian, Bactrian, and Uyghur Turkic (Skjaervø 1996; Kara 1996a). The Hebrew script was used to write Ladino and Yiddish, as well as Judaeo-Arabic (Hary 1996). The Arabic script spread with Islam and was modified to write Persian, Pashto, Urdu, Sindi, Ottoman Turkish, Malay, and other languages (Kaye 1996). While these languages do not share the semantic privileging of consonants found in Semitic and other Afroasiatic languages, the scripts used to write them continue to underspecify vowels. In many languages using these three scripts, Arab, Hebrew, and Aramaic loan-words are written in their original, rather than their locally adapted, forms. Everywhere the Arabic script has been adopted to write local languages, the active use of the Arabic language and texts is closely associated with Islamic religious practices.

The first alphabet was developed among Greek speakers, probably between 800 and 775 BC. Close similarities in forms, names, and values of letters confirm that the Greek alphabet was derived from the Phoenician consonantary—letters that were not needed to write Greek consonants being used to write vowels, which in Greek, unlike Phoenician, occurred at the beginning of words (Swiggers 1996b; Voegelin and Voegelin 1961:63–65). In Archaic Greek writing, vowels were sometimes omitted postconsonantally when they were the same as the vowel following the consonant in that consonant's name (Justeson and Stephens 1993:5). Eventually, however, all vowels were indicated consistently. A western variant of the Greek alphabet was soon transmitted to Italy, where it was used to write numerous languages and its letters developed a new set of forms, names, and values (Bonfante 1996). Hereafter the Greek and Roman alphabets were to dominate European writing.

In ancient times the Greek alphabet spread east to provide writing systems for various languages in Asia Minor: Phrygian, Pamphylian and Sidetic, Lycian, Lydian, and Carian (Swiggers and Jenniges 1996). In the fourth century AD, the Greek alphabet was adapted for writing the final stage of the ancient Egyptian language, known as Coptic. This script continues to be used to record the liturgical language of the Coptic Church. Initially Greek alphabetic writing was employed to specify the pronunciation of magical names written in late ancient Egyptian ritual papyri (Ritner 1996b:287). Later, when it was used to record whole texts, it clarified the pronunciation of the large numbers of foreign names and terms that occur in Egyptian Christian literature. The abandonment of hieroglyphic and demotic writing marked a clear break with Egypt's pre-Christian past and soon made the reviled non-Christian literature of earlier times totally inaccessible. The Gothic alphabet, which was invented in the fourth century AD to write a Germanic language spoken in Eastern Europe, is now believed to have the Greek alphabet as its only source (Ebbinghaus 1996). The Armenian and Georgian alphabets were freely modeled on the Greek one at about the same time (Holisky 1996; Sanjian 1996). The Greek alphabet spread north with Orthodox Christianity and in its Cyrillic form was used to write a number of Slavic languages: Bulgarian, Macedonian, Serbian, Ukrainian, Belarusian, and Russian. More recently it was adapted to write a number of non-Slavic languages of the Soviet Union (Cubberley 1996).

The Roman alphabet was used with considerably less variation to write the vernacular languages of the Roman Catholic portions of medieval Europe and has since been spread around the world by European colonists and employed by Christian missionaries to record the languages of many non-literate peoples. A major exception to its latter use was the creation by missionaries in the nineteenth century of syllabaries to provide writing systems for various Canadian aboriginal languages – a development inspired by the rapid spread of literacy following the invention of the Cherokee syllabary (Gleason 1996; Nichols 1996).

A highly variant form of the Roman alphabet was the runic futhark, which is first attested in Denmark in the second century AD and spread into Britain, Norway, and Sweden, being used in some areas until the thirteenth century. While claims of autonomous origin were once made, formal parallels suggest that it was invented in Denmark by someone familiar with the Roman and one or more northern Italic alphabets (Elliot 1996; H. Williams, this volume). The Ogam alphabet, which is the earliest known writing system in Ireland, where it was used from the fifth to seventh centuries AD, appears to have been inspired by the Roman alphabet, but differs radically from it in the form, sound values, and sequences of letters (McManus 1996). It may have been based on less knowledge of the Roman alphabet than was the runic one. Both the runic and Ogam scripts seem particularly well suited for carving on wood and stone; a feature they both share with the

Aramaic-derived Turkic Orkhon script from eighth-century AD Mongolia (Kara 1996a:536–539).

Although it is frequently claimed that the alphabet was invented only once, this is not the case. Alphabets have been created as a result of the systematic addition of vowels to the Arabic script used to write the Kurdish, Kashmiri, and Uyghur languages (Kaye 1996:749, 753, 759). The Aramaic Uyghur script, which was likewise largely alphabetized, inspired the Mongolian alphabet and it in turn provided the basis for the Manchu alphabet created in AD 1599 (Kara 1996a:545–554). Nevertheless, in many languages for which it is important to specify vowels, alphabets have not replaced consonantaries.

The Korean Hankul script, promulgated in AD 1446 for the use of common people, is a phonemically based alphabet in which consonants and vowels are grouped to form syllable blocks that superficially resemble Chinese characters. While it has been suggested that the inventor of this script was aware of various forms of Mongolian phonographic writing, no available script offered a precedent for the high level of organization and the sophisticated phonological analysis incorporated into Hankul. Hankul continued to be regarded as a low-status script until the twentieth century, when a "mixed script" style emerged in which morphemes of Chinese origin continued to be written in Chinese characters while native Korean words and grammatical endings were written in Hankul. Students in South Korea still learn approximately 1,800 logograms (King 1996:219–226; Sampson 1985:120–144).

I have found no evidence of alphabets giving rise to consonantaries or any other form of writing, except in situations of stimulus diffusion when they have sometimes inspired the development of syllabaries or complex semasiographies. In Egypt, alphabetic writing was replaced by a consonantary, but only when the Coptic language was superseded by Arabic. Today, in Tajikistan the Cyrillic alphabet is being challenged by the Arabic consonantary as a consequence of Islamic nationalism, while in some other former Soviet republics it is threatened with replacement by the Turkish or Roman alphabets (Comrie 1996:783–784).

There are four documented inventions of alphasyllabaries. Old Persian cuneiform, which appears to have been devised for the trilingual inscription of Darius I (550–486 BC) at Bisitun, used twenty-two signs to signify consonants followed by the letter *a*, and three vowels to write *a*, *i*, or *u* in word-initial position, long *a*, and *i* or *u* following any consonant (in which case the *a* that inherently followed the consonant was suppressed). Nine consonants took a different form before *i*, *u*, or both. Old Persian also employed seven logograms and a word divider. This script is thought to have been devised by individuals familiar with the Aramaic consonantary and the Ionic Greek alphabet (Justeson and Stephens 1993:30–36; Testen 1996).

Of much greater historical importance are the South Asian and Southeast Asian scripts derived from Brahmi, which was in use in Sri Lanka and India at least as early as the fourth or fifth centuries BC (Allchin 1995:176–179, 209–216, 335–337; Coningham *et al.* 1996). Some Indian scholars maintain that the Brahmi and closely related Kharoshthi writing systems are of wholly Indian origin and may be derived from the Indus script. Similarities in shapes and sound values between letters in the Aramaic and Kharoshthi scripts, and to a lesser degree in Brahmi, indicate knowledge of Aramaic writing, perhaps derived from Middle Eastern merchants. Nevertheless, the highly distinctive principles that structure these Indian scripts and the extremely systematic development of their sign forms suggest that Brahmi and Kharoshthi were elaborated by Indian scholars. Both scripts consist of a set of basic signs representing consonants and consonant clusters followed by the vowel *a*. These signs are modified by diacritics to represent consonants followed by other vowels or by no vowel. Although the basis of these scripts is an *aksara*, or graphic syllable, the syllables are composed of alphabetic units (Justeson and Stephens 1993:9–10; R. Salomon 1996). While Kharoshthi was used only in what is now Pakistan and eastern Afghanistan and died out in ancient times, Brahmi became the source of the indigenous scripts used to write all the languages of South Asia, as well as many in Tibet, Central Asia, and Southeast Asia (Burmese, Karen, Shan, Mon, Khmer, Thai, Lao, Malay, Javanese, and some Philippine languages [Daniels and Bright 1996:384–484]). Brahmi thus constitutes one of the major "parent" scripts of the world. In the course of its spread, the phonology and writing styles, but not the basic principles, of the script have varied considerably.

The third alphasyllabary is the Meroitic script, which was created in the Sudan in the third century BC to write the principal language of the kingdom of Kush. This script was developed from the Egyptian full or group writing that the Meroites previously had used to write names and words from their own language in texts that they composed in ancient Egyptian. They employed fifteen signs to represent consonants followed by *a*; four to indicate *e*, *i*, and *o* after consonants, as well as word-initial *a*; four to write specific syllables; and a word divider. This was the most economical of all the alphasyllabaries, using a total of only twenty-four signs (Justeson and Stephens 1993:39–40; Priese 1973).

The final alphasyllabary was developed in Ethiopia in the fourth century AD from the South Arabian consonantary that was used to write Ge'ez.

As the number of people who used Ge'ez as a second language increased and more specification of vowels became desirable, the consonantary was turned into an alphasyllabary by using each of the basic letters to represent a consonant plus *a* and adding diacritics to these basic signs to represent consonants followed by other vowels. This writing system later was used to record other Ethiopian languages, including Amharic (Haile 1996).

These four alphasyllabaries, despite their similar organizing principles, cannot be traced back to a common source. Two (Old Persian and South Asian) were developed by scholars who appear to have been familiar with the Aramaic consonantary and it has been suggested that the idea of an alphasyllabary might have been transmitted from India to Ethiopia in the context of the extensive sea trade between those two regions (Justeson and Stephens 1993:10). The Meroitic script developed too late to have been inspired by Persian sources during the Persian occupation of Egypt. Three of these systems represent efforts to supply vowels to new scripts that were being created with consonantaries as a model. The fourth appears to have resulted from extending a specialized syllabary used to write individual Meroitic words to write the whole language.

Discussion

We can now consider to what extent the development of writing displays some sort of evolutionary patterning. Since the earliest recording by means of visible signs, new writing systems have been created on the basis of varying degrees of knowledge of existing ones. Hence comparing various sequences provides an optimal basis for generalizing about the evolution of writing (Fig. 3.1).

It is now clear that, contrary to what was once widely believed, writing had multiple origins and developed in a far from unilinear fashion. Of the four best-known early writing systems (there may have been a few others), at least three (Sumerian, Shang Chinese, and Maya) appear to have developed completely independently of one another. While Sumerian writing may have influenced the early development of the ancient Egyptian system, these two scripts are based on significantly different principles and evolved slowly in separate cultural contexts. While four independent, or nearly independent, cases do not constitute a large sample of early scripts, comparing them permits more effective generalization about how such scripts were conceived than would be possible if all of them stemmed from a common source.

Semasiography, or the use of signs as mnemonic devices to represent ideas, is widespread in small-scale societies. Some of these societies also use signs

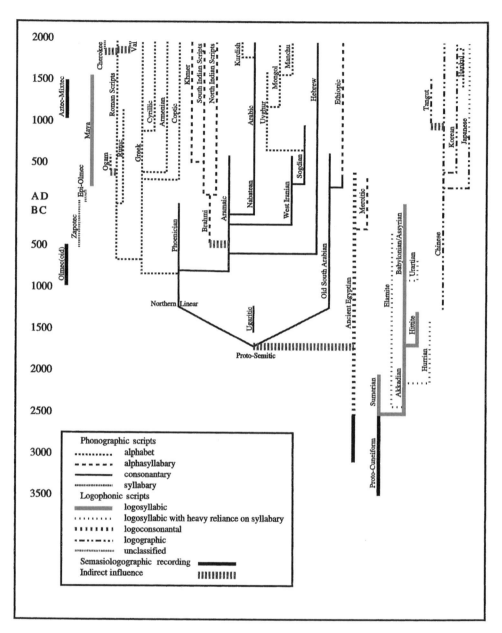

Fig. 3.1 Some historical relations among script types.

logographically to record names. A particular semasiographic system (more than one of which may be used simultaneously) is limited to recording information about a specific cultural domain. Since such systems record mainly ideas rather than language, their interpretation requires learning in advance and remembering what information was encoded.

As societies grew more complex, some (but not all) developed more systematic semasiologographies to record various categories of information, including numerical data. Some of these systems employed logograms more extensively and extended their use phonetically to clarify readings and record aspects of speech that were difficult to represent logographically. As this occurred, some semasiologographies evolved into writing systems that were capable of recording languages. The now well-documented development of Sumerian-Akkadian and ancient Egyptian writing demonstrates that semasiologographic recording can evolve into logophonic writing systems, but not apparently directly into phonographic ones. This suggests that in the evolution of writing systems the representation of words has cognitive priority over the representation of sounds (Daniels 1996b:585). The argument that semasiographic systems are not forerunners of writing is true only in the sense that systems that record speech are derived from the originally quite restricted logographic, rather than from the mnemonic, components of semasiologographic systems. All comprehensive writing systems are irreversibly committed to the representation of speech.

While each of the early writing systems came to record speech by expanding the use of its signs both semantically and phonetically, the reduction of ambiguity required the extensive use of phonetic indicators. Because of that, these scripts are often called logosyllabic, following Gelb. Gelb's usage disguises, however, the variation inherent in the ways phonetic representation was achieved in these scripts. Two of them, Sumerian and Maya, did use numerous signs to record syllables. Ancient Egyptian, however, disregarded vowels and concentrated on representing consonants, thus producing a logoconsonantary. Chinese created a separate character for each morpheme but to render such a script manageable had to incorporate phonetic indicators into most characters. Chinese is best described as a logographic system with a systematically built-in phonetic component.

It has been suggested that logophonic writing is most likely to develop for languages that have many single-syllable morphemes and much morphemic homophony, such as Chinese and Sumerian, or basic root forms that are readily isolatable, such as Egyptian and Maya (Daniels 1996b:585; Justeson 1986:451–452). It has also been proposed that only an uninflected language, such as Chinese, is likely to be written in a primarily logographic script (Sampson 1985:148). Such arguments do not, however, appear to explain why the Inka or Yoruba did not develop scripts or why Aztec recording remained at the semasiologographic level (Rogers 1995:37–38).

Scripts that are wholly or predominantly phonographic developed later than logophonic ones. It also appears that phonographic scripts did not develop without some knowledge of existing logophonic ones. Finally, three of the four well-known logophonic systems were eventually replaced by already established phonographic scripts. There also seems to be a general tendency for writing systems to become less logographic and more phonographic when they are used to write new languages. This was true for Akkadian by comparison with Sumerian and still more so for most of the cuneiform scripts that were derived directly or indirectly from Akkadian to write non-Semitic languages. The disjuncture between Egyptian writing and the West Semitic consonantaries that it may have inspired was even greater. In East Asia logographic writing has remained extremely important, dominating Chinese writing to the present and still playing a major role in Korean and Japanese scripts, alongside a locally invented alphabet in Korea and syllabaries in Japan.

Despite these trends, there is no evidence that a well-developed logophonic script ever evolved directly into a predominantly phonographic one. Ancient Egyptian hieroglyphic writing, which utilized about 700 signs in the Middle Kingdom, became more esoteric in the Greco-Roman period (332 BC – AD 400), when its signs increased until they numbered over 5,000 prior to the script becoming extinct (Ritner 1996a:74). Reversing earlier trends toward greater phonography, in the late second and first millennia BC the use of logograms in Babylonian cuneiform expanded to over 85 percent of words in divinatory, astronomical, and other technical records (Cooper 1996:53). In the seventh and sixth centuries BC the Babylonian language and its cuneiform script were superseded as a *lingua franca* in the Middle East by the Aramaic language and consonantary – although conservative priests and scholars continued to use Babylonian cuneiform into the first century AD.

It is also not true that logophonic scripts develop into syllabic ones and syllabic scripts in turn into consonantaries and alphabets. There is no confirmed example of a logophonic script giving rise to a mainly syllabic one. There are also no examples of syllabaries developing into alphabets, consonantaries, or alphasyllabaries, supporting Sethe's (1939) conclusion that syllabic scripts represent an evolutionary dead end. In China an informal syllabary was constituted to transcribe foreign words and in Japan syllabaries were invented to help write Japanese more clearly, but in these cases logographic writing did not disappear. In the Middle East the earliest purely phonemic scripts were the consonantaries that appear to have been inspired by the consonantal method of representing sounds in ancient Egyptian. This development, however, did not occur in Egypt and there is no evidence that Egyptians played any active part in it. Since most purely phonemic forms of writing are derived from West Semitic consonantaries, this raises the question of whether this form of writing would eventually have supplanted logophonic scripts in Egypt and the Middle East had the Egyptian logoconsonantary not existed.

The Aramaic, Hebrew, and Arabic consonantaries have been adapted to write numerous languages in the Middle East, Central Asia, South Asia, and Southeast Asia. Consonantaries have been transformed into alphabets in Greece and Central Asia, and for a few languages written in the Arabic script. Consonantaries have also served as a point of departure for the development of alphasyllabaries in Persia, India, and Ethiopia. The Kushites used a highly restricted system for indicating vowels as well as consonants that they had employed to represent words from their own language, Meroitic, in records that they had composed in ancient Egyptian to create an alphasyllabic script for writing their own language. The Koreans devised an alphabet to write Korean, although this development perhaps was inspired in part by knowledge of Mongolian alphabetic writing. Yet, while consonantaries have given rise to alphabets and alphasyllabaries, there are no examples of alphabets or alphasyllabaries giving rise to consonantaries. This appears to confirm Gelb's (1963:238) argument that vowel indication is superior to consonantaries because it makes it easier to record exact nuances of language, little-known dialectical forms, new words, and foreign names and words. All these operations become more important as international communications expand. Consonantaries and alphabets frequently give rise to syllabic writing but only when the inventor of the syllabary does not understand the nature of the writing system that is being replicated.

It is not true that at a given level of social and political evolution different societies possess "very similar" writing systems (Coe 1992:260–261). Phonography has advanced much further in West Asia and Europe than in East Asia. Today South Koreans are actively considering the merits of eliminating logographic elements from their script. Yet, while some Japanese and Chinese use the Roman alphabet to enter information into computers, neither people is ready to abandon their traditional script. Special reasons, such as a high degree of homophony, the need to access old documents and, in the case of China, radical speech variation are offered as explanations for this phenomenon. Similar practical considerations have prevented the rational phonemicization of many alphabetic scripts, including English. It is also clear that heavily logographic scripts have not impeded the development of mass literacy or, in Japan, the high consumption of published material and the functioning of a modern industrial economy. This supports

Unger and DeFrancis' (1995:54–55) argument that the difference between largely logographic and phonographic scripts pales into insignificance by comparison with their similarities.

There is considerable historical evidence of cultural conservatism in the use of writing systems. Once formed, scripts tend to persist over long periods without major changes. Gelb (1963:165) has argued that the vested social and economic interests of scribal and political elites in early civilizations may have been responsible for maintaining scripts that were difficult to learn. It has been suggested that the early Japanese "were not interested in evolving an easy system, or one that could be written quickly or read simply and unambiguously. Such values and goals were totally absent from ancient Japanese society" (R. Miller 1967:100). Some logophonic scripts were claimed to be divine revelations; hence knowing them was an esoteric privilege that was not to be shared widely (Daniels 1996c:5; Diringer 1962:14; Ritner 1996a:73). In China, Korea, and Japan, more simplified, phonographic versions of scripts have traditionally been regarded as appropriate only for the use of women, children, and the lower classes (Daniels 1996b:583; King 1996:218, 226; J. Smith 1996:212). Under these conditions, selective pressure was against rather than for simplifying writing systems.

These conservative values may explain why major shifts toward phonographic writing occurred mainly when scripts were adopted by foreign peoples who were not yet bound by firmly established cultural traditions or by social and political interests relating to literacy (Gelb 1963:165). Yet, even if it is true that phonographic scripts are more easily learned and hence more "democratic" than logographic ones, this does not mean their use is less influenced by cultural considerations. The Indian alphasyllabary diffused with Indian culture and Hindu and Buddhist religious practices throughout Southeast Asia. Arabic writing has spread with Islam, and the varied religious and cultural loyalties of Slavic-speaking peoples have continued to be expressed by their use of either the Roman or the Cyrillic alphabet. Major shifts in the use of scripts in Iran and India have generally accompanied the introduction of new religions. Likewise, whatever the practical advantages of the use of the Roman alphabet for writing Turkish may be by comparison with the Arabic script used previously, its replacement of the Arabic script in 1928 was a symbol of modernization and secularization.

Even when major technical changes are not involved, the decision to use a new script or substantially alter an old one involves the negotiation of identity. Scripts may be borrowed with only minimal changes to adapt them for writing another language as a sign of respect for the donor culture. On the other hand, scripts may be altered considerably in outward form to turn them into expressions of local identity. This may have been the case with the Georgian and Armenian alphabets as well as with the runic and Ogam scripts, although in the two latter cases adaptation for writing on a new medium also may have been involved. Scripts are technologies but they are also heavily impregnated with cultural values that do not relate directly to their practical role as a means of communicating.

Provided it is used with appropriate caution, the development of writing systems offers a model for trying to understand changes in other forms of material culture. Writing is more symbolic than most tools and more technologically driven than expressive art. It therefore displays in a balanced fashion the tendencies that are present to varying degrees in all other aspects of material culture. It is clear that the development of writing systems everywhere has been influenced by considerations of efficiency, which have promoted increasing reliance on phonography at the expense of logography. Yet the survival of heavily logographic scripts in modern industrial societies indicates that the superior efficiency of alphabets, and of phonography, has been ethnocentrically overrated by Western scholars. It is also obvious that religious, political, ethnic, and class loyalties, as well as cultural beliefs and preferences, have played an important role in both resisting and bringing about changes in scripts.

This accords with the view that all material culture is a product of knowledge systems that are inherited from the past and transformed as a result of considerations of technical efficiency, social interests, and cultural factors. Except with those aspects of material culture for which practical considerations play a preponderant role in shaping change, choices made in the remote past are likely to continue to influence cultural patterns, often over long periods, until major countervailing considerations come into play (Sahlins 1976; Trigger 1998). Technological efficiency can only be measured in relation to specific social needs, even if such calculations must inevitably take account of practical considerations relating to energy expenditures. On the other hand, class interests and cultural values also influence cultural change and often play a significant role in blocking it. In the case of writing systems, phonography has sufficient selective value to play an increasing role over time, but not enough importance to ensure that this has occurred equally in each family of historically related scripts. Cultural values have inhibited change sufficiently that most fundamental innovations in the nature of writing systems have occurred when scripts were being adapted for writing new languages.

In other aspects of material culture, the balance between practical and cultural considerations will be different and in each instance it must be determined empirically. This can be done only by comparing the nature of change in a variety of different cultural settings. Nothing is likely to be more detrimental to an objective understanding of change than assuming in advance the extent to which practical and cultural considerations play a role in shaping particular categories of material culture. Doing so is all the more dangerous if these assumptions become incorporated into classifications, which in turn reinforce such speculations.

Acknowledgments
This paper has been updated and revised for this publication. It was originally published under the same title in the *Norwegian Archaeological Review* (1998 [30]:39–62), and is reprinted with the permission of the editors and publishers of that journal.

PART II

Case Studies of Primary and Secondary Script Formation

4 | Babylonian beginnings: the origin of the cuneiform writing system in comparative perspective

JERROLD S. COOPER

> Because the messenger's mouth was heavy and he couldn't repeat (the message),
> The lord of Kulaba patted some clay and put words on it, like a tablet –
> Until then, there had been no putting words on clay.
> (From the Sumerian epic poem *Enmerkar and the Lord of Aratta*)

The recent appearance of two comprehensive treatments of early writing and its precursors in Babylonia affords me the relative freedom to provide here a more personal recapitulation of a by now familiar story, and to retell it with emphasis on a comparative perspective.[1] The story has changed dramatically since my earliest involvement with it in the mid 1960s. Then, I. J. Gelb's diffusionist model of writing's origin held sway: writing was invented in Babylonia just before 3000 BC, very soon stimulated the development of writing in nearby Egypt, and by means not well understood eventually stimulated the development of writing in China some 1,500 years later (Gelb 1963). Mesoamerican writing was not true writing, as Eric Thompson never tired of telling us, and need not be considered (Thompson 1972). And if Thompson's authority did not suffice, Gelb offered with a flourish as added proof (the logic of which escaped me then as it escapes me now) the deficient level of Maya metallurgy (Gelb 1963:58).[2]

Several decades later, everything has changed: the spectacular progress in the decipherment of Maya has established beyond all doubt that writing was invented independently at least twice (Old World and New); much greater knowledge of Chinese prehistory has made any dependence of Chinese writing on Near Eastern stimulus highly unlikely; and examples of writing in Egypt have been found that very well may pre-date the earliest writing from Mesopotamia. If it is certain that writing was invented more than once, as the Mesoamerican evidence compels us to believe, it could well have been invented four times. Many scholars working on early writing systems today would be happy with the proposition that Sumerian, Egyptian, Chinese, and Maya were all created in response to local needs and without stimulus by pre-existing writing systems from elsewhere (see Michalowski 1994:53).[3]

The bureaucratic origins of writing

What *were* the local needs to which writing responded? In each case, with the possible exception of Maya, writing was a response to increasing social and political complexity. I have long believed that the particular aspect of that complexity that led to the invention of writing was administrative, tracking income, disbursements, and transfers within large organizations, be they what we might call palace, temple, or community (Cooper 1989).[4] Whereas there can be little argument with this proposition based on the evidence from ancient Babylonia, where no clear use of writing for display or religious purposes appears for a half-millennium after writing's invention there, the case for Egypt, China, and Mesoamerica is less obvious. The surviving early written material from each of those regions is religious, political, for elite display, or a combination of these; except for Egypt, administrative texts have not been found.

The reason is simple: in Mesopotamia, the primary writing material was clay, virtually indestructible. It does not rot, and fire only makes it more durable. In Egypt, administrative records would have been kept on papyrus or other perishable materials, which would not have survived in the Nile flood plain, where administrative archives would have been located; the tags and cursive writing on pots identifying the source and nature of funerary offerings are the only surviving evidence for early Egyptian bureaucracy. In China, records would have been kept on silk or on wood strips, and in Mesoamerica, on bark paper or palm leaves. These, too, are perishable and would not have survived. What has survived are texts that were painstakingly engraved in stone, bone, or shell, or painted for display on architectural elements or pottery, not surfaces that would have been used for the rapid cursive writing necessary for efficient administration. Indirect evidence for administrative record-keeping in each of these cultures suggests that cursive documents were indeed produced at least as early as the surviving texts on durable materials (Cooper 1989; Postgate, Wang, and Wilkinson 1995).

Because the Mesopotamian writing surface was so durable, we can have confidence in the picture of writing's origin in Babylonia which has emerged from the last several decades of study. The Late Uruk period, roughly the last third of the fourth millennium BC, was a time of great population increase in Babylonia, during which the first true city emerged at Uruk, together with an increasingly hierarchical sociopolitical structure whose ability to mobilize labor and resources is best evidenced by the massive monumental structures excavated at Uruk (Nissen 1988; Liverani 1998). Glyptic and other art of the period portray a figure with distinctive headgear and clothing, depicted as

The origin of the cuneiform writing system 73

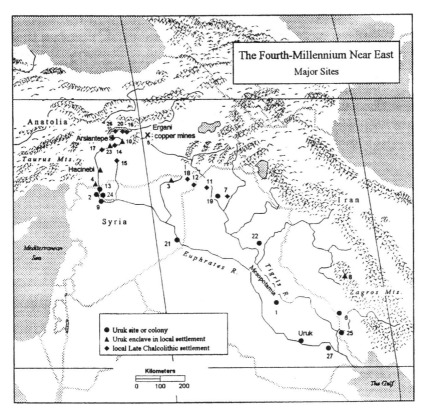

Fig. 4.1 The Near East in the Uruk period. Important Uruk Expansion sites include Abu Salabikh (1), Ur (27), Susa (25), Godin (6), Nineveh (19), Jebel Aruda (2), and Habuba Kabira (9) (Stein 1999:95, fig. 6.4).

larger than other humans, hunting, fighting in battle, overseeing the torture and execution of prisoners, and engaged in ritual activities, certainly a ruler (Amiet 1961:pls. 43–47; Pittman 1994:183, 186).[5] And the appearance of artifacts and architecture typical of Uruk at sites ranging in an arc from southwestern Iran across upper Mesopotamia to northern Syria has been seen as evidence for a strong southern Mesopotamian presence or even domination in these areas (see Fig. 4.1; Algaze 1993; Liverani 1998; Stein 1999; Rothman 2001; Englund, this volume).

The organizational and administrative challenge posed by this level of social and political complexity led to experiments with a variety of devices to enhance accounting and accountability (Nissen, Damerow, and Englund 1993: ch. 4; Pittman 1993; Pollock 1999:172; Englund, this volume). The clay tokens used as counters had been around for millennia (Schmandt-Besserat 1992), and the cylinder seals (Fig. 4.2) used with clay to seal closures of

Fig. 4.2 A cylinder seal and a modern impression of it (courtesy Musée du Louvre).

various kinds – on vessels, bundles, doors – were in principle the same as the stamp seals known from earlier periods.[6] New was the inclusion of tokens in clay bullae, which could be sealed and marked on the outside with impressions of the tokens within (Fig. 4.3), and clay tablets, sometimes sealed, with numerical signs (Fig. 4.4), signs whose prototypes can clearly be seen in certain of the simpler types of tokens (Englund 1998:48–50 and 214; Glassner 2000:146–157).[7] All of these devices are found both at Uruk and in the areas of northern Mesopotamia, Syria, and Susiana (southwestern Iran) where the Uruk Expansion manifested itself. A further device, however, which Englund calls "numerico-ideographic tablets" (Fig. 4.5), is found only at Uruk and in Susiana. These consist of "simple numerical notations" with "the inclusion of one, at most two of a group of ideograms, common to both regions, which represent discrete objects"; for Englund, they are "the missing link between numerical notations . . . and the mixed notations of numerical signs and ideograms which mark the inception of proto-cuneiform" (Englund 1998:51, 53, 214f.).

That the bullae and numerical tablets were found throughout the region of the Uruk Expansion, but "numerico-ideographic" tablets are found only at Uruk and in Susiana corresponds to the archaeological consensus that the Babylonian presence was more strongly felt and somewhat longer lasting in Susiana than in northern Mesopotamia and Syria. It is only when this presence disappears from Susiana as well, at the very end of the Late Uruk

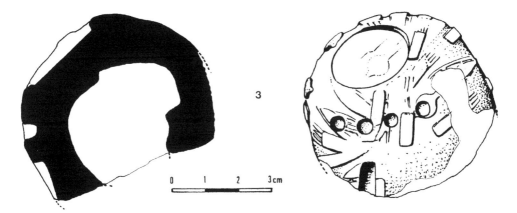

Fig. 4.3 Sealed hollow clay bulla from Susa. Inside it were four spherical clay tokens and one cylindrical token, corresponding to the impressions on its surface (Le Brun and Vallat 1978:45, fig. 3:3).

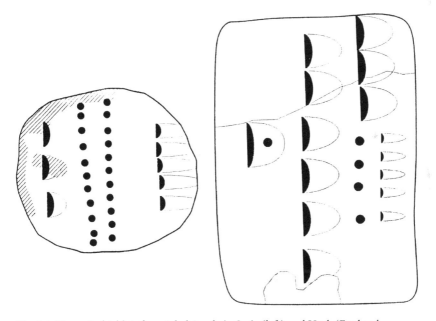

Fig. 4.4 Numerical tablets from Jebel Aruda in Syria (left) and Uruk (Englund 1998:51f., figs. 13 and 15).

period (c. 3200 BC), that tablets with complex numerical entries and a repertoire of many hundreds of signs (Fig. 4.6) appear at Uruk only. The irony that writing seems to be invented at Uruk just as the influence of Uruk itself in neighboring areas contracts has not been lost on scholars, but neither has it been adequately explained.

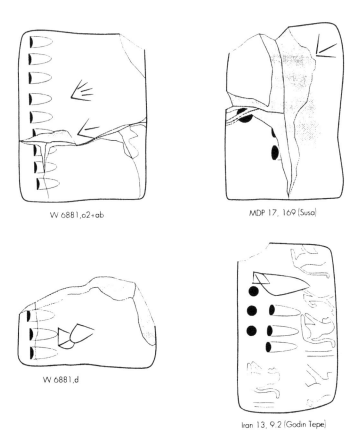

Fig. 4.5 "Numerico-ideographic" tablets from Uruk (left), Susa, and Godin (Englund 1998:54, fig. 16).

This earliest phase of writing at Uruk is known as Uruk IV, because it seems to correlate with the end of the archaeological phase so designated; the full flowering of archaic writing occurs in the following Uruk III phase, part of what is called in Babylonia the Jemdet Nasr period (c. 3200–3000 BC). This phase manifests a highly complex accounting system, and the accounts themselves reveal transactions involving very large quantities of a great variety of goods as well as a very elaborate bureaucracy (cf. Englund 1998:61). In addition, the archaic writing that is known from Uruk alone at the end of Uruk IV spread throughout Babylonia in the Jemdet Nasr period.[8]

Although archaic writing, which Englund aptly calls "proto-cuneiform," evolved noticeably from Uruk IV to Uruk III and continued to develop and change for the next several millennia (see below), we are confronted from its beginning with a fully elaborated system of logographic and

Fig. 4.6 Uruk IV cattle receipts (Englund 1998:154 and 156, figs. 52 and 53).

numerical-metrological signs, something entirely different from the far simpler tokens, bullae, and seals that originated in earlier periods (cf. Algaze 2001:213). The proto-cuneiform system draws on the one hand from the rude system of numerical notation of the tokens, and on the other from a long tradition of pictorial and symbolic representation known especially from glyptic art (cf. Buccellati 1981). The first step in combining the two on a clay tablet is represented by the sealed numerical tablets, and Englund's numerico-ideographic tablets may represent the first step in using the stylus to create representations of commodities. There are, however, no further incremental steps in the process. The idea that commodities, titles, names, and transaction types could be represented graphically led almost immediately to the elaboration of an entire system of signs, and, in contrast to the very simple enumeration of the earlier numerical tablets, we are confronted with an irrationally exuberant metrological system with over a dozen different sets of numerals for recording amounts of various kinds of discrete objects, weights, area, liquid and dry measures and time (Englund 1998:111–127).

For a system of writing with around 900 signs, complex numerical-metrical conventions and intricate bookkeeping formats to be useful, its utilization had to be uniform, necessitating years of more or less formalized instruction and the creation of teaching aids. In fact, the only non-administrative archaic texts that exist are what scholars call lexical texts, lists of words arranged by topic or category (Fig. 4.7), comprising just over 10 percent of the approximately 6,000 archaic tablets. Englund (1998:ch. 5) has also identified a small number of school writing and accounting exercises. Schools and schooling imply a substantial social investment, which could have been justified only if writing was successfully accomplishing the administrative tasks for which it was invented.[9]

In Egypt, too, the earliest writing was administrative in nature, and the early writing system exhibits many of the characteristics known from later Egyptian writing (Dreyer 1998:181f.).[10] In contrast to Mesopotamia, however, writing in Egypt was also used for display purposes very early on, and so the question of the reason for writing's invention there is not as simple to answer as in the case of Mesopotamia. Here, I think, we must be careful to separate the reason for writing's invention from the other uses to which it was put once it had been invented. If we compare the administrative needs of a growing state with the requirements of a nascent royal ideology, it seems reasonable, though, of course, not necessary, to presume that the logophonetic Egyptian writing system would have been devised for the administrative bureaucracy, and that royal display alone could have been very effectively accomplished with a highly sophisticated iconography that was not language-bound.[11] Once invented, however, Egyptian writing was very soon put to work in the service of the king by the ideologues.

China's earliest written materials are short dedicatory inscriptions on bronze vessels, and records on bone and shell of divination performed with the very objects on which the records are found. As in Mesopotamia and Egypt, early Chinese writing (Boltz 1994; F. Bottéro, this volume) is not a partial or rudimentary system; it manifests most of the features of mature Chinese writing. Would a writing system have been invented to identify the donor of a vessel when the clan emblems in use for millennia in China

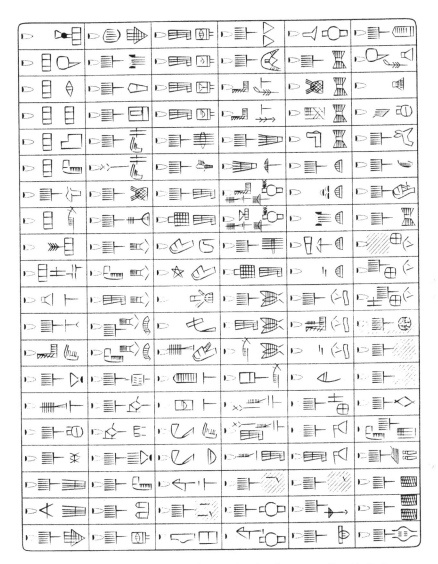

Fig. 4.7 Archaic list of offices and professions (Englund 1998:104, fig. 32). Each entry is preceded by the numeral 1, signifying "item."

would probably have sufficed?[12] Certainly, writing could not have been invented to make after-the-fact records of divination, since the records were not essential to the divinatory acts themselves, and not all shells and bones used for divination were inscribed.[13] Again, I think we are confronted by secondary, albeit early, uses of a writing system whose invention was sparked by the organizational needs of a growing Shang polity.

Although the earliest Maya writing is preceded by state formation, it may be difficult to argue persuasively that Maya script was invented to meet the state's administrative needs. The existence of earlier, as yet undeciphered Mesoamerican scripts, a long iconographic tradition of symbolic representation in that area, and the highly complex and culturally very important calendrical system common to Mesoamerica, with documented roots deep in the first millennium BC, suggest that here we may indeed – but I personally think not – have a writing system that developed for "religious" purposes, though not for royal commemoration.[14] Yet whatever the origins of Maya writing, it would soon have been co-opted by the bureaucracy, as represented in Maya art by the "accountant scribe" writing on leaves (Houston 2000:148).

To summarize, then, if we are looking for a common context for the invention of writing, a context which must also justify the social and economic investment required to propagate and maintain a writing system, we would do well to generalize from the Mesopotamian example and look to the administration of the kinds of organizations and polities that emerge in increasingly complex societies. The implications of this generalization, and the possible Maya exception, will be explored in my conclusion.

Writing, language, and speech

In his contribution to this volume, Bruce Trigger makes the important point that in their earliest stages, early writing systems were not the full writing systems that they became. This development is particularly obvious for Sumerian cuneiform (Cooper 1996:43–45) and Egyptian (Baines, this volume), where the gradual addition of grammatical and syntactic capability can be observed over centuries, as it can for Maya (Houston 2000:145–147). Early Sumerian and Egyptian, in their beginnings, were probably no more versatile than Inka khipu (cf. Larsen 1988:183–187), perhaps even less so, and Elizabeth Boone's (2000:ch. 3, and in this volume) discussion of the narrative strategies of Mexican pictography reminds one strongly of the way early Egyptian palettes deploy proto-hieroglyphs and iconography (Assmann 1994:19f.).[15] All of these early systems express language, but only in highly restricted applications, and all depend to some degree on non-linguistic features – tablet format, string placement, figural representation, institutional context – for their interpretation.[16]

Although there seems to be a small amount of phonetic writing in proto-cuneiform,[17] there is no certain expression of Sumerian grammatical affixes until the archaic tablets from Ur, *c.* 2800 BC, that is, four centuries or so after the invention of proto-cuneiform. This absence of grammar did

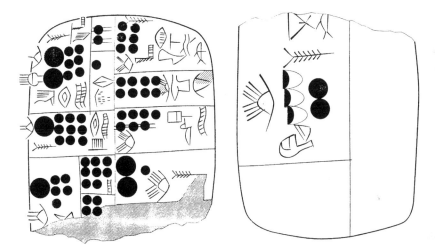

Fig. 4.8 Uruk III tablets with complex column formats. Top: account of male and female workers from Uruk (Englund 1998:177, fig. 65). Bottom: grain account over eight-year period from Uqair (Englund 1996:no. 1).

not impair the utility of proto-cuneiform, because its use was restricted to administrative accounts; even today, grammar has little or no role to play in ledgers. Syntax, too, was scarce or non-existent. Individual entries and summary remarks were enclosed in cases (rectangular boxes) on tablets, and these cases could be arranged in vertical columns, but within cases the placement of signs was arbitrary, except that numerals came first.[18] In fact, it is only after 2400 BC that the sequence of signs within cases consistently corresponded to the linguistic sequences they represented.

The role of grammar and syntax in ordering language and rendering it intelligible was performed for the archaic administrative tablets by format. In the Uruk III phase, a rich repertoire of subcases, subcolumns, and varying

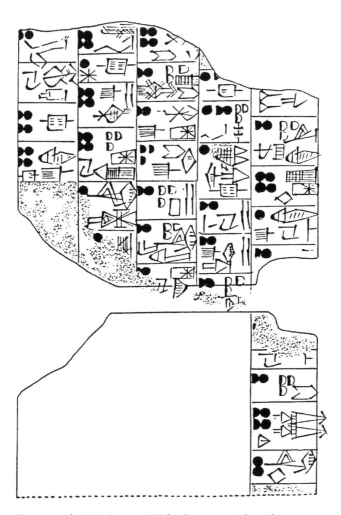

Fig. 4.9 Archaic Ur (c. 2800 BC) land account with uniform column format (Burrows 1935:no. 87).

column width was developed to denote the relationships between entries and groups of entries (Fig. 4.8; Englund 1998:56–64; M. Green 1981), but by the next documented phase of cuneiform writing, the archaic tablets from Ur, when Sumerian grammatical elements begin to be expressed, these complex formats disappear in favor of columns of uniform width (Fig. 4.9), a format that becomes standard for cuneiform tablets throughout the following several millennia. It is not that Sumerian bookkeeping becomes less complex in later periods, but rather that the written expression of grammar and syntax enables complex relationships to be expressed with language rather than format.[19]

Only around 2700 BC do the first royal inscriptions begin to appear in Babylonia (Cooper 1986); literature appears a century or so later (Krebernik 1998:317–325), and letters around 2400 BC (Michalowski 1993a; Kienast and Volk 1995).[20] The same gradual increase in expression of grammar and syntax, and the concomitant increase in variety of written genres that more precise linguistic expression makes possible, have been observed for Egyptian (Baines, this volume), and Houston (2000) has described the increase in phoneticism and grammatical expression in Maya texts over several centuries. The syntactic complexity of many early Chinese texts can probably be explained by the fact that our earliest Chinese texts are late Shang (Boltz 1994:31) and were preceded by centuries of development in the earlier Shang. That graphic systems, but not khipu, developed to the point that their potential for linguistic expression was unrestricted – that is, they could be used to record anything that a writer might think to express – suggests that graphic markings possessed a range and versatility comparable to the human vocal tract, suitable for expressing the full extent of language, a versatility that khipus (and certainly tokens!) lacked, however well suited they were for certain restricted uses.[21]

Let us return to Trigger's point that no early writing system was the full writing system it eventually became – that is, each was able to fully express language only after centuries of development. The reason is that no writing system was invented, or used early on, to mimic spoken language or to perform spoken language's functions. Livestock or ration accounts, land management records, lexical texts, labels identifying funerary offerings, offering lists, divination records, and commemorative stelae have no oral counterparts. Rather, they represent the extension of language use into areas where spoken language cannot do the job. Goody (1977:78) has aptly identified writing's major functions as decontextualization and storage, and it is through these capacities that written language asserts a superiority over spoken language. Only after long experience using writing for things that cannot be done orally do societies begin to apply writing to oral domains such as messages and literary narratives. Even then, though, these written forms produce dialects of their own, which both develop features that never appear in spoken language, and maintain features long obsolete in spoken language.[22] Therefore, it seems useful to disregard the obvious chronological primacy of speech over writing, and, for all societies that use writing, to prefer Vachek's model of language with two distinct (if overlapping) subsets, spoken language and written language, to Saussure's model of language as spoken language only, where writing "exists for the sole purpose of representing" that spoken language (Vachek 1939 and 1973; Saussure

1959:23; cf. Cooper 1989; Sproat 2000:209–212; and Robertson in this volume).

The Babylonians themselves, however, were Saussurians. In the myth of *Enmerkar and the Lord of Aratta* cited as an epigraph to this chapter, Enmerkar, legendary ruler of Uruk, invented writing in order to send a long and complicated message to the ruler of Aratta, his adversary on the Iranian plateau.[23] The recipient, much like Lévi-Strauss' (1974:296) unwitting Indian chief, studied the tablet carefully, then burst out in frustration, "It's wedges!" (Vanstiphout 1989; cf. Alster 1995:2321).[24] For the author(s) of this myth at the beginning of the second millennium BC, writing began as an aid for transmitting oral messages, a remedy for the messenger's restricted memory, or, if we take the text literally, his limited eloquence. For the author's ancestors 1,000 or so years earlier, writing had little or nothing to do with oral discourse; it was an administrative technology that extended the denotative versatility of language into realms that had previously been served only by the drastically more limited devices of tokens and seals.

Iconicity and its loss

Archaic proto-cuneiform signs are overwhelmingly pictographic (Fig. 4.10, "Archaic Uruk" column), as are early Egyptian, Chinese, and Maya graphs.[25] In Peircean terms, they are either icons, images of what they signify (as in Fig. 4.10[1]), or indexes, pointing in some way to what they signify, often by metonymy or synecdoche, or instrumentality (Fig. 4.10[5]). Very few are purely symbolic, having only an arbitrary, conventional relationship to what they signify, as do the array of signs used for sheep and goats, composed of cross, circle, and various combinations and alterations thereto to distinguish age, grade, and sex (as in Fig. 4.10[6]–[7]; M. Green 1980; Englund 1998:148–150). Whereas a relatively small number of archaic signs are clearly identifiable, such as certain animal heads or pottery vessel shapes (Fig. 4.11), most are so schematic that either the source of the image can only be identified when the meaning is known (as Fig. 4.10[5], clearly a foot only once the meaning "to go, stand" is known), or the image cannot be identified at all. A prime cause of our inability to identify so many images is that in the periods after 2600 BC, when we can much more fully understand cuneiform texts, those signs are no longer used for the objects they originally represented, but, rather, are used for other, probably rebus-derived, words. For example, the sign AK (Fig. 4.11) contains no visual clue to its later meaning "to make,

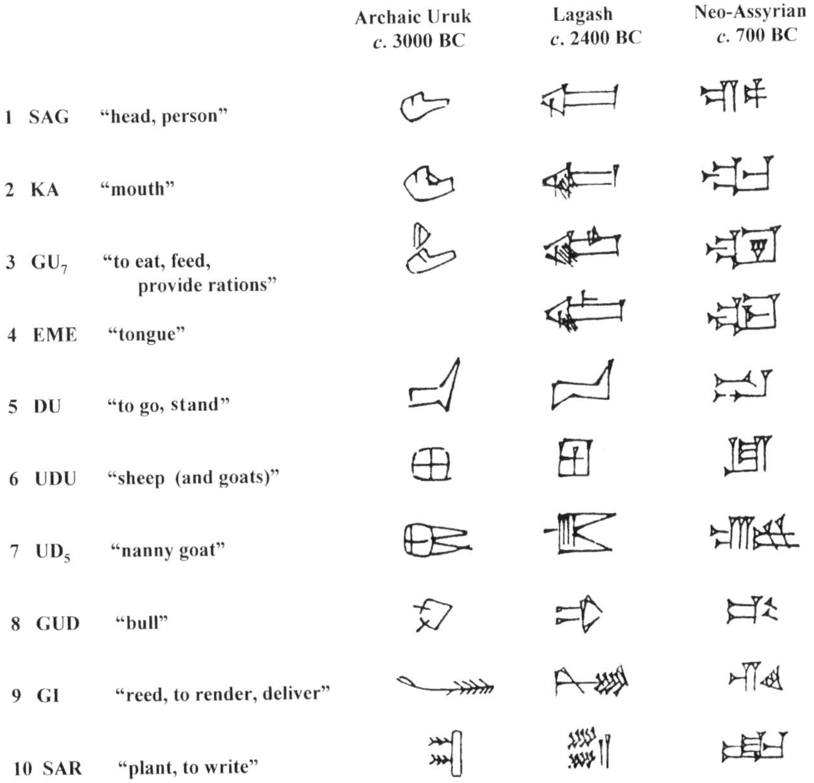

The origin of the cuneiform writing system 85

			Archaic Uruk c. 3000 BC	Lagash c. 2400 BC	Neo-Assyrian c. 700 BC
1	SAG	"head, person"			
2	KA	"mouth"			
3	GU₇	"to eat, feed, provide rations"			
4	EME	"tongue"			
5	DU	"to go, stand"			
6	UDU	"sheep (and goats)"			
7	UD₅	"nanny goat"			
8	GUD	"bull"			
9	GI	"reed, to render, deliver"			
10	SAR	"plant, to write"			

Fig. 4.10 The construction and evolution of cuneiform signs.

do"; Englund (1998:135), based on the sign's occurrence in archaic contexts, speculates that it represents "a container made of matted reeds."[26]

Proto-cuneiform signs are schematic because the archaic scribes quickly learned that the most efficient method of inscribing signs on clay was not to drag a pointed stylus through the clay to draw a sign, but to compose a sign out of lines impressed with rapid strokes of a stylus having a wedge-shaped tip and sharpened edge. The resulting lines have a characteristic wedge-shaped ("cuneiform") head and tapering tail.[27] Signs were thus composed predominantly out of straight lines, though dragging and pulling the stylus made it possible to make curved lines, and a series of short curved lines could create a circle. Already from phase IV to III at Uruk a straightening of curved lines can be observed, as well as a reduction in the possible direction of wedges and lines to correspond to the flow of the writing (see Englund 1998:72 and fig. 22). As Fig. 4.10 shows, curved lines disappear by 2400 BC, and, over time, the wedge head becomes wider, the number of lines in

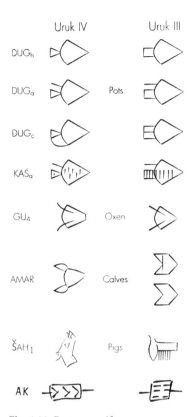

Fig. 4.11 Proto-cuneiform pictographs based on vessels and animal heads, and the sign AK (from Englund 1998:fig. 22; Green and Nissen 1987:no. 2).

a given sign are often reduced, and in first millennium Assyria there is a drastic reduction in oblique lines and wedges. It is also clear from Fig. 4.10 that the schematic pictograms of archaic Uruk become in later periods abstract symbols with no visual link whatsoever to what they signify (cf. Cooper 1996:40).

Not only do cuneiform signs take on a completely abstract appearance after the archaic period (Uruk IV–III / Jemdet Nasr), but there is no evidence that the users of cuneiform ever associated a sign's abstract shape with the object the sign designated. Rather, when the name of the sign was used in a metaphor or simile, it was the shape of the sign itself that was meant (Lieberman 1977). And if in the archaic period a few signs, especially those whose pictographic basis is the emblem or insignia of the god or office the sign represents, resemble those same objects as they are portrayed in glyptic

Fig. 4.12 From the Stela of the Vultures, Eanatum of Lagash (25th-century BC). The inscription runs along the top above the soldiers' heads, along the band dividing the upper from the lower register, and in the space beneath Eanatum's spear on the lower right (courtesy Musée du Louvre).

and other art (cf. Glassner 2000:ch. 8), in following periods cuneiform diverges utterly from Mesopotamian artistic convention. Whether on the 25th-century BC Stela of the Vultures from Lagash (Fig. 4.12), or on the walls of the 9th-century BC palace of Ashurnasirpal II of Assyria (Fig. 4.13), text and image remain entirely distinct.[28]

This is completely different from what we find in Egyptian and Maya, where the brush and pen enabled the retention of a detailed iconicity in the script for formal purposes even as cursive scripts were developed as well; in

Fig. 4.13 Ashurnasirpal II of Assyria (9th-century BC), flanked by attendants, on wall of palace at Nimrud (ancient Kalkhu). The lengthy cuneiform inscription forms an indistinct band beginning below the attendants' waists and below the king's knee (courtesy British Museum).

Egypt, a more schematic cursive is as old as writing itself. As a result, there is an iconic interplay between text and art in Egypt and Mesoamerica that is totally absent in Mesopotamia.[29] Also, in both Egypt and Mesoamerica, the iconicity of the signs became ever more elaborate in certain contexts, in the later Egyptian cryptographic writings and the increasing use of Maya head signs (see below).

In China, too, writing was done with the brush, but the pictorial content of the script followed the Mesopotamian pattern and not the Egyptian and Maya one. Early Chinese characters are obviously pictographic, but, as with archaic cuneiform, most characters are already quite schematic, unrecognizable unless you already know what they mean, or, in the case of indexical characters or rebus writings, what object the character represents (cf. Boltz 1996:Table 14:1; F. Bottéro, this volume). As the script developed, the characters became, like cuneiform signs, entirely abstract, and although calligraphy became a fine art in China, and can be combined with painting in the same work, the two are kept very separate, with little visual interplay. Yet, unlike ancient Mesopotamia where the original pictographic content of the sign seems to have been entirely lost in later periods, the Chinese have remained conscious of the iconic basis of characters which to an outsider look entirely abstract.

Semantic and phonetic elements in early writing systems

All early "pristine" writing systems use both semantic and phonetic elements in their construction, but the amount of phoneticism can vary drastically. The basis of phonetic writing is rebus, the use of a sign to represent a homonym or near homonym, as in Fig. 4.10(10), the sign for *sar* ("plant") (turn the sign 90° clockwise to see the plants growing out of a field or bed) used to write the homonym *sar* ("to write"). Whereas this particular rebus can not be confirmed as early as the archaic period, the use of the sign for *gi* ("reed") (Fig. 4.10[9]) to write an accounting term associated with Sumerian *gi* ("to render, return, deliver"), or possibly *gin* ("to confirm") is common in the archaic texts.[30] The same principle can be used to write sounds alone, either as a clue to the reading of a sign or group of signs, as in Fig. 4.10(4), where the sign for mouth is modified with *me* to represent the word *eme* ("tongue") something having to do with the mouth and containing the syllable *me*; or, to express a grammatical element, as in the Sumerian *dingir-ra* ("of the god"), writing *dingir* ("god") logographically, but using the sign RA phonetically to express the genetive suffix -*a(k)*.[31] The first of these phonetic uses is probably present in the archaic tablets;[32] the second probably does not occur until c. 2800.[33]

The rarity of phonetic writing in archaic cuneiform contrasts markedly with the systematic exploitation of phoneticism in early Egyptian and early Chinese writing.[34] From the beginning, Chinese writing used semantic components to disambiguate rebus spellings, resulting in the compound characters that account for over 90 percent of all Chinese characters. These compound characters are, in Boltz's terms, +S(emantic) and +P(honetic).[35] Early cuneiform also combines single characters to create compounds, but these are almost always +S+S, as Fig. 4.10(3) (head/mouth + ration/food = gu_7 ["to eat, feed, provide rations"]). Compound signs of the +S+P type, as Fig. 4.10(4) (mouth + ME = *eme* ["tongue"]), become more frequent after the archaic period, but remain in the minority.[36] Completely phonetic compounds, such as *ba-al* ("to dig") or *ḫa-lam* ("to destroy") are rarer still. Except for a distinct group of texts in the early second millennium BC that consistently utilizes unorthographic phonetic spellings, Sumerian uses logograms to write substantives, adjectives, and verbs, and reserves phonetic writing for grammatical particles and affixes, as well as foreign names and words. This is very different from Egyptian writing, which is primarily phonetic, with a heavy dose of semantic determinatives, and also different from Classic Maya, in which all classes of words can be written logographically, phonetically, or with a combination of logograms and phonograms (Houston 1989:38–40).[37]

In addition to creating +S + S (Fig. 4.10[3]) and +S+P compounds (Fig. 4.10[4]), and using rebus writings (Fig. 4.10[9]–[10]), Sumerian cuneiform has a large number of multivalent signs, that is, signs which each have more than one reading and meaning. The additional readings are usually based on semantic association. The sign KA (Fig. 4.10[2]) = Sumerian *ka* ("mouth"), itself derived from SAG (Fig. 4.10[1]) = Sumerian *sag* ("head, person") by the addition of supplemental diagonal lines, can, at least by the middle of the third millennium BC, be read dug_4 ("to speak"), *inim* ("word"), *gù* ("sound"), kir_4 ("nose"), and *zú* ("tooth")[38] Or, DU (Fig. 4.10[5]) = *du* ("to go") also has the values *gub* ("to stand") and *túm* ("to bring"). What is important to remember, however, is that Sumerian writing is logophonetic and not ideographic. In context, a sign that is not being used phonetically or as a determinative is a logogram, standing for a specific word in the Sumerian language. So, for example, DU in a given text is meant to be read either *du* or *gub* (and there will often be contextual hints or phonetic complements to help one decide which); it cannot simply be understood as something you do with your feet. The sign KA in a context requiring a body part must be either *ka* ("mouth"), kir_4 ("nose"), or *zú* ("tooth"). When decontextualized, however, these signs are indeed ideograms: KA is a sign used for words having to do with the mouth and its products or actions, and an adjacent organ ("nose"); and DU is a sign used for verbs involving the feet. This is the only sense it which it is proper to speak of ideograms in Sumerian as we know it in post-archaic periods, and this is probably true for archaic proto-cuneiform as well.[39]

Economy and prestige in logophonetic writing systems

The Sumerian, Egyptian, and Maya writing systems all employ logograms – word signs – and phonograms – signs that have a phonetic value only, which can be used to spell out a word without using a logogram, to complement a logogram by giving a phonetic hint to its reading, to express a bound morpheme, or to do a combination of the last two.[40] All three systems also use semantic classifiers, "unread" signs which point to the proper reading of a word by specifying its semantic category.[41] In cuneiform, such determinatives occur with nouns only.

In Sumerian cuneiform, phonetic writing of some grammatical affixes begins early in the third millennium BC, but it is not until the beginning of the second millennium BC that all or most grammatical affixes are consistently expressed. Nouns, adjectives, and verbs, as stated above, are regularly written with logograms. In Egyptian, logographic writing is rare;[42] most writing is phonetic, with a good deal of redundancy, and extensive use of determinatives with verbs as well as nouns. Maya writes grammatical affixes phonetically, and can increasingly substitute phonetic writings of nouns and verbs for logographic writings, or use phonetic complements with logograms. Despite the obvious capability to write texts entirely phonetically in each of these systems, however, none developed a purely phonetic orthographic norm.

This resistance to a purely phonetic orthography which would have greatly simplified these writing systems suggests that certain ideological biases in favor of traditional logophonetic writing were working against Gelb's "principle of economy aiming at the expression of linguistic forms by the smallest possible number of signs" (Gelb 1963:69 and 251; cf. Coulmas 1994:262f.). A similar opportunity to develop a phonetic orthographic norm seems to have been passed up in China, for the same reasons (Boltz 1994:168–177). When the Sumerian cuneiform system was adapted to write the Semitic Akkadian language (see Cooper 1999b), the prestige attached to Sumerian logograms led to a mixed system in which Sumerograms (Sumerian logograms in an Akkadian text) appear with or without phonetic complements in context with other words written entirely phonetically. The Sumerograms were, of course, read in Akkadian, as the phonetic complements indicate. In some dialects and text genres, Akkadian writing is overwhelmingly phonetic, but in others there is a good deal of logography, especially in administrative and legal texts, with their stock phrases, and in scientific texts. It may be thought that a certain economy is involved, that is, one can write the Akkadian word *šarru* ("king") with the single-sign Sumerogram LUGAL rather than using two phonograms to spell out *šar-ru*, but there are many cases where this is not so. For example, the common Sumerographic writing Ì.LÁ.E ("he shall pay") uses no fewer signs than its phonographic equivalent *i-ša-qal*; the Sumerogram for "ear", GIŠ.TÚG.PI, uses three signs to the two for the same word phonographically written, *uz-nu*; and the frequently used

Sumerogram for "horse," ANŠE.KUR.RA is far more complicated to write than the phonetic Akkadian *si-su*.[43]

Even though Sumerian was no longer spoken after the early second millennium BC, there is no diminution in the use of Sumerograms in later Akkadian. In fact, late first-millennium Akkadian divinatory and astronomical texts can be 85 percent Sumerograms (Civil 1973:26), and first-millennium Akkadian scribal culture exploited and played on the Sumerian potentiality of cuneiform signs to a much greater degree than did scribes writing in Akkadian 1,000 or more years earlier when Sumerian was still spoken (cf. J. Bottéro 1992:ch. 6). This tendency of scribal culture to complicate rather than simplify writing systems is found in the late Egyptian cryptographic writings (Ritner 1996a:81), the proliferation of head variants in later Classic Maya, the enormous inflation of characters in scholarly Chinese (Mair 1996:200), and the infusion of new *kanji* into Japanese at various moments in Japanese history (Seeley 1991).[44] Japan today, perhaps the most technologically advanced country in the world, zealously maintains a writing system that is probably the world's most difficult to learn, a telling reminder of the ideological investment a culture has in its traditional script. Economy and efficiency do not inevitably win out over complex traditional modes, either in the present or in the ancient societies in which writing first evolved.

The limits of a comparative study of writing systems

The preceding discussion has used the origin and development of cuneiform writing in Babylonia as a heuristic for elucidating some commonalities among the four pristine early writing systems, Sumerian cuneiform, Egyptian, Chinese, and Maya (and its Mesoamerican forebears). I have argued that, with a possible Maya exception, the invention of writing in each of these cultures was a response to increasing socio-economic complexity, because, in Goody's (2000:25) words, "the more complex the organization of the state and the economy, the greater the pressure toward the graphic representation of speech," although I would here substitute "language" for his "speech." Other important commonalities among these systems include the differences in each between written and spoken language, especially in the early stages of the writing systems, but continuing into later stages as well; the pictographic basis of the early sign repertoires; the use of both semantic and phonetic elements from a very early stage; and the resistance to simplification, especially the resistance to replacing logophonetic writing with a solely phonetic system. We have also, however, seen great differences between these systems in the range of early uses to which writing was put; the retention or loss of iconicity in the script; the quantity of phoneticism; and the way in which phoneticism was employed. Comparison will not generate a set of early writing system universals much beyond the rather general ones that I have indicated. Comparison *will* often help us to understand a puzzling feature in one system by identifying a better-understood analogue in another, and the differences in writing systems that comparison reveals enable a better understanding of the individual systems in their own right.[45]

The way writing is generally defined – as a graphic representation of language that, ultimately, can be used for any sort of linguistic expression – and the use of writing as a marker of higher civilization has created a certain anxiety among colleagues who study complex cultures that did not have writing as so defined. The Inka are always cited as the great exception to the rule that would make writing a marker of complexity. The astonishingly versatile khipu were accounting devices as accurate and specific as the proto-cuneiform tablets from Uruk, and I believe Gary Urton's assertion that they could keep track of dozens of different actions, objects, recipients, and donors. They may even have been used to send short messages and record sequences of events, which was not done in Mesopotamia until many centuries after writing's invention there. A system of knots and threads, however, has limits that a graphic system does not, and I seriously doubt that the khipu ever achieved the linguistic flexibility of the writing systems we have been considering.

Rather than attempt to gain the acceptance of khipu into the club of genuine writing systems, would it not be more productive to study and appreciate the khipu for what they actually are? Their limitations might help us to understand better just what kind of capacities were needed when a society reached a certain level of complexity, and we might look for the reasons that record-keeping took a non-graphic route in the Andes, whereas in comparable situations elsewhere bureaucrats took to making marks on flat surfaces.[46]

Boone's plea (2000:29, and this volume; cf. Sproat 2000:212) "for a more encompassing definition of writing . . . that embraces nonverbal systems" is explicitly ideological: if writing "is seen as a basic element of civilized society . . . how can we deny that the Aztecs and Mixtecs had writing?" Therefore, we must redefine writing to include the Mexican pictographies she studies. In her own words, however, "such a broadening blurs the important distinction between phonetic writing and other forms." I would say much in the same way that Gelb's (1963) insistence on broadening the definition of syllabary to include the Semitic alphabet blurred the distinction between that alphabet and all other syllabaries (and masked the Semitic alphabet's similarity to other alphabets). Again, should we not, rather, try to understand how those limited Mexican pictographies met the needs of what were surely civilized societies?[47] Indeed, given the historical context of the Mixtec and Aztec systems, should we not, with Houston, try to integrate what he calls "the great divide between varieties of Mesoamerican writing" into our ideas about writing's origins and development? Especially intriguing is Houston's notion that the Mexican pictographic systems do not represent a regression from the full phonetic writing of the Maya, but rather a more effective integration of art and writing, resolving a "tension persisting since late Olmec times" (Houston 2001).

In any case, my argument would never be that writing, or any other single characteristic, is an obligatory marker for complex societies or civilizations. Rather, writing is a response, but not the only possible response, to problems raised by complexity (cf. Larsen 1988; Pollock 1999:171f.). My plea here is for a flexible approach to the question of writing and civilization. We should not be so eager to discover universal characteristics of complex societies that we stretch our definitions of those characteristics in order to insure that they fit all known complex societies. It is enough to say that writing *usually* arises as societies become more complex, to admit exceptions, and to use those exceptions to understand better precisely what needs writing arises to fulfill, and how such needs came to be met in a few instances by other means.

Notes

1. Babylonia refers to southern ancient Mesopotamia, beginning just above the bottleneck formed by the Tigris and Euphrates near modern Baghdad. The southern part of Babylonia, from the ancient religious capital of Nippur to the Persian Gulf, is Sumer, and the northern part of Babylonia is Akkad. Assyria is the region in northern Mesopotamia around modern Mosul and Erbil.

    Englund (1998) is a thorough treatment of the origin and archaic phases of cuneiform by the scholar who best knows the material. Glassner (2000) is a wide-ranging discussion of early writing and its origins in Babylonia, whose concerns are more theoretical than Englund's. See, too, Englund's contribution to this volume.

2. Gelb was certainly the most methodologically rigorous study of writing systems of its time, despite a few lapses, and this rigor together with his lucid

presentation make for an intellectually exciting read. For critiques of Gelb from recent theoretical perspectives, see Coulmas (1994:271–273), and Trigger in this volume.

3. Françoise Bottéro, in this volume, revives the idea of stimulus diffusion from the ancient Near East to China, but, for me, the only problem area is the possibility of stimulus diffusion in the case of Egyptian and Sumerian. Because both systems trace their origins to the last third of the fourth millennium BC, a time when elements of southern Mesopotamian culture diffused throughout western Asia (the so-called "Uruk Expansion"), and because certain Mesopotamian art motifs and the cylinder seal (a hallmark of Mesopotamian culture) appear in Egypt at that time, it is difficult to dismiss the idea of diffusion entirely. The recent finds of very early writing (or its precursors) in Egypt have even led some to suggest the stimulus went from Egypt to Babylonia, and not vice versa (Dreyer 1998:182), but this seems unlikely (cf. Englund 1998:79, n. 166). Neither Mesopotamian nor Egyptian chronology at such early periods is precise enough to allow any definitive determination of "who was first." In any case, Egyptian and Sumerian writing are so utterly different, both formally and conceptually, that if any stimulus diffusion occurred, it was purely the idea that graphic marks could be used to express elements of language. Compare the novel variation on this notion by Pettersson (1996:80f.), and Baine's discussion in this volume.

4. Michalowski (1994:56) is reluctant to cede the role of writing's inventors to the bean counters. I trust that my arguments here will elicit from him an "Alas, it is so!" A similar reticence in Glassner (2000) is nicely dealt with by Selz (2000:171, n. 7, 195; see also Algaze 2001). Likewise, Baines' insistence in this volume on the symbolic aspects of an administrative system and the writing it entails is not inconsistent with my emphasis on the "practical" needs of the administrators which led to the invention of that writing.

5. Compare Glassner (2000:270–272), who wants to see in these representations not a single ruler figure but a variety of different high officials, and imagines that Uruk was ruled by an assembly in which these officials served. These scenes, however, are typical of royal art for the next two-and-a-half millennia, and there is no good reason to deny that the protagonist in them in this period is also an autocratic ruler.

6. Note, however, that there is no evidence that these tokens represent a uniform system, nor has it been accepted that what Schmandt-Besserat calls complex tokens were the prototypes for later non-numerical cuneiform signs. See the critiques of Zimansky (1993), Michalowski (1994:54f.), and Glassner (2000:ch. 4). Further illustration of the tokens appears in Englund's contribution to this volume, Fig. 5.10.

   For the change from stamp to cylinder seal, see Nissen (1977). For the uses of cylinder seals, see Collon (1987:ch. 13).

7. Englund distinguishes between "early" numerical tablets, which do not follow the bundling rules known from later texts, and "later" ones, which do. Glassner

conflates under the rubric "writing" the representation of numbers alone with the slightly later writing of signs for words.

8. For the short-lived proto-Elamite writing system that developed in Susiana, influenced by but different from the Babylonian writing system, see Englund in this volume.

9. The advantage that writing gave southern Mesopotamia over surrounding areas is well described by Algaze (2001); the administrative, organizational, and cognitive utility of writing served to accelerate the very processes that gave birth to it.

10. But compare with the important distinctions drawn by Baines (this volume) between the earliest Egyptian writing and slightly later stages of that writing system.

11. For the term *logophonetic* rather than *logosyllabic*, see below, and Cooper (2000).

12. For these emblems and their relation to early Chinese writing, see Boltz (1994:44–52).

13. "The writing recorded not what was about to be divined but what had been. Its purposes, therefore, were at least partly historical and bureaucratic . . ." (Keightley 1978:45). For uninscribed oracle bones, see Poo (1998:27).

14. Note Houston's remark (2000:146) that "depictions of kings long preceded explicit, monumental, *textual* description of them."

15. Note, however, that Assmann's claim there that in Sumerian writing "iconicity did not play a particularly great role since the signs were very abstract from the beginning" is incorrect.

16. Pettersson (1996:ch. 5) would extend the comparison of the early stages of Sumerian cuneiform with Inka khipu or Aztec pictography. For him, the early stages of later full writing systems were not language based, that is, the signs were not read phonetically, and early Egyptian phonetic writing was based on a misunderstanding of what early Sumerian writing was doing. This is part of a larger argument against privileging oral language over graphic or gestural language, which goes far beyond the argument in this chapter for understanding spoken language and written language as complementary expressions of language. For Pettersson, this view assumes the chronological primacy of spoken language and the position of spoken language as the basis of written language. He, on the other hand, considers gestural and early graphic communication to have been independent of spoken language.

17. *Contra* Englund (1998:73–81), and his strong statement in this volume; cf. Cooper (1999a:87–91), Glassner (2000:ch. 7), Selz (2000:170, n. 4, 181, 186, and 199).

18. The cases later develop into horizontal lines of script; cf. Cooper (1996:38f.).

Although it is customary to publish archaic tablets with their columns oriented vertically and from left to right on the obverse (see Englund 1998:ch. 4.1 for details), as tablets were read in later periods, we know from the orientation of

the archaic pictographs that the tablets were originally read turned 90° clockwise (see below), so that the columns would have been read horizontally beginning at the top right corner of the obverse.
19. For later as well as archaic Sumerian bookkeeping techniques, see Nissen *et al.* (1993).
20. It is somewhat peculiar that it takes four or five centuries for writing to be used for royal display. There are inscribed stone monuments in Babylonia as early as *c.* 2900 BC (Gelb, Steinkellar, and Whiting 1991), but these deal exclusively with land transfers; Wilcke (1995) identifies one of these as a possible royal inscription of sorts.
  Englund (1998:99–102) has argued, unconvincingly in my opinion, that one of the archaic lexical texts is a literary text. See also Westenholz (1998), who shares Englund's view of at least the first few lines of the text, and is preparing an edition.
21. Urton (1998:428–430) speculates that some khipu actually did express the Aymara language, including grammatical markers. He bases this on the use of the imperfect indicative in Spanish translations of khipu-makers' interpretations of khipus. Because the Spanish imperfect indicative was regularly used in the colonial period to translate the Aymara grammatical markers "for knowledge through language and/or nonpersonal knowledge," he assumes that such markers were encoded in the khipu themselves. But perhaps, rather, those markers were introduced by the khipu-makers in their oral interpretation to indicate that what they were telling was derived not from their own experience, but from the khipu. Similarly, there is an alternative interpretation to Urton's claim at the Sundance seminar that the stones the khipu-makers are reported to have used when reading out the khipus represented binary arrays used to decode the khipus. Urton's source says the khipu-makers placed "some stones on the ground by means of which they preformed their accounting together with the khipu." Could the stones not simply be counters to aid in calculation?
22. See Baines (this volume) on the Egyptian narrative infinitive, and cf. Michalowski (1994:59f.).
23. For the legends of Enmerkar and other rulers of Uruk, see Alster (1995) and Glassner (2000:ch. 1), and now Vanstiphout (2003).
24. Glassner (2000:ch. 1) provides a very different interpretation of the myth: clever, but for me, unconvincing.
25. By "pictographic" I mean only that the signs are images of things or parts of things, that is, the term as I use it has no implication for how the signs operate in the writing system. The archaic signs in Fig. 4.10 are given in the conventional orientation used in later periods; turn 90° clockwise for the original orientation.
26. Englund (1998:80f.) suggests that one reason it is so difficult to correlate a sign's pictographic form with its later meaning is that archaic proto-cuneiform was not invented for Sumerian, but for another, unknown language. When the Sumerians adopted cuneiform *c.* 2900 BC for their own language, they would

have used the phonetic values of the signs in the earlier language for rebuses in their own language. This is a strong argument to contend with (see also Englund in this volume), but wrong, I think; see Cooper (1999a). Whittaker (2001) takes up Englund's argument, and proposes that the unknown language is Indo-European, but compare Rubio (1999).

27. Numerals were inscribed using different styluses with a round cross section. For the problem of archaic styluses, see Glassner (2000:157f.).
28. The single intriguing exception is the small group of eighth- to seventh-century BC "inscriptions" (royal names plus titles), the so-called "Assyrian Hieroglyphs," treated in Finkel and Reade (1996).
29. For Egypt, see Assmann (1994).
30. For the difficulty in interpreting this term, see Englund (1998:76f.).
31. When a Sumerian word ends in a consonant, a following vowel is often expressed phonetically with a sign that repeats the final consonant, as in *dingir-ra* = *dingir* + *a(k)*; compare Cooper (1996:43).
32. This is disputed by Englund (1998:77, n. 158; cf. Cooper 1999a:89–91 and Glassner 2000:189–192).
33. For possible phonetic expression of grammatical affixes in the archaic tablets, see Glassner (2000:192, 210).
34. See the contribution of Baines to this volume, and Boltz (1994).
35. See Françoise Bottéro's contribution to this volume for some possible +S + S Chinese compound characters.
36. As in Chinese, the +P element in the Sumerian compound could also be chosen for its semantic value. Thus DU ("to go") + KAS = kas_4 ("to run"), but KAS is also the sign used to write Sumerian *kaskal* ("road").
37. Semantic determinatives are also used in cuneiform, but not to the extent that they are in Egyptian; see Cooper (1996:43, 53).
38. For the various supplemental marks and changes in orientation that can be used to create new signs with new values, see Glassner (2000:ch. 7).
39. Englund (1998) and Pettersson (1996) would disagree. For the question of ideogram versus logogram, see Gelb (1963:106f.).
40. I use the terms *logophonetic* and *phonogram/phonographic* instead of the more common *logosyllabic* and *syllabogram/syllabic* to accommodate Egyptian, which uses signs phonetically to express consonants only, not syllables. See Cooper (2000).
41. For Egyptian, see Ritner (1996a:76f. and 79f.); for cuneiform, Cooper (1996:43); for Maya, J. Harris and Stearns (1997:34).
42. Or, rather, Egyptologists describe many writings as phonetic (the triliterals) that in other systems might be considered logographic; see Ritner (1996a:75).
43. Logographic writing does have some practical advantage in scientific texts, making them easy to scan to locate specific phenomena; see the example in Cooper (1996:54).

44. Compare with Houston (2000:152) on the "hyper-refinement" of Classic Maya courts and "locating Maya writing within a calligraphic sensibility that was as much aesthetic as practical."
45. See Cooper (1999b) for the use of aspects of early Japanese writing to understand better some aspects of cuneiform writing in Babylonia and Syria in the mid third millennium BC.
46. Urton asked the same question in his Sundance presentation, but his answer seems to beg the question. Other early civilizations in addition to those in Peru and Bolivia also "worked in three-dimensional textile . . . technology," but did not use it for record-keeping.
47. Boone now (this volume) does precisely this, and abandons the broader definition of writing she proposed earlier (Boone 2000).

5 | The state of decipherment of proto-Elamite

ROBERT K. ENGLUND

With the ongoing publication of the proto-cuneiform texts by the collaborators of the project Cuneiform Digital Library Initiative (CDLI), we are achieving a more substantial basis for the continuing discussion of the early development of writing in Mesopotamia.[1] Cuneiform is a system of writing with a history of over 3,000 years of use, and can boast of a text corpus unparalleled in number and breadth before the invention of the printing press. Cuneiform offers, moreover, a unique view of the earliest stages of development of an advanced writing system. In a career spanning over thirty years, Denise Schmandt-Besserat has published and discussed the significance of a means of accountancy employed in the ancient Near East that represents a clear precursor of the first proto-cuneiform tablets. Small clay objects unearthed in prehistoric strata were termed "tokens" by Schmandt-Besserat, who wished to underscore their use as markers in an ancient system of bookkeeping. These clay objects consist on the one hand of simple geometrical forms, for instance cones, spheres, etc., and on the other, of complex shapes or of simpler, but incised, forms. Simple, geometrically formed tokens were found encased within clay balls (usually called "bullae") dating to the period immediately preceding that characterized by the development of the earliest proto-cuneiform texts; these tokens most certainly assumed numerical functions in emerging urban centers of the late fourth millennium BC. Indeed, impressed signs of an array of numerical systems found in proto-cuneiform accounts represented, in both form and function, many of the archaic tokens, so that the forerunner role of the simple tokens in the development of writing in Mesopotamia belongs, as the editor of this volume would understand the term, to the "core knowledge" of modern cuneiformists.

The spate of new proto-cuneiform tablets on the London markets deriving from post-Kuwait-War Iraq, including over 400 new texts of both Uruk III and Uruk IV period date, reputedly from the ancient city of Umma, have increased the size of the proto-cuneiform corpus to over 6,000 tablets and fragments containing more than 38,000 lines of text.[2] Two elements provide us with a relatively firm understanding of the contents of many of the earliest cuneiform documents. First, there is an evident continuous paleographic and semiotic progression of the cuneiform sign repertory into periods, beginning with the Early Dynastic IIIa period c. 2600–2500 BC, whose administrative and literary documents are increasingly comprehensible. Second and more importantly, a scholastic tradition of many centuries of compiling and copying lexical lists, ancient "vocabularies," helps bridge the gap between proto-historical and historical context. It should also not be forgotten that the seventy years in which a limited but quite involved circle of Sumerologists has worked on proto-cuneiform have resulted in a number of tools helpful in continuing research – including the first Uruk sign list of Falkenstein (1936) and its revision by M. Green and Nissen (1987) – but also in a growing number of primary and secondary publications by, among others, Friberg (1978–1979, 1982, 1997–1998), M. Green (1980, 1981), M. Green and Nissen (1987), Charvát (1993, 1998), and the members of the CDLI. Despite such research tools enjoyed by those involved in the decipherment of proto-cuneiform, no definitive evidence has been produced that would identify the language of proto-cuneiform scribes. The onus to make the case one way or the other would appear to rest with specialists in the field of Sumerology, since, given its later linguistic presence and the strong cultural continuity in southern Babylonia, Sumerian must be the favorite candidate for an eventual decipherment. Yet neither the evidence for possible multivalent use of signs in the archaic period, nor, for instance, the more sophisticated argument of a unique connection between Sumerian number words and the sexagesimal numerical system – a notational system which appears to be attested already in the token assemblages of the prehistoric clay bullae – have sufficient weight to convince skeptics.[3] On the contrary, it seems that a strong argument from silence can be made that Sumerian is not present in the earliest literate communities, particularly given the large numbers of sign sequences which, with high likelihood, represent personal names and thus should be amenable to grammatical and lexical analyses comparable to those made of later Sumerian onomastics.[4]

Despite these uncertainties in the proto-cuneiform record, many factors make the interpretation of the earliest phase of writing in Mesopotamia a very rewarding study. In Mesopotamia we are favored with a substantially unbroken tradition of writing in both form and function through a period of three millennia, including most importantly an exceedingly conservative tradition of so-called "Listenliteratur," that is, of compilation and transmission of thematically organized word lists beginning with those of the earliest, Uruk IV-period phase of writing; we count large numbers of inscribed tablets and fragments from archaic Babylonia, now approximately 6,000, which for purposes of graphotactical analysis and context-related

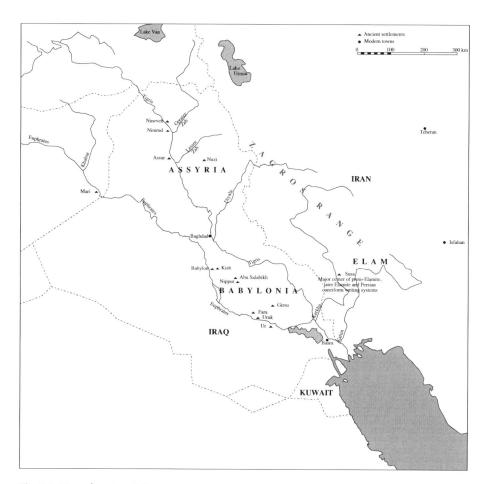

Fig. 5.1 Map of western Asia.

semantic categorization of signs and sign combinations represents a text mass of high promise; and assuming populations in Babylonia were relatively stable through time, we can utilize language decipherments from texts of later periods in working hypotheses dealing with the linguistic affiliation of archaic scribes.

Against this backdrop, the task of deciphering early texts from Persia seems all the more daunting. Although these texts have played an historically minor role relative to early cuneiform, the late nineteenth- to early twentieth-century French excavations of Susa (Fig. 5.2) made that script the first archaic Near Eastern writing system known to us. A quarter of a century before British–American excavators of Jemdet Nasr and German excavators of Uruk unearthed their proto-cuneiform tablet collections, de Morgan's archaeological earth-moving machine sent to the Louvre examples of an

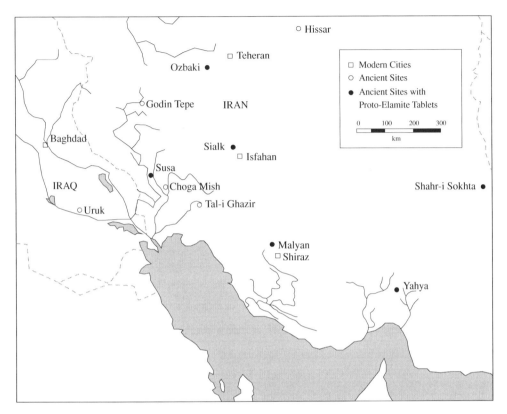

Fig. 5.2 Major sites of Late Uruk and proto-Elamite inscriptions in Persia.

evidently very early writing system which, based on a presumed genetic relationship to texts of the later-attested Elamite-speaking peoples of the Susiana plain, has been only conventionally named proto-Elamite.[5] The proto-Elamite corpus numbers just over 1,600 pieces, with around 10,000 lines of text, that is, about a quarter as many as from Babylonia (still, it represents a large amount of material compared to the relatively humble inscriptions of Linear A or of early Harappan).[6] The publication of tablets appears to have proceeded with little understanding of the text corpus and the accounting system it represented, and with little attention paid to an accurate representation in hand copies of the texts themselves.[7]

Accompanying sign lists were published with scant thought given to the high number of signs and the likelihood that the upwards of 5,500 signs in the final list attached to a primary publication by Mecquenem (1949) contained large numbers of sign variants. The list published by Meriggi (1971–1974) attempted to solve this problem by including under discrete headings presumed variant graphs and so arrived at a total of less than 400 sign entries. Unfortunately, that list was itself laced with incorrect identifications and graphic forms of many signs, in part reflecting the wayward decision of the author to opt to follow the original orientation of the proto-Elamite tablets, rather than the established conventional one. This, added to the fact that seemingly all of the signs were published as mirror images, and that the important numerical sign systems were defectively organized, makes the Meriggi list a research tool of limited value.[8] However, proto-Elamite inscriptions have been, and will remain, highly problematic in a discussion of writing because they represent a very unclear period of literacy, possibly beginning around 3300 and ending around 3000 BC, after which, unlike Mesopotamia, no writing tradition existed that might have served to reflect light back upon this earliest phase. The few so-called "Linear Elamite" inscriptions from the late Old Akkadian period, that is, from a period some eight centuries after the proto-Elamite age, exhibit little graphic and no obvious semantic connection to the earlier writing system.[9]

Still, the proto-Elamite writing system exhibits high potential and, but for its uniqueness as a largely undeciphered script of an entirely unknown dead language, has some features which might have made it an even better candidate for decipherment than proto-cuneiform. Among these are a substantially more developed syntax evident in a linear "line of sight" in the writing practice (see below), and in an apparently more static graphotactical sign sequence.

Description

Proto-Elamite clay tablets – to date, no known examples of the script have been found on other materials – exhibit a relatively straightforward and standardized format throughout their history. Entries on the obverse face of a tablet usually began in the upper left corner with a general heading, followed by one or more individual entries. These were inscribed in lines from top to bottom kept in columns defined, if at all, by the shank of the stylus pressed along the length of the tablet. No apparent organizing importance was attached to the end of these columns; the notation of a particular entry often began in a column at the bottom of a tablet, and continued at the top of the adjoining column. This phenomenon is particularly obvious in the many examples of numerical notations spread across two such "columns."[10]

Their clearly recognizable, standardized structure divides proto-Elamite administrative texts into three major sections (Fig. 5.3a). Many texts begin with a *heading*, a sign or a sign combination which qualifies all transactions recorded in the text and which never contains a numerical notation. The

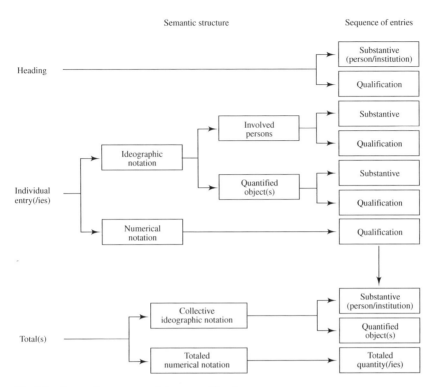

Fig. 5.3a Semantic structure of the proto-Elamite accounts.

clear formal structure of the following individual text entries allows their isolation from the headings and appended summations. These individual entries consisted of, first, a series of ideographic signs representing persons or institutions involved in the account, followed by signs representing objects qualified by further ideograms and by numerical notations. The sign combinations seem to indicate a possibly spoken sequence of substantive followed by qualification, as is also the case with the object designations and the numerical notations themselves.

Multiple-entry documents in the proto-Elamite corpus range in complexity from a simple linear sequence of entries of exactly the same type to involved accounts recording the consolidation of numerous primary accounts. A simple example may on the one hand be found in an account from the records of animal husbandry offices consisting of one or more entries representing numbers of animals moving from the care of one person or office to the next. On the other hand, texts may be highly structured, with up to three identifiable levels of hierarchy, reflecting, for instance, the organizational structure of a labor unit.[11]

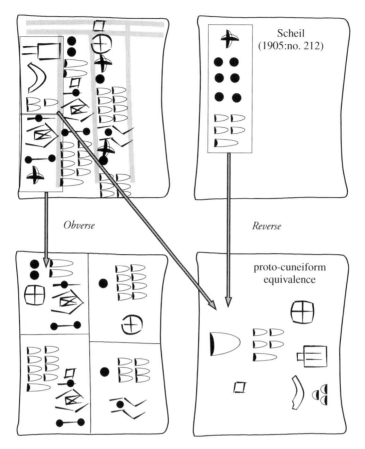

Fig. 5.3b Correspondence of proto-Elamite and proto-cuneiform accounts.

Particular entries, of a higher order which we call totals, contain summations of numerical notations from all or some entries together with collective ideographic notations. Since all entries seem to contain numerical notations, the syntax of these texts would seem more to represent the structure of a system of bookkeeping than the division of a spoken language into distinct semantic units, although within strings of ideographic signs we must anticipate such as-yet-undeciphered semantics.[12]

The first attempts to establish a clear relationship between the proto-Elamite and proto-cuneiform scripts were concentrated on the conformity between the number signs and numerical systems used in the respective scripts. This conformity is already suggested by the fact that, contrary to the ideograms, the proto-Elamite and the proto-cuneiform numerical signs exhibit the same sign forms (Fig. 5.4). More importantly, the

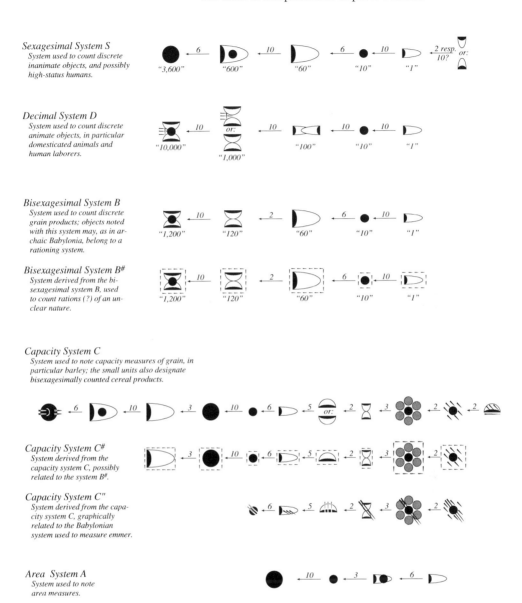

Fig. 5.4 Numerical systems attested in proto-Elamite accounts.

sequence of the basic signs (i.e., the combinations of vertical and oblique impressions of a round stylus) in the proto-Elamite numerical notations corresponds to that of the proto-cuneiform notations, thus indicating that the scribes of the proto-Elamite texts used numerical systems with at the very least the same quantitative order as the proto-cuneiform texts. Further, proto-Elamite numerical signs exhibit the same arithmetical ambiguity as the proto-cuneiform numerical signs, in that the numerical value of a particular sign differs according to its specific context of application. The exact quantitative relationships between the various members of an assumed system exhibited by the proto-Elamite text corpus could be inferred in many cases only by this analogy. When examined according to summations in the texts, however, these relationships stood in exact conformity with the relationships of the proto-cuneiform numerical systems.

One difference between proto-cuneiform and proto-Elamite numerical systems has already been noted in earlier treatments. In addition to the sexagesimal and the bisexagesimal systems well known from the proto-cuneiform administrative texts as numerical systems used to count discrete objects, a strictly decimal system was used in certain areas of application. Aside from six possible but unlikely exceptions, this numerical system finds no parallel in the proto-cuneiform corpus.[13]

An important result of our analysis of the proto-cuneiform numerical systems was the determination of ideograms which indicate in the texts the objects of the bookkeeping activities; this resulted in the confirmation that the numerical systems had distinctive areas of application. A comparably systematic analysis of the areas of application of proto-Elamite numerical systems has not yet been undertaken because of, in large part, the difficulty of identifying the semantic function of the signs.[14] A previous publication explored the numerical notations of proto-cuneiform accounts according to probability analysis in an attempt to isolate all systems employed in archaic Babylonian bookkeeping.[15] The same statistical method applied to the corpus of proto-Elamite texts allows us to reject confidently the presumption that the accounts record a hitherto unknown numerical system. The only exception would appear to be the surface area system identified in only one example (see Fig. 5.9). This tablet might represent a physical import from Babylonia.

The *sexagesimal system* (see Fig. 5.5) used in Mesopotamia for most discrete objects, including domestic and wild animals and humans, tools, products of wood and stone and containers of in some cases standard measures, is also well attested in the Susa administrative texts, although with an obviously restricted field of application.[16] The few discrete objects counted with the proto-Elamite sexagesimal system that can with some plausibility be identified include vessels and other products of craftsmen, and, it seems, humans of high status, but exclude animals and dependent laborers. Few tablets contain sufficiently preserved accounts to allow of a clear calculation of individual entries combined in a summation. For instance, Scheil

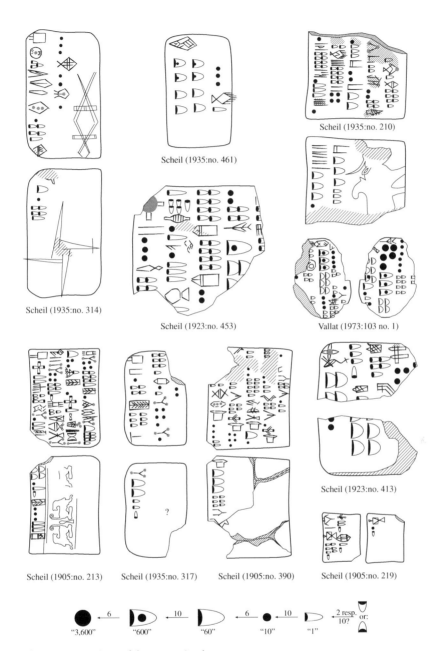

Fig. 5.5 Attestations of the sexagesimal system.

(1935: no. 314) consists of four entries on its obverse surface representing 15, 30, 20 and 10 units; thus the total on the text's reverse surface is to be considered a sexagesimal notation of N_{34} N_{14} $5N_1 = 75$ (counting presumed beer vessels).[17] Scheil (1905:no. 219) contains the individual entries $6\frac{1}{2} + 2\frac{1}{2} + 1\frac{1}{2}$ totaling, on its reverse surface, N_{14} $N_8 = 10\frac{1}{2}$. Other texts, though not completely preserved, retain individual entries which are compatible only with a sexagesimal interpretation of the texts' numerical system. For instance, the obverse of Scheil (1905:no. 213) consists of three entries of counted $M149_a - [13] + 10 + 10 = 33$ ($3N_{14}$ $3N_1$, rev. line 2) units – and five of counted $M376 - 12 + 45\frac{1}{2} + 90 + 47 + 67 =$ or $251\frac{1}{2}$ ($4N_{34}$ N_{14} N_1 N_8) units (reducing one of the obverse entries by 10); likewise, Scheil (1935:no. 317) may be reconstructed obv. N_{14} $4N_1$ / $6N_1$ / $7N_1$ / N_{14} $1N_1$ / $5N_{14}$ / N_{14} [$4N_1$ N_8] / $2N_{14} = 2N_{34}$ $2N_1$ N_8 (counting several presumable categories of humans). Both accounts appear to deal with humans of high status.[18] In other cases, numerical signs in large notations exhibit sequences which in all likelihood are sexagesimal, for example Scheil (1935:no. 461) with $4N_{48}$ $4N_{34}$ $3N_{14}$, and Vallat (1973:103 no. 1) with rev. i 2 $5N_{45}$ $3N_{48}$ $4N_{34}$ $5^{!?}N_{14}$ $8N_1$, are both evidence of large sexagesimal notations, the former text counting vessels, the latter among other commodities a sign very close to proto-cuneiform TI and thus possibly designating a large number of "bows and arrows."[19]

The *decimal system* (Figs. 5.6a–b) was used to count discrete objects in proto-Elamite texts; it has no proto-cuneiform counterpart. A handful of texts offer fully reconstructable calculations of counted objects with summations on reverse tablet surfaces and thus a clear interpretation of the absolute values represented by the individual signs of the system. For example, Scheil (1923:no. 45), contains individual entries on the obverse surface representing $94 + 69 + 147 + 44 + 50 + 112 + 75$ subsumed in a notation on the reverse surface equaling 591 ($5N_{23}$ $9N_{14}$ N_1) of counted M388 (⌐⊃).[20] For individual groups of small cattle (M346, ✈), Scheil (1905:no. 212; also Nissen *et al.* 1993:93–95) in like manner records notations representing $22 + 9 + 18 + 16$ head, subsumed in a notation on the reverse surface equaling 65 ($6N_{14}$ $5N_1$).[21] Accounts such as Scheil (1935:no. 205; Fig. 5.6a) with the sequence

$N_{51} \leftarrow N_{23} \leftarrow N_{14} \leftarrow N_1$,

for instance in line 1, N_{51} $7N_{23}$ $7N_{14}$ $4N_1$ (and see the accounts Scheil [1923:nos. 19, 86, 105, and 275–277]), confirm the structure of the numerical system as reconstructed in Fig. 5.6a, while the use of the sign N_{54} as the bundling unit above 1,000 is evident in only two texts, Mecquenem (1949: no. 31) and an unpublished Susa account in the Louvre. Each exhibits the use

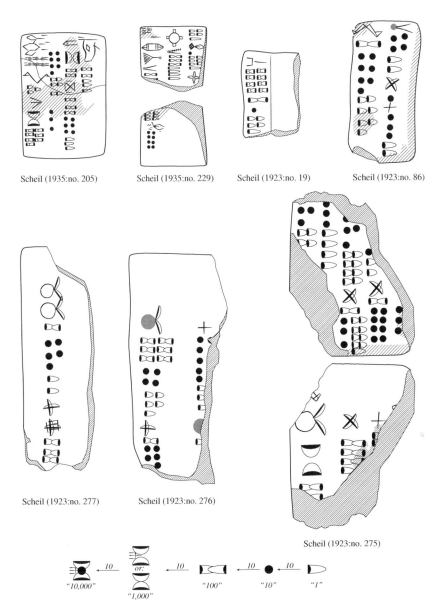

Fig. 5.6a Attestations of the decimal system.

of this number sign qualified with a graph resembling the proto-cuneiform sign GAL, "large." Although it would be tempting to imagine a relationship with Semitic /riba/ attested in the Ebla corpus, it would seem more likely that the graph is a form of gunification[22] used to differentiate this system clearly from the bisexagesimal system and its higher value signs N_{51} and N_{54} representing 120 and 1,200, respectively.

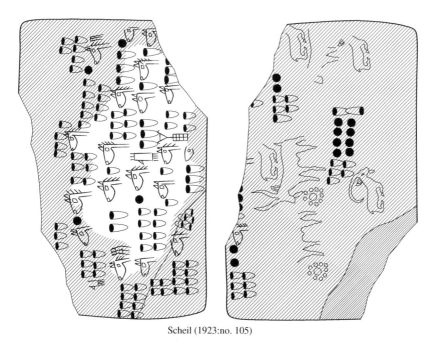

Scheil (1923:no. 105)

Fig. 5.6b Attestations of the decimal system.

The proto-cuneiform sexagesimal system was used to register *all* discrete objects with the exception of rations. Its field of application is shared in archaic Persia by the proto-Elamite sexagesimal system presumably loaned directly from Mesopotamia, and by a native proto-Elamite decimal system restricted to living beings, including animals *and* humans of low status. This categorization may be taxonomically relevant in our understanding of the world view of ancient Persians. Mesopotamian tradition established a dual gender system of animate and non-animate, whereby non-animate objects included animals and, charged with some ambivalence, occasionally household chattel and state slave laborers.[23] The proto-Elamite sexagesimal system may have been used to count objects of high, the decimal system to count objects of low, prestige. As an import from what was seen as a culturally advanced population, the sexagesimal system and the objects it was used to qualify might have enjoyed the status of prestige and power; the native decimal system may have been relegated to a qualifier of low-prestige humans and animals, in substantially the same fashion as Late Uruk Babylonian scribes treated dependent laborers KUR_a and SAL in their accounts. These were recorded with a tablet format wholly parallel to that employed in the bookkeeping of domesticated animals; the only difference between the two types of accounts was the inclusion of personal names in those concerning laborers (Englund 1998: 176–180).

It should be noted that both the sign representing 1,000 (N_{51}) and that representing 100 (N_{23}) in the proto-Elamite corpus, as well as apparently a spate of other numerical signs including N_{28} ($\frac{1}{4}$ N_{39} in the grain capacity system) and N_{34} ("60" in the sexagesimal and bisexagesimal systems), were used ideographically, or perhaps more likely phonetically in contexts strongly suggesting they formed parts of personal designations.[24] This frequent usage of numerical signs in non-numerical and non-metrological context should form a particular target of future attempts to reach a language decipherment of the proto-Elamite writing system.

The *bisexagesimal system* (Fig. 5.7) shows only minor differences in its structure and field of application relative to the same system in proto-cuneiform accounts. It was used to record barley rations and other cereal products in the form of discrete objects.[25] These barley products were themselves represented by numerical signs from the lower size registers of the grain capacity system, for instance in the text Scheil (1923:no. 421) with N_{30c} qualified by a bisexagesimal notation including $4N_{51}$ and $2[+n]N_{14}$, or in the text Scheil (1935:no. 50), with N_{30d} followed by a notation representing 120 + 60 units.[26] Other grain products are represented by a combination of low-register capacity signs and an ideogram, for instance the sign contained in the texts Scheil (1905:no. 388, and 1935:nos. 27, 125, 386) in Fig. 5.7.[27] Further, as in proto-cuneiform texts, proto-Elamite records of grain products can evidently insert grain equivalents of processed items. For example, the text Scheil (1905:no. 388) records various vessels that are followed by notations in the sexagesimal system and accompanied by dry grain products qualified in the bisexagesimal system. All entries were transferred into a grain capacity notation on the reverse surface of the tablet. A sufficient number of these accounts will permit us to determine the capacity typologies of the vessels used in proto-Elamite administration.[28]

There is no evidence of a proto-Elamite system comparable to the derived proto-cuneiform bisexagesimal system B* characterized by the addition of horizontal and vertical strokes to individual members of the related signs. Instead, proto-Elamite shows a derivation from the basic system in that an entire bisexagesimal notation can be framed with discontinuous strokes (therefore conventionally and mnemonically referred to as $B^{\#}$). The basic and this derived system can be added together, for instance in the account Scheil (1935:no. 27), combining $4N_{51}$ $4N_{14}$ + $[N_{34\#}$ $2N_{14\#}]$ + $6N_{51}$ + $N_{34\#}$ (520 + 80 + 720 + 60) in a common total N_{54} N_{51} N_{34} (1380), in contrast to the bisexagesimal systems in proto-cuneiform documents. The use of the proto-Elamite $B^{\#}$ system exclusively with grain products, and its graphic similarity to the derived proto-Elamite grain capacity system $Š^{\#}$ (see below)

114 Robert K. Englund

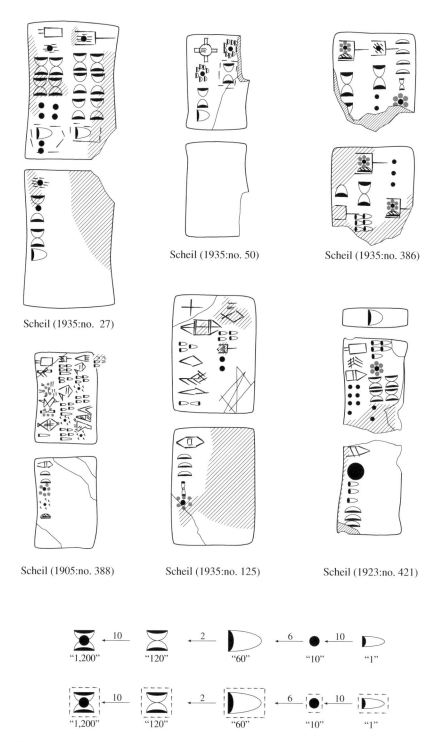

Fig. 5.7 Attestations of the bisexagesimal system.

The state of decipherment of proto-Elamite 115

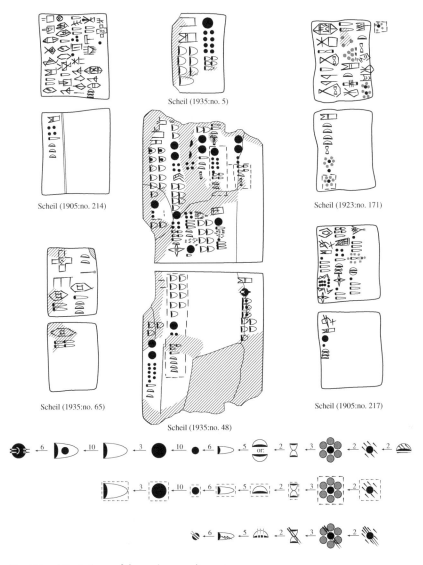

Fig. 5.8a Attestations of the grain capacity system.

suggests that $B^{\#}$ was used to register grain products containing amounts of grain recorded in the derived $Š^{\#}$ system. This would therefore imply that the basic system B recorded unprocessed grains, the derived system $B^{\#}$ products of those grains, including flour or simply cracked barley, along with breads and possibly malts.

One primary and two derived *grain capacity systems* (Fig. 5.8a) employ signs of the sexagesimal system, yet with entirely different arithmetical

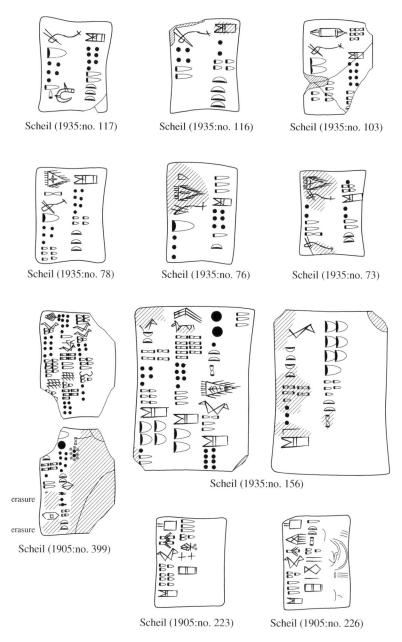

Fig. 5.8b PLOW = $2N_{39b}$, YOKE = $2\frac{1}{2} N_{39b}$ ($\frac{1}{2} N_1$).

values.[29] This system is as well attested in the proto-Elamite as in the proto-cuneiform sources, and seems to have the same field of application. In particular, the small units of the system are, in the same manner as in Mesopotamia, used as qualifying ideograms for grain products, thus denoting the quantity of grain in one unit of the product (Fig. 5.7). Contrary to the complex proto-cuneiform system of fractions represented by signs of the system below N_{39}, units in the proto-Elamite system are multiples of each other, including linearization down to $\frac{1}{12}$ and $\frac{1}{24}$ of N_{39b}.[30] Accounts such as Scheil (1935:no. 48) with the sequence

$N_{48} \leftarrow N_{34} \leftarrow N_{45} \leftarrow N_{14} \leftarrow N_1 \leftarrow N_{39b} \leftarrow N_{24}$,

and Scheil (1923:no. 171) (both Fig. 5.8a) with the sequence

$N_{39} \leftarrow N_{24} \leftarrow N_{39c}$,

clearly demonstrate the correspondence between the Babylonian and Persian basic systems. Numerical capacity systems derived from the primary system are as common in proto-Elamite texts as are such systems in proto-cuneiform. Best attested is the system $\check{S}^{\#}$, which seems related to the framed bisexagesimal system and probably is the functional equivalent of the proto-cuneiform system $\check{S}^*$ used to qualify measures of processed grain. A further derived system with individual signs in a notation qualified with two or more additional impressed bars is graphically similar to the proto-cuneiform system $\check{S}E''$, which, based above all on its resemblance to the later Sumerian sign *zíz*, has been interpreted to represent measures of emmer wheat.[31] Evidence concerning the absolute size of measures represented by the signs of the proto-Elamite grain capacity systems is, as with proto-cuneiform, very meager. Although the occurrence of both beveled-rim bowls and very nearly the same numerical systems for grain measures in archaic Persia as in Mesopotamia might indicate that the absolute volumes these numerical signs represented were the same in both administrative centers, we must remember that the proto-Elamite grain capacity system includes a sign in the lower range less than $\frac{1}{2}$ as large as the smallest arithmetically determined member of the proto-cuneiform system. A mean value of 0.6 liters for the beveled-rim bowls in Susa would have the smallest measure corresponding to just 0.15 liter, a measure which seems too small in an administration concerned with, at the least, measures of daily rations.[32] Numerous proto-Elamite texts indicate, moreover, that the signs representing worker categories were equated to $\frac{1}{2}$ of a basic unit of grain. If these texts followed Babylonian tradition, they most likely recorded the regular monthly rations of dependent workers, so that $\frac{1}{2}$ ⌓ should

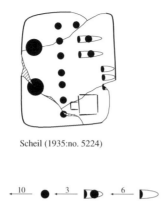

Fig. 5.9 Attestations of the area system.

approximately correspond to a one-month ration for a worker in contemporaneous Mesopotamia. Proto-Elamite grain numerical signs might therefore have represented measures roughly twice as large as those in Mesopotamia.[33]

A substantial number of proto-Elamite accounts attest to a standardized relationship of a given amount of grain recorded in the grain capacity system to a discrete number of objects qualified as YOKE (M54) or PLOW (M56; Fig. 5.8b). For instance, Scheil (1935:no. 117) contains two numerical notations qualifying M56 and the "gur" sign M288 (⊠▭). The first records 111½ M56, the second $7N_{14}$ $2N_1$ $3N_{39b}$, that is, $223N_{39b}$ of grain, corresponding to exactly $2N_{39b}$ grain per M56. On the other hand, the large account Scheil (1935:no. 156) contains in its summation the notations M54 $2N_{51}$ $5N_{23}$ $3N_{14}$ N_1, or 2,531 M54, followed by M288 $7N_{34}$ $5N_1$ $2N_{39b}$ N_{24}, or $6,327½N_{39b}$, resulting in the exact relationship of $2½N_{39b}$ ($= ½N_1$) per M54. Peter Damerow and I have interpreted these texts as representing grain distributions for the sowing of fields, whereby M54/YOKE is a sign for seeding workmen or workmen and their plow animals, M56/PLOW a sign for a measure of plowed and sowed field (Damerow and Englund 1989:57–58, no. 159).

Among the proto-Elamite texts, only Scheil (1935:no. 5224) contains a notation which may have been written in a numerical system used to register *surface measures* (Fig. 5.9). The diagrammed system assumes that the sign representing "10 BÙR" ("BUR'U") in the proto-Elamite corpus replaced the normal sign N_{50} of proto-cuneiform documents, although it must be remembered that its unique occurrence might act as evidence *against* the

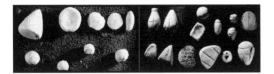

Fig. 5.10 Examples of simple (left) and complex (right) "tokens" from Uruk (digital images courtesy of CDLI).

use of this Babylonian system in Persia, given also the fact that we have reason to believe that the sign M56 discussed above may have served as a measure of arable land, registered in the sexagesimal system.[34] Format and text layout of Scheil (1935:no. 5224), moreover, give the impression of a true proto-cuneiform tablet, so that one might suspect that despite its possibly irregular use of the sign N_{45} this text was imported from Babylonia.

Precursors

Western Persia has been of particular interest to historians of early Mesopotamian history, since as Babylonian hinterland it always enjoyed a very close – oftentimes a desperately close – relationship with the early civilizations of the river plains. Indeed, as a more immediate source of items of trade and plunder, Persia was a natural partner of southern Mesopotamia, more so than ancient Syria to the northwest. For this reason, the Uruk Expansion of the fourth millennium BC is best attested in the Persian settlements of Susa, Choga Mish, and Godin Tepe. Above all, Susa demonstrates in its archaeological record a development parallel to that of Uruk, so parallel in fact that one might wonder who was influencing whom. In this Late Uruk period of shared culture, the most striking diagnostic features were the common use of seals and the development of writing as an administrative tool.

H. Nissen (1983:83–98, 1999:41–50) has emphasized the prehistoric means of administrative communication which in part led to the development of proto-cuneiform, including the use of stamp and then cylinder seals. He makes these claims in part on the basis of material presented in an array of articles and now a monograph by D. Schmandt-Besserat (1992), according to which archaic cuneiform derived from a prehistoric Near Eastern system of administration characterized by the use of small clay markers she terms "tokens" (see Fig. 5.10). The Susiana finds of both simple and complex tokens from the latter half of the fourth millennium BC represent possible evidence of a borrowing from southern Mesopotamia during the Late Uruk period, a prehistoric phase at the close of which the

Fig. 5.11 Examples of sealed (top), sealed and impressed (middle) bullae, and a "numerical" tablet (all from Susa – top: Sb 1932; middle: Sb 1940; bottom: Sb 2313; digital images courtesy of CDLI).

proto-cuneiform writing system was developed in Uruk. Schmandt-Besserat goes on to cite evidence of the close relationship between Uruk and Susa in the period immediately before the first Uruk IVa tablets, characterized above all at both of these centers by the insertion of tokens into clay balls, the outer surface of which was decorated with the impression of a cylinder seal. The next step in this scheme is the impression of those same tokens on the outer surface of the balls. Finally, immediately before the emergence of pictography, a flat, token-less clay tablet replaced the function of the earlier balls (Fig. 5.11).

Stratigraphically insensitive work at Susa by the mining engineers de Morgan and de Mecquenem – both laboring in a less sophisticated era of

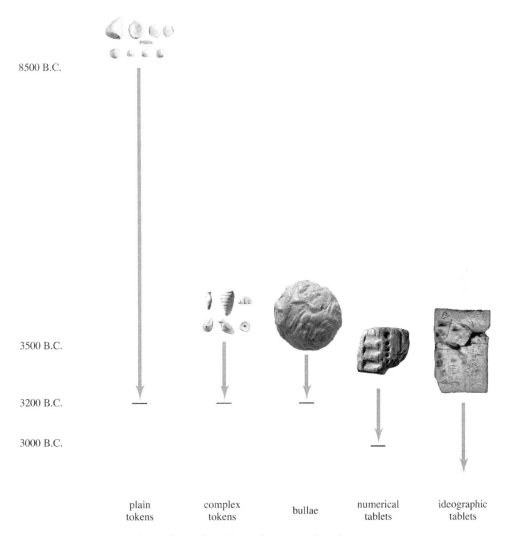

Fig. 5.12 Development of cuneiform, after Schmandt-Besserat (1992).

archaeological method – heavily disturbed the evidence we might expect from the single largest Persian settlement of the fourth millennium BC. The scheme devised by Schmandt-Besserat (Fig. 5.12) nevertheless fits well with the stratigraphic sequences outlined by Le Breton (1957:79–124) and improved upon by subsequent excavations at Susa and other Late Uruk and proto-Elamite sites in Persia.[35] Thus, the bullae with enclosed tokens derive primarily from level Susa 18, numerical tablets from level 17, and proto-Elamite tablets from 16–14. Architectural seriation by German archaeologists at Uruk has presented us with a confusing chronology from the

Babylonian locus of these developments. Neither the context of the bullae W 20987 from Uruk (Damerow and Meinzer 1995:7–33 + pls. 1–4) nor that of the numerical tablets from the area of the so-called "Red Temple" was undisturbed in antiquity, so that at the most we can state that the evidence from Uruk does not contradict that from Susa.[36]

Accordingly, Uruk and Late Uruk precursors of writing in Mesopotamia and Persia can be tentatively divided into a *period of early tokens* prior to *c.* 3500 BC, in which simply formed geometric clay counters were used in an ad hoc fashion to record simple deliveries of goods, primarily grain and animal products of local economies. This was followed by a *period of clay envelopes*, *c.* 3500–3400 BC, in which these same geometric clay counters with some further ideographic differentiations were enclosed in clay envelopes, and these envelopes were covered with impressions from cylinder seals. The outer surfaces of some envelopes were impressed with counters in a one-to-one correspondence to the enclosed pieces. The subsequent *period of early numerical tablets*, *c.* 3400–3350 BC, is characterized by flat and rounded clay tablets, sealed and unsealed, that were impressed with counters or with styli cut and shaped to imitate counters, thus representing numerical notations. In the *period of late numerical tablets*, *c.* 3350–3300 BC, flat and rectangular-shaped sealed clay tablets were impressed with styli to record numerical notations. Finally, during the last Late Uruk *period of numero-ideographic tablets*, *c.* 3300 BC, flat and rectangular-shaped sealed clay tablets were impressed with styli to record numerical notations and one, or at most two, ideograms. All ideograms represented the objects of the transaction, including sheep and goats and products derived from them, above all textiles and dairy oils (Englund 1998:214–215).

The Late Uruk loan

Interestingly, numerical tablets found in Susa coincide, according to more recent French examination of Susa stratigraphy, with the retreat of the cultural influence exerted by southern Babylonia over Persia and Syria *c.* 3300 BC, that is, at precisely the moment when Uruk succumbed to administrative pressures and began keeping complex written records. Sufficient evidence may be found in the proto-Elamite texts to support this moment in time, corresponding to the architectural level IVa at Uruk, as the period of final direct contact between Uruk and Susa. In the first place, there is general evidence that the proto-Elamite accounting system was strongly influenced by proto-cuneiform, including, in a sequence of increasing importance, the use of

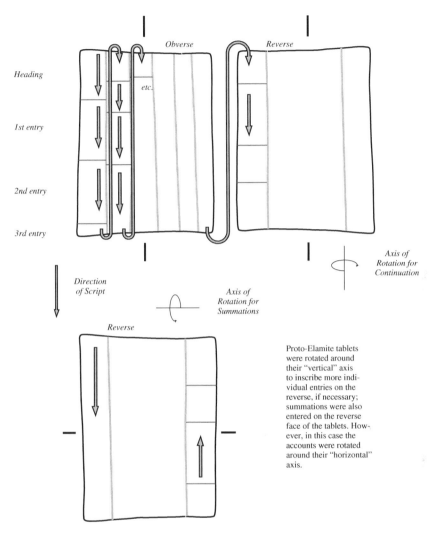

Fig. 5.13 Complex tablet rotation among proto-Elamite tablets (Scheil 1905:no. 4997).

- the same material for writing (clay and evidently a reed or wood stylus);[37]
- the same tablet format (usually c. 3:2) relative to the direction of writing;
- seals on the surfaces of bullae and the earliest texts (numerical tablets), whereas seals were not used later, when presumably ideograms replaced them in function;
- comparable accounting formats, according to which summations of numerical data on accounts were, as a rule, recorded on the reverse face of the tablets;

- the same rotation of tablets (simple and complex, Fig. 5.13). When more space for separate entries was required than available on the obverse of a tablet, the scribe continued these entries on the reverse, flipping the tablet over on its vertical axis. Totals were then inscribed by returning to the obverse face of the tablet and flipping it on its horizontal axis, as was normal practice in texts which had only such totals on their reverse faces;[38]
- the same numerical signs and sign systems, but including the derivative use of bisexagesimal signs for the 1,000 and 10,000 steps of the decimal system found only in Elam (the sign for "100," ▷◁, itself follows the productive method of placing two signs in opposition to form the next bundling step in the system); and of
- the same sign repertoires for humans and animals, including collective designations (Fig. 5.14). For instance, the proto-Elamite tablet Scheil (1923:no. 45), contains an account of various groups of persons qualified with the sign M388 (▷▷), totaling 591, as noted on the reverse of the text (Fig. 5.15). We have found very similar representations of persons designated KUR_a in the often discussed "slave labor" accounts of Uruk and Jemdet Nasr. Moreover, further qualifications of related signs (Fig. 5.14), for instance the fact that the proto-Elamite sign closely resembling the proto-cuneiform sign TUR is itself qualified with signs which seem clearly to represent male and female slaves, would seem to indicate a borrowing of these signs and sign combinations from Mesopotamia.

Susa stratigraphy and a relative chronology between Babylonia and the Susiana have helped generally to date the inception of the proto-Elamite system of writing to the Jemdet Nasr / Uruk III phase of Mesopotamia. It was noted above that the linearity and the apparently developed separation of semantics and syntax of proto-Elamite writing are evidence of a more advanced system than that of proto-cuneiform, in which much of the syntactical burden of the texts was carried by a complex format consisting of cases and subcases. This historical argument further supports a relative sequence of Uruk IV texts from Babylonia followed by Uruk III texts in the same region and, contemporaneously, proto-Elamite texts from Persia. However, if we attempt to define more precisely the period of borrowing, then several features of proto-Elamite script are suggestive of contact between Susa and Uruk during the early Uruk IVa period. These include:

- use of N_{39b} (◠) in grain capacity notations, as was the rule in proto-cuneiform texts from the earliest writing phase, following which

The state of decipherment of proto-Elamite

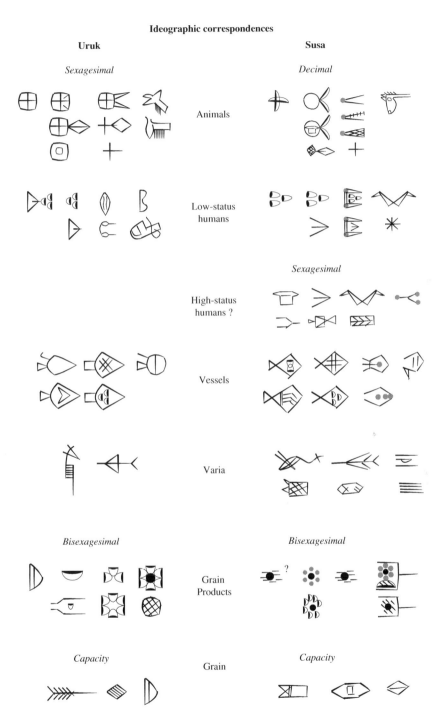

Fig. 5.14 Semantic and graphic correspondences between proto-cuneiform and proto-Elamite ideograms.

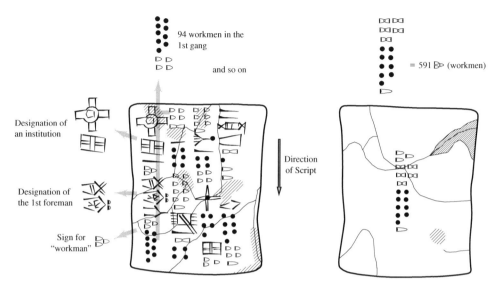

Fig. 5.15 Scheil (1923:no. 45), an account of 7 labor gangs, totaling 591 workmen.

(in the Jemdet Nasr/Uruk III period) Babylonian scribes used exclusively the inverted sign form N_{39a};[39]
- use of the same dividing lines formed with the shank of a stylus. This is a feature known only, but generally, in the numerical tablets from both Uruk (IVa) and Susa (17, Fig. 5.16);
- the same high occurrence of apparent sign variants as an indication of inchoate standardization (this may in fact be a means for the internal dating of the proto-Elamite tablets in a relative sequence, since we should expect to find more and more agreement on particular graphs, as is the case in Uruk).
- the same earliest ideograms. The most telling evidence of continuing contact between Uruk and Susa into the earliest phase of writing is found in a comparison of a number of tablets from both cities which combine the elements of numerical tablets (numerical notations, seal impressions, stylus shank dividers) with one, and at most two, apparent ideograms. I count about a dozen of these texts from unclear Uruk find spots – the stratigraphy of tablets from that settlement is impossible to reconstruct – including both purely numerical and ideographic tablets of phase IVa (Fig. 5.17), and several from Susa, Godin, and possibly Sialk in Persia (Fig. 5.18). A simple comparison (Fig. 5.20) of the signs found in this context would seem to show that at least in the case of this first block at the top the same sign is found in both centers.[40] Note that although the topmost signs would correspond nicely with a type of "complex" token found in nearly all token

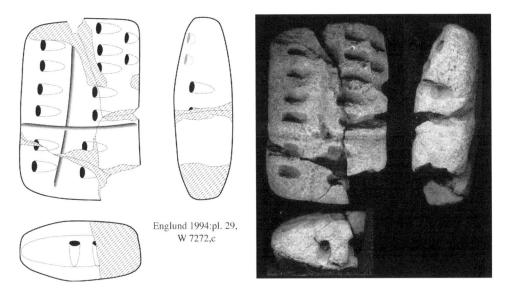

Fig. 5.16 Stylus shank case dividers on a numerical tablet from Uruk (digital image of original courtesy of CDLI).

deposits and equated by Schmandt-Besserat and others to the later sign KU_3 ("precious metal"), such tokens are more likely to represent the fraction "$1/2$" of a metrological unit from the archaic liquid capacity system based on a ceramic vessel containing butter oil (Englund 1998:168, fig. 61).

Conclusion

The prospects of discovering script characteristics that could lead to a decipherment of proto-Elamite are not great, but there are some areas of promise. In the first place, the proto-Elamite texts do contain sign sequences which are distinctly longer than the average of those from Mesopotamia. The texts are therefore more likely to contain language-based syntactical information than the very cursory notations in proto-cuneiform documents. There is, however, a more important, second point. Statistical analysis of text transliterations should point toward meaningful sign combinations of a fixed sign sequence which could reflect speech (Fig. 5.20). Further, the "proto-Elamites" are not entirely foreign to us. We can assume that they were a people who used a decimal system to count discrete objects, and some of their number words, in particular the words for "hundred" and "thousand," may have been used syllabically. In proto-Elamite accounts, the numerical notations *follow* counted objects and their qualifications. This deviation stands in contrast to Mesopotamian tradition (we have of late seen only one

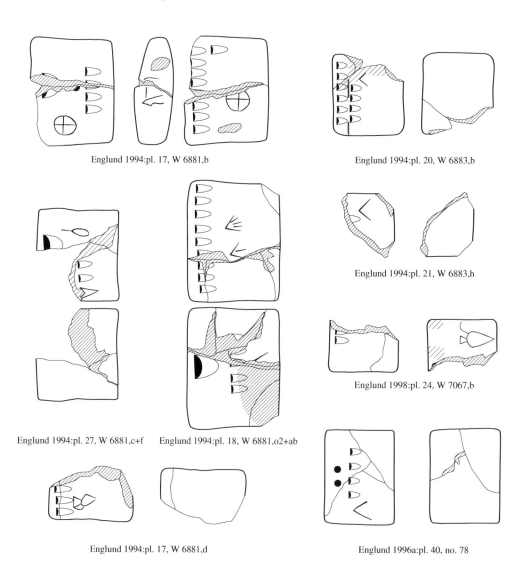

Fig. 5.17 Uruk "numero-ideographic" texts.

other example of such a convention, namely in the 24th-century BC accounts from Syrian Tell Beydar), and more importantly in contrast to the first ideographic tradition in Persia itself, that is, in the numero-ideographic tablets from Susa and Godin Tepe presumably imposed on the local population by Babylonian accountants.[41] We might therefore speculate that our so-called "proto-Elamite" derived from a language whose numerical qualifications were post-positional.

A first step in the reevaluation of the proto-Elamite text corpus is necessarily the electronic transliteration of all texts. CDLI staff have completed

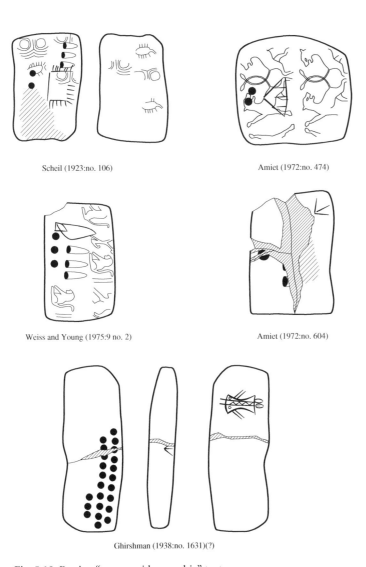

Fig. 5.18 Persian "numero-ideographic" texts.

this task, and are now beginning a new graphotactical examination of the texts. The following list demonstrates the use to which these data might be put. The proto-Elamite sign M371 (two round impressions connected by a single stroke) appears in the accounts in initial, intermediate, and final position, in altogether over 300 attestations.[42] As seems evident from attestations of the sign in initial and final position, it represents a discrete object counted in the sexagesimal or decimal system. A quick check of the sources confirms that the system is in fact sexagesimal. Scheil (1905:no. 391), for instance, contains clear sexagesimal notations ($1N_{34}$, $2N_{34}$) of

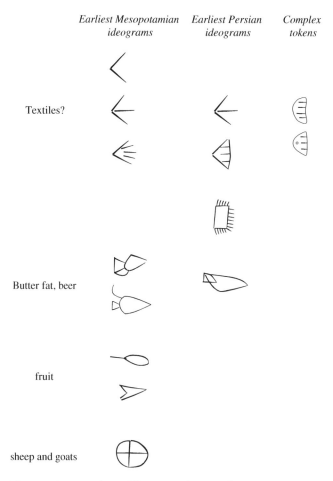

Fig. 5.19 A comparison of "numero-ideograms" in Mesopotamia and Persia.

objects including M371. Scheil (1923:no. 94) and other accounts imply that M371 is related to the proto-Elamite sign for male laborers (M388), possibly – since M371 is not reckoned in the decimal system – in a supervisory capacity.

1) *M371 in initial and final position*

Scheil (1935:no. 107)	O0101	**INIT&FINAL**M371
Scheil (1923:no. 139)	O0102	**INIT&FINAL**M371 [ ]
Scheil (1923:no. 162)	O0102	**INIT&FINAL**M371 $1N_1$
Mecquenem (1949:no. 029)	O0103	**INIT&FINAL**M371 $2N_1$
Scheil (1923:no. 299)	O0104	**INIT&FINAL**M371 $1N_1$
Scheil (1935:no. 5207)	O0104	**INIT&FINAL**M371 $1N_{39b}$
Scheil (1935:no. 5196)	O0104	**INIT&FINAL**M371 $3N_1$

Scheil (1935:no. 020)	O0105	INIT& FINAL**M371** $1N_{14}$
Scheil (1935:no. 264)	O0106	INIT&FINAL**M371** $1N_{14}$ $2N_1$
Scheil (1923:no. 248)	O0108	INIT&FINAL**M371** $2N_1$
Scheil (1935:no. 052)	O0109	INIT&FINAL**M371** $1N_1$
Scheil (1923:no. 437)	O0110	INIT&FINAL**M371** [ ]
Scheil (1935:no. 329)	O0110	INIT&FINAL**M371** $1N_1$
Scheil (1905:no. 215)	O0111	INIT&FINAL**M371** $1N_1$
Scheil (1935:no. 002)	O0114	INIT&FINAL**M371** $1N_{14}$
Scheil (1935:no. 0335)	O0118	INIT&FINAL**M371** $2N_1$ $2N_{39b}$
Scheil (1935:no. 342)	O0123	INIT&FINAL**M371** $6N_1$
Scheil (1923:no. 292)	O0217	INIT&FINAL**M371** [ ]
Scheil (1905:no. 391)	R0102	INIT&FINAL**M371** $1N_{34}$
Scheil (1935:no. 342)	R0104	INIT&FINAL**M371** $1N_{14}$ $8N_1$

2) *M371 in initial position, sorted according to following signs*

Scheil (1935:no. 218)	O0109	INIT**M371** $M3_b$ $2N_1$
Scheil (1905:no. 343)	O0112	INIT**M371** M9 INTER**M371** $M3_c$ $2N_1$
Scheil (1923:no. 121)	R0101	INIT**M371** M9 FINAL**M371** $2N_{39b}$
Scheil (1935:no. 5019)	O0103	INIT**M371** M9 FINAL**M371** $1N_1$
Scheil (1905:no. 344)	O0105	INIT**M371** M32 M96 $M329^?$ [ ]
Scheil (1935:no. 5206)	O0105	INIT**M371** $M36_o$ $1N_{14\#}$
Scheil (1935:no. 256)	O0102	INIT**M371** M54 $1N_{14}$ $7N_1$
Scheil (1923:no. 474)	O0103	INIT**M371** M139 $M296_c$ [ ]
Scheil (1905:no. 213)	O0109	INIT**M371** $M207_a^?$ M376 $4N_{14}$ $7N_1$
Scheil (1935:no. 311)	O0109	INIT**M371** M218 $1N_1$
Scheil (1923:no. 450)	O0105	INIT**M371** M218 M220 $M132_b$ M263 $2N_1$
Scheil (1905:no. 380)	O0105	INIT**M371** M263 [ ]
Scheil (1935:no. 468)	O0103	INIT**M371** M263 $2N_1$
Scheil (1905:no. 293)	O0111	INIT**M371** M263 M96 X M243 X [ ]
Scheil (1905:no. 292)	O0109	INIT**M371** $M295_k$ $M66^?$ M376 $1N_{8a}$
Scheil (1905:no. 389)	O0103	INIT**M371** $M298^?$ $4N_{14}$ $4N_{39b}$
Mecquenem (1949:no. 014)	O0102	INIT**M371** M325 M376 $4N_{14}$
Scheil (1905:no. 243)	O0106	INIT**M371** $M332_d^?$ M218 $1N_1$
Scheil (1905:no. 204)	O0106	INIT**M371** M346 $2N_1$
Scheil (1923:no. 292)	O0242	INIT**M371** $M370_c$ $1N_1$
Scheil (1923:no. 292)	O0241	INIT**M371** INTER**M371** $M124_c^?$ $1N_1$
Scheil (1923:no. 345)	O0102	INIT**M371** M376 $5N_1$
Scheil (1935:no. 284)	O0109	INIT**M371** M387 [ ]
Scheil (1935:no. 5037)	O0102	INIT**M371** M387 M9 $M264_b$ $3N_1$
Scheil (1935:no. 5207)	R0102	INIT**M371** X M118 M9
Scheil (1935:no. 5055)	O0111	INIT**M371** X M131 M263 X $1N_1$
Scheil (1905:no. 319)	O0110	INIT**M371** X M218 $1N_1$
Scheil (1905:no. 5002)	O0109	INIT**M371** X M218 $1N_{39b}$
Scheil (1905:no. 300)	R0101	INIT**M371** X X M218 X $1N_1$

3) *M371 in intermediate position, sorted according to immediately preceding signs*

Scheil (1923:no. 112)	R0116	M387 M372$_a$ M388 M296$_c$ M1 **INTERM371** M317 1N$_1$
Scheil (1905:no. 290)	O0110	X M1 **INTERM371** M1 1N$_1$ [ ]
Scheil (1923:no. 112)	R0114	M51 M388 M302$_e$ M3$_b$ **INTERM371** M317 1N$_1$
Scheil (1923:no. 112)	O0113	M112$_o$ M388 M24$_c$ M3$_b$ **INTERM371** M317 1N$_1$
Scheil (1905:no. 316)	R0107	M9 **INTERM371** M54 [ ]
Scheil (1935:no. 330)	O0109	M9 **INTERM371** M218 3N$_{14}$ 4N$_1$
Scheil (1905:no. 213)	O0104	M149$_a$ M246$_g$ M9 **INTERM371** M376 4N$_{14}$ 5N$_1$ 1N$_?$
Scheil (1905:no. 267)	R0105	M318$^?$ M9 **INTERM371** M288 4N$_1$ 4N$_{39b}$
Scheil (1935:no. 401)	R0103	M364 M9 **INTERM371** M288 1N$_1$
Scheil (1905:no. 240)	O0102	M377 M124$_a$ M48$_d$ M9 **INTERM371** M301$^?$ X **INTERM371** M348 1N$_{39b}$
Scheil (1923:no. 468)	O0106	X M9 **INTERM371** M288 1N$_{14}$
Scheil (1905:no. 311)	O0108	X M24 **INTERM371** M376 M370 X [ ]
Scheil (1935:no. 472)	O0109	M32 **INTERM371** M317 1N$_1$
Scheil (1905:no. 4999)	O0103	M263$_a$ M33 **INTERM371** M288 6N$_{14}$ 1N$_1$
Scheil (1923:no. 023)	O0103	X M33 **INTERM371** M288 3N$_1$
Scheil (1905:no. 369)	O0102	M181 M38$_a$ **INTERM371** M269$_d$ 1N$_1$
Scheil (1905:no. 369)	O0106	M38$_l$ **INTERM371** M264$_a$ 1N$_1$
Scheil (1935:no. 400)	O0102	M54 **INTERM371** M243$_g$ 1N$_1$
DE (1989:no. 11)	O0116	M388 M72 **INTERM371** M346 6N$_1$
Scheil (1923:no. 059)	O0102	M237 M263 M73$_q$ **INTERM371** M288 2N$_{14}$ 1N$_1$
Scheil (1935:no. 218)	O0102	M75$_h$ **INTERM371** M3$_c$ 1N$_1$
Scheil (1905:no. 258)	O0102	[ ] M388 M57$_c$ M96 **INTERM371** M288 4N$_1$ [ ]
Scheil (1923:no. 414)	O0106	M240$_i$ M132$_a$ M99 **INTERM371** M288$_k$ 1N$_1$
Scheil (1905:no. 240)	O0103	M110 **INTERM371** M346 M24 M434 M68$^?$ M266 M241 1N$_{39b}$
Scheil (1923:no. 292)	O0170	M388 M218 M110 **INTERM371** M3$_b$ 1N$_1$
Scheil (1923:no. 292)	O0221	M388 M387 M263$_a$ M110 **INTERM371** M352 M3$_b$ 1N$_1$
Scheil (1905:no. 267)	O0102	M124$_a$ **INTERM371** M9 M288 2N$_1$ 4N$_{39b}$
Scheil (1923:no. 157)	O0107	M124$_a$ **INTERM371** M9 **INTERM371** M288
Scheil (1935:no. 017)	O0102	M128$_d$ **INTERM371** X M290$_c$ 1N$_{14}$
Scheil (1905:no. 4997)	R0106	X M388 M139 **INTERM371** M291 M388 M373 1N$_{14}$ 1N$_1$
Scheil (1923:no. 217)	O0102	M145$_a$ **INTERM371** M297 1N$_{39b}$
Scheil (1935:no. 033)	O0102	M196 M147$_e$ M145$_a$ **INTERM371** M56 M288 3N$_1$

Source	Code	Text
Scheil (1935:no. 0295)	O0104	M388 M145$_a$ **interM371** M154
Scheil (1935:no. 4766)	O0106	M106 M323 M388 M145$_a$ **interM371** M36 4N$_1$
Scheil (1905:no. 351)	O0102	M388 M146 **interM371** M297 2N$_{14}$
Scheil (1905:no. 319)	R0112	M139 M388 M146$_b$ **interM371** M263 M218 M346 1N$_{14}$ 4N$_1$
Scheil (1905:no. 241)	O0102	M325$_d$ M388 M146$_b$ **interM371** M29$^?$ [ ]
DE (1989:no. 11)	O0111	M388 M206$_b$ **interM371** M346 7N$_1$
Scheil (1935:no. 400)	O0109	M132 M48 M219 M218 **interM371** M377$_e$ M390 **final**M371 1N$_1$
Scheil (1905:no. 292)	O0110	M311$_b$ M388 M218 **interM371** M218 [ ] [ ]
Scheil (1923:no. 292)	O0204	M388 M219 **interM371** M3$_b$ 1N$_1$
Scheil (1935:no. 129)	O0102	M305 M388 M222 **interM371** M387 M20 M263$_a$ 8N$_1$
Scheil (1935:no. 271)	O0102	M305 M388 M226$_c$ **interM371** M264$_h$ 1N$_1$
Scheil (1923:no. 153)	O0109	M124$_a$ M372 M229$_h$ **interM371** M132$_a$ X M218 M288$_f$ [ ]
Scheil (1923:no. 112)	O0109	M387$_1$ M372$_a$ M388 X M229$_m$ **interM371** M317 1N$_1$
Scheil (1923:no. 112)	R0102	M51 M388 M218 M229$_n$ **interM371** M317 1N$_1$
Scheil (1923:no. 185)	O0112	M233 **interM371** M288 1N$_1$
Scheil (1905:no. 391)	O0102	M157 M374 M9 M388 X M233$_b$ **interM371** M149$_a$ 8N$_1$
Scheil (1905:no. 212)	O0103	M342$^?$ M388 M4 M235$_a$ **interM371** M346 2N$_{14}$ 2N$_1$
Scheil (1935:no. 218)	O0113	M4 M240 **interM371** M54 8N$_1$
Scheil (1923:no. 292)	O0167	X M240$^?$ **interM371** M3$_b$ M388 [ ]
Scheil (1935:no. 340)	O0106	M377 M254$_c$ **interM371** M297 1N$_{30c}$
Scheil (1905:no. 309)	O0103	[ ] M351 M255 **interM371** M288 [ ]
Scheil (1905:no. 205)	O0104	M218$_a$ M259$_c$ **interM371** M223 X 1N$_1$
Scheil (1905:no. 353)	O0102	M305 M388 M218 M259$_m$ **interM371** M33 M66$^?$ M346 3N$_1$
Mecquenem (1949:no. 024)	O0103	M291 **interM371** M320 1N$_1$
Scheil (1935:no. 4758)	O0102	M175 M181 M124$_c$ X M297 **interM371** M297 M377 X X M124 M226$_f$ M101 X X 1N$_1$
Mecquenem (1949:no. 030)	O0102	X M376 M388 M364 M317$_c$ **interM371** M288 2N$_1$
Scheil (1905:no. 222)	O0102a	M365 M388 M57 M318$_a$ **interM371** M388 4N$_1$ [ ]
Scheil (1905:no. 205)	O0103	M102$_d$ M318$_a$ **interM371** M297 M150$_d$ 1N$_1$
Scheil (1923:no. 345)	O0101	M9 M318$_b$ **interM371** M321$_a$ [ ]
Scheil (1923:no. 317)	O0102	M388 M9 M318$_b$ **interM371** M36$_b$ [ ]

Scheil (1923:no. 148)	O0102	M388 M218 M364$^?$ M320$_h$ **interM371** M288$_i$ 4N$_{14}$ 2N$_1$
Scheil (1923:no. 043)	O0108	M240 M347 **interM371** M217$_c$ 1N$_1$
Scheil (1923:no. 490)	R0106	M387$_a$ M377$_e$ M347 **interM371** M288 1N$_1$
Scheil (1905:no. 4994)	O0107	M111 M388 M387N M318$_a$ X M377$_e$ M347 **interM371** M36$_e$ 5N$_1$
Scheil (1935:no. 353)	O0108	M218 M266 M373 **interM371** M101 M266 M283$_e$ X M266 3N$_1$
Scheil (1905:no. 258)	O0105	M380 **interM371** M38$_i^?$ M295$_s^?$ M218$_a$ 4N$_1$
Scheil (1905:no. 4997)	O0107	M388 **interM371** M117 M68$_d^?$ 1N$_{14}$ 1N$_1$
Mecquenem (1949:no. 031)	O0102	M388 **interM371** M263 M314$_f$ X X M301 M372 X [ ]
Scheil (1923:no. 159)	O0103	M195 M388 **interM371** M387 X [ ]
Mecquenem (1949:no. 004)	R0107	X M388 M263 M390 **interM371** M288 2N$_1$
Mecquenem (1949:no. 037)	O0109	M377$_e$ M390 **interM371** M388 M377$_e$ X X [ ]
Scheil (1935:no. 5218)	O0102	M388 M146$_b$ M377$_e$ M390 **interM371** M54 1N$_1$
Scheil (1905:no. 4996)	O0103	M263 X X M390 **interM371** M288 1N$_{14}$

4) *M371 in intermediate position, sorted according to following signs*

Scheil (1905:no. 290)	O0110	X M1 **interM371** M1 1N$_1$ [ ]
Scheil (1923:no. 292)	O0170	M388 M218 M110 **interM371** M3$_b$ 1N$_1$
Scheil (1923:no. 292)	O0204	M388 M219 **interM371** M3$_b$ 1N$_1$
Scheil (1935:no. 0298)	O0102	X M377 M263 X **interM371** M3$_b$ [ ]
Scheil (1923:no. 292)	O0167	X M240$^?$ **interM371** M3$_b$ M388 [ ]
Scheil (1935:no. 218)	O0102	M75$_h$ **interM371** M3$_c$ 1N$_1$
Scheil (1923:no. 098)	O0111	M96 X **interM371** M9 1N$_{30c}$
Scheil (1923:no. 157)	O0107	M124$_a$ **interM371** M9 **interM371** M288
Scheil (1905:no. 267)	O0102	M124$_a$ **interM371** M9 M288 2N$_1$ 4N$_{39b}$
Scheil (1905:no. 353)	O0102	M305 M388 M218 M259$_m$ **interM371** M33 M66$^?$ M346 3N$_1$
Scheil (1935:no. 4766)	O0106	M106 M323 M388 M145$_a$ **interM371** M36 4N$_1$
Scheil (1923:no. 317)	O0102	M388 M9 M318$_b$ **interM371** M36 [ ]
Scheil (1905:no. 4994)	O0107	M111 M388 M387N M318$_a$ X M377$_e$ M347 **interM371** M36$_e$ 5N$_1$
Scheil (1935:no. 5218)	O0102	M388 M146$_b$ M377$_e$ M390 **interM371** M54 1N$_1$
Scheil (1905:no. 246)	O0119	[ ] X **interM371** M54 1N$_1$
Scheil (1905:no. 316)	R0107	M9 **interM371** M54 [ ]
Scheil (1935:no. 218)	O0113	M4 M240 **interM371** M54 8N$_1$

Scheil (1935:no. 033)	O0102	M196 M147$_e$ M145$_a$ INTERM371 M56 M288 3N$_1$
Scheil (1935:no. 353)	O0108	M218 M266 M373 INTERM371 M101 M266 M283$_e$ X M266 3N$_1$
Scheil (1923:no. 357)	O0105	X INTERM371 M112$_f$ M36$_o$ 4N$_1$
Scheil (1905:no. 4997)	O0107	M388 INTERM371 M117 M68$_d^?$ 1N$_{14}$ 1N$_1$
Scheil (1923:no. 153)	O0109	M124$_a$ M372 M229$_h$ INTERM371 M132$_a$ X M218 M288$_f$ [ ]
Scheil (1905:no. 306)	O0103	[ ] INTERM371 M141 M54 X 1N$_{39b}$
Scheil (1905:no. 391)	O0102	M157 M374 M9 M388 X M233$_b$ INTERM371 M149$_a$ 8N$_1$
Scheil (1935:no. 0295)	O0104	M388 M145$_a$ INTERM371 M154
Scheil (1935:no. 5043)	O0103	M388 X INTERM371 M154$_r$ [ ]
Scheil (1923:no. 043)	O0108	M240 M347 INTERM371 M217$_c$ 1N$_1$
Scheil (1905:no. 293)	O0112	X INTERM371 M218 1N$_{14}$
Scheil (1935:no. 330)	O0109	M9 INTERM371 M218 3N$_{14}$ 4N$_1$
Scheil (1905:no. 292)	O0110	M311$_b$ M388 M218 INTERM371 M218 [ ] [ ]
Scheil (1923:no. 292)	O0109	X INTERM371 M218 M376$_a^?$ 1N$_1$
Scheil (1905:no. 205)	O0104	M218$_a$ M259$_c$ INTERM371 M223 X 1N$_1$
Scheil (1923:no. 073)	O0120	M218 M259$^?$ INTERM371 M223$_c$ M218 2N$_1$
Scheil (1935:no. 400)	O0102	M54 INTERM371 M243$_g$ 1N$_1$
Scheil (1905:no. 319)	R0112	M139 M388 M146$_b$ INTERM371 M263 M218 M346 1N$_{14}$ 4N$_1$
Mecquenem (1949:no. 031)	O0102	M388 INTERM371 M263 M314$_f$ X X M301 M372 X [ ]
Scheil (1905:no. 369)	O0106	M38$_l$ INTERM371 M264$_a$ 1N$_1$
Scheil (1935:no. 271)	O0102	M305 M388 M226$_c$ INTERM371 M264$_h$ 1N$_1$
Scheil (1905:no. 369)	O0102	M181 M38$_a$ INTERM371 M269$_d$ 1N$_1$
Scheil (1905:no. 258)	O0102	[ ] M388 M57$_c$ M96 INTERM371 M288 4N$_1$ [ ]
Scheil (1905:no. 267)	R0105	M318$^?$ M9 INTERM371 M288 4N$_1$ 4N$_{39b}$
Scheil (1905:no. 309)	O0103	[ ] M351 M255 INTERM371 M288 [ ]
Scheil (1905:no. 4996)	O0103	M263 X X M390 INTERM371 M288 1N$_{14}$
Scheil (1905:no. 4999)	O0103	M263$_a$ M33 INTERM371 M288 6N$_{14}$ 1N$_1$
Scheil (1923:no. 023)	O0103	X M33 INTERM371 M288 3N$_1$
Scheil (1923:no. 059)	O0102	M237 M263 M73$_q$ INTERM371 M288 2N$_{14}$ 1N$_1$
Scheil (1923:no. 185)	O0112	M233 INTERM371 M288 1N$_1$
Scheil (1923:no. 468)	O0106	X M9 INTERM371 M288 1N$_{14}$
Scheil (1923:no. 490)	R0106	M387$_a$ M377$_e$ M347 INTERM371 M288 1N$_1$
Scheil (1935:no. 401)	R0103	M364 M9 INTERM371 M288 1N$_1$
Mecquenem (1949:no. 004)	R0107	X M388 M263 M390 INTERM371 M288 2N$_1$
Mecquenem (1949:no. 030)	O0102	X M376 M388 M364 M317$_c$ INTERM371 M288 2N$_1$

Source	Object	Content
Scheil (1923:no. 148)	O0102	M388 M218 M364$^?$ M320$_h$ INTERM371 M288$_i$ 4N$_{14}$ 2N$_1$
Scheil (1923:no. 414)	O0106	M240$_i$ M132$_a$ M99 INTERM371 M288$_k$ 1N$_1$
Scheil (1905:no. 4997)	R0106	X M388 M139 INTERM371 M291 M388 M373 1N$_{14}$ 1N$_1$
Scheil (1905:no. 351)	O0102	M388 M146 INTERM371 M297 2N$_{14}$
Scheil (1923:no. 217)	O0102	M145$_a$ INTERM371 M297 1N$_{39b}$
Scheil (1935:no. 340)	O0106	M377 M254$_c$ INTERM371 M297 1N$_{30c}$
Scheil (1905:no. 205)	O0103	M102$_d$ M318$_a$ INTERM371 M297 M150$_d$ 1N$_1$
Scheil (1935:no. 4758)	O0102	M175 M181 M124$_c$ X M297 INTERM371 M297 M377 X X M124 M226$_f$ M101 X X 1N$_1$
Scheil (1923:no. 112)	O0109	M387$_l$ M372$_a$ M388 X M229$_m$ INTERM371 M317 1N$_1$
Scheil (1923:no. 112)	O0113	M112$_o$ M388 M24$_c$ M3$_b$ INTERM371 M317 1N$_1$
Scheil (1923:no. 112)	R0102	M51 M388 M218 M229N INTERM371 M317 1N$_1$
Scheil (1923:no. 112)	R0114	M51 M388 M302$_e$ M3$_b$ INTERM371 M317 1N$_1$
Scheil (1923:no. 112)	R0116	M387 M372$_a$ M388 M296$_c$ M1 INTERM371 M317 1N$_1$
Scheil (1935:no. 472)	O0109	M32 INTERM371 M317 1N$_1$
Mecquenem (1949:no. 024)	O0103	M291 INTERM371 M320 1N$_1$
Scheil (1923:no. 345)	O0101	M9 M318$_b$ INTERM371 M321$_a$ [ ]
Scheil (1905:no. 212)	O0103	M342$^?$ M388 M4 M235$_a$ INTERM371 M346 2N$_{14}$ 2N$_1$
DE (1989:no. 11)	O0111	M388 M206$_b$ INTERM371 M346 7N$_1$
DE (1989:no. 11)	O0116	M388 M72 INTERM371 M346 6N$_1$
Scheil (1905:no. 240)	O0103	M110 INTERM371 M346 M24 M434 M68$^?$ M266 M241 1N$_{39b}$
Scheil (1923:no. 292)	O0221	M388 M387 M263$_a$ M110 INTERM371 M352 M3$_b$ 1N$_1$
Scheil (1905:no. 213)	O0104	M149$_a$ M246$_g$ M9 INTERM371 M376 4N$_{14}$ 5N$_1$ 1N$_?$
Scheil (1905:no. 311)	O0108	X M24 INTERM371 M376 M370 X [ ]
Scheil (1935:no. 129)	O0102	M305 M388 M222 INTERM371 M387 M20 M263$_a$ 8N$_1$
Scheil (1923:no. 159)	O0103	M195 M388 INTERM371 M387 X [ ]
Scheil (1905:no. 222)	O0102a	M365 M388 M57 M318$_a$ INTERM371 M388 4N$_1$ [ ]
Mecquenem (1949:no. 037)	O0109	M377$_e$ M390 INTERM371 M388 M377$_e$ X X [ ]

5) *M371 in final position, sorted according to preceding signs*

Scheil (1923:no. 120)	O0132	X M3$_b$ FINALM371 1N$_1$
Scheil (1935:no. 286)	O0103	M9 FINALM371 1N$_1$
Scheil (1923:no. 292)	O0182	M9 FINALM371 2N$_{39b}$
Scheil (1923:no. 240)	O0110	M4 M9 FINALM371 1N$_1$
Scheil (1905:no. 362)	O0103	M29$_a$ M9 FINALM371 [ ]
Scheil (1923:no. 194)	O0103	M96$^?$ X M251$_b$ M9 FINALM371 1N$_1$
Scheil (1905:no. 272)	R0114	M120 M9 FINALM371 3N$_1$
Scheil (1935:no. 0333)	O0110	M124$_a$ M48$_c$ M9 FINALM371 1N$_1$
Scheil (1923:no. 270)	O0102	M218 X M9 FINALM371 [ ]
Scheil (1905:no. 271)	O0103	M251$_c$ M9 FINALM371 4N$_{39b}$
Scheil (1905:no. 267)	O0105	M318$_b$ M9 FINALM371 2N$_1$ 3N$_{39b}$
Scheil (1905:no. 293)	O0106	M325$^?$ M9 FINALM371 2N$_{14}$
Scheil (1923:no. 435)	O0107	X M9 FINALM371 [ ]
Scheil (1905:no. 311)	O0107	M124$_a$ M370 M24$_a$ FINALM371 [ ]
Scheil (1905:no. 4997)	O0112	M388 M373 M24$_a$ FINALM371 1N$_{14}$
Scheil (1923:no. 053)	O0102	M9 M24$_d$ FINALM371 1N$_1$
Scheil (1923:no. 299)	O0103	M24$_d$ FINALM371 [ ]
Scheil (1923:no. 230)	O0105	M32 FINALM371 1N$_1$
Scheil (1923:no. 436)	O0109	M32 FINALM371 1N$_1$
Scheil (1905:no. 293)	O0116	M251$_c$ M32 FINALM371 1N$_{14}$ 1N$_1$
Scheil (1905:no. 206)	O0104	M24 M33 FINALM371 1N$_{39b}$
Scheil (1923:no. 073)	O0108	M33 FINALM371 1N$_{14}$
Scheil (1935:no. 5222)	R0101	X M33 FINALM371 1N$_1$
Scheil (1923:no. 120)	O0119	M387$^?$ M387$^?$ M388 M272 M66 FINALM371 1N$_1$
Scheil (1905:no. 342)	O0103	M263 M94$_o$ FINALM371 [ ]
Scheil (1923:no. 246)	R0101	M99 FINALM371 1N$_1$
Scheil (1923:no. 387)	O0106	M99 FINALM371 1N$_1$
Scheil (1923:no. 279)	O0113	M124$_a$ M57 M99 FINALM371 1N$_1$
Scheil (1905:no. 267)	O0109	M131 M99 FINALM371 1N$_1$ [ ]
Scheil (1905:no. 362)	O0106	X M99 FINALM371 2N$_1$ 1N$_{39b}$
Scheil (1935:no. 330)	R0103	M1 M388 M99 X FINALM371
Scheil (1905:no. 353)	O0103	M104 FINALM371 1N$_2$
Scheil (1923:no. 144)	O0106	M110 FINALM371 1N$_1$
Scheil (1905:no. 286)	O0108	X M110$_a$ FINALM371 9N$_1^?$
Scheil (1923:no. 435)	R0103	X M352N M387$_a$ M122 FINALM371 1N$_{45}$ 6N$_{14}$
Scheil (1923:no. 292)	O0121	M124$_b$ FINALM371 1N$_1$
Scheil (1923:no. 031)	O0108	M153 M145$_a$ FINALM371 2N$_1$
Scheil (1905:no. 300)	O0108	X M145$_a$ FINALM371 2N$_1$
Scheil (1935:no. 5040)	O0103	M146 FINALM371 [ ]
Scheil (1923:no. 073)	O0112	M146 FINALM371 1N$_1$
Scheil (1923:no. 093)	O0105	M153 FINALM371 1N$_1$
Scheil (1905:no. 276)	O0107	X M218 FINALM371 3N$_1$
Scheil (1935:no. 4835)	O0104	M296 M388 M96 M225 FINALM371 1N$_1$
Scheil (1905:no. 350)	O0103	X M229$_o$ FINALM371 1N$_{14}$

Scheil (1905:no. 258)	O0103	[ ] X M4 M233$_c$ FINALM371 5N$_1$
Scheil (1905:no. 212)	O0104	M139 M4 M235$_a$ FINALM371 9N$_1$
Scheil (1905:no. 276)	O0108	M251$_i$ FINALM371 1N$_{8a}$
Scheil (1935:no. 054)	O0108	M254$_c$ FINALM371 1N$_1$
Scheil (1923:no. 292)	O0171	M370 M288 FINALM371 [ ]
Scheil (1923:no. 446)	R0102	M291 FINALM371 [ ]
Scheil (1935:no. 272)	O0105	M9 M318$_b$ FINALM371 1N$_{14}$ 4N$_1$
Scheil (1935:no. 272)	O0108	M24$_d$ M318$_b$ M318$_b$ FINALM371 [ ]
Scheil (1935:no. 400)	O0108	M24$_d$ M318$_b$ M318$_b$ FINALM371 1N$_1$
Scheil (1923:no. 094)	O0109	M387$_a$ M388 M9 M318$_b$ FINALM371 1N$_1$
Scheil (1935:no. 181)	O0104	M9 M318$_c$ FINALM371 1N$_{14}$
Scheil (1935:no. 052)	O0105	M29$_a$ M377$_e$ M347 FINALM371 [ ]
Scheil (1923:no. 446)	O0104	M347 FINALM371 1N$_1$
Scheil (1905:no. 272)	O0109	M377$^?$ M347 FINALM371 1N$_1$
Scheil (1935:no. 054)	O0111	M354 FINALM371 1N$_1$
Scheil (1935:no. 252)	O0109	M219 M380 FINALM371 2N$_1$
Scheil (1905:no. 276)	O0105	M386$_a$ M380 FINALM371 2N$_1$ 1N$_{8a}$
Scheil (1923:no. 392)	O0102	X M380 FINALM371 3N$_1$
Scheil (1935:no. 330)	O0105	M254$_a$ M380$_b$ FINALM371 3N$_{14}$ 2N$_1$
Scheil (1923:no. 073)	O0107	M263 M381 FINALM371 3N$_1$
Scheil (1935:no. 284)	O0107	M387$_c$ FINALM371 1N$_1$
Scheil (1923:no. 016)	O0106	M357 M388 M262 M390 FINALM371 1N$_1$
Scheil (1905:no. 274)	O0105	M68 M409 FINALM371 2N$_1$
Scheil (1923:no. 292)	O0138	M124$_a$ M430 FINALM371 1N$_1$
Scheil (1905:no. 4997)	O0106	M388 M24$_c$ M460 FINALM371 1N$_{14}$ 1N$_1$

Fig. 5.20 Example of graphotactical analysis of the proto-Elamite sign Meriggi 371.

At first sight, the sign sequences in entries including M371 seem without recognizable structure or repetition, and in fact there is no immediately striking pattern in the data. This may be an indication that we have been too optimistic in anticipating fixed sign sequences representing, for instance, linguistically meaningful personal names, other proper nouns, or even phonetic elements of spoken language. With a range of between one and fourteen, and a mean of around five non-numerical signs in this long list, any existing pattern should emerge. Nonetheless, interesting elements in the writing system do appear. For instance, three texts in §2 (Scheil 1905:no. 343, 1923:no. 121, 1935:no. 5019) contain the sign M371 twice, separated by just one sign. In each case, this is the sign M9, consisting of two horizontal strokes and possibly denoting as in Babylonia a sense of "doubling" (cf. Scheil 1923:no. 157, obv. vii for the same phenomenon in intermediate position). In the case of M371 in intermediate position, the list exhibits a strong relationship between the referent of M371 and those of a number of other signs, including M9 (double stroke, also found regularly in the position immediately preceding M371 when the latter is in final position, §5), M288 (the "GUR" sign as a general representation of a measure of grain), and M388 ("KUR" representing a male dependent laborer). We also do not need the explicit proof of Scheil (1923:no. 112) rev. 16 (**M387** M372$_a$ M388 M296$_c$ M1 **M371** M317 1N$_1$) with both M387 ("100" in the proto-Elamite decimal system, used ideographically) and M371 in the same line to dispose of the idea that the two signs might be graphic variants, based on a possible association between M388 and M376 (three circular impressions connected by incised strokes) and, for instance, between KUR$_a$ and 3N$_{57}$ in the proto-cuneiform texts.[43] A simple comparison of the sign sequences, above all the sign clusters in which M371 is found, makes their association, let alone an allographic relationship between the two, highly unlikely. Further short patterns of sign sequence are in these lines; we are hopeful that a comparison of all such patterns in the proto-Elamite corpus will allow us to formulate some general rules of sign application and so to begin an informed speculation about the nature of the ideographic writing system and its possible relationship to the language of proto-Elamite scribes. For it seems unlikely that they, or their archaic Babylonian brethren, should have been entirely successful in hiding their linguistic affiliation behind the evident formulaic bookkeeping symbols of our earliest texts.

Current work on the proto-Elamite corpus thus can draw on both internal data from the Persian documents, and on comparative data from Babylonia. The Babylonian comparisons pose again the question of the ultimate relationship between the two writing systems. Clearly, proto-Elamite must be reckoned among those cases of secondary script origin known from many non-literate regions in contact with literate cultures. Yet it is too facile to declare that Susa imported this idea of writing, along with some few direct loans, at a time when Babylonia had passed into a second writing phase at least several generations after the origin of proto-cuneiform in Uruk IVa. It is evident from our data that those elements which are direct, or nearly direct, loans from Babylonian tradition, for instance the numerical sign systems used in grain measures, point to a period within, or at the beginning of, and not at the conclusion, of the initial writing phase Uruk IVa. Moreover, the examples of numero-ideographic accounts demonstrate that both centers employed the same signs at the earliest phase of writing development. At this moment, direct loans from Babylonia were frozen in the proto-Elamite system, whereas they were still subject to paleographic variation in Babylonia. In the case of the number sign N$_{39}$, Uruk scribes of the Uruk IV period had not agreed upon one or the other of two possible forms, N_{39a} (⌒) and N_{39b} (⌒; this latter sign form might derive from the use of thumbnails to represent units smaller than the basic unit in grain metrology notations during the period of numerical tablets). By the beginning of the following period Uruk III, standardization had dictated the use of only N_{39a}. Persian accountants chose the equally plausible variant N_{39b} from the Uruk IV pool of signs.

This and other comparable agreements in the proto-Elamite syllabary point to a rapid development of a full writing system once its advantages in the administration were understood. One of the more important tasks ahead of us will be an attempt to eliminate from the current proto-Elamite sign list as many of the very numerous variant forms as possible. We count over 1,900 discrete signs in 26,320 sign occurrences in our transliteration data set, clustered around approximately 500 basic forms. Of the 1,900 forms, however, more than 1,000 occur just once, another 300 only twice in the texts. These numbers are a clear indication that the writing system as it has been transmitted to us was in a stage of flux, in which a scribal tradition had been unable to care for standardization of characters. Nonetheless, these numbers also tell us that the proto-Elamite system, like that of Babylonia, probably consisted of a mix of ideograms and syllabograms and comprised altogether between 600 and 900 discrete signs.

Chronologically, the proto-Elamite system fits well into the development and expansion of Babylonian proto-cuneiform. We may picture the Uruk expansion into Persia and Syria during the fourth millennium, characterized in the history of writing by the appearance of a systematic means of accounting through manipulation of small clay counters whose form indicated both numerical and ideographic qualities. This administrative tool crossed the barrier into transaction representation on one two-dimensional surface, namely on numero-ideographic tablets, when Uruk tradition was still strong in Persia, but the succeeding withdrawal of Babylonian influence, occasioned by developments in the south of Mesopotamia we cannot see, left Persian scribes to their own devices. An apparently continuous administrative apparatus, and a highly adaptable bureaucracy, formed the basis for the development of the proto-Elamite writing system that on its surface seems very foreign, but that on closer inspection reflects much of its Babylonian heritage.

In the meantime, debates continue about the populations which might have been in contact with or even existing within the region of ancient Persia. Given later linguistic evidence, it is likely that an indigenous, Elamite-speaking population was living there in the latter half of the fourth millennium. And clearly elements from the Babylonian south must have had close, possibly adversarial contact with local peoples. There may, however, have been much more population movement in the area than we imagine, including early Hurrian elements and, if Whittaker (1998:111–147), Ivanov, and others are correct, even Indo-Europeans.[44]

Notes

Vector images of proto-Elamite texts included in the present study are for the most part based on the hand copies of their original editors. Tablets in the figures have been collated according to inspections of originals (with sincere thanks due to Beatrice André for her permission to collate the published proto-Elamite texts and to inspect the unpublished Susa tablets housed in the Louvre) or photos. In the illustrations, areas shaded but not enclosed within a line represent surface abrasions, those also within a contour line represent broken surfaces that therefore contain no traces of damaged signs. The question of original tablet orientation will, for reasons given in previous publications, not be addressed here; all copies (unless otherwise noted, at 75 percent of original size) depict tablets as prescribed by publication conventions, that is, rotated 90° counter-clockwise from their original position. Transliterations of numerical notations are based on the treatment of their respective number sign systems by Damerow and Englund (1989:18–28).

1. This initiative (supported by the National Science Foundation under Grant #0000629) represents a natural expansion of the goals of the project Archaische Texte aus Uruk, directed over the last twenty-five years by Hans Nissen of the Free University of Berlin. The CDLI (http://cdli.ucla.edu/) studies all available Mesopotamian administrative texts of the late fourth and the third millennia BC. Babylonia and the Susiana were bound by a close interrelationship during this period, seen above all in the evident borrowings of Babylonian cultural diagnostic ware, including the writing tradition, by Persia. Since the time of the early excavations of both regions, researchers have as a consequence included both proto-Elamite of the late fourth and early third millennia BC, and linear Elamite of the late Old Akkadian period, in their discussions of cuneiform development. The web data set of the CDLI will soon include a full presentation of the proto-Elamite material, drawing on the files and publications of the collaborators Damerow and Englund (1989) and Friberg (1978–1979), and on the electronic transliterations, based on the sign list of Meriggi (1971–1974; the list proper was published in vol. II), now completed by staff member Jacob Dahl. Sign designations, for instance "M388," follow the numbering of the Meriggi list.

2. Together those represent the last phase of the Late Uruk period in Mesopotamia and date to *c.* 3200–3000 BC. Lawler (2001b:32–35, 2001c:36–38) has reported on recent excavations in Iraq, and the wholesale plunder of both Umma, modern

Djokha, and the neighboring Umm al-Aqirib. The history of the 2003 invasion and subsequent occupation of Iraq by US–British forces, with apparent wholesale plunder of established and recent excavation sites, is now being written. According to M. van Ess in Lawler (2001a:2419), the chronology of the proto-cuneiform periods in Uruk might have to be adjusted two centuries backward based on radiocarbon dating of Uruk charcoal remains. See below, n. 36, and J. Cooper's contribution in this volume.

3. See Englund (1988:131–133, n. 9, and 145–146, n. 18, 1998:73–81). A troubling tendency to simplify this discussion to a matter of tendentious speculation can be discerned in the more recent publications of some close to, and many at a fair distance from, the topic. Krebernik (1994:380–385) gave a measured appraisal of possible rebus values of signs in the proto-cuneiform repertoire in his review of M. Green and Nissen (1987); the phonetic readings identified by Steinkeller (1995:689–713, 1995–1996:211–214) are, on the other hand, heavily speculative and in some instances reckless. When, however, these identifications reach the level of treatments twice removed from the original documents, for instance that of Glassner (2000), we are confronted with such statements as "MAŠ+GÁNA – the two signs form a ligature – is *incontestably* [emphasis mine] a loan from the Akkadian *maškanu*, 'area of threshing, small agricultural establishment'" (Glassner 2000:210), which, although a direct borrowing from Steinkeller (and, incidentally, an indirect borrowing from M. Green, one of the original editors of the sign list [Green and Nissen 1987]), is nonetheless an indication of an unnecessarily cavalier attitude toward the proto-cuneiform texts. We need to be aware that the self-indulgent transmission of fantastical etymologies from publication to publication can engender an environment of mistrust with respect to the rigor of a field otherwise prone to great attention to detail.

4. Isolatable personal names are most evident, for instance, in the accounts of "dependent workers" SAL and KUR$_a$ in such proto-cuneiform texts as Englund and Grégoire (1991:nos. 212–222), and Englund (1998:177, W 20274,2 and 23999,1). Of course, we cannot determine in any convincing way the nature of name-giving in the archaic period, particularly insofar as this conservative cultural trait is transmitted through large numbers of "dependent workers" who will have been both ethnically and linguistically diverse, yet it seems out of character that *not one* of the sign combinations evidently representing humans in these texts can plausibly be interpreted as conforming to standard Sumerian practice, whereas the numbers of personal designations from the Early Dynastic I–II period texts from Ur (*c.* 100–200 years after the end of Late Uruk [Burrows 1935]) that are susceptible to such morpho-syntactical and even phonetic analysis is not small (di Vito 1993:23–24; Englund 1998:80, n. 168).

5. Hinz (1987:644) interpreted the indigenous geographical designation *ḫa(l)tamti* identified in much later texts to mean "god's land" from *ḫal* ("land") and tamt ("[gracious] lord"); "Elam" may be an Akkadianized rendering of these terms influenced by *elûm* ("to be high"). "Proto-Elamite" is an artificial term derived

from this geographical designation usually used to describe an historical phase in the Susiana plain and the Iranian highlands situated to the east of Mesopotamia, generally considered to correspond to the Jemdet Nasr / Uruk III and ED I periods in Mesopotamia, but possibly, based on considerations discussed here, to be dated earlier, to the Uruk IVa period. It is represented in Iran by the levels Susa 16-14B (including, possibly, part of 17A) and corresponding levels from other sites (in particular Yahya IVC, Sialk IV.2, and Late Middle Banesh [Banesh Building Level II]). It may be dated to *c.* 3300–3000 BC. The complex stratigraphy of Susa and its relevance to the chronology of the proto-Elamite period will not be considered here (for the French excavations, see N. Chevalier and E. Carter in Harper, Aruz, and Tallon [1992:16–19, 20–24]; Carter and Stolper [1984:103–132]); levels determined in the acropolis excavations of 1969–1971 are cited as generally accepted standards (cf. Le Brun 1971:163–216, and Dittmann 1986a, 1986b:332–366; "Susa 17" = "Susa Acropolis I 17").

6. For proto-Elamite, there are 208 tablets in Scheil (1905), including 2 tablets edited in Scheil (1900), 490 in Scheil (1923), 649 in Scheil (1935), and 50 in Mecquenem (1949), and approximately 40 in various articles (Mecquenem 1956:202; Vallat 1971:figs. 43 and 58, 1973:103; Stolper 1978:94–96). Some 100 unpublished fragments from Susa are in the collection of the Louvre, and 20 more in the Museum of Archaeology and Ethnology of the University of São Paulo. The Teheran Museum, finally, presumably houses all Susa texts from more recent (post- 1950) excavations, the proto-Elamite texts from Tall-i Malyan, of which an unclear number remain unpublished, as well as those from Tepe Yahya and Ozbaki; the collection of the Ecole Biblique, Jerusalem, contains 9 Susa texts presumably deposited there by the Dominican and Susa epigraphist V. Scheil. One proto-Elamite text has been discovered in the estate of Edith Porada (generously reported by M. van der Mieroop; its publication is planned by J. Dahl). See Damerow and Englund (1989:2, n. 4).

7. No more than two texts from the entire collection can be assigned with any likelihood to a non-administrative, perhaps school-exercise, context (Scheil 1923: no. 328; 1935:no. 362).

8. In the absence of a better alternative, however, it has served as the provisional basis for the electronic transliterations entered by CDLI staff insofar as the non-numerical signs are concerned; numerical signs have been transliterated according to the Uruk sign list published in M. Green and Nissen (1987:335–345). See n. 1 above.

9. Meriggi followed three primary assumptions in his analysis of proto-Elamite. First, he presumed it was a genetic relative of later Elamite represented by Linear Elamite of the late Old Akkadian period (in other sources described as "proto-Elamite B"). Second, he believed that isolatable proto-Elamite personal names were written syllabically. Third, he followed an implied rule that the proto-Elamite writing system represented language in rather strict sign sequences. The consequence of this line of thought was to allow the decipherer to test in the

proto-Elamite corpus syllabic readings of signs derived from a list of graphically comparable signs of both periods. See Meriggi (1971–1974, I: 172–220, 1975:105). Although a graphotactical analysis of the proto-Elamite script would seem to deliver some data of statistical interest (see Fig. 5.20), the results of Meriggi's efforts offer little encouragement. There are numerous exceptions to an implied rule of standardized sign sequence, as noted already by W. Brice (1962–1963:28–29 and 32–33). Further, seeming graphic correspondences are notoriously inaccurate and can only be pursued as an avenue of decipherment within the framework of a continuous writing tradition such as that of Babylonia, but even then must be considered highly tentative. Certainly, the use of signs must be shown to derive from comparable text genres and from within parallel contexts in the texts. Given the span of over 800 years unaccounted for between proto- and Old Elamite; given the fact that Linear Elamite was employed only following a period of Old Akkadian domination to record local royal events; and given the high probability of the use in proto-Elamite personal names of logographic signs whose later syllabic values might be seen in the Linear Elamite period, there is, as Gelb (1975:95–104) has also stated, little reason to be optimistic about an eventual language decipherment of proto-Elamite.

10. Notations in the metrological cereal capacity system $\check{S}^{\#}$ (see the discussion below) form a notable exception to this rule. The entire notation was encased in a rectangle of etched strokes; longer notations in $\check{S}^{\#}$ which could not be accommodated in the remaining space at the bottom of a column were moved to the next column, thus leaving a space in the preceding one.

11. See, for example, the treatment of Scheil (1905:n. 4997) in Nissen, Damerow, and Englund (1993:78–79).

12. Damerow and Englund (1989:15) have noted that the semantic structure of the proto-Elamite texts proves their close conceptual relationship to the proto-cuneiform corpus. Generally, proto-Elamite headings correspond to proto-cuneiform account colophons; entries in proto-Elamite documents correspond to "cases" of proto-cuneiform texts (Fig. 5.3b). It must be kept in mind, however, that the semantic hierarchy of proto-cuneiform texts is frequently represented directly by the graphical arrangement of cases and subcases, while the hierarchical structure of individual proto-Elamite entries is already on the whole a semantic construction. This latter contrast between the semantic and the syntactical structure of the two writing systems – the more developed separation of semantics and syntax evident in the proto-Elamite texts – is a strong indication of the antecedence of the proto-cuneiform corpus.

13. Englund (1994:pl. 26), W 7204, d edge i 1: ⌈$5N_{23}$⌉ [ ], W 20649 (unpublished), obv. i 1: [ ] ⌈$1N_{23}$?⌉ $2N_{34}$ ⌈$3N_{14}$⌉ [ ]; Damerow and Englund (1987:pl. 60), W 22115,9 rev. i 2: $1N_{23}$ $1N_{48}$; Cavigneaux (1991:143), W 24189, obv. ii 2: $7N_{23}$ [ ] ⌈BU_a⌉ X [ ] and obv. ii 3: $3N_{23}$ [ ] $1N_1$ X [ ]; an unpublished tablet from the current antiquities market, finally, has rev. iii 1: $2N_{23}$ $6N_{34}$ $I\check{S}_a$ X A

[ ] (this tablet carries the CDLI identifier "P006379"). In the absence of either a meaningful numerical sign sequence including N_{23} (proto-Elamite: "100") – N_{23} in the examples listed above should not be followed by N_{34} ("60" in the sexagesimal system) or N_{48} ("600") – or, for instance, of numerical notations including $6 + N_{14}$ ("10") that cannot be explained as having derived from the capacity or the area systems, no proto-cuneiform notations can be considered likely decimal qualifications.

14. The main reason for this difficulty is the interruption of the paleographic tradition in Elamite sources: later Elamite texts, with the exception of the few Old Elamite linear texts, were written with Babylonian cuneiform. The most successful method in the semantic decipherment of proto-cuneiform signs, namely the establishment of paleographic continuity between archaic and later periods, is thus not applicable in proto-Elamite research. Most of the proto-Elamite ideograms, moreover, are of a substantially more abstracted form than proto-cuneiform ideograms, whose pictographic character is often helpful in semantic analysis; the semantic analysis of proto-Elamite is consequently largely dependent on the examination of contextual sign usages. Proto-Elamite texts do, however, exhibit the same close connection between numerical systems and the nature of the objects quantified by numerical notations. This connection may well help in future research to establish more correspondences between proto-Elamite and proto-cuneiform ideograms than has been possible heretofore (see below, Fig. 5.14).

15. See Damerow and Englund (1987:121–123 and, for instance, 149, n. 20 and 150–151 n. 32).

16. The derived system S′, whose function in archaic Mesopotamian documents has not been satisfactorily explained, seems not to have been used in proto-Elamite texts.

17. Although formally the notation could derive from the bisexagesimal systems, for which see directly, there are sufficient indications that all such vessels were counted sexagesimally.

18. Possible representations of high-status humans include the signs M57, M72, M149, M291, M317, M320, and M376 (Fig. 5.14). Affiliation of particular representations to the category of sexagesimally counted high-status humans must be demonstrated through the identification of clearly sexagesimal notations on the one hand, and of semantic subsets and sets qualified by general ideograms on the other. For example, the mentioned texts (Scheil 1905:no. 213 and 1935: no. 317 [Fig. 5.5]) record in numerous obverse entries groups of objects designated M149 and M376; in the former account, subtotals of the reverse face distinguish between the two objects in numerical notations that both appear to derive from the sexagesimal system, while in the latter the two are subsumed under the collective ideographic designation M376 clearly counted sexagesimally. Such texts as Scheil (1905:no. 315) contain combinations of the sign M376 with both M72 (female laborer) and M388 (male laborer) in sequences comparable to that

of the same two signs with M291. M291 (⟶) seems evidently, in the laborer rationing account (Scheil 1905:no. 4997; Nissen *et al.* 1993:77–79), to represent a foreman semantically corresponding to Sumerian *ugula*, a representation of two sticks. This sign M291, together with M72, M57, and M317, is also generally qualified in Scheil (1905:no. 390 [Fig. 5.5]) as a member of the class of objects designated by the sign M317 and qualified sexagesimally.

19. Totaling 20,098 units. Compare the text Scheil (1923:no. 453), in which the same sign is also qualified with a large sexagesimal notation. Two Uruk IV period accounts from the proto-cuneiform corpus contain similarly large sexagesimal notations of TI: the text Englund (1994:pl. 86, W 9656,g) with a notation on its reverse surface representing 1910+ units as a total of individual entries on the tablet obverse recording a possible distribution of TI to the administrative elites at Uruk (see Englund 1994:49), and W 21742 (Englund and Nissen 2001:pl. 79) with a notation representing 740. These numbers would tend to support the interpretation offered here of the numerical notations in Vallat (1973:103, n. 1), which could only be seriously challenged on the basis of the inclusion in the copy by the text's editors of six instead of the presumptive five N_{14} signs. If, after all, correct, $6N_{14}$ would point to a possible notation in the capacity system. The immediately following notation of eight N_1 signs would, however, exclude this interpretation (in the capacity system $6N_1 = N_{14}$). The only accounts with very large sexagesimally counted objects from Uruk record the undeciphered object DUR (later Sumerian: "rope"). See Englund (1998:117, fig. 40).

20. Fig. 5.15 below, and Nissen *et al.* (1993:75–77). The sign M388 must be interpreted to be the proto-Elamite counterpart of proto-cuneiform KUR_a (⬥), both representing male dependent laborers. See in particular Damerow and Englund (1989:55–57).

21. For other examples see Damerow and Englund (1989:24, n. 75).

22. This term refers to the addition of a series of strokes to a cuneiform sign to signal a semantic variation from the meaning represented by its basic form.

23. Gender markers in Sumerian were embedded in the grammar with separate pronominal elements representing animate and inanimate subject/object, and were not evident in any known use of numerical systems, including number words.

24. For example, N_{28} impressed as a header of two subsections in the account Scheil (1905:no. 213), in Fig. 5.5. See also the impression of N_{34} on the edge of the tablet Scheil (1923:no. 421), below, Fig. 5.7.

25. Our limited understanding of the proto-Elamite object designations makes it impossible to know whether the proto-Elamite bisexagesimal system also qualified numbers of other, possibly ration products, such as cheeses and fresh fish, as was the case in proto-cuneiform texts. See Damerow and Englund (1987:132–135).

26. A calculation of the text would in fact require that the damaged part of this notation be reconstructed as $N_{14}\,8N_1$, since subtracting the initial grain capacity

notation from the total results in $2N_{14}\ 4N_1\ 3N_{39b}$, which divided by the grain product N_{30c} ($\frac{1}{6} N_{39b}$) results in 498 units. A correction of the total to ... $4N_{39b}^!$ would allow a reconstruction of ... $2N_{14}\ [4N_1]$ in the same entry.

27. This sign M36 forms a functional equivalent to the sign GAR in the proto-cuneiform corpus which is the pictographic representation of the Late Uruk beveled-rim bowl serving as a rationing unit of one man-day in archaic administration. Its pictographic referent might be a measuring can with a handle used in ration distribution, presumably into the same beveled-rim bowls (BRBs) as in Uruk, since they are found in comparable numbers at Susa and other Late Uruk Persian settlements.

28. For some preliminary identifications, see Damerow and Englund (1989:26–27, n. 86).

29. See Damerow and Englund (1989:18–20) for a short description of the history of research in the decipherment of the proto-Elamite grain capacity system, long believed to reflect a decimal structure in archaic Persia, but also in Babylonia, where there was in fact no decimally structured numerical system whatsoever. Assyriological adherence to this indefensible decimal interpretation of the Late Uruk grain capacity system remained unbridled until the Swedish mathematician Jöran Friberg (1978–1979) demonstrated the relationship $N_{14} = 6$(not 10!)N_1 in grain notations of both administrative centers.

30. Note that the sign N_{30c} in the proto-Elamite corpus misled Damerow and Englund (1987) in their treatment of the proto-cuneiform systems to include this sign as a variant of the sign N_{30a} (⊠, N_{30c} absent the central impression). Through the appearance of the text Nissen, Damerow, and Englund (1991:14, no. 4.3) – and now confirmed in unpublished accounts in the Norwegian Schøyen collection – N_{30c} has been shown to represent in proto-cuneiform documents a measure of grain equivalent to $\frac{1}{10}$, and not $\frac{1}{6}$, of the measure represented by the sign N_{39}, as is the case in archaic Persia.

31. The reverse side of the text (Scheil 1923:no. 419), with a discrete notation including signs with both two and three additional bars, suggests that the number of bars employed with a notation in the proto-Elamite system $\check{S}''$ was optional. We have followed Vaiman (1974:21–22) in this interpretation of the sign as a measure for emmer wheat. See Damerow and Englund (1987:139–140), Englund (1998:120), etc.

32. Cf. Beale (1978:289–313), with a range of around. 0.4–0.9 liters for archaic Persia.

33. The same argument is made to manipulate the absolute volume of the Old Sumerian sìla upward. See Englund (1990:xv–xvi).

34. See Damerow and Englund (1987:142) for a discussion of the same phenomenon in the ED I texts from Ur. If true and if the equivalence of $2N_{39b}$ to 1 unit of M56 represents seed grain, then the land measure would correspond to approximately $\frac{1}{2}$ to 1 Babylonian *iku*, based on a seeding rate of around 10–20 *sìla*/liters per *iku*.

35. For publications, see Le Brun (1971:163–216, 1978a:61–79, 1978b:57–154, 1978c:177–192), Stève and Gasche (1971), Dollfus (1971:17–162, 1975:11–62), Sumner (1974:155–180, 1976:103–114 and pls. I–III), Lamberg-Karlovsky, in Damerow and Englund (1989:v–xiii). The proto-Elamite component of the Yahya excavations has in the meantime been published (Lamberg-Karlovsky and Potts 2001). Glassner (2000:54–66) offers an excellent review of the pertinent excavations.

36. Englund (1994:12–16). See now D. Sürenhagen (1993:57–70, 1999), according to whom the earliest phase of the proto-cuneiform system of writing is pushed back to the Uruk V period and thus possibly a century or more earlier than commonly accepted. Recently performed radiocarbon datings in Heidelberg (Lawler 2001a:2419) might result in even greater adjustments in our chronology. These considerations are to be noted with regard to the recent publications of G. Dreyer (J. Baines, this volume, and Lawler [2001a:2418–2420]) concerning the age of the inscribed Egyptian tags from predynastic Abydos.

37. This judgment is based on the form of the signs as shown in photos available to me. Through inspection of the originals it should be possible to determine the material of the stylus by examining the butt end, and often simply the lateral surface of the individual impressions. Such wedges on proto-cuneiform tablets often exhibit the grain of the original stylus and thus indicate the use of wood or reed (we can assume that some professionals carried styli made of ivory or precious metal; note the description in Gudea Cylinder A iv 25 // v 22 of the silver stylus used by the goddess of writing, Nisaba: gi dub-ba kù NE-a šu im-mi-du$_8$// gi dub-ba kù NE šu bí-du$_8$-a).

38. This method of record-keeping is a good indication that, like Babylonian texts, the proto-Elamite accounts were stored with this information immediately visible, in baskets or shelves akin to modern filing cabinets.

39. Note also the signs N$_8$ and N$_8$ *inversum* (⌓) representing half of a discrete unit in the sexagesimal system; the latter sign is not found in proto-cuneiform documents.

40. The sign from Godin Tepe has been discussed by Michel, McGovern, and Badler (1993:408A–413A) and Badler (2000:48–56), who proposed an identification with the cuneiform sign representing a jar of beer. Archaic pictography, however, would support an identification of the sign with a jar of butter oil, if the numerical notation is in fact sexagesimal; it cannot, though, be ruled out that this sign has no clear referent, and that the notation in fact derives from the grain capacity system.

41. See Ismail (1996) and Lebeau and Suleiman (1997).

42. The list in Fig. 5.20 has been cleansed of uninformative attestations with breaks and otherwise disturbed lines. The fullness of the remaining entries will hopefully be excused in the interest of a complete representation of the context of one proto-Elamite sign. DE = Damerow and Englund; O0101 = "obverse face, column 1, line 1" (generally including just one column on tablet surfaces,

see above, "Description"); INIT = initial position, INTERM = intermediate position, FINAL = final position; X = unidentifiable sign, $^?$ = conjectural.

43. And compare with the following (Scheil 1923:no. 120, obv. 19, Scheil 1923: no. 159, obv. 3, Scheil 1923:no. 248, obv. 10, etc.).

44. Rubio (1999:1–16) has reviewed recent publications, and the pioneering initial work by Landsberger on possible substrate lexemes in Sumerian, and concludes that the fairly extensive list of non-Sumerian words attested in Sumerian texts did not represent a single early Mesopotamian language, but rather reflected a long history of *Wanderwörter* from a myriad of languages, possibly including some loans from Indo-European, and many from early Semitic.

6 | The earliest Egyptian writing: development, context, purpose

JOHN BAINES

In this chapter I attempt to model a social and functional context for the initial development of the Egyptian writing system; and to present and explore the earliest attestations of Egyptian writing, its possible antecedents, and the nature of the system that produced these examples and was developed further in the following couple of centuries. Of these two aspects, the society produced the writing and has logical priority, but not very much can be said about it. I focus more on the material itself, which is relatively recently published and needs to be discussed before a context can be modeled.

In stating the issues in terms of society and then of writing system, I also raise the question of the relationship of writing and language. Even though writing systems represent language, along with other data, and have been developed from their various points of departure to focus more and more on language, that is not necessarily what writing was intended to notate at its point of origin. Most definitions of what constitutes "full" writing state that it notates a language. More precisely, they require either that it should do this through both phonetic (whole-word, syllabic, or phonemic) and semantic elements, or that in "purer" and generally later forms it should restrict its primary repertory of signs – as against layout, spaces, and such elements – to the phonemic (for more inclusive approaches to definition, see below).[1]

Yet unless those who originated several scripts were rather inefficient, language cannot have been what they principally aimed to record, because their inventions existed for centuries before they were modified to notate it effectively. If their initial goal was not extensive notation of language, a script could still have developed later from a partial representation of language to a fuller representation that was applicable to a much wider range of contexts, while all along retaining its position in a society and fulfilling its existing roles, as well as acquiring new ones. Even where scripts expanded greatly in systematic aspects and in range of use, it may be extremely difficult to determine when they achieved a relatively full notation of language, including its grammar. For the Egyptian and Mesopotamian scripts, such a point was reached perhaps half a millennium after their first appearance (I return later to this matter). The structure of scripts that were secondary inventions, and were stimulated by existing models that notated language quite fully, may not need to be interpreted with non-linguistic factors in mind. In contrast, "primary" scripts that could not look to a language-notating model must be seen in different terms, whether or not their inventors knew of a model of "writing," in the broadest sense of a system for recording information indirectly through the combination of "signs" belonging to a specific repertory.[2] Among such systems I include here, but only here, methods of notation and transaction of the kind argued for by Denise Schmandt-Besserat in her much-criticized hypothesis about the use of tokens in the prehistoric Near East (1992; see reviews, for example, by Michalowski 1993b; Zimansky 1993; also Englund, this volume).

Such a largely non-linguistic point of departure may give an improved perspective on what the earliest writing was intended to do and how it operated. How can one model a partly or wholly non-linguistic point of departure for writing? The functions of the earliest writing can be summarized abstractly under the headings of communication – which is presumably valid for all writing – and display (Baines 1989). Information might be stored in writing in a permanent form that was not intended specifically to communicate, even though its use would imply that it could one day be looked at. Such writing remains within the category of communication, even if the communication is hypothetical because no specific audience is addressed. Practices like inscribing Shang oracle bones may have some of that character (e.g. Keightley 1999; also Bagley, and F. Bottéro, this volume). "Utilitarian" communication, such as that of administrative documents, is at one theoretical pole among purposes of writing and is exemplified by the thousands of Late Uruk period tablets discovered at Uruk. One should not, however, force this identification of the tablets' function into an assertion that they were focused exclusively on communication or that what they did was to increase efficiency by storing and imparting information. Rather, their introduction created new institutions for information storage and accountability, forming something that probably had prestige and symbolism through its mere existence and that went beyond the communicative "need" that is likely to have provided much of the stimulus for its creation.[3] As with many modern bureaucratic institutions, there is no reason to think that the proliferation it rendered possible was anticipated when it was created, or that it necessarily increased efficiency.

The two purposes of communication and display are not in opposition, because display seeks to communicate. Pictorial representation, which is a precondition for most original inventions of writing systems, also communicates, but in different ways. Modes of display may be very unlike writing, while writing that is incorporated into display often cannot be read in normal conditions – for example, because it is too small or inscribed in too remote a position, or not decipherable because the audience would not be literate, or because it is interred and serves the hereafter rather than this world. Giorgio Raimondo Cardona (1981), in particular, reviewed an extraordinary range of such usages. In all these contexts, knowledge that writing is present, that it is meaningful, and that it is exclusive may be as relevant for the actors as any specific verbal content or instrumental function it might possess. Exclusivity merges into secrecy, and writing systems can be used almost as easily to make things secret as to make them known. As the symbolic salience of writing increases, the potential for secrecy or mystification in the service of status and cultural association increases; one need only think of the widespread use of Latin in public inscriptions in the modern world.

This polar spread from communication to display is prominent in discussions of what stimulated the invention of writing. Opinions on where the focus lay vary for different cases. The clearest polarity is between Mesopotamianists, who stress communication, and Mesoamericanists, who focus on display. More broadly, changing views of the purpose of writing relate to developments in the interpretation of historical societies, which have been moving toward greater emphasis on the constitutive roles of complex symbolic and high-cultural forms. Here Egypt, where from the first an elaborate display form of writing coexisted with a more "communicative" one that had simpler sign forms but the same principles of notation, offers a paradigm for comparison with other societies.

I return briefly to these issues after presenting the earliest writing discovered in Egypt and discussing how far it can be deciphered, whether any particular notational system can be identified in it, and how far it recorded language. I have studied the next phase of writing's development, down to the 3rd dynasty, in a little more detail elsewhere (for dates, see Chronological Table [Table 6.1]).[4]

The earliest Egyptian writing

Excavations since the late 1970s in the late Predynastic and Early Dynastic elite and royal necropolis of Abydos in Upper Egypt – Cemeteries U, B, and Umm el-Qaʿab – have increased the amount of early Egyptian writing available for study, extending its range back in time probably by more than a century, as well as revealing an unsuspected style of material and generally stimulating renewed interest.[5] Systematic work by Jochem Kahl on the entire early sign repertory has placed research on a solid basis (1994; see Baines

Table 6.1 Chronological table: Predynastic and Early Dynastic Egypt, periods and rough dates

Merimda (Delta)	c. 5000
Badari (Nile Valley)	c. 4500
Naqada I ("Amratian," Nile Valley)	c. 4000
Early Buto (Delta)	c. 4000
Maʿadi (Delta)	c. 3800
Naqada II ("Gerzean," Nile Valley, later all Egypt)	c. 3500
IIc (Hierakonpolis Tomb 100)	
IId2 (cultural uniformity of Egypt; end of Maʿadi culture)	
Naqada III (late Predynastic and dynasty 0)	c. 3200
IIIa2 (tomb U-j at Abydos)	
IIIb (dynasty 0)	
IIIb2 or IIIc (= 1st dynasty)	c. 2950
Early Dynastic Period	
1st dynasty	c. 2950–2775
2nd dynasty	c. 2775–2650
3rd dynasty	c. 2650–2575
Old Kingdom	c. 2575–2150
4th–8th dynasties	

All dates are BC. Palestinian Early Bronze I corresponds approximately with late Naqada II / Naqada III; correspondences between Egypt and Late Uruk Mesopotamia (late fourth millennium) are disputed.

1997b) and goes far beyond what had been achieved before (Kaplony 1963), although materials from the earliest stage were not yet available to him. Broadly, Cemetery U dates to Naqada II and early Naqada III, Cemetery B to Naqada III b /dynasty 0, and Umm el-Qaʿab to the 1st–2nd dynasties (see below for the context of these in terms of societal change). By the time of Cemetery B, written sources from elsewhere in Egypt increase in number. The material from Hierakonpolis in the south is very significant, although its quantity is smaller. Many Egyptologists attribute priority in the development of the state and civilization to Hierakonpolis, but I believe that its prominence is more a result of patterns of preservation in desert environments than of a predominant role.

In 1989 the excavators Günter Dreyer and Ulrich Hartung found tomb U-j, a royal tomb of Naqada IIIa that is a century or more older than those in Cemetery B.[6] The tomb contained many objects bearing inscriptions. This is the largest and the oldest early group of inscribed artifacts so far found in Egypt and is now magisterially published and analyzed by Dreyer, Hartung, and Pumpenmeier (1998b; imported pottery in Hartung [2001]).

The material is difficult to analyze and of uncertain interpretation. Although limited, the writing system appears well formed. This is unlikely to have been the first material ever written, and it has prompted the excavators to search for earlier antecedents to writing (see Hartung 1998a, 1998b) and to reexamine the widespread assumption that diffusion of the idea of writing from Mesopotamia stimulated its invention in Egypt. Two sets of radiocarbon dates have been obtained; one puts the Abydos material slightly later than the Uruk IV tablets (Boehmer *et al.* 1993), the other – which the excavators prefer – slightly earlier (Görsdorf, Dreyer, and Hartung 1998; cf. Joffe 2000). The hypotheses of Dreyer and Hartung are thus maximalist, placing the first Egyptian writing both significantly earlier than others have suggested and before the normal dating of the oldest known Mesopotamian writing. Within Egypt, they point for earlier material to a few signs on late Naqada II pottery, a century or so before tomb U-j, and to the designs on sealings of early Naqada III, some of them from tomb U-j. They suggest that the former are the earliest preserved examples of writing, which would thus have been invented in late Naqada II (accepted by Kahl 1994:156–161). The sealings do not themselves include writing, but they have a partly comparable appearance and would fit well in a context of practice in which writing existed and was integrated with pictorial decoration and patterned designs. In this chapter I do not follow this proposed Naqada II date for writing's invention, for which the evidence seems to me to be insufficient, and opt for Naqada III.

The finds fall into two categories. First, nearly 200 small bone and ivory tags (Fig. 6.1; typically 1.5×1.25 cm), drilled in one corner, normally the top right, had perhaps been tied to bales of cloth or other high-value grave goods that were later robbed (no doubt along with many further lost tags). Most of the inscriptions on the tags are attested in several examples; around forty different inscription types are known (Fig. 6.2). Technical features show that the material was to some extent "mass-produced"; Dreyer *et al.* (1998b:137) suggests that areas of bone were inscribed by incising with many copies of the same group of signs, scored with a grid, and then separated along the grid lines. The inscriptions were colored black after the signs had been incised. The tags bear either numerals or between one and five representationally based signs that would be termed "hieroglyphs" in the context of later writing; for simplicity I also use that term here. The majority have two hieroglyphs. In all but a few possible cases (Dreyer *et al.* 1998b: nos. 86–102; two different inscriptions each attested in a number of examples), numerals and hieroglyphs appear not to occur together on the tags, in a

Fig. 6.1 Selection of bone tags from tomb U-j at Abydos. Naqada IIIa period. Average height c. 1.5 cm (courtesy Deutsches Archäologisches Institut).

Fig. 6.2 Samples of four tag designs from tomb U-j at Abydos. After Dreyer *et al.* (1998b:nos. 67–69, 103–105, 134–135, 142–143). Nos. 67–69 and 103–105 are, respectively, examples of the same design. The back of no. 69 shows a scoring line that derives from the production process (see text). Dreyer proposes that the design of nos. 134–135 signifies "east" and that of nos. 142–143, "west" (see text, courtesy Deutsches Archäologisches Institut).

pattern of separation similar to that which Stephen Houston (2000:147–149) posits for early Mesoamerican writing.

Second, more than 100 relatively ordinary ceramic jars, all of the "wavy-handled" type, bore large single or paired signs painted on their walls. A precise total of jars cannot be established because the material is broken and looted; here too, multiple examples of the same inscriptions survive. The principal contents of the jars may have been oils or fats, presumably commodities of high value.[7]

The numerals on the tags include single digits in groups of up to twelve (written either horizontally or vertically), the sign for 100, and 100 + 1 (Dreyer *et al.* 1998b:113–118). The later notation system for numbers includes a sign for 10, and by the Early Dynastic Period writings of 10–90 using from one to nine signs for 10 were common. No counting base other than 10 is attested from Egypt, so that the use of units up to 12 – which cannot favor 12 as a base because 11 should then be the highest number expressed in single digits – is not likely to point to any different system. The pattern on the U-j tags suggests instead that the digits encode a complex form of numeration. Dreyer *et al.* (1998b:140) cites parallels with third-millennium cloth lists, in which horizontal strokes stand for 10 and vertical ones for 1. The system could also have worked like later grain records, where the units often stood for multiples of their literal values (e.g. Gardiner 1957:§266).[8]

The hieroglyphic signs represent armed human figures, mammals and an emblematic ox head or bucranium, birds, reptiles, a scorpion, fish, plant elements, geographical features and temporal concepts such as "night," and some man-made elements, notably a schematized "palace façade," a throne type, and a shrine (for a full list, see Dreyer *et al.* 1998b:138). The order and combination of the pairs of signs on the tags are variable, and for that reason alone the system is likely to constitute a "script" with an orthography distinguishing different entities, most of them notated by sign pairs (for further discussion of the entities, see below). In terms of later iconography, the man-made elements form the most striking group: the throne and façade were central symbols of kingship, while the shrine was the sacred building of Upper Egypt. These signs demonstrate that the script exploited a well-formed visual culture that had much in common with that of later times, and that was associated with similar political institutions, notably kingship.[9] Some other signs, such as the scorpion, an elephant, and a jackal, are also likely to have carried great symbolic weight. The number of signs attested is not more than a few dozen (Dreyer estimates about fifty); while there is no means of assessing what proportion of the total then in use they constitute, nothing points to its having been very much larger.

The selection of models for signs is revealing in other ways. The numerical preponderance of the animate world can be compared with the prevalence of birds, in particular, among the signs in commonest use in later periods. This detailed exploitation of fauna for signs probably relates to folk categories. In third millennium Egypt knowledge of such domains was prominent, as was an encyclopaedic high-cultural recording of them that was as often pictorially as textually organized (e.g. Edel 1961–1963; Brovarski 1987). I suggest that this was a deliberate, culturally laden strategy for developing a script. In many cases other ways of encoding the same information according to the same principles could no doubt have been found. The strategy's prime aims are not likely to have been quick legibility, for which general criteria were presumably not available, or simple differentiation, which can hardly be aided by the use of numerous bird signs, but rather something like modeling distinctions of meaning in terms of suitable domains (whether those distinctions were in the entities that the signs recorded or were phonemic).[10] As the script developed further, the range of models for signs, and of domains from which they were taken, increased and the focus on fauna lessened.

Not very many signs on the tags are identical with later hieroglyphs, but the difference between the U-j material and its successors may be minor, particularly since several forms are not distinct enough to be evaluated one way or another. The signs with the best claim to be the same as later ones are some birds; a stretch of water, later uniconsonantal š; and possibly a cobra, later *d̠*. Thus, the most promising cases could be uniconsonantal signs, but the material is so sparse that this correspondence may be a matter of chance. Usage of these signs in the U-j system need not have been the same as later usages of comparable signs.

The signs on the jars (Figs. 6.3, 6.4) are very large in relation to what they are written on, being up to half the height of the vessel walls (which are 22–37 cm high), and they could have been identified from a distance; the world over, writing is seldom as large as this. The forms are rougher than those on the tags and are best termed "cursive," but their scale suggests that they constitute some sort of display and do not only convey information. The scale contrasts strongly with the tiny tags, as well as with the still more miniaturistic sealings from the tomb, which had been impressed upon the mud closures of imported pottery (Hartung 1998b; Hartung in Dreyer *et al.* 1998b:108–112; Hartung 2001:216–238). There is considerable overlap in the representational repertories of the signs on the tags and on the pottery.

The earliest Egyptian writing 159

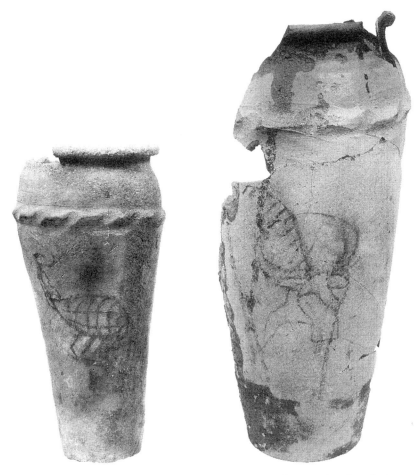

Fig. 6.3 Two sample wavy-handled pots with inscriptions from tomb U-j at Abydos. The sign on the left pot (height of vessel 25.7 cm) represents a scorpion and that on the right pot (height of vessel 33.5 cm) a bucranium on a pole with a palm frond or similar ornament; for drawings of the signs, see Fig. 6.4 (courtesy Deutsches Archäologisches Institut).

The scorpion and the bucranium, for example, are evidently the same signs in the two different styles of writing. Numerals are not attested on the pottery.

It would be possible to see the signs on the jars as different from those on the tags and as constituting a system of "potmarks" rather than "writing." I prefer to assume that the content of the two groups of material is not the same and that the signs differ because of differences in inscriptional content, medium, and graphic style. Moreover, the jar signs are not like the potmarks widely known from later Naqada III and the 1st dynasty (Helck 1990; van

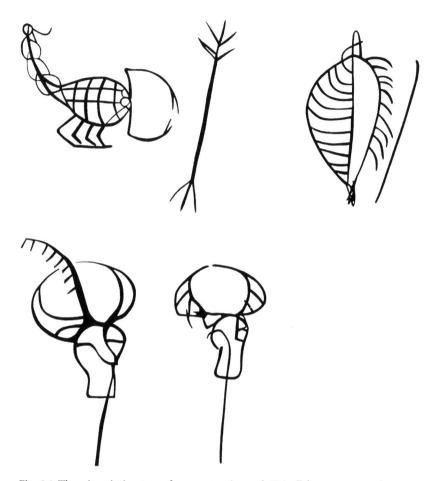

Fig. 6.4 Three inscription types from pottery in tomb U-j; all fragmentary and completed from parallel examples in the tomb: (a) scorpion and tree (?); (b) seashell and vertical stroke; and (c) bucranium in two variants, with and without added frond (?; see Fig. 6.3). Drawings after Dreyer *et al.* (1998b:figs. 33a, 40, 45, courtesy Deutsches Archäologisches Institut).

den Brink 1992). If the U-j signs were forerunners of the marks, typology and style would have changed radically, and there is no evidence for such a shift.

I therefore believe that the two media and modes of inscription of the U-j material belong to the same overall system and constitute two graphically distinct, but systematically almost identical and mutually convertible forms. Comparable duality, plurality, and convertibility is known from later Egyptian writing; the modern names for the principal script forms are "hieroglyphic" and "hieratic." Many scripts in other civilizations have had numerous different realizations, but Egyptian may be the clearest case where this characteristic was integral from the start. The complex as a whole constitutes "writing," on the broad definition used at the beginning of this chapter, which sidesteps the issue, to which I return later, of how far this stage of writing recorded "language."

Discussion

Many questions arise, several of which I address briefly. Why was this writing system with its two forms invented? What is the content of these extremely brief inscriptions? How do they notate what they write? How far can they be deciphered? How similar is their notation to that of the next significant attestations of writing, a century or more later? For the last of these, one can hardly avoid applying later readings of hieroglyphs experimentally and thus risking circularity.

Hypotheses about the content of speculatively deciphered or undeciphered material are notoriously problematic; the following should be read with that in mind. Dreyer (e.g. Dreyer *et al.* 1998b:89, 145) proposes that the motivation for inventing writing was administrative/economic, that the content of the tags and jar inscriptions is of that character, and that the invention took place within a rapidly developing administration. As an example he points to imports as requiring administrative supervision. The discovery in tomb U-j of hundreds of Palestinian vessels of a distinctive "export" ware not attested in its place of origin is evidence for the significance of long-distance trade connections in the economies of both regions (Hartung in Dreyer *et al.* 1998b:92–107; Hartung 2001). The Palestinian imports themselves are uninscribed, no doubt because the writing system was not in use outside Egypt, but the sealings were associated with the imported pottery. The seals' distinctive style and the pictorial motifs on them, which do not include writing itself, would presumably have marked them as being Egyptian. The seals may also have conveyed specific information about ownership or responsibility, more probably through the range of types in use than through specific "legibility" of the designs. They could have been applied in Palestine – the simplest option, which implies the presence of some Egyptians there – or in Egypt.

Controversially, Dreyer argues that Egypt became politically unified at the same time as its material culture became a unity, at the end of Naqada II (IId2, first suggested by Werner Kaiser [for example 1990]; others place this development later). As noted above, he dates the invention of writing to Naqada IIc, before the posited political unity. Writing would be an early creation of complex society and a century or so later – the interval from Naqada IIc to IIIa – the "state" would, one supposes, have extended the system to meet perceived administrative needs. Both the jar inscriptions and the tags would be records of the provenances of deliveries from estates or productive units throughout the country. Dreyer *et al.* (1998b:139) deciphers groups as signifying, for example, the places "Abydos" (his nos. 53–56, 59–60) and "Bubastis" (nos. 103–104), and "West" (nos. 142–143). The unnamed owner of the estates would be the king. Some groups or individual signs on the tags could be royal names, as Dreyer *et al.* (1998b:140–143) suggests for an elephant, a falcon, and a scorpion, all of which are also attested on the pottery.[11]

This general interpretation is plausible if one accepts the institutional premise of complex estate holdings in the period – whether or not all of Egypt was a single polity – but in detail it raises problems. The values Dreyer proposes for the signs and the methods by which he derives them are comparable with those of dynastic times, but few values are the same as later ones (the following examples are from Dreyer *et al.* 1998b:138–145). He proposes that simple concepts are written in elaborate, otherwise unknown ways. Thus, he interprets a group consisting of a sign later signifying "night" (normally as a classifier rather than notating a specific word), a snake (perhaps the later *d*), and a schematic form of desert/mountain, as "West," that is, "mountain (at the edge of the Nile Valley) of night" (Fig. 6.2, right). He identifies a counterpart for "East" in a group he interprets as "mountain of light," the latter written with a sign depicting an ibis (Dreyer *et al.* 1998b:143; a later sign of a different ibis writes the root *3ḫ* "luminescent"). He then suggests that these are the names of settlements or estates – presumably "(estate of the) West" rather than just "West." None of this has clear parallels. Most later Egyptian words for "West" are straightforward and relate to a common Afroasiatic root for "right" (*jmn*), while words for "East" are more variable because East was "left" and often inauspicious. Dreyer's readings here are therefore as hypothetical as the institutions to which he suggests they refer. He uses basically the same approach for the signs on jars, interpreting a sign representing a tree as "estate" or "plantation" (proposing the reading *š*, which does not have a later parallel), and taking the accompanying, more variable sign as a king's name (Dreyer *et al.* 1998b:84–91). The best attested of these signs is a scorpion, which could be the name "Scorpion" referring to the king buried in tomb U-j.[12] Other signs include a seashell, a fish, a bucranium on a pole, birds, and boats. As with the hieroglyphs, the presence of man-made objects in the repertory is significant; the mounted bucranium is also surely a religious symbol (Dreyer *et al.* 1998b:47–73).

Dreyer *et al.* (1998b:181) interprets the signs on the tags as exhibiting all the basic principles of notation of later writing: semagrams/logograms that write whole words; phonograms, including uniconsonantal and biconsonantal signs, with some used as "phonemic complements," that is, additional signs that reinforce the reading of a multiconsonantal sign; and determinatives, whose function is approximately to assign the word groups they terminate to semantic classes (also termed "taxograms," "semagrams," "classifiers," etc.; see Loprieno [1995:13]; for a new approach, McDonald [2002]). He believes that the writing of a sign twice for the dual and three times for the plural is also attested.[13] While this is evidently the case with numerals and likely for other elements, the linguistic distinction between "2 *x*," using a number, and a grammatical dual, that is, a word with a specific dual morphology, cannot be confirmed in the surviving material, and is elusive at least until the 1st dynasty.

Dreyer's interpretations are impressive and consistent, and they encompass not only the writing but also a model of its institutional setting. The material is, however, meager and probably insufficient to confirm or refute his results. Apart from this general difficulty, there are specific problems, for example with his reading "Basta" (modern Tell Basta / Bubastis in the Nile Delta) for the group IBIS + THRONE. Here, the bird is not the same as the one later used to write *b3*, while the proposed reading does not fit normal Egyptian syllable patterns, in which the throne should read *s°t*, with the vowel coming between the two main consonants, rather than $*C(˘)stV(')$, as the reading *ba3sta* would require.[14] Orthography on the tags differs from that on the jars, because the jars generally have one or two signs only. Single signs might notate the names of kings, as they often did in dynasties 0–1, and Dreyer suggests that a number of the signs on the jars do so. Some evidence from other sources may support this interpretation (see below), which has the corollary that both writing and the symbolism and representation of royal titles were transformed in the century or so between tomb U-j and dynasty 0, when rulers were buried in the nearby Cemetery B. By then, royal names were written in a rectangle at the top of the "palace façade" hieroglyph and other words are attested in orthographies that clearly use the script's later principles.

If Dreyer's readings are correct, the inventors or developers of the script visible in the U-j material created a complex, effective, and culturally portentous means of representing the Egyptian language, constituting a representation of a limited range of lexemes, rather than a representation of concepts in a pictographic or more purely pictorial or graphic form that would be termed writing only on a wide definition, like that of Elizabeth

Boone (this volume; see also Boone 2000:29–31).[15] It is possible to envisage an alternative to Dreyer's interpretation: the earliest writing could have worked in a different way from that of late dynasty 0, which shows effects of a reform that was followed by further reforms that led eventually to a more or less stable system 400 or 500 years after tomb U-j, in the late 2nd or early 3rd dynasty (see Kahl 1994:161–163). In that case, the U-j finds fit the Boone definition better than the narrow one. I believe that the material is too exiguous to establish which of these approaches is the right one. Nothing on the tags or pots unquestionably requires a reading that would work only through the Egyptian language. Such a decisive example might or might not happen to be present within a small sample of inscriptions like that from tomb U-j. The case is less clear even than that of the altogether larger corpus of Uruk IV writing, where it is still controversial whether it records Sumerian (no other language is in question) or no specific language (see n. 28). Nothing points to the U-j script's writing any language other than Egyptian. Unlike cuneiform, the later Egyptian script was hardly ever used to write other languages. Like Mayan writing (Houston 1994b), it carried enormous ideological weight and formed a "closed" system integrated with its particular, self-consciously unitary culture.

Whether or not Dreyer's specific readings of the U-j material are accepted, his identification of the tag inscriptions' general content is extremely plausible. The inscriptions cannot well name products or qualities, either of which would need only a more restricted set of terms than is suggested by the number of signs and combinations attested; they therefore most plausibly notate names of some kind. Since prestigious symbols are used as signs, these are likely to refer to prestigious entities like royal estate names. That inference might seem illogical for a script, like much later Egyptian, in which the relationship between sign form and content is arbitrary, so that, for example, as a logogram a throne could notate something other than itself, while as a phonogram it might notate a pair of consonants in a word that did not mean "throne" (if phonograms existed at this stage). The link between prestige and writing is, however, plausible in this case, because the signs themselves are connected with a developing system of pictorial representation that was restricted in usage and in what it depicted, as well as being constrained within iconographic conventions of decorum (e.g. Baines 1985:277–305, 1989). The choice of models for signs was therefore probably not arbitrary, neither in the case of the fauna discussed earlier nor in that of the artifacts and symbols. Moreover, the notion of completely arbitrary exemplars for signs is probably inappropriate to a repertory that retains a significant degree of iconicity.

The likely prominence of names among the entities recorded raises once again the question of how names are notated, a problem that is one motor in the elaboration of phonemic writing and more broadly of writing in general (see, for example, Boone 2000). If names are composed of largely non-abstract words in language, they may be encoded either directly or through rebus, but if their sounds have no other meaning, different methods may be needed. Later Egyptian names are mostly meaningful utterances but they include significant numbers of short forms and apparently meaningless syllables, as well as complex concepts that could not be notated directly. Dreyer's proposed readings of names in the earliest writing are all meaningful, and so cannot show whether the system possessed phonemic elements, or indeed notated language in any precise sense. The earliest names that are unquestionably written with phonograms date to the 1st dynasty, after the system's first reform.[16] More generally, the material fits with the general importance of naming among the functions of the earliest writing: numerical information is less salient than names, and commodity identifications are absent until just before the 1st dynasty.

Names often consist of more than one lexeme and may not in themselves favor any particular notational method. The possible example of "West" cited earlier could be an instance of multiple elements notating a single concept, perhaps in default of an available simpler form, or through some type of symbolic avoidance. It cannot be known how such a notation would have been realized in speech: the relationship between the complex notation and the relatively simple entity notated could have been indirect. The system of graphic notation need not have been thought of as closely paralleling spoken language, because their functions were different.

Finally, the relation of the U-j writing to where it was inscribed and used calls for comment. Dreyer *et al.* (1998b:84, 138–139) remarks, as I have above, that the tags and the jar inscriptions cannot record the contents of the groups of material or containers to which they were attached; the only exceptions would be the numerical tags, which may have made explicit something that could not be seen at first glance in the material. Understanding the inscriptions therefore relied on the association of context and content. A tag attached to a bundle was visibly [Bundle X] + [Name/indication of provenance]. "Syntax" was provided by the object itself and the meaning was associative (as Stephen Houston points out to me). Similar usages seem to occur in the earliest writing of a number of traditions. Perhaps only when systems had evolved further was writing capable of conveying meaning in a less context-dependent manner. Context-dependence may also correlate in part with the possible language-independence I discuss below.

The societal and iconographic context

The U-j material needs to be set in the archaeological and societal context of its period.[17] The Naqada II period, which began before the invention of writing, saw a marked differentiation of wealth and the emergence of complex societies, regional polities, and at its end a uniform material culture throughout Egypt. This process has been characterized in the literature as the formation of a centralized state or as the creation of a regional interaction sphere among polities that was later followed by the formation of a unitary state (contrast Kemp [1989:19–46] with Kaiser [1990]).

Whether or not a single polity of Egypt emerged before the end of Naqada II, the Naqada III period essentially continues the development of the same repertory of material culture. It is characterized by increased social inequality, a simplification of non-elite material culture, increasing size of elite tombs, the proliferation of luxury goods, the appearance of specific symbols of rulership, and finally writing (see, conveniently, for example, Bard 2000).

In some ways, more can be said about developments in pictorial representation than about their social context. Complex forms of representational art that developed in Naqada I and the first half of Naqada II are known from textiles (Donadoni Roveri and Tiradritti 1998:168–169, no. 77), pottery, and the wall painting of Hierakonpolis Tomb 100 (e.g. Midant-Reynes 2000:169–210). The last of these shows a marked contrast between sophisticated content and rapid execution, suggesting that more highly wrought works existed in other media and contexts, perhaps in shrines and elite dwellings (see Wengrow and Baines 2004). The characteristic decorated pottery of Naqada II (D-Ware) was made of desert marl probably extracted in Wadi Qena across the river from Naqada. The ware, which was painted before firing (Payne 1993:98–101), is likely to have been made locally and traded in relatively large quantities throughout Egypt. Its decorative repertory intersects in places with later motifs, notably emblems of deities and perhaps of one or two provinces (nomes) from the dynastic period. Like the Tomb 100 painting, it is relatively simple in execution. Both D-Ware and the more traditional, mostly undecorated black-topped red ware (B-Ware) ceased to be made at the end of Naqada II. Part of their position in a hierarchy of values was taken by luxury stone vases and by representational carving, notably on ivory among surviving materials.[18] These developments signal increasing social inequality and a withdrawal of pictorial forms from non-elites.

Thus, writing was probably invented during a period when pictorial representation that was accessible to relatively many people had recently disappeared. As in many societies, representation was a scarce resource, and it may have become heavily sacralized. The use of pictorial forms in writing therefore marks it as a product of the central elite, who were presumably those who appropriated pictorial representation, in an intensification of their control of material and symbolic resources that was in part articulated through the system of decorum (for related arguments, see Baines and Yoffee [1998, 2000]). It is difficult to be specific about the pictorial context for writing: the surviving material with which it might be compared is sparse and much of it cannot be dated because it comes from secondary contexts or from the early twentieth-century art market. Finds in Cemetery U at Abydos (references in n. 5) confirm that the earliest writing was broadly contemporaneous with the initial development of the style and iconography which led into that of dynastic times. Compositions regularly included some hieroglyphs, for example as identifying captions, as was true of all later Egyptian pictorial representation.

These parallels with other domains of material culture bring out how "advanced" the U-j writing is in content and in pictorial conventions. Its sign forms were almost certainly designed to mesh with pictorial representation, and perhaps for that reason were not close to the cursive signs used on pottery at the same date, even though signs could be transposed between the two. The difference between writing and representation still remains clear, and was exploited no later than dynasty 0 to create an intermediate form that I term "emblematic personification," in which various pictorial elements including hieroglyphs were given human arms to make them capable of pictorial action (Baines 1985:41–63; compare Gardiner's interpretation of an emblematic group [1957:§5]). These hieroglyphs convey values integral to Egyptian ideology.

The cursive sign forms are essentially what might be expected in quick versions of hieroglyphs written with brush and ink or paint. In the U-j material their representational basis remains clear, perhaps in part because of their large scale and the fact that any given inscription consists of only one or two signs. One can imagine their being used in smaller variants for different purposes, but nothing of the sort survives.

The U-j writing has few parallels. Dreyer (1995) has suggested that secondary graffiti on a group of colossal statues from Koptos offer rough-carved versions of some of its forms (see also Dreyer *et al.* [1998b:175–179]; for a different view, see Kemp, Boyce, and Harrell [2000]). Tomb U-j itself produced hardly any pictorial material and no inscribed objects apart from those discussed above. Everything precious had been robbed, so that one should allow for the original presence of such materials in the tomb. In style, the U-j writing is very similar to a detail on the Hunters' Palette, of unknown

168 John Baines

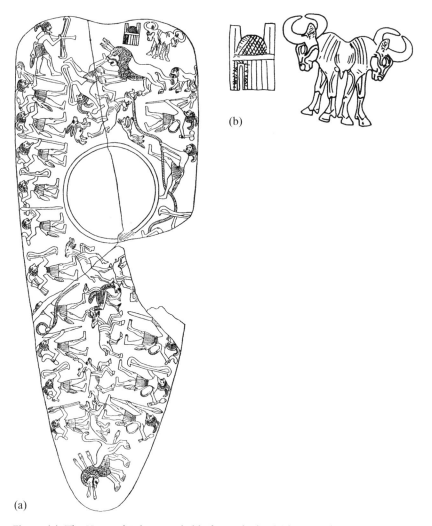

Fig. 6.5(a) The Hunters' Palette, probably from Abydos (either temple or necropolis). Naqada IIIa period (?). Height *c.* 64 cm. Siltstone. British Museum EA 20790, 20792, Louvre E 11254. Drawing after W. Smith (1949:111, fig. 25). **(b)** Detail of the design of building and double bull at the top of the Hunters' Palette. Drawing by Christine Barratt; after Baines (1995:112, fig. 5, p. 151).

date and provenance, at the top of which are two signs, of a double bull and a building, that probably signify the king but cannot be read (Fig. 6.5(a); Asselberghs 1961:figs. 122–124). Another relevant example is a palette in the Metropolitan Museum of Art that bears the "Horus Name" of a king in the form known from later times but in a more archaic style (Asselberghs 1961:fig. 170). Both of these are typologically earlier than the palettes from

The earliest Egyptian writing 169

Fig. 6.6 The Scorpion Macehead, main decorated area, from Hierakonpolis Main Deposit. The only writing preserved is the pair of signs in front of the central figure of the king, but no more than a third of the decorated area is preserved. Dynasty 0. Height *c.* 30 cm. Limestone (Oxford, Ashmolean Museum E 3632; drawing by Marion Cox, courtesy Ashmolean Museum).

later dynasty 0 and could be as old as tomb U-j (compare ivories found in Cemetery U at Abydos: Dreyer *et al.* [1993:plates 6d–f]). The Hunters' Palette example is almost identical with later material, such as the Scorpion Macehead (Fig. 6.6), in its siting and relation to the pictorial decoration, and is best explained as a piece of writing that uses otherwise unattested signs. The graffiti on the colossi include several of the same signs as the U-j pottery, supporting the distinction between types of writing, and on Dreyer *et al.*'s interpretation (1998b:178–180) extending its chronological range both back in time and down into dynasty 0.

The two types of writing in tomb U-j are the first examples of the consistent Egyptian practice of using distinct forms for different purposes. Hieratic, the everyday form executed in ink – present from the first but often so termed only in its later forms – no doubt constituted the overwhelming mass of writing, but because its media were perishable, much less of it is known than of hieroglyphic. Hieratic sign forms are less clearly representational than hieroglyphic ones, but complex signs and signs employed soon after their first introduction resemble one another more closely in the two script forms than do simpler and more widespread ones. Signs that require detail in order to be distinguished from one another in hieroglyphs, such as a number of types of bird, are distinguished in hieratic by different stroke patterns; many came to resemble their hieroglyphic counterparts very little. Nonetheless, from the invention of the script to the first millennium BC, the two forms remained commensurable and one could be transposed into the other.[19] Because of the prestige of hieroglyphs, which were integral to the cultural norms that form parts of the overarching system of decorum, I would expect essential innovations to have been focused on hieroglyphs while affecting the two forms together. Cursive scripts later acquired a life of their own, but the two types did not depart far from each other until the first millennium BC – altogether outside the period considered here.

All the written material of this earliest attested stage comes from a royal burial place, as does that from the next century or so, with the addition of some pieces dedicated in temples (pieces from the early twentieth-century art market are probably from one or other of those contexts). This pattern of preservation relates in the first instance to the nature of the Egyptian terrain and the siting of accessible monuments. Settlements with palace complexes are almost entirely unknown, but are likely to have been the prime contexts of the use and further development of writing, even if a significant proportion of it was intended for sacred and mortuary purposes. What is known may thus reflect only a subset of early uses of writing. Alternatively, writing may have been largely a royal prerogative and its administrative functions restricted to that domain. The U-j material, however, appears to be administrative – that is, it attached information to deliveries. The instrumental utility of adding provenance information to bolts of cloth and jars deposited in a royal burial is uncertain. Display purposes are conceivable, for example in the prestige of its being known that their deposition was administered through a complex, relatively novel procedure. The practice does not in itself point toward there having been a system of administration in writing that extended outside the sphere of the inner elite. For example, no pottery inscribed in the same manner is known from other cemeteries of the Naqada IIIa period, which suggests that other containers, products, and recipients of deliveries were treated in other ways.[20]

Both in what it notated and in the social contexts of its use, writing in Naqada III seems to have been an extremely limited system, despite the large investment of creativity, as well as symbolic and material resources, involved in its invention. This does not mean that it was not valuable for administration, display, or both, but rather that its most important aspect was that it formed part of a complex of visual high culture which was of overriding value for the central elite. Wider applications were probably not sought until significantly later, nor was its potential systematically investigated and exploited. The creation and maintenance of the institutions necessary to maintain writing – which must be posited even though the material is so sparse – and to reform it during dynasty 0 are equally significant.

I therefore believe that the focus on narrowly practical administrative purposes in some explanations of the origins of writing is reductive (for example Postgate, Wang, and Wilkinson 1995). It is not possible to establish that writing was "necessary" to the administration of states such as those of Uruk period Mesopotamia. In Egypt, the range of administration supported by writing seems to have been restricted, while the Mesopotamian system seems to have been invented near the end of the Uruk growth phase. These points in no way imply that the invention was unimportant. Rather, for Egypt some areas of administration mattered far more than others. Symbolic aspects were at least as significant as practical ones.

Notation in the early script

As indicated, it is uncertain how the script notated the entities it recorded, that is, whether this was done through specifying lexemes, or whether the focus was on the entities rather than lexemes.[21] In the U-j case, the groups on the tags might signify a lexeme (like *3bdw* ["Abydos"]) or might point more directly to a particular estate or productive unit. On a narrow and probably irrelevant definition, the latter procedure would be "proto-writing" rather than writing.[22] The script was hardly used later to write any language except Egyptian, the dominant language of the country, but in the period of political and cultural coalescence when it was invented, more languages – now entirely unknown to us – are likely to have been present and a largely language-independent notation could have had advantages (for possible evidence, see, for example, n. 10 here). The idea of language-independence has traditionally been resisted by historians of Egyptian writing and of writing in general, perhaps in part because it eludes verification or falsification (for discussion around an instance of another perspective, see F. Salomon [2001]). It may nonetheless be viable for a system with a limited repertory of signs and range of usage, like that of U-j with its perhaps 50–100 signs. The close relation between hieroglyphic writing and pictorial contexts may not have suggested any need for linguistic notation, even though it opened the way toward it; at this stage, cursive writing too remained nearly as iconic as hieroglyphic. Both writing styles seem also to have been closely tied to the contexts in which they were inscribed, so that context-dependence is as important a factor as language-dependence or -independence. As indicated below, by the 1st dynasty the notion of language-independence becomes largely irrelevant. Here, hieroglyphic Egyptian, Hittite (Luwian), and Maya glyphs show one approach to developing scripts and integrating them with high culture; Mesopotamian and Chinese writing show another. The vast Mesopotamian Uruk IV sign repertory may have come to strain memory insofar as it was a primarily graphic system and not strongly representational. This difficulty does not apply to the U-j writing, with its smaller number of much more representational signs. Moreover, East Asian writing systems show that vast sign repertories that have far from straightforward connections with their linguistic realizations can readily be held in memory.

One issue here is the means by and extent to which writing was "invented" at a single moment in the way that Marvin Powell (1981), for example, posits for Mesopotamia (see Michalowski [1996] for a more cautious view). The moment of invention of the Egyptian system is inaccessible, but one could imagine that a notation was devised to record a small range of entities and numbers with a few dozen signs, as attested no doubt incompletely from tomb U-j. Such a notation could be created quite quickly, incorporating some already existing symbols into its sign repertory. The attested system is so limited that a diverse purpose or usage need not be posited for it.

In dynasty 0 the writing system was reformed to extend its capacity to record specific lexemes, insofar as that had not been possible before. The number of signs in use proliferated greatly (repertory: Kahl [1994]), reaching perhaps more than 1,000 before reducing again to a few hundred in the mid third millennium. Language itself was adapted to writing: by the early 1st dynasty the "narrative infinitive" was introduced as a method of presenting events, notably those after which years were named, without recording continuous discourse.[23] While, in writing, the narrative infinitive remained important for headings and other specialized purposes for more than three millennia, there is no reason to suppose that it was a spoken linguistic form – except inasmuch as the spoken mimicked the written, which it certainly did in some contexts. Rather, the narrative infinitive owed its existence to the dominance in writing of tabular and pictorial forms of recording and

The earliest Egyptian writing 173

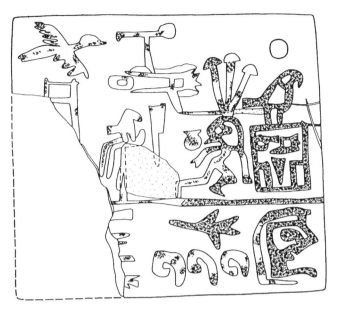

Fig. 6.7 Tag of Narmer from Umm el-Qaʿab Cemetery at Abydos (uncontexted find). Mixed writing and emblematic representation. The upper register shows a catfish, which writes the Nar- (nʿr-) element in the king's name, smiting a northern foe, while the full form of the name is written on the extreme right. The lower register probably specifies a quantity of oil. Late dynasty 0. Height 3.65 cm, width 4 cm. Material not stated, probably bone. Drawing after Dreyer et al. (1998a:139, fig. 29, with photograph pl. 5c).

the absence of written continuous discourse. This interaction of writing and language probably fostered the script's general usefulness, but until the rationalization of the late 2nd/3rd dynasties it was not often used to record the full grammatical range of language. When full discourse was written, tabular forms very gradually lost their preeminence.

Another development was in mixed pictorial–linguistic forms that exploited all the hieroglyphic script's potential for expressing meaning, perhaps building on the style of the earlier Hunters' Palette (Fig. 6.5; see above). From the end of dynasty 0 these forms are prominent on the larger tags which succeeded the miniature ones of tomb U-j (Figs. 6.7, 6.8) and which mostly contain year names and designations of produce, notably oils.[24] The compositions of the tags range as far as the wholly pictorial (for example Dreyer et al. 1998a: pl. 12d–e), while paralleling the more linguistic formulations of year names preserved on the 5th dynasty Palermo Stone, which preserves fragments of a consolidated display version of royal annals (for example

Fig. 6.8 Wooden tag of Aha from Cemetery B at Abydos, tomb complex of Aha. Mixed writing and pictorial representation. The lowest register specifies oil and probably other products. The principal events of the top register seem to be the manufacture of a cult image together with a visit to the temple of Neith at Sais in the Nile Delta. 1st dynasty. Height not given. Present location not known. After Petrie (1901:pl. X:2).

Wilkinson 2000, with erroneous dating of the object itself). The transformation in comparison with the U-j tags is remarkable. These pictorial and written display forms no doubt related closely to modes of temple decoration that must have formed the core of the system of pictorial and inscriptional decorum (Baines 1989). At the same time, there was a proliferation of uses of writing on such objects as seals (Kaplony 1963). More widespread administrative applications probably developed in the 1st dynasty – papyrus was invented no later than its middle years (Baines 1983:575 with 593, n. 4) – although little can be dated precisely. Thus, writing's range of uses increased greatly after its first reform, both in enhanced symbolic potential and in practical applications; but continuous discourse and full syntax were not notated for another couple of centuries. Instead, there was a great development of tabular and pictorial forms, comparable in some respects with that described by Boone (this volume) for Mesoamerica, and in others with usage in early Mesopotamian cuneiform (e.g. Michalowski 1996:35–36; Cooper, this volume).

If the role of reforms – such as the one in dynasty 0 – in the pattern of the script's development is appreciated, it becomes possible to set writing's initial appearance better in context, principally by discarding assumptions about its uses that are based on later, more versatile forms. The system that was first invented – in the only stage that could be termed a pure "invention" – was very limited and could not have been exploited for practical purposes without prior knowledge of the context and of the repertory of what was notated; it was far from being a self-sufficient means of communication. Its cultural salience could have been as important as anything else about it. Its inventors could not have foreseen that it would later develop into a nearly universal recording medium. That is something that was appreciated by subsequent reformers, but probably only those of a much later period. The reforms of dynasties 0/1 and of the late 2nd/3rd dynasties proceeded a step at a time. Not until the Middle Kingdom (after $c.$ 2000 BC) was the range and relative freedom of use of writing at all comparable with that of the modern world (cf. Baines 1983).

Influence from outside?

Increased evidence for early Mesopotamian and Egyptian writing has made it, if anything, more difficult to assess which was invented first and whether one depended on the other. These questions should be approached in terms of the earliest attested systems – and neither of these is the oldest writing that ever existed in its area.[25] Precursors of written notation (of non-language-dependent items and numbers rather than of words) in the form of numerical tablets and tokens incorporated into bullae are evident in Mesopotamia rather than Egypt, while the Egyptian Delta (e.g. Faltings 1998), and in different ways the Nile Valley, demonstrate Near Eastern connections from about 4000 BC onward. The artistic motifs that link Egypt to Late Uruk Mesopotamia and Iran are of uncertain import here because they cannot be dated precisely in relation to the appearance of writing (e.g. Joffe 2000; Moorey 1987; H. Smith 1992; Teissier 1987). It has been assumed almost automatically that the influence ran from Mesopotamia to Egypt rather than the other way around (e.g. Pittman 1996). Although the newly discovered older written material in Egypt makes this priority less clear, the reverse possibility has hardly been entertained. The further argument for stimulus diffusion from Mesopotamia, which is that the assumption that there were two inventions of writing in the same region of the world within a century or two of each other stretches coincidence, is weak. It is equally possible that the two civilizations came, by different routes but in the same general period, to invent comparable systems of notation, both of which later developed into full writing. So long as it cannot be established whether the Mesopotamian or the Egyptian system is older, it remains prudent to study the two separately.[26]

In relation to how the first writing was invented, the most important recent change in opinion is the view, which has developed particularly in relation to the Uruk IV system, that its notation of language is at most very limited; some of those who work with it term it "proto-writing" rather than "writing" (e.g. Damerow 1999b). As a system, the U-j writing has a different character and greater artistic potential, but overall it is at least as limited. The proposed stimulus diffusion therefore remains possible, but the stimulus would be awareness of a complex recording system rather than of the representation of language.[27] Perhaps the only prerequisite for inventing a system like the U-j writing is the insight – itself an enormous leap forward – that there could be a recording system using signs derived from pictorial representation and relating to entities in new ways; the signs would be assembled in pairs or groups on primarily non-pictorial principles and would incorporate, or work with, numerical information. The more elaborate Uruk IV writing could be described as just such a recording system. As Jerrold Cooper emphasizes (this volume), early Mesopotamian and Egyptian writing perform different functions from spoken language and should not be assimilated closely to it. Moreover, while writing might represent language in the sense that a linguistic formulation preceded the creation of any particular piece of writing, it does not follow that the piece itself notated specific words; and a performance or realization of the piece – a "reading" – might use yet other words. The earliest writing in Mesopotamia and Egypt was no doubt enveloped by human use of language and mobilized by means of it, but it does not follow that it focused upon and operated directly through the notation of uniquely identified words of language. The linguistic focus of research and concern with "decipherment" may have blinded scholars to the possibility that this writing worked in different ways.[28]

For the theory of script development, the main point here is that the way in which each system notates language must be studied separately. Second-millennium BC inventions of writing in the Near East, such as Aegean linear scripts or Ugaritic, took place in an environment where phonemic notation was widespread, whereas no such presupposition can have existed in the late fourth millennium, simply because there was no prior writing. The notation of specific features of language, such as the phonemes of particular groups of lexemes, was integral to the development of the earliest systems after, not during, their initial invention. Those earliest systems may not have been full writing on the strong definition that writing encodes language, but that definition is not very relevant here, since it was hundreds of years before anything like continuous discourse was notated. Here, Chinese, with its seemingly more rapid evolution into a full language-recording system, may present a different picture from Mesopotamia, Egypt, and probably Mesoamerica, but there too it is highly unlikely that samples of the very first writing have been discovered (see Bagley, this volume).

Lexical structure of language in relation to writing system

Scholars such as Peter Daniels argue that the conceptual leap of inventing writing occurs most easily where the subset of the lexicon that is written is largely monosyllabic. Establishing the rebus principle and identifying sign/graph with unit of meaning and unit of sound are thought to be more intuitive in these cases than where there is no such easy correspondence, as is the case in polysyllabic languages, particularly inflected ones. William Boltz (2000) remarks further that the Chinese system has remained "frozen" at the stage of development in which there is, at least in theory, such a correspondence, despite the growth of polysyllables after the script's invention. Daniels also uses the monosyllabic argument in support of a priority of Mesopotamian writing over Egyptian, since Sumerian is held by some to be, to a limited extent, monosyllabic. It is worth reviewing the implications of these points, while bearing in mind that the view that particular language types affect the invention of writing pays little regard to the social and intellectual context in which that invention took place.

While those who invented Mesopotamian writing were probably Sumerian speakers, their linguistic environment was almost certainly multilingual, and they might have had an interest in creating a system that crossed linguistic boundaries – if they gave the matter any thought. If, however, they did not focus strongly on words, a desire for language-independence would hardly be relevant to the initial invention, whereas later developments that incorporated characteristics of a particular language had to face the issue of how best to do that. Nonetheless, even Uruk IV writing may provide evidence for the incorporation in the script of some Sumerian phonemic elements, while scholars generally accept that one or more Semitic languages were spoken in the society in addition to Sumerian.[29] Notating some elements through verbal association is different from aiming at a general encoding of language.

In relation to early Egyptian, and especially to the monosyllabic hypothesis, one question that arises here is: what sort of analysis of the language would the script's developers in dynasty 0 and later – as opposed to the inventors of the U-j system – have had to make in order to reach the result they did and to express adequately what they needed to record of the Egyptian language? In order to provide a context, I review a couple of features of Egyptian.

Unlike some scholars' views of part of Sumerian, Egyptian lexemes are in no way monosyllabic.[30] Egyptian is an Afroasiatic language, forming a separate subfamily closest to Semitic and sharing the latter's tri- and bi-consonantal root structures but not its complex verbal conjugations. In languages like Egyptian, vowels are more variable than consonants and words are formed with syllabic and consonantal prefixes and suffixes. To explain the prevalence of consonantal scripts in the notation of Egyptian and Semitic by saying that vowels are irrelevant to meaning in such languages is wrong, because vowels very often convey the semantic distinctions between similar forms. Nonetheless, the relative stability of the consonantal base might have attracted people seeking to represent elements of language by means of a limited range of signs, many of which notated more than a single phoneme (in contrast, for example, to the very much larger number of graphs in Chinese). Both early Egyptian and much of the earliest Semitic writing, in cuneiform and in the early second-millennium BC "Protosinaitic" script, used words as pure lexemes without syntax and were closely context-dependent. In such usages vowels may have been more dispensable than in continuous discourse (plenty of continuous Semitic writing also largely dispenses with vowels). When specific words rather than entities began to be notated in Egyptian, signs were devised to represent consonantal features ranging from single consonants to whole roots. Uniconsonantal signs could write brief elements like prepositions, as well as being in principle universally applicable, while triconsonantal signs were linked to particular lexical roots.[31] Since homophonous roots are fairly common in Egyptian – no doubt often distinguished in speech by vowels and syllable pattern – linking triconsonantal signs to roots was advantageous for clarity in reading (homophony was not as prevalent as in Sumerian or Chinese). Biconsonantal signs, the largest category of phonemic signs, were probably derived by rebus from biconsonantal roots. They were used much more widely than triconsonantal signs in the orthography of words unrelated to the root from which their consonantal values derived, but their application was not universal, and unlike uniconsonantal and triconsonantal signs, an appreciable number of them are homophones.

Together with most Egyptologists, I term all these sign types "consonantal." Although I. J. Gelb in particular argued that they represent syllables rather than consonants (1963:75–81, 201), this view has tended to be discounted, because it has more advantages for Gelb's theory of a unilinear evolution from logogram through syllabogram to alphabet than for analyzing how the Egyptian script works. While Egyptian phonograms generally take syllable boundaries into account (see n. 14), Gelb's position is problematic because the script does not notate vowel quality or quantity. In keeping with Gelb's hypothesis, Wolfgang Schenkel has suggested (1976) that Gelb's syllables could be "script syllables" rather than syllables of the language itself, but this notion too is difficult: a "script syllable" would have to include zero among its vowels, since the position of vowels changes with prefixation and suffixation while the core signs used to write a root remain the same. This is a greater variability than is normally found in syllabic scripts where, for example, vowel position before or after a consonant is generally a basic distinguishing feature. More than a millennium later the Egyptians introduced a special "syllabic orthography," mainly to write non-Egyptian names. This included a rudimentary notation of vowels, using one or more hieroglyphs for each syllable on the CV pattern (e.g. Hoch 1994:487–512). This innovation suggests strongly that the Egyptians understood their traditional writing system as not being essentially syllabic – or as being unlike syllabic cuneiform – especially since syllabic orthography had Old and Middle Kingdom forerunners that were more "consonantal" and rather closer to standard orthography (e.g. Osing 1976). Syllabic orthography is likely to have been directly or indirectly influenced by cuneiform, perhaps after Egyptian awareness of it increased with more active contacts with Syria-Palestine in the early second millennium BC.

The Egyptian script of the early 1st dynasty and later possessed a wide range of phonograms and specifically recorded only consonantal skeletons. Those who enlarged the U-j system into this fuller form must have exploited the rebus principle – which as Dreyer states is likely to be present already in U-j – and must have analyzed some of the language's phonological characteristics in order to discard vowels. An essential feature of the notation of continuous discourse in Egyptian is the presence of determinatives, which greatly facilitate the identification of word boundaries. They were also sometimes used – for example in classificatory boxes – in the tabular presentation of complex materials typical of the Early Dynastic Period and Old Kingdom. Determinatives are relatively unimportant to early writing because it did not record discourse: in pictorial compositions, or in the labeling of objects, the context "determined" what was written – often a single word – and determinatives are largely absent.[32] Dreyer's proposal that determinatives may be present in the U-j material is not argued on specific evidence and remains inconclusive (Dreyer *et al.* 1998b:181, more cautiously phrased on p. 139).

Similarly, the "phonetic complements" he finds are uncertain, if only because his readings of the groups as a whole are hypothetical.

Analysis of the forms of lexemes, including their phonology, contributed to the development from proto-writing to writing, when encoding needed to be extended to cover elements in language that were not previously notated, and some general applicability needed to be introduced without increasing the number of signs excessively. At this next stage, fully syntactic language with continuous discourse was still not an issue, because most writing consisted of brief notations that were organized as much visually or by context as by linguistic consecution. In Egypt, the stage of continuous discourse, the third and final one on the model I adopt here, seems to have been reached in the later 2nd dynasty, 400–500 years after the U-j system was devised (Baines 1999a:28–30). In Mesopotamia – where there are significant gaps in the evidence – the parallel change came after a comparable interval. Moves to subsequent stages of both scripts were reforms, not gradual developments. At least in Egypt, the writing of discourse may have been restricted initially to specific domains: it is first attested in a statement of what a god did for a king and in speeches that caption figures of deities (Baines 1997a:132 with n. 8).

Those who developed the Egyptian system decided to limit its notation to roots, optionally including affixes, and to ignore the internal variation that vowels underwent in particular word forms. They therefore possessed a notion of a "root."[33] In some sense they must have made a distinction between consonants and vowels. Another rule was almost more important: enough of a word should be written to enable identification, whether logographically or phonemically, but there was no requirement to represent all its consonants explicitly, while the "weak" ꜣ, j (values in this period uncertain, see n. 5), and w could be omitted – and thus seem to have been perceived as a distinct category (for detail, see Kahl [1994]). Some "phonological" analysis therefore contributed to the reform. "Complementing," in which extra written consonants reinforced the reading of a word whose root was expressed by a bi- or triconsonantal sign, was optional. Words could be written with logograms that did not in themselves indicate a specific reading; this method of notation was later often marked by a "logogram indicator" stroke.

The inventory of signs was not closed: new signs could be introduced at will, although this did not happen very much. During the Early Dynastic Period many signs went out of use, as can be seen from a comparison of Kahl's list (1994) with Gardiner's core set for rather later periods (1957). The majority of consonantal hieroglyphs can be related to roots that supplied their original values. Once principles of derivation had been established, devising new signs for the general range of content that needed to be encoded was the principal task. Among basic elements, almost the full range of uniconsonantal signs is attested by mid 1st dynasty (Kahl 1994:70–71), when the repertory of biconsonantal signs seems still to have been relatively limited. This suggests that the developers envisaged notating not just whole words and semantic units but increasingly their phonemic constituents, and that they aimed to create a system that was in principle universally applicable.

Thus, the specifically linguistic analysis involved in extending the Egyptian script exceeded the recognition, posited by Daniels and Boltz for Sumerian and Chinese respectively, of syllables as semantic units ("words") and of the rebus principle. In particular, it required a concern with "philology," that is, with analyzing word structures and identifying some primarily grammatical elements, such as prepositions and pronoun suffixes, that were written mainly with consonantal signs and without determinatives and thus did not conform with general orthographic patterns. How much such analysis had been involved in devising the U-j system is uncertain. Be that as it may, linguistic analysis is possible without writing, as is shown especially by the Indian grammatical school with its main exponent Pāṇini (c. fifth century BC), who worked before writing was introduced in India and whose sutras were transmitted for many centuries before being written down.[34] While the secondary elaboration of Egyptian writing in dynasties 0/1 was an enormous intellectual achievement and guided the system's development in specific directions, it may not tell us anything particular about the previous introduction of complex visual recording or proto-writing, that is, about the U-j system, which was itself a stupendous leap into a new system of communication. The patterns along which the Sumerian and Chinese scripts developed were no doubt influenced by the character of the languages they wrote, but in all cases the original point of departure could have had less to do with language than with recording and with creating a self-standing system that was parallel, but not coextensive, with language.

This relation of writing to non-continuous discourse is relevant to another feature of Egyptian. There seems to have been no strong principle of "economy" that might have led to the discarding of signs that were dispensable in the notation of words. Had such a principle existed, the system might conceivably have been reduced to a smaller number of signs or even to uniconsonantal ones, but that would have made the script more difficult to read, except by those who had not yet learned it properly. Such a strategy is not likely to have had any appeal for as long as continuous discourse was not recorded, because a script that records words outside the context of discourse needs abundant cues if it is to be read with ease. In later periods a reduction of the repertory would have been if anything still less appealing, for both cultural and practical reasons. Redundancy helps to form identifiable fixed groups and to reduce multivalence.

The disadvantages of uniconsonantal orthography as perceived by third-millennium Egyptians may be visible in the uninterpretable names of prehistoric kings inscribed in the first register of the 5th dynasty Palermo Stone, which use many such signs (e.g. T. Wilkinson 2000:fig. 1): at that date other types of document wrote exotic names by means of large numbers of uniconsonantal signs, in a specialized orthography of a different character (e.g. Osing 1976). The writings of the names on the Palermo Stone may have been devised as opaque forms that demonstrated their own obscurity. We now know that names which might have belonged in that register of the stone – that is, rulers' names of the Naqada III period and dynasty 0 – were originally written in a different way. The uniconsonantally written names on the stone are therefore fictitious, at least in their orthography. They may, however, fit with some earlier practice, if only coincidentally: many Early Dynastic inscriptions, especially on seals, that make no sense and constitute pseudo-writing created for prestige, use numerous uniconsonantal signs (e.g. Fig. 6.9; Kaplony 1963:III, figs. 435–720; compare Kahl 1994:16–18). In the Old Kingdom Pyramid Texts, the orthography of some magical spells against snakes that may be collections of sounds rather than conventionally meaningful discourse has an exceptionally high proportion of uniconsonantal signs, perhaps in part as a mystification or token of their portentousness (Kammerzell 2001:123–125). Thus, in Early Dynastic and Old Kingdom Egypt, uniconsonantal orthography seems to have been an obscurantist device rather than a form of writing that was intended to be easier to read than the normal mixture of categories of sign.

Language type may influence profoundly the direction in which scripts develop subsequent to invention, as has been true of many reforms of orthography around the world, but it may be largely irrelevant to writing's original invention and should therefore not be invoked in arguments about where this occurred. The very different early forms and uses of writing in Mesopotamia and Egypt act more as "communicative systems" (see, e.g. Michalowski 1990) than as representations of language. The argument for the influence of lexical structure of language on choices in script structure may be applicable to developments in Mesopotamia after writing's initial appearance, and it may apply to Chinese at a still earlier stage in the latter's development (but a later absolute date), but neither case relates closely to

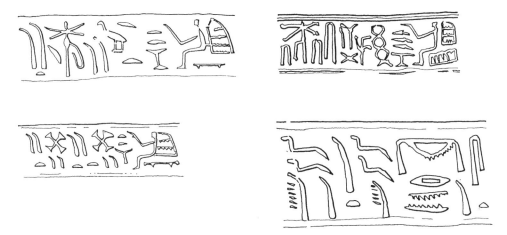

Fig. 6.9 Sample cylinder seals of the 1st–2nd dynasties with unintelligible pseudo-writing. All but one are organized partly as scenes, with a seated figure at the right, and thus are semi-pictorial. British Museum EA 65853 (top L), 66812 (top R), 65872 (bottom L; all black steatite, height 1.9, 1.6, 1.5 cm), 36462 (bottom R; wood, height 2.8 cm). All unprovenanced. Drawings by Richard Parkinson, copyright British Museum. Publication with different drawings: Spencer (1980:nos. 423, 446, 432, 414).

Egyptian because of the difference in language type and the greater range of phonogram types the Egyptian script possessed after its reform in dynasty 0, quite apart from its focus on such features as the iconicity of hieroglyphic signs.

Numerous writers have asserted that without a preexisting script or knowledge from outside, those who developed writing past initial forms like that of the U-j system could not have achieved such feats as distinguishing consonants from vowels. These arguments are not persuasive, particularly when it is probable, as in Egypt, that many or all of the phonemic and taxonomic features of the script were secondary developments. The developers of writing there were surely more intelligent than the generality of their modern interpreters, and their enterprise was centrally important to the elites of which they were members. Unlike more recent Western thinkers about language, they did not record their ideas in any surviving form other than the script itself. Not only is there no reason why they should have done so, but also the writing systems they created were not intended for expressing such matters, which did not become topical in writing until altogether later. This absence of explicit linguistic theory has parallels in other domains of the ancient societies in which meta-terminology was absent. This does not mean that people did not think about and discuss these things, but that if they did so – as is known to have been done in ancient India – it was in different ways from those of the more recent West.

Conclusion

All this leaves both the initial purpose of the invention of writing in Egypt and the precise nature of its earliest forms there no more certain than before. The discovery of tomb U-j has taken the understanding of early Egypt and its writing forward enormously, but unless significantly more material is found, I doubt whether it will be possible to establish a generally agreed interpretation of its inscriptions. The notion of "decipherment" may not be relevant to material of this sort because "readings" are unlikely to be clearcut. The find remains fundamentally important for comparative study of the invention of writing, which it opens up to less teleological and linguistically focused analysis. More positively expressed, it encourages interpretation of the system in terms of the forms and capabilities it exhibits, rather than those of a more encompassing, generally later, system.

The U-j writing also sets the question of the function of the writing and the interests it served in a new light. The Mesopotamian Uruk IV writing could have been used for mass administration, although it seems to me to be uncertain whether this was done, while the poorer attestation of writing after Uruk III could suggest that the institutions it created were not completely indispensable. The U-j writing was more clearly an ultra-restricted form. Nothing points to its having spread far beyond ceremonially tinged royal administration and central artistic forms (compare Kahl 1994:158–161). The integration of scribal status with elite display in the subsequent Early Dynastic Period (notably in the relief panels of Hezyre [Wood 1978]) suggests that for centuries the process of writing carried such prestige that mastery of it was prized for its own cultural value. For Hezyre, whose tomb and titles demonstrate that he was one of the leading members of society, the mastery was in the king's service. A comparable status for writing lower down the elite scale can be seen in the pseudo-inscriptions mentioned above. There are archaeologically better-founded parallels for elite artistic and scribal status among the Maya (Houston 2000:149–155; Inomata 2001) or in the Late Bronze Age Aegean (Bennet 2000), where the evidence comes from settlements rather than burials and so offers a more rounded picture.

Both these parallels and the U-j material itself emphasize the salience of complex elite institutions, like those of writing, in the archaeological record. From this perspective, the first question to ask is not so much what function writing had in the wider society, but who it served at the center and how it contributed to patterns of social inequality and access to symbolic resources, including those of administration, in early states. Early writing is part of the elite appropriation, reformulation, and invention of prestigious representational and symbolic forms in emergent civilizations. Perhaps only in retrospect could its notation of language be seen, with the eyes of the philologist, as a uniquely privileged aspect of the system even at the time of its first invention.

Postscript

New interpretations of the U-j writing have appeared since this chapter was sent for printing. Francis Amadeus Karl Breyer, "Die Schriftzeugnisse des prädynastischen Königsgrabes U-j in Umm el-Qaab: Versuch einer Neuinterpretation" (*Journal of Egyptian Archaeology* 88, 2002, 53–65), suggests some alternative readings. Jochem Kahl, "Die frühen Schriftzeugnisse aus dem Grab U-j in Umm el-Qaab" (*Chronique d'Egypte* 78, 2003, 112–135), offers other readings and proposes to reject Dreyer's hypothesis that many of the tags and pot inscriptions contain royal names (see pp. 162, 163 here). These arguments tend in a different direction from my own, but should be reported here because some of them represent clear improvements on Dreyer's initial readings.

p. 164 here: Kahl (2003) no longer argues that writing was invented in Naqada II.

Acknowledgments

I should like to thank Stephen Houston in particular for organizing the marvellously stimulating conference on "The First Writing" at Sundance in April 2000, for being patient over the delivery of this chapter for the resulting volume, and for his very suggestive comments on the penultimate draft, many of which I have incorporated more or less as he made them. I am grateful to Bill Boltz, Mark Collier, Peter Damerow, Esther Flückiger-Hawker, and numerous others for supplying me with references and for discussing related issues. I also owe a great debt to the late Jeremy Black and Richard Parkinson for commenting valuably on a very imperfect draft, and to Bob Bagley for greatly clarifying the final text.

Notes

1. Those studying Near Eastern systems tend to use "sign" (not in a semiotic sense), Sinologists "graph," and Mayanists "glyph." If all three terms denote something like "minimal bounded entity in a (complex, non-alphabetic) script," it matters little which is adopted, and I retain "sign" here. "Graph" and "glyph" have the advantage of not intersecting with usages in semiotics.

2. This is the point of departure that Albertine Gaur (1995) sees, correctly in my opinion, for the invention of writing. Her brief sketch is very valuable despite inaccuracies, as is the conclusion – as against the rather opaque argument – of Roy Harris (1986).
3. I assume that the Mesopotamian archaic list of professions had an ideological role, even if not a very salient one. For this and comparable material, see Nissen, Damerow, and Englund (1993:22–24, 105–115); Englund (1998:86–106).
4. Baines (1999a; short version Baines 1999b). For an excellent survey of Egyptian writing, its varieties and uses, see Parkinson (1999).
5. See, for example, Kaiser and Dreyer (1982); Dreyer, Hartung, and Pumpenmeier 1993; Dreyer *et al.* (1990, 1996, 1998a, 1998b, 2000).

   In what follows, I use the standard consonantal transcription of Egyptian into latin script. The values to be attributed to a number of consonants for early periods, notably j (*yodh*), ʿ, and $ʒ$ (traditionally ʿayin and glottal stop), are very uncertain. This problem need not affect the discussion here; review: Loprieno (1995:28–37).
6. The designation U-j indicates that this is a constructed brick tomb in Cemetery U (pit tombs are assigned numbers rather than letters).
7. Almost all the stone vessels had been looted (Dreyer *et al.* 1998b:14, 169–170).
8. The likely use of the later cubit (*c.* 525 mm) as the design module for a box of imported cedarwood, presumably from Lebanon, is relevant here (Dreyer *et al.* 1998b:165–167).
9. Here one can go beyond Baines (1995:95–121), which was originally composed before the discovery of tomb U-j.
10. Signs representing parts of the human body are another case of special and distinctive treatment: the values of several of them are not those of the Egyptian words but relate to Semitic vocabulary, as in *d* written with a hand, *yad* in Semitic but *ḏrt* in Egyptian (Lacau 1970:esp. 145–146). This pattern suggests some kind of classificatory avoidance, either in language or in the script, and might also point to the presence of more than one spoken language in Egypt in the period of the script's formation.
11. Kahl (2001) shows that the majority of the elephant signs are wrongly identified. I would prefer to read as a jackal the second of the proposed "elephant" types that he reassigns, rather than as his Seth animal, but in either case the elephant becomes less prominent in the inventory of signs.
12. Not to be confused with the Scorpion of the well-known Scorpion Macehead (Fig. 6.6), one of the premier decorated objects of the end of dynasty 0.
13. The equivalence of "3" and plural is probably attested in iconography from as early as Naqada IIc; see, e.g., Schäfer (1986 [1974]:155, fig. 142).
14. See Kahl (1994:87–94) on the significance of syllables for the script's organization. The assumed consonant cluster *$ʒst$ in this hypothetical form is itself problematic.

15. Where possible I avoid the term *word* because its status in linguistics is vexed, using it mainly for word groups in the developed Egyptian script.
16. I exclude the dynasty 0 king "Irihor" here because the reading of his name is very uncertain (for his identification, see Kaiser and Dreyer [1982:232–235]). Phonographic writings were widespread by the time of the personal names on stelae from subsidiary burials in the complex of King Djer of the early 1st dynasty (Petrie 1901: pl. XXVI).
17. See, for example, Midant-Reynes (2000). I treat aspects of the symbolic and artistic context in more detail in Baines (2003), focusing on evidence probably dating to dynasty 0. It is not possible here to present the social context in detail or to cite extensive bibliography. For the latter, see Hendrickx (1995), with annual updates in the journal *Archéo-Nil*.
18. Stone vases of the succeeding Early Dynastic Period are catalogued by Ali el-Khouli (1978); there is no comparable collection for Naqada II–III – see more generally Aston (1994). The largest body of ivories is from the "Main Deposit" at Hierakonpolis, most of which is of Naqada III and 1st dynasty date (e.g. Quibell 1900; Quibell and Green 1902; B. Adams 1974). The Naqada II and especially Naqada III display repertory may have included metal vessels, but these are not securely attested until the 1st dynasty. The decorated pottery studied by Bruce Williams (1988) is not closely relevant here, because the majority is from the Nubian A-Group rather than from Egypt itself, and may date from a little later than he proposes.
19. "Cursive hieroglyphic," a form used only for religious texts and a literary training composition, came between the two main variants. It largely disappeared when hieratic and hieroglyphs drew apart in the first millennium BC.
20. The material so far known from elsewhere in Cemetery U is very meager: see, e.g. Dreyer *et al.* (1998b:80–83).
21. The numerals are on tags that do not bear non-numerical signs and it is not certain what they enumerate, but their mode of notation must be different from that of the hieroglyphs and of the cursive writing on the pots. As many will have experienced, written numbers are in any case insulated from the linguistic context in which they may be set. They are, for example, typically the last element that someone will learn to "read out" in the surrounding language of a foreign-language text.
22. Compare especially the approach of William Boltz (1994:44–51; I return to this matter below). Boltz points to what may be clan insignia of the much earlier Chinese Dawenkou culture and later parallels on Shang period bronzes as possible forerunners of writing. The latter, however, are contemporaneous with much less representational graph forms of the oracle bone writing, so that the situation is a little different from Egypt, where fully pictorial forms were retained within the hieroglyphic script, even though writing operated on different principles from pictorial representation. See also Bagley (this volume).

23. There seems to be no published study of this form, which is marked in weak verbs by a *-t* ending. Whereas the earliest examples of *ms(t)* ("making [a cult statue]") do not exhibit the *-t* (e.g. Petrie 1901:pls. III:2, 4; IIIA:5–6, X–XI [drawings]), the probable 5th dynasty summary on the Palermo Stone does have it, as also in *ḫʿt* ("appearing [by the king]") (T. Wilkinson 2000:fig.1), illustrating how a full notation of flexions was only gradually introduced. Nonetheless, the later writing confirms that the narrative infinitive is not simply a writing of the verb without syntax, but a precise adaptation of language. Attention to flexion is attested by no later than the mid 1st dynasty in the writing of a feminine passive participle with *-t* ending in the name *mrjt-njt* ("Beloved of Neith"); normally vocalized "Meritneith" (e.g. Petrie 1900:frontispiece).
24. See, for example, Dreyer *et al.* (1996:pl. 5c) and Petrie (1900:pl. II:4 = X:1) – both reign of Narmer, probably end of dynasty 0; material of the reign of Aha (beginning of the 1st dynasty) is cited in n. 23.
25. Glassner (2000:62–68) comes nearest to doing this, but mixes radiocarbon dates with those of archaeological periods.
26. See also Cooper (this volume). On possible connections between Mesopotamia and Egypt through Syria in the Late Uruk period, see, e.g. Englund (1998:79, n. 166, with a perhaps over-precise chronology).
27. Compare Glassner (2000:62–66), who sees the possible diffusion as better sited in his proposed pre-Uruk IV writing stage.
28. One might draw the analogy, familiar to readers of scholarly books, of oral presentations of an academic paper. Often these are made on the basis of complete written texts, but the words pronounced, while covering much the same ground as what is written, may be entirely different. As it happens, the system used to notate the paper (modern writing) encodes language, but this is almost incidental to its function as an aide-mémoire for the presentation.
29. For example, note Michalowski (1996:35) and Steinkeller (1995), but disputed by Englund (1998:73–75); see also Cooper (this volume). I am not persuaded by Englund's argument (1998:77–91) that Sumerian might have overlain an "Archaic" language in Mesopotamia. This seems to assume an isomorphism of language and culture for which neither later Mesopotamia nor general patterns of language spread in complex societies offer a close parallel. On these issues, see further Rubio (1999).
30. For a description, see Loprieno (1995). Egyptian was distantly related to the Semitic language or languages spoken alongside Sumerian in Mesopotamia. There is no evidence that those languages influenced the recording of language in the first few hundred years of Mesopotamian writing; when Akkadian and other Semitic languages were written nearly a millennium later, they were pressed into the existing pattern of Sumerian cuneiform. See Cooper (this volume).
31. This linkage might suggest that the category of the triconsonantal sign is dispensable and such signs should be termed "logograms." However, the patterns of phonemic supplementation and addition of determinatives to these signs to

form orthographic groups suggest strongly that they were perceived as consonantal.
32. On the intersection of pictorial representation and writing, see works of Henry George Fischer (e.g. 1974, 1986). The two are intimately linked but, unlike Fischer, I believe that they are in principle distinguished compositionally, except in cryptography and allied procedures, which include deliberate play with representational and linguistic categories.
33. It would be a matter for investigation how far they also had a notion of "derived forms" such as nouns. Verbal roots are the ones that emerge clearly in the writing system. The structure of Egyptian words focuses strongly on verbs, as is true of many Afroasiatic languages. Perception of roots as part of the comprehension of spoken discourse seems probable to those for whom these languages are not mother tongues. Whether that was true of native speakers of Egyptian is impossible to say.
34. See, for example, Hinüber (1989) for the introduction of writing in India, perhaps in the third century BC. The suggestion of John Sören Pettersson (1996:126–130), that Pāṇini was probably aware of alphabetic writing even though it was not used in India in his period, seems forced, and "awareness" is hardly a sufficient basis for his argument. Similarly, Jack Goody's position (e.g. 2000:26–46) that Indian transmission must have been influenced by writing probably takes too unitary an approach to the potential for the use of memory and verbal argument in different societies.

7 | Anyang writing and the origin of the Chinese writing system

ROBERT W. BAGLEY

The earliest Chinese writing known to us, dating from about 1200 BC, is preserved on bronze vessels and divination bones unearthed at the Anyang site in north China. At the moment we first encounter it, the Anyang script has a repertory of several thousand characters, well standardized in graphic form, and it is full writing, able to record connected discourse. To explain the sudden appearance of a full-fledged writing system a number of different hypotheses have been proposed. Ranging from outside stimulus to overnight invention, all are shaped by the same awkward fact, namely that clear precursors for Anyang writing have not been found.

To an archaeologist, constantly reminded of what survives in the soil of north China and what does not, the lack of precursors looks more like an archaeological lacuna than a clue to origins. Steps toward writing in the centuries before 1200 BC might be unknown to us simply because the writing was done on perishable materials that have vanished; or those steps might have been taken at sites that archaeologists have not yet fully explored. Limited to one city and one or two narrow functions, our sample of second-millennium writing is unrepresentative in crucial ways. It cannot be assumed to represent the place or time of the script's invention, or to represent the full range of functions that writing served at Anyang, or to exhibit the function that at some earlier stage prompted the invention of writing. Nor does it tell us how many places besides Anyang used writing.

To explore these questions we must sift the evidence that we have – both epigraphic and archaeological – for clues to what once existed. In this effort, comparisons with the history of writing in the Near East are indispensable in suggesting possibilities that might not otherwise occur to us. Later periods in Chinese history might also be used comparatively, of course, but they can only show us what existed later in the history of Chinese writing; Mesopotamia and Egypt show us ways in which early stages can differ from late stages. No amount of indirect or comparative evidence can make up for the lack of pre-Anyang epigraphic materials; unless archaeologists are someday able to provide those, we may never be able to say much about the invention of the Anyang script. Still, research on the origins of Mesopotamian writing in recent decades has changed our ideas about what the immediate precursors of writing might look like. It is conceivable that, armed with a knowledge of the Mesopotamian record, archaeologists in China might find clues hitherto unrecognized. In drawing attention to the weakness of existing hypotheses, the present chapter aims not to discourage investigation but to redirect it into more promising channels. To make the best use of the evidence we have, we must go beyond hypotheses tailored to the contours of a merely accidental archaeological sample.

The Anyang epigraphic corpus

Let us begin with an overview of the sample, so as to form an idea of what it can tell us about origins and an idea of what is missing from it. Our first evidence for Chinese writing comes from the last capital of the Shang dynasty, modern Anyang, and belongs to the last two centuries of the second millennium BC, the so-called Anyang period, corresponding to the reigns of the last nine Shang kings.[1] Wu Ding, first of the nine, lived around 1200 BC. Inscriptions on divination bones survive in great quantities from his time, along with very brief inscriptions on bronze ritual vessels, and it is possible that the practice of inscribing both bronzes and divination bones originated in his reign.

Divination inscriptions

Although divination by cracking heated animal bones is known from many places in China and long precedes the Shang dynasty, inscribed bones come overwhelmingly from the Anyang site. At Anyang both turtle shells (usually the undershell, the plastron) and bovine scapulas (shoulder blades) were used. Heat applied to hollows carved on one side of the bone or shell produced cracks on the other side from which the omen's response to a previously announced question was read. The hollows were shaped so as to ensure that the crack would always have the form shown in Fig. 7.7a, but what feature of the crack gave the oracle's answer is not known.[2] To give an accurate idea of the size of the Anyang oracle-text corpus is not easy. Counts of bones are not very meaningful, since most are broken pieces bearing only a few characters. Only a handful of inscriptions have more than fifty characters. The great bulk of the corpus has been reproduced actual size in a multi-volume compendium that runs to about 5,000 folio pages.[3]

Wu Ding's inscriptions are the earliest and hence the chief concern of the present chapter. They are also the most varied and the most numerous, amounting to half the entire corpus. The example shown in Fig. 7.1, a

Fig. 7.1 Rubbing of a turtle plastron. Reign of Wu Ding, c.1200 BC. After Zhang (1962:no. 247).

rubbing of a plastron, has the special interest that it involves a person known not just to readers of the oracle texts but also to archaeologists: she was a consort of Wu Ding named Lady Hao ("lady" being a title for royal women), and hers is the richest Shang tomb ever found. The inscription on the left half of the plastron is a slightly abbreviated version of the inscription on the right half, with the question put in negative form. Let us look at the positive version on the right half. This begins at top right and reads in vertical columns. The first two characters give the date, a particular day in a

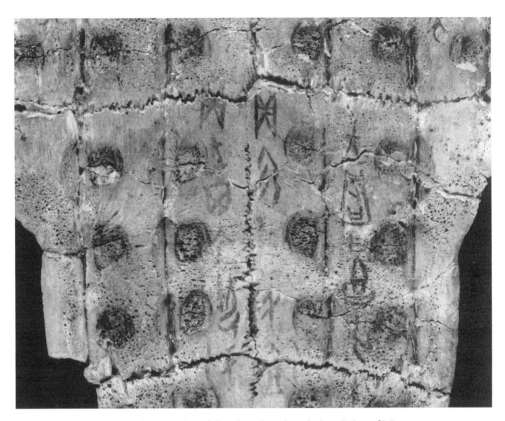

Fig. 7.2 Turtle plastron (*Yibian* 3380) with brush-written inscription. Reign of Wu Ding, c.1200 BC. (Photograph courtesy of Institute of History and Philology, Academia Sinica.) On brush-written oracle inscriptions, see *Kaogu* (1991[6]):546–554, 572).

cycle of six ten-day weeks (the first character is the day of the week, the two together fix both day and week). The third character, which refers to the act of divining, depicts the crack in a heated plastron or scapula that gave the oracle's response to a question (compare Fig. 7.7[a]). The fourth graph is the name of the official who is performing the divination, on this occasion a man named Que, one of more than 30 diviners at Wu Ding's court (about 120 are known from the Anyang period as a whole). After his name comes the word "divines" or "poses the question." Up to this point the inscription follows a standard formula; it says "Crack-making on the day *jiashen*, Que divines."

The question follows. It begins with the name "Lady Hao," though a break in the plastron has obliterated the upper part of the graph for "lady" (it can be seen complete in the negative version of the inscription, at the top of the second column from left). The name "Hao" is clearly legible

Fig. 7.3 Rubbing of a turtle plastron. Reign of Wu Ding, c.1200 BC. After Zhang (1962:no. 207).

Fig. 7.4 Huayuanzhuang Dongdi H3, a pit containing divination shells and bones excavated at Anyang in 1991 (shown crated for removal in a mass). The deposit dates from Wu Ding's reign and includes both royal and non-royal divinations. It also mixes inscribed and uninscribed pieces: of 755 complete turtle shells, fewer than 300 are inscribed. (The total count of 1,558 shells and shell fragments includes 574 with writing. Of 25 pieces of bone, 5 have writing.) See preliminary excavation report (*Kaogu* 1993[6]:488–499). Illustration after *Yinxu* (2001:pl. 24).

at the top of the next column; it is a compound formed by combining the graphs for "woman/mother" and "child." Next is the graph "childbearing" followed by the graph "lucky." The question ends here. It reads: "Lady Hao's childbearing lucky?"

Most oracle inscriptions end at this point, with the statement of the question.[4] This one continues, without punctuation or visible break, stating first the king's interpretation of the omen and then what actually happened.

The two graphs at the bottom of the second column say "the king prognosticates." (The graph for "prognosticate" depicts a scapula with a divination crack on it and, below the crack, a mouth; perhaps the logic of the character is "the crack on the bone speaks.") The plastron has replied to the question about Lady Hao's childbearing, and the king gives his interpretation of its answer: "If the child is born on a *ding* day, lucky; if on a *geng* day, vastly auspicious." The king has identified two days of the week (any week) as lucky. Since a crack presumably could not say much more than "auspicious" or "inauspicious," extracting information about particular days required a series of questions, like our game of Twenty Questions.[5] Perhaps the diviner announced the question and cracked the bone separately for each of the ten days of the week. The cracks are not easy to see in the rubbing, since most of them coincide with later breaks in the plastron, but they were numbered, and the numbers are legible near the plastron's lower edge: the numbers one to five on the left side, one to six on the right (the number five looks like Roman numeral X).[6] The inscription thus seems to be giving us only a digest of a divination process that involved a whole series of spoken questions, crackings, and royal interpretations. When a prognostication is recorded, it is almost always the king rather than the diviner who makes it. Perhaps the diviner kept track of a series of questions and responses (the numbering of the cracks would have helped him), and the king pronounced a verdict on the accumulated body of information.[7]

After the king's forecast the inscription concludes by recording what actually happened: "Three weeks and one day later, on the day *jiayin*, the child was born. Not lucky. It was a girl." Since *jiayin* was neither a *ding* day nor a *geng* day, this disappointing news might be said to fulfill the king's prediction. As a rule, when an outcome is recorded, it is consistent with the forecast. This part of the inscription is conventionally referred to as the verification, though we cannot be sure that its only purpose was to confirm the correctness of the forecast.

Whether the king's questions were answered by the bone itself or by spirits who spoke through the bone is not certain (see Keightley 1999:245, 247). It is clear, however, that these interrogations did not take place in writing. Since the graphs of the inscriptions sometimes avoid the cracks in the bone, the divination ritual was over by the time the inscription was carved. In lengthy inscriptions the layout and uniform handwriting often give the impression that the question, the forecast, and the outcome were carved at one time, as one continuous text. Probably only the crack numbers and crack notations (see note 6) were carved at the time of the divination. In the present example, the concluding portion of the inscription could not be written until Lady Hao's child was born, thirty-one days after the divination, and it is possible that none of the inscription was carved until then (if the first part was carved earlier, it was certainly carved by the same hand). After performing the divination on the day *jiashen*, the diviner may well have kept the plastron, along with a separate record of the question and the king's interpretation of the oracle's answer, for thirty-one days or more. Then, when he knew the outcome, he summarized the information he had recorded and sent the summary together with the plastron to a carver who transcribed it onto the bone. Since divinations by Que are carved in several distinct hands, and inquiries by several different diviners are sometimes carved in a single hand, diviners and carvers were different people.

Bones were sometimes revisited at intervals for a series of divinations about a single topic. On the tenth day of every week the fortune of the coming week was divined by asking the question "Week without disaster?" Sometimes the diviner returned to the same bone to ask this question, week after week, for many weeks. (Over the same period he might revisit other bones for divinations on other topics.) When forecasts and outcomes were not recorded, these weekly questions leave a curious record: ". . . On the day *guiwei* divining, week without disaster? On the day *guisi* divining, week without disaster? On the day *guimao* divining, week without disaster? . . ." Perhaps these were less questions than wishes. Nevertheless the oracle sometimes replied that disaster would come, and the inscription confirms that it did: "Five days later, indeed there came from the west a messenger bearing bad news. Zhi Guo reported that the Tufang have attacked our eastern border and seized two settlements. The Gongfang likewise invaded our western border lands."[8] A single bone may in this way narrate two or three weeks of enemy attacks. Whether or not an answer to the "week without disaster" question appears on the bone, the diviner must have been keeping a log that recorded questions, forecasts, and eventual outcomes, noting down the raw data from which a summary for carving might or might not later be made.

The narrative of attacks just quoted comes from a Wu Ding inscription. (The diviner is Que, as in the inquiry about Lady Hao's childbearing; diviner names are an important dating criterion. On another bone a different diviner asks about a campaign to be led jointly by Zhi Guo and Lady Hao, who figures in several inscriptions as an army commander.) Wu Ding divined about a wider range of topics than his successors did, including the childbearing of his consorts, the fortune of the coming week, dreams, weather, warfare (enemy attacks, raising troops, issuing orders to commanders), and much more. In his reign and later, however, the topic divined most often by far was sacrifice, sacrifice to a range of spirits but above all to the spirits of the royal ancestors. Ancestors were referred to by two-character posthumous names. The first character was often a kinship term; the second was always a day name, the day of the week on which the ancestor normally received sacrifice. "Father Jia" was the father or uncle of the king who so addressed him, and he received sacrifice on *jia* days, i.e., the first day of the week. Timing seems to have been vitally important in the rituals of sacrifice. A prominent feature of Anyang inscriptions – not only oracle texts but also the few lengthy bronze inscriptions written at the very end of the period – is carefully and sometimes elaborately specified dates.

What can the oracle inscriptions tell us about the Anyang script and its uses? Who was the audience for them and who was literate in ancient Anyang?

As to the script, specialists are agreed that it is full writing at the moment when we first encounter it; that is, a Shang scribe could probably have written pretty much anything he could say. In three-part inscriptions like the one about Lady Hao's childbearing, the opening is formulaic but questions and outcomes are not; there is nothing formulaic about Zhi Guo's report of enemy attacks. In the nature of the sample, not even the fullest accounts of outcomes range outside the king's consultations with the spirits – there are no poems or tax registers on these bones – but their language is flexible enough to confirm the existence of a writing system capable of doing much more. Estimates of the number of characters in the oracle script vary from 3,000 to 5,000 (the uncertainty arises from the difficulty of deciding whether two characters that differ slightly represent different words or only differences of handwriting). There is a certain amount of orthographic variation, but the signs are constructed and executed with obvious refinement and regularity, and on balance the impression is one of standardization.[9] Handwriting differs from one carver to another, but, in Wu Ding's reign particularly, the carvers are very accomplished.[10] The Wu Ding inscriptions moreover have a system for naming the sixty days of the calendrical cycle and a fully developed system of numeration.[11]

Why were these inscriptions made? Since the question was not recorded until after the divination was performed, the inscription was not a part of the divination process. That divining did not require writing is abundantly clear from the fact that most bones and plastrons found at Anyang, not to mention all divination bones from earlier sites, have scorch marks and cracks but no inscriptions. The spirits who spoke through the cracks did not need to read a question written on the bone, nor presumably did they need afterwards to be told what the king predicted or what actually happened. The bones are normally found in large pit deposits, disposed of in bulk, suggesting that they had been kept above ground for some time (Fig. 7.4). Might we suppose that the diviners kept an archive of cracks and prognostications, precedents to help them interpret cracks? This seems unlikely, since most inscriptions record only the question, and most bones do not even record that; well over half of the plastrons in the deposit shown in Fig. 7.4 are uninscribed.[12] The purpose behind the inscriptions is as much a puzzle as the divination process itself.

Especially in Wu Ding's reign, the inscriptions are often so painstakingly and beautifully executed as to suggest that they were meant for display of some kind.[13] Scholars who have tried to replicate the divination and carving process say that the shell and bone are very difficult to carve. The draftsmanship of the inscription on Lady Hao's plastron (Fig. 7.1) betrays clearly enough a medium in which straight lines are easier to cut than curves, but it shows also a practiced carver who managed to form handsome characters despite all difficulties (compare the various occurrences of the left-hand component of Lady Hao's name, a kneeling woman, which serves also as the left-hand component of the character "lucky"). Other Wu Ding inscriptions were executed more laboriously still. In Fig. 7.3, for instance, while the inquiries at bottom left and right are written as usual, the one at the top consists of much larger characters that imitate the plump and fluid lines of brush-and-ink writing (compare the actual examples of Wu Ding brush writing shown in Figs. 7.2 and 7.15).[14] Moreover the carved characters of the inscriptions were often embellished with inlays of black pigment or vermilion; sometimes the divination cracks themselves were carved deeper and then inlaid. Occasional inscriptions were brush-written in ink or vermilion rather than carved (Fig. 7.2).

If the inscriptions, or some of them, were meant for display, the audience for the display must have been privileged and small. Inscribed objects a foot or so high are not public monuments; the audience they addressed is likely to have been a literate inner circle around the king.[15] In Egypt, where spectacular writing was a vital ingredient of royal display, literacy was a normal part of the education of the highest class, the king included: "elite status was completely identified with literacy."[16] In Mesopotamia, though writing was slow to assume a function in royal art, most rulers and officials are likely to have been literate.[17] Maya scribes sometimes identify themselves as members of the royal family (for example as younger sons of rulers).[18] At Anyang, literacy was probably an essential job qualification for the royal relatives and nobility who served as high officials, and the king no doubt received the same education his relatives did. Since a literate king would probably imagine his deceased ancestors as literate, the royal ancestors could have been the audience, or part of it, for whom the oracle bones were carved and embellished.

In summary, the oracle inscriptions were not a part of the divination process, and they seem to have had less to do with record-keeping than with some sort of display, but the motive and audience for the display remain elusive. Divination bones found at sites other than Anyang, though mostly uninscribed, show that the ability to divine was not confined to the Anyang king.[19] This makes it difficult to suppose that the king's inscriptions served merely to advertise that he was in touch with the spirits. Lady Hao's plastron is the record of a disappointment; why did the king display that? Surely not just to announce his success in prognosticating. Neither for the finely written and embellished oracle inscriptions nor for the more routine ones has any convincing function been suggested.

Bronze inscriptions

Though the inscriptions on Anyang bronzes cannot compare with the oracle texts in length or number, they differ interestingly in content, authorship, and audience. The divinations of which we have a written record were performed and recorded for the king.[20] By contrast bronze ritual vessels were used by all the elite for presenting offerings to their deceased ancestors. The inscriptions on vessels, or at least the ones we can interpret, identify the person who commissioned the vessel or the ancestor who would be offered food or drink in it.[21]

Like the practice of carving inscriptions on divination bones, the practice of casting inscriptions on bronzes seems to have been an innovation of Wu Ding's reign. Typical are the inscriptions on bronzes from Lady Hao's tomb, excavated by Anyang archaeologists in 1976. The tomb contained 200 bronze vessels, most of them inscribed, most with Lady Hao's name only. If we compare the rubbings shown in Fig. 7.5 with Lady Hao's name as written on the plastron (Fig. 7.1, top of the second column from the left), we notice several differences. First, the line quality of the bronze inscriptions is more fluent. The bronze caster reproduced in metal an original that had been

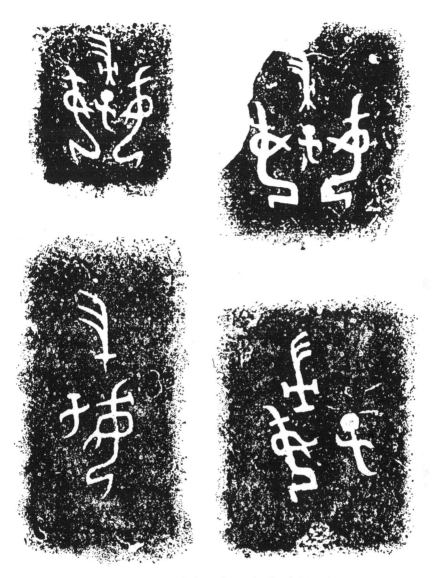

Fig. 7.5 Inscriptions of bronze vessels from the tomb of Lady Hao, Anyang, c.1200 BC. After *Yinxu Fu Hao Mu* (1980:figs. 29.2, 27.8, 35.3, 35.8).

executed in clay, and for the scribal artist working in soft clay, imitating the curving lines of brush-and-ink writing was much easier than it was for the oracle-bone carver. Second, the four versions of the name in Fig. 7.5 differ from each other and from the oracle-bone form. The graph "lady" is written in four slightly different ways; the graph for "woman" has an extra stroke (a hairpin?) at the top that is missing from the bone form; the third and fourth of the bronze versions are mirror-images of each other;[22] and the graphs are not spaced like successive characters of a text but composed into a sort of monogram, an Anyang counterpart of the fancy initials we sometimes put on silver tableware or linen napkins. This is most obvious in the first version, where the scribe has repeated the "woman" element and created something approaching a picture. In the last two versions we assume that the woman and child occur together simply because they are the components of the character *hao*, but in the first we seem to see not an orthographic relationship but a family scene, two women with a child between them. The graph "lady" may not function as part of the picture, but it certainly does function as part of the monogram: nothing in the layout of this inscription tells us how many words we are dealing with.

The designers of these monograms seem to have been playing with the iconic content of the graphs in an almost Egyptian way. An Egyptian artist painting or carving fine hieroglyphs was always conscious of their iconic element, which he might enhance with as much depictive detail as the glyph size allowed (the reeds of a mat, the barbs of a feather) or exploit in subtler and deeper ways (Davies 1987:10–20; Baines 1989). Fundamental to Egyptian writing throughout its history, these artistic options were relinquished early in China. Rapid execution with brush and ink promoted cursive forms, and the iconicity of the script diminished sharply after the Anyang period, the last vestiges disappearing in a major script reform of the third century BC. Though iconic content mattered to the artists who wrote Anyang bronze inscriptions, calligraphers of later times gave their attention to line quality and character structure.[23]

The bronze inscriptions in Fig. 7.6 come from a small tomb contemporary with Lady Hao's. The first two consist of the character "son," here signifying "prince," followed by a graph showing fish in water (modern reading *yu*). This Prince Yu, a son of Wu Ding, is mentioned often in the Wu Ding oracle texts.[24] In oracle texts, however, the character for his name has only two components, the "water" element and a single fish, and the fish is drawn with less internal detail (Fig. 7.7[b]).[25] As in the writing of Lady Hao's name, the scribe devising a fancy monogram for Prince Yu's bronzes has converted a graphic combination, "water" + "fish," into something playfully suggestive of fish in water.

The inscriptions shown in Figs. 7.6(c) and 7.6(d) come from other bronzes found in the same tomb. The first is a graph composed of a circle with two footprints above it. In the oracle script this writes the word "attack" (Fig. 7.7[d], modern *zheng*; in the disaster inscription quoted above, the Tufang "attacked" the eastern border). Here, however, it seems to be a name. In Fig. 7.6(d) the graph for a rank conventionally translated as "marquis" has

Anyang writing and the origin of Chinese writing 203

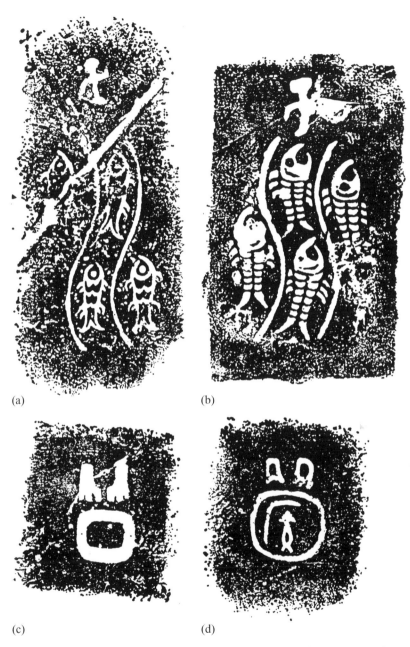

Fig. 7.6 Inscriptions of bronze vessels from Xiaotun M18, a tomb near Lady Hao's, Anyang, c.1200 BC. After *Kaogu xuebao* (1981[4]:496).

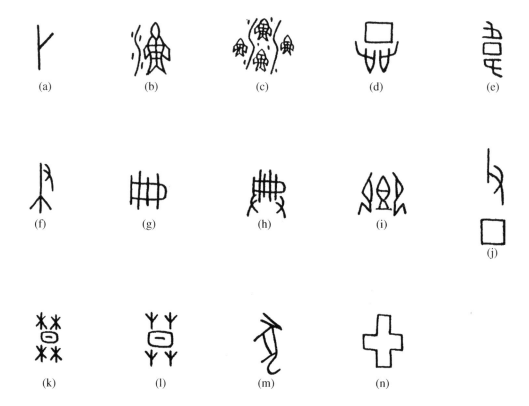

Fig. 7.7 Oracle-bone characters, after Shima (1971): (a) *bu* ("divination"); (b, c) *yu* (proper name; "to fish"); (d) *zheng* (proper name; "to attack, subdue"); (e) *wei* (proper name; "to guard"?); (f) *yu* ("writing brush"); (g) *ce* ("document"); (h) *dian* ("document, record"); (i) *xiang* (name of a ritual feast); (j) *Fu Ding* ("Father Ding"); (k, l) *mu* ("dusk"); (m) *quan* ("dog"); and (n) *ya* (a rank).

been written inside the circle. Presumably we can read the combination as "Marquis of Zheng," but this is not the way the title would be written if it occurred in an oracle inscription; the scribe has again designed a monogram. A bronze axe of unknown provenance shows a scribe playing with the graph *zheng* in another way (Fig. 7.8). Axes were for some reason often made with large circular openings in their blades; the designer of this one reduced the size of the normal opening and added a pair of feet adjacent, punning on shapes to make an inscription.

A different character, modern *wei*, has the form in the oracle script of two feet walking around a circle (Fig. 7.7[e]; carved on bone, a circle becomes a square). In the bronze inscription in Fig. 7.9 the scribe has added two more feet and placed inside the circle a graph composed of two hands holding a

Fig. 7.8 Bronze axe. Probably thirteenth or twelfth century BC. Height 32.7 cm. (Courtesy of the Freer Gallery of Art, Smithsonian Institution, Washington, DC; accession no. F1946.5.)

Fig. 7.9 Inscription of a bronze vessel, twelfth century BC, in the Musée Cernuschi, Paris. After Luo (1937:12.57.1).

document (Fig. 7.7[h]; the document by itself is Fig. 7.7[g]). In oracle texts the graph *wei* occurs mainly as a name, for instance as the name of one of Wu Ding's diviners, but later meanings include "surround" and "guard," and the structure of the graph hints that some such meaning is the original one, the one the graph was devised to convey. On the analogy of Fig. 7.6(d) we might guess that Fig. 7.9 combines the name Wei with some sort of scribal title, but it seems possible that a play on the idea of guarding the documents is also involved. Whatever the correct interpretation, it is clear that the designer has used characters of the regular script to compose a monogram that, as a whole, does *not* constitute a character of the script.[26]

A few of the bronzes from Lady Hao's tomb are inscribed with one of her posthumous names. The inscription in Fig. 7.10 calls her "Mother Xin," the name by which her sons directed sacrifices to her (on *xin* days, the eighth day of the week).[27] Anyang bronze inscriptions, royal and non-royal alike, often include such dedications naming the ancestor who will be offered food or drink in the vessel.

Figs. 7.11 and 7.12 show ancestor dedications from later in the Anyang period. In Fig. 7.11, the pronged rectangle at the bottom of the inscription may be equivalent to some character of the regular script, but its identity is uncertain. Just above it is the name of an ancestor, Father Gui (*gui* is the last day of the week). The graph at the top of the inscription is probably the name of a ritual feast offered to Father Gui; occurring on many bronzes, it shows two seated figures reaching toward a vessel.[28] Play with iconic content is especially obvious here; comparison with the oracle-script equivalent (Fig. 7.7[i]) shows how much the calligrapher has enhanced the depictive

Anyang writing and the origin of Chinese writing 207

Fig. 7.10 Inscription of a bronze vessel from the tomb of Lady Hao, Anyang, c.1200 BC. After *Yinxu Fu Hao Mu* (1980:fig. 25.2).

quality of the graph. Similarly in the graph "father" he has drawn a very delicate hand that does not quite touch the droplet-shaped element it holds; usually the two components are fused (compare Fig. 7.12 and also the oracle-bone form seen in Fig. 7.7[j]).

These elegant graphs designed for casting in bronze are the closest approaches to pictorial art that Anyang artists ever made. Nothing remotely like the picture of two feasting men in Fig. 7.11 seems to have existed outside the writing system.[29] It follows that one of the needs writing was called upon to serve elsewhere in the ancient world did not exist in China. In Egypt, Mesopotamia, and Mesoamerica, the use of writing for display was intimately bound up with representational art, with the labelling or captioning of pictures and statues, but at Anyang there were no pictures or statues to label. Pictures are in equally short supply in the Erligang culture, the immediate ancestor of the Anyang civilization.[30] In other parts of the world

Fig. 7.11 Inscription of a bronze vessel, eleventh century BC. Avery Brundage Collection, Asian Art Museum of San Francisco (accession no. B60B1046). (Courtesy Asian Art Museum).

nascent writing systems seem to have drawn on preexisting pictorial art for some of their signs, but if this happened in China, we have no evidence of it. It may be that a strong pictorial tradition is not really a prerequisite for the invention of a script.

In Fig. 7.12 a dedication to Father Ding is preceded by a clan sign identifying the family to which Father Ding and his descendant belonged.[31] A few such signs may be unrelated to writing; that is, they may be something more like a family crest than a name. Many more are elegantly designed names constructed from characters of the regular script (Fig. 7.12), and still others may be constructed from characters but so transformed that we do not know how to analyze them (Fig. 7.13). For the one in Fig. 7.12, oracle-script versions of the components are shown in Fig. 7.7(k),(l),(m), and (n). The sun among trees is "dusk," the animal below is "dog," and the cartouche that surrounds them is in some oracle-bone contexts a title or rank. Many bronze emblems include this last element, some of them spectacular works of the designer's art (Fig. 7.13).[32]

In the reigns of the last two Anyang kings we encounter a very few bronzes whose inscriptions go beyond ancestor dedications to include actual narrative text.[33] The example shown in Fig. 7.14 begins at top right with a day date, *yihai*, second day of the second week, and concludes with a

Fig. 7.12 Inscription of a bronze vessel, eleventh century BC. Gugong Bowuyuan, Beijing. After Yu (1957:no. 274).

lengthier date "in the sixth month, in the king's sixth year, on an Yi day."[34] The text framed by these dates involves three persons. The first, whose name immediately follows the day date, is Bi Qi. The second is a person with the title *zuoce* ("maker of documents"; compare the graph *ce* ["document"] at the top of the second column with the oracle-bone equivalent shown in Fig. 7.7[g]). *Zuoce* was evidently a title for high-ranking scribes, perhaps the title of a specific court official. The scribe's name, perhaps to be read "Zhizi," follows his title. The third person, mentioned at the top of the third column, is dead: he is Ancestor Gui, named after the day on which he receives offerings (such as the beer that will be presented in this vessel). The text that connects

Fig. 7.13 Inscription of a bronze vessel, twelfth or eleventh century BC. After *Shanghai Bowuguan Cang Qingtongqi* (1964:no. 13).

the three people tells us how the vessel came to be made: "Bi Qi gave the Zuoce Zhizi [some kind of] jade, whereupon [Zhizi] made Ancestor Gui's ritual vessel."[35]

The maker of the vessel – that is, the person who commissioned it – was the scribe Zhizi.[36] Since inscribed bronzes were costly objects, he was certainly a man of high rank. Bi Qi was his superior or was acting on behalf of his superior the king. In some sort of court ceremony, probably as a reward for distinguished service of some kind, Bi Qi has made an award to Zhizi. The graphs specifying the award include the "jade" determinative, so it was probably something made of jade. This event was so important to Zhizi that he cast a bronze to inform his ancestor of it. The inscription is located inside the vessel and was surely intended for the same recipient as the beer. Similar inscriptions were made in large numbers in the Western Zhou period (late eleventh century to 771 BC). Often much longer than their Shang prototypes, and more varied in content, some describe a court ceremony in which the vessel's maker was honored with gifts and appointed to an office or a fief; occasionally we are told that a court officer with the title *zuoce* read out a written document of appointment, one copy of which was kept by the king, the other given to the maker, who quotes from it in his inscription.[37]

In the draftsmanship of Zhizi's text we notice a rather close approximation to brush writing: compare Figs. 7.2 and 7.15, and also the oracle inscription shown in Fig. 7.3 (where the imitation of brush writing was more painfully achieved). Beneath the characters of the text, and distinct in size and composition, is the same clan sign that in Fig. 7.12 accompanies a dedication to Father Ding. Zhizi and his Ancestor Gui must have been members of the same family as Father Ding and his son. Older and far more common than long texts like Zhizi's, inscriptions that consisted only of a clan sign and an ancestor dedication probably supplied the nucleus around which long inscriptions grew.

Like the oracle texts, the bronze inscriptions are display texts, but it seems rather clearer in the case of the bronzes that the display is addressed to the dead. Inscriptions on bronzes buried with the person to whom they were dedicated can only have been read by the deceased; once the funeral was over, no one but Lady Hao saw the inscription her sons wrote for her (Fig. 7.10). Other bronzes were used above ground in sacrifices unconnected with funerals, presumably, and if those vessels had inscriptions, a living audience could have read them. But Anyang bronze inscriptions do not acknowledge such an audience; they do not even confirm the existence of vessels made for use above ground. Only in the second century of the Zhou period do we begin to encounter inscriptions which conclude "May sons and grandsons forever treasure and use this vessel," implying that long use by the living is the purpose for which the vessel was cast and that posterity is a part of the acknowledged audience for the maker's report of his achievements.[38]

An illiterate elite would not be likely to make a practice of communicating with its deceased in writing, nor would it be likely to employ scribal artists to make those communications beautiful. Zhizi, of course, was literate by profession (perhaps we are seeing his own handwriting in Fig. 7.14), but literacy seems a reasonable presumption also for the other aristocrats who commissioned lengthy inscriptions. Admittedly such inscriptions appear only at the very end of the Anyang period, and only in small numbers; the far more numerous bronzes inscribed only with an emblem and an ancestor dedication do not tell us much about their owners.[39] Yet the fact remains that beautiful writing, something never achieved without effort, and in the case of the oracle inscriptions achieved only with painful effort, is conspicuously present from the moment of our first encounter with the Chinese script. Heavy investment in fine writing implies an audience able to appreciate it

Fig. 7.14 Inscription of the *Zuoce Zhizi you*. Eleventh century BC. Gugong Bowuyuan, Beijing. After Yu (1957:no. 273).

and willing to supply the resources for it. In a society where literacy was confined to menial scribes serving illiterate masters, writing would never have become a vehicle of elite display. If the aristocrats of Lady Hao's time put only their monograms on their bronzes, rather than lengthy inscriptions like Zhizi's, this might mean not that they were illiterate but only that bronze inscriptions had not yet been conceived as serving any purpose beyond dedicating a vessel to the service of a particular ancestor or family. Several dozen of the emblems on bronzes correspond to diviner names, and diviners certainly were literate. Late Anyang inscriptions like Zhizi's might reflect not an increase in literacy but new ideas about communicating honors to the ancestors (repeatedly, each time the vessel was used: the ancestors must be regularly fed *and* reminded). For all we know, the gift that prompted Zhizi's inscription might itself be a late Anyang innovation in court ceremony.

Other inscriptions

Along with oracle texts and bronze inscriptions, the Anyang site has yielded a scattering of other bits of writing. The examples described below are grouped by writing surface.

Bone and shell

A few inscriptions carved on bone or shell are not divinations. A bone from the foreleg of a tiger bears the following text, carved and then inlaid with tiny pieces of turquoise: "On the day *xinyou* the king hunted on the slopes of Mount Ji and caught a large and ferocious tiger. It was the tenth month in the king's third year, on a Xie day."[40] The bone is evidently a trophy of a royal exploit, and the king's proud inscription uses the same dating formula as the scribe Zhizi's boast of honors received, both men being concerned to fix the event in time: fully eleven of the twenty characters in the king's inscription are specifying the date. Zhizi's text was meant to accompany offerings to one of his forebears, indeed the main reason for casting the bronze may have been to deliver the message to Ancestor Gui. The audience for whom the king's inscription was intended is not clear.

Three more inscriptions occasioned by royal hunts are known, two on deer skulls and one on the rib of a rhinoceros. Although the rib bears a date in the king's sixth year, its inscription seems not to have been written for the king, for the statement that he caught a rhinoceros is followed by the announcement of a gift made to a person named Zai Feng. Since the king would be unlikely to mention in an inscription of his own a gift made to a subordinate, the person who had the bone inscribed was probably Zai Feng. By analogy with bronze inscriptions recording royal gifts, we might guess that Zai Feng distinguished himself in the hunt and was honored by the king. Perhaps he assisted in the capture of the rhinoceros and was awarded part of the slain animal, including the rib he inscribed.

A few inscribed fragments of human skull have been found at Anyang. On one of them the inscription speaks of sacrificing the chief of the Renfang to a royal ancestor. Like the tiger's foreleg, perhaps, the skull is a sort of royal hunting trophy, but with the important difference that the victim is explicitly dedicated to an ancestor.

One of the lengthiest of all Anyang texts, only partly preserved, is carved on a scapula.[41] About fifty characters survive but the inscription may originally have been twice that length. It mentions a military expedition, kinds and amounts of booty, and the capture of two enemy chiefs followed by their sacrifice to three royal ancestors. Nothing in the surviving part of the inscription suggests that this is a divination text, though it might just be a lengthy report of an event that had been forecast. Whatever its exact nature, however, it is unlikely to be the primary record of the events it mentions. Scribes probably accompanied the king on his campaigns and kept detailed records of the plunder secured and the numbers of the slain. The text carved on the bone might have taken from those records just the information needed for a particular celebratory purpose.

Oracle bones and shells sometimes bear short notations that record not divinations but deliveries.[42] On scapulas a typical one reads: "On the day *guihai*, X requisitioned from Y ten scapula pairs. Recorded by Z." The name Z is that of a Wu Ding diviner. Turtle shells, which may have come from farther away, bear notations of the form "X sent in [a certain number of] plastrons." The numbers are large – one or several hundred, even 1,000. Oracle-bone scholars have sometimes spoken of these shipments as "tribute" sent by distant statelets to an Anyang overlord, but it seems more probable that some form of trade or exchange is in question (if the shells came from the Yangzi region, as seems possible, the supposed Anyang overlordship is very unlikely). Notations occasionally also record some sort of preparation or consecration of the plastrons, often performed by a royal consort: "Wo brought in 1,000; Lady Jing ritually prepared 30. Recorded by Que." (Que is the diviner who enquired about Lady Hao's pregnancy in Fig. 7.1.) Notations of both kinds date chiefly from Wu Ding's reign. They have the appearance of purely administrative records kept by a divining establishment that obviously was consuming vast quantities of bone and shell.

Jade and stone

A number of jade and stone objects bear short inscriptions, sometimes incised, sometimes written with brush and ink. A jade halberd blade (*ge*) from Lady Hao's tomb bears an incised inscription of six characters worded

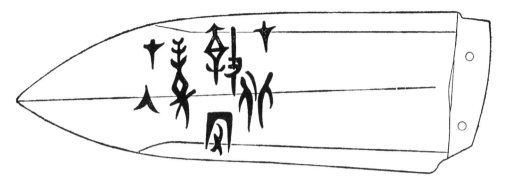

Fig. 7.15 Jade *ge* blade with brush-written inscription from Xiaotun M18, a tomb near Lady Hao's, Anyang, *c.* 1200 BC. Length 20.5 cm. After *Kaogu xuebao* (1981[4]:504).

like the provenance notation on a divination shell: "Lufang X sent in five *ge*." Lufang is identified by the suffix *fang* as a polity distinct from Shang; X may be the name of a person connected with it. Lady Hao seems to have been a collector of jades – her tomb contained over 700, including 39 *ge* blades of assorted shapes and sizes – and it is conceivable that this inscription had the prosaic function of noting the provenance of a particularly handsome specimen. Or perhaps Lufang X had the inscription carved to ensure that Lady Hao would not forget his gift.[43]

The inscription on the blade shown in Fig. 7.15, which comes from the same tomb as the bronze inscriptions of Fig. 7.6, is brush-written in vermilion.[44] The first part is obliterated and what survives is difficult to interpret, but if vermilion was not an everyday ink, we might at least guess that this inscription was less prosaic in purpose than Lady Hao's.[45] Whatever its content, it illustrates nicely the line quality of brush writing. The Chinese writing brush is held vertically, as shown in an oracle-bone graph that depicts it (Fig. 7.7[f]). The line it makes widens and narrows as the brush is pressed more or less firmly against the writing surface; individual strokes often begin with a sharp point where the tip of the brush was laid against the surface, and end similarly where the brush was lifted from the surface.

Our sample of Anyang writing thus includes three rather distinct script styles. Brush writing, which bone (Fig. 7.3) and bronze (Fig. 7.14) inscriptions sometimes imitate, was surely the regular script of the Anyang period. The oracle-bone script adapts the regular script for easier engraving on an intractable material (compare "Father Ding" in Figs. 7.12 and 7.7[j]).[46] The bronze inscriptions, cast from originals written in clay, required no such adjustment. The earliest ones have a wiry line, less variable in width than the line drawn by the brush but no less smoothly curved (Figs. 7.5, 7.10), and later examples often show the same debt to the soft clay medium (Fig. 7.11). But the long bronze inscriptions that appeared toward the end of the Anyang period tended to borrow mannerisms from brush writing or even to imitate it exactly. Zhizi's inscription (Fig. 7.14) probably reproduces his brush-written draft quite closely: by comparison with the barely modulated lines of Fig. 7.10 the characters are more fluid and less tense, and line width sometimes varies ostentatiously (for example in the character at top right).[47] Even in Fig. 7.5 the line quality cannot be entirely independent of brush writing. Drawing curved lines in clay – lines that, in order to produce the neat and deep characters we see on bronzes, had to be excavated rather than just plowed – was not effortless and certainly not quick. The signs of proto-cuneiform, which show Mesopotamian writing at its most iconic, were also written on clay, and a glance at them will persuade us at once that the neatness and fluidity of the characters on bronzes were not automatic consequences of writing in clay but required effort comparable to that which put decoration on a vessel's exterior. Cuneiform, the less iconic script that succeeded proto-cuneiform, is even less like the bronze inscriptions. Written by dragging or impressing a stylus, these Near Eastern scripts give us a good idea of the sort of handwriting that is easy and natural in the medium of soft clay.[48] The extent to which the inscription in Fig. 7.14 differs in appearance from cuneiform is perhaps a rough measure of its debt to brush writing.

Pottery

A few bits of writing, never more than half a dozen characters, have been found brush-written or incised on Anyang pottery.[49] The graph done in black ink on the potsherd illustrated in Fig. 7.16 shows very clearly the modulated line quality natural to writing with a soft brush. It was probably written on the sherd rather than on the unbroken pot (on the pot it would have been upside down).[50] The sherd shown in Fig. 7.17 is inscribed in vermilion.

Wood or bamboo slips

One feature conspicuously shared by the whole of the epigraphic corpus just surveyed is the durability of the writing surface. We have no example of what must have been the everyday writing surface at Anyang, the *ce* of wood or bamboo slips. Nevertheless there is no reason to doubt that the oracle-bone character for *ce* (Fig. 7.7[g]) depicts the object that later went under that

Anyang writing and the origin of Chinese writing 217

Fig. 7.16 Potsherd from Anyang with inscription brush-written in ink. After Li Ji (1956:pl. 22).

name, a row of slender strips of wood or bamboo tied together with string, forming a sort of mat that could be rolled up into a scroll. Actual examples survive abundantly from the fifth century BC onward; the characters are written on the slips with brush and ink in vertical columns (Fig. 7.18).[51]

Given the complete disappearance of other wood and bamboo objects at Anyang – the timbers of wooden tomb chambers have left no trace beyond impressions in the soil – it is no surprise that *ce* have not survived burial conditions there. Unfortunately, the loss inevitably affects our understanding of the writing that survives. The greater the loss, the less representative our sample.

The bias of the sample

The materials that have preserved Anyang writing for us are bone, bronze, jade, and pottery. Whatever writing was done on perishable materials has perished. Is the loss likely to be great or small? The inscriptions that we have are mostly connected with divination or with offerings to ancestors.

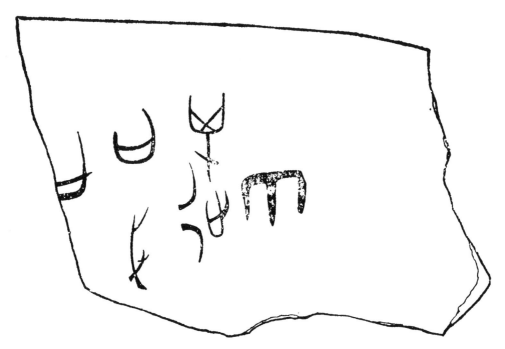

Fig. 7.17 Potsherd from Anyang with inscription brush-written in vermilion. Length of top edge about 15 cm. After *Kaogu* (1989[10]:900).

Is it possible that writing was limited to the religious purposes of a narrow court circle? Or were religious purposes the only ones that called for durable media? If writing was confined mainly to bone and bronze, with only occasional use of bamboo slips for incidental purposes (for example, for drafting bone or bronze inscriptions), then our epigraphic sample is representative – representative, in particular, of the functions Anyang writing served. On the other hand, if the bulk of Anyang writing was on bamboo slips, then their loss has left us with a badly skewed sample, as though our own civilization were struck by some paper-destroying plague that left no writing behind except the Latin inscriptions on buildings.

Many separate lines of argument converge on the conclusion that the losses are substantial. The existence of three script styles, for instance, is suggestive. Oracle-bone, bronze, and brush-and-ink scripts are not mechanical changes of hand as the scribe moved from one medium to another, they are carefully cultivated styles of writing. No matter how poorly the brush script may be represented in our sample, the fact that bone and bronze inscriptions sometimes imitate it argues that it had a kind of primacy. Why would display inscriptions on important objects imitate the ductus of an everyday script written on a material of no intrinsic importance or value? If

Anyang writing and the origin of Chinese writing 219

Fig. 7.18 Bamboo *ce* from Mawangdui tomb no. 1, Changsha, Hunan province, *c.* 168 BC. The document is an inventory of the contents of the tomb in which it was found. After *Changsha Mawangdui Yihao Han Mu* (1973, II:pl. 270).

brush writing was a more frequent sight than bone or bronze inscriptions, and if it was the medium in which the literate learned to read and write, familiarity alone could have made it the standard form of the script. But perhaps something beyond familiarity was involved: perhaps the scribe's skillful handling of the brush had established an aesthetic of brush writing. As anyone who has tried to control a Chinese writing brush knows, long training and practice lie behind the inscriptions seen in Figs. 7.2 and 7.15. The scribes who wrote those texts had practiced hands, and their investment of effort argues that brush writing was an important skill. If display inscriptions in bone and bronze imitate qualities that are specific to brush writing, sometimes with obvious effort (Fig. 7.3), then I think we must infer that fine writing in the medium of brush and ink was recognized and that its qualities were consciously valued.

Another line of argument asks what functions we might reasonably expect writing to have served at Anyang. Are there types of document that we do not have, but that we can be confident must have existed? To the extent that we see them as probable or inevitable, functions absent from our sample are arguments for the loss of whole categories of document. The functions surveyed in the next section might all be invoked here, with varying degrees of confidence, but in one category, at least, our confidence can approach certainty: one very substantial body of texts whose existence at Anyang we cannot doubt has left no trace in the archaeological record. Scribes who used a writing system that employed 3,000 or more characters had to keep lists of those characters. In Mesopotamia, lists of words occur at the very first appearance of writing; in the earliest finds of tablets they are the only texts besides bookkeeping records.[52] They constitute a substantial fraction of the written corpus throughout the history of the cuneiform script, and they are found all over the Near East, at almost every site that has yielded tablets of any kind. In the oldest lists the signs are grouped by meaning, and this remained a standard list type in later periods. The semantic groups include trees and wooden objects (all qualified by the sign for "wood"); metal objects; clays and pottery; animals; and so on. This is, of course, how Xu Shen's dictionary of Chinese, compiled in the first century AD, was organized: it sorts characters into 540 groups, each distinguished by a semantic determinative (such as the sign for "wood").[53]

Mesopotamian lexical lists would not survive in such abundance – 10 percent of the archaic corpus at Uruk (Englund 1998:82, 86–87) – if they were only reference works. They were instruments of pedagogy as well, and they reach us in the form of student copies. Transmitting a writing system to the next generation is not a casual undertaking, and in Mesopotamia clay tablets have preserved for us every stage of the training, starting with clay blanks shaped by pupils learning how to make a tablet.[54] Surviving exercise tablets show the beginner learning to use the stylus by practicing first a single cuneiform wedge over and over, then combinations of two or three wedges, then the correct formation of whole signs. Then the pupil wrote out lists of names, lists of words grouped by meaning, and literary compositions. These texts might be copied, written out from memory, or taken from a teacher's dictation. For beginners the teacher wrote out a line or two at the top of a small tablet and the student reproduced it below. Larger tablets sometimes have a left-hand column containing a model written by the teacher and a much-erased and reused right column in which the student practiced copying it. Apart from these left-column model texts, surviving literary texts are, to judge by the errors they contain, without exception the work of students: Sumerian literature has come down to us in the form of schoolboy exercises.

Lacking the smallest archaeological clue to how Wu Ding's diviners acquired their literacy, and having long forgotten our own kindergarten days, we depend on comparative evidence to remind us that literacy is the result of schooling. The evidence from Mesopotamia and Egypt suggests that scribal training could take place in several settings: at the palace, for the children of kings and favored nobles; in large units of administration (palace, temple), which needed a steady supply of clerks and overseers to replenish the ranks of their own bureaucracies; and in private homes, where a scribe might prepare his own children for the family trade or might take apprentices from other families wishing to give their sons entrée into the life of a scribe. Even a low-level scribe had an enviable life (so the school texts assure us), and a man who combined literacy with other talents might rise to high position. The word "scribe" does not describe one social class or one employment; in Mesopotamia the title was claimed by a wide range of people, from petty bookkeepers to high officials, city governors, even rulers (Nissen *et al.* 1993:106–109). By the same token, scribal training taught not just literacy but the other skills required for a variety of scribal employments – arithmetic, bookkeeping, standard legal and administrative forms, and more.[55]

The literature copied by Mesopotamian schoolboys includes myths, hymns to gods and kings, dialogues, and many other genres, but the most entertaining texts are probably those that speak directly to the schoolboy's life. The best-known of these was composed around 2000 BC:

Son of the tablet house, where have you been going since early childhood?
I have been going to the tablet house.
What did you do in the tablet house?
I read my tablet aloud, I ate my lunch,
I made a tablet, and finished my writing exercise.
After I was let out of school, I would go home and my father was sitting there.
I recited my daily exercises for him,
Read my tablet aloud; my father was pleased.

Further on:

I went in and sat down, and my teacher read my tablet. He said "There's something missing!"
And he caned me.
One of the people in charge said "Why did you open your mouth without my permission?"
And he caned me.
The one in charge of rules said "Why did you get up without my permission?"
And he caned me.
The gatekeeper said "Why are you going out without my permission?"
And he caned me.
The keeper of the beer jug said "Why did you get some without my permission?"
And he caned me.
The Sumerian teacher said "Why did you speak Akkadian?"
And he caned me.
My teacher said "Your handwriting is no good!"
And he caned me.[56]

Or as an Egyptian school text puts it: "A boy's ears are on his back." Can we doubt that such scenes were replayed many times at Anyang? Even though the normal practice of the Mesopotamian school was to dissolve exercise tablets in water and reuse the clay (Tinney 1998:49), a practice which argues that the exercise tablets found by archaeologists are only odds and ends that survived by accident, scribal training in Mesopotamia has left us a huge mass of writing. The Anyang writing system could not have functioned without lexical lists and school exercises, yet we have not the slightest trace of either.[57] And if those texts have vanished entirely, we must reckon with the possibility of other losses equally different in character from the mainly ritual and divinatory texts that did survive.

Functions of writing at Anyang

If we must assume that significant amounts of Anyang writing have been lost, and that writing on durable surfaces does not adequately represent writing on perishable surfaces, what might the lost texts have been? What documents can we reasonably suppose to have been written at Anyang? Let us try to form an idea of the range of needs Anyang writing might have served before attempting to identify the one most likely to have motivated the invention of the writing system.

In the early Mesopotamian epigraphic corpus, the overwhelming majority of texts are records bearing on the control of production and distribution in agriculture, animal husbandry, and crafts. What emerges from them is a rather frightening picture of administrative control; we must hope that the rise of civilization was not like this everywhere. Yet even if not at Mesopotamian levels of intensity, the administration documented in Mesopotamia is likely to have existed at Anyang. The Anyang court too had to manage its agricultural base, and it needed scribes to keep muster rolls for troops, organize conscript labor, and operate the bronze foundries and other large craft enterprises.[58] To these might be added, at least as possibilities, land survey, contracts, trade, and other commercial applications, many of which would require systems of measure. It is frustrating indeed that we can only compile dry lists of such administrative needs. In Mesopotamia the actual documents survive, and they make compelling reading.[59]

Scribes at the Anyang court probably kept non-administrative records as well. Diviners wrote the divination log from which the bone inscriptions were digested, and they needed other documents that were seldom or never carved on bone, such as genealogies of the ancestors who received sacrifice and schedules of sacrifices. Scribes might also have kept a running record of the king's military campaigns, hunts, and other activities. Perhaps the elaborate dates that appear in a few bronze inscriptions toward the end of the Anyang period draw on such a record. The dates not only specify the king's reign year but also mention some notable event: "It was when the king subdued the Renfang, it was the king's fifteenth year, on a Yong day"; "In the eleventh month, in the king's twentieth year, on a Xie day, when a pig was sacrificed to Wu Yi's consort Bi Wu."[60] Here the Renfang campaign and the sacrifice to Bi Wu (which must have been a ritual of some importance) help to fix the year or day. In both Mesopotamia and Egypt, year dates of the same kind were used from a very early time, and, in both places, lists of the year names were kept, constituting a brief chronicle: "The year when Sargon went to Simurrum ... The year when Naram-Sin conquered X and Abullat, and felled cedars in Mt Lebanon" (Postgate 1992:40). The events used to identify years were often religious: "The year in which Ishme-Dagan installed the copper statue of Ninurta for the Eshumesha on its high dais" (Postgate 1992:118). In Egypt too, "many years were named for rituals, probably because rituals were predictable: they both gave shape to the record and could be anticipated and perhaps proclaimed as a year's name even at its beginning."[61] Perhaps the Anyang court kept a similar record of year names.

Letters appear in the Mesopotamian archaeological record toward the end of the third millennium – they are among the earliest texts to write connected discourse – and while the first examples are mostly official communications that look like a simple extension of existing administrative practice, within a few centuries correspondence of all kinds is abundant, from private letters to formal diplomatic exchanges between rulers.[62] Might the Anyang court have corresponded with other cities and rulers? Until recently it was assumed that the Anyang king had nobody to correspond with; traditional historiography maintained that the Anyang dynasty ruled the only civilized state of its day, and this made it easy to interpret the lack of writing from other places as evidence that writing, like civilization, was an Anyang monopoly. But archaeology in the last few decades has so thoroughly disproved the notion of an Anyang monopoly of civilization that we would be well advised to think more cautiously about its apparent monopoly of writing. Major city sites have been discovered in Sichuan province, and strong evidence for bronze-using civilization has been found in the middle Yangzi region as well.[63] To assume that other cities were illiterate merely because no texts have been found would be very unsafe.[64] At Anyang we have lost all the inscriptions that were not carved on divination bones or cast on bronze ritual vessels. What inscriptions could we hope for from the city at Sanxingdui in Sichuan, which has not yielded bones used for divination and which, though it cast bronze on a lavish scale, did not make ritual vessels? The evidence from archaeology increasingly suggests that we should visualize north and central China in the Anyang period as a mosaic of small states; it would not be strange if the rulers of those states exchanged written messages. The disaster inscription quoted earlier stated that Zhi Guo reported to Wu Ding an invasion by the Gongfang and the seizure of two settlements by the Tufang. A writing system capable of recording his report on the bone was capable also of making the original report.

Cities might also have been linked by the correspondence of merchants, a category heavily represented in the Near Eastern corpus.[65] Certainly the city of Anyang belonged to an extensive trade network. It can only be chance that we have merely a few brief records of a traffic in divination bones and luxury goods – notations like "X sent in 250 shells" and "X sent in five *ge*." If the receipt of five jade blades warranted a notation on Lady Hao's *ge*, what masses of records must we imagine for the trade in copper, tin, and lead? The metals trade was geographically extended, reaching to mines 500 kilometers and more to the south and southwest, and its volume was enormous, far beyond anything known elsewhere in the ancient world. If a note was made of the requisitioning of ten scapulas, what records must have existed for the quantities of charcoal requisitioned by the bronze foundries? When we see the complex accounting that in Mesopotamia tracked the production of a simple commodity like beer (which was produced at Anyang too), it is difficult to imagine the Anyang bronze industry functioning without an army of literate clerks. Nor can we take it for granted that all trade and industry were in the hands of the court. In the Near East, private trading enterprises, contracts, and correspondence are well attested. The bias of our sample of Anyang writing focuses our attention on the court, but we should hesitate to conclude that no one outside the court could read and write.

Scholars who believe that Anyang writing was a monopoly of the court, or even of the court's divining establishment, might argue that the varied uses of writing surveyed above belong only to the much later periods from which actual examples survive. Restricted use at Anyang is perfectly plausible, it has been argued, because in both Mesopotamia and Egypt, the earliest writing is confined to a very limited range of uses – in Mesopotamia, administrative record-keeping, in Egypt, administration and royal display. What such comparisons overlook is that in both places restricted use belongs to a time when the writing systems were very far from writing connected discourse: they were mnemonic systems, not the full writing we see in the Wu Ding oracle texts. The linguistic capacity evinced in the oracle texts is something that in Mesopotamia and Egypt postdates the first writing by at least half a millennium. Because Anyang writing is the earliest we know, we have slipped into the habit of thinking of it as early, but it is in no way undeveloped.[66]

In Mesopotamia and Egypt writing originated in contexts in which a lexicon unequipped to transcribe speech was a perfectly functional technology for narrower uses, such as recording specific bits of information for bookkeeping purposes.[67] The gradual expansion of the technology to record more linguistic detail went hand in hand with its acquisition of new functions: adding a few verb endings to make a balance sheet a bit clearer enabled someone to imagine that adding a little more linguistic detail would make it possible to record still more information. When this had gone far enough, writing could leap from the accountant's ledger to radically different uses. The expansion from bookkeeping to letter-writing took centuries, but by the time it was complete, and full writing was available, writing was employed for a very wide range of purposes. Without the pressure of new needs, or the lure of new possibilities, full writing would never have come into being.[68]

Comparison with these well-charted developments in the Near East argues that the writing system we encounter in the Wu Ding oracle texts is the end product of a gradual spread to a broad range of applications. Surely Anyang scribes did not create a lexicon of 3,000 characters just so that they might occasionally supplement a divination record with a note of what actually happened. The idea that writing in China was confined to the ritual context in which we first encounter it, though firmly embedded in the literature, has no basis.[69] Since the writing system we encounter at Wu Ding's court is full writing, with capabilities that in Mesopotamia and Egypt did not develop until half a millennium after the invention of writing, the comparative evidence from the Near East does not give us any reason to expect a restricted range of use; quite the contrary. The ability to write connected discourse is attested for us only by a few oracle texts with lengthy verifications, but it must have developed under the pressure of other needs.

Origins

The most natural explanation for the abrupt appearance of full writing in Wu Ding's reign is an abrupt decision to inscribe durable surfaces. Perhaps diviners had been keeping logs for generations before Wu Ding for some reason commanded that digests of the log entries be carved on some of the bones; perhaps writing suddenly appears on our radar screens because of a royal whim. We might choose a word less frivolous than "whim" if we understood better the purpose behind Wu Ding's inscriptions. Yet almost any motive might seem disproportionately small when for us it has the momentous effect of lifting the curtain on a finished writing system.

Once we decide that Wu Ding's writing is not the first, we face the awkward reality that we do not know when, where, or why the Chinese script was invented. In particular, having no idea how many decades or centuries of development lie behind the Wu Ding script, we cannot assume that the prehistory of the script unfolded at the Anyang site. Do earlier inscriptions survive undiscovered at some other site? Or have they all perished? For whatever reason, we do not have pre-Anyang inscriptions, and, in their absence, attempts to explain the origin of the Chinese writing system have taken three main forms.[70]

Stimulus diffusion

A first line of argument proposes that Chinese writing depended somehow on ideas from Mesopotamia. Fifty years ago, at a time when Western archaeologists believed that significant elements of the Anyang culture originated in the Near East, philologists like I. J. Gelb, convinced that writing is an invention too difficult to have been made twice, explained its sudden advent in China as the result of stimulus diffusion from Mesopotamia (Gelb 1963:214, 219). By 1960, however, Chinese archaeologists had discovered the

Erligang culture, and this supplied local antecedents for so many features of the Anyang civilization that, for most scholars, outside influence ceased to be an explanatory option. Civilization in China was certainly not a transplant from the Near East. Yet neither was China's isolation in antiquity so absolute as was commonly claimed twenty or thirty years ago. F. Bottéro's revival of the possibility of stimulus diffusion (this volume) is a healthy reminder that, knowing nothing of the pre-Wu Ding history of the script, we should keep an open mind about formative stages. On the other hand, no one has yet detected convincing traces of outside influence in Anyang writing; and as Daniels points out, it is not easy to see how the partly syllabic cuneiform script of, say, 1500 BC, whose signs were by then devoid of iconic content, could have provided the starting point for logographic Anyang writing with its distinctly iconic signs.[71] Moreover, the argument from difficulty of invention no longer seems as strong as it once did. Better understanding of Mesoamerican writing has made it easier (and necessary) to believe in multiple independent origins of writing: however difficult the invention may be, it was made at least twice. And perhaps it is not quite so impossibly difficult. The shift in recent decades from a purely philological view of the history of writing to a more functional one has made the intellectual accomplishment seem less improbable, less of a fluke. The Mesopotamianists are, I believe, prepared to imagine that administrative needs of the sort that led to writing in their part of the world could do the same thing elsewhere.[72]

Clan signs

A second hypothesis, the oldest and most persistent, suggests that we have indeed lost the precursors of the Anyang script but that we know what pre-Anyang writing looked like because the so-called clan signs on Anyang bronzes imitate it. The emblems on bronzes, in other words, preserve the archaic script in fossilized form. In this view, the river with four fish in Fig. 7.6(a),(b) is not an artist's elaboration of the regular-script graph (Fig. 7.7[b]), it is the "more realistic pictograph" from which the regular graph, by a process of simplification and abstraction, was derived.[73]

But the invention of writing is not a story of pictures gradually shrinking into signs. Identifying precursors that are a little more like pictures brings us no closer to understanding the invention of the script. Moreover, even if Anyang graphs were preceded by more pictorial forms – and they need not have been[74] – there is no reason to suppose that the emblems on bronzes, because they are more pictorial, *are* those earlier forms. The graph at the top of Fig. 7.11 is a more detailed picture than its oracle-bone equivalent (Fig. 7.7[i]), but I doubt that the scribe who drew it was faithfully reproducing a pre-Anyang character form. He is more likely to have been adding pictorial content to the regular graph because his assignment was to produce a handsome inscription for an emblematic purpose. The artist who designed Fig. 7.6(b) added some extra fish for the same reason. A pictorial form is not ipso facto an archaic form.

Might the emblems on bronzes instead be a clue to the *functional* precursors of writing? Did writing originate in emblems that marked ownership? Is it possible that, at some decisive moment, clan signs that previously were marks of identification with no fixed reading were suddenly reinterpreted as signs standing for the (spoken) names of their owners? It is not easy to see why this would happen. What would the reinterpretation achieve? Why would it matter to anyone? It would matter only if some visionary looking at a clan sign saw and pursued the possibility of graphic representation of language, and the use of signs as identifying marks does nothing to motivate such a leap or make it easy. As Cooper (this volume) observes, marking ownership does not by itself seem to supply a strong motive for the invention of writing. In the Near East, seals served the purpose long before writing arose and continued to do so long after. Nor does the use of clan signs to attach names to objects suggest an institutional context in which we can imagine someone devising and putting into use a *repertory* of signs.[75]

In any case, if clan signs were in any way ancestral to writing – that is, if we suppose that Anyang writing somehow emerged from an earlier practice of marking ownership with clan signs – then it is puzzling that we have no trace of those earlier clan signs. When it was first proposed that Anyang bronze emblems are fossils of more archaic writing, pre-Anyang sites and bronzes were unknown. They are now known in abundance. Hundreds of Erligang bronzes have been unearthed, and, with one or two possible exceptions,[76] none bears anything resembling a clan sign, and none has any other writing.[77] Nor have Erligang sites yielded other artifacts bearing clan signs. If at some pre-Wu Ding stage the use of clan signs was prevalent enough to motivate the invention of a writing system and to supply its first graphs, why are they not more conspicuous in the archaeological record? Unlike other precursors we might imagine for the Anyang script, such as administrative records, clan signs are things which, if they existed, we would expect to find on durable materials.

In the absence of any suitable repertory of signs on pre-Anyang bronzes, a number of authors have proposed the emblems incised on a small group of

Anyang writing and the origin of Chinese writing 229

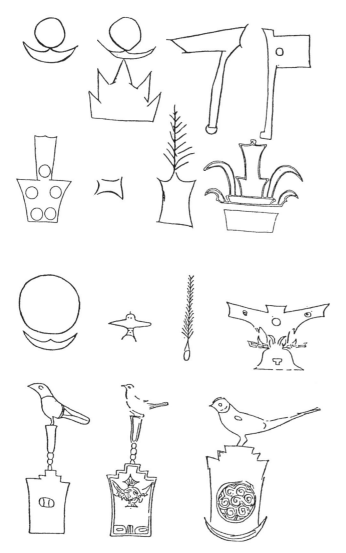

Fig. 7.19 Emblems from Dawenkou pottery (top) and Liangzhu jades (bottom). Neolithic, third millennium BC. After *Wenwu* (1987[12]:75); Li Xueqin (1985:157).

Neolithic jades and pots from coastal areas of eastern China as precursors of the Anyang script.[78] The emblems in question, a total of ten or twelve distinct designs, occur on perhaps two dozen artifacts from the Dawenkou and Liangzhu cultures (Fig. 7.19). Yet these designs bear little resemblance to any Anyang emblem or graph; they certainly do not represent an iconographic repertory from which Anyang graphs were drawn. Nor are the cultures that produced them close to Anyang in time or space. Dawenkou and Liangzhu belong to the third millennium BC; they have no special connection with the late second-millennium Bronze Age civilization of central north China. Attempts to derive Anyang writing from material so remote merely underline the lack of precursors where we ought to find them, in the archaeological culture immediately ancestral to Anyang, the Erligang culture.

Sudden invention of full writing

A third hypothesis is sudden invention, "sudden" in this context meaning swift enough to have left no archaeological trace. Mesopotamian writing emerged from complex non-linguistic bookkeeping and took half a millennium or more to reach the point of recording continuous discourse; but must all writing systems develop gradually? Might we instead suppose that in China a few gifted court officials – diviners perhaps – discovered the principles of phonetic representation, saw the value of a sign system that could represent language, and elaborated a full lexicon immediately? Perhaps we have no writing before Wu Ding because there was none; perhaps writing was invented in his time and had yet to spread beyond the ritual context in which it was invented.[79]

Since the writing system when we first encounter it is capable of writing connected discourse, the possibility we are exploring is sudden invention of *full* writing – invention within a generation or so of the lexicon of several thousand graphs attested by the Wu Ding oracle inscriptions. What might that look like? What would have to happen, and how might it happen? In part these are questions about the discovery of techniques for the graphic representation of language. On a purely technical level, what is involved in turning mute signs, clan emblems for instance, into a lexicon capable of full writing?

To examine this question let us envisage the stage just preceding the invention of Chinese writing as follows. A collection of signs of some kind has been formed – perhaps clan signs, perhaps notations connected with divination, perhaps something else. Probably most of the signs are drawings of the things they stand for, though a few might point to a meaning in some less direct way or be purely arbitrary. A kneeling human figure might signify a woman, a circle with a central stroke might signify the sun, a drawing of a dog would signify a dog. The number of these signs (dozens? hundreds?), and how systematically the collection of signs is organized, will depend on the function they are serving. Let us assume the existence of some such collection, however, and let us ask what would be required to convert it into the writing system we know from the Wu Ding inscriptions.

Fast or slow, the conversion requires the discovery and application of the same ideas. First, signs that originally stood for things must be reinterpreted to stand for words: the drawing of a dog no longer signifies a dog but instead the word "dog," the drawing of a hand signifies not a hand but the word "assist." Second, because the reinterpretation does not yield much more than a collection of depictable nouns and verbs, ways must be found to extend the reach of the sign repertory to a larger portion of the language (for full writing, the entire language). This must somehow be done without making the repertory impossibly unwieldy. A collection of several thousand completely unrelated signs would strain the best memory; both writer and reader would have to work from a code book. In Egypt, Mesopotamia, and China alike, keeping the sign repertory manageable while extending its scope seems to have relied on much the same small set of strategies. Making new signs by modifying or combining existing signs had clear mnemonic value. And rather than make a distinct sign for each word of the language, individual signs were allowed multiple uses (which the reader would discriminate according to context): a sign could be borrowed for its sound, or it could be used to write a word different in sound but related in meaning. The first option is rebus writing, writing with puns: if we were devising a writing system for English, the graph we used for "sun" could be borrowed to write the word "son." (Such phonetic loans bind the writing system to the sounds of a particular language, though in practice they seem not to have been limited to exact homonyms but to be used more freely, as though we were to borrow the graph for "sun" to write "stun.") In the second option, semantic borrowing, the graph for "sun" might be borrowed for its sense rather than its sound to write the semantically related word "day" (here it does not matter whether we are writing English or Chinese).

Compound characters are abundantly represented in the oracle texts, as are characters used multivalently, i.e., semantic and phonetic loans (F. Bottéro, this volume). The compounds were formed by a variety of processes, several of which have analogues in cuneiform.[80] Some combine a semantic element with a graph borrowed for its phonetic value; compounds of this type were to be very prominent in the later history of the script.[81] Others combine two signs, both chosen for their semantic value, neither contributing a phonetic clue to the word signified.[82] The thinking behind compounds is seldom transparent, however, making it difficult even to count them. Do we analyze Fig. 7.7(k) as a compound of the graphs for "tree" and "sun," or is it a pictograph of the sun setting among trees? Whatever the exact fraction, a perusal of the index to Shima's concordance of the oracle texts suggests that compounds constitute the bulk of the lexicon.[83]

In summary, creating the writing system that we know from the Wu Ding oracle texts involved (1) reinterpreting an initial repertory of signs that previously lacked fixed readings, and (2) by the strategies just described, extending the reach of that repertory to cover something close to the full vocabulary of the spoken language. *Sudden* invention would mean doing this more or less punctually. The sudden inventor of *full* writing is someone who says to himself, "If we take these signs to represent not things but words for things; and if we can find ways to extend the sign repertory from depictable things to the whole vocabulary of the language without making it unmanageable; then we can write anything we can say" – and who then does extend the sign repertory to the whole language.

How difficult would this be? And where would the difficulties lie? Older accounts of the origin of writing commonly assume that full writing follows more or less automatically from the discovery of principles: principles are difficult, exploitation is easy and obvious. Yet it is not at all clear that the principles of phonetic representation should be great obstacles. Punning is well known in nonliterate societies; for the inventors of writing, the rebus principle may have lain ready to hand, available for use the moment a need arose. Qiu Xigui argues the point convincingly, mentioning nonliterate societies in which objects (for example a *doumen* leaf) are sent as conventionalized messages, the message (*doumen* ["adorn (yourself)"]) being a pun on the name of the object.[84] In such messages signs are representing sounds, of course, and we can easily imagine other contexts in which phonetic values might become attached to signs more systematically. For a preliterate bookkeeper who manipulated a few pictographs to keep track of sheep and pigs, the association between the pig sign and the word "pig" might well have become habitual (how many different words could he have had for referring to the sign?). If the repertory of pictographs grew large (for example, at a higher level of administration tracking a wider range of commodities), having fixed names for them might have been distinctly useful. In the right setting, therefore, the attachment of sounds to signs and the rebus use of signs might come about easily enough. If there is an intellectual difficulty in the graphic representation of words, surely it lies not in the principles themselves but in imagining what can be accomplished by their systematic application.

The evidence from Mesopotamia and Egypt argues that discovering principles and exploiting them are two very different things. In both places the principles were understood and applied by 2900 BC, centuries before connected discourse was written.[85] Why the delay? The answer is surely that the varied uses for writing that we take for granted were not immediately obvious to the people who first grasped the principles. Full writing was the byproduct of a gradual discovery of new applications. We need not suppose that, because the development to full writing took 500 years in Mesopotamia and Egypt, it also required 500 years in China. The nature of the Chinese language, which spared the inventors the problem of deciding how to represent affixes and inflections, makes the orthography of Chinese a good deal simpler than that of Sumerian or Akkadian or Egyptian, and we might on this account imagine the Chinese inventors having an easier time of things. Yet whatever the importance of such advantages, they do not lower the threshold at the moment of invention: *sudden* invention of a writing system like Wu Ding's presupposes an inventor who, in a society that lacked even the concept of writing, was able to envisage a literate future and proceed directly to it. Never having seen anything closer to writing than, say, clan emblems, this person would have had to imagine the usefulness of a written counterpart to spoken language and then devise the comprehensive repertory of signs necessary to achieve it. The inventor of writing was the author of the first lexical list; if he invented full writing at one stroke, he was the author of a comprehensive lexical list. Moreover, he had not only to compile a lexicon of 3,000 graphs but also to persuade others to learn it. All this is uncomfortably visionary. It has a teleological flavor, requiring the inventor to imagine a world utterly beyond his experience.[86]

An unmotivated leap from signs with no fixed reading to Wu Ding's comprehensive lexicon is surely too improbable. The scenario described above must somehow be broken down into a sequence of smaller, more intelligible steps; we must introduce intermediate stages, stages in which the lexicon was more limited in scope. The moment we try to do this, the necessity for taking function into account becomes obvious: a lexicon unable to transcribe continuous discourse must be serving some other function. In protoliterate Mesopotamia, for example, terse notations could keep detailed records because they were made on standardized bookkeeping forms and dealt with a limited range of activities; information carried by format and context did not need to be expressed linguistically.[87] An analysis that leaves function out of account actually *requires* sudden invention of full writing, because halfway stages have no apparent reason to exist.[88] Yet even in the scenario just described the need to consider function is apparent, for the repertory of signs that provided the starting point in that scenario must itself have served some purpose. Why did someone assemble the initial sign repertory? The Mesopotamian and Egyptian cases argue forcibly that the invention of writing turns not on philological principles but on context and function.[89]

Contexts of invention

Instead of focusing on principles for relating signs to language, therefore, let us turn our attention to functions that in China might have motivated the steps of a staged development. We need to imagine both a *raison d'être* for a limited initial repertory of signs and a context in which that lexicon could grow. In Mesopotamia, beyond question, the initial repertory arose from the recording of administrative transactions; the point of departure for writing was non-linguistic bookkeeping. In the earliest Egyptian material, administrative record-keeping is seen alongside another use, royal display, the two functions being served by two scripts.[90]

For Chinese writing the starting points most often suggested are clan signs and the divination ritual. For reasons discussed already, an origin in clan signs seems unlikely. In particular, such signs do not appear on pre-Anyang bronzes and may not have existed before Wu Ding's time. Might the first steps toward writing have been taken in the realm of divination and sacrifice? Can we think of a need connected with divination that might have inspired a small repertory of signs and provided the narrow context of use in which it was functional?[91]

At Wu Ding's court, sacrifice was the main topic of divination, and sacrifice to the ancestors was incessant. The complex royal ancestral cult we see in his inscriptions is not likely to have been entirely his own creation; perhaps it had been elaborated gradually during his dynasty's rise to power. If we imagine Erligang diviners having to deal with an increasingly complicated round of sacrifices, one that required auspicious days to be determined in advance for more and more ancestors and sacrifices, it is easy to suppose that sooner or later they would want records of some kind, a way to keep track of dates in particular.[92] With only a few dozen signs they could have labelled bones with dates, names, and the oracle's response ("lucky"/"unlucky"), and they could then have used the bones as mnemonics to help them make the right sacrifices at the right times. (Of course, since oracle bones before Wu Ding are not inscribed, the labels we are imagining would have had to be kept separately from the bone, perhaps on a diagram of the bone.) None of this presents any special difficulty. On the other hand it might not have been especially obvious either. Written notations are not the only possible way to store the information the diviners needed, perhaps not even the most convenient. Filing bones relating to different ancestors or different days in different locations might have been just as effective.

More important, even if we were to suppose that Erligang ritual specialists devised a system of labels in the process of elaborating the royal sacrifices, we would still face the problem of understanding how that system grew into the full writing we know from Wu Ding's inscriptions. Diviners needed lists of ancestors and schedules of rituals, but these do not require the ability to write grammatical sentences. And while Wu Ding's inscriptions sometimes contain continuous discourse, it is by no means evident that they had a pressing need for it. No more than half the bones used for divination at Anyang were inscribed with the question, and only a small fraction of those were inscribed also with prognostication and outcome. Lengthy oracle texts are neither so abundant nor so obviously indispensable as to supply a convincing motive for developing a lexicon of several thousand graphs. If a sign system ancestral to Anyang writing did originate in crack notations, its expansion to full writing must still have been driven by needs outside the realm of divination. Given that divination normally functioned without writing, and that the nine Anyang kings' practice of inscribing some of their bones was quite exceptional in the wider history of scapulimancy, it is hard to see the invention of writing as a response to needs arising from divination.

The early histories of other writing systems suggest two other contexts of invention that we should consider, administration and display. In Egypt, though administrative applications were important enough to inspire a cursive script at a very early stage, the arena in which writing was invented may well have been royal display (Baines, this volume). In Mesoamerica too, display was an early and central function of writing (Houston, this volume, ch. 10). Since our sample of Anyang writing consists overwhelmingly of display inscriptions, these are suggestive comparisons. Yet it is difficult to see display as having played a role in the invention of the Chinese script, if only because, as argued above, the script must have been invented well before bones and bronzes were ever inscribed. Wu Ding may have initiated the use of writing for display purposes, but writing itself must precede him.

At least on present evidence, therefore, none of the possible starting points for Chinese writing just reviewed – marking ownership, keeping divination records, royal display – seems to offer a compelling alternative to an origin along Mesopotamian lines in administrative record-keeping.[93] As a default hypothesis this has the special attraction that an administrative setting helps to make the invention comprehensible. A writing system depends for its existence on a script community prepared to learn it, employ it, and transmit it to the next generation, and that script community must be serving functions important enough for someone to be willing to support it. The inventor of writing must be in a position to impose his vision on others; the invention must take place in a setting capable of exploiting it. In Mesopotamia, it is clear, a bureaucracy engaged in complex accounting *preceded* writing.

Writing began as a new accounting device that turned out, in the very long term, to have extraordinary potential.

Applied to China before Wu Ding, the default hypothesis might go something like this. In an already well-organized administrative setting, such as could have been provided by the Erligang state, an initial repertory of signs arose in the service of some kind of record-keeping. The signs need not at first have stood for words, but as the recording system expanded to include more detail or to deal with a wider range of activities, they came to do so, they were used multivalently, and they were joined by new signs. Eventually the growing capacity of the system brought it to the stage of full writing that we know from the Wu Ding inscriptions. What length of time is embraced by the word "eventually" is hard to say. A limited system adequately serving limited functions would not be expanded until some purpose for the expansion was envisaged. When a need was perceived, however, expansion could have been conscious and swift (and accompanied by a corresponding expansion of the scribal establishment that performed the new functions). When Wu Ding ordered the carving of divination inscriptions he gave the writing system a new application, but not one that necessarily motivated any essential step in its development. Display writing on bones and bronzes looks like the adoption for new purposes of a writing system already well developed in the service of other needs.

Comparison with Mesopotamia gives us only a hypothesis, not a proof, but it is a hypothesis that suggests interesting lines of investigation. It should for instance persuade us to widen our search for the precursors of Anyang writing. Instead of looking for signs more pictorial than the ones on the oracle bones, we should be looking for functional precursors of writing, including perhaps systems of numeration like the token systems of the Near East. Those precursors, if they survive, are likely to be found at pre-Anyang sites. With its wealth of inscriptions Anyang has monopolized the thinking of archaeologists no less than palaeographers, yet the evidence of archaeology is clear that state formation and the formation of a spectacular elite artistic tradition happened earlier. Just how writing is related to social and political organization is an unsettled question, but it is hard to imagine that the Erligang state, briefly an empire, functioned without it.

Acknowledgments

Warmest thanks to Stephen Houston for inviting me to the wonderful gathering at Sundance, encouraging me to write something, and reading my drafts. I am very grateful also to John Baines and Jerrold Cooper, who answered a stream of questions and made detailed comments on drafts; their patience with a trespasser in their fields was exemplary. Ken'ichi Takashima graciously answered questions about the oracle texts, and my last revision benefited greatly from Michael Nylan's comments and from a reading of Olivier Venture's dissertation, of which he kindly gave me a copy. For stimulating conversations over the years and indeed for my introduction to the problem of origins, I am indebted to William Boltz. And finally, I owe special thanks to the graduate students in my Spring 2003 seminar, David Liu, Kyle Steinke, and Wang Haicheng, who read drafts and made invaluable suggestions during a memorable semester we spent reading and talking about writing.

Notes

1. Toward the end of the eleventh century BC the Shang dynasty was succeeded by the Zhou, which for the next two and a half centuries (until the end of the Western Zhou period in 771 BC) ruled an empire that stretched across north China. What territory the Anyang kings controlled is uncertain, but it was much smaller. Our sample of Western Zhou writing is no larger than our sample of Anyang writing, but it is rather different, consisting of often lengthy bronze inscriptions found at widely scattered sites. For a survey of Anyang and pre-Anyang archaeology see Bagley (1999).
2. Scorched hollows can be seen in Fig. 7.2, which shows what was, from the turtle's point of view, the inner side of the undershell (the rubbings in Figs. 7.1 and 7.3 are from the outer sides of those plastrons). In Fig. 7.3 one of the divination cracks is clearly legible: just below the main inscription and to the right of the plastron's central axis is a small graph consisting of a square with a cross inside; the horizontal line above this graph and the vertical line to the right of it are the divination crack.
3. Keightley (1999) is a good general account of the oracle inscriptions; Keightley (1997) translates a range of examples. Keightley (1978), now outdated in parts, is a handbook of oracle-bone studies. For a basic introduction to the ancient script see Moore (2000).
4. Many of the statements put to the oracle by the diviner in fact seem not to be questions (see n. 7). I have nevertheless used the word "question" in preference to the more non-committal word "charge" mainly because, in inscriptions like the present one, the underlying impulse is at least partly interrogative and the oracle has responded with information. For several reasons, including the fragmentary state of most bones, good statistics are hard to come by, but certainly at least half of the oracle inscriptions are questions (or rather charges) alone, with no mention of forecast or event (Keightley 1978:41, n. 67).

5. In fact, the back of the plastron is carved with a slightly more detailed version of the king's forecast: "If the child is born on a *ding* day, lucky; if on a *geng* day, vastly auspicious; if on the day *renxu*, not auspicious." The king has somehow elicited information about one specific day, *renxu*, the thirty-ninth day after the day *jiashen* on which the divination was performed.
6. Crack 1 on the left side and crack 2 on the right are also inscribed with the two characters "second report," a notation that dropped out of use after Wu Ding's time. In later reigns the crack notations "auspicious," "greatly auspicious," and "vastly auspicious" (but never "inauspicious") occur instead.
7. No single interpretation of the Anyang divination process quite fits all the inscriptions. In many cases, as here, the king seems genuinely to be seeking information (his prognostication shows that he obtained very specific information); sometimes he seeks information to guide future action (for instance when he enquires about plans for a military campaign, or when he tries to determine an auspicious day for a particular sacrifice). In other cases the question seems both to seek an answer and to express a wish that the king hopes the spirits will grant (Will the coming week be without disaster? Will Lady Hao not die because of her pregnancy?). Recent scholarship has also stressed that many divinations should not be understood as questions at all (Keightley 1997:51–54; Qiu 1989; Takashima 1989). Given this variety, and hence the variety of purposes that we lump together under the single word "divination," it may be wrong to expect a single *raison d'être* to account for all of the oracle inscriptions. (Shifts of purpose are clearly implied by the changes of divination practice that can be observed in the reigns after Wu Ding's.) It might be added that in the realm of divination, even the simplest request for information can have deeper and perhaps unacknowledged motives; prognostication can for instance disguise and thereby facilitate a process of decision-making (Lloyd 2002:22–23). If the question is "Shall we raise 5,000 men and attack the Tufang?" then deciding that the oracle's answer was "Yes" is tantamount to deciding to undertake the expedition. The king and his diviners, discussing the interpretation of the omen, might then be the king and his council, deciding what to do; and the final decision, the prognostication, would naturally be reserved for the king himself. The king must also have reserved for himself the right to ask questions on important subjects (a younger brother who made his own divinations and announced different answers would be a threat).
8. From a scapula illustrated and discussed by Keightley (1999:242). If both of the attacks mentioned are being reported by Zhi Guo, then he might be speaking about borders of his own.
9. F. Bottéro (this volume) takes orthographic variation to mean that the script is at an early stage of development, but I am not sure that the variation she describes is significantly greater than is encountered in much later periods.
10. The oldest inscriptions from Wu Ding's reign, those of the so-called Dui-group diviners, are less neatly written than later ones (Venture 2002a:220),

perhaps because they represent early experiments in putting divination records on bone.

11. As Wang Haicheng reminds me, this abstract numerical system, in which numbers are separate from the things counted, is an important and by no means obvious achievement (see Damerow 1999b; Nissen, Damerow, and Englund 1993:ch. 6). Houston interestingly observes that "Most early scripts use word signs bundled with systems of numeration that probably had a different and far more ancient origin" (Houston 2004).

12. Though the ratio of inscribed to uninscribed Anyang bones is uncertain (excavators sometimes ignore uninscribed bones), it is probably less than one (Keightley 1978:166, n. 5).

13. Keightley (1978:46, n. 90) reserves the term "display inscription" for a particular subset of the bones, but his definition seems arbitrary (that is, I am not certain that a Shang king would have made the same distinction), and I prefer to leave open the possibility that some other subset or indeed all of the oracle inscriptions served display purposes. Perhaps even the bones that were not inscribed should be understood in this way. The inscribed and uninscribed shells in Fig. 7.4 were presumably buried together because they had been kept together, and if they were treated alike before burial, the reason might be that they testified alike to rituals performed, communication achieved.

14. All the inscriptions on this plastron have to do with sacrifice to royal ancestors. Why one of them (translated in Keightley 1997:37) was singled out for special treatment is not obvious, but Hu Houxuan argues that the inscription in question – one of a series – concerns an ancestor of particularly high status to whom Wu Ding offered special sacrifices (Hu 1970, vol. III, "Buci Xia Yi Shuo"). As on Lady Hao's plastron, the diviner in Fig. 7.3 is Que.

15. Including the diviners: though they are never mentioned in the oracle texts in connection with activities other than divination (Venture 2002a:66, n. 156), they might well have been powerful courtiers whose responsibilities, advisory or other, went beyond the posing of questions. That they came from families of high status is suggested by the occurrence of many of their names as emblems on bronze vessels (Bagley 1987:245–247; Keightley 1999:237). Literacy would have extended down to mundane scribes and clerks, of course, but the display was not for them.

16. Baines (1983:580). On the king's literacy, see Baines and Eyre (1983:77–81); Baines (1983:589). Writing in royal display: Baines (1989), and this volume. Palace schools for royal children: Lesko (1999:887); R. Williams (1972:215, 216).

17. On elite literacy in Mesopotamia see Cooper (1992:110); Michalowski (1994); Nissen *et al.* (1993:107); Baines and Eyre (1983:81); Wilcke (2000). Cooper (this volume) dates the first royal inscriptions in Mesopotamia around 2700 BC, four or five centuries after the invention of writing.

18. D. Stuart (1995:ch. 3), Coe and Kerr (1997:36–38, and ch. 3), and Inomata (2001).

19. A very few inscribed bones have been unearthed at places other than Anyang. Of particular interest is a recent find of eight inscribed plastrons of Shang date at Daxinzhuang in Shandong province, a site that had previously yielded a good many uninscribed bones and shells (*Zhongguo wenwu bao*, 18 April 2003, p. 1). By far the largest find outside Anyang is 300 inscribed fragments (along with 17,000 uninscribed), of borderline Shang-Zhou date, unearthed in Zhou territory in Shaanxi province (Qiu 2000:68–69; Venture 2002a:ch. 1 passim, and ch. 5, pp. 208–212).
20. A few inscriptions show that at Wu Ding's court divinations were occasionally performed for persons of high rank other than the king; the pit illustrated in Fig. 7.4 contained examples. Such inscriptions are not so far known from later reigns.
21. Bronze weapons occasionally bear inscriptions like those on vessels. Since extant weapons come from tombs and occasionally have inlays of turquoise that would not have survived hard use, their purpose is likely to have been more ritual or display than practical, and their inscriptions thus may not differ much in purpose from the inscriptions on vessels.
22. The right-facing and left-facing versions of Lady Hao's name occur with about equal frequency in the oracle texts (Shima 1971:139–141). They do not seem to occur together in a single inscription, however, even though oracle texts that state the question in both positive and negative form sometimes use mirror-reversed characters in the two statements.
23. The iconic sources of certain basic character components are remembered to this day, presumably because they have mnemonic value – children are taught "this is a horse, this is a roof" – but no uninstructed observer shown those characters could possibly guess what they are supposed once to have represented. Cooper (this volume) notes a similar but even more complete loss of iconicity in cuneiform, again in the interest of efficient execution. In Egypt, retaining iconicity for artistic purposes required maintaining a separate cursive script for other purposes.
24. See Keightley (1999:270–271). The tomb from which the bronzes come may not be Prince Yu's; the excavation report says that the occupant may have been female (*Kaogu xuebao* 1981[4]:493).
25. In oracle texts the name Yu occurs twice written with four fish (Fig. 7.7[c]), forty times written with one fish (Fig. 7.7[b], Shima 1971:240). The handwriting in Fig. 7.7 is that of a modern oracle-bone scholar, but it represents the oracle script faithfully enough for the purposes of the present discussion.
26. The cross-shaped graph at the top of Fig. 7.9 is the ancestor of a character that in later periods means "spirit medium," but the exact nature or function of persons so described in the oracle texts is unclear. The bronze from which this inscription comes is probably a generation or two later than Wu Ding's time.
27. The inscription includes a third element, upper left, variously interpreted as a title or a ritual.

28. In the oracle-bone version of the graph (Fig. 7.7[i]), the element flanked by the figures resembles the oracle-bone graph for the name of a particular type of ritual vessel.
29. Thote (2003) contrasts Anyang bronze inscriptions with Anyang bronze decoration, noting that the pictorial elements present in the first are entirely absent from the second. In bronze and other media the Anyang civilization produced art in abundance, and pictures play no role in it. Chinese civilization in fact had little in the way of pictorial art for the next half-millennium. Only in the sixth century BC do pictorial designs appear on a few bronze vessels, line drawings that include, among other things, scenes of feasting (Thote 2001:218–221). These are, apart from Anyang bronze inscriptions, the earliest pictures from China known to me.
30. On the Erligang culture see Bagley (1999:165–171). The Erligang type site is located at the modern city of Zhengzhou, 160 kilometers south of Anyang.
31. Though it has become common to apply the term "clan sign" to all boldly written emblems on bronzes, the description is sometimes suspect, if not demonstrably wrong. It is plausible enough in the present case, but other emblems clearly refer to individuals rather than kinship groups ("Prince Yu"), and at least a few are likely to be names of rituals (the upper element in Fig. 7.11). The inscription on a large axe in the Museum of Far Eastern Antiquities, Stockholm, consists of the ancestor dedication "Father Yi" accompanied by an emblem that shows an axe above a headless human figure (Karlgren 1952:pl. 5). Here the emblem must refer not to Father Yi's clan but rather to the offering which the inscribed object provides for him.
32. In Egyptian, certain enclosing signs – one for "fortress," one for "settlement," one for buildings, and the serekh (and later the cartouche) for a king's name – may function as semantic determinatives for the names they enclose (Fischer 1989:64). If this analogy applies to Fig. 7.12, the contents of the cartouche would have a reading while the cartouche itself did not. The contents do in fact look like two characters in sequence, for the dog is upended; this is the orientation of the character "dog" in continuous text (compare Fig. 7.7[m]), not the orientation of a real-world dog with its feet on the ground. The character for "dusk" is written sometimes with trees (Fig. 7.7[k]) but more often with grass (Figs. 7.7[l], 7.12), an alternative with less obvious iconic motivation.
33. About a dozen of these inscriptions (listed and discussed in Bagley [1987:521–536]) include dates in a king's reign year. In the oracle texts, dates of this form occur only in the last two Anyang reigns.
34. The last character in the third column is the number "six." The character for "month" begins the fourth column; the third character in that column is "king," the last is "day." The character before "day" is Yi, the name of a ritual, one of a series of five offered in successive weeks. In dates of this form, naming the ritual may serve to fix the week (Keightley 1999:260–261).

35. For an idea of the evidence and arguments deployed to decipher Shang and Zhou inscriptions, see Moore (2000:27–29, 39–47); Djamouri (1997:215–224). In Fig. 7.14, "six," "month," "day," and "king" are all quite close to modern forms, but most Anyang graphs are not so easily related to later characters.
36. Late Anyang and early Zhou award inscriptions are sufficiently patterned in form as to leave no doubt that in the present example it is Zhizi, not Bi Qi, who is the descendant of Ancestor Gui and the person who commissioned the vessel.
37. See Falkenhausen (1993). Viewed as a display text condensed from a lengthier separate record, the bronze inscription becomes parallel to the oracle inscription condensed from the diviner's log.
38. The evidence of these inscriptions is corroborated archaeologically by hoards of bronzes buried at the end of the Western Zhou period, which often contain bronzes made generations apart. At Anyang no such hoard is known; bronze vessels are seldom found anywhere but in tombs, and the vessels from a tomb seldom show much spread in date. The bronzes from Lady Hao's tomb that bear her name may all have been cast for her funeral by her husband. Venture (2002a, 2002b), who argues that bronze inscriptions were not addressed to the dead, does not sufficiently allow for shifts of purpose between Anyang and late Western Zhou.
39. Most of the inscriptions on Anyang-period bronzes from sites other than Anyang are equally short, meaning that their geographic distribution has no clear implication for the wider use of writing.
40. Xie is one of the five rituals (see n. 34 above). The bone, now in the Royal Ontario Museum, is illustrated in Bagley (1987:525; q.v. for the rhinoceros bone mentioned below, now in the Historical Museum, Beijing). The characters resemble the boldly carved characters at the top of Fig. 7.3, which imitate brush writing.
41. Qiu (2000:62, fig. 6); Chen Mengjia (1956:pl. 16); Venture (2002a:141, n. 24). The other side of this bone bears part of a sixty-day calendar. Many such lists of the day names of the six-week cycle are known (Venture 2002a:165). Puzzlingly, some are incomplete (e.g. Moore 2000:30, fig. 3.7) or more than complete (i.e., they repeat part of the cycle); these may have been carving practice. Others, complete and finely carved, may have been calendars for the diviners' use.
42. See Keightley (1978:11–12, 15–17, 113, 1999:281). The examples I quote are Keightley's.
43. The inscription is reproduced in *Yinxu Fu Hao Mu* (1980:136, fig. 75.3). A chimestone from Lady Hao's tomb has an incised inscription of similar form saying "X sent in stone" (*Yinxu Fu Hao Mu* 1980:198–199, and pl. 170.2). Three chimestones said to be from Anyang published in a 1940 collector's catalogue have two-character (musical?) inscriptions instead (Yu 1940:2.17–2.19). On Lady Hao's jade collection see Bagley (1999:197–202).
44. Color photographs of the blade are reproduced in *Yinxu Yuqi* (1982: pls. 21–22).

45. In a survey of Anyang inscriptions on jade and stone, Chen Zhida interprets this one as having to do with warfare (Chen 1991:67). Also written in vermilion are the inscriptions on six small and slender stone tablets unearthed from a late Anyang burial in 1991 (*Kaogu* 1993[10]:900, fig. 6). Each tablet is inscribed with the name of a different ancestor: Ancestor Geng, Ancestor Jia, Ancestor Bing, Father Xin, Father [illegible], Father Gui. For jade fragments inscribed in vermilion from another group of Anyang tombs see *Wenbo* (1996[5]:3–13).
46. Postgate, Wang, and Wilkinson (1995:477–478) describe the oracle-bone script as "cursive," a description I do not understand.
47. If the scribe used brush and ink to write the inscription on a piece of soft clay and then carefully excavated the ink-covered parts, he could reproduce the ductus of brush writing exactly.
48. The first proto-cuneiform signs were incised with a pointed stylus, but this technique soon gave way to a neater and faster one that used a stylus of triangular section to impress rather than incise the clay. As sign forms were further altered for the sake of still more efficient execution (e.g., by the elimination of curved lines), the last vestiges of iconicity were lost and the cuneiform script came into being. See photographs in Nissen *et al.* (1993): for proto-cuneiform, frontispiece and pp. 37, 45; for fully developed cuneiform, pp. 60, 64, 81, 84. On the relationship between writing tool and script, see pp. 118–119.
49. *Yinxu de Faxian yu Yanjiu* (1994:248–255), Li Ji (1956:ch. 7, and pls. 21–22). The material Li publishes includes both writing and potmarks likely to be unrelated to writing.
50. I am grateful to Wang Haicheng for pointing this out to me. The graph is the name of a sacrifice which the king made annually; it is borrowed to signify "reign year" in dates like that seen in Fig. 7.14 (last line, fifth character).
51. A great many *ce* dating from the last few centuries BC have come from waterlogged tombs in south China, where wet and stable burial conditions sometimes preserve perishable materials extremely well (including occasional manuscripts on silk, a fabric that did exist at Anyang). In the Han period the administration of newly conquered desert regions in the northwest left documents on *ce* that have survived under arid burial conditions in large quantities. On archaeological finds of manuscripts see Tsien (1962:ch. 5) and E. Wilkinson (2000:chs. 18–19). The standard direction of Chinese writing, in vertical columns as opposed to horizontal lines, might have arisen from writing on slips held one by one in the hand and bound into *ce* only after they had been written on.
52. See Englund (1998:ch. 5), Nissen *et al.* (1993:chs. 13–14), and Civil (1995). Such word lists, organized semantically, are known from Egypt as well, but there they were normally written on papyrus, and apart from one Old Kingdom fragment (Brovarski 1987), the earliest surviving examples are of Middle Kingdom date (Parkinson 1999:61–62; R. Williams 1972:219).
53. On Xu Shen's dictionary see the article by William Boltz in Loewe (1993:429–442).

54. Tinney (1998), with excellent illustrations. Civil (1995:2313) mentions tablets with instructions on how to prepare a tablet.
55. On schooling and school texts in Mesopotamia and Egypt, see Civil (1992, 1995), Tinney (1998), Nissen *et al.* (1993:ch. 13), Michalowski (1991:51–53), McDowell (1996, 1999:ch. 4, 2000), Lesko (1999), Baines (1983:580–581), and R. Williams (1972:218).
56. First two lines of first extract here quoted from Nissen *et al.* (1993:109), remainder from Tinney (1998:48). In the end the teacher is invited to the pupil's home, fed, flattered, and won over.
57. A few bone inscriptions have been interpreted as carving practice (e.g. inscriptions with meaningless repetitions of a graph). It should be said explicitly that these do not show a carver learning to write: practice bones are not school exercises.
58. Keightley (1999:282–288) reviews a number of such record-keeping needs.
59. Postgate (1992) and Nissen *et al.* (1993) give a vivid sense both of the range of the Mesopotamian texts and of their wealth of concrete detail.
60. Examples from Bagley (1987:521–536). See also the scribe Zhizi's inscription in Fig. 7.14.
61. Baines (in preparation). See also Baines (1983:576).
62. See Michalowski (1993a) and Postgate (1992:66, 68). For a wide range of early second-millennium examples see Dalley (1984).
63. The spread of bronze-using civilization to regions outside north China took place during the Erligang period, the two or three centuries preceding Wu Ding. The archaeological record of this period shows an expansion and then a retreat of northern culture, perhaps the material trace of a short-lived empire; the retreat was followed by the rise of civilized local powers (see Bagley 1999:165–180). If the administration of an Erligang empire employed writing, it could have bequeathed it to the local courts that arose in its wake. (In Mesopotamia the spread of writing from its point of origin – probably Uruk – to other cities took place within about two centuries of the invention, at first in the form of bookkeeping.) On local cultures in the Yangzi region, see Bagley (1999:171–175, 208–219) and, for more information on Sichuan, Xu (2001). A few bits of undeciphered writing likely to be at least as early as Wu Ding are known on pottery from an early Bronze Age site in Jiangxi well to the south of the Yangzi (Bagley 1999:171).
64. Under the next dynasty, the Zhou, bronzes with lengthy inscriptions are found all over north China; literacy was geographically widespread, however circumscribed in social class, and the inscriptions themselves moreover assure us of the existence of other documents written on other materials by quoting from them (Falkenhausen 1993). Yet if it were not for their practice of inscribing bronze vessels and a very few divination bones, we would have no evidence that the Zhou had writing at all.
65. For merchant correspondence, which becomes abundant early in the second millennium BC, see Larsen (1989:132–134) and Postgate (1992:ch. 11).

66. As Boltz (1986:424) puts it: "In one important respect the scripts of the OBI [oracle-bone inscriptions] and the Shang bronzes . . . are identical. Both reflect a fully developed writing system, identical in the principles of its structure and operation with modern Chinese, though formally, of course, very different from it. There is, in other words, nothing 'primitive' or 'rudimentary' about the writing already in its earliest attested form."

67. See Cooper (this volume). For the origin of writing in Mesopotamia see Nissen (1985), Nissen *et al.* (1993, e.g. pp. 29–30), and Englund (1998). M. Green (1981, 1989) supplies more detail on certain points; Damerow (1999a) adds a theoretical perspective. For Egypt, see Baines (this volume).

68. Postgate (1984, 1992:especially ch. 3) and Larsen (1989) survey the expanding functions of writing over the 3,000-year history of the cuneiform script; Postgate (1992:66) supplies an instructive summary in chart form. For Egypt, see Baines (1983:especially pp. 574–579); Baines and Eyre (1983); and Baines (1988:194–204; this traces expanding use and growing range of text types down to the end of the Old Kingdom). Baines (this volume) sees the development in Egypt as a jerky one, with invention around 3200 BC followed by major "reforms" a few centuries later in dynasty 0 and again toward the end of dynasty 2 around 2700 BC. Such a model may apply equally well in Mesopotamia (compare Damerow 1999a:14–15; Postgate 1984:15; Houston, this volume, ch. 1).

69. The supposed special connection of writing with religious ritual has sometimes even been taken as a deep and significant feature of ancient Chinese culture (see, for example, Lewis 1999:14–15). Yet the only argument for this special connection is the scarcity of non-divination texts, and while it is perfectly true that little besides divination texts has survived, to infer that little besides divination texts ever existed is a fault in logic. If we applied the same argument – "the writing we have is all the writing that existed" – to the following period, we would conclude that all Western Zhou writing was done on bronze vessels. It is as though the archaeologist of a paperless future decided that Latin-speaking North Americans invented writing for the purpose of inscribing buildings.

70. A few other suggestions will not be discussed here. A number of scholars have sought to establish a high antiquity for the Chinese script by matching Neolithic potmarks with the simplest oracle-bone graphs (crosses, arrows, parallel lines, and other simple shapes) and then declaring the potmarks to be ancestors of Anyang writing; Demattè (1996) is a Western-language statement of arguments common in the Chinese literature. These arguments, which may or may not explain a few sign forms but certainly do not explain a writing system, have been criticized elsewhere (Djamouri 1997:210–211; Qiu 2000:30–33; cf. Glassner 2000:210–215). A recent discussion of seventh-millennium finds from Henan Jiahu is vulnerable to similar criticisms (and others), despite the authors' protestations to the contrary (Li Xueqin *et al.* 2003). Qiu Xigui (2000:10–12) sees the invention of writing as involving the gradual reinterpretation of the components of a storytelling picture under the influence of language; to mention only one objection, his model for "primitive writing," taken from ethnography, is Naxi

pictography, which is unlikely to have been insulated from the Chinese writing system in use around it. Keightley (1989:192–199) implausibly suggests that Chinese writing originated in the measurement needs of Neolithic carpenters and jadeworkers.

71. Daniels (1992:94–95). No doubt aware of this difficulty, in the chart at the front of his 1963 book Gelb tentatively derived Chinese from proto-cuneiform by way of proto-Elamite and the Indus script. See also Houston (this volume, ch. 1) on dubious recent claims for a Central Asian source.

72. See Cooper (this volume) and Postgate *et al.* (1995). This is not to underrate the intellectual achievement or to say that there is anything simple or automatic about a development from bookkeeping to writing. Nevertheless it is the great strength of recent accounts of the origin of cuneiform that they supply an institutional setting in which the intellectual steps are both motivated and exploitable (Damerow 1999a; M. Green 1981; Nissen 1985; Nissen *et al.* 1993).

73. This hypothesis goes back at least to the 1940s; for a recent presentation see Qiu (2000:39–40, 42, 45–46, 65–66). Qiu writes (p. 40): "During the formative process of the Chinese script, most of these clan emblems undoubtedly were transformed into characters." Among his examples are the fish-and-water graphs shown in Figs. 7.6(a), (b), and 7.7(b).

74. That is, nothing requires the inventors of a writing system to begin with graphs more pictorial than those seen in Fig. 7.1. (On the role of iconicity in early scripts see Cooper [1996:4, and this volume] and M. Green [1981:346].) To my eye, the first proto-cuneiform signs have rather less iconic content than the oracle-bone graphs, though this might only be because the latter are more familiar to me.

75. The need to write personal names has often been mentioned as an important motive for stripping signs of semantic value and using them strictly for phonetic representation (see, e.g., Gelb 1963:66–67). But if I understand the point correctly, this need to write names is a motive not for the first steps toward writing but for using the signs of an already existing system for their phonetic values alone, i.e., for exploiting the rebus principle (compare Cooper 1996:42).

76. The most likely, a vessel from Zhengzhou that predates Wu Ding's reign by fifty or a hundred years, bears on the otherwise undecorated portion of its neck the figure of a turtle (Bagley 1987:87, fig. 77). Though the turtle is three times repeated, in alignment with three units of decoration below it, its prominence and isolated placement invite the suspicion that it is something distinct from the decoration; and among the inscriptions of Anyang bronzes are a few with little turtles in the position of a clan sign (Boltz [1986:422] shows an example accompanied by a dedication to Father Yi).

77. Perhaps half a dozen items have been suggested as possible pre-Anyang inscribed bronzes (see, e.g., *Kaogu* [1988(3):246–257, 218]), but all are borderline cases in one way or another – either the bronze is not certain to be so early, or the device on it is not certain to be writing, or the inscription looks like a modern

forgery (Bagley 1987:210, n. 1). All indications are that the idea of inscribing bronze was new in Wu Ding's time.

78. See for instance Qiu (2000:33–40) and Boltz (1986:432–434). Note that the inscriptions accepted by Postgate *et al.* (1995:468) as Neolithic writing are in fact of uncertain archaeological context, date, and even authenticity.

79. This scenario is sometimes proposed explicitly (see references in Qiu 2000:44), more often simply assumed. Boltz has urged it in a series of publications (1986, 1994, prolegomena and part 1, 1999:109–123, 2000:15–16 and 29–30, n. 21, 2001).

80. On Chinese character-formation processes see F. Bottéro (this volume) and Qiu (2000). Perhaps because most syllables were words, the writing system seems to have insisted fairly stringently on a one-to-one correspondence between syllables and graphs. When a word was written using two or more distinct elements (e.g., the *hao* of Lady Hao's name), the elements were almost always formed into a single graphic unit. Rare exceptions in Anyang and early Zhou inscriptions – two syllables written as one graph or one syllable written as two separate graphs – were eliminated in later periods. In cuneiform too, new words were written by modifying or combining old signs, but cuneiform orthography did not insist that one word should be written with one sign: phonetic complements and semantic determinatives could be separate signs, and words could be written syllabically (Cooper 1996, especially pp. 41–43; M. Green 1989:45–51). The largely consonantal orthography of Egyptian is even further removed from Chinese.

81. On semantic+phonetic compounds see Qiu (2000:51–53). Boltz (1986, 1994, 1996, 1999, 2000, 2001) maintains that this is the only way Chinese ever formed compound characters, but his view has no basis that I can see, and it is contradicted by examples analyzed by F. Bottéro and Qiu (see n. 82).

82. See F. Bottéro (this volume) and Qiu (2000:185–203). A possible example is the graph "prognosticate," which depicts a scapula with a crack and a mouth (Fig. 7.1, last character of second column from right). In early cuneiform such compounds seem to have been much more common than semantic+phonetic compounds (Cooper, this volume). By some estimates they were more common in the Anyang script too.

83. Keightley (1989:200, n. 20) notes that Shima (1971) "was able to classify nearly all oracle-bone graphs under 164 'radicals' of his own devising." See also Djamouri (1997:219–222).

84. Qiu (2000:6). Daniels (1992) and Boltz (2000) have suggested that the rebus principle was most readily discovered in "monosyllabic" languages (viz., Chinese and Sumerian) because they contained many homonyms, but it is hard to imagine that the advantage was significant; punning is not confined to monosyllabic languages. Boltz (2000:15) surely goes too far when he suggests that writing arose in China in Wu Ding's time because a (hypothetical) evolution of the language toward monosyllabicity at that point triggered the discovery of rebus.

Compare Houston (this volume, ch. 1) and Baines (this volume) on the relation between writing system and lexical structure of language, and see n. 85 on the limited importance of rebus in early stages.

85. Cooper (1996:42–43); Baines (1999b:882). Rebus was used only to a limited extent in early cuneiform (Cooper, this volume), even though in the Mesopotamian linguistic environment it offered advantages that may not have been important in Chinese: it allowed the writing of grammatical affixes to nouns and verbs, and it allowed a writing system devised for the Sumerian language to write non-Sumerian names and then the unrelated Akkadian language (just as the Chinese writing system was eventually adapted to write Japanese) (Cooper 1996:43–55). Houston (this volume, ch. 10) raises doubts about the importance of rebus in early Maya writing as well.

86. Teleology is sometimes explicit in discussions of the origin of the Chinese script. Qiu Xigui for instance assumes that the steps he describes were taken by inventors whose aim from the first was full writing and who were casting about for ways to achieve it (Qiu 2000:6). If the inventors of the Chinese script began with so clear a grasp of the possibilities of writing, we would have to wonder where they got it. From the Near East?

87. Another possible function for writing that does not supply full linguistic detail is to serve as an aid to oral performance, providing mnemonics for a knowledgeable reader who fills in the gaps (Cooper 1992:117; Daniels 1992:93–94; Houston 1994a:29–31; Houston, this volume, ch. 1; Larsen 1987:219).

88. As Boltz's three-stage account of the origin of the Chinese script illustrates (see, e.g., Boltz 1986:table on p. 429 and comments on p. 432). Taking as starting point his conviction that all compound characters originated by the addition of determinatives to unit characters (see n. 81), Boltz posits a first stage in which unit characters were used to write what they depicted; a second stage in which they were used multivalently (i.e., as semantic or phonetic loans); and a third stage in which determinatives were added to clarify multivalent usage. But these stages collapse into one unless distinct functions can be specified for them. In other words, for the stages to have any reality, there would have had to be a narrow initial context of use in which the limited repertory of unit characters was a functional recording system; then a somewhat expanded context, wide enough to need to use characters multivalently but narrow enough for multivalent use to be unambiguous; and finally a still wider context in which ambiguities arising from multivalent use required the addition of determinatives. Without some account of context, a hypothetical sequence of sign-forming processes does little to explain the invention of writing.

89. The point is made eloquently by Cooper and Baines in their contributions to the present volume, as well as by Damerow (1999a), Nissen (1985), and Nissen *et al.* (1993). "The development of writing cannot be adequately described on the technical level of coding information only" (Damerow 1999a:13). It seems possible that scholars who take a strictly philological approach to the

origin of writing have been disposed to view phonetic representation as a major intellectual obstacle because, inattentive to the role of function and context, they see no other explanation for the infrequency with which writing systems have been invented.

90. Baines (this volume). The correlation of different scripts with different functions, seen to a limited extent in Anyang inscriptions, is of course very marked in Egypt, where the hieroglyphic script was an artistic form maintained entirely for display purposes (Davies 1987:ch. 2; Baines 1983:583; Baines, in preparation).

91. Boltz (2000:29–30, n. 21) has recently suggested this possibility; earlier he favored Dawenkou emblems as the likely starting point (1986, 1994).

92. Of course, if they had a writing system already, as seems likely, these needs would have been met before they arose.

93. Thus, in the case of China at least, I agree with Postgate *et al.* (1995).

8 | Writing on shell and bone in Shang China

FRANÇOISE BOTTÉRO

The first known Chinese writing is the script found in the shell and bone inscriptions dating from around the thirteenth century BC (late Shang dynasty).[1] Another category of documents, the bronze inscriptions, existed at the same time. These inscriptions also have great importance for the history of writing in China.[2] Nonetheless, because the bone inscriptions are more numerous for the Shang period, I will limit my discussion to that writing system, trying to show how it works, and how it records the language (see also F. Bottéro 1996, 2001; Keightley 1978, 1999; Vandermeersch 1977; Zhang Bingquan 1988).

Specialists usually call the bone inscriptions oracle-bone inscriptions (OBI) because they essentially record acts of divination, yet the fact that the texts were inscribed after the act of divination suggests strongly that the writing was not addressed to the spirits nor was it a means for communicating with the Other world. The bones used for divination were not always inscribed, and in any case pyro-scapulomancy (fire-augury on shoulder blades) existed before writing in the Neolithic period and continued in use, mainly without inscription, after the Shang dynasty.[3]

More than 150,000 pieces of inscribed bones have been found up to now, some of them bearing only a few graphs, and the longest with more than 100 signs. Nonetheless, it must be emphasized that only between a third and a quarter of the 4,500 signs of the shell and bone inscriptions have been successfully deciphered.

Encoding the Chinese language

Chinese writing is said to have pictographic origins (Tang Lan 1981:87). Indeed, some of the OBI graphs depict things from the visible world, but the pictographic aspect of the OBI should not impede a proper scholarly analysis of its real nature. There are in fact several general devices for encoding words or linguistic units in the OBI writing system as illustrated below.

Pictographs

The term *pictograph* is used here to mean a graph that encodes a word (or a linguistic unit) through the medium of depiction. Strictly speaking, the Shang characters are "symbols," not pictographs, but the term manages to convey a sense of how some graphs represent words. This is the case for graphs depicting a tree, a cowrie, the moon, the sun, a hand, a mouth, a tooth, a sheep, a fish, a field, a bed, a door, etc., and respectively encoding these words. No matter what the earlier history of these signs as symbols, they are used in OBI as components of a real writing system: that is they stand for linguistic signs or, in linguistic terminology, for a signifier and a signified (a pronunciation and a meaning). As symbols standing for words or morphemes, the graphs do not need to be completely realistic. Some characters, for example, represent animals in quite an unnatural way, being rendered vertically; after all this is not drawing, but rather linguistic representation.

Phonograms

The rebus use of graphs is well attested in grammatical particles: the graph for "bird" is used to represent the copula, that of "basket" a modal particle, that of "wheat" the verb "arriving," etc. In fact, most of the pictographs could also be used as phonograms. More than 80 percent of the pictographs represent other words, ranging from patronyms, toponyms, clan names to sacrificial names. The "hand" graph was used to write the words *right hand, to have*, the name of a sacrifice, as well as the coordinating conjunction "and"; the "nose" graph represented *nose, self,* and *from*; the graph for "fire" sometimes recorded the terms *calamity, disaster*, while the graph for "cauldron" was used to convey *to divine*. Many other examples may be found. It seems that there were only a few pictographs not used for their phonetic value. As far as I know, this is true for "sun," "moon," and *bu* ("cracking"). In this system, "pictographs" as well as other graphs could either express their pronunciation (a phonetic value) or their meaning (a semantic value). In other words, a "pictograph," as I use the term here, was not just an image, it also represented a sound. It not only gave shape to a linguistic sign but could also stand for a phonological segment and thus be deployed as a rebus or a phonogram.

Abstract signs

Another set of graphs gives more or less abstract representations. Even though there is a pronounced tendency among Chinese scholars to explain the shape of these graphs and give them a figurative value, it is extremely difficult to establish what they represented. Graphs recording numbers, space ("above," "below") as well as time (cyclical characters), belong to this type. Cyclical characters (*ganzhi*) were used to record days, and eventually years, by combining two sets of 10 and 12 signs which constitute a total of 60 binomes (see the example below).

Grapheme combination

Another important way of encoding words was by means of combining graphemes. Theoretically, all simple graphs could be joined together to form compound graphs, but we need to make a clear-cut distinction between three kinds of combinations. First, there is what looks to be a combination but is actually a simple sketch representing an experience, a gesture, or an action. The word meaning "to capture," *huo* 🖾 (獲) (which can also stand for a toponym, or a patronym), is represented by the graphemes "hand" and "bird."[4] This compound graph is found in sentences that are not necessarily related to the capture of birds, but could also involve pigs, fish, deer, etc.:

丁卯卜王大獲魚
ding-mao-crack-making-king-greatly-capture-fish
"Crack-making on *ding-mao*, the king will get an important capture of fish."

Other examples include the graph for "raising," "presenting," "to carry," "to realize," "to hold," *xing* 🖾 (興); it depicts four hands (sometimes two) pulling or holding something. Another is a graph that indicates "to chase," "to hunt," "a pursuit," *zhu* 🖾 (逐) (see below, p. 257); it is composed of a foot, along with an animal that can be a pig, deer, rabbit or horse.[5] The sole stable element in this graph is the foot, but it would not be reasonable to think of it as the phonophoric (sound-bearing) element since it appears in many different graphs with varying pronunciations (more than fifty by my count). A system that would allow one graph to have so many values would be too cumbersome to be effective. Finally, there is a graph meaning "to give birth," *yu* 🖾 (育 / 毓), which combines the elements "woman (person)" and "baby."[6] It would be difficult to argue for a phonophoric element within the graph, as there is little chance that a semantic element + a phonetic element would correspond exactly to the combination of the graphs for woman and baby, both of which are deployed in a pictorial image of birthing. To put this another way, it would be more complicated, even less persuasive, to imagine a phonetic combination for this kind of graph rather than simply depicting or roughly sketching the action they represent.

Some grapheme combinations represent another step in the direction of greater abstraction and heightened complexity of sign combination. For example, in the graph for "mouse," *shu* 𣇤 (鼠), we can distinguish two signs, that for "small" and another for a particular animal. "Male animal" is represented by the sign for "male" linked to the drawing of an animal: thus (a) "male" + "cow," (b) "male" + "pig," (c) "male" + "sheep," etc. The same pattern allows scribes to indicate the female sex of an animal. Unfortunately, except for "male" + "cow," which stands for present-day *mu* 牡 ("male"), and "female" + "cow," which records present-day *pin* 牝 ("female"), we do not know how to pronounce the other characters. They did not survive as graphs in later versions of Chinese script and so cannot be deciphered. As a result, it is hard to say whether they were graphic variants for "male" and "female" in general, or whether they were read differently, designating in each case a special type of male animal or female animal. Both interpretations compete among Chinese scholars (Yang Fengbin 1993). In another example, "dental caries," *qu* (齲), we can clearly distinguish the graphemes "tooth" and "worm." This graphic construction shows how the Shang people imagined a cavity. Indeed, it seems that they were not the only people to think this way. Mesopotamian scribes had the same kind of representation for the rotting of teeth. Today, a popular expression in modern Chinese for "tooth decay" is *chong ya* 虫牙 ("worm-tooth") = "hollow-tooth."

What should be noticed here is that none of these characters bear any phonophoric element within their graphic structure. They use the pictographic, the sketch, or the combination devices to represent a particular reality. The fact that they can be analyzed today into more than one grapheme is probably responsible for the assertion by North American scholars (Boodberg 1957 and Boltz 1994:72, 149) that this kind of compound without a phonophoric element does not exist. With respect to this issue, I disagree with William Boltz (1994:149) who, following Peter Boodberg (1957), rejects "compound characters that do not have a phonophoric element within their graphic structure." As I have tried to show, the pictograph device was also applied to compound characters, some of which could involve more abstract tableaux or scenes sketching the essentials of a meaning, such as the woman and the baby for "giving birth." I do not see why the Shang scribes would have limited the use of pictographic processing to simple signs. Again, it would be more complicated to imagine a phonetic combination for this kind of graph than to roughly outline what they represented in the minds of people of that time. These signs were not very numerous, but they made use of an important device that existed in other writing systems, including proto-cuneiform in Mesopotamia.

A second kind of compound graph combines a semantic and a phonophoric element. Later in the development of Chinese script, this will become the most productive way to create unambiguous characters, but in the Shang period the process was not yet applied systematically. These characters usually represent women's names, river names, or the names of sacrifices. A good example is the name of Lady Jing, 井𠂤, recorded by the grapheme for "woman" and the phonophoric element *jing* 井. A second example is "river," *he* 𣱵 (河), which is also the name of the divinity of the river. It combines "water" with the phonophoric element *ke* 可. Note that, in the Chinese script, the phonophoric element does not need to be a perfect homophone; the end-rhyme is sufficient to recall the word. In this example, the phonophoric element bears the same end-rhyme, whereas the initials were different but homorganic (meaning they had the same point of articulation). In Baxter's historical reconstructions (Baxter 1992:771), the phonophoric element should be read **khajʔ*, while "river" was **gajʔ*. A third example is *he* 龢 (龢), representing a sacrificial name. It is composed of a "flute," 龠, and the phonophoric element *he* 禾 ("ear of cereal"). Yet another instance would be "to fish," *yu* 漁, which is sometimes composed of the following elements: "water" + one "fish" or "water" + four "fish," or a "(fishing) net" + "fish," the fish corresponding to the phonophoric element (see below). Finally, there is the symbol for the "phoenix," *feng* (鳳), whose graph has been borrowed for "wind" and which combines a "bird" and a phonophoric element 凡.

The third type of compound employs repetitions of identical graphic elements. Some graphemes representing countable things can appear two, three, or even four times within a single graphic structure. This device is still in use today: the graph written with one tree, *mu* 木, means "tree" – the "one-tree" graph can express the singular ("one tree") as well as the plural ("trees"); the graph written with two trees, *lin* 林, means "wood," while the graph written with three trees, *sen* 森, means "forest." These characters have different pronunciations, so we cannot deduce that there is a secure phonophoric element. Obviously, we have here a purely mental construction. In OBI, the three graphs exist as well, but it is not certain whether they represent the same words since *lin* stands for the name of a tribe, whereas the meaning of the sentences with *sen* ("forest") tends to be unclear.

The graphs with one, two, three, and four sheep coexist. They seem to have different meanings, but it is uncertain whether they represent a difference in quantity. According to some sentences, the "three-sheep" graph seems to be equivalent to the "four-sheep" graph, making it likely that they are graphic variants of a toponym. The same process applies to combinations of one and two insects or snakes, etc. On the other hand, the reduplication of the graph "man" 🰀 means "to follow" if written with the same orientation – 从 – and "north" (probably "back") if written in opposite directions: 北.

Before concluding the first part of my chapter, I will give an example of a sentence to show the way the oracle was consulted and the way the declaration was recorded on bone or shell. First comes the date, with two cyclical characters giving the day the divination was made, followed by the name of the diviner in charge of the oracle, then the content of the oracle, and, finally, the verification, in this case a month later, of what really happened. As shown, the inscription reproduces the syntactic organization of Chinese language. For this reason, I find it impossible not to acknowledge that OBI recorded spoken language.

甲申卜Que貞婦好娩不其嘉三旬又一日甲寅娩允不嘉惟女 (*Guo* 1982:14002 recto) *jia-shen*-crack-making-Jue [name of diviner]-divine-Lady-Hao-delivery-negation-future modal-happy-three-decade-and-one-day-*jia-yin*-deliver-indeed-negation-happy-auxiliary-girl
"Crack-making on *jia-shen* day [day 21]. Jue [Que] divined: the delivery of Lady Hao will not be a happy event. Three decades and one day later on *jia-yin* day [day 51], she delivered [a baby], indeed it was not a happy event, it was a girl."

Graphic variants

Having described the different devices used by the Shang scribes to encode words or linguistic units in their language, I will now present the different types of graphic variants in OBI. I believe allographs are extremely useful for understanding the OBI writing system as well as for determining its stage of development within script evolution.

One of the characteristics of this writing is that it allows many graphic variants, that is different graphs standing for the same morpheme (same meaning and same pronunciation). As we have seen for the characters meaning "male animal," complex matters of decipherment are at stake here. Some morphemes can be represented by different graphs, but, at the same time and for various reasons – phonetic and semantic links as well as graphic resemblance – one graph can also stand for different morphemes. This is the case for the graphs "sun" meaning also "day," and "moon" which also signifies "month." In such a complex system, it is crucial to ensure that we are really dealing with graphic variants and not with different characters or words.

As in any other script, some graphic variants result from diachronic evolution. However, the Chinese system also has a good number of synchronic variants. I have counted some nine different types of the latter in OBI. The following list contains samples of these, giving first the modern *pinyin* transcription, second the meaning of the character in OBI, third the modern character, and finally different ways of writing the graph in oracle bone script.

(1) The first set consists of graphic variants written in opposite directions (we find the same phenomenon in Egyptian hieroglyphic writing [Davies 1994:112]). Such variants are linked to the symmetrical arrangement of texts on turtle plastrons:

er "ear" 耳
yin "officer" 尹

(2) Graphs representing the same thing but seen from a different angle:

gui "tortoise" 龜
ju "cart" 車

(3) Graphic variants that combine the same elements but in a different order:

pin "sacrifice's name" 品
xiang "to inspect" 相
zhu "name of a person or a tribe" 貯

(4) Graphic variants that combine different quantities of elements:

yu "to fish" 漁
fu "sacrifice"[7] 福 (a) (b) (c) (d) (e) (f)
she "to shoot an arrow" 射
bing "illness" 病

(5) Some use an equal number of elements, yet one of these components will shift while still retaining membership in the same semantic category

(e.g., graphic elements designating human beings, quadrupeds, etc., can be freely exchanged). In other words, the varying element is a semantic one. It can be "man" for "woman"; "pig," "horse," "deer," or "tiger" for any quadruped, and so on:

zhu "to hunt"   逐
lao "pen"   牢

yu "to give birth, chief, ..."[8] 毓 / 育 (a)   (b)   (c)   (d)

(6) The phonetic element may vary on occasion:

lu "valley, foot of a hill" 麓   [= 林 ("forest") + 彔 (lù toponym)]
                                  [= 林 ("forest") + 鹿 (lù ("deer"))]

(7) The presence or absence of a phonetic element may create variants:

feng "phoenix, wind"   鳳
xing "star"   星
yi "the following day"   翌

(8) The presence or absence of a semantic element may create variants:

zhen "to divine"   貞
ge "to arrive"   各
jing "women's name"

(9) Some of the variants can be represented by completely different characters.

wu "five"   五   (Zhu 1992:39)
zi "the first of the twelve Earthly Branches"   子

The graphic variants enable us to deduce interesting information about the OBI writing system. They help us to understand the details of graph structure and the varying principles of graph formation (pictographic, phonetic, combination of both, etc.). As I have emphasized in another article (F. Bottéro 2001), if certain graphic variants are indications of scribal liberty, that freedom is nevertheless limited by the readability of the texts. The addition of a phonetic or semantic element into a graph can be seen as a means of disambiguating the graph or reducing the opacity of the text. To me, the need for disambiguating graphs suggests strongly that these documents were meant to be read.

Still, the existence of allographs using distinct devices to represent a single word shows that this writing was not yet fixed or standardized. The absence of a phonetic element in some graphs ("phoenix," "star," "following day," etc.) demonstrates that the use of what will become the favored way to create Chinese characters – the combination of a semantic and a phonophoric element – is just beginning at this time. Shang writing was obviously close to its time of origin (see Bagley, this volume).

Conclusion

The Chinese script is obviously an original system of signs created to record an ancestral form of the Chinese language. Linguistic units are encoded by a certain number of devices that can also be found in other writing systems. In contrast with other early writing systems of the Old and the New World, however, the first documents in China reproduce continuous language.[9]

The origins of writing in China are problematic. Chinese scholars tend to date their writing back to the Neolithic period arguing that the signs found on pottery are quite similar in shape to those of the OBI.[10] As William Boltz has shown, this is a rather improbable proposal. First, there is no indication that the function or the meaning of these few Neolithic marks was the same as that of the Shang graphs; second, ". . . it would appear virtually impossible that the nascent seeds of writing could have germinated in the mid-fifth millennium BC but not grown into anything approaching a real writing system until more than three thousand years later" (Boltz 1994:38).

On the other hand, as the characters written with a brush would suggest,[11] it is quite possible that other perishable writing surfaces existed as well, especially when considering the difficulty of inscribing the bones (see Bagley, this volume). The survival of materials such as bone, shell, bronze is probably a consequence not only of their durability but also of the specific nature of their contents.

Still, if Chinese writing were invented earlier than the OBI, it could not have been very much earlier. First, it is hard to find any social requirements for writing prior to the Shang dynasty. Second, as we have seen, the graphic style of the Shang script, with its rather pictographic shape, strongly suggests a writing close to its first steps or its beginning, as do the numerous graphic variants. Last but not least, it is only several centuries later that literature, epistolary, and private writing appear in China.

Here, we must consider the chronological sequence of the successive appearance of different scripts in the Old World. Chinese writing is definitely the youngest of the group. It appears around the thirteenth century BC, about 1,700 years after the inception of writing in Mesopotamia. There was thus more than enough time for the Chinese to benefit from the progress of other civilizations. If the graphic elements used in the Chinese writing system were not borrowed from any other known script, and are of truly Chinese origin, the *idea* of writing is likely, in my opinion, to have come from the West. The opposing hypothesis of an independent invention of writing in China is difficult to sustain. It implies that China was isolated, that Chinese people lived without any contacts with the rest of the world or without any external influence, in other words, without any cultural exchange, a rather improbable state of affairs. In contrast, the hypothesis of a diffusion of the idea of writing proper from the West would help in understanding why, in China, we do not find any rudiments or any real first steps of writing, and why it suddenly appears during the Shang dynasty as a full and complete system for transcribing the spoken language. It would be erroneous to think that the diffusion of the idea of writing equates to direct influence from archaic Mesopotamian writing. Rather, it means that the Chinese received the idea that a visual system of signs could be used for recording spoken language. To me, this hypothesis seems more promising or credible than the hypothesis of an independent invention of writing in China. But of course new discovery may shed more light on this question.

Notes

1. Since written documents play an important role in different fields (e.g. history, anthropology, archeology, etc.), and accordingly are subject to diverging approaches, a clarification seems necessary here. The fact that writing enables us to visualize, fix, and record our thoughts is possible only via the intermediary of language, a crucial fact often neglected. The present chapter insists on this linguistic perspective as a fundamental prerequisite to a proper study of writing.
2. The pronunciation of the Chinese characters is given in *pinyin*, the phonetic system of transcription adopted in February 1958 by the People's Republic of China.
3. According to Hu Houxuan, at least an equal number of fragments were found without characters as were found with in the first forty years after the discovery of oracle bones (Wang Yuxin 1989:106). The earliest evidence of pyro-scapulomancy may be dated to around 3500 BC (Keightley 1978:3). The inscription of the

divinatory content on the bones is an innovation by the Shang. In 1977, about 300 inscribed bones (out of 17,000 fragments) of the Western Zhou dynasty (eleventh to eighth century BC) were discovered in Shanxi Zhouyuan, north China.

4. According to reconstructions of Old Chinese pronunciation by Baxter (1992), neither the "bird" nor the "hand" were phonophoric or sound-bearing: "to capture" (獲 *huo*) was pronounced *wrak, "bird" (隹 *wei*) was pronounced *ljujʔ, "hand" (手 *shou*) was *hjuʔ or *wji (k)s (又 *yòu*). The asterisk indicates an unattested reconstructed form, ʔ stands for a glottal stop, [i] represents a central *i*.

5. As a verb, this character is usually followed by an object representing an animal that is not necessarily the same as the one in the graph for "hunt": it can be a buffalo, pig, deer, moose, tiger, etc. This is illustrated by the following example – 貞王往逐麋獲 (Guo 1982:10347 recto) "Divination: the king goes hunting deer. There is a capture" – in which the animal of the graph "hunt" is a pig, the object of the capture is a deer, and the animal in the graph "capture" is a bird.

6. The *yu* graph also records the name of an ancestor, a "chief," as well as *hou* ("descendant, heir"). This is an intriguing graph because of its graphic variants. In some graphs there is a man or a human being replacing the woman, sometimes the baby is upside down, at other times not (see above, p. 257).

7. The character *fu* 福 can be written with the phonophoric element *fu* 畐 (b) sometimes replaced by the semantic element *you* 酉 representing the pictograph of a "vase" as in (c), (d), and (e). Two hands holding the vase appear in some graphs as in (b), and (e), along with the sign for "altar" 丅 as in (e) and (f), and the sign for "roof, edifice" as in (d) and (f). Even though compound characters may include a semantic and a phonophoric element (b), there are still other ways to represent them that do not necessarily require a phonophoric component. Rather, they use a combination of semantic elements. This is another reason why I think the existence of semantic compounds cannot be denied.

8. In some graphs – (a) – and (d) – the "woman" element is replaced by "man," or "human being." Initially, I assumed that solely the graph with a woman and a baby issuing out of the mother's body (b) meant "giving birth." After checking all the sentences written with the different graphs of *yu*, this turned out to be untrue. The graphs could all communicate any of the meanings of *yu* ("ancestors, chief, give birth") or *hou* ("descendant, heir"), etc.

9. The study of early writing systems shows that the first writing did not precisely record spoken language. Proto-cuneiform writing was an *aide-mémoire* (J. Bottéro 1987:132); in the texts of early Egypt "continuous language was not written" (Baines, this volume), and the proto-Elamite texts "seem to represent more the structure of a system of book-keeping than the division of a spoken language into distinct semantic units" (Englund, this volume). As for Maya script, it "cannot be regarded as completely faithful to spoken language. Like other Mesoamerican systems, Maya writing represents a laconic script, omitting

some elements obligatory in spoken language and providing ample leeway for improvised readings and oratorical expositions on terse passages" (Houston 1994b:2450).

10. Specialists distinguish two types of Neolithic signs found on pottery: (1) marks that resemble scratches consisting of a few strokes arranged geometrically; and (2) emblems or pictographs (with some found on jade objects) (e.g. Cheung Kwong-yue 1983; Boltz 1994:35–38).

11. Some of them were not necessarily meant to be incised (Keightley 1978:46–47, and Venture 2002a:52–53).

9 | Reasons for runes

HENRIK WILLIAMS

Compared to ancient classical scripts, the old Germanic runes are a young and unsophisticated relative from a remote corner of the world. Runes may be called young, since, at the time when they first appear, almost all major writing systems in the world were already invented. The runic script may also be thought unsophisticated or uncomplicated in several respects. First, it is alphabetic and thus does not include the large sign lists and heavy logographic component of other scripts discussed in this volume. Yet, even here, runic writing is a somewhat unrefined member of its class. It does not, for example, fully utilize the inherent abilities of alphabetic systems. There is no doubling of graphemes to denote long phonemes, and features such as word division and marking of nasals before homorganic consonants are optional. Second, even the execution of runic inscriptions is often inelegant: letters are incised with a broad range of tools in almost any kind of material, some of which are less than ideal media for writing, such as metal and stone. The texts are short, often only a word or two in length, and sometimes uninterpretable even by readers of that time. Even worse is that there are so irritatingly few runic inscriptions, only a couple of hundred from the first half-millennium of our era, even if we count generously. Third, runic inscriptions are not associated with a group of people otherwise renowned for cultural achievements. The Germanic tribes in southern Scandinavia and the northern part of the European continent are not, for good reasons, counted among the classical civilizations, at least not if we demand impressive buildings, extensive written texts, and a central organized society as evidence of a culture with claims to be great.

The number and shapes of the runic letters are well established (Table 9.1). This chapter will explore the setting for the invention and first use of the runes. It elaborates on thoughts in two earlier articles of mine (H. Williams 1996, 1997). The issues I want to address are: (1) where were the runes first used? (2) when were the runes invented? (3) from which alphabet were the runes derived? (4) how was the derivation made? (5) to what uses were the runes put? and (6) why were the runes invented?

Table 9.1 The oldest runic letters (*c.* AD 150–800). Number, shape, order, and the division into three groups are evidenced by fifth-century inscriptions of the rune-row (the futhark). The names (designations), their meaning, and the sound value of the individual runes are derived from ninth-century and later manuscripts. The derivations from Roman letters (third column) are found in H. Williams (1996).

Number	Rune	(From Roman letter)	Phonemic value	Germanic name (reconstructed)	Translation
1	ᚠ	(F)	f	*fehu*	cattle
2	ᚢ, ᚢ	(V)	u	*uruz*	ox
3	ᚦ	(D)	θ (th)	*þurisaz*	giant
4	ᚨ	(A)	a	*ansuz*	god
5	ᚱ	(R)	r	*raido*	riding
6	<	(C)	k	*kaunan*	ulcer
7	ᚷ	(X)	g	*gebo*	gift
8	ᚹ	(P)	w	*wunjo*	joy
9	ᚻ	(H)	h	*hagalaz*	hail (stone)
10	ᚾ	(N)	n	*naudiz*	need
11	ᛁ	(I)	i	*isaz*	ice
12	ᛃ	(G)	j	*jeran*	year
13	ᛇ	(Z)	ç (ch)?	*ihwaz*	yew
14	ᛈ	(K)	p	*perþo?*	?
15	ᛉ	(Y)	z	*algiz*	elk
16	ᛊ, ᛋ	(S)	s	*sowilo*	sun
17	ᛏ	(T)	t	*tiwaz*	the god Týr
18	ᛒ	(B)	b	*berkanan*	birch twig
19	ᛖ, ᛗ	(M)	e	*ehwaz*	horse
20	ᛗ	(E)	m	*mannaz*	human
21	ᛚ	(L)	l	*laguz*	liquid
22	◊	(O)	ŋ (ng)	*ingwaz*	the god Ing
23 or 24	ᛟ	(Q)	o	*oþalan*	inherited land
24 or 23	ᛞ	Innovation	d	*dagaz*	day

Where were the runes first used?

The oldest dated artifact with an undoubted runic inscription is the bone comb from Vimose on the Danish Island of Funen (Fig. 9.1). The object probably dates to the second half of the second century AD. Other early inscriptions have been found on old Danish territory from Schleswig in present-day northern Germany to Scania, now in southern Sweden. But

Fig. 9.1 Bone comb from Vimose, Denmark.
The inscription reads **harja**, a personal name.
(Picture: Nationalmuseet, Copenhagen.)

there are also a number of early, rune-inscribed spearheads with eastern Germanic provenance from the early third century. From this we may draw the conclusion that the runes had to be invented no later than *c.* AD 150. The fact that a not-so-small number of roughly contemporary inscriptions appear in a rather large area is very suggestive and will be discussed more fully below.

When were the runes invented?

The answer to this question is that we simply do not know. Many scholars have tried to pinpoint the time when the runes were invented by establishing the literary culture from which they were borrowed. Different answers may be offered depending on which writing system is posited as the source of the runes. Very much hinges on the time span allowed between the invention itself and the oldest known examples of the runic script in use. Those allowing a long period between the actual invention of the runes and their first recorded usage may posit an older Mediterranean area as the source of runes. In this vein the archaic Greco-Roman alphabet has been proposed as a plausible donor (see most recently Antonsen [1989:144–155]). Few runologists have been convinced by this proposal, and most scholars tend to narrow the gap between invention and recorded usage. The effect has been to favor either the Roman alphabet as the source of the runes or the late North Italic (sometimes called Etruscan) alphabets used by Celtic tribes in the Alpine region. The Roman origin tends to be favored by Scandinavians whereas German- and English-speaking scholars often lean toward a North Italic source. My personal feeling is that this question should really be saved for last; it is, after all, the solution to the entire complex of problems and should pivot on how the other questions are answered.

From which alphabet were the runes derived?

Again, this question can really only be answered after many other problems are resolved. However, I want to point out that attempts have been made to approach the problem from two directions, that is cultural and alphabet-historical. The culture "on top" at the time when runes began to spread was, of course, Roman. A number of scholars, myself included, have argued for the probability that Roman influence was strong long before and after the runes started to appear, and that the runic source alphabet therefore most likely is the same as the one used for writing Latin. There is no real consensus, however, regarding exactly which kind of Latin writing was a pattern for the runes or at what exact time and place the invention occurred. Most (but not all) scholars agree that if only we could show that runes came from the Roman letters the problem would have been solved, but most (yet again not all) declare that it is not possible to find a perfect fit between letters and runes. One example should suffice: the rune ᚹ looks like a Latin <P> but actually represents /w/, whereas the rune for /p/, ᛈ, does not look like any Latin letter.

For this reason people have gone shopping for another classical script, one that is easier to reconcile with the actual shapes of the runic symbols. Hence the derivation from Greek and and North Italic alphabets. Chronological problems do arise, however, and there has been no greater success at proving a convincing absolute correspondence between individual runes and letters in these possible source alphabets. There has been an inevitable tendency toward explaining deviations by various ad hoc developments. And, of course, the greater the time span allowed between the invention of the runes and the oldest extant inscriptions, the greater the possibility for changes to occur in the shapes of the runes.

These difficulties have led most level-headed runologists to refrain from supporting one theory over another. Indeed, the problem has very little significance for the kind of runic philology most of us practice in the field. Not even when interpreting the earliest runic inscriptions does it seem important whether the runic symbols themselves are ultimately derived from one alphabet or another. When discussing the history and culture of the Germanic tribes, however, the origin of the runes is of utmost importance and must be addressed by scholars from all disciplines. It should go without saying that runologists cannot abstain from participating in this work.

I have tried to make my own contribution to the search for the runic origins. I accept the commonly held view that one cannot ignore Roman influence in Germania during the first few centuries AD. I find that one cannot dismiss the Roman alphabet as the most likely source of the runes, although it is still an open question which version of Latin script we are dealing with. It is known for a fact that men from the Germanic tribes were held hostage in the Roman empire and served in the Roman armies, which must have given plenty of opportunity for contact with writing. Roman soldiers (presumably also those with Germanic roots) were taught writing, and it is also likely that people in the Germanic provinces had some more-or-less peaceful experience with the script of the occupying Roman army. These possible influences would most likely establish the cursive or provincial forms of Roman letters as the origin of runes (see Rausing 1992 and Quak 1996, respectively). The runes do not give a cursive impression at all, however. Problems even arise when using provincial forms in the derivations. Runes certainly look exceedingly epigraphic (i.e., cut rather than painted) and immediately strike one as more like monumental Roman letters used epigraphically than any cursive or provincial writing. This is why I follow other scholars in using the full 23-character alphabet of the classical Latin script as the sole source for the 24 runic graphemes.

How was the derivation made?

There is a proverb which I like tremendously: "If it walks like a duck and talks like a duck, it is probably a duck." Unfortunately, one cannot use this common-sense approach when deciding on the origin of the runes, at least not all of then. If we return to our runic ᚹ we find that it does indeed walk like a duck, that is, it *looks* like a Roman <P>, but it does not talk like a duck, since it does not have the phonemic value /p/. This is the reason why this rune has been given all kinds of fanciful derivations, and consequently the search for the origin of the runes veers off on a wild goose (or duck!) chase. I, on the other hand, was the first to argue that even if ᚹ does not fully behave as a duck, it most definitely does not behave like any other known bird. Therefore we seem obliged to be satisfied with only the first part of the famous saying: "If it walks like a duck, it probably *is* a duck."

I follow the principle that if a rune looks identical or very close to a Roman letter, it is most likely derived from that same letter. In judging likeness one has to take into account certain graphemic rules which are evident from how the runes were formed.[1] The rules are simple and absolute and may untechnically be summarized in five points:

(1) A runic grapheme is made up of a full-length vertical line and/or lines of various length that are neither vertical nor horizontal, but diagonal.
(2) The diagonal lines may not proceed further up nor lower down than the verticals.
(3) The diagonal lines never issue exclusively from the bottom of the verticals, but are applied starting from the top, cf. ⌈ (*l*) and ⋂ (*u*).
(4) Two diagonal lines may be combined to form angles, which may be vertical or horizontal; three joined diagonal lines form a diagonal "crook."
(5) Runes made up of angles only reach full height if stacked on top of each other, cf. < (*k*), ⧖ (*j*), ◇ (*ŋ*), and ⧨ (*s*), respectively.

These rules deriving runes from letters leave us with only two more or less problematic cases: ᛗ and ᛞ.[2] The first of these may be shown to be a derivative of <E> (see H. Williams 1996:214f.). Thereby all 23 Roman letters are exhausted as donor signs. Since the inventor of the runes felt the need for 24 graphemes, one had to be made up: ᛞ. The process is rather straightforward and presents no insurmountable problems. Of course, the result bears only a poor resemblance to the known sound values of the runes; at least eight runic graphemes do *not* represent the phoneme they should have done if my model were correct. By studying what happened to the Roman letters in the process, however, one may discover something interesting. All five of what we may call "unnecessary" letters in the Roman alphabet were used for phonemes or phoneme clusters with no equivalents in Latin; that is <K>, <Q>, <X>, <Y>, and <Z> were used for /w/, /ŋ/, /j/, /ç/, and /z/, respectively, as was the invented rune for /d/. Why the extant runes do not show this state of affairs, but rather a state where these very graphemes plus ᛗ and ᛗ have been switched, was not within my power to discover. My suggestion (see H. Williams 1996:217) has been that the "mix-up" took place separately after the creation of the runes, albeit very early, when the runic writing system had to survive independently of any reference to its Roman parent. I did write: "Although this mix-up might be unintentional, I have tried to show that it is by no means arbitrary" (H. Williams 1996:217). I should have realized that if the switching process were non-arbitrary, it must have taken place simultaneously with the process of creating the runes as we know them. Whoever was responsible for the "mix-up" obviously knew very well which runes corresponded to unnecessary letters in the Roman alphabet, and the subsequent switch must therefore have been intentional in spite of what I claimed. It took someone better linguistically initiated than myself to sort out the possibilities. I refer to a joint article by John Robertson and myself, where he proposes what I consider to be a brilliant solution to the final stage of this problem, namely, the devising of new signs according to a linguistic process of analogy.

To what uses were the runes put?

Most of the early runic inscriptions appear on high-prestige artifacts such as the spearheads mentioned earlier, but also commonly on women's brooches (Fig. 9.2). It is interesting to note that the inscriptions, as such, do not seem to have had a very public function at first. The brooches were all inscribed in places where the runes would be hidden from everyone when the ornament was used, and only a person handling the item itself could read its text. On the other hand, one could not claim that the inscriptions were intentionally hidden on brooches; the best surfaces for inscribing are the non-ornamental ones, facing the back of the brooch or the plain sides, which were less visible than the decorated fronts. It could be argued that on a spearhead the inscription was displayed more openly, perhaps not to the enemy who at most beheld it briefly before it was plunged into a tender part of his body, but probably to fellow warriors when comparing weapons or when exhibiting them at other occasions.

That runic inscriptions were not intentionally hidden is also borne out by comparing the spearheads with inscribed shafts of various kinds, chapes, shieldbosses, buckles, and other details of equipment, as well as the odd comb and wooden box which have been found. This lack of seemingly secretive purposes accords well with the absence of any evidently occult inscriptions in the earliest material. One gets the impression that any difficulties encountered when trying to decipher an inscription are due more to incompetence on the part of the rune writer than to any conscious desire to mislead the reader or challenge her or his wits.

The impression of openness is strengthened by a look at the contents of the earliest runic texts. It is very common to find only one word, usually a name. In most cases the name probably denotes the owner of the inscribed artifact or the writer of the runes, possibly identical with the donor. There are many possible explanations for why a person's name appears on an item, but if it is the owner's name, one reason might well be the sheer delight in having one's name in writing. On spearheads the names seem to refer to the weapon itself: *Prober, Router, Goal-pursuer, Whiner*. However, three spearheads with the same name, *Wagnijo* ("the mover"), probably bear the name of the spearmaker. Simple makers' formulae do occur. Sometimes an

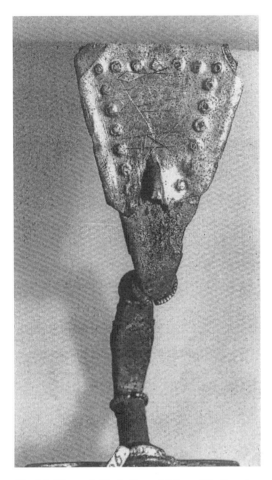

Fig. 9.2 Woman's fibula (brooch) from Himlingøje, Denmark. The inscription reads **hariso**, a personal name. (Picture: Nationalmuseet, Copenhagen.)

epithet of some kind is added to the name: for example *W. the well known*. There are a very few texts of more than two words, but they are always obscure, not least because of damage to the object.

I have lingered a while on the nature of the earliest inscriptions for the reason that many scholars have advocated and some still advocate a wholly different approach. Dennis H. Green, for example, claims that "instead of transmitting a communication the runes appear to have been used to conceal it, to wrap it up in mystery and magic" (1994:35). Neither Green nor any earlier scholar has presented any real evidence that runes were used for such concealment. I believe much of the reason for the fixation with the putatively esoteric side of runes depends on old interpretations of the inscriptions that were riddled with the spirit of magic. Another contributing factor is the word *rune* itself, which is still universally considered to be full of occult meaning. Lately, however, this view has been challenged, very convincingly so, in my opinion, by Christine Fell in a most important work (1991). She demonstrates that the cognates of the word *rune* did not carry a pagan meaning for the Anglo-Saxon Christians. The connection with "magic, incantation, charm, superstition, pagan belief, etc." was actually imported with the Scandinavian invasions in the ninth century onwards. Influence from the Continent must also be taken into account (Fell 1991:228). We are still waiting for a similar study to be carried out on Scandinavian material, but it seems clear that the runes themselves were considered as a gift from the gods in that region, at least around the year 500, since the Swedish runestone from Noleby talks about "divine rune" with the same words as were in the Old Norse Poetic Edda from the thirteenth century (but used roots from pagan times [Jansson 1987:9]). Even so, however, there is nothing that directly connects divine origin with magic, nor is there any evidence of how runes were viewed during the first couple of centuries of their use, other than that they were utilized as a perfectly plain and serviceable means of writing.

For obvious reasons it is very difficult to come to any conclusions about the social and cultural context of these earliest inscriptions, the purpose of the runic texts, or the status of writing in Germanic society. Yet the *lack* of certain kinds of texts is most illuminating. By studying what runic writing was *not*, we may get hints of what it *was*. We may thus note the complete absence of any inscriptions dealing with cult, administration, literature, law, and so on. Later on, there are a few inscriptions which may have to do with cult and literature, but even counting these poor remnants one cannot escape the conclusion that Germanic culture was oral in principle, and that whatever purpose writing served it was not anything remotely similar to Latin literacy of the time. On this point I concur with Bengt Odenstedt (1990:173), the author of the latest monograph on this topic, who ends his book with the conclusion: "The art of writing was a luxury which Germanic people had seen Romans practise and which they no doubt envied and tried to imitate, with very little success."

This vacuum of sophisticated or lengthy inscriptions cannot be due to chance. As Anders Bæksted (1952:134) has shown, the extant inscriptions must be representative of the whole corpus, even though it cannot make up more than a fraction of what was originally produced. One should also note that the nature of the inscriptions seems to remain unchanged for approximately two centuries. If the datings are at all correct, we do not enter a new stage until around the year AD 400, when an era of changes in language, contents, medium, and style is inaugurated. This later stage, however, need not concern us here. Suffice it to say that the earliest inscriptions appear toward the end of the second century, in the form of an explosion around the year AD 200, and that the inscriptions are quite simple at first with no great variation as to their content.

Why were the runes invented?

We may now start speculating on possible reasons behind the creation of the runes. It has been noted that runic inscriptions spring up almost simultaneously in southern Scandinavia and northern Germany and Poland. It can be suggested that "strongly Roman-influenced" (Stoklund 1996:114) centers in southern Scandinavia, with a possible hub on the Danish main island of Zealand, were responsible for the spread of the runes, if not necessarily the invention of the runes themselves. I have earlier leaned toward the view that the runes were created some time during the first century AD. I did point out a couple of extremely short first-century inscriptions which could represent the proto-runic stage I assumed reigned for a short time (H. Williams 1997:191). As it turns out, one of these inscriptions does not contain a positive rune-like symbol, as was first believed (Dietz, Marold, and Jöns 1996:184f.), which leaves us with very slender evidence indeed, and evidence pointing to Germanic experimentation with Roman letters that does not necessarily constitute a proto-runic stage. The final nail in the coffin of a first-century origin for runes may prove to be an observation in a yet-unpublished work by the Swedish settlement historian Stefan Brink.[3] He suggests that the runes were invented in one of two periods, either the first half of the first century or the century spanning the year AD 200. He observes that "many objects with runic inscriptions occur in wealthy graves around ca. AD 200. If runes were known and used before this time, one would expect to find some prestigious objects with similar runic inscriptions in graves from the Early Roman Iron Age (especially AD 1–50) . . . , but there are non[e]." Following Stoklund he discusses the power centers of Denmark at the end of the second century. If we accept the hypothesis that runes were spread from romanized centers in northern Germania, it would explain the distribution and chronology of the earliest finds. A later parallel might be the bracteates that start to appear in the fifth century AD. These are imitations of Roman medallions, some of which were given to Germanic chieftains. Gradually the bracteates become more and more Germanicized in iconographic style, and runes also soon replaced letters. If we return to the earliest stage, I will venture the speculation that some differences between runes and Roman letters may be due to a conscious Germanic desire to make something separate of their script and not just to mimic the Latin writing system. We cannot prove any degree of conscious striving in this direction, unless it be the deviations from the Latin letter values discussed above. Many of the objective differences between runes and letters may have practical reasons only, but one cannot help but wonder at other alternatives. The unique and non-alphabetical order of the runes is one point of interest; the use of meaningful names for the runes is another (Table 9.1; see also H. Williams 1997:181–183).

The question of why the runes were invented must be answered by studying how they were used, and I have tried to show that it was not for very advanced purposes. The Germanic tribes were under Roman influence for centuries and more or less directly exposed to the art of writing. In my opinion the most likely theory is that someone invented the runes in the first half of the second century AD and that this invention was soon embraced and possibly adapted by the highest class in Germanic society. This class chose to mark various objects with runes, often to manifest ownership or donorship. There were, however, other aims at play as well. Spearheads were given names and marked accordingly, and markers' formulae are also well represented. A tentative division of the types of artifacts carrying runic inscriptions might be one that separates owned/given objects such as brooches, named objects such as weapons, and, lastly, manufactured objects such as equipment details and utensils. Of these, only the second group lends itself easily to interpretations beyond the mundane. If a spearhead is named *Prober* it may certainly be done so with magical functions in mind. We need to voice two reservations, though, before accepting this possibility with all its implications. Objects may be given names for other purposes; that is, just because a boat is called *Speedy* does not prove that its owner believes in the power of magic. Moreover, even if there is a magical intent behind the name as such, this fact proves nothing about the magic of the text itself or the graphemes used to write it. All scripts may certainly be employed for supernatural purposes without inherently imbuing the textual medium with such properties.

All in all, I cannot escape the impression that runes were used for very limited purposes. I believe that Anders Bæksted came very close to the truth when he stated that runes really did not have any practical function (1952:134, 137). Perhaps their function as a concrete manifestation of visible speech was all that mattered. Even the act of writing gibberish is very powerful. Just having your own name on an object, or the name of whoever fashioned it or gave it to you, is intrinsically satisfying for social and psychological reasons. Owning or giving away such items must have been an efficient means of marking alliances and group membership.

With the view of the earliest runic inscriptions that I have outlined in the latter part of this chapter, there follows a shift in attitude toward the nature of runic origins. There are originally neither magical nor practical inducements for inventing or using runes. This should come as no surprise, since the same is true for some other scripts as well. Rex Wallace (1989:123) observes: "Precisely how and for what purpose(s) Latins first learned the art of writing remain something of a mystery." He also finds evidence to suggest "that writing was acquired by the wealthiest families as a symbol of prestige" (Wallace 1989:123).

A "symbol of prestige" is a good enough reason for runes, also.

Notes

1. The best graphemic analysis of the older runes is found in Antonsen (1978).
2. In my original presentation I described the derivation of ʞ from K as problematic, since I could not explain why this shape failed to be maintained as *K. At the Sundance symposium a student at Brigham Young University, Christy Barber, was kind enough to point out that my own graphemic rules would forbid such a development. A rune *K would contain a full-length vertical line, I, plus a vertical angle, 〈, but single angles are never allowed to be of full height. Therefore the rune had to consist of a full-length vertical line plus two horizontal angles, i.e. I + ˅ + ∧. I wish to thank Ms. Barber for her sharp insight.
3. The following extracts are from an e-mail message sent by Dr. Brink to the author, March 2000, and quoted with his permission.

10 | Writing in early Mesoamerica

STEPHEN D. HOUSTON

From about 500 years before Christ until the beginning of the Common era, the peoples of Mesoamerica innovated, used, and developed a series of graphic systems that encoded language: in short, they created "writing" where none existed before, almost certainly in isolation from Old World inputs. That such systems were writing by any definition of the word (cf. Damerow 1999b:4–5; Gelb 1963:58) is now beyond dispute, especially in the case of Maya script (Coe 1999). This chapter reviews how these developments came about in the initial centuries of script generation in Mesoamerica, challenges misconceptions held by specialists within this region and those outside – that Maya is the earliest script, that Maya is monosyllabic, that all relevant scripts are well understood (cf. Boltz 2000:4, 15; DeFrancis 1989:50) – and offers a set of perspectives that builds on, and responds to, valuable earlier treatments (e.g., Coe 1976; Justeson 1986; Justeson and Mathews 1990; Marcus 1976b; Prem 1971). It begins by reviewing basic concepts and problems and then addresses the iconographic and onomastic basis of Mesoamerican writing, along with three major traditions, Zapotec, Isthmian, and early Mayan, none of which supports an optimistic prognosis for full interpretation.

Basic concepts and problems

A necessary step in understanding the development of writing systems in Mesoamerica is to sort out basic approaches. How, for example, do we model script development? Most such attempts involve attention to three features: space, time, and script boundary (Coe 1976; Justeson *et al.* 1985; Justeson and Mathews 1990; Marcus 1976b; Prem 1971, 1973). The first two features are self-explanatory – when and where a writing system was used. The third simply means that certain scripts share enough features to be regarded as distinct systems. They may, and usually do, have internal variability, but that heterogeneity is of an entirely different order in comparison to the attributes of other writing systems. A script with pronounced boundaries will have attributes that immediately distinguish it from its neighbors in time and space; a script with weaker boundaries will need closer scrutiny before it can be clearly defined.

One way of understanding such boundaries is in terms of "open" and "closed" writing systems (Houston 1994b). Eric Wolf first applied these labels in an entirely different context, to certain kinds of peasant societies (1955:462). "Open" implied a near-constant state of interaction with other societies, "closed" quite the opposite, having the connotation of a marked state of isolation. As with any social typology, the terms do not correspond precisely to any one society, nor are they altogether successful in characterizing the actual history of peasant communities (Monaghan 1995:61–62; Wolf 1986:327). They do, however, emphasize an important point, that some properties of societies – or writing systems – transcend or supersede local conditions while others accentuate them. The irony is that terms which fail to work for Wolf's peasants may apply persuasively to writing systems: thus, an "open" writing system serves the needs of diverse cultures and languages; a "closed" one relates to a *particular* culture, language, or set of related languages (Houston, Baines, and Cooper, 2003) – it will tend toward greater linearity as a relatively clear record of language as well as greater self-sufficiency or abstraction in graphic terms. In some respects, this distinction seems to operate across a continuum, but there are also indications of a fundamental divide in strategy, an "open" script being far more likely to require pictographic aids, a "closed" one, with fuller commitment to linguistic transparency, having the capacity to occur on its own, within a closed frame that excludes such aids.

In general, the writing systems used in the eastern part of Mesoamerica have a "closed" nature. They are maladroit in recording other, unrelated languages but supremely effective in reproducing their own, often including many linguistic and syntactic nuances. Mayan script or glyphs exemplify this class of writing system and represent standing proof against Ignace Gelb's claim that writing in the New World was "limited" by its failure to use "*systematic* phonography" (Gelb 1963:59; emphasis in original; as many have pointed out, Gelb expressed little but contempt for New World civilizations, which could not "stand comparison with the Oriental cultures" he esteemed [Gelb 1963:58]; this attitude can also be found among some archaeologists of the time, including the prominent Old World specialists V. Gordon Childe and Mortimer Wheeler [Hawkes 1982:278]). Few foreign words appear in Mayan script. When they do, the words are garbled, and have already been loaned and phonologically massaged into a Mayan language, in this instance Yukatek (Taube and Bade 1991; Whittaker 1986). In contrast, "open" writing systems are found with some abundance in western Mesoamerica. Most contain elements that make sense only in particular languages, leading Janet Berlo to describe these words as "embedded texts" that exist within narrative pictographies (Berlo 1983:2–17). Yet, to a strong extent, these scripts and the information they contain could probably be understood across language boundaries. A Mixtec pictorial, for example, can be easily glossed in English without doing violence to its general meaning (e.g. Byland and J. Pohl 1994:176; van der Loo 1994:84). Some time ago, David Kelley made a similar observation, suggesting that the translinguistic nature of these scripts made special sense in societies emphasizing "economic or historical information," so that tribute rolls could be compiled and interpreted in several different languages (Kelley 1976:166). Kelly also pointed out that, rather than being "primitive," these scripts admirably suited the needs of their societies, an early instance in which Ignace Gelb's evolutionism came under negative scrutiny.

It is striking that the earlier the scripts in Mesoamerica, the more likely they are to be "closed." One of the so-called "Danzantes" from Monte Albán, Oaxaca, of uncertain date but probably from a century or so before Christ, displays a long sequence of non-calendrical signs in single-column order, a good illustration of the transparent linguistic commitment in closed systems (Fig. 10.1[a]; Urcid Serrano 2001:fig. 4.47). A similar, relatively long sequence occurs on La Venta Monument 13, perhaps the earliest linear text in Mesoamerica, dating to about 500 BC or, according to some estimates, a few centuries later (Fig. 10.1b; Karl Taube, personal communication, 2002). At Monte Albán, texts from c. AD 450 to 800 become acutely "open," and earlier experiments with linear text disappear aside from long sequences of day signs and superposed registers of paired couples (Zaachila Stone 1; Masson and Orr 1998; Urcid Serrano 2001:fig. 6.9). Even later texts from this area have lost their "closed" quality entirely and appear to be little different from documents elsewhere in Postclassic Mesoamerica, regardless of language zone (e.g. the Lienzo de Guevea; Seler 1906). Similarly, Isthmian writing of the Tehuantepec and surrounding regions is patently "closed" because of its long linear texts, a pattern that continues well into the middle of the first millennium AD, as on Cerro de las Mesas Stela 8 (Stirling 1943). Later texts from the general region drop this "closed" quality and monumental inscriptions become, as in Veracruz, severely reduced to a system of dates serving as nominal glyphs (Wilkerson 1984:110–114).

Certain choices were doubtless made by script communities in response to events and influences of a broader sort. In the last few years scholars have become increasingly aware that, far from being devoid of writing, the great

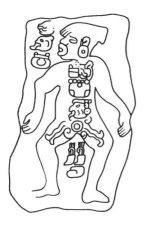 

Fig. 10.1 Early linear texts: (a) Monte Albán Danzante, MA-D-55 (Urcid Serrano 2001:fig. 4.47); (b) La Venta Monument 13 (Coe 1968:148, after drawing by Miguel Covarrubias).

Mexican city of Teotihuacan possessed an elaborate emblematic script that appeared to combine isolated word signs of a nominal and titular nature with pictographic or narrative settings. This iconographic property is precisely what made the signs hard to identify at first (Taube 2000b:15). Teotihuacan script began to flourish about AD 350 to 450, so its dates are suggestive in view of developments in Mesoamerican scripts. The city is known to have exercised a profound impact on areas far distant, including the Valley of Oaxaca (e.g. the Lápida de Bazán; Taube 2000b:fig. 30.d). Thereafter, many areas under Teotihuacan influence employed glyphic styles that were decidedly "open," including spare nominal signs at El Tajín, Veracruz (Kampen 1972:figs. 32–38), apparent titles and name glyphs at Xochicalco, Morelos (Berlo 1989:30–40), painted glyphs at Cacaxtla (Foncerrada de Molina 1982), as well as sites as far distant as Chichen Itza, Yucatan, where non-Maya signs seem to label non-Maya personages (Maudslay 1889–1902, III:pls. 38, 45–47, 49–50; Morris, Charlot, and Morris 1931:311).

The question before us, and one that is inherently difficult to answer, is whether this new strategy reflected a historical practice emanating from the pluralistic, polyglot polity centered on Teotihuacan. An exact sequence of choices is impossible to reconstruct, but it is plausible that Teotihuacan, whose memory was strongly cherished in Mesoamerican tradition, established a practice that became dominant in areas most directly under its influence. Those examples of Teotihuacan writing that are the most "closed," i.e., linear, with many signs, including what may be quotative particles, occur closest to the Maya region, on mirror backs and other objects from the

Fig. 10.2 Linear Teotihuacan script (Taube 2000b:20, 34–35, fig. 27).

Pacific coast of Guatemala (Fig. 10.2; Taube 2000b:20, 34–35, fig. 27). A working hypothesis might be that the more polyglot the elites of an area – the Pacific Coast of Guatemala (Maya, Xinca, Pupuluca, and Pipil [?] [Chinchilla Mazariegos 1996:533–534, 550]), Chichen Itza (Maya and Nahuatl [?]), Cacaxtla (Mayan and other indeterminate languages?) – the more inclined they would be to use "open" script and to underscore its relation to Teotihuacan, the preeminent, multi-ethnic Mesoamerican civilization of the first millennium AD. Only among the Maya does "closed" script continue to flourish, and then in codices that could be consulted by relatively few people (Houston *et al.* 2003). Maya glyphs expired soon after the Spanish conquest, while "open" forms in Mexico continued to find a role in colonial court cases and, in general, as a preferred means of formal indigenous expression (Boone 2000:245–249).

Another issue in conceptualizing early writing in Mesoamerica is how to present its development in graphic form. One approach is to group scripts by attribute, some having bars and dots for numbers, others making use of the Maya Long Count (a place-notational system that implied a mythogenic account as its starting point), yet others a list of more subtle traits, including the shape of day signs and double column formats (Justeson *et al.* 1985:table 16). These tabulations intersect with space and time to help create block-like flow charts whose outlines indicate script boundaries (see above) but whose arrows, issuing laterally or debouching into later scripts, indicate the influence of one script on another (e.g. Prem 1973:fig. 1; Urcid Serrano 2001:fig. 1.2).

Typologies of script directly involve historical traditions. For some scholars, these blocks of writing systems can be boiled down to two major legacies, both emerging from iconographic traditions of the Early and Middle Formative periods, in a time roughly coincident with the first half of the first millennium BC. One has been described as "Oaxacan," the other as "Southeastern," in large part because of their zone of initial florescence (Justeson *et al.* 1985:38; Justeson and Mathews 1990:107). However, given the evidence in favor of dramatic breaks *within* script traditions, as "open" conventions of writing dominate "closed" ones, this distinction between Oaxacan and Southeastern traditions seems misleading. Scripts are concrete practices that associate with communicative strategies: they are not Darwinian organisms that inherit attributes but, in a sense, Lamarckian entities that acquire such attributes during their period of use.

One of the primary problems here may be the use of biological metaphors, including "offshoot," "descendant," "branches," "descend," "co-evolved" (Justeson and Mathews 1990:107, 113, 120). Such language is evocative but, on closer reflection, unhelpful. Communicative systems, graphic or otherwise, do not operate in the same way as biological organisms with fixed packages of DNA. Rather, they change in tandem with other systems of communication, and in response to historical circumstances. Still, choices made at earlier times clearly affected later outcomes, making it necessary to recognize scripts as traditional practices that have both inertial tendencies and a propensity to particular directions of change. For example, having become "open," central Mexican script does not return to linearity and syntactic specificity until the advent of a new model – Roman script – as may be seen in the early Colonial Codex Xolotl (Dibble 1980). This document, a form of cartographic history, contains long sequences of hieroglyphs, some still difficult to understand, that differ substantially from far more abbreviated texts of an earlier date (Houston and Taube 2000:fig. 13c). It seems unlikely that this form of writing derives from some poorly documented script tradition. Instead, it probably patterns itself on the lengthy phonic writing that had become available from the Spaniards. Nonetheless, the Codex continues to operate within an indigenous idiom, an example of subtle copying that persists, for sociolinguistic reasons, in emphasizing local practices.

Another problem in looking at script origins and development in Mesoamerica is a basic one of sampling. For the Maya, thousands of texts are available from the Classic period, but from the earliest periods, those most relevant to this book, the sample is exceedingly small and heterogeneous (see Bagley, this volume). Although isolated texts from a variety of locations in the highlands of Guatemala share a few signs, no credible argument can be made for a complete overlap of systems. The incised text on Kaminaljuyu "Stela" 10, actually a throne fragment, which probably dates to around the time of Christ, shares at most three signs with Isthmian script (Fig. 10.3; MS49, MS101/103, MS129; Macri and Stark 1993). Connections with the later Maya signary are just as weak, involving no more than a few glyphs, none in any explainable order: one sign, identical to later *winik* ("person") or *winal* ("unit of 20 days") glyphs, does not appear in contexts that are obviously pertinent to those readings. The few other texts from the same site, such as Kaminaljuyu Stela 21 (Parsons 1986:fig. 157), are short and display no demonstrable overlap with the longer text from Stela 10. What this means is that scholars cannot easily determine patterns of sign equivalence or allography (substitutable forms), what the overall system might have looked like, or how the script might have functioned. It is not even clear that these texts belong to the same system or to a cluster of highly localized scripts. Worse, most of these early texts have been shifted from their original position or appear on unprovenanced portable objects, making it difficult to establish that particular texts belong to a more or less synchronous system. The period in which we most want to understand Maya writing – that of its coalescence and broader use – is the time in which the dating is the least secure. Zapotec script is in no better position, in that monuments can only be dated to, at best, 250-year spans calibrated by rather gross archaeological phases rather than by internal dating (e.g. Urcid Serrano 2001:4, fig. 4.16).

The two difficulties – poor sampling and uncertain chronology – suggest that an appropriate analogy might be the ever-wavering interpretation of hominid fossils (Tattersall 1995:229–246). Every year, seemingly, new finds of unexpected morphology appear, with dramatic consequences for any statement of evolutionary relationship. Recent chronometric dates of Javanese specimens of *Homo erectus* push the diaspora from Africa ever further back than hitherto suspected; fresh finds of aberrant Australopithecines in Kenya point to early evidence of upright posture. Some would even suggest that the fossil record – the analogue of a corpus of surviving texts – represents "only about three percent of all the primate species that have ever existed" (Tattersall 1995:231). The earlier one goes, the more sketchy the

Writing in early Mesoamerica 281

Fig. 10.3 Kaminaljuyu "Stela" 10 texts (after rubbing supplied by Albert Davletshin).

narrative that can be devised, a sobering reminder of the taxing issues in understanding the early writing of Mesoamerica. At some point the analogy fails: palaeoanthropologists deal with the residue of biological evolution and vastly enlarged frameworks of time. Yet the example of such research should guide us to an attitude of expectant humility. Unexpected discoveries may dramatically revise current beliefs, as happened with the discovery of the

Isthmian La Mojarra Stela 1 in 1986 (Winfield Capitaine 1988). The present sample of early texts neither is representative nor adequately reveals broader patterns of development.

There are two final methodological problems. One is the persistent temptation to use the known to explain the unknown, extending understandings from a better-understood script to one that is less well understood. In studying early scripts this can be an overwhelming enticement. In the first place, we naturally use whatever tools are available and, in the second, we often hope that historical connections existed between writing systems, one contributing elements to another. Thus, the closer the scripts in time and space, the more reasonable the assumption that similar signs had similar values, a glyph in Isthmian having the same reading or iconic motivation as a sign in Maya that, perhaps, looks like the Isthmian example. A linked assumption is that these correlations become more credible if, supposedly, one system (Isthmian) led to the other (Maya) or vice versa. This approach and all the premises it involves must be treated with the greatest possible caution. Simple forms, such as those for hills or other elements that relate to understood iconography, are one thing; ones that rely more on the eye-of-faith and comparisons between signs of uncertain iconic origin are another (see below, for discussion of the Isthmian problem). At present, many specialists working with Isthmian were trained in Mayanist scholarship (e.g. L. Anderson 1993; Macri and Stark 1993; Justeson and Kaufman 1993, 1997, 2001a, 2001b). This becomes disquieting when patterns in the better-known Maya script are discerned in Isthmian. Is interpretive bias truly under control? It might be better to start with a presumption that no such correlations exist and then make each plausible case as carefully as possible. Another method is comparing later Maya glyphs with earlier ones. The presumption of connection is stronger, obviously, but carries with it palpable dangers when the resemblances appear to be forced. The earlier the Maya writing, the more imprudent this approach (see below).

A final methodological problem is the tendency in Mesoamerican and Maya studies to accept glottochronological estimates at face value or with only minimal adjustment (Grube 1994:185; Justeson *et al.* 1985:14, 58, 61–62). Glottochronology is a statistical procedure introduced into Mexican linguistics by Morris Swadesh (1967) and later implemented in Maya research by Terrence Kaufman (1974). It purports to date language change according to several questionable assumptions, almost none of which is given credence in other linguistic regions (e.g. Nurse 1997:366, commenting on Africa). One articulate critic working with Mesoamerican materials has repeatedly drawn attention to the deficiencies of the method and the inherent dangers in accepting its dates (Campbell 1984:4). In Mesoamerica, other data, when available, point consistently to conclusions that diverge from those of glottochronology. Glottochronology and lexicostatistics can be used to propose an initial breakup of Uto-Aztecan between 5,000 and 6,000 BP, while other, more persuasive measures suggest an approximate date millennia later (J. Hill 2001:929). Classic Maya writing, which offers exquisite temporal control, indicates problems with prior glottochronological estimates, in this case involving not a shortened but a deepened chronology for the detachment of certain language "branches" (Houston 2000; Houston, Robertson, and Stuart 2000).

The entrenchment of glottochronology in Mesoamerican studies should be a cause of real concern. One worry is that it supplies what are likely to be misleading chronological brackets. By following its conclusions, epigraphers can expect *a priori* to see particular linguistic features in script in one period and not others. By this means a problematic method has come to establish the parameters of acceptable inference, transforming them from a set of hypotheses to a category of hard evidence. For archaeologists, there is another concern that is even more troubling, namely, attempts by linguists to correlate cultural periods and language change (e.g. Josserand 1975; Kaufman 1976). The possibility of tautology is great, especially when scholars align glottochronological estimates with ceramic periods. Lying behind the alignment is a more subtle implication of causality, in that change in language is assumed to explain, or to be explained by, change in artifacts. Yet, there is no reason to think that shifts in ceramic inventory, the usual means of distinguishing periods, would have any linkage to language break-up or phonological shifts.

Linguistic correlations are especially relevant to the Olmec civilization, which coalesced during the last centuries of the second millennium BC on the Gulf Coast of Mexico. The Olmec phenomenon is widely assumed to have been formed and spread by Mixe-Zoquean speakers (Campbell and Kaufman 1976; see below). The reasoning is that many broadly disseminated words for plants, maize preparation, and some ritual and calendrical terms are probable loans from Mixe-Zoquean into other, contiguous languages. The Olmec and, by extension, Mixe-Zoquean speakers would have dominated the "mother civilization" or *cultura madre* that disseminated these elements. This proposal has direct bearing on the Isthmian or so-called "Epi-Olmec" script for the reason that the distribution of that writing system roughly accords with the colonial distribution of Mixe-Zoquean languages and, far earlier, with the presence of objects and sculptures that employ Olmec artistic conventions. Thus, the proposal specifies linguistic and cultural continuity in a large region over a period of some 2,500 years. The claim is viable but must remain tenuous in the absence of independent lines of evidence.

Iconography and first writing

The first, broadly distributed system of codified symbols or iconography occurred within Olmec civilization or, put more conservatively, within a particular style that swept across Mesoamerica, especially in the Middle Preclassic period (*c.* 900 to 500 BC). There is much debate about the nature of these symbols, principally as to whether they possessed exclusively local meanings or formed part of a pan-regional system that transcended geographic regions and ethnic and linguistic groups, perhaps going even beyond the boundaries of Olmec civilization itself (cf. Flannery and Marcus 1999:13; Taube 1995). The consistent and patterned use of motifs, often in relation to complex pictorial designs, suggests strongly that the first view, although endorsed by many archaeologists, is misinformed. At the same time, the symbols would have had to have been understood locally. Otherwise there would scarcely have been any motivation to use them. An over-emphasis on regionalism, however, fails to take account of the consistency that informs much of the system, particularly in the Middle Formative period.

Codified symbols represent an important first step, although not an inevitable one, to the creation of writing. Such signs, often iconic in origin, with recognizable referents in nature or artifacts, have been excised from their pictorial context, a hand depicted in isolation from an arm, a headdress from the body that wore it (Justeson and Mathews 1990:90–93). Olmec iconography has long been known to express a *pars pro toto* principle, in which a part implies, or stands for, a larger whole. This enables a certain economy of representation and permits the clustering of elements that imply yet more complex, if implicit, orderings. But it would be incorrect to see such clusterings as writing per se which, following most authors in this volume, can be defined as graphs that record elements of language. In Olmec iconography, the juxtaposition of elements refers to spatial organization, place names, and icons of centrality, including directional symbolism: the elements exist, not as text, but as features of a landscape, including primordial, cosmic ones (Reilly 1995:38–39). In this sense, these images or graphs might be best described as *emblems*, which join elements into meaningful arrangements yet do not clearly record sound.

One such emblem is recorded, like so many of its kind, on a greenstone celt (Fig. 10.4[a]; Tate and Reilly 1995:pl. 127). The emblem combines two major

Writing in early Mesoamerica 285

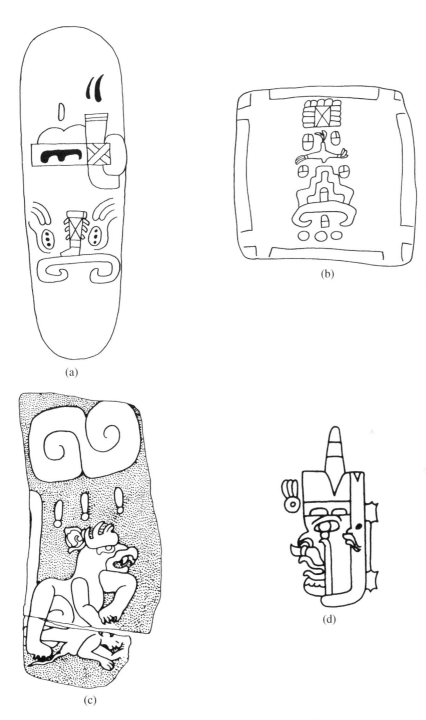

Fig. 10.4 Olmec icons: (a) toponym (Tate and Reilly 1995:pl. 127); (b) another toponym (Tate and Reilly 1995:pl. 131); (c) cloud icon, Chalcatzingo Monument 31 (Taube 1995:fig. 24c); and (d) emergence cleft (Taube 2000a:fig. 2f).

elements. At the bottom is a place name indicated by a lower leg with ankle and shin lashings, a curl that probably represents the bottom of a "hill" sign, and symmetrically placed elements that resemble vegetal growth. A headdress appears above. The arrangement recalls later Mesomerican place names, in which a specific toponym occurs above the hill. The headdress may indicate dominion over that location. Another incised object, also of greenstone, shows a more elaborate hill sign surmounted by vegetation with directional symbolism and a headdress (Fig. 10.4[b]; Tate and Reilly 1995:pl. 131). The importance of these objects is that they demonstrate the Olmec origin of signs that continue throughout the development of Mesoamerican writing systems: (1) hills to indicate specific place names, and (2) headdresses to designate lordly titles. A third sign that continues from Olmec times into the Maya Postclassic is one that stands for "clouds" (Fig. 10.4[c]; Reilly 1996); others would be the symbol for "wind," often worn as a T-shaped jewel around the neck (Karl Taube, personal communication, 1999), and a convention for "birth" that expresses a metaphor taken from vegetal emergence (Fig. 10.4[d]). It is also firmly established that both the Olmec and the Classic Maya perceived stela as celts or adzes driven into the ground (Porter 1992), a revealing instance of Olmec play with scale and monumentality (see Hung 1995:4, for a culturally informed definition of these concepts).

A knowledgeable viewer could look at these elements and attach a word to them. However, that procedure of lexical identification would be irrelevant to apprehending the full meaning of the emblem. Places and titles linked to them could be understood in any language, a benefit of an "open," inclusive system of communication that bridged many different groups. Yet the elements are not sequenced. They have no fixed reading order. Only the overall emblem, each part taking meaning from the whole, makes sense of its constituents. As a consequence, if writing is the recording and ordering of lexemes, then this is not writing. It does not possess true linearity that can be made to record expandable syntax. It is, however, a necessary precursor to script, consisting of codified signs that are organized systematically and employed consistently over wide areas. An iconographic "community," including people versed in an arcane system of signs, would logically prefigure a script "community" that learns and uses writing.

An argument has been made that celts themselves contributed to the formation of script in Mesoamerica (Justeson and Mathews 1990:94–97). The columnar disposition of emblems on greenstone objects, compressed and framed by the narrow edges of the celts, supposedly led to segmentation and vertical sequencing "homologous to . . . clause-level conceptual structures of language" (Justeson and Mathews 1990:94). There is little question that the earliest texts in Mesoamerica appeared in vertical columns. The Maya double-column format is relatively late in the development of Maya glyphs and, in any case, simply represents a division of a single column into two parts, read with a general vertical drift but with horizontal scanning within rows of the column.

The assertion, however, that rectangular formats, whether on stela or celts, led to glyphic columns is almost impossible to prove. It is true that the columnar arrangement of early Chinese script may derive from the bamboo sticks on which, hypothetically, it was recorded (Gaur 1992:50). Once made, however, the decision to dispose texts vertically, with reading order from top to bottom, will *always* yield rectangular texts, longer than they are wide. The double-column format would have resulted in texts that were squarer in outline; the presence of hieroglyphs on stairway risers and, later still, across lintel faces contributed to an opposing tendency toward horizontal arrangements of text. Texts accompanying images with many figures (scenes probably influenced by mural art or screenfold book compositions) used both vertical and horizontal dispositions freely; unfortunately, the chronology and orientation of text placement is a subject that has yet to be studied rigorously and systematically in Maya glyphs. There is a cross-cultural tendency for texts to be read top-to-bottom. Ogam from Celtic areas of the British Isles is a rare exception, and even that eventually traverses down the right-hand side of the stone on which it is carved (McManus 1991). Perhaps a more compelling motivation for this general reading order has less to do with the origin of script on celts and stelae than a primeval human propensity for scanning the head first, where identity, emotional orientation, and intent are recognized and evaluated, and then down the body, which signals less of such matters. This would in itself encourage the cross-cultural tendency toward top-to-bottom rather than bottom-to-top reading orders.

Another claim is that Middle Preclassic (or Formative) period seals record textual elements arranged in linear fashion. These elements appear on small clay or stone cylinders that, when dipped in paint, were rolled across skin, paper or other ductile materials (Justeson *et al.* 1985:fig. 2; Kelley 1966; Lee 1969:71–87; Tate and Reilly 1995:297; Taube 1988:43). Some images of Olmec bodies show finely incised designs that may, in the original, have been produced in this fashion, a seal imparting its design to skin; yet other designs were more likely to have been tattoos, in which multiple faces interplayed on the skin of the tattooed, as identities shifted and merged (Tate and Reilly 1995:140, 221, 268). Most likely, these tattoos were made, as in Polynesia, with black or red pigments and picked out with small bone or wood combs, chisels or sharks' teeth (Gell 1993:246–247; see comb from Tlapacoya, Basin of Mexico [Niederberger 2000:177], and hafted shark tooth from Manatí, Veracruz [Ortiz and Rodríguez 2000:fig. 20]). Virtually all the designs that can be easily interpreted are purely iconographic, and the lone example thought to be a text, from the highland Mexican site of Tlatilco, shows a well-known icon of centrality, a flower, and a deity head (Reilly 1994:242–243). Repetition of the design as it rolled out on the receiving surface would have made it difficult to determine where the "text" began.

Names and bodies

In Mesoamerica, the body marked and advertised personhood. Signs in headdresses identified people, and clothing accorded with rank (Kelley 1982; Houston and Stuart 1998). In general, depictions of actions signaled personal category. Captors could be contrasted with captives by means of distinct, stylized gestures and relative positioning. These features persisted throughout the Precolumbian period, but found their origin in the iconography of sculptures from the transition between the Early and Middle Formative periods (*c.* 900 BC) and perhaps some centuries before. Here, in glyphic markers of personal identity, lay the origins of Mesoamerican writing (D. Stuart 1995).

Among the clearest examples are the monumental sculptures from the Olmec site of San Lorenzo. The celebrated colossal heads of this settlement (Fig. 10.5; e.g. Monuments 1, 2, 4, 5, 17), most dating to the period between 1150 and 900 BC, show marked differences in their headdresses. It has been suggested that these differences correspond to portraiture, each head relating to a different ruler (Diehl and Coe 1995:23; independent observation by David Grove). At San Lorenzo, some represent birds, others distinctive tassels and beadwork. Monuments dating to *c.* 900 to 600 BC at La Venta, Tabasco, also display conspicuous differences in headgear (e.g. Altar 5), making it likely that they performed a similar identifying function. A series of sensitively carved masks from Río Pesquero, Veracruz, extend only to the lower forehead, as though they could be coupled with substitutable or interchangeable headdresses (Tate and Reilly 1995:pl. 31, 187–192). This may also explain the bald or clean-shaven pates on other Olmec pieces, which appear to have been supports or mannequins for perishable clothing and other identifiers (Tate and Reilly 1995:pls. 8–10, 22). The plainness of these images, as in the wooden sculptures from El Manatí, Veracruz (Ortiz and Rodríguez 2000:figs.19–24), may simply reflect their

Fig. 10.5 Nominal elements in headdress, San Lorenzo Monument 2 (Coe and Diehl 1980, I:fig. 425).

use as grounding for elaborate, distinguishing adornments of less enduring form.

Not all headdresses in Olmec imagery, however, fit this pattern. Some are general ornaments indicating the presence or impersonation of certain deities (Taube 1995:107–108). Such god impersonations occur in the Oxtotitlan painting from Guerrero, Mexico (Grove 1970), where an individual appears within the plumage and head of a quetzal bird (Taube 2000a:304). Another complication stems from the evidence itself. There is insufficient redundancy of names from monument to monument to demonstrate that the headdresses are purely nominal in function. Still, the view that these represent names remains the best possibility, in part because this practice accords with later headdresses among the Maya and Mixtec, peoples who often used such headgear to record names (Houston and Stuart 1998). One of the earliest uses of nominal signs from the Maya area occurs on Kaminaljuyu Monument 65 (Parsons 1986:fig. 149), in which three lords on thrones display headdresses with variable glyphic elements, including a sign that also occurs in Isthmian script (MS28). Each lord has, to either side, a kneeling captive, a few shown naked in a common Mesoamerican convention for humiliation; all but one of these captives bear nominal glyphs. The limited content of the monument makes any supposition of its meaning difficult to prove, but it seems likely that the scene shows consecutive rulers, underscoring their prowess in warfare (Kaplan 2000:191). A crucial point is that, if correctly identified as names, the headdresses would be *lexemic*, that is, they would inherently correspond to words or strings of words (D. Stuart 1995). These signs would differ from writing only in the sense that they had not yet detached physically from the persons they identified. To put this differently, the signifier (the name) remained in the same existential field as the signified (the person so identified). They were tethered to one another, and not floating to the side as glyphic captions would begin to do somewhat later in Mesoamerica.

The physical detachment of signs from the body set the stage for texts to appear. Recording of lexemes occurred in headdresses. Yet the first decoupling of identifiers from the body did not take place until the Middle Formative period, between 900 and 600 BC. A stela from Amuco, Guerrero, although imprecisely provenanced, shows a figure in Olmec style with a detached sign to viewer's left of the headdress (Paradis 1981:fig. 4). Nonetheless, the important point is that the existential divide between signified and signifier remained porous throughout the history of Mesoamerican script. In Maya writing, nominal glyphs could easily detach from text and shift back into the existential field of the image. In this, glyphs belong firmly to the category of iconic scripts such as Egyptian hieroglyphs or Luwian, and contrast with those scripts, such as cuneiform and Chinese, which begin iconically and shift within a few centuries to progressive degrees of abstraction (see Bagley, Baines, Englund, and F. Bottéro, this volume; note, however, that "abstraction" may exist partly in the eye of the beholder, as later users of Chinese continued to recognize some iconicity in signs [William Boltz, personal communication, 2000]). The sustained iconicity of Maya glyphs and Egyptian hieroglyphs requires some explanation, for which several possibilities come to mind: (1) iconicity assists sign recognition, especially in cases where the inventory of signs is great, as in heavily logographic systems; and (2) iconicity reflects an aesthetic impulse to downplay the seam between text and image, especially in systems that prize pictorial displays.

Given the high number of logographs in cuneiform, an abstract, non-iconic system, the first explanation is less compelling than the second, although a case can be made that higher levels of iconicity promote some limited literacy in a general population, a jaguar head (as part of a ruler's name) thus being made broadly recognizable (Houston 1994a:37; Kubler 1973:162). The second explanation, which emphasizes a predominant pictorial orientation, does not account for the cursive, abstract forms of Egyptian writing, which existed alongside hieroglyphs for millennia. Yet it is consistent with the use of iconic signs in areas meant for perusal by more than one person, namely, in more "public" settings of text reception.

Perhaps the most compelling view would be to see the sustained iconicity of hieroglyphic scripts as an existential statement that a signifier carried with it the divisible essence of the signified, or, to put this another way, objects created by artifice could also embody less tangible properties, such as vitality and identity, that were not devised by the artificer. The person crafting the image became less an illusionist, a mimetic specialist, than a theurgical practitioner who infused the inanimate with inherent animation (Belting 1994:6; Besançon 2000:55–57; Freedberg 1989:76–81; Kris and Kurz 1979:71–90). Three propositions follow from this. One is ontological, that matter and spirit are not so easily separable in some traditions; another is that neither matter nor spirit is necessarily valorized over the other; and the third is that the injection of animation and vitalization requires an act or series of acts, whether that of image-making or of ritual consecration – the image has a beginning and, in its mutilation or decay, an end. This is precisely the opposite of orthodox Christian tradition, which exalts the spiritual over the material, sometimes to the point of indulging in iconoclastic destruction (Besançon 2000:123–126).

The ontological fusion of spirit and matter accounts for a wide variety of practices in ancient Mesoamerica. Jade beads were thought from Olmec times on to contain the breath and soul force of people, the intrinsic value of this rare material being consistent with vitality itself (Houston and Taube 2000:267). One of the earliest known glyphs, a T-shaped sign for "wind," first becomes apparent on Olmec pectorals hung over the lungs and heart (Karl Taube, personal communication, 1999). Similarly, among the Classic Maya, a good deal of greenstone jewelry appears to contain ancestral references: this is especially clear in the belt ornaments that display the head-depictions and names of ancestors, usually above a suspended set of three celts, each colliding with the other in percussive, musical fashion, possibly in allusion to ancestral speech (D. Stuart, Houston, and Robertson. 1999). Such assemblages go back well into the Late Preclassic period (c. 400 BC to AD 100), although there they appear to commemorate deities rather than kings (e.g. Nakbe Stela 1 [Sharer 1994:fig. 3.5]). Other Classic Maya depictions of ancestors, often only partly embodied, with head, one arm, and the upper torso, also occur as pectorals, worn in the same place as wind-jewels, as though the ornaments equated to ancestral essence (D. Stuart *et al.* 1999). In all such objects, matter seems to have blended with vitality and spirit. Sustained iconicity in Mesoamerican writing may well have expressed a profound disinclination to separate the icon from the existential world in which it originated and in whose life force it shared. A token of this may be the Mesoamerican and, indeed, nearly universal tendency of heads in hieroglyphic scripts to face the direction of reading (here, to the left), as though addressing an actual interlocutor.

If writing is (1) a graphic representation of language, (2) detached from the body of its referent, and (3) disposed into linear sequences that can theoretically expand into greater degrees of syntactic complexity, then writing first appears in Mesoamerica in the century between 600 and 500 BC, as attested on La Venta Monument 13 (Fig. 10.1[b]). This sculpture occurs in a late deposit at La Venta, but, to judge from its upright position, which makes little sense in terms of its image, the carving is likely to have been reset from other locations or carved on an older sculpture, a frequent problem with Olmec sculptures (Drucker, Heizer, and Squier 1959:40). The *terminus ante quem* for the monument – the date before which it must have been carved – should be more or less coincident with the Palangana phase at San Lorenzo, Veracruz, at somewhere between 600 and 400 BC (Coe and Diehl 1980, I:202; Lowe 1989:59; cf. Pye and Clark 2000:fig. 2, for temporal brackets of 600 to 500 BC). For stylistic reasons, Karl Taube prefers a date even later, to the Late Preclassic period (personal communication, 2002). Monument 13 is unusual for its reversed orientation. This may indicate its original, architectural placement toward readers coming from the right and a suggestion that it had a twin, now lost, with the more usual, left-facing reading order. The glyphs include a human footprint to indicate movement – a convention that becomes common from the first millennium on (e.g. a painted text in a cave at El Puente, Tepelmeme de Morelos, Oaxaca [Urcid Serrano 2001:fig. 1.7a]) – and three signs to record what may be a name. Each glyph block equates to a single sign, an archaic pattern that persists throughout most of early Mesoamerica. One sign resembles a tri-lobate blood scroll found in early Zapotec images as well, although without all the same, butterfly-like embellishments (e.g. J. F. Scott 1978:D-47, D-57, J-100).

The La Venta inscription has only one possible contemporary: Monument 3 of San José Mogote, from the Zapotec-speaking area of Oaxaca, Mexico (Marcus 1992:36–38). Monument 3 shows an eviscerated captive and appears to name him with a date in the 260-day sacred calendar; it was common practice in Mesoamerica to assign nominals on the basis of propitious birth dates, even though the day sign identification at San José Mogote remains controversial (cf. Urcid Serrano 2001:184). The date of Monument 3 may be c. 600–500 BC, although some regional specialists dispute this assignment, suggesting a date some few centuries later, perhaps even 200 BC or beyond (Cahn and Winter 1993). The literature on the two sculptures, one from the Olmec "heartland," the other from the Zapotec Highlands, veers between those authorities claiming priority for one monument over the other (Marcus 1992:41–42), but little can be done at present to resolve the question: an earlier date for La Venta Monument 13 would establish a connection to Olmec nominal icons at lowland sites like San Lorenzo; an earlier date for San José Mogote would suggest a more complex origin for script in Mesoamerica – certainly, the style of that monument is distinct from Olmec antecedents. What is striking is that such innovations only came into existence at the *end* of La Venta as a major center and San José Mogote as a regionally distinguished settlement (Flannery and Marcus 1996:139). Similarly, Maya script only begins to flourish at a time when major Formative centers began to collapse (see below). It may be that experiments in communicative practices found a purchase at times of transition rather than when traditional habits held sway.

This section cannot end without addressing recent claims for "Olmec writing" at about 650 BC in La Venta, Tabasco (Pohl, Pope, and von Nagy 2002). The finds consist of two incised greenstone objects of small size. The "signs" are rounded, as Mesoamerican hieroglyphs tend to be, but do not appear to form continuous text or correspond to elements from later scripts, contrary to claims by the authors. The more cautious view of these two objects – a caution not evident in the massive publicity generated by journalists (e.g. www.newscientist.com/news/news.jsp?id=ns99993151) – is that the finds are suggestive yet inconclusive. The stronger likelihood is that they are iconic elements.

Zapotec writing

In the final half of the first millennium BC, writing appeared in relatively small quantity in and around the Valley of Oaxaca, an area known historically to have been associated with the Zapotec language, a sub-branch of the Otomanguean family (Caso 1928:9; Hopkins 1984). The script was used in varying quantities over a period spanning roughly 500 to 400 BC and on to the tenth century AD. Its general themes have been known for some time: disemboweled, castrated, and bloodied captives in various states of agony or post-mortem repose, and, slightly later, apparent conquest slabs memorializing defeated sites along with mummy bundles (García

Moll, Patterson Brown, and Winter 1986; A. G. Miller 1995:fig. 85; Urcid Serrano 2001:fig. 2.6; Whittaker 1992; Winter 1994), culminating in sculptures relating genealogies of a limited sort. Only one monument, from Tomb 9, Xoxocotlan, appears to commemorate a long series of bearded ancestors (Urcid Serrano 2001:fig. 2.3; see also Marcus 1983a). Such beards or long hair also characterize ancestors (*mam*) in Maya script (David Stuart, personal communication, 1998).

The singular property of Zapotec writing is that it can barely be shown to record the Zapotec language or an earlier form of it, likely as that supposition might be: that is, there are few if any direct clues from the script itself to indicate its linguistic connection to Zapotec (Urcid Serrano 2001:21–22). The most comprehensive monograph yet to appear, by Urcid Serrano (2001), devotes over a third of its pages to reconstructing the hieroglyphic calendar, with many details still undecided. Under such conditions, the likelihood of reading the non-calendrical portions of the script seems limited and discussions of its content indecisive. Some longer sequences of signs appear, including strings that repeat from text to text (Urcid Serrano 2001:fig. 6.9), but in few cases can even rebus or homophonic signs be linked to Zapotec terms. The signs themselves very occasionally take suffixes that might assist in decipherment (Urcid Serrano 2001:fig. 6.5), and Urcid Serrano has attempted to demonstrate the existence of logographs in two nominal sequences (Urcid Serrano 2001:figs. 6.3, 6.4). These do not appear to be provable on present evidence, yet they do improve on prior efforts to read Zapotec inscriptions. These treat such texts as non-linguistic sets of icons, from which the reader is meant to infer a story that passes in silence over Zapotec syntax and morphemes (see Marcus 1983c:179, commenting on the Lápida de Bazán). From the perspective of decipherment, the great difficulty with Zapotec inscriptions, especially the longer ones, is that signs are often *sui generis*, with little possibility of contextual control over meaning. There is little to no evidence of syllabic or phonetic signs that would confirm readings, the script exhibiting instead a high number of intractable logographs. In such cases, clear instances of rebus alone will demonstrate the validity of a reading.

The most persuasive argument as to content is simply that calendar names designate people or their ancestors (Marcus 1983a:150–152). Another is Alfonso Caso's productive insight that places and their capture constitute a pivotal part of the textual record in the Valley of Oaxaca (Caso 1947). Joyce Marcus has used this insight to suggest that some place names found at the key Zapotec center of Monte Albán correspond to much later place names recorded by the Aztecs in the Codex Mendoza, a sixteenth-century tribute

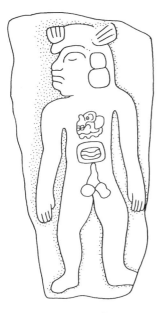

Fig. 10.6 Danzante from Monte Albán (after J. F. Scott 1978:D-59).

document (Marcus 1976a). It is safe to say that, aside from her students, who have detected evidence of these conquests in excavations outside the Valley (e.g. C. Spencer 1982), many epigraphers reject her supposition that relatively common place names (e.g. "Hill of the Bird," "Hill of the Jaguar") exactly match four toponyms in conquest slabs from Monte Albán (Marcus 1983b:107–108; cf. Urcid Serrano 2001:62). At least two of these place names differ fundamentally from their Aztec parallels in smaller signs that go unremarked by Marcus (an unidentifiable suffix in the case of "Cuicatlán," arrows in the case of "Tototepec").

It is puzzling that the largest corpus of early Zapotec images, the so-called "Danzantes" that represent dead or mutilated captives, have, out of a total of some 317 such figures, only about 6 with calendrical names, although many other apparent nominals occur (approximately 39) (Fig. 10.6). If calendrical names are the dominant pattern, why are they comparatively rare in early naming practices of this region? Some of the Danzantes have a repeated element in their captions, usually in final position of a short, two-glyph string (e.g. J. F. Scott 1978:D-2, D-6, D-8, D-22, D-86, D-130, E-1?, J-90, M-2). This consists of a circular element with four or five dots placed over a stick, but its meaning is unknown. It may serve as a title. On present review, one doubts that much progress can be made with Zapotec writing, barring substantial new discoveries (Urcid Serrano 2001:442). A plausible, even probable explanation is in place that day names refer to people, that the inscriptions record earlier forms of Zapotec language, and that much of the imagery is martial and sanguinary, but there is insufficient redundancy of evidence or data of an independent sort to confirm these views. What can be stated with more certainty is that, like other early scripts, the system begins with exceptionally short texts that appear to function as labels, and then, some centuries later, it inches toward longer, syntactically complex texts that culminate in the Teotihuacan-influenced Lápida de Bazán or Monte Albán's SP-1 (Urcid Serrano 2001:fig. 4.3). Thereafter, the script shifts toward an "open" system in a more polyglot Valley of Oaxaca, and the "closed" trajectory comes to a halt. At this point, the "memory load" of a sculpture lies less in text than in accompanying iconography and the mind of the knowledgeable beholder.

Isthmian writing

Even rarer than "Zapotec" writing is Isthmian writing, a script employed in and around the Isthmus of Tehuantepec in the first few centuries after Christ. One example, from the Middle to Late Formative Alvarado Stela 1, Veracruz, Mexico, may be its first appearance (I. Bernal 1969:62, fig. 8; Medellín Zenil 1960; Winfield Capitaine 1988:26; Karl Taube, personal communication, 1998), but no more than a handful of legible texts are known: La Mojarra Stela 1 (Winfield Capitaine 1988), the Tuxtla Statuette (Fig. 10.7; Holmes 1907; Méluzin 1987), the O'Boyle Mask (Méluzin 1995), a pottery fragment from Chiapa de Corzo (Winfield Capitaine 1988:fig. 15b), and a small number of connected texts, some little more than calendrical (e.g. Chiapa de Corzo Stela 2 [Lee 1969:fig. 60], and the El Sitio celt [Navarrete 1971]). A new text, from a private collection, has also just come to the attention of scholars (Michael Coe, personal communication, 2002, from a drawing by David Joralemon). It contains eighty-six signs disposed into six columns, all in excellent state of preservation, evidently on the reverse of a mask in Teotihuacan style.

Some authors prefer to label the script "Epi-Olmec" on the assumption that it descends from the users of Olmec iconography, believed in turn to be speakers of Mixe-Zoquean languages because of the present-day distribution of such speech in the same general zone ("Mije-Sokean" in some usage [Justeson and Kaufman 1993:1703]). Nonetheless, "Isthmian" is a better label. It does not presuppose descent from Olmec icons, yet it does indicate the geographical range of most texts. Virtually all texts can be dated to a few centuries from Christ because of the consistent, interpretable use of

Fig. 10.7 Tuxtla Statuette (Winfield Capitaine 1988:23, corrected against original by Houston).

Long Count notations, ranging from 10 December 36 BC (Chiapa de Corzo Stela 2) to 15 March, AD 162 (Tuxtla Statuette), in the Julian Calendar (Coe 1957; Stirling 1943; Winfield Capitaine 1988:fn. 4). Although the inscriptions are eroded, it may be that the system continued into the Early Classic period in Veracruz, a speculation reinforced by the apparent style of the new mask, which would date to this period (e.g. Cerro de las Mesas [M. Miller 1991]).

The Isthmian writing system is exceptional for several reasons. First, it appears *ex nihilo*, in fully developed form, a feature that could easily be disproved by finding more texts of earlier date. Second, the sample is shockingly small given the geographic dispersion of the system. Nevertheless, this range may be misleading. It should be kept in mind that the examples with secure provenance come from an area separated by only a few dozen kilometers; given its small size, the Chiapa de Corzo sherd could easily have traveled from this zone to interior Chiapas (Winfield Capitaine 1988:fig. 1), and the Chiapa de Corzo stela and its peers are insufficiently preserved to signal clearly that they belong to this writing system. (John Clark cautions, however, that the sherd is a ware local to its find spot, personal communication, 2002; he also points out that the area in question was under heavy Maya influence at the time.) The shared use of bar-and-dot numeration may not be adequate for this determination. The limited quantity, however, must still be compared with the many thousands of Maya texts and hundreds of Zapotec inscriptions. Third, relatively few signs are identifiable as icons, and most seem instead to be highly abstract, angular, and codified forms, without the rounded, calligraphic quality of Maya signs. In other words, the tendency may be away from iconicity and toward the abstraction found in cuneiform and later Chinese. Fourth, like the Maya system, Isthmian writing is clearly "closed," with even longer passages than appear in Early Maya script; at the outset, the rhetorical pattern differs from the more abbreviated segments of Maya text, which tend to less prolix passages punctuated and separated by dates and toponymic referents. In view of patterns elsewhere in Mesoamerica, this would suggest something other than a polyglot milieu. In addition, the relation to attendant iconography has a greater imbalance than in other Mesoamerican systems, since the imagery which appears with texts is highly limited and static.

The largest question is whether Isthmian is decipherable, as two scholars have claimed in several publications (Justeson and Kaufman 1992, 1993, 1997, 2001a, 2001b). Inherently, the chances would seem small, as several key criteria for decipherment are absent: (1) a biscript, a text that is written in two different systems; (2) a large corpus; (3) transparent links to iconography, with the possibility of discovering semantic controls over proposed decipherments; (4) a known language; and (5) a well-understood cultural setting (Coe 1995). The initial publications on the Isthmian "decipherment" were nearly impossible to evaluate because methods and steps toward translation were left opaque (Justeson and Kaufman 1992, 1993, 1997; Justeson and Kaufman do refer to a volume entitled *The Decipherment of Epi-Olmec Hieroglyphic Writing and Mixe-Zoquean Comparative Linguistics*, said to be "in press" as of 1993 [Justeson and Kaufman 1993:1711, fn. 29]). A recent presentation, issued in schematic form as a workbook but more fully as a word-for-word transcript (Justeson and Kaufman 2001a, 2001b), has clarified the premises and conclusions of this work. It also shows, inadvertently, and as will be explained in another forum, that the script does not appear to be decipherable with currently available materials (Robinson 2002).

Early Maya writing

Of all the scripts in Mesoamerica, Maya writing is in the most advanced state of decipherment, although, to be sure, many signs are not yet fully understood. The present corpus of inscriptions and painted or modeled texts is difficult to quantify but reaches into the thousands, somewhat in the range of runic texts in Scandinavia (Sawyer 2000:7). The first Maya texts date to around the time of Christ, the last, depending on whether one restricts the sample to longer, non-calendrical examples, to the sixteenth century and perhaps slightly beyond (Houston *et al.* 2003). Such an extended range of dates has led to several errors of interpretation. The first might be described as the "synoptic fallacy," the notion that properties of the script in one period can explain its properties in another and that the script can be seen in a condensed fashion, all periods of use conflated together. A strong tendency in current Mayanist scholarship is to acknowledge that the script changed over time. The Maya introduced new signs, jettisoned others, or reinterpreted them in new ways, their original iconic motivation having been lost (Grube 1990, 1994; Lacadena 1995). These principles of sign change derive from conditions – often taking place at the rupture between the Early and Late Classic periods, but also earlier still – in which, as David Stuart and I see it, the Maya changed their views about the iconic motivation of certain signs (the "reinterpretation principle"), begat glyphs from other glyphs ("extension principle"), and employed rebus to engender consonant + vowel syllables ("syllabification principle"). The second fallacy is a variant of the first. It is the "retroactive conceit" that later, better-understood inscriptions can be used to explain murky, earlier ones. The main problem here is that, for all the successes of Maya decipherment, almost all apply to the Classic and especially the Late Classic period, and to texts from certain regions. In contrast, the earliest Maya texts are notoriously challenging to interpret.

In part, such challenges stem from the sampling issues mentioned before, but they may also reflect the existence of highly fragmented "script communities," the social groupings that employ, teach, and learn particular writing systems or versions of scripts. If small in number of participants and limited in geographical extension, such groupings would create texts that might not be easily intelligible to readers of other, related scripts. Disruptions in such script communities could result in lapses of understanding and lead to innovations (see above). A second obstacle to interpretation is the high number of word signs or logographs in the earliest texts; these can be more resistant to decipherment than syllables. A third obstacle involves the lack of clear narrative structure, i.e., a sequencing of events with temporal closure, a conspicuous beginning, middle, and end, and the creation, suspension, and resolution of episodes. In later inscriptions, multiple dates assist with such sequencing, but these are not present in texts before about AD 400 (Balakbal Stela 4 [Morley 1937:pl. 178c]; Tikal "Hombre" [Fahsen 1988]), leading to long chains of glyphs that cannot always be parsed with ease. The onset of such temporally punctuated narrative appears to correlate with an intense episode of contact with the great Mexican center of Teotihuacan (S. Martin and Grube 2000:29–31). It is uncertain whether this correlation has a causal basis, yet there does seem to be a pronounced shift from a focus on one moment to many, implying a new kind of historical or recollective mode.

With Maya glyphs it is useful to understand that they are very much a "secondary" invention, centuries after the isolated text at La Venta and the first inscriptions in the Zapotec corpus. The Maya dating system, of the so-called "Long Count" or place-notational system, was adopted a few hundred years after its first appearance in texts to the south and west (Coe 1957), albeit with new specifications of the temporal periods in question, a set of clarifications and additions possibly induced by the cross-linguistic or trans-cultural borrowing of a system devised by other peoples. The columnar format, too, is consistent with Isthmian. Nonetheless, at an early date, the script transparently records Mayan languages, to judge by the use of ergative pronouns in Preclassic inscriptions (e.g. Covarrubias 1957:fig. 94; Proskouriakoff 1974:fig. 12.1).

Another misconception is the "statist" perception of early Maya texts, that they only come into existence for the administrative, competitive, and propaganda needs of states or other forms of complex society (Marcus 1992:435; Postgate, Wang, and Wilkinson 1995). To some extent, this claim is impossible to evaluate. A large part of the output of scribes may have been in perishable form, such as on palm leaves, a form of script or notation attested iconographically in Classic contexts (Houston 2000:148–149; wooden objects, including inscribed boxes, occur infrequently, usually in very special conditions of preservation, but their existence points to a vanished corpus of similar texts). Still, the great majority of early texts in the Maya Lowlands are on portable objects and not easily read by more than a few people at a time. If the aim is "propaganda," a reductive and anachronistic term, then only a handful could have read such texts, and, necessarily, the message would have been abridged in its readership. There are some exceptions – possible names on building façades (see below) or petroglyphs on rock faces or cave walls, as at San Diego, Guatemala, and the earlier carving at Loltun, Yucatan – but even a public monument such as El Mirador, Stela 2, which dates to the Late Preclassic period (c. 300 BC to AD 150), has a text with minutely incised glyphs that can only be seen at close distance (Hansen 1991:fig. 4, also from author's examination of the original; published drawings of the monument are deficient). Despite the monumental context, the scribal mentality behind such an inscription points to a predominant orientation toward diminutive scales of presentation. However, this does not seem to have been true in adjacent areas of southern Mesoamerica, including the highlands and piedmont of Guatemala, El Salvador, and Chiapas, Mexico, where monuments show bolder, more easily visible statements in three-dimensional form (Coe 1976; Orrego Corzo 1990 – but see small glyphs on Kaminaljuyu "Stela" 10).

The relation between lowland Maya script and the few instances of writing in highland and piedmont areas in and around the base of the Yucatan peninsula continues to be debated. Isolated signs, especially one corresponding to "person" or a unit of twenty days, occur both in secure Maya inscriptions and at Chalchuapa, El Salvador, and Kaminaljuyu, Guatemala (D. Anderson 1978:fig. 2). Similarly, a small number of Isthmian signs occur in the text of "Stela" 10 of Kaminaljuyu, including one from the new mask ("Stela" 10: F8), but the signs are otherwise distinct, with a more calligraphic quality that is common to Maya signs (Kaminaljuyu Stela 21, Chinchilla Mazariegos 1999:fig. 230). In general, this and other texts, including a somewhat earlier isolate from El Porton, Guatemala (Sedat 1992; Sharer and Sedat 1987:pl. 18.1), perhaps dating to Middle to Late Preclassic transition, at *c.* 400 to 300 BC, are impossible to read aside from their limited calendrical content. The occasional fresh find, such as a short text of uncertain temporal context at Abaj Takalik (Stela 53, inverted in Orrego Corzo [1990:pl. 11]), does little to augment the meager corpus. Those inscriptions that seem interpretable at present are the nominal glyphs found on captives and lords on Kaminaljuyu Monument 65. For now, these texts do not provide any unambiguous clues about the linguistic affiliation of scribes: the supposed *huun* spelling on Kaminaljuyu "Stela" 10, considered to be a clear reflection of a particular branch of Mayan languages, is probably a sign for "wind" that comes from a distant, Olmec source in Mesoamerican iconography; the "wind" symbol is also documented at Kaminaljuyu in other sculptures (Houston and Taube 2000:fig. 5a; cf. Grube and Martin 2001:II-26). With all of these texts, excepting the enigmatic inscription from El Porton – Does it show iconography? Is it an isolate without successors? – chronological priority of Maya Lowlands over the piedmont and highland zones or vice versa cannot be established with current controls (e.g. Parsons 1986:128; Proskouriakoff 1950:fig. 36d; cf. Mora-Marin, 2001:13, who accepts an early date for Kaminaljuyu "Stela" 10 at *c.* 200 to 100 BC). At best, it would seem that a broad area used hieroglyphic writing at about the same time, but little can be said about its content, apart from a few calendrical dates.

Aside from these equivocal data, there is nevertheless a number of early Maya texts that are identifiable as such by grammatical elements, such

Fig. 10.8 Dismembered captive, possibly from Tikal, on unprovenanced altar, Petén, Guatemala (after photograph by Houston).

as distinctive pronouns and suffixes, and by recognizable Maya signs in interpretable contexts. These can be divided into three earlier periods: Period IA (*c.* 100 BC to AD 150), Period IB (*c.* AD 150 to 250), and Period II (*c.* AD 250 to 500 [Houston 2000:table I]). Period IA represents the inception of writing in the lowland Maya area. As Michael Coe confirmed in 1966, it contains clear evidence of the historical content that prevails in Classic-era inscriptions of 500 years later (Coe 1966:15). Some of the clearest evidence for early nominals comes in fact from names associated with captives, as on stuccoed column altars from Río Azul (see imperfect renderings in R. M. Adams [1999:fig. 3–33], who assigns a date that appears, on stylistic grounds, to be far too late; see also G. Stuart [1987]). Another early captive, shown gutted and dismembered on an unprovenanced altar from Petén, Guatemala, may correspond to the founder of the Tikal dynasty (Fig. 10.8; S. Martin and Grube 2000:26). Yet, Maya script does not coincide with the local inception of complex society, which, in the Lowlands, antedates the development of glyphs by several centuries (Hansen 1998:63): i.e., there is solid evidence that Maya writing did not coincide with the inception of massive architecture, itself reflecting large changes in society and the organization of labor. The only exceptions might be the deity faces that abound on the façades of Preclassic buildings, from about 300 BC on (Freidel and Schele 1988:fig. 2.3; Hansen 1990:158–172, 1998:81–82). There is a possibility that some of these are royal names (David Stuart, personal communication, 2000), but many are certainly geo-mythic labels for buildings or their multiple, godly denizens. The suggestion that these Preclassic façades, especially at the site of El Mirador, represent the beginnings of king lists attested at sites like Calakmul is not credible (cf. Stanley Guenter, personal communication, 2000; see list in S. Martin 1997). Key elements of those names are missing, and there is little reason to think that the names and deity heads are one and the same. Conceptually, a probable descendant of such building embellishments are the Early Classic cache vessels that display deity heads of approximately similar form (e.g. Land, Nicholson, and Cordy-Collins 1979:pls. 127–128). The Classic Maya explicitly regarded some ceramic pots as "houses," and so the trope may have been applicable to cache vessels as well (Houston 1998:349–352). In no case do these vessels display head-variants of royal names. Parenthetically, the proposal that a Maya glyph from El Mirador, Guatemala, occurs on a sherd dating to 300 to 100 BC is not feasible, as the sign in question is a common floral motif rather than a glyph (Demarest 1984:90–91; compare with Lee [1969:fig. 43e], for a non-glyphic design of similar date from Chiapa de Corzo, Chiapas).

The earliest, unambiguous Maya texts, from about 100 BC to AD 150, occur on small objects that were presumably of intrinsic value, consisting of carved greenstone, several heirlooms recycled from Olmec lapidary products (Coe 1966; Schele and Miller 1986:119–120, pls. 31, 32). This portability means that their eventual find-spots are not securely their places of manufacture, although a large number do appear to concentrate in Belizean sites. Without exception, these texts manifest marked equivalences between single glyphs and single glyph blocks: a glyph fills the outline of a block, with few to no attempts at further compression of signs. The pattern shifts when more grammatical elements make an appearance and texts achieve a greater condensation of sound and meaning: the Dumbarton Oaks Pectoral, for example, has, as an early text from about the time of Christ, 24 glyph blocks and about 32 individual glyphs (Coe 1966:fig. 11); of the 34 legible glyph blocks on the "Hombre de Tikal," dating to AD 406, there are about 101 individual glyphs, a far different ratio (Fahsen 1988:fig. 4; the cadencing of glyphs within blocks has yet to be studied systematically in the Maya corpus). Another feature of early texts, including those in Phase IB and into Phase II, is that they seem to consist in large part of deity heads, arranged in no certain order (El Bellote, Tabasco, bowl [Easby and J. F. Scott 1970:fig. 26, pl. 168]; Kendal, Belize, bivalve facsimile [Gann 1918:pl. 16a, Schele and Miller 1986:79, pl. 10]; the Kichpanha, Belize, bone [Gibson, Shaw, and Finamore 1986:fig. 5]; the Pomona, Belize, earflare [Hammond 1987, Justeson, Norman, and Hammond 1988:fig. 3.1]; unprovenanced stone sphere, private collection; and unprovenanced bowl of later date; see also Berjonneau and Sonnery [1985:pl. 320], and Abaj Takalik Monument 11 and Altar 12 [Orrego Corzo 1990: lam. 21, 22]). Such lists of deities may correspond to the local gods mentioned at a number of Maya cities (Houston and Stuart 1996:302). Perhaps the supernaturals are named here as owners of an object, godly invocations, or as incantatory cues for those reading the text (see Monaghan and Hamman 1998). The syntactic opacity makes nearly any interpretation at once possible and undemonstrable. The relevant observation is that such lists are less like writing than a spatial disposition of deities, a pattern apparent on the two displays from Abaj Takalik.

Other kinds of texts are more likely to be "name-tags," the by-now well-known inclination of Maya scribes to label the owners or makers of objects. Some texts start with what appear to be elements of the "Primary Standard Sequence," a formula that indicates the offering of an object or the text on an object (e.g. Dumbarton Oaks Pectoral [Coe 1966:fig. 11, A1-B1]; Diker Bowl, A2 [Coe 1973:27]; Kerr Photograph 8279). In comparison to later patterns, such examples on early texts would seem to be correctly interpreted, although many of the suffixes remain obscure. Another pattern in early inscriptions includes a distinctive "fish-like" head with, in clearer examples, something that resembles a subfixed [ne] or [ni] syllable; in fact, this "syllable" may be part of the logograph, as almost exactly the same set of elements occurs in a deity list from the Kendal, Belize, jade (A3 [Schele and Miller 1986:79]). Mora-Marín (2000:figs. 46, 49, 2001:7; Grube and Martin 2001:II-33) interprets the head-sign as an "antipassive" verb, sometimes followed by a "patient" and "agent," and, on occasion, another head with element protruding from the brow. Such sophisticated parsing is wishful thinking, as none of the elements are confidently deciphered.

There is limited but not overwhelming evidence of rebus in the early use of a pocket gopher head, /baah/, to record the term for "image," /baah/ (Houston and D. Stuart 1998). To an arresting degree, in view of the importance assigned to rebus within script development in general (DeFrancis 1989:50; Hansell 2002:129–130), such signs are hard to find in early Maya writing, although this may only reflect current ignorance. More likely, the most common signs are what William Boltz calls [P+, S+], in that they contain both sound, [P], and meaning, [S] (Boltz 1994:19). A homophone, strictly speaking, would involve a sign in which an alternate meaning of a similarly or identically sounding word is communicated by the first meaning; thus, as in Shang script, "image" (*dzjangx*) is conveyed by the depiction of an "elephant" (*dzjangx* [Boltz 1994:61]). There must have been a stage in which de-semantization took place [S-]. Then, the scribes either found a replacement meaning (a homophonic rebus) or they chose not to find a semantic replacement (a syllable). Maya indulgence in such homophones may have become more common in the Classic period, as in the comparatively late interchangeability of signs for the homophones "sky," "snake," and the number "four" (Houston 1984). A better way of looking at Maya script is not that it makes heavy use of rebus but that it is thoroughly saturated with logography (D. Stuart 1995). This may reflect cultural and sociolinguistic choices rather than mere phonic efficiency: as in other scripts, such as Women's Script of Southern Hunan, China, logographs (signs emphasizing a semantic component) may have been privileged over signs stressing sound (Chiang 1995:130–131). The very first syllabic sign, in which meaning has been stripped from sound ([P+, S-]), may occur as a complement [wa] to a logograph [WAY] (Covarrubias 1957:fig. 94), but they are sporadic. Instances of pre-vocalic [ya], a pronominal prefix on a logograph for "night" [AK'AB], probably appear in early contexts as well (Grube and Martin 2001:II-28, 31), although one wonders whether the [ya] sign derived from, rather than antedated, these particular spellings.

The earliest morphological suffixes fall into two classes and make their debut early in Phase IB: (1) signs that record vowel complexity by means of CV syllables, among the first known in glyph-final position (e.g. [TZUTZ-ma] > /tzutz-*j-oom/, Dumbarton Oaks celt [Schele and Miller 1986:pl. 22], dating to *c*. AD 120, if perhaps in retrospective reference [Houston, Stuart, and Robertson 1998]); and (2) morphosyllables that record VC forms that, unlike syllables, are [P+, S+] and thus communicate meaning (Houston *et al.* 2000). The two most common morphosyllables are instrumentals, /-Vb/, that permit actions to take place (e.g. [wa-WAY-VB] [Covarrubias 1957:fig. 94], for "place/thing that allows sleeping"; see also Proskouriakoff [1974:fig. 12.1]), and /-Vl/ suffixes used in possessive constructions (Proskouriakoff 1974:fig. 12.1). Such signs allow considerable flexibility with the vowel, which must be inserted by the reader. They also record derivational or inflectional meaning. At a far later date they become, at times, CV syllables. The first true syllables are likely to have been prefixes rather than suffixes. Their iconic origin is unclear, but later syllabic signs derive from Mayan and Ch'olan words (/CV'/ or /CVh, CVy/) in a process of limited acrophony (Justeson 1989:33). There is no reason to think that the Maya adopted syllabic elements from other languages, such as those, whichever they might be, recorded in highland, piedmont, and Isthmian texts.

The appearance of a label, a "wind" sign to designate a pectoral (see also Laporte and Fialko 1995:fig. 19), in a position just after the "fish-face," may indicate some morphological function for the face, perhaps as a pronoun (/ni/, for "my"?). It cannot be the third-person ergative pronoun /u/ or its prevocalic variant /yu/, both of which are documented in early Maya texts from the Preclassic period (e.g. Covarrubias 1957:figs. 94; Proskouriakoff 1974:figs. 12.1, 7). A noteworthy feature of most of these texts is that codification of glyphs has begun. There is still a great deal of variation, however, as though the script communities were relatively fragmented: one text, from an adze in an Early Classic cache vessel, is strikingly loose in its incision and columnar reading (Grube and Martin 2001:II-28; Thompson 1931:pl. 33; note, however, that the style-date of this text may be later than commonly thought; its illegibility should not be taken as proof of antiquity).

By this point, Maya texts passed into a phase of more complete development, Phase IB, from about AD 150 to 250, and bridging into the Early Classic Period, Phase II (AD 250 to 550). A full repertoire of glyphic instruments existed to record language and its subtleties. Nonetheless, the chronological problems mentioned before must always be kept in mind. A few texts are clearly early, such as the Dumbarton Oaks Pectoral and the Peabody Museum statuette (Fig. 10.9; Coe 1973:25). Yet, there are grave pitfalls in assigning dates to later pieces, as the fragmented script communities may by their nature upset rigid chronologies inferred from the appearance or nonappearance of particular attributes. For example, the so-called Hauberg "stela," long thought to be an early example of Maya script, is almost certainly an anachronism (cf. Schele 1985; independent observation by Alfonso Lacadena, personal communication, 1997), as may be the Diker Bowl. What is even less conspicuous is the exact linguistic affiliation of these early texts (Houston *et al.* 2000). Unlike texts from the Early Classic period (Phase II in script development), there is little intrinsic evidence that weighs in favor of a particular language or language branch of the Mayan family. Whether this was intentional or not is uncertain. It may be that greater linguistic salience appeared only when scribes became more ambitious rhetorically, when they needed to amplify their range of expression. The shift to monumental texts, as presaged in the brief cave text at Loltun and the later San Diego, Guatemala, wall-face, came only after an earlier predisposition toward small glyphs.

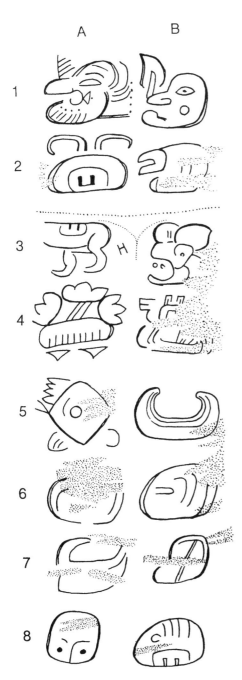

Fig. 10.9 Peabody Museum statuette (Coe 1973:pl. 1).

General lessons from early Maya texts include the growing doubt that such inscriptions arose from a need to broadcast royal messages to wide audiences. Another feature is the system's apparent cultural and linguistic autonomy even at an early date; only the problematic text from Kaminaljuyu "Stela" 10 shows linkages to Isthmian. From the outset, the rounded contours hint at a calligraphic basis, now lost apart from a proto-Classic / Early Classic list of day signs from a vase found at Tikal (Laporte and Fialko 1995:fig. 34) and a destroyed mural text from Structure B-XIII at Uaxactun (A. Smith 1950:fig. 47). The overall chronology of early Maya texts is still fluid, yet there is a sense that texts came into existence with relative speed around the time of Christ. The actual pace of developments is nonetheless impossible to gauge until the chronology achieves greater clarity. The heavy theological content of the early texts, including a preponderance of references to deities, suggests that script was motivated as much by revelatory insight as technocratic efficiency. Much like other writing systems, then, Maya script commences as a system that is somewhat intransigent to interpretation, economical in phrasing, and temporally unmoored, unlike later Maya texts which concern themselves intensely with chronological anchors. Fixed times appear to be less momentous than a timeless invocation of supernatural verities or declarations of possession. As is true for early Chinese inscriptions, the physical linkage with objects remains strong, a means by which words become concrete and enduring by attaching themselves to substantial, palpable things (Robert Bagley, personal communication, 1999).

Coda

The promise of Mesoamerican data as a source on the first writing is only partly fulfilled: the earliest scripts are either isolates, possibly without successors (La Venta Monument 13, El Porton Monument 1), or almost unreadable from a considered and cautious perspective. Most emanate a general sense of their meaning yet without the specificity that distinguishes those Maya decipherments from the Classic period. A call for more texts may or may not be met – scholars should not hold their breath – nor is it clear that the act of thinking harder will harvest a better crop of insights. The evidence is intrinsically poor and patchy. Some points can be made, however. The early writing systems of Mesoamerica embraced a "closed," ethnically discrete quality that was only displaced with the advent of trans-cultural polities such as Teotihuacan. They coalesced within group acts of codification, prefigured by Olmec iconography, to which words were eventually attached and then detached to form graphic captions with explanatory syntax. As iconic, hieroglyphic systems, they preserved an existential strand to the world. This persistent bond is what made the systems distinctive in the history of script and underscored their partnership to other communicative devices in ancient Mesoamerica.

Acknowledgments

I thank John Clark, Michael Coe, Alfonso Lacadena, Robert Sharer, David Stuart, and Karl Taube for their useful comments on earlier drafts of this chapter.

PART III

Epilogue

11 | Beyond writing

ELIZABETH HILL BOONE

In a volume dedicated to the origins of writing and to the development of scripts in different parts of the world, this chapter may seem incongruous, for it deals not with writing but with not-writing. It considers those graphic forms of communication that are not linguistically based and thus do not record speech, but instead record other areas of knowledge and understanding. Those that concern me here are non-writing and beyond writing, because they are graphic systems that developed in the place of writing to serve similar record-keeping and epistemological ends. Whereas the first writing lies at the beginning of the conceptual and technological world that is writing, my concern is with the other end. These are situations where language writing does not effectively serve a culture or a group within it and the members develop alternative forms of graphic communication to serve their record-keeping needs. Either they consciously develop non-language systems as alternatives to writing or they merely choose not to adopt writing and instead follow another path. The graphic forms they develop nevertheless stand in the place of writing and occupy the same (or very similar) social niches as writing otherwise would.

In this volume, the editor and other authors define writing as language recorded graphically, because their concerns are the development of linguistically based script and the relation between the graphics of these scripts and the linguistic elements they represent. This is a valid definition of writing, and indeed the most generally accepted one, and it allows them to focus on the extremely interesting problems of how language is represented graphically and how scripts developed to do this. Because my own interests, however, are in those forms of graphic communication that do not represent language, I have elsewhere (1994) argued for an expanded definition of writing as "the communication of relatively specific ideas in a conventional manner by means of permanent, visible marks." This definition embraces semasiographic or non-verbal as well as verbal systems and allows scholars like me to address different kinds of questions about writing, questions that focus more on the graphic nature of representation and record-keeping and on the culturally specific social roles of writing. The danger of accepting this broad definition is that its very breadth can dilute or obscure questions that specifically attend the development of speech writing. The danger of not accepting it is that the non-linguistic systems cannot contribute to the discussion because they are ignored; moreover, the distinction between writing and non-writing carries, unconsciously or not, certain value judgments that raise phonetic writing above other forms of communication.

The usual definition of writing arises from our own training, which values writing over image making. Specialists in childhood development in Europe and the United States have found that very young children draw and write equally, that their general graphic activity is an amalgam of ideographic imaging, scribbling, and the first attempts at drawing letters. By four or five years of age, this graphic activity bifurcates into iconic representation (or drawing) and writing with conventional symbols (Krampen 1986:80–82).[1] The school system nurtures and trains children's alphabetic writing as communication, while it allows drawing to develop naturally as self-expression. The rules of speaking and writing are taught, but not many rules are taught for seeing and image making. Concurrently, children's books, which begin as picture books, gradually lose their illustrations and increase their alphabetic texts. This means that we emerge from our education thinking that writing is the principal mechanism of graphic communication and the partner of thought, while the visual arts are reduced to an agreeable skill for "entertainment and mental release" (Arnheim 1971:3; Kress and van Leeuwen 1996:15).

The last few decades, however, have seen a growing interest in non-phonetic graphic systems of communication, an interest that both acknowledges the ubiquity of images and recognizes that non-verbal visualizations, rather than principally alphabetic ones, are crucial to thought. Attention is being turned to the semasiographic systems that support the sciences, mathematics, logic, music, dance, and statistical analysis, for in these areas where prose writing fails to record effectively the kinds of information these fields use, alternative communication systems developed naturally. Historians and philosophers of science and mathematics, in particular, are investigating their semasiographic codes to understand how notations, diagrams, and other graphics govern analysis and interpretation in their own disciplines.[2]

This inquiry into the range of graphic codes naturally requires us to detach writing from its dependence on speech. Building on pioneering work by linguists like William Haas (1976), investigators and theorists from the realms of art history (Elkins 1999), semiotics (Roy Harris 1995; Rotman 1993, 1995), linguistics and language (Crump 1990; Gaur 1992; Larsen 1988; Twyman 1986), anthropology (Aveni 1986; Wrolstad and Fisher 1986), graphic design (Kress and van Leeuwen 1996), and the sciences (especially Drake 1986; Owen 1986) are proposing a broader view of writing, one that focuses more on writing's communicative function and less on its relation to language. Whereas a number of scholars recognize that even the most developed forms of speech writing fail to record the entirety of the linguistic code, others argue that writing's relation to speech is beside the point: that written language has its own autonomy as a communication system separate from its connection to spoken language (Derrida 1976:3, 6–9, 30–59, 88; Roy Harris 1995:4; Wrolstad and Fisher 1986:ix). The point being made is that writing should be recognized and studied as a graphic communication system rather than solely as a speech-recording system. As Brian Rotman (1995:390) describes it, writing is "any systematized graphic activity that creates sites of interpretation and facilitates communication and sense making." The focus is on the "set of practices . . . associated with an inventory of written forms" which unites the writer and reader over the object that is written (Roy Harris 1995:56, 64, 113).

My own interest in this topic comes from my research on Mexican pictorial codices, specifically the painted books of the Aztecs, Mixtecs, and their neighbors outside the Maya world. Although the Maya did develop speech or sound writing through a hieroglyphic script that represents words logographically and syllabically and that reproduces phrases and sentences, the Aztecs and Mixtecs did not. The Aztecs, like the central Mexican peoples before them, interacted with the Maya and must have known about their hieroglyphic script, but they chose not to adopt it.[3] Instead, their writing was fundamentally pictorial, consisting of images structured to create visual messages that sometimes parallel spoken language but do not usually record it (Fig. 11.1). The elements of their graphic vocabulary appear as figural representations, icons, and symbols. This vocabulary does include word referents – nominal glyphs that record place names and appellatives, and symbols that can be voiced as specific words – but these logographic elements are only part of the larger graphic system. The syntax is fundamentally spatial, where meaning is created and directed by structure and by the principles of sequence, proximity, inclusion, and exclusion. I call this system "Mexican pictography."

One could study this system and not call it writing were it not that the Aztecs themselves conceptualized it as writing. Their pictography occupied the cultural space of writing in their society. The acts of writing and painting shared the same verb in Aztec Mexico, *tlacuiloliztli*, and their books were painted books. Aztec legends about their ancient origins tell of the importance of books (*amoxtli*, literally "glued paper") as containers of knowledge

Fig. 11.1 The Codex Féjerváry-Mayer, a religious and divinatory codex from Aztec Mexico.

and guides for living. Their ancient leaders, their sages or *tlamatinime* (literally "knowers of something"), were "owners of books" and "possessors of writings." The metaphor for writings or books, *in tlilli in tlapalli*, translates literally as "the black [ink], the red [ink]" but is always used for its larger meaning; it was also the metaphor for knowledge or wisdom. Thus, an exposition on books and knowledge strings together a sequence of related words – the black, the red, the paper, the painting, the knowledge – to build to a larger understanding.[4]

The range of books was great in Aztec Mexico (Glass 1975:28–37; Boone 1998:150–155). Religious books included divinatory almanacs that pointed the way to correct living, protocols for rituals, guides to dream interpretation, astronomical records and predictions, and books of song and oration. The histories recorded both the mythological and secular past and included cosmogonies as well as biographies and genealogies. Documents concerning the practical side of life included maps, tax and tribute lists, accounts of private property, and the transcripts of court proceedings. The Aztecs looked to these books and records as permanent repositories of information.

It is only the figural and spatial nature of Aztec writing and its relative independence from language that exclude it from traditional definitions of writing. A number of scholars have persisted in trying to find language writing in Aztec pictography by concentrating on the name signs that represent personal names and places logographically or phonetically (Dibble 1971, 1973; Nicholson 1973; Prem 1969–1970, 1992; Prem and Riese 1983). Although this approach tells us about indigenous phoneticism and logography and explains the formation of name signs, it ignores almost all of Aztec pictography except the appellatives and place names, and it essentially compares Aztec writing to what it is not. Thus, it does not advance our understanding of the graphic system as a whole.

If we are to progress in understanding Aztec pictography as well as the other non-writing systems, if we are to appreciate their characteristics and virtues, I believe we must reconceptualize our position. This means turning away from limiting comparisons with phonetic writing, and focusing on how non-writing systems operate.

Semasiographic systems

Graphic or semasiographic systems succeed over phonetic systems because they employ shape and two-dimensional space directly to create meaning. Because their messages are not processed through auditory and verbal channels but are cognitively accessed through sight, recognition is both more immediate and free from any constraints of language; one can grasp the meaning of a shape, for example, without knowing its name. Haas (1976:206) recognizes the special abilities of semasiographic systems when he says that they "afford us an easy survey of complex messages, and [give] quick and precise references from any given point to other parts of a message." Because graphics bypass speech, they are unconstrained by the strict linearity inherent in speaking and speech writing. Graphic images have the desirable quality of revealing at a single moment a complete entity, all the while allowing details to reveal the complexities of different parts. This holistic presentation allows a reader to see how the parts relate to each other, while the details provide bold and subtle distinctions in meaning. Graphic systems are ideal for representing complex structures and for communicating relationships among variables. They function both as storage mechanisms for information and as research instruments, the means by which data are analyzed and interpreted. Semasiographic systems have the added characteristic of internationalism: because they are independent of language, they are readable by all who know the canons of the system, regardless of the language they speak.[5]

As early as 1971, Rudolf Arnheim argued that visual perception was crucial to human cognition and that individuals relied on perceived images to structure their thinking. In essence, he contended that humans thought visually rather than verbally and that graphic images are crucial to thinking and the development of knowledge.[6] In challenging the widespread view that humans think linguistically, he argued that, although "language helps thinking" by "stabilizing and preserving intellectual entities" in words and phrases, "detached theoretical thinking can function without words" (Arnheim 1971:228, 236, 229). Instead:

The mind, reaching far beyond the stimuli received by the eyes directly and momentarily, operates with the vast range of imagery available through memory and organizes a total lifetime's experience into a system of visual concepts . . . The visual medium is so enormously superior [to language] because it offers structural equivalents to all characteristics of objects, events, relations. The variety of available visual shapes is as great as that of possible speech sounds, but what matters is that they can be organized according to readily definable patterns, of which the geometrical shapes are the most tangible illustration. The principal virtue of the visual medium is that of representing shapes in two-dimensional and three-dimensional space, as compared with the one-dimensional sequence of verbal language. The polydimensional space not only yields good thought models of physical objects or events, it also represents isomorphically the dimensions needed for theoretical thinking. (p. 232)

$$\frac{1}{2}\sum_{\mu\nu} \sqrt{-g} \cdot \frac{\partial g_{\mu\nu}}{\partial x_\sigma} \Theta_{\mu\nu}$$

Fig. 11.2 Algebraic notation for "the momentum (or energy) imparted by the gravitational field to the matter per unit," from Albert Einstein's general theory of relativity (Einstein 1996:163).

Arnheim pointed toward visual thinking in mathematics and science, where visual models evoke understandings that are not otherwise representable. Practitioners in these disciplines and in logic and design have now come to reinforce and expand his position. Eugene Ferguson (1977:827) points out that "Thinking with pictures ... is an essential strand in the intellectual history of technical development." He explains that non-verbal thought is a central feature in engineering design, whereby the mind's eye of the designer and inventor calls up, analyzes, modifies, and assembles visual images to create the structures and machines of Western technology (Ferguson 1977:834–835). Mathematics, physics and other sciences, logic, music, and statistics are just a few of the disciplines where knowledge is developed by visual thinking. Inscribing or writing graphically usually accompanies this practice.

Mathematics and physics

In mathematics and physics, algebraic notation and diagrams largely replaced phonetic writing when it became increasingly impossible to state in ordinary language what was being proposed about the physical realities of the universe (Fig. 11.2; Drake 1986:136, 138, 139, 154). These graphic systems grew out of the need to represent their subject matter concisely and completely, and because they developed naturally from the problem at hand, they can describe phenomena more appropriately or fully than is initially known. Stillman Drake (1986:139) notes that Galileo did not use newly introduced algebraic equations in his work "because they implied more than he could prove to be rigorously true," although these implications were usually found to be true later. Successful algebraic equations can imply laws that are only later established otherwise, which is why algebraic notation has proved to be such a powerful aid to physical discoveries (Drake 1986:153–154).

Mathematics and physics are both fields where experimental thinking is impossible without its graphic expression, for experiments unfold only by the concurrent activities of thinking and inscribing (Barwise and Etchemendy 1996; Rotman 1993:25, 33, 84; 1995:392, 395, 397). As Brian Rotman (1993:x) notes, "mathematical thinking is always through, by means of, in relation to the manipulation of inscriptions. Mathematics is at the same time a play of imagination and a discourse of written symbols." Mathematical, or algebraic, inscriptions are a particular kind of writing, composed of graphic elements (numbers, letters, and symbols) that have been assigned individual meanings, which are arranged according to a complex set of rules and procedures. There is no attempt to reproduce the sounds of spoken language or, indeed, to record anything that is extramathematical; it is an inscription system perfectly adapted to mathematics and physics.

Music and dance

In like manner the notational systems of music and dance were developed specifically to serve these fields, fields where prose writing is relatively useless. The kind of musical notation established in Western Europe and now widely used focuses on musical features not grasped by other systems (Fig. 11.3); these include note, pitch, intensity, loudness, and such temporal elements as speed, rhythm, pause, and duration (McCawley 1996). In music, just as in mathematics and physics, the creative act of thinking accompanies and is inseparable from the physical act of inscribing.

In dance, three basic kinds of systems have been developed. One records the human figure as seen from the audience, moving through time, with time progressing horizontally (Fig. 11.4). Another records the human figure as viewed from above, moving through space, as in a map with footprints on the floor (Fig. 11.5). A third records the human figure from the individual body's perspective, moving through time but not specifically through space (Fig. 11.6; Farnell 1996; Guest 1984; McGuinnes-Scott 1983). This latter system, called "Labanotation" after Rudolf Laban who invented it, emphasizes such features of dance actions as the direction, vertical level, and timing of the action, as well as the part of the body moving, all of which are presented through time (Guest 1984:84; Hutchinson 1966; Laban 1974). Because music is usually integral to dance, and timing always is, most of the dance systems also embrace or accommodate musical notations. Dance notational systems, in contrast to musical notation, are not widely used today – much dance is still communicated directly from teacher to student – perhaps because a single preferred system has not emerged, and each separate system carries its own specific syntax and vocabulary of signs. Still, these notational systems are able to record complex movements in space and over time and preserve them permanently.

Beyond writing 321

Fig. 11.3 The opening of stanza 2 of the Dumbarton Oaks Concerto by Igor Stravinski, 1938 (photograph courtesy of Dumbarton Oaks).

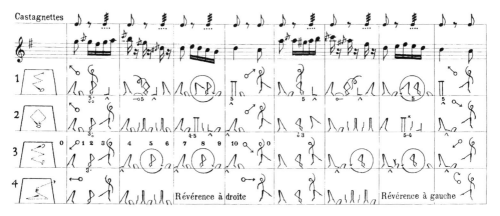

Fig. 11.4 Dance notation recording profiles of motion for four dancers, reading left to right, accompanied by the score (Tufte 1990:117).

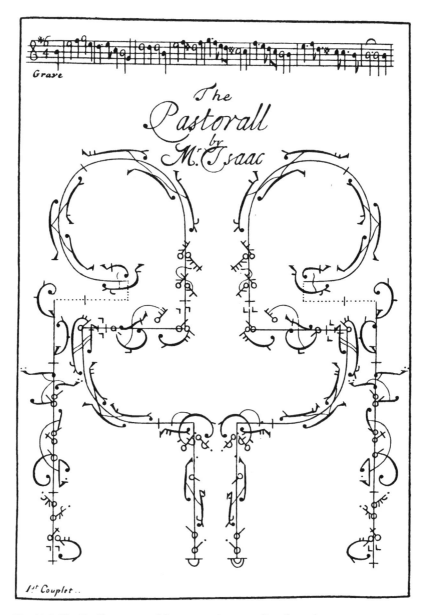

Fig. 11.5 The Feuillet system of dance notation recording the early eighteenth-century dance "The Pastorall." It concentrates on the footwork, knowing the torso and arms will follow conventionally (Guest 1984:fig. 10.1).

Beyond writing 323

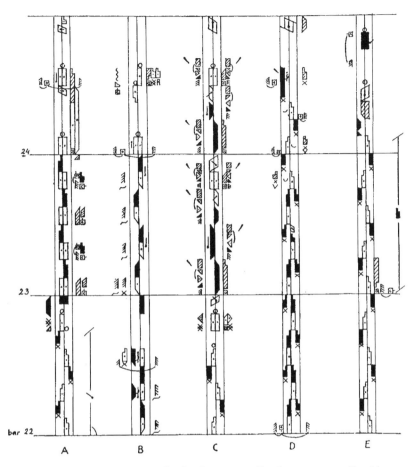

Fig. 11.6 Labanotation: notation for five dancers, reading bottom to top. On either side of the central vertical line representing the body's center, the defined areas identify fields of the body (support, leg, torso, arm, head), and geometric forms indicate the actions (Guest 1984:fig. 12.10).

Logic

Some realms of logic, especially that of relations, employ logic diagrams in problem solving because they can express relationships more sharply than prose. Venn Circles, developed in the late nineteenth century by logician John Venn to diagram the logic of syllogisms, are a prime example (Fig. 11.7). "The result was a diagrammatic method so perfectly isomorphic with the Boolean class algebra, and picturing the structure of class logic with visual clarity, that even a nonmathematically minded professor could 'see' what the new logic was all about" (Gardner 1982:29–31, 39). The intersection of

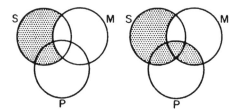

Fig. 11.7 Venn circles used to express relationships such as "no S is M" (Gardner 1982:40).

three circles, for example, can show relationships like "no S is M," or "some of S is P and some of S is MP." As Martin Gardner (1982:28–29) points out:

In logic a good diagram has several virtues. Many individuals think with far greater ease when they can visualize an argument pictorially, and a diagram often makes clear to them a matter which they might have difficulty grasping in verbal or algebraic form... A good diagrammatic method is capable of solving certain logic problems in the same efficient way that a graph may be used for the solution of certain equations.

Indeed, logicians working with diagrams have found that these visual presentations can reveal problems in the propositions and constructs that were expressed verbally, and this pushed thinkers to go further than they might otherwise (e.g. Allwein and Barwise 1996:vii–viii; Kress and van Leeuwen 1996:53).[7]

Chemistry

The diagram proves especially powerful in the sciences, particularly in chemistry, which is dominated by problems of structure and the relationships of discrete parts to each other (Drake 1986:150). In order to identify and enumerate these discrete parts and explain the relations among them, chemists developed many different kinds of graphics, each with its own ability. Most basic is the molecular formula (e.g., H_2O for water or C_6H_6 for benzene), which lists the elements and quantities in a molecule, but is silent on the relationships between them (Fig. 11.8). Instead, molecular structure is expressed in diagrams and models. Structural diagrams record the differences in bonds between particular atoms, as in the benzene molecule of Fig. 11.9, with its hexagonal arrangement of six carbon and six hydrogen atoms (Atkins 1987:8; Drake 1986:151; see also Hoffmann and Laszlo 1989:24; Hoffmann 1990); the bonds can also be simplified in a line diagram that ignores the hydrogen and carbon atoms and shows only the carbon–carbon bonds (Fig. 11.10).

But shape matters in chemistry. Molecular structure involves the three-dimensional arrangement of atoms in space, and this structure is crucial for

Fig. 11.8 Molecular formula for benzene, which is composed of six carbon atoms and six hydrogen atoms.

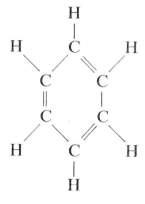

Fig. 11.9 Structural diagram of benzene molecule (Pauling 1967:117).

Fig. 11.10 Structural diagram of benzene showing the carbon bonds but omitting the hydrogen atoms (Pauling 1967:121).

understanding a molecule's function. In compounds that have the same elements in the same proportions, differently arranged atoms produce entirely different properties. Even identical but mirror-image arrangements can differ dramatically (Harrison 1991; Hoffmann and Laszlo 1989:26; Hoffmann 1990). A notorious example of the latter is the molecule for the sedative thalidomide, which exists in both right-handed and left-handed shapes; the left-handed version is benign, whereas the right-handed version can cause congenital deformations, as it did to so many babies whose mothers had taken thalidomide in the early 1960s before its danger was known (Atkins 1987:174). The spatial arrangement of atoms in molecules is usually depicted through the familiar ball-and-stick model (Fig. 11.11), which clarifies the bonding arrangement, or the simpler stick model which show the bonds but omits the balls representing the atoms. The space-filling model (Fig. 11.12) tends to obscure bonds between atoms, although it is volumetrically more realistic.

In particularly large and complex molecules, such as proteins, these models prove too confusing. For example, hemoglobin, the oxygen transporter in our blood, has some 10,000 atoms; it is composed of 4 intricately folded

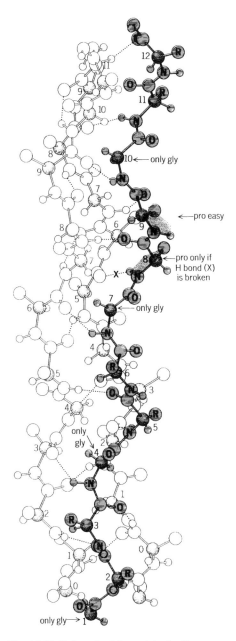

Fig. 11.11 Ball-and-stick model of collagen, composed of three left-handed single-chain helixes that wrap around each other with a right-handed twist (Dickerson and Geis 1969:42).

Fig. 11.12 Space-filling model of collagen (Schulz and Schirmer 1979:72).

polypeptide chains (2 α chains and 2 β chains) packed together in a tetrahedral arrangement, each chain embracing an oxygen-binding site (Dickerson and Geis 1983:7; Perutz 1964:64; Stryer 1988:150–151). Stick models of hemoglobin are so dense as to be nearly unreadable, even when the four chains and binding sites are distinguished by color; space-filling models would tell us even less. Instead, chemists interested in the overall structure of hemoglobin represent the chains as ribbons or cords, which clarifies their relative placement, the location of the binding sites, and the overall symmetry (Fig. 11.13). The great variety of notations and models in chemistry, which is only sampled here, arose because each one was designed to capture some particular aspect of a molecule under study; each model therefore suits some purposes better than others (Hoffmann 1990:192; Hoffmann and Laszlo 1989:28; Stryer 1988:4–5).

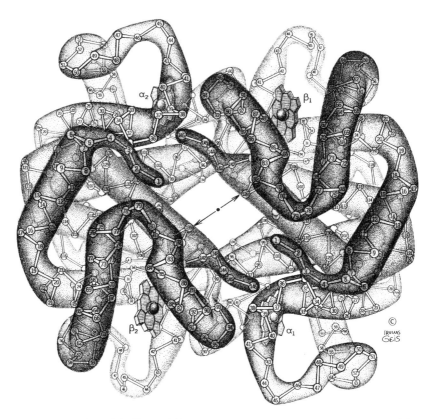

Fig. 11.13 Cord model of hemoglobin concentrates on its quaternary structure and the shapes and intertwining spatial relationships of the four subunits (drawing by Irving Geis [Armstrong 1989:100]).

These models serve chemistry because "structure is generally more effectively depicted than described" (Drake 1986:153). Although most scientists use visual imagery in problem solving to sort and organize data and find analogies – essentially to think – chemists are distinctive because their images are so predominately representational (Hoffmann and Laszlo 1989:33–35). Chemical models picture the properties of their subjects and allow them to be inspected and analyzed. The very complex three-dimensional models required to understand DNA, for example, developed out of schematic notation for representing the nature of attachments between atoms and between atoms and molecules (Drake 1986:153). It was James Watson's and Francis Crick's correct modeling of DNA in 1953 as a double helix around a central axis that enabled them to explain its structure (Fig. 11.14). The model was crucial to solving the problem in the first place, for their theory of DNA structure was the model itself (J. Watson and Crick 1953a, 1953b).

Beyond writing 329

Fig. 11.14 James Watson and Francis Crick with their three dimensional stick model of DNA, 1953 (McClelland and Dorn 1999:fig. 15b).

As Stillman Drake (1986:153) points out, "special notations [and models] may become equivalent to theories and serve science in the place of words and sentences."[8]

Data analysis

Diagrams, graphs, charts, and tables are the partners of thought on material and pragmatic/operational levels also. Such graphics as pie charts, flow charts, scatter graphs, bar graphs, network diagrams, maps, tables, and the like are not simply the means of presenting information to others, they are instruments for controlling and understanding the data in the first place. With the need to cope with increasingly large amounts of information (like census data, sales results, and geographic distributions, for example), analysts turn to graphics to consolidate and compare it. Behind every graphic presentation of ideas, countless draft and discarded images served to hone the problem solving (Bertin 1983:4; R. L. Harris 1999:3; Murgio 1969:13).[9]

The range of business graphics is great; some forms are highly textual whereas others are purely visual. Closest to prose text is the simple list, which has the virtues of condensation, enumeration, and comparison (Fig. 11.15). When two or more lists of similar data are being presented and compared,

SMITH ROBERT GEORGE	PFC	AR	11 JUN 45	02 JAN 66	CLEVELAND	OH	4E	52
SMITH ROBERT HAROLD	SP4	AR	27 OCT 46	24 JAN 67	WARMINSTER	PA	14E	73
SMITH ROBERT JAMES	SSGT	AR	16 DEC 45	18 APR 68	ALBANY	NY	50E	41
SMITH ROBERT JEREMIAH	CPL	AR	16 MAY 47	29 SEP 67	BUFFALO	NY	27E	32
SMITH ROBERT JOE	SP4	AR	04 JUL 44	21 MAR 67	JACKSONVILLE	FL	17E	14
SMITH ROBERT JOHN	A1C	AF	15 OCT 42	25 JUN 65	SCARBORO	ME	2E	19
SMITH ROBERT JOSEPH	PFC	MC	04 AUG 48	26 AUG 68	COLUMBUS	GA	46W	34
SMITH ROBERT JR	PFC	AR	20 MAR 45	26 MAY 66	PHILADELPHIA	PA	7E	111
SMITH ROBERT L	SGT	AR	30 JUN 37	25 AUG 66	MILLINGTON	TN	10E	44
SMITH ROBERT LEE	SP4	AR	06 NOV 43	29 JAN 66	WELCH	WV	4E	115
SMITH ROBERT LEE	SSGT	AR	22 AUG 32	25 MAY 68	CHILLICOTHE	OH	67W	6
SMITH ROBERT LEE	LCPL	MC	09 JAN 46	31 MAY 68	MONROE	MI	62W	17
SMITH ROBERT LEE	PFC	MC	28 MAR 46	02 SEP 68	CINCINNATI	OH	45W	28
SMITH ROBERT LEE	PFC	AR	06 OCT 43	30 DEC 69	CHICAGO	IL	15W	111
SMITH ROBERT LEE JR	LCPL	MC	31 JUL 45	04 MAR 66	NEWPORT NEWS	VA	5E	110
SMITH ROBERT LEWIS	PFC	AR	05 APR 48	06 JUN 68	SMITHLAND	KY	59W	15
SMITH ROBERT LINDO	PFC	AR	22 JAN 40	17 FEB 66	SANFORD	NC	5E	43
SMITH ROBERT LOUIS	CPL	AR	27 MAY 47	08 MAR 67	ANGIER	NC	16E	42
SMITH ROBERT MICHAEL	SGT	AR	11 NOV 48	10 MAR 70	PEORIA	IL	13W	108

Fig. 11.15 A partial list of deceased veterans named "Smith," from the Directory of Names at the Vietnam Veterans Memorial. Given are the name, rank, service, birthdate, deathdate, home town, and panel and line number locating the name on the memorial (Tufte 1990: 43).

their data are better arranged in a table (Fig. 11.16), where the framework of horizontal and vertical axes makes the parallels explicit (R. L. Harris 1999:8; Wright and Fox 1970:234–235). Tables are more efficient even than lists for presenting some kinds of precise information clearly at a glance. Psychologists studying the effectiveness of different presentational formats for conveying instructions found that individuals used tables and flow charts more easily than prose or lists of short sentences (Wright 1980; Wright and Reid 1973). Where lists and tables tend toward specificity and precision, charts and graphs excel at summarization (Fig. 11.17); they transform quantities into shapes and locations that can be easily read. Charts and graphs rely on spatial relationships, where the two-dimensional field is divided up in some predetermined way, and the meaning of a graphic form depends on its location within that space (R. L. Harris 1999:123). Maps and diagrams drawn to scale rely on this principle. Conceptual diagrams, such as Venn circles, are not usually quantitative and do not provide much detail. Instead they provide a graphical overview of relationships between two or more elements, and are thus usually used as explanatory or summary diagrams (R. L. Harris 1999:100).

Technical instruction and safety

In the fields of technical instruction and safety, images have come to be used over words and prose statements because they are direct, concise, and international. They communicate relatively simple information quickly to a broad audience of individuals from different cultures, ages, and backgrounds

LEVEL	VERBAL LANGUAGE	MATHEMATICAL LANGUAGE	GRAPHIC LANGUAGE
1	ALPHABET	ALPHANUMERIC SYMBOLS	CONTEXTS
	PUNCTUATION MARKS		ENTITIES
		OPERATORS	ATTRIBUTES
		OPERATORS	OPERATORS
2	WORDS	NUMBERS	FIGURES
		VARIABLES	
		CONSTANTS	
3	PHRASES	EXPRESSIONS	ASSOCIATIONS
	CLAUSES		COMPARISONS
4	SENTENCES	EQUATIONS	STATEMENTS
		IDENTITIES	
		INEQUALITIES	
5	PARAGRAPHS	SYSTEMS OF EQUATIONS	ARGUMENTS
6	COMPOSITIONS	ALGORITHMS PROOFS	PRESENTATIONS

Fig. 11.16 Table organizing verbal, mathematical, and graphic language into the steps that lead from basic parts to conceptual exposition (Owen 1986:171, fig. 8.17).

who share knowledge of these special codes. Road signs and directions in transportation facilities like airports must communicate quickly and unequivocally to people in motion, advising where and how to go or not go. The message carriers therefore have to be straightforward and concise.

They employ both representational (figural) codes and symbolic codes (color, shape, conventional symbols). For example, color coding on pipes signals such information as temperature and content; a cigarette encircled in red with a red diagonal across it instructs people not to smoke. In road signs, color and shape work together to indicate the general nature of the message being given: a rectangle advises, a yellow triangle warns, an inverted yellow triangle warns to yield, and a red hexagon commands to stop. On these colored shapes, words and numbers are then added to specify the speed limit, tell of men working or rocks falling, etc. The information-bearing elements in simple systems like these usually work independently or in combination with a few other elements; it is a feature of these systems that their elements are not woven together into complex grammatical structures, so that they

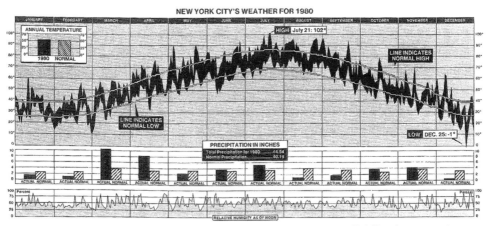

Fig. 11.17 Timeline diagram of New York City's weather in 1980 effectively summarizes 2,220 numbers (Tufte 1983:30).

are easy to understand intuitively. Their very simplicity is what makes them so effective.

The broad range of graphic systems in use today arose because of the failure of phonetic writing to encode and communicate in an effective way the concepts and data required in these fields. Having adopted alphabetic writing for general purposes, our society has turned to auxiliary systems for those things alphabetic writing cannot do. Some systems – such as algebraic notation or musical notation – are often called special-purpose systems, because they developed specifically to serve the needs of their specialized fields. Their dominance in these fields has in turn given rise to distinctive kinds of literacies, shared by practitioners worldwide but not by the general public (Drake 1986:136; H.-J. Martin 1994:493; Wrolstad and Fisher 1986:131).

Technology and graphics

The explosion of graphic use is partially due to the revolution in electronics technology, which is greatly changing the way we write, read, and think. Fast-moving developments in video and computer graphic technology make graphic expression easier than ever before. Whereas the typewriter suppressed graphic writing, computer graphics programs, coupled with the menu and the mouse, facilitate a newer visual expression, one that often relies on tables, charts, diagrams, and other images.

The computer, with its vast storage capabilities, is also changing the fundamental concepts of writing, reading, and thinking. Within the context of information processing, writing has come to mean the inputting of data via a program that exists to receive and analyze it. It is the program that reads the information according to its own protocols, and it is the program that analyzes the data to yield answers to questions it is asked. Systems that allow a dialogue between user and database enable the database to learn from the user at the same time that the user learns from the database. Answers, when expressed, can take the form of numbers, words, tables, charts, or diagrams. Computers with compatible programs can also transport the information to other computers, who read the electronically written messages being sent, analyze them, and accomplish the activities appropriate to them. The computer, then, is not simply an instrument for writing, it has also become the reader, the thinker, and the writer itself (Barwise and Etchemendy 1996:14; Gaur 1992:208; R. Harris 1995:163; H.-J. Martin 1994:463–506; Rotman 1995:413)

The computer's ability to accomplish searches that are beyond human limits has already led to new ways of thinking mathematically. Brian Rotman (1995:412) points out that chaos theory and fractal geometry have come about because the computer can create "previously undrawable kinds of diagrams, [and] somewhat differently, [can] witness proofs . . . that exist only as computer-generated entities."[10] In the realm of biochemistry, advances in computer hardware and software have made gene research feasible. Detectors now collect X-ray diffraction data about the composition of molecules and sub-molecular units, and special graphics programs translate these diffraction patterns into structural models that can be manipulated and analyzed in simulated three-dimensional space on the computer screen; "substrates and inhibitors can be fitted into enzymes, [and] DNA-building proteins docked into DNA, all by the manipulation of a joystick" (Brandon and Tooze 1991:vi). The computer as a reading, analyzing, and writing machine, accomplishes these tasks outside the realm of writing as traditionally defined. It challenges us to reconceptualize writing as information storage and reading as information retrieval (Gaur 1992:7, 14, 33, 206).

Just at the point when Western culture is spreading alphabetic writing throughout the globe, advanced thinkers in that culture are abandoning it for other conceptions and forms of writing and are opting to use other systems for recording and manipulating knowledge (Clanchy 1979:8; Derrida 1976:3–4, 9–10). Music and choreography never used alphabetic writing, and mathematics and science have largely outgrown it.

Models of the graphic catalogue

Of those who have looked at the range of graphics systems, only a few have attempted to organize or categorize them beyond the traditional division between phonetic writing and other systems, whether these non-writing codes are called semasiographic, discourse, or original systems (as per Haas 1976:131–208; A. Hill 1967:94; Sampson 1985:29). Charles Owen (1986:156–159), who was principally interested in diagrammatic systems, ordered graphics in a continuum from the most symbolic or abstract to the most realistic. Those with the greatest degree of abstraction also had the greatest grammatical structure; such are alphabetic writing and mathematical notation. At the other end, those with the most representational power have less innate structure; such are, according to Owen, movies and television. He located diagramming in the middle of this range.

The limits of this bi-polar model are that it is too restrictive and too linear, for it judges systems not by their operational features but only by their degree of abstraction or pictorial realism and by the level of complexity of their grammars. In this continuum, a system is either more abstract or less abstract than its neighbor. It also comes too close to the old "word versus image" dichotomy, where graphic codes are judged according to their relationship to alphabetic writing.

More useful, I feel, is James Elkins' (1999) organization of the "domain of images," as his book is titled. Elkins critiques the word-and-image model and instead offers up a tripartite model of "writing," "notation," and "picture." Here, Writing in its purest sense is alphabetic writing, Notation refers to systems like algebraic notation, and Picture is the "image" of word-and-image (Elkins 1999:85–89). Elkins conceptualized them using Venn circles, each circle representing one of the three intersecting spheres (Fig. 11.18). Although Elkins (1999:89–91) ultimately abandoned this simpler triad for a seven-fold division of the graphic domain, I find his trilobed model to be the better heuristic device for analyzing graphic systems. Its three lobes – writing, notation, and picture – are natural realms that reflect the way we interpret graphics. Together they form a roughly triangular shape that circumscribes the full catalogue of graphics in its great variety. I admire the model's simplicity and spatial configuration, which allow one to locate all graphic codes in or between one or more of these realms. Thus, mathematical and musical notation cluster along with chemical formulae and Labanotation in the notational realm, whereas chemical diagrams fall closer to the pictorial lobe, although some still contain notational elements. Between Picture and Writing are the hieroglyphic scripts, such as Maya, which, because it is increasingly syllabic in its late forms (see Houston, this

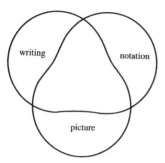

Fig. 11.18 James Elkins' (1999:80) trilobed model of the graphic catalogue.

volume, ch. 10), is closer to Writing than, say, early Egyptian hieroglyphs, which are logographic and iconic (see Baines, this volume, and Robertson, this volume). Between Picture and Notation are diagrams and models, charts and graphs, although these may also have a smattering of writing. It is here also that Aztec and Mixtec pictography is found, but somewhat closer to Picture than are strict diagrams, and in the area that overlaps with Writing.

Mexican pictography

Like so many graphics, Mexican pictography is a mixed system that, depending on its genre, shares organizational features with several other systems. The historical genre of Aztec and Mixtec writing is predominately linear; it carries a narrative that is either organized by time (as in an annals, Fig. 11.19) or by event (as in the Mixtec *res-gestae* genealogical histories), or that plays out in multiple tracks over the space of a map (as in the cartographic histories). Although the map-based histories are more diagrammatic than the other two, their stories still unfold like the others over time and space and thus have a temporal and linear quality to them. One reads them from the beginning to the end, as one reads phonetic writing or a musical score. Historical pictography is thus a little closer to Writing and Notation.

The pictography represented by the religious and divinatory codices, however, is much more diagrammatic. The religious and divinatory codices do not normally present narratives, although they may contain elements that refer to familiar and distant stories.[11] Instead, the divinatory codices are largely composed of individual almanacs that bring units of the divinatory calendar together with their governing forces; they also prescribe and describe rituals appropriate to these units and forces. In a purely abstract sense, their purpose is to record discrete elements, organize these elements

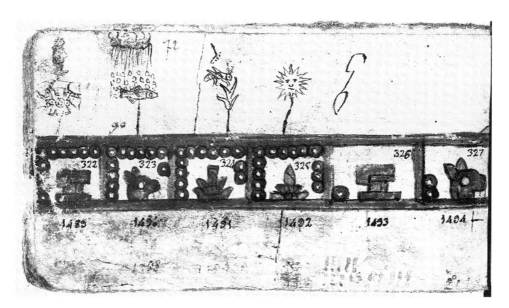

Fig. 11.19 Section of the annals history in the Codex Mexicanus (72), which records natural and climactic phenomena for the years 10 House (left) to 2 Rabbit (right). An earthquake rocked the land in 10 House, in 11 Rabbit there was a hailstorm so severe that the fish in the lake died, a plague of grasshoppers descended to devour the corn in 12 Reed, and 13 Flint was parched by drought (courtesy of the Bibliothèque Nationale, Paris).

structurally, and explain the relationships between the different parts. In this sense, they share the purpose of many graphics that support chemistry, logic and statistical analysis, which is to specify elements, show how they are organized, and explain the relationships between them. They thus have much in common with the kind of conceptual diagramming found in chemistry and logic, and with tabular and list graphics otherwise found in statistical analysis.

Meaning in the almanacs is created by picturing the 260 days of the ritual count together with their mantic, or prophetic, influences (the gods, forces, etc., that govern them) in ways that establish systems of correspondence. The count is composed of 20 day signs – represented by animals (e.g. Crocodile, Serpent, Jaguar) and a few plants (e.g. Reed, Flower) and natural phenomena (e.g. Movement, Rain) – and the numbers 1 through 13, so that each day has both a sign and a number. Figural images associated with the signs and numbers are the basic message-carrying units, but their message is controlled by the way in which they are organized. The almanacs employ structure, space, sequence, proximity, and the properties of inclusion and exclusion to convey meaning.

In the 100 or so extant almanacs, one sees three basic organizational schemes employed to link time to its influences: the list, the table, and the diagram. The list organizes material according to sets arranged in a sequence. The table is in many ways a complex list, for it presents data in sets and in multiple sequences; it achieves meaning both by the sequences and by the intersection of the horizontal and vertical axes.[12] The diagram presents material as a form or shape; it conveys meaning according to the iconic or symbolic value of that form and the parts of which the form is made. Variations and blendings of lists, tables, and diagrams add presentational richness to the divinatory books.

List

The simplest way to relate a series of things to another series of things is in a list, particularly in a list where there is a clear correspondence between the elements put into association. In this kind of graphic, the elements of one set are presented sequentially, usually in a line, and subsidiary elements are then put into direct association with them. When lists like this involve time, specialists in information graphics refer to them as Sequence Charts or Time Lines, which consolidate and display time-related information (R. L. Harris 1999:347, 417). In its simplest form, the list links one temporal unit with one mantic element, as a one-on-one correspondence. Lists, however, can also group several units of time with a single mantic element.

A basic list is the almanac that spans Codex Borgia 22b–24, which associates the twenty day signs with their patrons or mantic scenes (Fig. 11.20). Each day sign is provided with its own cell (always outlined in red), and the patron or divinatory scene associated with it is located in the cell along with the day sign. The day signs are listed sequentially in a boustrophedon pattern, beginning in the lower right with Crocodile and running left along the bottom register to Rabbit, then continuing right along the middle register to Jaguar, and then left along the upper register until the signs finish with Flower. The almanac's principal goal is to link each day sign with its specific mantic elements. The use of the cell achieves this linkage perfectly, because it physically encloses the elements and thereby relates them unambiguously.

Space within the cells does not itself carry meaning, except where elements of individual mantic scenes are united as in a tableau. The different occupants of the cell do not interact spatially, but simply appear *with* one another. The organizing elements are the red lines forming the cells, which function to include those elements that are pertinent and to exclude all others; this means that the relationship of each part to the others is clear. The list format,

Fig. 11.20 Almanac listing the twenty day signs and their patrons or mantic influences, Codex Borgia 22b–24 (reconfigured from 1993 edition).

Beyond writing 339

Fig. 11.21 Almanac grouping the twenty day signs with six travelers, Codex Borgia 55 (1993 edition).

featuring cells of equal size, also ensures that each temporal unit has the same weight.

A variation on the basic list is the grouped list, where several day signs are grouped together in association with a single mantic unit. Such a grouped list appears on Borgia 55, where the twenty day signs are associated with a series of six traveling or walking supernaturals (Fig. 11.21); the almanac is thought to signal the fate of one taking a journey (Anders, Jansen, and Gareia 1993:297; Seler 1963, II:129–136). The almanac begins in the lower right with Crocodile and runs left, right, and left in a boustrophedon pattern up the three registers, finishing with Flower in the upper left. The principle of adjacency links the grouped day signs to the traveler just above them. The day sign boxes are also painted tan or gray and have footprints on them, which effectively transforms them into the very roads on which the supernaturals walk, so that the supernaturals walk on the road of time. A

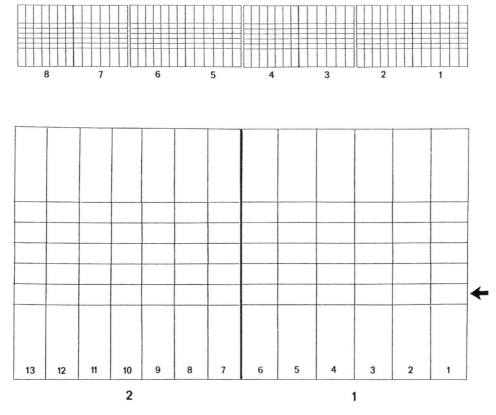

Fig. 11.22 Diagram of the *in extenso* almanac presenting the 260 days of the cycle in 5 registers that span 8 pages, reading right to left, Codex Borgia 1–8 (1993).

further variation can occur when some of the signs in the grouped list are replaced by disks, which simply stand in for the more elaborate signs.

Table

These lists of the 20 day signs are repeatable. When lists repeat themselves, they are most efficiently presented as a table. Indeed, the table format is the way the great *in extenso* almanacs are presented. These large almanacs are called *in extenso* because they picture all 260 days of the cycle: they repeat the sequence of 20 day signs 13 times. Clearly of major importance, *in extenso* almanacs open and occupy the first eight pages of three divinatory codices.[13] In them, the day signs are sequentially listed in five horizontal registers that span the full 8 pages, or 4 two-page spreads (Fig. 11.22). Each two-page spread contains 13 days (called a *trecena*). In the Borgia the day signs begin

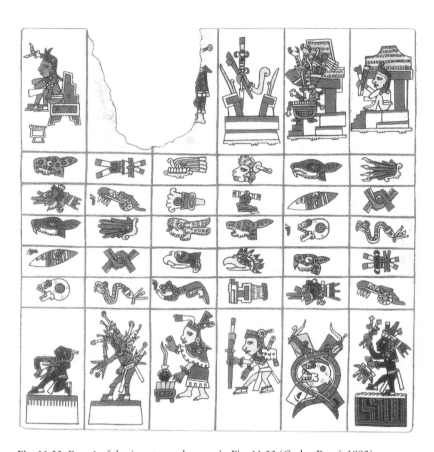

Fig. 11.23 Page 1 of the *in extenso* almanac in Fig. 11.22 (Codex Borgia 1993).

in the lower right and read right to left; after reaching the end on page 8, they jump back to the next higher register on page 1 and read again right to left, so that the sequence flows like lines of a prose text.[14] Above and below the five registers are elements, figures, and scenes that give meaning to the day signs (Fig. 11.23). They are controlled by red grid lines that create the horizontal registers and the vertical columns that unite and separate the day signs and elements. Because the mantic elements are located above and below, the days take their meanings from their columnar axes and share the fates at the top and bottom. Thus, in the first column, Crocodile, Reed, Serpent, Movement, and Water share the association with the man seated in a temple holding a bone awl and maguey spine used in bloodletting, and below with the priest who holds similar instruments and an incense pouch (he also walks on water). These are surely days for ritual bloodletting. The relative position of a day in the column may associate it more to one scene than the other when the messages differ. The upper days in the second column, for example, may relate more to the eagle descending into a precious vessel (above) than to the skull, crossroads, and coral snakes that signal malevolent or destructive forces (bottom).

Although the horizontal registers are not assigned specific mantic associations, the reader sees that each 2-page spread represents the 13 days of a trecena and thus knows that the numbers 1 through 13 are automatically attached to these days. The first column on the right page carries the implicit number 1, the second column 2, the third column 3, and so forth (Fig. 11.22). As the reader opens the almanac to other pages, he or she notes correspondences between the mantic elements associated with each position. Although there is a great deal of variation in the fates from column to column, some themes and elements tend to reappear in certain positions.

As in the simple list of the 20 day signs and their attributes, this table uses the cell, here more fully developed as a grid, to separate and unite the days and fates. Spatial location functions within the columns to relate the days to the elements below and above, and space implicitly links columns in the same relative position from trecena to trecena, so that the second days of the different trecenas carry some associated meanings. The table, more so than the simpler list, shows patterns and multi-directional relationships. The nuances of these kinds of relationships would be impossible to render in words and sentences. What the painter has provided is a complex system of correspondence that allows the user to extract shades of meaning from the grid.

Diagram

The third basic structure for almanacs is the diagram. Diagrammatic almanacs are organized with respect to a form or image that expresses a conceptual truth, and the day signs or other temporal units are then located on or around this image. In such diagrammatic almanacs, the red cells and grids are usually absent, which means that the principles of inclusion and exclusion that operate with lists and tables are not in play. Instead of red lines that unite and separate elements, space functions actively to associate or disassociate the various components. Location, proximity, and relative position become important.

Page 1 of the Codex Féjerváry-Mayer is the most-often reproduced page of all the Mexican codices (Figs. 11.24, 11.25). It is both a cosmogram of the Aztec world and a 260-day almanac, in which other almanacs are also embedded. Around a central figure of Xiuhtecuhtli ("Turquoise Lord"), the lord of the year and of time, the painter arranged the 260 days of the

Beyond writing 343

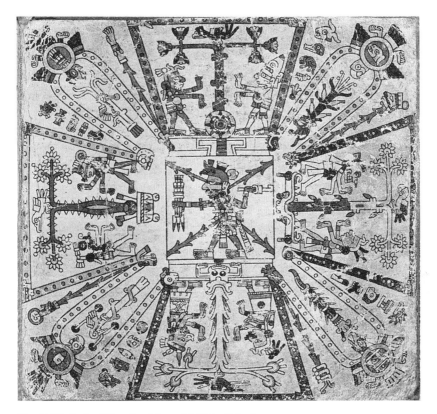

Fig. 11.24 Codex Féjerváry-Mayer 1 (1971 edition).

ritual calendar in a multi-colored ribbon that defines a Formée Cross (often called a Maltese Cross). The cross's broad arms are oriented toward the four cardinal directions, with East at the top. Narrower loops between the arms are oriented toward the intercardinal points. The 260 days flow along this ribbon in 20 groups of 13 days, the trecenas. Each trecena is represented by the first day sign of the period followed by 12 disks that stand in for the other 12 days. Beginning with the first day (Crocodile), the count reads counterclockwise around the cross: the first five trecenas are associated with the East and Northeast, the second five with North and Northwest, the third 5 with West and Southwest, and the fourth 5 with South and Southeast.

Each arm of the cross, and thus each direction, has it own color: red in the East, yellow in the North, blue in the West, and green in the South. Within the frame of each arm appear the two lords, the directional tree, and the bird that are associated with that direction. These nine lords – two in each direction and Xiuhtecuhtli in the center – are the Nine Lords of the Night, who in other contexts influence the fates of the days in sequence. The

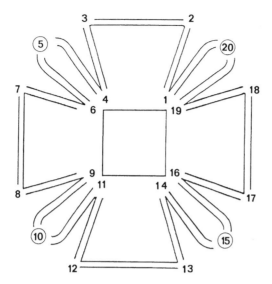

Fig. 11.25 Diagram of the 260-day almanac on Féjerváry-Mayer 1 (1971).

intercardinal loops have their own plants and animals, and they are topped with birds flying toward the center. Within the birds' bodies, circles around the day signs Rabbit, Reed, Flint, and House distinguish these day signs also as yearbearers. Beside the birds, dismembered body parts of the deity Tezcatlipoca ("Smoking Mirror," god of rulership and divination) release blood that flows toward Xiuhtecuhtli in the center, as if the body of the god of divination were nourishing the lord of time at the center. A second set of trecena day signs along the intercardinal loops associates the *trecenas* with the directions in yet another pattern.

In this one complex and masterful presentation the painter has used the regular passage of the 260-day ritual count and the continuity of the trecenas to recreate the physical space of the cosmos with its cardinal directions, cosmic trees, birds, and the lords who rule those directions. As it passes, time moves from one part of the cosmos to another, absorbing the mantic meaning associated with each direction. Thus, the ribbon of time describes the cosmos as a physical and geographical entity; at the same time the physicality of the cosmos inscribes time with mantic meaning. This single diagram, interpreted as a temporal and spatial map of the cosmos, shows how inextricably time is linked to space in the Aztec mind.

We might think of this diagram as a purely Mesoamerican phenomenon, but others elsewhere also created diagrams to describe the physical, spatial,

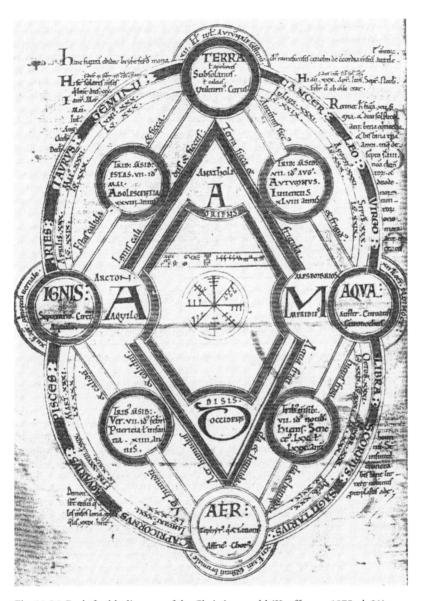

Fig. 11.26 Byrhtferth's diagram of the Christian world (Kauffmann 1975:pl. 21).

and qualitative properties of their world. A general comparison can be made with a version of Byrhtferth's diagram from an eleventh-century text book of natural science, now in St. Johns College, Oxford (Fig. 11.26). The diagram shows the harmony of the physical and physiological fours, the elements, directions, seasons, humors, and the like, to construct a cosmogram of the eleventh-century Christian world. In function and basic structure it is not unlike Féjerváry-Mayer p. 1, because the zodiac and months trace a route around the outer ring, thus encircling the world. Diagrams such as these succeed because they are the clearest way we have to depict structures – structures of thought, structures of understanding, and structures of the world.

These kinds of visual presentations – the list, the table, and the diagram – with their layers of meaning and their nuances, yield rich and multivalent interpretations. Moreover, they do so with an economy that is particular to the realm of graphic communication. The calendar priests saw at a glance the associations and correspondences of the days and mantic elements (both subtle and direct), and these they weighed and judged in order to fashion their thick interpretations.

If we were to replace these pictorial almanacs with prose texts, we would need very many words and phrases to explain all the elements exactly and to specify the intricacies of their relationships. The prose text would tend to privilege one interpretation over the others and thereby limit and harden the message into a partial truth. This would constrict any interpretation. Additionally, the words and phrases would be meaningful in only a single spoken language, which would obviously limit the interpretation to speakers of that language.

Instead, the painted text presents the individual elements within an organized arrangement, which allows the diviner to see relationships and associations and to draw out the most appropriate reading for his subject. Graphic writing systems like these Aztec almanacs codify knowledge by depicting the structures of cosmic and social reality.

Contemporary and ancient graphic systems make it clear that alphabetic writing is only one form of writing. Although language writing has proven to be the most adaptable of all systems for recording a wide range of informational genres – which is why it has been so universally adopted – it is not the best form for recording some kinds of information. Graphic systems work much better than speech writing at showing structures. They are very good at explaining the relationships of elements to each other, regardless of whether these elements are objects, concepts, or qualities. They allow one to understand systems of correspondence and to derive meaning from the operation of these systems. By receiving this structured knowledge, the reader of the semasiographic code can comprehend the different parts, understand their organization, judge the relevance of these relationships, and then develop his or her interpretation accordingly.

Notes

1. Krampen (1986) reports on studies conducted in the 1950s–1980s on the graphic marks of European and Turkish children.
2. See Drake (1986), Ferguson (1977), Harrison (1991), Hoffman (1990), Hoffman and Laszlo (1989), Lynch (1985), Owen (1986), Pimm (1987), Rudwick (1976), Ruse (1990), Wimsatt (1990); see also the discussion in Elkins (1999:31–33).
3. Although there is no evidence that the libraries of Mexico-Tenochtitlan contained Maya codices or that a Maya manuscript painter journeyed to the Aztec capital, Aztec imperial reach extended well into Maya territory, and there was considerable communication between the two groups. Aztec merchants regularly traveled to distant Maya trading centers, including Xicalanco and Potonchan on the Gulf Coast, Naco and Nito in Honduras, and Zinacantan in highland Chiapas (Sahagún 1950–1982, bk. 9:17–21; Scholes and Roys 1968:24, 27, 320; Berdan 1978; Gasco and Berdan 2003). The Aztecs housed a garrison in Zinacantan, and established a tribute province in Xoconochco on the Pacific coast of Guatemala to yield luxury goods for Tenochtitlan's elite (Remesal 1964, 1:376; Berdan 1996; Gasco and Berdan 2003). Moreover, Nahua speakers in Tabasco had Maya women in their households, Doña Marina or La Malinche being a prime example (Díaz del Castillo 1956:66–67). The first reports of Spaniards appearing off the Yucatan coast came via the Maya to the Aztecs in 1518 (Codex en Cruz 1981:panel 3a). Such open lines of communication mean that the Aztecs would surely have known about Maya hieroglyphic writing, just as the Maya knew about Aztec gods and divinatory almanacs and incorporated such elements into their own codices (Coe 1973:151; Taube and Bade 1991; Boone 2003; Just n.d.; Victoria Bricker, personal communication).
4. For *tlacuiloliztli* and *amoxtli* see Molina (1970:second pagination 120), León-Portilla (1992:317). For the metaphors and sages, see Sahagún (1959–1982, bk. 10:29–30, 190); also discussed in Boone (2000:24–27; n.d.)
5. See Bertin (1983:2–3); Brice (1976:43), Drake (1986:147, 151–153); Haas (1976:206); Martin (1994:6, 488–494).
6. See also Murgio (1969:14), who does not, however, develop this argument.
7. For the uses of diagrams in reasoning, see also Barwise and Etchemendy (1996); Eklund, Ellis, and Mann (1996).
8. Wimsatt (1990:112, 113) also presses this point; see also Ruse (1990).
9. For the range of graphics diagrams, see the classic work by Karsten (1923), as well as Murgio (1969), R. L. Harris (1999).
10. See also Harris (1995:163), Gaur (1992:208).
11. The exception is the narrative section in the Codex Borgia (29–46).
12. I thank Stephen Houston (personal communication) for reminding me that lists and tables "cluster logically" but that diagrams are "a different interactional order." It is an important distinction. Houston further suggests that diagrams appear to be exceedingly ancient in Mesoamerica (e.g. cosmograms on Olmec

celts). Lists may be equally old, however – they are at least as old as the Long Count, which is a vertical list – but the earliest surviving lists are the inscriptions on Stelae 12 and 13 at Monte Albán.

13. Borgia, Cospi, and Vaticanus B. The term "*in extenso*" was coined by Nowotny (1961:229–230).
14. The cognate almanacs in the Vaticanus B and Cospi read left to right, because the relevant side of these manuscripts begins on the left. Thus, like the Borgia, their *in extenso* almanacs read from the outside in, beginning with the bottom row.

12 | Final thoughts on first writing

STEPHEN D. HOUSTON

The temptation to offer a "conclusion" to an edited volume is great but unprofitable: the authors herein have already accepted that task individually, and with far greater authority than the editor. It would also be tedious to summarize the chapters. Interested readers should turn directly to the papers for their rich content. What this coda can do is to pinpoint areas of agreement and disagreement, thus indicating the way to future work of a comparative nature.

The points of agreement included the supposition that cultural and historical setting matter. The mechanistic views of script origin, which see writing systems coming into existence because of particular linguistic properties, are not at all persuasive: the accounting systems discussed by Jerrold Cooper and Robert Englund, the onomastic and calendrical patterns in Mesoamerican data, the offertory and tributary (?) records from the earliest texts in Egypt – these are the product of human needs, variously felt but uniformly concerned with an enduring, graphic record. This is not to negate the philosophical stance taken by John Robertson, who discerns in writing a bridge between auditory and visual dimensions, and a bundle of potentialities bestowed by attempts to move from iconic (visual) to symbolic (linguistic) modes. It may be that in Peircean perspectives lie logical, philosophical verities that transcend culture and history. At stake here, and as discussed in the chapter by Robertson, are the relative importance of "rebus" or homophonic elements that link graphically malleable icons (like, in the Maya case, a pocket gopher or *baah*) with more abstract words that are inherently difficult to depict (*baah* or "body / self / reflexive pronoun"). Nevertheless, a number of authors underscored the centrality of rebus (F. Bottéro), others felt it less important in their scripts (Houston).

Another matter of agreement was the enormous difficulty in understanding the earliest texts, be they proto-Elamite, Egyptian, Mesoamerican, or runic. Scattered words; numbers with isolated, probable word signs or logographs; ancestral forms with unclear tethers to later evidence: the legacy of this period is patchwork, inherently unapproachable because of its paucity of texts, early stages of codification, and sociolinguistic setting that may have involved exceedingly small numbers of literates or – a more apt word – "scribal adepts." Robert Bagley leaves us with a bleak but plausible picture of a script whose early stages are simply not present; in partial disagreement, Françoise Bottéro discerns a script not far from its time of inception. She deduces this from what appear to be high numbers of graphic variants, a looseness of signary that also marks the U-j texts from Egypt, although Bagley has doubts about the degree of graphic variation in Shang script. In either case, however, Bagley and Bottéro concur that Shang script was unusually developed, without the halting stages and impenetrable quality of other "first writing." For my part I expressed skepticism that early Mesoamerican texts would ever be fully understood, or all of its perishable expressions recovered. Englund's brilliant exposition of the proto-Elamite system, its logographic meaning hedged and defined roughly by distinct numbering systems and analogies with a "parent" script elsewhere, at once amazed me with its ingenuity and stunned me with the challenge of making substantive advances in the absence of further information. The systematic method employed by Englund and Bottéro will surely form the touchstone of work in other regions, as toil continues apace in sign cataloguing and pattern detection.

Participants in this book mostly shared the perception that the earliest scripts were, if not embryonic, then at least of a special nature. It would be drastically wrong to see them in terms of systems they would become or engender at a later date. On this Bagley and John Baines are firm. As mentioned in the introduction, the episodes of script development may highlight universals, especially the feature that the first writing did not fully record the nuances of language. That content was communicated elsewhere, by acts of memory or oral disquisition: whether these scripts intersected with orality is less clear in the Mesopotamian case, strongly so in Mesoamerica. Still, at the risk of seeming over-abstract, I assert that the *materiality* of script differed by cultural setting: Mesoamerican texts contained a vital essence, at times a fetishistic quality that obtained in Egypt as well. I would hazard a guess that these existential, ontological beliefs about writing, even if supplemented by purely pragmatic functions, established differences between traditions of writing systems. (An absolute divide between such attitudes is unlikely, however, to judge by the long record of varied usage in Egypt.) These scripts are the ones that, above all, retained a relation to Robertson's visual world.

Yet, we must attempt to account for why language (Robertson's auditory, linguistic dimension) began to play a strong role only some generations after the earliest writing. Was there a crumbling of memory and a need to transfer cybernetic load from the restrictions of the human brain to clay, stone, and bronze? A development of new genres of literary and historical expression? Changes in linguistic geography and patterns of multilingualism or prestige language? In all of this we are compelled to ask, what was the "script community" like that used and transmitted these signs to new generations? Our sketchy information from deep antiquity makes this question nearly impossible to answer. A presentation at Sundance by Gary Urton raised, for the editor, an intriguing possibility, that khipu was a "script" that had completely non-iconic origins: Urton himself made a strong case for its extraordinary intricacy of encoding, perhaps of linguistic elements (see also F. Salomon 2001; Quilter and Urton 2002; Urton 2003).

A topic that came up repeatedly was the pacing and nature of script origins. As the one extreme, it appears likely that runic came into existence rapidly, a condition that may well apply to all syllabic, consonantal, or alphabetic systems. Here there may well have been a "creator." As explained in the introduction to this book, a single syllable or other, exclusively phonic element does little good without its other, logical companions, the sounds that would complete the system. In contrast, logographic scripts can be as limited in content as the scribes wish it to be, the prime directive being to record certain words, often in connection with quantities. I believe that most numbering systems built on trajectories that were different from, if often bundled with, phonic writing, or [+P, +S], [+P, −S] systems, to use William Boltz' classification. My suspicion is that most numbering systems were of greater antiquity, the first to arrive and among the last to go.

Now to the differences. In the first place, the Mesoamerican evidence may not yet have sunk in, despite editorial efforts on my part. There is still a slight tendency to understand the Mesoamerican evidence as synchronic, or to see Maya script as a "primary" invention or whatever descriptive might be used. Maya writing is not any of these. Despite being an invention of a certain group of language speakers, and bound with Maya civilization in all its finery of dynastic display, it did not come first but was rather preceded by highly complex systems, such as Isthmian, that are not yet deciphered. Maya would thus be closer to proto-Elamite in its relation to the earliest script in Mesopotamia: not hugely later, but later nonetheless. The earliest Maya texts are, in addition, as linguistically equipped, with ergative pronouns, possessive suffixes, and instrumentals, as anything seen in Oracle Bone Inscriptions. The assertion that Maya script was not "true" or "full" writing is untrue, as any perusal of, say, the inscriptions of Palenque, Mexico, will show.

This is an unfortunate misconception. In a circulated paper, Peter Damerow (1999b) essentially suggests that "full" writing, in the sense of precise transcription of spoken language, is of single origin, emanating from somewhere in the Near East. He expresses this concept graphically by means of a "ground-zero" diagram that places cuneiform at the center of concentric circles of script invention that are progressively later in time and farther in distance. The inference, although not directly stated by Damerow, is that later developments exist in relation to a momentous burst of creative activity in the Near East. Bruce Trigger makes it clear in his contribution that these views, while still, perhaps, relevant to the enigmatic origins of Shang script, are inapplicable to the New World. To my thinking, the iconic origin of many scripts suggests local roots, as though emerging from preexisting pictorial traditions (although see Bagley, this volume).

A remaining point of division involves the "administrative" hypothesis or "statist" view, that writing is a necessary component of administration in early polities. That need is what led to writing. Bottéro endorses this perspective, as do, not surprisingly in light of their data, Cooper and Englund, although Cooper argues for a flexible approach to this matter. Nonetheless, he also believes that writing is a response to the predicament of "increasing socio-economic complexity" in human society. Trigger places an interesting spin on the "complexity" argument by stating that semasiographic and even limited logographic systems that "record names" may occur in "small-scale societies." The demands of involved administration and monitoring of human activity, however, soon require more explicit statements rendered into graphic records of language. This is a reasonable and justifiable claim.

The problem, as ever, is the information from Mesoamerica. The early scripts of that vast region are, to coin a word, highly "ethnogenetic," being related to, and helping to form, groups connected by shared cultural practices, traditions, and language. From available evidence, their role involved assertative displays of royal identity and martial puissance. In many cases it is unclear whether large polities existed in this area at the time of script inception, or, when they did exist, as in the Mirador Basin of northern Guatemala, whether they used writing to a full extent. The recent finds of Late Preclassic painted texts from San Bartolo, Guatemala, still date those remains to a time after the coalescence of those polities (William Saturno, personal communication, 2003); again, these glyphs, among the most important found in decades, are nearly impossible to understand beyond a few isolated elements. It seems possible that proto-Elamite came into existence in part as a distinct script in reaction to writing used by opposed groups in the Mesopotamian plain: thus, writing *qua* side-effect of competition and tension. Of course, there could have been ample quantities of perishable administrative documents in early Mesoamerica. But we simply have no evidence of them. These lacunae mean that a general theory of the administrative origins of writing remains hypothetical.

Where do we go from here? My suggestion is that there be more sociolinguistic modeling of how script creation and transmission took place, more compilation of texts (admirably in process by Englund and the CDLI team), and sheer, dumb luck, through the fortuitous discovery of more finds, as in Mesoamerica. The fossil analogy (Houston, this volume) holds: a fresh text may substantially alter the narrative of script origins in any one area. The reason the first writing will continue to intrigue us is that it forms an elastic and untameable frontier of knowledge, made wonderful and mysterious and enticing by the limits of evidence.

Acknowledgments
Jerrold Cooper and John Robertson commented on this chapter to my great benefit.

References

N.b.: Chinese archaeological journals cited in text by title: *Huaxia kaogu, Kaogu, Kaogu xuebao, Wenbo, Wenwu, Zhongguo wenwu bao.*

Adams, Barbara. 1974. *Ancient Hierakonpolis* and *Ancient Hierakonpolis: Supplement.* Warminster: Aris & Phillips.

Adams, Richard E. W. 1999. *Río Azul: An Ancient Maya City.* Norman, OK: University of Oklahoma Press.

Adams, Robert McC. 1996. *Paths of Fire: An Anthropologist's Inquiry into Western Technology.* Princeton, NJ: Princeton University Press.

Algaze, Guillermo. 1993. *The Uruk World System.* Chicago, IL: University of Chicago Press.

  2001. Initial Social Complexity in Southwestern Asia. *Current Anthropology* 42:199–233.

Allchin, Frank R. 1995. *The Archaeology of Early Historic South Asia.* Cambridge: Cambridge University Press.

Allen, James P. 2000. *Middle Egyptian: An Introduction to the Language and Culture of the Hieroglyphs.* Cambridge: Cambridge University Press.

Allwein, Gerard, and John Barwise, eds. 1996. *Logical Reasoning with Diagrams.* Oxford and New York, NY: Oxford University Press.

Alster, Bendt. 1995. Epic Tales from Ancient Sumer. In *Civilizations of the Ancient Near East*, ed. Jack M. Sasson. New York, NY: Scribner's, pp. 2315–2326.

Amiet, Pierre. 1961. *La glyptique mésopotamienne archaïque.* Paris: Centre National de la Recherche Scientifique.

Anders, Ferdinand, Maarten Jansen, and Luis Reyes García. 1993. *Los templos del cielo y de la oscuridad: oráculos y liturgia; libro explicativo del llamado Códice Borgia.* Accompanied by a facsimile of the codex. Graz: Akademische Druck- u. Verlagsanstalt; Madrid: Sociedad Estatal Quinto Centenario; Mexico, DF: Fondo de Cultura Económica.

Anderson, Dana. 1978. Monuments. In *The Prehistory of Chalchuapa, El Salvador*, Volume I: *Introduction, Surface Surveys, Excavations, Monuments, and Special Deposits*, ed. Robert J. Sharer. Philadelphia, PA: University of Pennsylvania Press, pp. 155–180.

Anderson, Lloyd B. 1993. *The Writing System of La Mojarra and Associated Monuments.* 2nd edn. 2 vols. Washington, DC: Ecological Linguistics.

Antonsen, Elmer. 1978. The Graphemic System and the Germanic Fuþark. In *Linguistic Method: Essays in Honor of Herbert Penzl*, ed. I. Rauch and G. Carr. Janua Linguarum Series Major 79. The Hague: Mouton, pp. 287–297.

　1989. The Runes: The Earliest Germanic Writing System. In *The Origins of Writing*, ed. Wayne M. Senner. Lincoln, NE: University of Nebraska Press, pp. 137–158.

Armstrong, Frank B. 1989. *Biochemistry*. 3rd edn. Oxford and New York, NY: Oxford University Press.

Arnheim, Rudolf. 1971. *Visual Thinking*. Berkeley, CA: University of California Press.

Ascher, Maria, and Robert Ascher. 1981. *Code of the Quipu*. Ann Arbor, MI: University of Michigan Press.

Asselberghs, Henri. 1961. *Chaos en beheersing: Documenten uit het aeneolitisch Egypte*. Documenta et Monumenta Orientis Antiqui 8. Leiden: E. J. Brill.

Assmann, Jan. 1994. Ancient Egypt and the Materiality of the Sign. In *Materialities of Communication*, ed. Hans Gumbrecht and K. Ludwig Pfeiffer. Stanford, CA: Stanford University Press, pp. 15–31.

Aston, Barbara G. 1994. *Ancient Egyptian Stone Vessels: Materials and Forms*. Studien zur Archäologie und Geschichte Altägyptens 5. Heidelberg: Heidelberger Orientverlag.

Atkins, P. W. 1987. *Molecules*. New York, NY: Scientific American Library.

Aveni, Anthony F. 1986. Non-Western Notational Frameworks and the Role of Anthropology in Our Understanding of Literacy. In *Toward a New Understanding of Literacy*, ed. Merald E. Wrolstad and Dennis F. Fisher. New York, NY: Praeger, pp. 252–280.

Badler, Virginia. 2000. The Dregs of Civilization: 5000 Year-Old Wine and Beer. Residues from Godin Tepe, Iran. *Bulletin of the Canadian Society for Mesopotamian Studies* 35:48–56.

Bæksted, Anders. 1952. *Målruner og Troldruner: Runemagiske Studier*. Nationalmuseets Skrifter, Arkæologisk-Historisk Række 4. Copenhagen: Gyldendal.

Bagley, Robert. 1987. *Shang Ritual Bronzes in the Arthur M. Sackler Collections*. Cambridge, MA: Harvard University Press.

　1999. Shang Archaeology. In *The Cambridge History of Ancient China: From the Origins of Civilization to 221 BC*, ed. Michael Loewe and Edward L. Shaughnessy. Cambridge: Cambridge University Press, pp. 124–231.

Baines, John. 1983. Literacy and Ancient Egyptian Society. *Man* n.s. 18:572–599.

　1985. *Fecundity Figures: Egyptian Personification and the Iconology of a Genre*. Warminster: Aris & Phillips; Chicago, IL: Bolchazy-Carducci.

　1988. Literacy, Social Organization, and the Archaeological Record: The Case of Early Egypt. In *State and Society: The Emergence and Development of Social Hierarchy and Political Centralization*, ed. John Gledhill, Barbara Bender, and Mogens Trolle Larsen. London: Unwin Hyman, pp. 192–214.

　1989. Communication and Display: The Integration of Early Egyptian Art and Writing. *Antiquity* 63:471–482.

1995. Origins of Egyptian Kingship. In *Ancient Egyptian Kingship*, ed. David O'Connor and David P. Silverman. Probleme der Ägyptologie 9. Leiden: E. J. Brill, pp. 95–156.

1997a. Kingship before Literature: The World of the King in the Old Kingdom. In *Selbstverständnis und Realität: Akten des Symposiums zur ägyptischen Königsideologie Mainz 15–17.6.1995*, ed. Rolf Gundlach and Christine Raedler. Ägypten und Altes Testament 36, Beiträge zur Ägyptischen Königsideologie 1. Wiesbaden: Otto Harrassowitz, pp. 125–186.

1997b. Review of Jochem Kahl, *Das System der ägyptischen Hieroglyphenschrift in der 0.–3. Dynastie. Die Welt des Orients* 27:170–173.

1999a. Scrittura e società nel più antico Egitto. In *Sesh: lingue e scritture nell'antico Egitto – inediti dal Museo Archeologico di Milano*, ed. Francesco Tiradritti. Exhibition catalogue. Milan: Electa, pp. 21–30.

1999b. Writing, Invention, and Early Development. In *Encyclopaedia of the Archaeology of Ancient Egypt*, ed. Kathryn Bard. London and New York, NY: Routledge, pp. 882–885.

2003. Early Definitions of the Egyptian World and its Surroundings. In *Culture through Objects: Ancient Near Eastern Studies in Honour of P. R. S. Moorey*, ed. Timothy Potts, Michael Roaf, and Diana Stein. Oxford: Griffith Institute, pp. 27–57.

in preparation. Writing and Society in Early Egypt. Manuscript in possession of author.

Baines, John, and C. J. Eyre. 1983. Four Notes on Literacy. *Göttinger Miszellen* 61:65–96.

Baines, John, and Norman Yoffee. 1998. Order, Legitimacy, and Wealth in Ancient Egypt and Mesopotamia. In *Archaic States*, ed. Gary Feinman and Joyce Marcus. Santa Fe, NM: School of American Research Press, pp. 199–260.

2000. Order, Legitimacy, and Wealth: Setting the Terms. In *Order, Legitimacy, and Wealth in Ancient States*, ed. Janet E. Richards and Mary Van Buren. New Directions in Archaeology. Cambridge: Cambridge University Press, pp. 13–17.

Bard, Kathryn. 2000. The Emergence of the Egyptian State (*c.* 3200–2686 BC). In *The Oxford History of Ancient Egypt*, ed. Ian Shaw. Oxford: Oxford University Press, pp. 61–88.

Barnett, William K., and John Hoopes, eds. 1995. *The Emergence of Pottery: Technology and Innovation in Prehistoric Societies*. Washington, DC: Smithsonian Institution Press.

Barwise, Jon, and John Etchemendy. 1996. Visual Information and Valid Reasoning. In *Logical Reasoning with Diagrams*, ed. Gerard Allwein and John Barwise. Oxford and New York, NY: Oxford University Press, pp. 3–25.

Bauer, Thomas. 1996. Arabic Writing. In *The World's Writing Systems*, ed. Peter T. Daniels and William Bright. New York, NY, and Oxford: Oxford University Press, pp. 559–564.

Baumgartel, Elise J. 1955. *The Cultures of Prehistoric Egypt*, Volume I, 2nd edn. Oxford: Oxford University Press.

Baxter, William H. 1992. *A Handbook of Old Chinese Phonology*. Berlin: Mouton de Gruyter.

Beale, Thomas. 1978. Bevelled Rim Bowls and their Implications for Change and Economic Organization in the Later Fourth Millennium B.C. *Journal of Near Eastern Studies* 37:289–313.

Belting, Hans. 1994. *Likeness and Presence: A History of the Image Before the Era of Art*. Chicago, IL: University of Chicago Press.

Bennet, John. 2000. Agency and Bureaucracy: Thoughts on the Nature and Extent of the Pylos Administration. In *Proceedings of the International Conference on the Mycenaean Palatial System, Cambridge, 1–3 July 1999*, ed. J. T. Killen and S. Voutsaki. Cambridge Philological Society Supplementary Volume. Cambridge: Cambridge Philological Society, pp. 25–37.

Bennett, Emmett L. 1996. Aegean Scripts. In *The World's Writing Systems*, ed. Peter T. Daniels and William Bright. New York, NY, and Oxford: Oxford University Press, pp. 125–133.

Berdan, Frances F. 1978. Ports of Trade in Mesoamerica: A Reappraisal. In *Cultural Continuity in Mesoamerica*, ed. David Browman. The Hague: Mouton, pp. 179–198.

1996. The Tributary Provinces. In *Aztec Imperial Strategies*, ed. Frances F. Berdan, Richard E. Blanton, Elizabeth H. Boone, Mary G. Hodge, Michael E. Smith, and Emily Umberger. Washington, DC: Dumbarton Oaks, pp. 115–136.

Berjonneau, G., and J.-L. Sonnery. 1985. *Rediscovered Masterpieces of Mesoamerica: Mexico–Guatemala–Honduras*. Boulogne: Editions Art 135.

Berlo, C. Janet 1983. Conceptual Categories for the Study of Texts and Images in Mesoamerica. In *Text and Image in Pre-Columbian Art: Essays on the Interrelationship of the Verbal and Visual Arts*, ed. Janet C. Berlo. British Archaeological Reports International Series 180. Oxford: British Archaeological Reports, pp. 1–39.

1989. Early Writing in Central Mexico: *In Tlilli, In Tlapilli* before AD 100. In *Mesoamerica after the Decline of Teotihuacan, AD 700–900*, ed. Richard A. Diehl and Janet C. Berlo. Washington, DC: Dumbarton Oaks Research Library and Collection, pp. 19–47.

Bernal, Ignacio. 1969. *The Olmec World*. Berkeley, CA: University of California Press.

Bernal, Martin. 1987. *Black Athena: The Afroasiatic Roots of Classical Civilization*, Volume I: *The Fabrication of Ancient Greece, 1785–1985*. London: Free Association Books.

Bertin, Jacques. 1983. *Semiology of Graphics: Diagrams, Networks, Maps*. Madison, WI: University of Wisconsin Press.

Besançon, Alain. 2000. *The Forbidden Image: An Intellectual History of Iconoclasm*. Chicago, IL: University of Chicago Press.

Binford, Lewis R. 1962. Archaeology and Anthropology. *American Antiquity* 28:217–225.

Bloomfield, Leonard. 1933. *Language.* New York, NY: Henry Holt.

Bodel, John. 2001. Epigraphy and the Ancient Historian. In *Epigraphic Evidence: Ancient History from Inscriptions*, ed. John Bodel. London: Routledge, pp. 1–56.

Boehmer, Rainer M., Günter Dreyer, and Bernd Kromer. 1993. Einige frühzeitliche 14c-Datierungen aus Abydos und Uruk. *Mitteilungen des Deutschen Archäologischen Instituts, Abteilung Kairo* 49:63–68.

Boltz, William G. 1986. Early Chinese Writing. *World Archaeology* 17:420–436.

  1994. *The Origin and Early Development of the Chinese Writing System.* American Oriental Series Volume 78. New Haven, CT: American Oriental Society. Reprinted with corrections, 2003.

  1996. Early Chinese Writing. In *The World's Writing Systems*, ed. Peter T. Daniels and William Bright. New York, NY, and Oxford: Oxford University Press, pp. 191–199.

  1999. Language and Writing. In *The Cambridge History of Ancient China*, ed. Michael Loewe and Edward L. Shaughnessy. Cambridge: Cambridge University Press, pp. 74–123.

  2000. *Monosyllabicity and the Origin of the Chinese Script.* Preprint 143. Berlin: Max-Planck-Institut für Wissenschaftsgeschichte.

  2001. The Invention of Writing in China. *Oriens Extremis* 42:1–17.

Bonfante, Larissa. 1996. The Scripts of Italy. In *The World's Writing Systems*, ed. Peter T. Daniels and William Bright. New York, NY, and Oxford: Oxford University Press, pp. 297–311.

Boodberg, Peter. 1957. The Chinese Script: An Essay on Nomenclature (The First Hecaton). *Bulletin of the Institute of History and Philology* 29:113–120.

Boone, Elizabeth Hill. 1994. Introduction: Writing and Recording Knowledge. In *Writing without Words: Alternative Literacies in Mesoamerican and the Andes*, ed. Elizabeth H. Boone and Walter D. Mignolo. Durham, NC: Duke University Press, pp. 3–26.

  1998. Pictorial Documents and Visual Thinking and Postconquest Mexico. In *Native Traditions in the Postconquest World*, ed. Elizabeth Hill Boone and Tom Cummins. Washington, DC: Dumbarton Oaks, pp. 149–199.

  2000. *Stories in Red and Black: Pictorial Histories of the Aztecs and Mixtecs.* Austin, TX: University of Texas Press.

  2003. A Web of Understanding: Pictorial Codices and the Shared Intellectual Culture of Late Post-Classic Mesoamerica. In *The Postclassic Mesoamerican World*, ed. Michael E. Smith and Frances F. Berdan. Salt Lake City, UT: University of Utah Press, pp. 207–221.

  n.d. *In Tlamatinime*: The Wise Men and Women of Aztec Mexico. In *Painted Books and Indigenous Knowledge in Mesoamerica: Manuscript Studies in Honor of Mary Elizabeth Smith*, ed. Elizabeth Hill Boone. New Orleans, LA: Middle American Research Institute, Tulane University (forthcoming).

Boone, Elizabeth Hill, and Walter D. Mignolo, eds. 1994. *Writing without Words: Alternative Literacies in Mesomerica and the Andes.* Durham, NC: Duke University Press.

Bottéro, Françoise. 1996. Les trente premières années du déchiffrement des inscriptions oraculaires (1903–1933). In *Écritures archaïques: systèmes et déchiffrement*, ed. Yau Shun-chiu. Paris: Editions Langages Croisés, pp. 73–98.

2001. Variantes graphiques dans les inscriptions sur os et écailles. In *Actes du colloque "Centenaire de la Découverte des Inscriptions sur Os et Carapaces,"* ed. Yau Shun-chiu. Paris: Editions Langages Croisés.

Bottéro, Jean. 1987. *Mésopotamie: l'écriture, la raison et les dieux.* Paris: Gallimard.

1992. *Mesopotamia: Writing, Reasoning, and the Gods.* Chicago, IL: University of Chicago Press.

Brandon, Carl, and John Tooze. 1991. *Introduction to Protein Structure.* New York, NY: Garland.

Brice, William C. 1962–1963. The Writing System of the Proto-elamite Account Tablets of Susa. *Bulletin of the John Rylands Library* 45:15–39.

1976. The Principles of Non-phonetic Writing. In *Writing Without Letters*, ed. William Haas. Manchester: Manchester University Press, pp. 29–44.

Brovarski, Edward J. 1987. Two Old Kingdom Writing Boards from Giza. *Annales du Service des Antiquités de l'Egypte* 71:27–52.

Brown, Gillian, and George Yule. 1983. *Discourse Analysis.* Cambridge: Cambridge University Press.

Buccellati, Giorgio. 1981. The Origin of Writing and the Beginning of History. In *The Shape of the Past: Studies in Honor of F. D. Murphy*, ed. Giorgio Buccellati and Charles Speroni. Los Angeles, LA: Institute of Archaeology and Office of the Chancellor, pp. 3–13.

Burrows, Eric. 1935. *Archaic Texts.* Ur Excavations Texts 2. London/Philadelphia, PA: British Museum (Harrison and Sons) / University Museum, University of Pennsylvania.

Byland, Bruce E., and John M. D. Pohl. 1994. *In the Realm of 8 Deer: The Archaeology of Mixtec Codices.* Norman, OK: University of Oklahoma Press.

Cahn, Robert, and Marcus Winter. 1993. The San José Mogote Dancer. *Indiana* 13:39–64.

Campbell, Lyle. 1984. The Implications of Mayan Historical Linguistics for Glyphic Research. In *Phoneticism in Mayan Hieroglyphic Writing*, ed. John S. Justeson and Lyle Campbell. Institute for Mesoamerican Studies, Publication 9. Albany, NY: State University of New York, pp. 1–16.

Campbell, Lyle, and Terrence Kaufman. 1976. A Linguistic Look at the Olmecs. *American Antiquity* 41(1):80–89.

Cardona, Giorgio Raimondo. 1981. *Antropologia della scrittura.* Turin: Loescher.

Carter, Elizabeth, and Matthew Stolper. 1984. *Elam: Surveys of Political History and Archaeology.* Berkeley, CA: University of California Press.

Caso, Alfonso. 1928. *Las estelas zapotecas.* Monografías del Museo Nacional de Arqueología, Historia y Etnografía. Mexico, DF: Talleres Gráficos de la Nación.

1947. Calendario y escritura de las antiguas culturas de Monte Albán. In *Obras completas de Miguel Othón de Mendizábal*, Volume I. Mexico, DF: Talleres Gráficos de la Nación, pp. 114–145.

Cavigneaux, Antoine. 1991. Die Inschriften der xxxii./xxxiii. Kampagne. *Baghdader Mitteilungen* 22:33–123, 124-163.

Changsha Mawangdui Yihao Han Mu. 1973. Beijing: Wenwu Chubanshe.

Charvát, Petr. 1993. *Ancient Mesopotamia: Humankind's Long Journey into Civilization*. Prague: Oriental Institute, Academy of Sciences.

1998. *On People, Signs, and States: Spotlights on Sumerian Society, c. 3500–2500 BC*. Prague: Oriental Institute, Academy of Sciences.

Chen Mengjia. 1956. *Yinxu Buci Zongshu*. Beijing: Kexue Chubanshe.

Chen Zhida. 1991. Shang Dai de Yu Shi Wenzi. *Huaxia kaogu* 2:65–69, 64.

Cheung Kwong-yue. 1983. Recent Archeological Evidence Relating to the Origin of Chinese Characters. In *The Origins of Chinese Civilisation*, ed. David N. Keightley. Berkeley, CA: University of California Press, pp. 323–391.

Chiang, William W. 1995. *"We Two Know the Script; We Have Become Good Friends": Linguistic and Social Aspects of The Women's Script Literacy in Southern Hunan, China*. Lanham, MD: University Press of America.

Childe, V. Gordon. 1925. *The Dawn of European Civilization*. London: Kegan Paul.

1950. The Urban Revolution. *The Town Planning Review* 21:3–17.

Chinchilla Mazariegos, Oswaldo. 1996. Settlement Patterns and Monumental Art at a Major Pre-Columbian Polity: Cotzumalguapa, Guatemala. Unpublished Ph.D. dissertation, Vanderbilt University.

1999. Desarrollo de la escritura en Mesoamérica durante el Preclásico. In *Historia General de Guatemala, Tomo I*, ed. Marion Popenoe de Hatch. Guatemala: Asociación de Amigos del País, Fundación para la Cultura y el Desarrollo, Guatemala City, pp. 557–562.

Chomsky, Noam, and Morris Halle. 1968. *The Sound Pattern of English*. New York, NY: Harper and Row.

Civil, Miguel. 1973. The Sumerian Writing System: Some Problems. *Orientalia* 42: 21–34.

1992. Education in Mesopotamia. In *Anchor Bible Dictionary*, Volume II, ed. David Noel Freedman. New York, NY: Doubleday, pp. 301–305.

1995. Ancient Mesopotamian Lexicography. In *Civilizations of the Ancient Near East*, ed. J. M. Sasson. New York, NY: Scribner's, pp. 2305–2314.

Clanchy, M. T. 1979. *From Memory to Written Record: England, 1066–1307*. Cambridge, MA: Harvard University Press.

Classen, Constance. 1993. *Inca Cosmology and the Human Body*. Salt Lake City, UT: University of Utah Press.

Codex Borgia. 1993. *The Codex Borgia: A Full-color Restoration of the Ancient Mexican Manuscript*, by Gisele Díaz and Alan Rodgers, with a new introduction and commentary by Bruce E. Byland. New York, NY: Dover.

Codex en Cruz. 1981. *Codex en Cruz*, ed. Charles Dibble. 2 vols. Salt Lake City, UT: University of Utah Press.

Codex Féjerváry-Mayer. 1971. *Codex Féjerváry-Mayer 12–14 M, City of Liverpool Museums*, intro. Cottie A. Burland. Graz: Akademische Druck- u. Verlagsanstalt.

Codex Mexicanus. 1952. Commentaire du Codex Mexicanus Nos. 23–24 de la Bibliothèque Nationale de Paris, ed. Ernst Mengin. *Journal de la Société des Américanistes* 41: 387–498. With facsimile of the codex published as a supplement to the *Journal*.

Codex Vaticanus B. 1972. *Codex Vaticanus 3773 (Codex Vaticanus B). Biblioteca Apostolica Vaticana*, intro. Ferdinand Anders. Graz: Akademische Druck- u. Verlagsanstalt.

Coe, Michael D. 1957. Cycle 7 Monuments in Middle America: A Reconsideration. *American Anthropologist* 59:597–611.

1966. *An Early Stone Pectoral from Southeastern Mexico*. Studies in Pre-Columbian Art & Archaeology 1. Washington, DC: Dumbarton Oaks Research Library and Collection.

1968. *America's First Civilization*. New York, NY: American Heritage.

1973. *The Maya Scribe and His World*. New York, NY: Grolier Club.

1976. Early Steps in the Evolution of Maya Writing. In *Origins of Religious Art and Iconography in Preclassic Mesoamerica*, ed. Henry B. Nicholson. Latin American Studies Series 31. Los Angeles, CA: University of California at Los Angeles, pp. 107–122.

1992. *Breaking the Maya Code*. London: Thames and Hudson.

1995. On *Not* Breaking the Indus Code. *Antiquity* 69:393–395.

1999. *Breaking the Maya Code*. Rev. edn. London: Thames and Hudson.

Coe, Michael D., and Richard A. Diehl. 1980. *In the Land of the Olmec*, Volume I: *The Archaeology of San Lorenzo Tenochtitlán*. Austin, TX: University of Texas Press.

Coe, Michael D., and Justin Kerr. 1997. *The Art of the Maya Scribe*. London: Thames and Hudson.

Collon, Dominique. 1987. *First Impressions: Cylinder Seals in the Ancient Near East*. London: British Museum Press.

Comrie, Bernard. 1996. Script Reform in and after the Soviet Union. In *The World's Writing Systems*, ed. Peter T. Daniels and William Bright. New York, NY, and Oxford: Oxford University Press, pp. 781–784.

Coningham, R. A. E., F. R. Allchin, C. M. Batt, and D. Lucy. 1996. Passage to India? Anuradhapura and the Early Use of the Brahmi Script. *Cambridge Archaeological Journal* 6:73–97.

Cooper, Jerrold. 1986. *Sumerion and Akkadian Royal Inscriptions, I: Presargonic Inscriptions*. American Oriental Society Translation Series Vol. I. New Haven, CT: American Oriental Society.

1989. Writing. In *International Encyclopedia of Communications*, Volume IV, ed. Eric Barnouw. New York, NY: Oxford University Press, pp. 321–331.

1992. Babbling on: Recovering Mesopotamian Orality. In *Mesopotamian Epic Literature: Oral or Aural?* ed. Marianna E. Vogelzang and Herman L. J. Vanstiphout. New York, NY: Edward Mellen, pp. 103–122.

1996. Sumerian and Akkadian. In *The World's Writing Systems*, ed. Peter T. Daniels and William Bright. New York, NY, and Oxford: Oxford University Press, pp. 37–57.

1999a. Sumer et Sumériens: questions de terminologie. *Supplément au Dictionnaire de la Bible* fascicle 72. Paris: Letouzey, pp. 78–93.

1999b. Sumerian and Semitic Writing in Most Ancient Syro-Mesopotamia. In *Languages and Cultures in Contact at the Crossroads of Civilizations in the Syro-Mesopotamian Realm*, ed. Karel Van Lerberghe and Gabriela Voet. Orientalia Lovaniensia Analecta 96. Leuven: Peeters, pp. 61–77.

2000. Right Writing: Talking about Sumerian Orthography and Texts. *Acta Sumerologica* 22.

Coulmas, Florian. 1989. *The Writing Systems of the World*. Oxford: Blackwell.

1994. Theorie der Schriftgeschichte. In *Schrift und Schriftlichkeit: ein interdisziplinäres Handbuch internationaler Forschung*, ed. Hartmut Günther and Otto Ludwig. Berlin: de Gruyter, pp. 256–264.

1996. *The Blackwell Encyclopedia of Writing Systems*. Oxford: Blackwell.

Covarrubias, Miguel. 1957. *Indian Art of Mexico and Central America*. New York, NY: Alfred A. Knopf.

Crump, Thomas. 1990. *The Anthropology of Numbers*. Cambridge: Cambridge University Press.

Cubberley, Paul. 1996. The Slavic Alphabets. In *The World's Writing Systems*, ed. Peter T. Daniels and William Bright. New York, NY, and Oxford: Oxford University Press, pp. 346–355.

Dalley, Stephanie. 1984. *Mari and Karana: Two Old Babylonian Cities*. London: Longman. 2nd edn. Piscataway, NJ: Gorgias Press, 2002.

Damerow, Peter. 1999a. *The Material Culture of Calculation: A Conceptual Framework for an Historical Epistemology of the Concept of Number*. Preprint 117. Berlin: Max-Planck-Institut für Wissenschaftsgeschichte.

1999b. *The Origins of Writing as a Problem of Historical Epistemology*. Preprint 114. Berlin: Max-Planck-Institut für Wissenschaftsgeschichte. (Also presented at symposium, "The Multiple Origins of Writing, Symbol, and Script," Center for Ancient Studies, University of Pennsylvania, 26 March; www.mpiwg-berlin.mpg.de/Preprints/P114.PDF)

Damerow, Peter, and Robert Englund. 1987. Die Zahlzeichensysteme der Archaischen Texte aus Uruk. In *Zeichenliste der Archaischen Texte aus Uruk*, ed. Margaret Green and Hans Nissen. Ausgrabungen der Deutschen Forschungsgemeinschaft in Uruk-Warka 11. *Archaische Texte aus Uruk 2*. Berlin: Gebrüder Mann Verlag, pp. 117–166 and tables 54–60.

1989. *The Proto-Elamite Texts from Tepe Yahya*. American School of Prehistoric Research Bulletin 39. Cambridge, MA: Harvard University Press.

Damerow, Peter, and Hans-Peter Meinzer. 1995. Computertomographische Untersuchung ungeöffneter archaischer Tonkugeln aus Uruk W 20987,9, W 20987,11 und W 20987,12. *Baghdader Mitteilungen* 26:7–33 and pls. 1–4.

Daniels, Peter T. 1992. The Syllabic Origin of Writing and the Segmental Origin of the Alphabet. In *The Linguistics of Literacy*, ed. Pamela Downing, Susan D. Lima, and Michael Noonan. Amsterdam: Benjamins, pp. 83–110.

1996a. Aramaic Scripts for Aramaic Languages. In *The World's Writing Systems*, ed. Peter T. Daniels and William Bright. New York, NY, and Oxford: Oxford University Press, pp. 499–514.

1996b. The Invention of Writing. In *The World's Writing Systems*, ed. Peter T. Daniels and William Bright. New York, NY, and Oxford: Oxford University Press, pp. 579–586.

1996c. The Study of Writing Systems. In *The World's Writing Systems*, ed. Peter T. Daniels and William Bright. New York, NY, and Oxford: Oxford University Press, pp. 3–17.

Daniels, Peter T., and William Bright, eds. 1996. *The World's Writing Systems*. New York, NY, and Oxford: Oxford University Press.

Davies, W. V. 1987. *Reading the Past: Egyptian Hieroglyphs*. London: British Museum.

1994. Les hiéroglyphes égyptiens. In *La naissance des écritures du cunéiforme à l'alphabet*. Paris: Editions du Seuil, pp. 102–181.

Davies, W. V., and Renée Friedman. 1998. *Egypt Uncovered*. New York, NY: Stewart, Tabori, and Chang.

DeFrancis, John. 1984. *The Chinese Language: Fact and Fantasy*. Honolulu, HI: University of Hawaii Press.

1989. *Visible Speech: The Diverse Oneness of Writing Systems*. Honolulu, HI: University of Hawaii Press.

Demarest, Arthur A. 1984. La cerámica preclásica de El Mirador: resultados preliminares y análisis en curso. *Mésoamerica* 7:53–92.

Demattè, Paola. 1996. The Origins of Chinese Writing: Archaeological and Textual Analysis of the Pre-dynastic Evidence. Unpublished Ph.D. dissertation, University of California at Los Angeles.

Derrida, Jacques. 1976. *Of Grammatology*, trans. Gayatri Chakravorty Spivak. Baltimore, MD: The John Hopkins University Press.

Diamond, Stanley. 1974. *In Search of the Primitive: A Critique of Civilization*. New Brunswick, NJ: Transaction Books.

Díaz del Castillo, Bernal. 1956. *The Discovery and Conquest of Mexico*, trans. and ed. Alfred P. Maudslay. New York, NY: Farrar, Straus and Cudahy.

Dibble, Charles E. 1971. Writing in Central Mexico. In *Handbook of Middle American Indians*, Volume X, ed. Robert Wauchope, Gordon Ekholm, and Ignacio Bernal. Austin, TX: University of Texas Press, pp. 322–332.

1973. The Syllabic-alphabetic Trend in Mexican Codices. *40th International Congress of Americanists, Rome–Geneva, 1972* 1:373–378.

1980. *Códice Xolotl.* 2 vols. Mexico, DF: Universidad Nacional Autónoma de México.

Dickerson, Richard E., and Irving Geis. 1969. *The Structure and Actions of Proteins.* Menlo Park, CA: W. A. Benjamin.

1983. *Hemoglobin: Structure, Function, Evolution and Pathology.* Menlo Park, CA: Benjamin/Cummins.

Diehl, Richard A., and Michael D. Coe. 1995. Olmec Archaeology. In *The Olmec World*, ed. Jill Guthrie. Princeton, NJ: The Art Museum, Princeton University, pp. 10–25.

Dietz, Martina, Edith Marold, and Hauke Jöns. 1996. Eine frühkaiserzeitliche Scherbe mit Schriftzeichen aus Osterrönfeld, Kr. Rendsburg-Eckernförde. *Archäologisches Korrenspondenzblatt* 26:179–188.

Diringer, David. 1962. *Writing.* New York, NY: Praeger.

Dittmann, René. 1986a. Seals, Sealings and Tablets. In *Ǧamdat Naṣr: Period or Regional Style?* ed. Uwe Finkbeiner and Wolfgang Röllig. Wiesbaden: Reichert Verlag, pp. 332–366.

1986b. *Betrachtungen zur Frühzeit des Südwest-Iran.* Berliner Beiträge zum Vorderen Orient 4. Berlin: Reimer Verlag.

Di Vito, Robert. 1993. *Studies in Third Millennium Sumerian and Akkadian Personal Names.* Studia Pohl, Series Maior 16. Rome: Editrice Pontificio Istituto Biblico.

Djamouri, Redouane. 1997. Ecriture et langue dans les inscriptions chinoises archaïques. In *Paroles à dire, paroles à écrire: Inde, Chine, Japon*, ed. Viviane Alleton. Paris: Editions de l'Ecole des Hautes Etudes en Sciences Sociales, pp. 209–240.

Doblhofer, Ernst. 1973. *Voices in Stone: The Decipherment of Ancient Scripts and Writings.* London: Granada Publishing.

Dollfus, Geneviève. 1971. Les fouilles à Djaffarabad de 1969 à 1971. *Cahiers de la Délégation Archéologique Française* 1:17–162.

1975. Les fouilles à Djaffarabad de 1972 à 1974. *Cahiers de la Délégation Archéologique Française* 5.11–62.

Donadoni Roveri, Anna Maria, and Francesco Tiradritti. 1998. *Kemet: Alle sorgenti del tempo.* Milan: Electa.

Drake, Stillman. 1986. Literacy and Scientific Notation. In *Toward a New Understanding of Literacy*, ed. Merald E. Wrolstad and Dennis F. Fisher. New York, NY: Praeger, pp. 135–155.

Dreyer, Günter. 1995. Die Datierung der Min-Statuen aus Koptos. In *Kunst des Alten Reiches: Symposium im Deutschen Archäologischen Institut Kairo am 29. Und 30. Oktober 1991.* Deutsches Archäologisches Institut, Abteilung Kairo, Sonderschrift 28. Mainz: Philipp von Zabern, pp. 49–56.

Dreyer, Günter, Joachim Boessneck, Angela von den Driesch, and Stefan Klug. 1990. Umm el-Qaab: Nachuntersuchungen im frühzeitlichen Königsfriedhof, 3./4. Vorbericht. *Mitteilungen des Deutschen Archäologischen Instituts, Abteilung Kairo* 46:53–90.

Dreyer, Günter, Eva-Maria Engel, Ulrich Hartung, Thomas Hikade, Eva Christiana Köhler, and Frauke Pumpenmeier. 1996. Umm el-Qaab: Nachuntersuchungen im frühzeitlichen Königsfriedhof, 7./8. Vorbericht. *Mitteilungen des Deutschen Archäologischen Instituts, Abteilung Kairo* 52:11–81.

Dreyer, Günter, Ulrich Hartung, Thomas Hikade, Eva Christiana Köhler, Vera Müller, and Frauke Pumpenmeier. 1998a. Umm el-Qaab: Nachuntersuchungen im frühzeitlichen Königsfriedhof, 9./10. Vorbericht. *Mitteilungen des Deutschen Archäologischen Instituts, Abteilung Kairo* 54:77–167.

Dreyer, Günter, Ulrich Hartung and Frauke Pumpenmeier. 1993. Umm el-Qaab: Nachuntersuchungen im frühzeitlichen Königsfriedhof, 5./6. Vorbericht. *Mitteilungen des Deutschen Archäologischen Instituts, Abteilung Kairo* 49:23–62.

1998b. *Umm el-Qaab I: Das Prädynastische Königsgrab U-j und seine frühen Schriftzeugnisse*. Deutsches Archäologisches Institut, Abteilung Kairo, Archäologische Veröffentlichungen 86. Mainz: Philipp von Zabern.

Dreyer, Günter, Angela von den Driesch, Eva-Maria Engel, Rita Hartmann, Ulrich Hartung, Thomas Hikade, Vera Müller, and Joris Peters. 2000. Umm el-Qaab: Nachuntersuchungen im frühzeitlichen Königsfriedhof, 11./12. Vorbericht. *Mitteilungen des Deutschen Archäologischen Instituts, Abteilung Kairo* 56:43–129.

Drucker, Philip, Robert F. Heizer, and Robert J. Squier. 1959. *Excavations at La Venta, Tabasco, 1955*. Bureau of American Ethnology Bulletin 170. Washington, DC: Smithsonian Institution.

Easby, Elizabeth K., and John F. Scott. 1970. *Before Cortés, Sculpture of Middle America: A Centennial Exhibition at the Metropolitan Museum of Art from September 30, 1970, through January 3, 1971*. New York, NY: Metropolitan Museum of Art.

Ebbinghaus, Ernst. 1996. The Gothic Alphabet. In *The World's Writing Systems*, ed. Peter T. Daniels and William Bright. New York, NY, and Oxford: Oxford University Press, pp. 290–296.

Edel, Elmar. 1961–1963. *Zu den Inschriften auf den Jahreszeitenreliefs der "Weltkammer" aus dem Sonnenheiligtum des Niuserre*. Nachrichten der Akademie der Wissenschaften in Göttingen, philol.-hist. Klasse 1961, 1963. 3 vols. Göttingen: Vandenhoeck & Ruprecht.

Einstein, Albert. 1996. *The Collected Papers of Albert Einstein*, Volume IV: *The Swiss Years: Writings, 1912–1914*, trans. Anna Beck. Princeton, NJ: Princeton University Press.

Eklund, Peter W., Gerard Ellis, and Graham Mann, eds. 1996. *Conceptual Structures: Knowledge Representation as Interlingua: 4th International Congress of Conceptual Structures, ICSS '96, Sydney, Australia, August 19–22, 1996: Proceedings*. Berlin and New York: Springer.

el-Khouli, Ali Abd el-Rahman Hassanain. 1978. *Egyptian Stone Vessels, Predynastic Period to Dynasty III: Typology and Analysis*. 3 vols. Mainz: Philipp von Zabern.

Elkins, James. 1999. *The Domain of Images.* Ithaca, NY, and London: Cornell University Press.
Elliott, Ralph W. V. 1989. *Runes: An Introduction.* Manchester: Manchester University Press.
Elliott, Ralph W. V., and Jean-Pierre Grégoire. 1991. *The Proto-Cuneiform Texts from Jemdet Nasr.* Materialien zu den frühen Schriftzeugnissen des Vorderen Orients 1. Berlin: Gebrüder Mann Verlag.
Elliott, Ralph W. V., and Hans Nissen. 2001. *Archaische Verwaltungstexte aus Uruk: Die Heidelberger Sammlung.* Archaische Texte aus Uruk 7. Berlin: Gebrüder Mann Verlag.
  1996. The Runic Script. In *The World's Writing Systems*, ed. Peter T. Daniels and William Bright. New York, NY, and Oxford: Oxford University Press, pp. 333–339.
Englund, Robert K. 1988. Administrative Timekeeping in Ancient Mesopotamia. *Journal of the Economic and Social History of the Orient* 31:121–185.
  1990. *Verwaltung und Organisation der Ur III-Fischerei.* Berliner Beiträge zum Vorderen Orient 10. Berlin: Reimer Verlag.
  1994. *Archaic Administrative Documents from Uruk: The Early Campaigns.* Archaische Texte aus Uruk 5. Berlin: Gebrüder Mann Verlag.
  1996. The Proto-Elamite Script. In *The World's Writing Systems*, ed. Peter Daniels and William Bright. New York, NY, and Oxford: Oxford University Press, pp. 160–164.
  1998. Texts from the Late Uruk Period. In *Mesopotamien: Späturuk-Zeit und Frühdynastische Zeit*, ed. Joseph Bauer, Robert Englund, and Manfred Krebernik. Orbis Biblicus et Orientalis 160/1. Freiburg: Universitäts-Verlag; Göttingen: Vandenhoeck & Ruprecht, pp. 15–233.
Fahsen, Federico. 1988. *A New Early Classic Text from Tikal.* Research Reports on Ancient Maya Writing 17. Washington, DC: Center for Maya Research.
Falkenhausen, Lothar von. 1993. Issues in Western Zhou Studies. *Early China* 18:139–226.
Falkenstein, Adam. 1936. *Archaische Texte aus Uruk.* Leipzig: Otto Harrassowitz.
Faltings, Dina. 1998. Ergebnisse der neuen Ausgrabungen in Buto: Chronologie und Fernbeziehungen der Buto-Maadi-Kultur neu überdacht. In *Stationen: Beiträge zur Kulturgeschichte Ägyptens*, ed. Heike Guksch and Daniel Polz. Mainz: Philipp von Zabern, pp. 35–45.
Farnell, Brenda. 1996. Movement Notation Systems. In *The World's Writing Systems*, ed. Peter T. Daniels and William Bright. New York, NY, and Oxford: Oxford University Press, pp. 855–879.
Fell, Christine H. 1991. Runes and Semantics. In *Old English Runes and their Continental Background*, ed. Alfred Bammesberger. Anglistische Forschungen, Heft 217. Heidelberg: Carl Winter, pp. 195–229.
Ferguson, Eugene. 1977. The Mind's Eye: Nonverbal Thought in Technology. *Science* 197:827–836.

Finkel, Irving, and J. Reade. 1996. Assyrian Hieroglyphs. *Zeitschrift für Assyriologie* 86:244–268.

Fischer, Henry George. 1974. Redundant Determinatives in the Old Kingdom. *Metropolitan Museum Journal* 8:7–25.

  1986. *L'écriture et l'art de l'Egypte ancienne: quatre leçons sur la paléographie et l'épigraphie pharaoniques.* Collège de France, Essais et Conférences. Paris: Presses Universitaires de France.

  1989. The Origin of Egyptian Hieroglyphs. In *The Origins of Writing*, ed. Wayne M. Senner. Lincoln, NE: University of Nebraska Press, pp. 59–76.

Flannery, Kent V., and Joyce Marcus. 1996. *Zapotec Civilization: How Urban Society Evolved in Mexico's Oaxaca Valley.* London: Thames and Hudson.

Foncerrada de Molina, Marta. 1982. Signos glíficos relacionados con Tlaloc en los murales de la batalla en Cacaxtla. *Anales del Instituto de Investigaciones Estéticas* 50(1):23–34.

Forsyth, Donald W. 1993. The Ceramic Sequence at Nakbe, Guatemala. *Ancient Mesoamerica* 4:31–53.

Freedberg, David. 1989. *The Power of Images: Studies in the History and Theory of Response.* Chicago, IL: University of Chicago Press.

Freidel, David, and Linda Schele. 1988. Symbol and Power: A History of the Lowland Maya Cosmogram. In *Maya Iconography*, ed. Elizabeth P. Benson and Gillett G. Griffin. Princeton, NJ: Princeton University Press, pp. 44–93.

Freidel, David, Linda Schele, and Joy Parker. 1993. *Maya Cosmos: Three Thousand Years on the Shaman's Path.* New York, NY: William Morrow.

Friberg, Jöran. 1978–1979. *The Early Roots of Babylonian Mathematics*, Volumes I–II. Göteborg: Department of Mathematics, Chalmers University of Technology and the University of Göteborg.

  1982. *A Survey of Publications on Sumero-Akkadian Mathematics, Metrology and Related Matters (1854–1982).* Göteborg: Department of Mathematics, Chalmers University of Technology and the University of Göteborg.

  1997–1998. Round and Almost Round Numbers in Proto-Literate Metro-Mathematical Field Texts. *Archiv für Orientforschung* 44–45:1–58.

Gager, John J., ed. 1992. *Curse Tablets and Binding Spells from the Ancient World.* Oxford: Oxford University Press.

Gann, Thomas W. F. 1918. *The Maya Indians of Southern Yucatan and Northern British Honduras.* Bureau of American Ethnology, Smithsonian Institution Bulletin 64. Washington, DC: Government Printing Office.

García Moll, Roberto, Donald W. Patterson Brown, and Marcus C. Winter. 1986. *Monumentos escultóricos de Monte Albán.* Munich: Verlag C. H. Beck.

Gardiner, Alan H. 1957. *Egyptian Grammar, Being an Introduction to the Study of Hieroglyphs.* 3rd edn. London: Oxford University Press for Griffith Institute, Oxford.

Gardner, Martin. 1982. *Logic Machines and Diagrams.* 2nd edn. Chicago, IL: University of Chicago Press.

Gasco, Janine, and Frances F. Berdan. 2003. International Trade Centers. In *The Postclassic Mesoamerican World*, ed. Michael Smith and Frances F. Berdan. Salt Lake City, UT: University of Utah Press, pp. 109–116.

Gaur, Albertine. 1987. *A History of Writing*. New York, NY: Charles Scribner's.

1992. *A History of Writing*. Rev. edn. New York, NY: Cross River Press.

1995. Scripts and Writing Systems: A Historical Perspective. In *Scripts and Literacy: Reading and Learning to Read Alphabets, Syllabaries, and Characters*, ed. Insup Taylor and David R. Olson. Neuropsychology and Cognition 7. Dordrecht, Boston, MA, and London: Kluwer Academic Publishers, pp. 19–30.

Gelb, Ignace J. 1963. *A Study of Writing*. 2nd edn. Chicago, IL: University of Chicago Press.

1975. Methods of Decipherment. *Journal of the Royal Asiatic Society* 1975: 95–104.

Gelb, Ignace, Piotr Steinkeller, and Robert Whiting, Jr. 1991. *Earliest Land Tenure Systems in the New East: Ancient Kudurrus*. Chicago: Oriental Institute.

Gell, Alfred. 1993. *Wrapping in Images: Tattooing in Polynesia*. Oxford: Oxford University Press.

Ghirshman, Roman. 1938. *Fouilles de Sialk près de kashan 1933, 1934, 1937*, Vol. I. Paris: Librairie Orientaliste Paul Geuthner.

Gibson, Eric C., Leslie C. Shaw, and Daniel R. Finamore. 1986. *Early Evidence of Maya Hieroglyphic Writing at Kichpanha, Belize*. Working Papers in Archaeology No. 2., San Antonio, TX: Center for Archaeological Research, University of Texas, San Antonio.

Giddens, Anthony. 1984. *The Constitution of Society: Outline of the Theory of Structuration*. Berkeley, CA: University of California Press.

Glass, John B. 1975. A Survey of Native Middle American Pictorial Manuscripts. In *Handbook of Middle American Indians*, Volume XIV, ed. Robert Wauchope and Howard F. Cline. Austin, TX: University of Texas Press, pp. 3–80.

Glassner, Jean-Jacques. 2000. *Ecrire à Sumer: l'invention du cunéiforme*. Paris: Editions du Seuil.

Gleason, Allan. 1996. Christian Missionary Activities. In *The World's Writing Systems*, ed. Peter T. Daniels and William Bright. New York, NY, and Oxford: Oxford University Press, pp. 777–780.

Goody, Jack. 1977. *The Domestication of the Savage Mind*. Cambridge: Cambridge University Press.

1986. *The Logic of Writing and the Organization of Society*. Cambridge: Cambridge University Press.

1987. *The Interface between the Written and the Oral*. Cambridge: Cambridge University Press.

2000. *The Power of the Written Tradition*. Washington, DC: Smithsonian Institution Press.

Goody, Jack, and Ian Watt. 1963. The Consequences of Literacy. *Comparative Studies in Society and History* 5(3):304–345.

Görsdorf, Jochen, Günter Dreyer, and Ulrich Hartung. 1998. ^{14}c Dating Results of the Archaic Royal Necropolis Umm el-Qaab at Abydos. *Mitteilungen des Deutschen Archäologischen Instituts, Abteilung Kairo* 54:169–175.

Gould, Stephen J. 1999. Introduction: The Scales of Contingency and Punctuation in History. In *Structure and Contingency: Evolutionary Processes in Life and Human Society*, ed. John Bintliff. London: Leicester University Press, pp. ix–xxii.

Gragg, Gene B. 1996. Mesopotamian Cuneiform: Other Languages. In *The World's Writing Systems*, ed. Peter T. Daniels and William Bright. New York, NY, and Oxford: Oxford University Press, pp. 58–72.

Green, Dennis H. 1994. *Medieval Listening and Reading: The Primary Reception of German Literature 800–1300*. Cambridge: Cambridge University Press.

Green, Margaret W. 1980. Animal Husbandry at Uruk in the Archaic Period. *Journal of Near Eastern Studies* 39:1–35.

    1981. The Construction and Implementation of the Cuneiform Writing System. *Visible Language* 15:345–372.

    1989. Early Cuneiform. In *The Origins of Writing*, ed. Wayne M. Senner. Lincoln, NE: University of Nebraska Press, pp. 43–57.

Green, Margaret W., and Hans Nissen, eds. 1987. *Zeichenliste der archaischen Texte aus Uruk*. Ausgrabungen der Deutschen Forschungsgemeinschaft in Uruk-Warka 11. Archaische Texte aus Uruk 2. Berlin: Gebrüder Mann verlag.

Grove, David C. 1970. *The Olmec Paintings of Oxtotitlan Cave, Guerrero, Mexico*. Studies in Pre-Columbian Art and Archaeology 6. Washington, DC: Dumbarton Oaks Research Library and Collection.

Grube, Nikolai. 1990. *Die Entwicklung der Mayaschrift*. Berlin: Verlag von Flemming.

    1994. Observations on the History of Maya Hieroglyphic Writing. In *Seventh Palenque Round Table, 1989*, ed. Merle G. Robertson and Virginia M. Fields. San Francisco, CA: Pre-Columbian Art Research Institute, pp. 177–186.

    1998. Speaking through Stones: A Quotative Particle in Maya Hieroglyphic Inscriptions. In *50 Years of Americanist Studies at the University of Bonn*, ed. S. Dedenbach-Salazar Sáenz, C. Arellano Hoffmann, E. König, and H. Prümers. Bonn: Verlag Anton Saurwein, pp. 543–558.

Grube, Nikolai, and Simon Martin. 2001. *The Coming of Kings: Writing and Dynastic Kingship in the Maya Area Between the Late Preclassic and Early Classic*. Austin, TX: Texas Workshop Foundation.

Guest, Ann Hutchinson. 1984. *Dance Notation: The Process of Recording Movement on Paper*. New York, NY: Dance Horizons.

Guo Moruo, ed. 1982. *Jiaguwen heji*. 13 vols. Beijing: Zhongguo Shehui kexueyuan lishi yanjiusuo.

Haas, William. 1976. Writing: The Basic Options. In *Writing Without Letters*, ed. William Haas. Manchester: Manchester University Press, pp. 131–208.

Haile, Getatchew. 1996. Ethiopic Writing. In *The World's Writing Systems*, ed. Peter T. Daniels and William Bright. New York, NY, and Oxford: Oxford University Press, pp. 569–576.

Halverson, John. 1992. Goody and the Implosion of the Literacy Thesis. *Man* 27:301–317.

Hammond, Norman. 1987. *The Sun Also Rises: Iconographic Syntax of the Pomona Flare.* Research Reports on Ancient Maya Writing 7. Washington, DC: Center for Maya Research.

Hansell, Mark. 2002. Functional Answers to Structural Problems in Thinking about Writing. In *Difficult Characters: Interdisciplinary Studies of Chinese and Japanese Writing*, ed. Mary S. Erbaugh. Columbus, OH: National East Asian Languages Resource Center, Ohio State University, pp. 124–176.

Hansen, Richard D. 1990. *Excavations in the Tigre Complex, El Mirador, Petén, Guatemala: El Mirador Series, Part 3.* Papers of the New World Archaeological Foundation 62. Provo, UT: Brigham Young University.

1991. *An Early Maya Text from El Mirador, Guatemala.* Research Reports in Ancient Maya Writing 37. Washington, DC: Center for Maya Research.

1998. Continuity and Disjunction: The Pre-Classic Antecedents of Classic Maya Architecture. In *Function and Meaning in Classic Maya Architecture*, ed. Stephen D. Houston. Washington, DC: Dumbarton Oaks Research Library and Collection, pp. 49–122.

Harper, Prudence, Joan Aruz, and Françoise Tallon, eds. 1992. *The Royal City of Susa: Ancient Near Eastern Treasures in the Louvre.* New York: Metropolitan Museum of Art.

Harris, John F., and Stephen K. Stearns. 1997. *Understanding Maya Inscriptions. A Hieroglyph Handbook.* 2nd edn. Philadelphia, PA: University Museum, University of Pennsylvania.

Harris, Robert L. 1999. *Information Graphics: A Comprehensive Illustrated Reference.* Atlanta, GA: Management Graphics; New York, NY, and Oxford: Oxford University Press.

Harris, Roy. 1986. *The Origin of Writing.* La Salle, IL: Open Court; London: Duckworth.

1995. *Signs of Writing.* London and New York, NY: Routledge.

Harrison, Stephen. 1991. What Do Viruses Look Like? *Harvey Lectures* 85:127–152.

Hartung, Ulrich. 1998a. Prädynastische Siegelabrollungen aus dem Friedhof U in Abydos (Umm el-Qaab). *Mitteilungen des Deutschen Archäologischen Instituts, Abteilung Kairo* 54:187–217.

1998b. Zur Entwicklung des Handels und zum Beginn wirtschaftlicher Administration im prädynastischen Ägypten. *Studien zur Altägyptischen Kultur* 26:35–50.

2001. *Umm el-Qaab II: Importkeramik aus dem Friedhof U in Abydos (Umm el-Qaab) und die Beziehungen Ägyptens zu Vorderasien im 4. Jahrtausend v. Chr.* Deutsches Archäologisches Institut, Abteilung Kairo, Archäologische Veröffentlichungen 92. Mainz: Philipp von Zabern.

Hary, Benjamin. 1996. Adaptations of the Hebrew Script. In *The World's Writing Systems*, ed. Peter T. Daniels and William Bright. New York, NY, and Oxford: Oxford University Press, pp. 727–742.

Hawkes, Jacquetta. 1982. *Adventurer in Archaeology: The Biography of Sir Mortimer Wheeler*. New York, NY: St. Martin's Press.

Hawkins, David. 1986. Writing in Anatolia: Imported and Indigenous Systems. *World Archaeology* 17:363–376.

Helck, Wolfgang. 1990. *Thinitische Topfmarken*. Ägyptologische Abhandlungen 50. Wiesbaden: Otto Harrassowitz.

Hendrickx, Stan 1995. *Analytical Bibliography of the Prehistoric and Early Dynastic Period of Egypt and Northern Sudan*. Egyptian Prehistory Monographs 1. Leuven: Leuven University Press.

Hill, Archibald A. 1967. The Typology of Writing Systems. In *Papers in Linguistics in Honor of Léon Dostert*, ed. William M. Austin. The Hague: Mouton, pp. 92–99.

Hill, Jane H. 2001. Proto-Uto-Aztecan: A Community of Cultivators in Central Mexico? *American Anthropologist* 103(4):913–934.

Hinüber, Oskar von. 1989. *Der Beginn der Schrift und frühe Schriftlichkeit in Indien*. Akademie der Wissenschaften und der Literatur, Mainz, Abhandlungen, Geistes- und Sozialwissenschaftliche Klasse 1989: 11. Wiesbaden and Stuttgart: Franz Steiner.

Hinz, Walther. 1987. Persia c. 2400–1800 BC. In *Cambridge Ancient History* Volume I, part 2, 3rd edition, ed. Iorwerth Edwards, Cyrus Gadd, and Nicholas Hammond. Cambridge: Cambridge University Press, pp. 644–680.

Hoch, James E. 1994. *Semitic Words in Egyptian Texts of the New Kingdom and Third Intermediate Period*. Princeton, NJ: Princeton University Press.

Hodder, Ian. 1991. *Reading the Past: Current Approaches to Interpretation in Archaeology*. 2nd edn. Cambridge: Cambridge University Press.

Hoffmann, Roald. 1990. Molecular Beauty. *Journal of Aesthetics and Art Criticism* 48(3):191–204.

Hoffmann, Roald and Pierre Laszlo. 1989. Representation in Chemistry. *Diogenes* 147:23–51.

Holisky, Dee A. 1996. The Georgian Alphabet. In *The World's Writing Systems*, ed. Peter T. Daniels and William Bright. New York, NY, and Oxford: Oxford University Press, pp. 364–369.

Holmes, William H. 1907. On a Nephrite Statuette from San Andrés Tuxtla, Vera Cruz, Mexico. *American Anthropologist* 9:691–701.

Hopkins, Nicholas A. 1984. Otomanguean Linguistic Prehistory. In *Essays in Otomanguean Culture History*, ed. Kathryn Josserand, Marcus Winter, and Nicholas A. Hopkins. Vanderbilt University Publications in Anthropology 31. Nashville, TN : Vanderbilt University, pp. 25–64.

Houston, Stephen D. 1984. An Example of Homophony in Mayan Script. *American Antiquity* 49(4):790–805.

1989. *Reading the Past: Maya Glyphs*. Berkeley, CA: University of California Press.

1994a. Literacy Among the Pre-Columbian Maya: A Comparative Perspective. In *Writing Without Words: Alternative Literacies in Mesoamerica and the Andes*, ed. Elizabeth H. Boone and Walter Mignolo. Durham, NC: Duke University Press, pp. 27–49.

1994b. Mesoamerican Writing. In *The Encyclopedia of Language and Linguistics*, Volume V, ed. R. Ascher and J. M. V. Simpson. Oxford: Pergamon, pp. 2449–2451.

1998. Classic Maya Depictions of the Built Environment. In *Function and Meaning in Classic Maya Architecture*, ed. Stephen D. Houston. Washington, DC: Dumbarton Oaks Research Library and Collection, pp. 333–372.

2000. Into the Minds of Ancients: Advances in Maya Glyph Studies. *Journal of World Prehistory* 14:121–201.

2001. Writing Systems: Overview and Early Development. In *Oxford Encyclopedia of Mesoamerican Cultures*, Volume III, ed. Davíd Carrasco. New York, NY, and Oxford: Oxford University Press, pp. 338–340.

2004 The Archaeology of Communication Technologies. *Annual Review of Anthropology* 33:223–250.

Houston, Stephen D., and David Stuart. 1993. Multiple Voices in Maya Writing: Evidence for First- and Second-person References. Paper presented at the 58th meeting of the Society for American Archaeology, St. Louis.

1996. Of Gods, Glyphs and Kings: Divinity and Rulership among the Classic Maya. *Antiquity* 70:289–312.

1998. The Ancient Maya Self: Personhood and Portraiture in the Classic Period. *RES* 33:73–101.

Houston, Stephen D., and Karl Taube. 2000. An Archaeology of the Senses: Perception and Cultural Expression in Ancient Mesoamerica. *Cambridge Archaeological Journal* 10(2):261–294.

Houston, Stephen D., John Baines, and Jerrold Cooper. 2003. Last Writing: Script Obsolescence in Egypt, Mesopotamia, and Mesoamerica. *Comparative Studies in Society and History* 45(3):430–480.

Houston, Stephen D., John Robertson, and David Stuart. 2000. The Language of Classic Maya Inscriptions. *Current Anthropology* 41(3):321–356.

2001. *Quality and Quantity in Glyphic Nouns and Adjectives.* Research Reports in Ancient Maya Writing 47. Washington, DC: Center for Maya Research.

Houston, Stephen D., David Stuart, and John Robertson. 1998. Disharmony in Maya Hieroglyphic Writing: Linguistic Change and Continuity in Classic Society. In *Anatomía de una civilización: aproximaciones interdisciplinarias a la cultura maya*, ed. A. Cuidad Ruiz, Y. Fernández Marquínez, J. M. García Campillo, M. J. Iglesias Ponce de León, A. Lacadena García-Gallo, and L. Sanz Castro. Madrid: Sociedad Española de Estudios Mayas, pp. 275–296.

Hsu, Cho-yun, and Katheryn M. Linduff. 1988. *Western Chou Civilization.* New Haven, CT: Yale University Press.

Hu Houxuan. 1970. *Jiaguxue Shang Shi Luncong Chuji.* Hong Kong: Wen You Tang.

Hutchinson, Ann. 1966. *Labanotation.* New York, NY: Theatre Arts Books.

Huxley, Julian. 1960. *Knowledge, Morality, and Destiny.* New York, NY: New American Library.

Inomata, Takeshi. 2001. The Power and Ideology of Artistic Creation: Elite Craft Specialists in Classic Maya Society. *Current Anthropology* 42:321–349.

Ismail, Farouk. 1996. *Administrative Documents from Tell Beydar (Seasons 1993–1995)*. Subartu 2. Turnhout: Brepols.

Jakobson, Roman. 1971a. On the Relation between Visual and Auditory Sign. In *Selected Writings II*. The Hague: Mouton, pp. 338–344.

 1971b. Visual and Auditory Sign. In *Selected Writings II*. The Hague: Mouton, pp. 334–337.

Jakobson, Roman, and Linda Waugh. 1990. Quest for the Ultimate Constituents. In *On Language*, ed. Linda R. Waugh and Monique Monville-Burston. Cambridge, MA: Harvard University Press, pp. 259–293.

Jansson, Sven B. F. 1987. *Runes in Sweden*. Stockholm: Gidlunds.

Joffe, Alexander H. 2000. Egypt and Syro-Mesopotamia in the 4th Millennium: Implications of the New Chronology. *Current Anthropology* 41:113–123.

Johnson, Matthew. 1996. *An Archaeology of Capitalism*. Oxford: Blackwell.

Josserand, J. Kathryn. 1975. Archaeological and Linguistic Correlations for Mayan Prehistory. *Actas del XLa Congreso Internacional de Americanistas* 1:501–510.

Just, Bryan, n.d. Concordances of Time: In Extenso Almanacs in the Madrid and Borgia Group Codices. Tulane University, unpublished manuscript.

Justeson, John S. 1976. Universals of Language and Universals of Writing. In *Linguistic Studies Offered to Joseph Greenberg*, ed. Alphonse Juilland. Saratoga, CA: Anma Libri, I, pp. 57–94.

 1986. The Origin of Writing Systems: Preclassic Mesoamerica. *World Archaeology* 17:437–458.

 1989. The Representational Conventions of Mayan Hieroglyphic Writing. In *Word and Image in Maya Culture: Explorations in Language Writing and Representation*, ed. William F. Hanks and Don S. Rice. Salt Lake City, UT: University of Utah Press, pp. 25–38.

Justeson, John S., and Terrence Kaufman. 1992. Un desciframiento de la escritura jeroglífica epi-olmeca: métodos y resultados. *Arqueología* 8:15–26.

 1993. A Decipherment of Epi-Olmec Hieroglyphic Writing. *Science* 259:1703–1711.

 1997. A Newly Discovered Column in the Hieroglyphic Text on La Mojarra Stela 1: A Test of the Epi-Olmec Decipherment. *Science* 277:207–210.

 2001a. *Epi-Olmec Hieroglyphic Writing and Texts*. Austin, TX: Texas Workshop Foundation.

 2001b. *The Proceedings of the Maya Hieroglyphic Workshop: Epi-Olmec Writing*. Transcribed by Phil Wanyerka. Austin, TX: Texas Workshop Foundation.

Justeson, John S., and Peter Mathews. 1990. Evolutionary Trends in Mesoamerican Hieroglyphic Writing. *Visible Language* 24(1):88–132.

Justeson, John S., and Laurence D. Stephens. 1994. The Evolution of Syllabaries from Alphabets: Transmission, Language Contrast, and Script Typology. *Die Sprache* 35:2–46.

Justeson, John S., William M. Norman, Lyle R. Campbell, and Terrence S. Kaufman. 1985. *The Foreign Impact on Lowland Mayan Language and Script*. Middle

American Research Institute, Publication 53. New Orleans, LA: Tulane University.

Justeson, John S., William M. Norman, and Norman Hammond. 1988. The Pomona Flare: A Preclassic Maya Hieroglyphic Text. In *Maya Iconography*, ed. Elizabeth P. Benson and Gillett G. Griffin. Princeton (NJ): Princeton University Press, pp. 94–151.

Kahl, Jochem. 1994. *Das System der ägyptischen Hieroglyphenschrift in der 0.–3. Dynastie*. Göttinger Orientforschungen IV: Ägypten 29. Wiesbaden: Otto Harrassowitz.

    2001. Die ältesten schriftlichen Belege für den Gott Seth. *Göttinger Miszellen* 181:51–57.

Kaiser, Werner. 1990. Zur Entstehung des gesamtägyptischen Staates. *Mitteilungen des Deutschen Archäologischen Instituts, Abteilung Kairo* 46:287–299.

Kaiser, Werner, and Günter Dreyer. 1982. Umm el-Qaab: Nachuntersuchungen im frühzeitlichen Königsfriedhof, 2. Vorbericht. *Mitteilungen des Deutschen Archäologischen Instituts, Abteilung Kairo* 38:211–269.

Kammerzell, Frank. 2001. Die Entstehung der Alphabetreihe: zum ägyptischen Ursprung der semitischen und westlichen Schriften. In *Hieroglyphen, Alphabete, Schriftreformen: Studien zu Multiliteralismus, Schriftwechsel und Orthographieneuregelungen*, ed. Dörte Borchers, Frank Kammerzell, and Stefan Weninger. Lingua Aegyptia, Studia Monographica 3. Göttingen: Seminar für Ägyptologie und Koptologie, pp. 117–158.

Kampen, Michael. 1972. *The Sculptures of El Tajín, Veracruz, Mexico*. Gainesville, FL: University of Florida Press.

Kaplan, Jonathan. 2000. Monument 65: A Great Emblematic Depiction of Throned Rule and Royal Sacrifice at Late Preclassic Kaminaljuyu. *Ancient Mesoamerica* 11:185–198.

Kaplony, Peter. 1963. *Die Inschriften der ägyptischen Frühzeit*. Ägyptologische Abhandlungen 8. 3 vols. Wiesbaden: Otto Harrassowitz.

Kara, György. 1996a. Aramaic Scripts for Altaic Languages. In *The World's Writing Systems*, ed. Peter T. Daniels and William Bright. New York, NY, and Oxford: Oxford University Press, pp. 536–558.

    1996b. Kitan and Jurchin. In *The World's Writing Systems*, ed. Peter T. Daniels and William Bright. New York, NY, and Oxford: Oxford University Press, pp. 230–238.

Karlgren, Bernhard. 1952. Some New Bronzes in the Museum of Far Eastern Antiquities. *Bulletin of the Museum of Far Eastern Antiquities, Stockholm* 24:11–26.

Karsten, Karl G. 1923. *Charts and Graphs: An Introduction to Graphic Methods in the Control and Analysis of Statistics*. New York: Prentice Hall.

Kaufman, Terrence. 1974. *Idiomas de Mesoamérica*. Seminario de Integración Social Guatemalteca Publicación 33. Guatemala: Ministerio de Educación.

    1976. Archaeological and Linguistic Correlations in Maya-land and Associated Areas of Meso-America. *World Archaeology* 8:101–118.

Kauffmann, Claus Michael. 1975. *Romanesque Manuscripts, 1066–1190.* A Survey of Manuscripts Illuminated in the British Isles, vol. 3. London: H. Miller.

Kaye, Alan S. 1996. Adaptations of Arabic Script. In *The World's Writing Systems*, ed. Peter T. Daniels and William Bright. New York, NY, and Oxford: Oxford University Press, pp. 743–762.

Keightley, David N. 1978. *Sources of Shang History: The Oracle-Bone Inscriptions of Bronze Age China.* Berkeley, CA: University of California Press.

1997. Shang Oracle-Bone Inscriptions. In *New Sources of Early Chinese History: An Introduction to the Reading of Inscriptions and Manuscripts*, ed. Edward L. Shaughnessy. Berkeley, CA: Society for the Study of Early China, pp. 15–55.

1999. The Shang: China's First Historical Dynasty. In *The Cambridge History of Ancient China: From the Origins of Civilization to 221 BC*, ed. Michael Loewe and Edward L. Shaughnessy. Cambridge: Cambridge University Press, pp. 232–291.

Kelley, David H. 1966. A Cylinder Seal from Tlatilco. *American Antiquity* 31:744–746.

1976. *Deciphering the Maya Script.* Austin, TX: University of Texas Press.

1982. Costume and Name in Mesoamerica. *Visible Language* 16(1):39–48.

Kemp, Barry J. 1989. *Ancient Egypt: Anatomy of a Civilization.* London and New York, NY: Routledge.

Kemp, Barry J., Andrew Boyce, and James Harrell. 2000. The Colossi from the Early Shrine at Coptos in Egypt. *Cambridge Archaeological Journal* 10:211–242.

Kienast, Burkhart, and Konrad Volk. 1995. *Die sumerischen und akkadischen Briefe.* Freiburger altorientalistische Studien 19. Stuttgart: F. Steiner.

King, Ross. 1996. Korean Writing. In *The World's Writing Systems*, ed. Peter T. Daniels and William Bright. New York, NY, and Oxford: Oxford University Press, pp. 218–227.

Krampen, Martin. 1986. On the Origins of Visual Literacy: Children's Drawings and Compositions of Graphemes. In *Toward a New Understanding of Literacy*, ed. Merald E. Wrolstad and Dennis F. Fisher. New York, NY: Praeger, pp. 80–111.

Krebernik, Manfred. 1994. Review of Green and Nissen (1987). *Orientalistische Literaturzeitung* 89:380–385.

1998. Die Texte aus Fara und Abū Solābīh. In *Mesopotamien: Späturuk-Zeit und Frühdynastische Zeit*, Josef Bauer, Robert K. Englund, and Manfred Krebernik. Orbis Biblicus et Orientalis 160/1. Freiburg, Switzerland: Universitätsverlag Freiburg Schweiz, pp. 237–427.

Kress, Gunther, and Theo van Leeuwen. 1996. *Reading Images: The Grammar of Visual Design.* London and New York, NY: Routledge.

Kris, Ernst, and Otto Kurz. 1979. *Legend, Myth, and Magic in the Image of the Artist: An Historical Experiment.* New Haven, CT: Yale University Press.

Kroeber, Alfred L. 1940. Stimulus Diffusion. *American Anthropologist* 42:1–20.

1948. *Anthropology.* 2nd edn. New York, NY: Harcourt, Brace.

Kubler, George. 1973. The Clauses of Classic Maya Inscriptions. In *Mesoamerican Writing Systems*, ed. Elizabeth P. Benson. Washington, DC: Dumbarton Oaks Research Library and Collection, pp. 145–164.

Kychanov, Evgenij I. 1996. Tangut. In *The World's Writing Systems*, ed. Peter T. Daniels and William Bright. New York, NY, and Oxford: Oxford University Press, pp. 228–230.

Laban, Rudolf. 1974. *The Language of Movement: A Guidebook of Choreutics.* Annotated and edited by Lisa Ullmann. Boston, MA: Plays.

Lacadena, Alfonso. 1995. Evolución formal de las grafías escriturarias mayas: implicaciones históricas y culturales. Unpublished Ph.D. dissertation, Universidad Complutense de Madrid.

Lacau, Pierre. 1970. *Les noms des parties du corps en Egyptien et en Sémitique.* Mémoires de l'Académie des Inscriptions et Belles-Lettres 45. Paris: Imprimerie Nationale / Klincksieck.

Lamberg-Karlovsky, Clifford Charles, and Daniel T. Potts. 2001. *Excavations at Tepe Yahya, Iran 1967–1975: The Third Millennium.* American School of Prehistoric Research Bulletin 45. Cambridge, MA: Harvard University Press.

Land, L. K., H. B. Nicholson, and Alan Cordy-Collins. 1979. *Pre-Columbian Art from the Land Collection.* San Francisco, CA: California Academy of Sciences.

Laporte, Juan Pedro, and Vilma Fialko. 1995. Un reencuentro con Mundo Perdido, Tikal, Guatemala. *Ancient Mesoamerica* 6(1):41–94.

Larsen, Mogens Trolle. 1987. The Mesopotamian Lukewarm Mind: Reflections on Science, Divination, and Literacy. In *Language, Literature, and History: Philological and Historical Studies Presented to Erica Reiner*, ed. Francesca Rochberg-Halton. New Haven, CT: American Oriental Society, pp. 203–225.

  1988. Introduction: Literacy and Social Complexity. In *State and Society: The Emergence and Development of Social Hierarchy and Political Centralization*, ed. John Gledhill, Barbara Bender, and Mogens Trolle Larsen. London: Unwin Hyman, pp. 173–191.

  1989. What They Wrote on Clay. In *Literacy and Society*, ed. Karen Schousboe and M. T. Larsen. Copenhagen: Akademisk Forlag, pp. 121–148.

Lawler, Andrew. 2001a. Destruction in Mesopotamia. *Science* 293:32–35.

  2001b. Iraq Opening Sets Off Scramble for Sites. *Science* 293:36–38.

  2001c. Writing Gets a Rewrite. *Science* 292:2418–2420.

Lebeau, Marc, and Antoine Suleiman. 1997. *Tell Beydar: Three Seasons of Excavations (1992–1994), A Preliminary Report.* Subartu 3. Turnhout: Brepols.

Le Breton, Louis. 1957. The Early Periods at Susa. *Iraq* 19:79–124.

Le Brun, Alain. 1971. Recherches stratigraphiques à l'Acropole de Suse, 1969–1971. *Cahiers de la Délégation Archéologique Française* 1:163–216.

  1978a. La glyptique du niveau 17B de l'acropole (campagne de 1972). *Cahiers de la Délégation Archéologique Française* 8:61–79.

  1978b. Le niveau 17B de l'acropole de Suse (campagne de 1972). *Cahiers de la Délégation Archéologique Française* 9:57–154.

  1978c. Chantier de l'Acropole I. *Paléorient* 4:177–192.

Le Brun, Alain, and François Vallat. 1978. L'origine de P'écriture à Suse L'origine. *Cahiers de la Dlégation Archéologique Française* 8:11–57.

Lee, Thomas A., Jr. 1969. *The Artifacts of Chiapa de Corzo, Chiapas, Mexico.* Papers of New World Archaeological Foundation 26. Provo, UT: Brigham Young University.

León-Portilla, Miguel. 1992. Have We Really Translated the Mesoamerican "Ancient Word?" In *On the Translation of Native American Literatures*, ed. Brian Swann. Washington, DC: Smithsonian Institution Press, pp. 313–338.

Lesko, Leonard H. 1999. Writing, Reading, and Schooling. In *Encyclopedia of the Archaeology of Ancient Egypt*, ed. Kathryn Bard. London: Routledge, pp. 885–887.

Lévi-Strauss, Claude. 1974. *Tristes tropiques.* New York, NY: Atheneum.

Lewis, Mark Edward. 1999. *Writing and Authority in Early China.* Albany, NY: State University of New York Press.

Li Chi [Li Ji]. 1977. *Anyang.* Seattle, WA: University of Washington Press.

Lieberman, Stephen J. 1977. The Names of the Cuneiform Graphemes in Old Babylonian Akkadian. In *Essays on the Ancient Near East in Memory of J. J. Finkelstein*, ed. Maria de Jong Ellis. Connecticut Academy of Arts and Sciences, Memoir 19. New Haven, CT: Connecticut Academy of Arts and Sciences, pp. 147–154.

Li Ji [Li Chi]. 1956. *Xiaotun, di san ben, Yinxu Qiwu: jia bian, Taoqi: shang ji.* Taibei: Institute of History and Philology, Academia Sinica.

Liverani, Mario. 1998. *Uruk, la prima città.* Rome: Laterza.

Li Xueqin. 1985. Kaogu Faxian yu Zhongguo Wenzi Qiyuan. *Zhongguo Wenhua Yanjiu Jikan* 2:146–157.

Li Xueqin, Garman Harbottle, Juzhong Zhang, and Changsui Wang. 2003. The Earliest Writing? Sign Use in the Seventh Millennium BC at Jiahu, Henan Province, China. *Antiquity* 77:31–44.

Lloyd, G. E. R. 2002. *The Ambitions of Curiosity: Understanding the World in Ancient Greece and China.* Cambridge: Cambridge University Press.

Loewe, Michael, ed. 1993. *Early Chinese Texts: A Bibliographical Guide.* Berkeley, CA: Society for the Study of Early China.

Loprieno, Antonio. 1995. *Ancient Egyptian: A Linguistic Introduction.* Cambridge: Cambridge University Press.

Lounsbury, Floyd G. 1989. The Ancient Writing of Middle America. In *The Origins of Writing*, ed. Wayne M. Senner. Lincoln, NE: University of Nebraska Press, pp. 203–237.

Lowe, Gareth W. 1989. The Heartland Olmec: Evolution of Material Culture. In *Regional Perspectives on the Olmec*, ed. Robert J. Sharer and David C. Grove. Cambridge: Cambridge University Press, pp. 33–67.

Luo Zhenyu. 1937. *Sandai Jijin Wen Cun.* N.p.

Lynch, Michael. 1985. Discipline and the Material Form of Images: An Analysis of Scientific Visibility. *Social Studies of Science* 15:37–66.

Machor, James L., and Philip Goldstein, eds. 2000. *Reception Study: From Literary Theory to Cultural Studies.* London: Routledge.

Macri, Martha J., and Laura M. Stark. 1993. *A Sign Catalog of the La Mojarra Script*. Pre-Columbian Art Research Institute Monograph 5. San Francisco, CA: Pre-Columbian Art Research Institute.

Mair, Victor H. 1996. Modern Chinese Writing. In *The World's Writing Systems*, ed. Peter T. Daniels and William Bright. New York, NY, and Oxford: Oxford University Press, 200–208.

Mann, Michael. 1986. *The Sources of Social Power*, Volume I: *A History of Power from the Beginning to AD 1760*. Cambridge: Cambridge University Press.

Marcus, Joyce. 1976a. The Iconography of Militarism at Monte Albán and Neighboring Sites in the Valley of Oaxaca. In *The Origins of Religious Art and Iconography in Preclassic Mesoamerica*, ed. Henry B. Nicholson. Los Angeles, CA: Latin American Center, University of California, Los Angeles, pp. 123–139.

1976b. The Origins of Mesoamerican Writing. *Annual Review of Anthropology* 5:35–67.

1983a. Lintel 2 at Xoxocotlán. In *The Cloud People: Divergent Evolution of the Zapotec and Mixtec Civilizations*, ed. Kent V. Flannery and Joyce Marcus. New York, NY: Academic Press, pp. 150–152.

1983b. The Conquest Slabs of Building J, Monte Albán. In *The Cloud People: Divergent Evolution of the Zapotec and Mixtec Civilizations*, ed. Kent V. Flannery and Joyce Marcus. New York, NY: Academic Press, pp. 106–108.

1983c. Teotihuacán Visitors on Monte Albán Monuments and Murals. In *The Cloud People: Divergent Evolution of the Zapotec and Mixtec Civilizations*, ed. Kent V. Flannery and Joyce Marcus. New York, NY: Academic Press, pp. 175–181.

1992. *Mesoamerican Writing Systems: Propaganda, Myth, and History in Four Ancient Civilizations*. Princeton, NJ: Princeton University Press.

Martin, Henri-Jean. 1994. *The History and Power of Writing*. Trans. Lydia G. Cochrane. Chicago, IL: University of Chicago Press.

Martin, Simon. 1997. The Painted King List: A Commentary on Codex-Style Dynastic Vases. In *The Maya Vase Book*, Volume V, ed. Justin Kerr. New York, NY: Kerr Associates, pp. 846–867.

Martin, Simon, and Nikolai Grube. 2000. *Chronicle of the Maya Kings and Queens: Deciphering the Dynasties of the Ancient Maya*. London: Thames and Hudson.

Masson, Marilyn A., and Heather Orr. 1998. The Role of Zapotec Genealogical Records in late Precolumbian Valley of Oaxaca Political History. *Mexicon* 20(1):10–15.

Maudslay, Alfred P. 1889–1902. *Biologia Centrali-Americana: Archaeology*. 5 vols. London: R. H. Porter and Dulau.

McCawley, James D. 1996. Music Notation. In *The World's Writing Systems*, ed. Peter T. Daniels and William Bright. New York, NY, and Oxford: Oxford University Press, pp. 847–854.

McClelland, James E., III, and Harold Dorn. 1999. *Science and Technology in World History: An Introduction*. Baltimore, MD: The Johns Hopkins University Press.

McDonald, Angela. 2002. Animal Metaphor in the Egyptian Determinative System: Three Case Studies. Unpublished D.Phil. dissertation, University of Oxford.

McDowell, Andrea. 1996. Student Exercises from Deir el-Medina: The Dates. In *Studies in Honor of William Kelly Simpson*, Volume II, ed. Peter Der Manuelian. Boston, MA: Museum of Fine Arts, pp. 601–608.

　1999. *Village Life in Ancient Egypt*. Oxford: Oxford University Press.

　2000. Teachers and Students at Deir el-Medina. In *Deir el-Medina in the Third Millennium AD, A Tribute to Jac. J. Janssen*, ed. R. J. Demarée and A. Egberts. Leiden: Nederlands Instituut voor het Nabije Oosten, pp. 217–233.

McGaw, Judith A. 1996. Reconceiving Technology: Why Feminine Technologies Matter. In *Gender and Archaeology*, ed. Rita P. Wright. Philadelphia, PA: University of Pennsylvania Press, pp. 52–75.

McGuinnes-Scott, Julia. 1983. *Movement Study and Benesh Movement Notation*. Oxford: Oxford University Press.

McManus, Damian. 1991. *A Guide to Ogam*. Maynooth Monographs 4. Maynooth: An Sagart.

　1996. Ogham. In *The World's Writing Systems*, ed. Peter T. Daniels and William Bright. New York, NY, and Oxford: Oxford University Press, pp. 340–345.

McNeill, William H. 1989. *Arnold Toynbee: A Life*. Oxford: Oxford University Press.

Mecquenem, Roland de. 1949. *Epigraphie proto-élamite*. Mémoires de la Délégation en Perse 31. Paris: Presses Universitaires de France.

　1956. Notes proto-élamites. *Revue d'Assyriologie et d'Archéologie Orientale* 50:200–204.

Medellín Zenil, Alfonso. 1960. Monolitos inéditos olmecos. *La palabra y el hombre: Revista de la Universidad Veracruzana* 16:75–97.

Melchert, H. Craig. 1996. Anatolian Hieroglyphs. In *The World's Writing Systems*, ed. Peter T. Daniels and William Bright. New York, NY, and Oxford: Oxford University Press, pp. 120–124.

Méluzin, Sylvia. 1987. The Tuxtla Statuette: An Internal Analysis of Its Writing System. In *The Periphery of the Southeastern Classic Maya Realm*, ed. Gary W. Pahl. Los Angeles, CA: Latin American Center, University of California, Los Angeles, pp. 68–113.

　1995. *Further Investigations of the Tuxtla Script: An Inscribed Mask and La Mojarra Stela 1*. Papers of the New World Archaeological Foundation 65. Provo, UT: Brigham Young University.

Meriggi, Piero. 1971–1974. *La scrittura proto-elamica I–III*. Rome: Accademia nazionale dei Lincei.

　1975. Der Stand der Erforschung des Proto-elamischen. *Journal of the Royal Asiatic Society* 1975:105.

Michalowski, Piotr. 1990. Early Mesopotamian Communicative Systems: Art, Literature, and Writing. In *Investigating Artistic Environments in the Ancient Near East*, ed. Ann Gunter. Washington, DC: Arthur M. Sackler Gallery, Smithsonian Institution Press, pp. 53–69.

1991. Charisma and Control: On Continuity and Change in Early Mesopotamian Bureaucratic Systems. In *The Organization of Power: Aspects of Bureaucracy in the Ancient Near East*, ed. McGuire Gibson and Robert D. Biggs. 2nd edn. Chicago, IL: University of Chicago Press, pp. 45–57.

1993a. *Letters from Mesopotamia*. Writings from the Ancient World 3. Atlanta, GA: Scholars Press.

1993b. Tokenism. *American Anthropologist* 95:996–999.

1994. Writing and Literacy in Early States: A Mesopotamianist Perspective. In *Literacy: Interdisciplinary Conversations*, ed. Deborah Keller-Cohen. Cresskill, NJ: Hampton Press, pp. 49–70.

1996. Cuneiform: Origins. In *The World's Writing Systems*, ed. Peter T. Daniels and William Bright. New York, NY, and Oxford: Oxford University Press, pp. 33–36.

Michel, Rudolph, Patrick McGovern, and Virginia Badler. 1993. The First Wine and Beer: Chemical Detection of Ancient Fermented Beverages. *Analytical Chemistry* 65(8):408A–413A.

Midant-Reynes, Béatrix. 2000. *The Prehistory of Egypt, from the First Egyptians to the First Pharaohs*, trans. Ian Shaw. Oxford and Malden, MA: Blackwell.

Millard, A. R. 1986. The Infancy of the Alphabet. *World Archaeology* 17:390–398.

Miller, Arthur G. 1995. *The Painted Tombs of Oaxaca, Mexico: Living with the Dead*. Cambridge: Cambridge University Press.

Miller, Mary E. 1991. Rethinking the Classic Sculptures of Cerro de las Mesas, Veracruz, Mexico. In *Settlement Archaeology of Cerro de las Mesas, Veracruz, Mexico*, ed. Barbara L. Stark. Institute of Archaeology Monograph 34. Los Angeles, CA: University of California, Los Angeles, pp. 26–38.

Miller, Roy A. 1967. *The Japanese Language*. Chicago, IL: University of Chicago Press.

Molina, Alonso de. 1970. *Vocabulario en lengua castellana y mexicana y mexicana y castellana*, ed. Miguel León-Portilla. 4th edn. Mexico, DF: Editorial Porrúa.

Monaghan, John. 1995. *The Covenants with Earth and Rain: Exchange, Sacrifice, and Revelation in Mixtec Society*. Norman, OK: University of Oklahoma Press.

Monaghan, John, and B. Hamman. 1998. Reading as Social Practice and Cultural Construction. *Indiana Journal of Hispanic Literatures* 13:131–140.

Montelius, Oscar. 1899. *Der Orient und Europa*. Stockholm: Königliche Academie der schönen Wissenschaften, Geschichte und Alterthumskunde.

Moore, Oliver. 2000. *Reading the Past: Chinese*. London: British Museum Press.

Moorey, P. R. S. 1987. On Tracking Cultural Transfers in Prehistory: The Case of Egypt and Lower Mesopotamia in the Fourth Millennium BC. In *Centre and Periphery in the Ancient World*, ed. Michael Rowlands, Mogens Trolle Larsen, and Kristian Kristiansen. New Directions in Archaeology. Cambridge: Cambridge University Press, pp. 36–46.

Mora-Marín, Davíd. 2000. Background to the Study of the Earliest Maya Writing. Ph.D. Question II, State University of New York at Albany.

2001. Late Preclassic Inscription Documentation Project. Report to the Foundation for the Advancement of Mesoamerican Studies, Inc. www.famsi.org/reports/moramarin/moramarin.html.

Morgan, Lewis H. 1907. *Ancient Society; or, Researches in the Lines of Human Progress from Savagery through Barbarism to Civilization.* Chicago, IL: Kerr. (originally published 1877).

Morley, Sylvanus G. 1937. *The Inscriptions of Peten*, Volume V, Part 1. Washington, DC: Carnegie Institution of Washington.

Morris, Earl, Jean Charlot, and Ann Axtell Morris. 1931. *The Temple of the Warriors at Chichen Itza, Yucatan.* Carnegie Institution of Washington, Publication 406. Washington, DC: Carnegie Institution of Washington.

Murgio, Matthew P. 1969. *Communications Graphics.* New York, NY: Van Nostrand Reinhold.

Nabokov, Peter. 1996. Native Views of History. In *The Cambridge History of the Native Peoples of the Americas*, Volume I:, *North America*, ed. Bruce G. Trigger and Wilcomb E. Washburn. Cambridge: Cambridge University Press. pt. 1, pp. 1–59.

Navarrete, Carlos. 1971. Algunas piezas olmecas de Chiapas y Guatemala. *Anales de Antropología* 8:69–82.

Nichols, John D. 1996. The Cree Syllabary. In *The World's Writing Systems*, ed. Peter T. Daniels and William Bright. New York, NY, and Oxford: Oxford University Press, pp. 599–611.

Nicholson, H. B. 1973. Phoneticism in the Late Pre-Hispanic Central Mexican Writing System. In *Mesoamerican Writing Systems: A Conference at Dumbarton Oaks, October 30th and 31st, 1971*, ed. Elizabeth P. Benson. Washington, DC: Dumbarton Oaks Research Library and Collection, pp. 1–46.

Niederberger, Christine. 2000. Ranked Societies, Iconographic Complexity, and Economic Wealth in the Basin of Mexico toward 1200 BC. In *Olmec Art and Archaeology in Mesoamerica*, ed. John E. Clark and Mary E. Pye. Studies in the History of Art 58. Washington, DC: Center for Advanced Study in the Visual Arts, National Gallery of Art, pp. 168–191.

Nissen, Hans. 1977. Aspects of the Development of Early Cylinder Seals. In *Seals and Sealings in the Ancient Near East*, ed. McGuire Gibson and Robert D. Biggs. Bibliotheca Mesopotamica 6. Malibu, CA: Undena, pp. 15–23.

1983. *Grundzüge einer Geschichte der Frühzeit des Vorderen Orients.* Grundzüge 52. Darmstadt: Wissenschaftliche Buchgesellschaft.

1985. The Emergence of Writing in the Ancient Near East. *Interdisciplinary Science Reviews* 10:349–361.

1986. The Archaic Texts from Uruk. *World Archaeology* 17:317–334.

1988. *The Early History of the Ancient Near East, 9000–2000 BC.* Chicago, IL: University of Chicago Press.

1999. *Geschichte Altvorderasiens.* Munich: R. Oldenbourg Verlag.

Nissen, Hans, Peter Damerow, and Robert Englund. 1991. *Frühe Schrift und Techniken der Wirtschaftsverwaltung im alten Vorderen Orient.* Berlin: Verlag Franzbecker and Max Planck Institute for Education and Human Development.

   1993 *Archaic Bookkeeping: Early Writing and Techniques of Economic Administration in the Ancient Near East.* Chicago, IL: University of Chicago Press.

Noble, David F. 1999. *The Religion of Technology: The Divinity of Man and the Spirit of Invention.* London: Penguin.

Nowotny, Karl Anton. 1961. *Tlacuilolli: Die mexikanischen Bilderhandschaiften, Stil und Inhalt, mit einem katalog der codex-Borgia-gruppe.* Berlin: Verlag Begr. Mann.

Nurse, D. 1997. The Contributions of Linguistics to the Study of History in Africa. *Journal of African History* 38:359–391.

O'Connor, M. 1996. Epigraphic Semitic Scripts. In *The World's Writing Systems*, ed. Peter T. Daniels and William Bright. New York, NY, and Oxford: Oxford University Press, pp. 88–107.

Odenstedt, Bengt. 1990. *On the Origin and Early History of the Runic Script: Typology and Graphic Variation on the Older* Futhark. Acta Academiae Regiae Gustavi Adolphi 69. Uppsala: Swedish Science Press.

Olivier, Jean-Pierre. 1986. Cretan Writing in the Second Millennium BC. *World Archaeology* 17:377–389.

Orrego Corzo, Miguel. 1990. *Investigaciones arqueológicas en Abaj Takalik, El Asintal, Retalhuleu, año 1988: Reporte no. 1.* Guatemala: Ministerio de Cultura y Deportes.

Ortiz, Ponciano, and María del Carmen Rodríguez. 2000. The Sacred Hill of El Manatí: A Preliminary Discussion of the Site's Ritual Paraphernalia. In *Olmec Art and Archaeology in Mesoamerica*, ed. John E. Clark and Mary E. Pye. Studies in the History of Art 58. Washington, DC: Center for Advanced Study in the Visual Arts, National Gallery of Art, pp. 74–93.

Osing, Jürgen. 1976. Ächtungstexte aus dem Alten Reich (II). *Mitteilungen des Deutschen Archäologischen Instituts, Abteilung Kairo* 32: 133–185.

Owen, Charles L. 1986. Technology, Literacy, and Graphic Systems. In *Toward a New Understanding of Literacy*, ed. Merald E. Wrolstad and Dennis F. Fisher. New York, NY: Praeger, pp. 156–187.

Paradis, Louise I. 1981. Guerrero and the Olmec. In *The Olmec and Their Neighbors: Essays in Memory of Matthew W. Stirling*, ed. Elizabeth P. Benson. Washington, DC: Dumbarton Oaks Research Library and Collection, pp. 195–208.

Parkinson, Richard B. 1999. *Cracking Codes: The Rosetta Stone and Decipherment.* London: British Museum Press.

Parpola, Asko. 1986. The Indus Script: A Challenging Puzzle. *World Archaeology* 17:399–419.

   1996. The Indus Script. In *The World's Writing Systems*, ed. Peter T. Daniels and William Bright. New York, NY, and Oxford: Oxford University Press, pp. 165–171.

Parsons, Lee A. 1986. *The Origins of Maya Art: Monumental Stone Sculpture of Kaminaljuyu, Guatemala, and the Southern Pacific Coast.* Studies in Pre-Columbian Art and Archaeology 28. Washington, DC: Dumbarton Oaks Research Library and Collection.

Pauling, Linus C. 1967. *The Chemical Bond.* Ithaca, NY: Cornell University Press.

Payne, J. Crowfoot. 1993. *Catalogue of the Predynastic Egyptian Collection in the Ashmolean Museum.* Oxford: Clarendon Press.

Peirce, Charles Sanders. 1931–1966. *Collected Papers of Charles Sanders Peirce*, ed. Charles Hartshorne, P. Weiss, and A. W. Burks. 8 vols. Cambridge, MA: Harvard University Press.

Perutz, Max F. 1964. The Hemoglobin Molecule. *Scientific American* 211(5): 64–76.

Petrie, W. M. Flinders. 1900. *The Royal Tombs of the First Dynasty, 1900*, Volume I. Egypt Exploration Fund, Memoir 18. London: Egypt Exploration Fund.

—— 1901. *The Royal Tombs of the Earliest Dynasties, 1901*, Volume II. Egypt Exploration Fund, Memoir 21. London: Egypt Exploration Society.

Pettersson, J. 1996. *Grammatological Studies: Writing and Its Relation to Speech.* Reports from Uppsala University Linguistics 29. Uppsala: Department of Linguistics.

Pimm, David. 1987. *Speaking Mathematically: Communication in Mathematics Classrooms.* London and New York, NY: Routledge and Kegan Paul.

Pittman, Holly. 1993. Pictures of an Administration: The Late Uruk Scribe at Work. In *Between the Rivers and Over the Mountains. Archaeologica Anatolica et Mesopotamica Alba Palmieri Dedicata*, ed. Marcella Frangipane. Rome: Dipartimento di Scienze Storiche Archeologiche et Antropologiche dell'Antichità, pp. 235–245.

—— 1994. Towards an Understanding of the Role of Glyptic Imagery in the Administrative Systems of Proto-Literate Greater Mesopotamia. In *Archives Before Writing*, ed. Piera E. Fiandra, G. G. Fissore, and Marcella Frangipane. Turin: Scriptorium, pp. 177–203.

—— 1996. Constructing Context: The Gebel el-Arak Knife, Greater Mesopotamian and Egyptian Interaction in the Late Fourth Millennium BCE. In *The Study of the Ancient Near East in the 21st Century: The William Foxwell Albright Centennial Conference*, ed. Jerrold S. Cooper and Glenn M. Schwartz. Winona Lake, IN: Eisenbrauns, pp. 9–32.

Pohl, Mary E. D., Kevin O. Pope, and Christopher von Nagy. 2002. Olmec Origins of Mesoamerican Writing. *Science* 298:1984–1986.

Pollock, Susan. 1999. *Ancient Mesopotamia.* Cambridge: Cambridge University Press.

Poo, Mu-Chou. 1998. *In Search of Personal Welfare: A View of Ancient Chinese Religion.* Albany, NY: State University of New York Press.

Pope, Maurice. 1966. The Origins of Writing in the Near East. *Antiquity* 40: 17–23.

—— 1975. *The Story of Decipherment: From Egyptian Hieroglyphic to Linear B.* London: Thames and Hudson.

Porter, James B. 1992. "Estelas celtiformes": un nuevo tipo de escultura olmeca y sus implicaciones para los epigrafistas. *Arqueología* 8:3–14.

Postgate, Nicholas. 1984. Cuneiform Catalysis: The First Information Revolution. *Archaeological Review from Cambridge* 3:4–18.

1992. *Early Mesopotamia: Society and Economy at the Dawn of History*. London: Routledge.

Postgate, Nicholas, Tao Wang, and Toby Wilkinson. 1995. The Evidence for Early Writing: Utilitarian or Ceremonial? *Antiquity* 69:459–480.

Powell, Marvin A. 1981. Three Problems in the History of Cuneiform Writing: Origins, Direction of Script, Literacy. *Visible Language* 15:419–440.

Prem, Hanns. 1969–1970. Aztec Hieroglyphic Writing System – Possibilities and Limits. *38th International Congress of Americanists, Stuttgart-München* (Munich: Klaus Rener) 2:159–165.

1971. Calendrics and Writing. In *Observations on the Emergence of Civilization in Mesoamerica*, ed. Robert F. Heizer and John A. Graham. University of California Archaeological Research Facility, Contribution 11. Berkeley, CA: University of California Press, pp. 112–132.

1973. A Tentative Classification of Non-Maya Inscriptions in Mesoamerica. *Indiana* 1:29–58.

1992. Aztec Writing. In *Supplement to the Handbook of Middle American Indians: Epigraphy*, ed. Victoria R. Bricker. Austin, TX: University of Texas Press, pp. 53–69.

Prem, Hans, and Berthold Riese. 1983. Autochthonous American Writing Systems: The Aztec and Maya Examples. In *Writing in Focus*, ed. Florian Coulmas and Konrad Ehlich. Berlin: Mouton, pp. 167–186.

Priese, Karl-Heinz. 1973. Zur Entstehung der meroitischen Schrift. *Meroitica* 1:273–306.

Proskouriakoff, Tatiana. 1974. *Jades from the Cenote of Sacrifice, Chichen Itza, Yucatan*. Memoirs of the Peabody Museum of Archaeology and Ethnology 10(1). Cambridge, MA: Harvard University.

Pye, Mary E., and John E. Clark. 2000. Introducing Olmec Archaeology. In *Olmec Art and Archaeology in Mesoamerica*, ed. John E. Clark and Mary E. Pye. Studies in the History of Art 58. Washington, DC: Center for Advanced Study in the Visual Arts, National Gallery of Art, pp. 8–17.

Qiu Xigui. 1989. An Examination of Whether the Charges in Anyang Oracle-Bone Inscriptions are Questions. *Early China* 14:77–114.

2000. *Chinese Writing*, trans. Gilbert L. Mattos and Jerry Norman. Berkeley, CA: Society for the Study of Early China.

Quak, Arend. 1996. Noch einmal die Latein-These. *Amsterdamer Beiträge zur älteren Germanistik* 45:171–179.

Quibell, J. E. 1900. *Hierakonpolis I*. Egyptian Research Account, Memoir 4. London: Bernard Quaritch.

Quibell, J. E., and F. W. Green. 1902. *Hierakonpolis II*. Egyptian Research Account, Memoir 5. London: Quaritch.

Quilter, Jeffrey, and Gary Urton, eds. 2002. *Narrative Threads: Accounting and Recounting in Andean Khipu.* Austin, TX: University of Texas Press.

Rausing, Gad. 1992. On the Origin of the Runes. *Fornvännen* 87: 200–205.

Ray, J. D. 1986. The Emergence of Writing in Egypt. *World Archaeology* 17:307–316.

Reilly, F. Kent, III. 1994. Cosmología, soberanismo y espacio ritual en la Mesoamérica del Formativo. In *Los olmecas en Mesoamérica*, ed. John E. Clark. Mexico, DF: Citibank, pp. 238–259.

1995. Art, Ritual, and Rulership in the Olmec World. In *The Olmec World: Ritual and Rulership*, ed. Jill Guthrie. Princeton, NJ: The Art Museum, Princeton University, pp. 27–46.

1996. The Lazy-S: A Formative Period Iconographic Loan to Maya Hieroglyphic Writing. In *Eighth Palenque Round Table, 1993*, ed. Martha Macri and Jan McHargue. San Francisco, CA: Pre-Columbian Art Research Institute, pp. 413–424.

Remesal, Antonio. 1964. *Historia general de las Indias Occidentales y particular de la gobernación de Chiapa y Guatemala*, vol. I. Biblioteca de Autores Españoles vol. 175. Madrid: Ediciones Atlas.

Ritner, Robert K. 1996a. Egyptian Writing. In *The World's Writing Systems*, ed. Peter T. Daniels and William Bright. New York, NY, and Oxford: Oxford University Press, pp. 73–84, 87.

1996b. The Coptic Alphabet. In *The World's Writing Systems*, ed. Peter T. Daniels and William Bright. New York, NY, and Oxford: Oxford University Press, pp. 287–290.

Robinson, Andrew. 2002. *Lost Languages: The Enigma of the World's Undeciphered Scripts.* New York, NY: McGraw-Hill.

Rogers, Henry. 1995. Optimal Orthographies. In *Scripts and Literacy*, ed. Insup Taylor and David Olson. Dordrecht: Kluwer, pp. 31–43.

Rothman, Mitchell S., ed. 2001. *Uruk Mesopotamia and Its Neighbors: Cross-Cultural Interactions in the Era of State Formation.* Santa Fe, NM: School of American Research Press.

Rotman, Brian. 1993. *Taking God out of Mathematics and Putting the Body Back in: An Essay in Corporeal Semiotics.* Stanford, CA: Stanford University Press.

1995. Thinking Dia-Grams: Mathematics, Writing, and Virtual Reality. *South Atlantic Quarterly* 94(2):389–415.

Rowlands, Michael J. 1989. A Question of Complexity. In *Domination and Resistance*, ed. Daniel Miller, Michael J. Rowlands, and Christopher Tilley. London: Unwin Hyman, pp. 29–40.

Rubio, Gonzalo. 1999. On The Alleged "Pre-Sumerian Substratum." *Journal of Cuneiform Studies* 51:1–16.

Rudwick, Martin J. S. 1976. The Emergence of a Visual Language for Geological Science, 1760–1840. *History of Science* 14:149–195.

Ruse, Michael. 1990. Are Pictures Really Necessary? The Case of Sewell Wright's "Adaptive Landscapes." In *PSA 1990*, ed. Arthur Fine, Micky Forbes, and

Linda Wessels. East Lansing, MI: Philosophy of Science Association, vol. II, pp. 63–77.

Sahagún, Bernardino de. 1959–1982. *Codex Florentine: The General History of the Things of New Spain*, trans. and ed. Arthur J. O. Anderson and Charles Dibble. 12 vols. Santa Fe, NM: School of American Research and the University of Utah.

Sahlins, Marshall. 1976. *Culture and Practical Reason.* Chicago, IL: University of Chicago Press.

Salomon, Frank. 2001. How an Andean "Writing Without Words" Works. *Current Anthropology* 42:1–27.

Salomon, Richard G. 1996. Brahmi and Kharoshthi. In *The World's Writing Systems*, ed. Peter T. Daniels and William Bright. New York, NY, and Oxford: Oxford University Press, pp. 373–382.

Sampson, Geoffrey. 1985. *Writing Systems: A Linguistic Introduction.* Stanford, CA: Stanford University Press.

Sanjian, Avedis K. 1996. The Armenian Alphabet. In *The World's Writing Systems*, ed. Peter T. Daniels and William Bright. New York, NY, and Oxford: Oxford University Press, pp. 356–363.

Saussure, Ferdinand de. 1959. *Course in General Linguistics.* New York, NY: Philosophical Library.

Sawyer, Birgit. 2000. *The Viking-Age Rune-Stones: Custom and Commemoration in Early Medieval Scandinavia.* Oxford: Oxford University Press.

Scancarelli, Janine. 1996. Cherokee Writing. In *The World's Writing Systems*, ed. Peter T. Daniels and William Bright. New York, NY, and Oxford: Oxford University Press, pp. 587–592.

Schäfer, Heinrich. 1986 [1974]. *Principles of Egyptian Art*, ed. Emma Brunner-Traut. Revised reprint; trans. and ed. John Baines. Oxford: Griffith Institute. 1st German edn. 1919, 4th edn. 1963.

Scheil, Vincent. 1900. *Textes élamites-sémitiques.* Mémoires de la Délégation en Perse 2. Paris: Ernest Leroux.

  1905. *Documents en écriture proto-élamites*, Mémoires de la Délégation en Perse 6. Paris: Ernest Leroux.

  1923. *Textes de comptabilité proto-élamites.* Mémoires de la Délégation en Perse 17. Paris: Ernest Leroux.

  1935. *Textes de comptabilité proto-élamites.* Mémoires de la Délégation en Perse 26-26S. Paris: Librairie Orientaliste Paul Geuthner.

Schele, Linda. 1985. The Hauberg Stela: Bloodletting and the Mythos of Maya Rulership. In *Fifth Palenque Round Table, 1983*, ed. Virginia M. Fields. San Francisco, CA: Pre-Columbian Art Research Institute, pp. 135–149.

Schele, Linda, and Mary E. Miller. 1986. *The Blood of Kings: Dynasty and Ritual in Maya Art.* Fort Worth, TX: Kimbell Art Museum.

Schenkel, Wolfgang. 1976. The Structure of Hieroglyphic Script. *Royal Anthropological Institute News* 15:4–7.

Schmandt-Besserat, Denise. 1992. *Before Writing: From Counting to Cuneiform.* 2 vols. Austin, TX: University of Texas Press.

Scholes, France V., and Eleanor B. Adams. 1968. *The Maya Chontal Indians of Acalan-Tixchel: A Contribution to the History and Ethnography of the Yucatan Peninsula.* 2nd edn. Norman, OK: University of Oklahoma Press.

Schulz, George, and R. Heiner Schirmer. 1979. *Principles of Protein Structure.* New York, NY: Springer-Verlag.

Scott, James C. 1976. *The Moral Economy of the Peasant: Rebellion and Subsistence in Southeast Asia.* New Haven, CT: Yale University Press.

1998. *Seeing Like a State: How Certain Schemes to Improve the Human Condition Have Failed.* New Haven, CT: Yale University Press.

Scott, John F. 1978. *The Danzantes of Monte Albán, Part II: Catalogue.* Studies in Pre-Columbian Art and Archaeology 19. Washington, DC: Dumbarton Oaks Research Library and Collection.

Sedat, David W. 1992. Preclassic Notation and the Development of Maya Writing. In *New Theories on the Ancient Maya*, ed. Elin Danien and Robert J. Sharer. University Museum Monograph 77. Philadelphia, PA: University Museum, University of Pennsylvania, pp. 81–90.

Seeley, Christopher. 1991. *A History of Writing in Japan.* Leiden: Brill.

Seler, Eduard. 1906. Das Dorfbuch von Santiago Guevea. *Zeitschrift für Ethnologie* 38:121–155.

1963. *Commentarios al Códice Borgia.* 2 vols. and facsimile. Mexico, DF: Fondo de Cultura Económica.

Selz, Gebhard. 2000. Schrifterfindung als Ausformung eines reflexiven Zeichensystems. *Wiener Zeitschrift für Kunde des Morgenlandes* 90:169–200.

Senner, Wayne. 1989. Introduction. In *The Origins of Writing*, ed. Wayne Senner. Lincoln, NE: University of Nebraska Press, pp. 1–26.

ed. 1989. *The Origins of Writing.* Lincoln, NE: University of Nebraska Press.

Sethe, Kurt H. 1939. *Vom Bilde zum Buchstaben: Die Entstehungsgeschichte der Schrift.* Leipzig: J. C. Hinrichs.

Shanghai Bowuguan Cang Qingtongqi. 1964. Shanghai: Shanghai Museum.

Shanks, Michael, and Christopher Tilley. 1987. *Social Theory and Archaeology.* Cambridge: Polity Press.

Sharer, Robert J. 1994. *The Ancient Maya.* 5th edn. Stanford, CA: Stanford University Press.

Sharer, Robert J., and David W. Sedat. 1987. *Archaeological Investigations in the Northern Maya Highlands, Guatemala: Interaction and the Development of Maya Civilization.* University Museum Monograph 59. Philadelphia, PA: University Museum, University of Pennsylvania.

Shi, Dingxu. 1996. The Yi Script. In *The World's Writing Systems*, ed. Peter T. Daniels and William Bright. New York, NY, and Oxford: Oxford University Press, pp. 239–243.

Shima Kunio. 1971. *Inkyo Bokuji Sōrui.* Rev. edn. Tokyo: Kyūko Shoin.

Shingler, John V. 1996. Scripts of West Africa. In *The World's Writing Systems*, ed. Peter T. Daniels and William Bright. New York, NY, and Oxford: Oxford University Press, pp. 593–598.

Sims-Williams, P. 1993. Some Problems in Deciphering the Early Irish Ogam Alphabet. *Transactions of the Philological Society* 91:133–180.

Sjoberg, Gideon. 1960. *The Preindustrial City: Past and Present.* Glencoe, IL: The Free Press.

Skjaervø, P. Oktor. 1996. Aramaic Scripts for Iranian Languages. In *The World's Writing Systems*, ed. Peter T. Daniels and William Bright. New York, NY, and Oxford: Oxford University Press, pp. 515–535.

Smith, A. Ledyard. 1950. *Uaxactun, Guatemala: Excavations of 1931–1937.* Carnegie Institution of Washington, Publication 588. Washington, DC: Carnegie Institution of Washington.

Smith, H. S. 1992. The Making of Egypt: A Review of the Influence of Susa and Sumer on Upper Egypt and Lower Nubia in the 4th Millennium BC. In *The Followers of Horus: Studies Dedicated to Michael Allen Hoffman 1944–1990*, ed. Renée Friedman and Barbara Adams. Egyptian Studies Association Publication 2, Oxbow Monograph 20. Oxford: Oxbow Books, pp. 235–246.

Smith, Janet S. 1996. Japanese Writing. In *The World's Writing Systems*, ed. Peter T. Daniels and William Bright. New York, NY, and Oxford: Oxford University Press, pp. 209–217.

Smith, Mary E. 1973. *Picture Writing from Ancient Southern Mexico: Mixtec Place Signs and Maps.* Norman, OK: University of Oklahoma Press.

Smith, William Stevenson. 1949. *A History of Egyptian Sculpture and Painting in the Old Kingdom.* 2nd edn. London: Geoffrey Cumberlege, Oxford University Press, for Museum of Fine Arts, Boston.

Spencer, A. Jeffrey. 1980. *Early Dynastic Objects.* Catalogue of Egyptian Antiquities in the British Museum 5. London: British Museum Publications.

  1993. *Early Egypt: The Rise of Civilisation in the Nile Valley.* London: British Museum Press.

Spencer, Charles S. 1982. *The Cuicatlán Cañada and Monte Albán: A Study of Primary State Formation.* New York, NY: Academic Press.

Sproat, Richard W. 2000. *A Computational Theory of Writing Systems.* Cambridge: Cambridge University Press.

Stein, Gil J. 1999. *Rethinking World Systems. Diasporas, Colonies, and Interaction in Uruk Mesopotamia.* Tuscon, AZ: University of Arizona Press.

Steinkeller, Piotr. 1995. Review of M. W. Green and Hans J. Nissen, *Zeichenliste der archaischen Texte aus Uruk* (1987). *Bibliotheca Orientalis* 52:689–713.

  1995–1996. Review of Englund and Nissen (1993). *Archiv für Orientforschung* 42/43:211–214.

Stève, Marie-Joseph, and Hermann Gasche. 1971. *L'Acropole de Suse.* Mémoires de la Mission Archéologique de Iran 46. Paris: Ernest Leroux.

Stirling, Matthew. 1943. *Stone Monuments of Southern Mexico.* Bureau of American Ethnology Bulletin 138. Washington, DC: Smithsonian Institution.

Stoklund, Marie. 1996. Runes. In *Roman Reflections in Scandinavia*, ed. Eva Björklund. Rome: "L'Erma" di Bretschneider, pp. 112–114.

Stolper, Matthew. 1978. Inscribed Fragments from Khuzistan. *Cahiers de la Délégation Archéologique Française* 8:89–96.

Street, Brian V. 1993. Introduction: The New Literacy Studies. In *Cross-Cultural Approaches to Literacy*, ed. Brian V. Street. Cambridge: Cambridge University Press, pp. 1–21.

Stryer, Lubert. 1988. *Biochemistry*. 3rd edn. San Francisco, CA: W. H. Freeman.

Stuart, David. 1995. A Study of Maya Inscriptions. Unpublished Ph.D. dissertation, Vanderbilt University.

  1996. Kings of Stone: A Consideration of Stelae in Ancient Maya Ritual and Representations. *RES: Anthropology and Aesthetics* 29/30:148–171.

Stuart, David, Stephen Houston, and John Robertson. 1999. *Recovering the Past: Classic Mayan Language and Classic Maya Gods*. Austin, TX: Texas Workshop Foundation.

Stuart, George. 1987. *A Carved Shell from the Northeastern Maya Lowlands*. Research Reports on Ancient Maya Writing 13. Washington, DC: Center for Maya Research.

Sumner, William. 1974. Excavations at Tall-i Malyan, 1971–1972. *Iran* 12:155–180.

  1976. Excavations at Tall-i Malyan (Anshan) 1974. *Iran* 14:103–114 and pls. I–III.

Sürenhagen, Dietrich. 1993. Relative Chronology of the Uruk Period. *Bulletin of the Canadian Society for Mesopotamian Studies* 25:57–70.

  1999. *Untersuchungen zur relativen Chronologie Babyloniens und angrenzender Gebiete von der ausgehenden Ubaidzeit bis zum Beginn der Frühdynastisch II-Zeit 1*. Studien zur Chronostratigraphie der südbabylonischen Stadtruinen von Uruk und Ur. Heidelberger Studien zum Alten Orient 8. Heidelberg: Heidelberger Orientverlag.

Swadesh, Morris. 1967. Lexicostatistic Classification. In *Handbook of Middle American Indians*, Volume V: *Linguistics*, ed. Norman McQuown. Austin, TX: University of Texas Press, pp. 79–115.

Swiggers, Pierre. 1996a. The Iberian Scripts. In *The World's Writing Systems*, ed. Peter T. Daniels and William Bright. New York, NY, and Oxford: Oxford University Press, pp. 108–112.

  1996b. Transmission of the Phoenician Script to the West. In *The World's Writing Systems*, ed. Peter T. Daniels and William Bright. New York, NY, and Oxford: Oxford University Press, pp. 261–270.

Swiggers, Pierre, and Wolfgang Jenniges. 1996. The Anatolian Alphabets. In *The World's Writing Systems*, ed. Peter T. Daniels and William Bright. New York, NY, and Oxford: Oxford University Press, pp. 281–287.

Takashima Ken'ichi. 1989. An Evaluation of the Theories Concerning the Shang Oracle-Bone Inscriptions. *Journal of Intercultural Studies* [Kansai University] 15–16(1988–1989):11–54.

Tang Lan. 1981. *Guwenzixue daolun*. Jinan: Qilu shushe.

Tate, Carolyn E., and F. Kent Reilly, III. 1995. Catalogue of the Exhibition. In *The Olmec World*, ed. Jill Guthrie. Princeton, NJ: The Art Museum, Princeton University, pp. 125–329.

Tattersall, Ian. 1995. *The Fossil Trail: How We Know What We Think We Know About Human Evolution*. Oxford: Oxford University Press.

Taube, Karl A. 1988. *The Albers Collection of Pre-Columbian Art*. New York, NY: Hudson Hills Press.

1995. The Rainmakers: The Olmec and Their Contribution to Mesoamerican Belief and Ritual. In *The Olmec World*, ed. Jill Guthrie. Princeton, NJ: The Art Museum, Princeton University, pp. 83–103.

2000a. Lightning Celts and Corn Fetishes: The Formative Olmec and the Development of Maize Symbolism in Mesoamerica and the American Southwest. In *Olmec Art and Archaeology in Mesoamerica*, ed. John E. Clark and Mary E. Pye. Studies in the History of Art 58. Washington, DC: Center for Advanced Study in the Visual Arts, National Gallery of Art, pp. 296–337.

2000b. *The Writing System of Ancient Teotihuacan*. Ancient America 1. Barnardsville, NC, and Washington, DC: Center for Ancient American Studies.

Taube, Karl A., and Bonnie L. Bade. 1991. *An Appearance of Xiuhtecuhtli in the Dresden Venus Pages*. Research Reports on Ancient Maya Writing 35. Washington, DC: Center for Maya Research.

Taylor, Isaac. 1883. *The Alphabet: An Account of the Origin and Development of Letters*. 2 vols. London: Kegan Paul, Trench.

Teissier, Beatrice. 1987. Glyptic Evidence for a Connection between Iran, Syro-Palestine, and Egypt in the Fourth and Third Millennia. *Iran* 25:27–53.

Testen, David D. 1996. Old Persian Cuneiform. In *The World's Writing Systems*, ed. Peter T. Daniels and William Bright. New York, NY, and Oxford: Oxford University Press, pp. 134–137.

Thompson, J. Eric S. 1931. *Archaeological Investigations in the Southern Cayo District, British Honduras*. Field Museum of Natural History, Publication 301. Chicago, IL: Field Museum of Natural History.

1972. *Maya Hieroglyphs Without Tears*. London: British Museum Press.

Thote, Alain. 2001. The Archaeology of Eastern Sichuan at the End of the Bronze Age. In *Ancient Sichuan: Treasures from a Lost Civilization*, ed. Robert Bagley. Princeton, NJ: Princeton University Press, pp. 202–251.

2003. Du message à l'image: le décor des bronzes Shang et Zhou. *Arts Asiatiques* 58:73–85.

Thwaites, Reuben G., ed. 1896–1901. *The Jesuit Relations and Allied Documents*. 73 vols. Cleveland, OH: Burrows Brothers.

Tinney, Stephen J. 1998. Texts, Tablets, and Teaching: Scribal Education in Nippur and Ur. *Expedition* 40:40–50.

Trigger, Bruce G. 1998. *Sociocultural Evolution: Calculation and Contingency*. Oxford: Blackwell.

Tsien, Tsuen-hsuin [Qian Cunxun]. 1962. *Written on Bamboo and Silk*. Chicago, IL: University of Chicago Press.

Tufte, Edward R. 1983. *The Visual Display of Quantitative Information*. Cheshire, CT: Graphics Press.

1990. *Envisioning Information*. Cheshire, CT: Graphics Press.

Twyman, Michael. 1986. Articulating Graphic Language: A Historical Perspective. In *Toward a New Understanding of Literacy*, ed. Merald E. Wrolstad and Dennis F. Fisher. New York, NY: Praeger, pp. 188–251.

Unger, J. Marshall, and John DeFrancis. 1995. Logographic and Semasiographic Writing Systems: A Critique of Sampson's Classification. In *Scripts and Literacy*, ed. Insup Taylor and David Olson. Dordrecht: Kluwer, pp. 45–58.

Urcid Serrano, Javier. 2001. *Zapotec Hieroglyphic Writing*. Studies in Pre-Columbian Art and Archaeology 34. Washington, DC: Dumbarton Oaks Research Library and Collection.

Urton, Gary. 1998. From Knots to Narratives: Reconstructing the Art of Historical Record Keeping in the Andes from Spanish Transcriptions of Inka *Khipus*. *Ethnohistory* 45:409–438.

2003. *Signs of the Inka Khipu: Binary Coding in the Andean Knotted-String Records*. Austin, TX: University of Texas Press.

Vachek, Josef. 1939. Zum Problem der geschriebenen Sprache. *Travaux du cercle linguistique de Prague* 8:94–104.

1973. *Written Language*. Janua Linguarum, Series Critica 14. The Hague: Mouton.

Vallat, François. 1971. Les documents épigraphiques de l'Acropole (1969–1970). *Cahiers de la Délégation Archéologique Française* 1:235–245.

1973. Les tablettes proto-élamites de l'Acropole (campagne 1972). *Cahiers de la Délégation Archéologique Française* 3:93–107.

1986. The Most Ancient Scripts of Iran: The Current Situation. *World Archaeology* 17:335–347.

van den Brink, Edwin C. M. 1992. Corpus and Numerical Evaluation of the "Thinite" Potmarks. In *The Followers of Horus: Studies Dedicated to Michael Allen Hoffman*, ed. Renée Friedman and Barbara Adams. Oxbow Monograph 20. Oxford: Oxbow Books, pp. 265–296.

van der Loo, Peter L. 1994. Voicing the Painted Image: A Suggestion for Reading the Reverse of the Codex Cospi. In *Writing Without Words: Alternative Literacies in Mesoamerica and the Andes*, ed. Walter Mignolo and Elizabeth H. Boone. Durham, NC: Duke University Press, pp. 77–101.

Vandermeersch, Léon. 1977. *Wangdao ou la voie royale: recherches sur l'esprit des institutions de la Chine archaïque*. 2 vols. Publications de l'Ecole Française d'Extrême Orient, vol. 108. Paris: Adrien-Maisonneuve.

Vanstiphout, Herman L. J. 1989. Enmerkar's Invention of Writing Revisited. In *Studies in Honor of Åke W. Sjöberg*, ed. Herman Behrens, Darlene Loding, and Martha T. Roth. Occasional Publications of the S. N. Kramer Fund 11. Philadelphia, PA: University Museum, University of Pennsylvania, pp. 515–524.

2003. *Epics of Sumerian Kings: The Matter of Aratta*. Writings from the Ancient World, vol. 20. Atlanta: Society of Biblical Literature.

Venture, Olivier. 2002a. Etude d'un emploi rituel de l'écrit dans la Chine archaïque (XIIIe–VIIIe siècle avant notre ère): réflexion sur les matériaux épigraphiques des Shang et des Zhou occidentaux. Thèse pour l'obtention du diplôme de Docteur de l'université Paris 7.

2002b. L'écriture et la communication avec les esprits en Chine ancienne. *Bulletin of the Museum of Far Eastern Antiquities, Stockholm* 74 (in press).

Voegelin, Charles F., and Florence M. Voegelin. 1961. Typological Classification of Systems with Included, Excluded, and Self-sufficient Alphabets. *Anthropological Linguistics* 3:55–96.

Walker, Willard B. 1996. Native Writing Systems. In *Handbook of North American Indians*, Volume XVII: *Languages*, ed. Ives Goddard. Washington, DC: Smithsonian Institution, pp. 158–184.

Wallace, Rex. 1989. The Origins and Development of the Latin Alphabet. In *The Origins of Writing*, ed. Wayne M. Senner. Lincoln, NE: University of Nebraska Press, pp. 121–135.

Wang Yuxin. 1989. *Jiaguxue tonglun*. Beijing: Shehui kexue chubanshe.

Watson, James D., and F. H. C. Crick. 1953a. Molecular Structure of Nucleic Acid: A Structure for Deoxyribose Nucleic Acid. *Nature* 171:737–738.

1953b. Genetic Implications of the Structure of Deoxyribonucleic Acid. *Nature* 171:964–967.

Watson, Patty Jo, Steven A. LeBlanc, and Charles Redman. 1971. *Explanation in Archeology: An Explicitly Scientific Approach*. New York, NY: Columbia University Press.

Weiss, Harvey, and Theodore Cuyler Young. 1975. The Merchants of Susa. *Iran* 13:1–18.

Wengrow, David, and John Baines. 2004. Images, Human Bodies, and the Construction of Memory in Late Predynastic Egypt. In *Egypt and its Origins: Study in Memory of Barbara Adam Proceedings of the International Conference "Origins of the State: Predynast and Early Dynast Egypt," Krakow 28th August–1st September 2002*, ed. Krzysztof M. Ciałowicz, Marek Chłodnicki, Renée Friedman, and Stan Hendrickx. Egyptian Prehistory Monographs 5. Leuven: Leuven University Press, pp. 1083–1115.

Westenholz, Joan. 1998. Thoughts on Esoteric Knowledge and Secret Lore. In *Intellectual Life in the Ancient Near East*, ed. Jiří Prosecký. Rencontre Assyriologique Internationale 43. Prague: Oriental Institute, pp. 451–462.

Wheatley, Paul. 1971. *The Pivot of the Four Quarters: A Preliminary Enquiry into the Origins and Character of the Ancient Chinese City*. Edinburgh: Edinburgh University Press.

Whittaker, Gordon. 1986. The Mexican Names of Three Venus Gods in the Dresden Codex. *Mexicon* 8(3):56–60.

1992. The Zapotec Writing System. In *Supplement to the Handbook of Middle American Indians: Epigraphy*, ed. Victoria R. Bricker. Austin, TX: University of Texas Press, pp. 5–19.

1998. Traces of Early Indo-European Language in Southern Mesopotamia. *Göttinger Beiträge zur Sprachwissenschaft* 1:111–147.

2001. The Dawn of Writing and Phoneticism. In *Hieroglyphen, Alphabete, Schriftreformen: Studien zu Multiliteralismus, Schriftwechsel und Orthographieneuregelungen*, ed. Dörte Borchers, Frank Kammerzell, and Stefan Weninger. Lingua Aegyptia-Studia Monographica 3. Göttingen: Seminar für Ägyptologie und Koptologie, pp. 11–50.

Wilcke, Claus. 1995. Die Inschrift der "Figure aux plumes" – ein frühes Werk sumerischer Dichtkunst. In *Beiträge zur Kulturgeschichte Vorderasiens: Festschrift für Rainer Michael Boehmer*, ed. Uwe Finkbeiner, R. Dittmann, and H. Hauptmann. Mainz: Verlag Philipp von Zabern, pp. 669–674.

2000. *Wer las und schrieb in Babylonien und Assyrien: Überlegungen zur Literalität im Alten Zweistromland*. Munich: Verlag der Bayerischen Akademie der Wissenschaften.

Wilford, John Noble. 1999. Discovery of Egyptian Inscriptions Indicates an Earlier Date for Origin of the Alphabet. *The New York Times on the Web*, 13 Nov.

2001. Rethinking a History That's Carved in Stone. *The New York Times on the Web*, 31 July.

Wilkerson, S. Jeffrey K. 1984. In Search of the Mountain of Foam: Human Sacrifice in Eastern Mesoamerica. In *Ritual Human Sacrifice in Mesoamerica*, ed. Elizabeth H. Boone. Washington, DC: Dumbarton Oaks Research Library and Collection, pp. 101–132.

Wilkinson, Endymion. 2000. *Chinese History: A Manual*. Rev. edn. Cambridge, MA: Harvard University Press.

Wilkinson, Toby. 2000. *Royal Annals of Ancient Egypt: The Palermo Stone and Its Associated Fragments*. Studies in Egyptology. London: KPI.

Williams, Bruce. 1988. *Decorated Pottery and the Art of Naqada III: A Documentary Essay*. Münchner Ägyptologische Studien 45. Munich: Deutscher Kunstverlag.

Williams, Henrik. 1996. The Origin of the Runes. *Amsterdamer Beiträge zur älteren Germanistik* 45:211–218.

1997. The Romans and the Runes – Uses of Writing in Germania. In *Runor och ABC: Elva föreläsningar från ett symposium i Stockholm våren 1995*, ed. Staffan Nyström. Opuscula 4. Stockholm: Sällskapet Runica et Mediævalia, pp. 177–192.

Williams, Ronald J. 1972. Scribal Training in Ancient Egypt. *Journal of the American Oriental Society* 92:214–221.

Wimsatt, William. 1990. Taming the Dimensions – Visualizations in Science. In *PSA 1990*, ed. Arthur Fine, Micky Forbes, and Linda Wessels. East Lansing, MI: Philosophy of Science Association, vol. II, pp. 111–135.

Winfield Capitaine, Fernando. 1988. *La Estela 2 de La Mojarra, Veracruz, México*. Research Reports on Ancient Maya Writing 16. Washington, DC: Center for Maya Research.

Winter, Marcus, ed. 1994. *Escritura Zapoteca prehispánica: nuevas aportaciones*. Oaxaca: Instituto Nacional de Antropología e Historia.

Wolf, Eric R. 1955. Types of Latin American Peasantry: A Preliminary Discussion. *American Anthropologist* 57:452–471.

——— 1986. The Vicissitudes of the Closed Corporate Peasant Community. *American Ethnologist* 13:325–329.

Wood, Wendy. 1978. A Reconstruction of the Reliefs of Hesy-Re. *Journal of the American Research Center in Egypt* 15:9–24.

Wright, Patricia. 1980. The Comprehension of Tabulated Information: Some Similarities between Reading Prose and Reading Tables. *Improving Human Performance Quarterly* October:25–29.

Wright, Patricia, and Kathryn Fox. 1970. Presenting Information in Tables. *Applied Ergonomics* 1(4):234–242.

Wright, Patricia, and Fraser Reid. 1973. Written Information: Some Alternatives to Prose for Expressing the Outcomes of Complex Contingencies. *Journal of Applied Psychology* 57(2):160–166.

Wrolstad, Merald E., and Dennis F. Fisher, eds. 1986. *Toward a New Understanding of Literacy*. New York, NY: Praeger.

Wrong, George M., ed. 1939. *The Long Journey to the Country of the Hurons*, Father Gabriel Sagard. Toronto: The Champlain Society.

Wu Hung. 1995. *Monumentality in Early Chinese Art and Architecture*. Stanford, CA: Stanford University Press.

Xu, Jay. 2001. Sichuan before the Warring States Period, and Bronze at Sanxingdui. In *Ancient Sichuan: Treasures from a Lost Civilization*, ed. Robert Bagley. Princeton, NJ: Princeton University Press, pp. 21–37 and 59–151.

Yang Fengbin. 1993. Cong pin mu deng zi kan jiaquewenzi de chouxianghua chengdu. In *Jiagu yuyan taohui lunwenji*, ed. Hu Houxuan. Wuchang guizishan: Huazhong shifan daxue, pp. 136–144.

Yinxu. 2001. Beijing: Wenwu Chubanshe.

Yinxu de Faxian yu Yanjiu. 1994. Beijing: Kexue Chubanshe.

Yinxu Fu Hao Mu. 1980. Beijing: Wenwu Chubanshe.

Yinxu Yuqi. 1982. Beijing: Wenwu Chubanshe.

Yoffee, Norman. 2001. The Evolution of Simplicity. *Current Anthropology* 42(5):767–769.

Yu Xingwu. 1940. *Shuang Jian Chi Gu Qiwu Tulu*. Beijing: n.p.

——— 1957. *Shang Zhou Jinwen Luyi*. Beijing: Xinhua Shudian.

Zhang Bingquan. 1962. *Xiaotun, di er ben: Yinxu Wenzi: bingbian*, part 2(1). Taibei: Institute of History and Philology, Academia Sinica.

——— 1988. *Jiaguwen yu jiaguxue*. Taibei: Zhonghua Xueshu.

Zhu Qixiang. 1992. *Jiaguxue luncong*. Taipei: Xuesheng Shuju.

Zimansky, Paul E. 1993. Review of Denise Schmandt-Besserat, *Before Writing*. *Journal of Field Archaeology* 20:513–517.

Index

Page numbers in italics indicate a reference to an illustration.

Abaj Takalik, Guatemala 301, 304
abstraction 298
Abu Salabikh, Iraq 73
Abydos, Egypt 154, *155, 156, 159, 160*, 162, 167, *168, 173, 174*
acrophony 16, *30, 31*, 29–31, 36
adjectives 91
administration 72, 80, 84, 91, 95, 117, 147, 151, 171, 184, 185, 223, 224, 228, 234, 270, 300
  accounting in service of 73, 89, 100, 103, 105, 106, 108, 112, 139, 140, 148, 151, 161, 349, 352
  Archaic Babylonian bookkeeping for 108
adverbs 53
Aegean 184
  Bronze Age 184
  scripts 176
  settlements 184
age grade 84
Akkad 94
Akkadian 52, 53, 63, 64, 142, 143
  language 91, 92, 188, 233
  Old 52, 53, 104, 141, 143, 144
  scribes 53
  writing 91, 92
Algaze, Guillermo 96
alphabet 16, 36, 37, 40, 41, 42, 43, 46, 49, 50, 51, 52, 53, 54, 55, 58, 59, 60, 61, 64, 65, 94, 179, 262, 264, 265, 266
  Archaic Greek 57
  Armenian 58, 67
  Cyrillic 58, 66
  Georgian 58, 67
  Gothic 58
  Greco-Roman 264
  Greek 265
  Ionic Greek 59, 60
  Italic 58

Latin 266, 267
Manchu 59
Mongolian 59, 65
North Italic 265
Ogam 58, 67
Roman 55, 57, 58, 59, 66, 264, 265, 266, 267
Semitic 94
Turkish 54, 59, 60, 61, 65, 66
alphasyllabary 54, 59, 60, 61, 65, 66
Alster, Bendt 97
Alvarado Stela 1 296
Amuco, Guerrero, Mexico 290
ancestors 291, 294
  speech of 291, 292
Andes 93
Anglo-Saxon 270
anthropology 314
Antonsen, Elmer 273
apprenticeship 6
Arabic 33, 45, 56, 57, 59, 65
  consonantary 55
  Judaeo- 57
  script 45, 66
Aramaic 45, 57, 59, 64
  consonantary 56, 57, 60, 61, 65
Aratta 84
archaeology 237
  of Anyang (China) *195, 201, 203, 207, 215, 217, 218*, 237
  cultural-historical 39, 63
  of pre-Anyang (China) 237
  postprocessual 39
archaeologists 222, 236
archives 72
Arnheim, Rudolf 318, 319
art history 314
Aryan peoples 42
Ashton, Alan 14

Asia Minor 57
  languages of (Carian, Lycian, Lydian, Pamphylian, Phrygian, Sidetic) 57
Asian Art Museum of San Francisco *208*
  Avery Brundage Collection in *208*
Assmann, Jan 96, 98
Assyria 86, 87, 94
  Ashurnasirpal II of 87, *88*
  "hieroglyphs" of 98
  language of 52, 53
Aston, Barbara 187
atoms 324, 325, *325*
Australopithecines 280
Aymara 97
Aztec (Mexican) 47, 94, 294, 295, 315, 317, 342, 344
  calendar priests 346
  days 337, 340, 341, 342, 343
  divinatory calendar 335
  god of divination 344
  Mexican precursors of the 315
  months 346
  painter 344
  pictography 96, 315, *316*, 317, 335, *336*, 338, *339*, *340*, *341*, *343*, 344
  views of cosmos 344

Babylonia 71, 72, 76, 83, 84, 94, 95, 96, 97, 99, 101, 102, 103, 108, 117, 119, 122, 124, 138, 139, 140, 141, 144, 147
  civilization of 119
  cuneiform in *85*, 145, 148
  hinterland of 119
  language of 52, 64
  plunder in 119
  river plains of 119
  scribes of 126, 139
  trade in 119
Bæksted, Anders 270, 272
Baghdad, Iraq 94
Bagley, Robert 14, 185, 187, 190, 237, 242, 244
Baines, John 11, 14, 48, 95, 96, 97, 98, 150, 186, 187, 236, 239, 244, 245, 246, 350
barbarism 40
Barber, Christy 273
Baxter, William 253, 254, 260
Beale, Thomas 147
Belize 303
Berlo, Janet 276

Bhartrhari 18
bibliography
biochemistry 333
biscripts 10
Bisutun carving 59, 60
  trilingual in 59
Black, Jeremy 185
Bolivia 99
Boltz, William 7, 14, 24, 26, 37, 38, 50, 89, 96, 98, 237, 243, 245, 247, 253, 254, 258, 304, 351
  monosyllabic theory of 7, 177, 181, 185, 187, 247
books 315, 317
  as biographies 317
  as cosmogonies 317
  as divinatory almanacs 338, *339*, *340*, *341*, *343*, 344
  as genealogies 317
  as maps 317
  as tribute lists 317
  for taxation purposes 317
  painted 315
Boone, Elizabeth 13, 14, 37, 80, 93, 99, 163, 164, 174, 313
Bottéro, Françoise 14, 95, 98, 227, 238, 247, 250
boustrophedon 339
Brice, William 144
Brigham Young University 4, 5, 273
Bright, William 4
Brink, Stefan 271, 273
British Isles 58, 286, 287, 291, 299, 300, 303, 305, 308
British Museum 4, 5
Broodberg, Peter 253, 254, 260
Buddhism 66
bullae 74, *75*, 100, 101, 120, *120*, 121, 123, 175
bureaucracy 72–80, 151, 152
Byrhtferth's diagram 345, *345*

Cacaxtla, Tlaxcala, Mexico 277, 278
Calakmul, Campeche 303
calendar dates 47
calligraphy 89, 298, 301, 308
captions 290, 295, 308
captives *277*, 289, 290, 292, 293, 295, *295*, 299, 302, *302*, 306
Cardona, Giorgio 152, 174, 177

Caroline Islands 55
  Woleaian language of 55
Caso, Alfonso 294
Celts 264, 286, 287
celts (adzes) 284, 286, 287
Central Asia 57, 65
  non-Semitic languages of (Bactrian, Parthian, Persian, Sogdian, Uyghur Turkic) 57
Cerro de las Mesas Stela 8 276
Chalcatzingo, Morelos, Mexico Monument 31 285
Chalchuapa, El Salvador 301
chaos theory 333
characters 51
charts 328, 329, 330, 333, 335
  flow 330
Charvát, Petr 101
chemists 324
Chen Mengjia 242
Chen Zhida 243
Chiapas, Mexico 297, 301
Chichen Itza, Yucatan, Mexico 277, 278
Childe V. Gordon 275
childhood development 314
  iconic representation in 314
  use of symbols in 314
China 40, 53, 59, 61, 65, 66, 71, 72, 78, 88, 89, 91, 95, 98, 190, 191, 202, 207, 208, 226, 227, 230, 231, 234, 236, 237, 241, 244, 247, 250, 258, 259
  archaeologists of 222, 236
  Bronze Age 244
  Chinese scholars of 251, 253
  Dawenkou culture 50, 187, 229
    emblems *229*
  dialects in 51
  Erligang culture 50, 207, 227, 228, 230, 234, 236, 241, 244
    bronzes 228
    diviners 234
    state 236, 244
    type site of Zhengzhou 241
  Erlitou period 50
  Han period 51, 243
    administration 243
  history of 190
  language of 51, 53, 63, 233, 250, 255, 258
    inflections in 233
    modern Mandarin 51
    relation of orthography to 233
    spoken 259, 260
    syllables in 51, 247
    verbs in 260
  Liangzhu culture 229, *229*
  Neolithic *229*, 250, 258
    carpenters 234
    jades 229
    jadeworkers 246
    marks 245, 258, 261
    pots 229
    writing 247
  North American scholars of 253, 254
  Northern 42
  pottery *217*, *218*, 258
  Shang 79, 83, 151, 250, 253, 254, 260
    period as mosaic of small states 224
  Western Zhou dynasty 210, 211, 242, 260
    Shang prototypes of 210
    writing of 237, 244, 245, 247
  Yangshao culture 50
    pottery of 50
  Zhou 237, 240, 242, 244
Chinese writing 3, 4, 7, 10, 20, 24, 26, 34, 37, 41, 49, 50, 51, 52, 53, 54, 59, 63, 64, 78, 84, 88, 89, 92, 96, 98, 172, 177, 178, 181, 182, 190, 191, 211, 226, 235, 238, 245, 246, 247, 250, 254, 256, 258, 259, 284–293, 298, 308, 350, 352
  abstract signs in 251–252
  animals in 252, 253, 254, 260
  clan emblems in 78, *229*, 251, 261
  compound graphs in 252, 253, 254, 260
  divinatory function of 78, 79, 250, 255
  diviners in 255
  evolution of 256
  grammatical particles in 251
    coordinating conjunction 251
    copula 251
    homorganic 253, 254, 258
    modal 251
  grapheme combination in 252–255
  graphemes in 252, 253, 254
  graph formation in 257
  graphic variants of 255–258, 260
  invention of 190, 259
    independent 259
  numbers in 252
  on bamboo 286, 287

Chinese writing (*cont.*)
  on bronze vessels 78, 187, *201, 203, 205, 206, 207, 208, 209, 210, 212*
  on oracle bones 78, 79, 96, 151, 187, 351
  on turtle shells 78, 79, *195*
  oracle bone inscriptions (OBI) 250, 251, 254, 255, 256, 257, 258
  oracles in 254, 255, 259
  patronyms in 251
  phonetic elements in 257
  phonophoric elements in 252, 253, 254, 260
  pictographic origins of 250, 253
  pictographs in 251, 253, 260, 261
  pronunciation of 252, 253, 254, 260
  rebus in 251
  relation of spoken language to 255
  river names in 253, 254
  sacrifices mentioned in 251, 254
  sacrificial names in 251, 255
  scribes of 253, 254, 255
  semantic elements in 257, 260
  sheep in 254, 260
  space notations in 252
  stimulus diffusion as origin of 190, 191, 198, 199, 200, 202, 207, 213, 214, 216, 217, 220, 222, 223, 224, 225, 226–227, 229, 230, 235, 236, 240, 241, 242, 259
  synchronic variants in 253, 254
  texts of 83
  time notations in 252
    days 252
    years 252
  toponyms in 251, 255
  turtle plastrons with *192, 193*, 194, *195*, 256
  women's names in 252, 253, 254, 260
    Lady Jing 253, 254
  Women's script of 305
  words in 251
Choga Mish, Iran 119
Ch'olti' (Maya) 33
Chomsky, Noam 45
Christenson, Allen 14
Christianity 270
  missionaries of 58
  Orthodox tradition of 58, 291
  Roman Catholic 58
  world view of *345*, 346
Civil, Miguel 243, 244

civilization 40, 41, 42, 66, 93, 94, 99, 153, 160, 175, 185, 207, 223, 226, 241, 262
  bronze-using 224, 244
  in China 227, 245
  New World 275
Clark, John 309
class interests 67
Codex Borgia 337, 338, *339*, 340, *341*
Codex Féjerváry-Mayer *316*, 342, *343, 344*, 346
Codex Mendoza 294
  as tribute document 294
Codex Mexicanus *336*
Codex Xolotl 279
codices 278
Coe, Michael 14, 239, 302, 309
cognition 318
Collier, Mark 185
Collon, Dominique 95
commodities 77
communication 40, 65, 67, 119, 151, 152, 175, 181, 224, 279
  display as 78, 97
  of royal ideology 78
  utilitarian 151
complexity 94, 166, 188
computers 65, 333
consonantary 42, 50, 54, 55, 56, 59, 64, 65
  Arabic 59, 65
  Aramaic 56, 57, 60, 61, 65
  linear 56
  northern linear 56
  Phoenician 57
  southern linear 56, 57
  unpointed 57
  West Semitic 42, 64, 65
consonants 41, 44, 45, 50, 54, 57, 59, 60, 61, 63, 65, 98, 163, 164, 178, 179, 180
  clusters 60
contingency 6
Cooper, Jerrold 14, 23, 71, 96, 98, 99, 142, 148, 176, 188, 228, 236, 239, 240, 245, 246, 349, 352, 353
Coulmas, Florian 95
covenants 10
Cretan Hieroglyphic 52, 55
Crick, Francis 328, 329, *329*, 330, 333, 335
cryptography 186, 189
culture
  change 67

conservatism of 66
values of 67
cuneiform 12, 23, 38, 52, 53, 56, 64, 71, 82, 84, 85, *85*, 86, 88, 89, 91, 92, 94, 95, 97, 98, 99, 100, 101, 102, *121*, 145, 146, 148, 178, 179, 216, 220, 227, 231, 240, 245, 246, 247, 290, 298
   archaic 119, 142
   archaic scribes of 102
   as bookkeeping 220, 224, 225, 232, 234, 235, 236, 246
   Babylonian 64
   Ebla corpus of 111
   gunification 111
   Hittite 53
   iconicity in 240, 243
   legal texts 91, 92
   lexical lists 78, 83, 97, 220, 222, 243
   literary texts 97
   Old Persian 59
   orientation of 97, 98
   proto-cuneiform 47, 52, 76, 77, 80, 84, 85, *86*, 90, 97, 100, 101, 102, 104, *105*, 107, 108, 110, 111, 113, 117, 118, 119, 120, 122, 124, 127, 139, 140, 142, 144, 145, 146, 147, 148, 216, 243, 246, 254, 260
      administrative texts 108, 141
      numerical signs 106, 107, 108, 117, 122, 145
      scribes 101
      sexagesimal system 112
   ration accounts 83
   stylus *127*, 220, 243
   Sumerian 23, 24, 38, 71, 80, 90, 91, 92, 95, 96, 98
   Sumerograms in
   syllabic 179
   tablets *75*, 77, 120, 220, 221
      archaic 80, 96, 98
   wedges in 148, 220
Cuneiform Digital Library Initiative (CDLI) 100, 101, 128, 141, 143

Dahl, Jacob 141
Dalley, Stephanie 244
Damerow, Peter 11, 12, 118, 141, 143, 144, 145, 146, 147, 185, 245, 351, 352
Daniels, Peter 4, 10, 52, 177, 181, 227, 246, 247
Darius I 59, 60
data analysis 328, 329–330

database 333
Daxinzhuang, Shandong, China 237, 240, 242, 244
decipherment 100, 104, 113, 124, 127, 143, 144, 147, 184, 294, 298, 299
   with biscripts 10, 298
   with Rosetta Stone 10
DeFrancis, John 38, 66
deixis 26, *26*
Demattè, Paola 245
Denmark 58, 271
determinatives (classifiers) 24–25, 49, 91, 98
diacritics 57, 60
diagrams 314, 319, 324, *325*, 329, 330, *332*, 333, 335, 336, 337, *344*, *345*, 342–346
diffusion 39, 42
   stimulus 43, 52, 55, 59
diplomatic exchanges 224
Diringer, David 41
discourse 334, 336
display 78, 97, 151, 152, 171, 290, 351
divination 47, 83, *192*, *193*, 194, *195*
Djamouri, Redouane 242, 247
Djokha, Iraq 142
DNA 328, *329*
Drake, Stillman 319
Dreyer, Günter 153, 154, *156*, 157, 161, 162, 163, 164, 165, 167, 169, 179, 187, 188

East Asia 54, 65
   secondary scripts of 54, 64
   societies of 41
Ebla corpus 111
Ecole Biblique, Jerusalem 143
Egypt 40, 42, 47, 48, 49, 50, 53, 61, 64, 65, 71, 72, 78, 88, 95, 98, 152, 153, 154, 157, 158, 161, 162, 166, 171, 175, 176, 177, 179, 180, 182, 183, 184, 186, 187, 188, 190, 199, 202, 207, 223, 225, 226, 231, 232, 233, 234, 235, 240, 243, 244, 245, 249
   Abydos 48, 148, 152, *155*, 169
      Cemetery B 152, 153, 163, *174*
      Cemetery U 152, 153, 167, 169, 186, 187
      necropolis 152
      Umm el-Qaʿab 152, 153, 163, *173*
   Afroasiatic roots in 50, 57, 64, 162, 189
   art market 169, 170, 186
   bureaucracy of 72
   cemeteries in 170

Egypt (*cont.*)
　Christian literature of 58
　chronology of 95
　　dynasty 0 153, 163, 164, 167, 169, *169*, 171, 172, 173, 175, 177, 181, 182, 183, 186, 187, 188, 245
　　1st dynasty 159, 163, 165, 172, 174, *174*, 179, 181, *183*, 187, 188
　　2nd dynasty 164, 173, 175, 180, *183*
　　3rd dynasty 164, 173, 175
　　5th dynasty 173, 182, 188
　　Early Dynastic 157, 179, 180, 182, 184, 187
　　Middle Kingdom 50, 57, 64, 175, 179, 243
　　Naqada I 166
　　Naqada II 153, 154, 161, 162, 166, 186, 187; pottery (B-Ware) 166; pottery (D-Ware) 154, 166
　　Naqada III 153, 154, *155*, 159, 162, 166, *168*, 170, 171, 182, 187
　　New Kingdom 50
　　Old Kingdom 179, 181, 182, 243, 245
　civilization of 153, 160, 175, 185
　cloth lists in 157
　Coptic Church of 58
　cryptography in 92
　deities of 166, 180
　Delta of 175
　Early Dynastic 152
　early hieroglyphs in 152–161
　　"Basta" 163
　　birds 157, 159, 162
　　boats 162
　　"Bubastis" 161, 162, 170
　　elephant 162, 186
　　estate names 164
　　falcon 162
　　fish 157, 162
　　ibis 162
　　jackal 186
　　ox head (bucranium) 157, 159, *160*, 162
　　ox head on pole *159*, 162
　　palace façade 157
　　plant 157, *159*
　　reptiles 157, 164, 167, 186
　　scorpion 157, 159, *159*, *160*, 162, 186
　　seashell *160*, 162
　　shrine 157
　　throne 157, 164
　　"West" 162
　elites of 152, 183
　　dwellings of 166
　　tombs of 166, 184, 187
　estates (plantations) in 162, 171
　fauna of 158, 164
　folk categories in 158
　graffiti of 167, 169
　grain records in 157
　hieroglyphs of 154, 158, 160, 161, 167, 170, 179, 187, 256
　high culture of 171
　history of 50
　Hunter's Palette from 167, *168*, 169, 170, 173
　iconicity in 164, 183
　iconography of 157, 164, 167, 186
　　decorum 164, 167
　　"emblematic personification" *173*
　ideology of 167, 186
　imported pottery in 158, 161
　jars of 157, 158, 159, 161, 162, 163, 170
　　for commodities 157, 165
　　for fat 157
　　for oil 157, 173
　　texts on 165
　kingship in 157
　kings of 162, 163, 168, *169*, 180, 182, 184
　　Aha *174*, 188
　　annals of 173
　　burials of 168, 170
　　Djer 187
　　"Horus Name" of 168, 170
　　"Irihor" 187
　　Narmer *173*, 188
　　prehistoric 182
　language of 56, 58, 60, 63, 64, 163, 164, 171, 177, 178, 186, 188, 189, 233
　　affixes 180
　　biconsonantal roots 178
　　consonantal prefixes 178, 179
　　consonantal suffixes 178, 179
　　consonants 163, 164, 178, 179, 180
　　Coptic 58, 59
　　flexion 188
　　homophones 178, 179
　　lexemes 163, 165, 171, 172, 176, 178, 180
　　lexical structure 182
　　morphology 163

nouns 189
phonology (syllables) 163, 165, 178, 179, 180
roots 178, 180, 189
spoken 165, 176, 189
syntax 165, 178, 180, 188
verbal conjugations 178, 188, 189
vowels 178, 179, 180, 183
weak verbs 188
words 178, 180, 181, 186, 188, 189
luxury goods in 166, 174
metal vessels in 187
names of 165
narrative in 97
Nile Valley in 175
palaces in 170
Palermo Stone from 173, 182, 188
palettes in 80
papyrus in 174
people of 56, 57, 64, 65
potmarks in 159
pottery of 159, *159*, *160*, 162, 164, 166, 167, 170, 187
Predynastic 152
provinces (nomes) in 166
Pyramid texts of 182
ritual papyri in 58
royal officials of 48
rulership in 166
school texts in 222
Scorpion Macehead from 169, *169*, 170, 186
scribes in 184, 200, 202, 240
sealings from 154, 158, 161, 174, 182, *183*
Seth animal in 186
settlements of 170
shrines of 166, 178
spells in 182
state organization of 153, 162, 171
stone vases in 166
tags (bone and ivory) in 154, *155*, *156*, 157, 161, 162
temples of 168, 170
textiles of 166, 170
titles in 163, 184
trade in 161
U-j tomb of 11, 48, 153, 154, 158, 160, 161, 162, 163, 164, 165, 166, 167, 169, 170, 171, 172, 173, 176, 178, 179, 180, 181, 183, 184, 186, 350

tags from 148, *155*, *156*, 157, 158, 159, 163, 164, 165, 171, 173, 174, 187
Upper 152, 157
writing in 3, 11, 26, 30, 34, 38, 48, 49, 50, 52, 56, 61, 63, 64, 71, 78, 80, 84, 87, 88, 89, 90, 91, 92, 95, 96, 98, 150, 152, 154, 160, 161, 164, 169, 171, 172, 175, 176, 177, 178, 179, 180, 181, 182, 183, 186, 187, 200, 202, 241, 290, 291, 335, 349
biconsonantals 163, 178, 181
cartouches 241
complex signs in 167, 170
consonantal 180, 186, 189
cursive 167, 172, 187, 235, 240
determinatives 163, 179, 188; semantic 241
discourse 173, 174, 178, 179, 180, 181, 182
hieratic 160, 169, 170, 187
iconicity in 240
logograms 163, 164, 179, 180, 188
multiconsonantals 163
"narrative infinitive" 172, 188
non-Egyptian names in 179
offertory 349
of names 187
on stelae 187
orthography 157, 178, 179, 181, 182, 189, 247
phonemic complements 163, 180, 188
phonemic signs 178, 180
phonograms 163, 164, 165, 179, 187
pictographs 163
prestige of 167, 169, 170, 173
proto-hieroglyphs 171, 176, 180, 181
pseudo-inscriptions 182, *183*, 184
rebus 165, 177, 178, 179, 181, 188
reforms in 164, 165, 180, 183
sacred function of 170
semagrams 163
semantic classes
sign repertory 152
syllabogram 179, 186
tributary 349
triconsonantals 178, 188
triliterals 98
uniconsonantals 178, 181, 182

Egyptians 40, 48, 54
Egyptologists 98, 153, 178
Einstein, Albert *319*
   relativity theory of *319*
Elam 42, 124
Elamite 53, 145
   Old 144
      linear texts 145
   palaeographic tradition in 145
   speakers of 103
Eldredge, Niles 6
el-Khouli, Ali 187
Elkins, James 334, *335*
   model of Notation 334, 335
   model of Picture 334, 335
   model of Writing 334, 335
El Manatí, Veracruz, Mexico 288
   wooden sculptures at 288
El Mirador, Guatemala 300, 303
   Stela 2 at 300, 303
El Porton, Guatemala 301
El Salvador 301
El Tajín, Veracruz, Mexico 277
emblems 284
emmer wheat 115, 117
empire 244
English 31, 32, 33, 34, 36, 45, 265, 276
   Old English 35
   spoken 45
   written 45, 63
Englund, Robert 74, 77, 78, 94, 95, 96, 97, 98, 100, 118, 141, 142, 143, 144, 145, 146, 147, 148, 186, 188, 243, 245, 349, 350, 352
Enmerkar 84
epigraphers 295
Erbil, Iraq 94
Ethiopia 56, 61, 65
Euphrates 94
Europe 42, 54, 58, 65
   medieval 58
   writing of 57
evolution 276
   cultural 39
   Darwinian frameworks of 41
   unilinear 42, 43
excavations 152, 153, 154, 157, 158, 161, 162, 166, 171, 175, 176, 177, 179, 180, 182, 183, 184, 186, 187, 188
expressive art 67

Falkenhausen, Lothar von 242
Falkenstein, Adam 101
Fell, Christine 270
Ferguson, Eugene 319
Finkel, Irving 98
Fischer, Henry G. 189
Flückiger-Hawker, Esther 185
Forsythe, Evie 14
fractal geometry 332–333
French 44
Friberg, Jöran 101, 141, 147
Funen, Denmark 263
futhark (runic alphabet) 35, 45, 58, 263

Galileo 319
Gardiner, Alan 180
Gardner, Martin 324
Gaur, Albertine 186
Gee, John 14
Ge'ez 56
Gelb, Ignace 6, 13, 40, 42, 43, 47, 54, 55, 63, 65, 66, 71, 91, 94, 95, 144, 178, 179, 246, 275, 276
   principle of "Unidirectional Development" 40, 52
   theory of unilinear evolution 179
German 265
   experimentation with runes 265, 271
Germany (Germania) 263, 266, 271
   chieftains of 271
   culture of 270
   language of 58
   people of 270
   provinces of 266
   Roman influence on 272
   society of 270, 272
   tribes of 266, 272
Glassner, Jean-Jacques 94, 95, 96, 97, 98, 142, 188
glottochronology 282, 283
glottography 44
glyphs 185, 186
Godin Tepe, Iran *73*, *76*, 119, 126, 128, 148
Goody, Jack 40, 83, 92, 189
Gould, Stephen Jay 6
grammatology 39
   evolutionary 40–43, 65
graphemes 266, 267, 272, 273
   rules of 273
graphs 185, 329, 330, 332, 334, 346

catalogues of 334–335
design of 315, 319
systems of 313, 314
technology of 332–333
graves 154, 157, 159, 184, 187, 271
Greece 42, 65
    alphabet of 42, 57, 58
    language of 34, 55, 57
    people of 42, 57
Green, Dennis 269
Green, Mary 60, 101, 143
Greenberg, Joseph 4
Guatemala 278, 280, 301
    highlands of 301
    Pacific coast of 278
    piedmont of 301

Haas, William 314, 318
Habuba Kabira, Syria *73*
Halle, Morris 45
Hamman, Byron 14
Hankul 59
Harris, John 98
Harris, Roy 186
Hartung, Ulrich 153, 154
headdresses 286, 288, 289, 290, 298
    lexemic 290
Hebrew 56, 57
Heidelberg University 142, 148
Henan Jiahu, China 245
Hendrickx, Stan 187
heterography 28, 29, 31–34, 36
Hezyre 184
Hierakonpolis, Egypt 153
    ivories from 187
    "Main Deposit" at *169*, 187
    Tomb 100 at 166
    wall painting 166
hieroglyphs 291, 292, 309, 315, 334
Himlingøje, Denmark *269*
Hinduism 66
Hinüber, Oskar von 189
Hinz, Walther 142
Hittite hieroglyphs 52, 55
homeostasis 34
Homo erectus 280–282
homonyms (homophones) 22, *22*, 23–24, 25,
    47, 49, 51, 65, 89, 93, 178, 179, 247,
    294, 305, 349
    near-homonyms 49

Houston, Anders 15
Houston, Hannah 15
Houston, Stephen 13, 14, 38, 83, 94, 96, 99,
    157, 185, 236, 239, 274, 349
Hu Houxuan 239, 259
human body 290
Hurons 44
Hurrian 53

Iberian scripts 55
    Phoenician influence on 55
icon (Peircean) 18, 19, 25, 26, 28, 29, *31*, 34, 36,
    38, 84, 291, 292, 294, 299, 315, 335, 349
iconicity 84, 87, 164, 183, 290, 291, 292, 298,
    299
    loss of 84–89, 93
iconographic community 286, 287
iconography 80
identifiers 290
ideographs 16, 25, 26, 27, 28, 36, 37, 38
index (Peircean) 18, 25, 26, 28, 36, 84
India 66, 181, 184, 189
    culture of 66
Indian grammatical school 181
Indo-European 53, 141
    peoples 42
Indus script 13, 52, 60, 246
industrial societies 67
Indus Valley 42
Inka 40, 63, 80, 93
Inomata, Takeshi 239
inscriptions 298, 299
instrumentality 84
internationalism 318
Iran 66, 143, 175
    highlands of 143
Iraq 42, 47, 48, 49, 52, 53, 119, 120, 122, 123,
    141, 142
    invasion of 142
    plunder of 142
Islam 57, 66
    nationalism in 59
Ismail, Farouk 148
Isthmian writing ("Epi-Olmec") 7, 13, 48, 274,
    276, 280, 282, 283, 290, 292, *297*,
    296–298, 300, 306, 308, 351
    bar-and-dot numeration in 298
    Chiapa de Corzo sherd 296, 297
    Chiapa de Corzo Stela 10, 297
    claims to decipherment of 298

Isthmian writing (*cont.*)
  El Sitio Celt 296
  La Mojarra Stela 1 282, 296
  Long Count notations in 297
  O'Boyle Mask 296
  signs in 298
  supposed relation to Mixe-Zoquean languages 296
  Teotihuacan Mask 296, 297, 301
  Tuxtla Statuette 296, *297*
Isthmus of Tehuantepec 276, 296
Italy 57
Ivanov, Vyacheslav 141

jade (greenstone) 284, 286, 291, 298, 303
Jakobson, Roman 16, 17, 18, 19
Janetski, Joel 14
Japan 54, 64, 65, 66
Japanese 34, 53, 65, 66, 92, 99
  kana 53
  kanji 53, 92
  words 53
  writing 41, 55
Jebel Aruda, Syria *73*, *75*
Jemdet Nasr, Iraq 76, 86, 102, 124
  British–American excavators of 102
Jiangxi, China 244
Jurchin 53

Kahl, Jochem 152, 180, 186
Kaiser, Werner 186
Kaminaljuyu, Guatemala 301
  language at 301
  lords at 301
  Monument 65 289, 301
  nominal glyphs at 301
  sculptures at 301
  "Stela" 10 from 280, *281*, 301, 308
  Stela 21 from 280
Kashmiri 59
Kaufman, Terrence 282
Keightley, David 237, 238, 239, 240, 242, 244, 246, 247
Kelley, David 276
Kendal, Belize 304
Kenya 280
Kerr, Justin 239
khipu (knotted ropes) 13, 40, 80, 83, 93, 96, 97, 351

  as non-iconic writing 351
  as record-keeping 99
Kitan 53
Koptos, Egypt 167, 170
  colossal statutes of 167, 169
Korean 33, 34, 53, 59, 64, 65, 66
  Hankul 59, 64
  words 59
Krebernik, Manfred 142, 148
Kroeber, Alfred 43, 54
Kurdish 59

Laban, Rudolf 320
Labanotation 320, *323*, 334
Lacadena, Alfonso 309
Ladino 57
Lagash, Iraq 87
  Stela of the Vultures from 87, *87*
Landa, Diego de 10
Landsberger, Benno 149
landscape 284
language 38, 44, 83, 294
  adjectives in 50, 53
  affixes of 50, 51, 91, 98
  dialects of 45, 83
  grammar in 81, 82, 90, 150, 334
  grammatical particles in 50, 53
  nouns of 50, 53
  pronouns of 48
  relation of writing to 150, 177–184
  spoken 20, 25, 27, 28, 29, 33, 37, 49, 52, 63, 83, 92, 96, 315, 320, 346
  syntax of 81, 82, 286, 287, 292, 315
  universals in 4
  verbs in 50, 53, 91
    medio-passive 33
    transitive 33
  written 96
Larsen, Mogens T. 244, 245
Latin 10, 152, 153, 154, 157, 158, 161, 162, 166, 171, 175, 176, 177, 179, 180, 182, 183, 184, 186, 187, 188, 265, 267, 272
  alphabet 266, 267
  letters 265, 266, 272
La Venta, Tabasco, Mexico 288, 292, 293, 300
  Monument 13 from 276, *277*, 292, 293
Lawler, Andrew 142
Lebanon 186
  cedarwood of 186
Lebeau, Marc 148

Le Breton, Louis 121
Lesko, Leonard 239, 244
letters 28, 56, 57, 267, 271
    Roman 265, 266, 267, 271, 272
Levant 10, 56, 179
Lévi-Strauss, Claude 84
lexemes 6
lexicon 177, 225, 233, 235
lexicostatistics 283
Li Chi (Li Ji) 50, 228, 236, 239, 240, 245, 246
Linear A (Minoan) 55
Linear B (Mycenaean) 55
Linear Elamite 104, 141, 143, 144
linearity 318
linguistics 314
lists 329, 330, *330*, 336, 337–340, 342, 346
    grouped 339
literacy 6, 41, 200, 211, 212, 213, 221, 239, 244, 290
    autonomous model of 6
    ideological model of 5–8
    kinds of 332
    Latin 270
    recitation 6, 8
literature 83
Liu, David 237
Loewe, Michael 243
logic 314, 319, 323–324, 336
    diagrams of 323
    of relations 323
    syllogisms 323
logicians 324
logographs (logograms) 6, 11, 16, 23, 26, 27, 28, 29, 30, 34, 36, 37, 38, 40, 41, 42, 44, 45, 46, 47, 48, 49, 50, 51, 52, 53, 54, 55, 56, 59, 60, 62, 63, 64, 65, 66, 67, 90, 91, 98, 262, 290, 294, 299, 304, 305, 349
logophones 45, 46, 48, 49–54, 55, 63, 64, 65, 66
Loltun, Yucatan, Mexico 300, 306
Loprieno, Antonio 186, 188
Louvre Museum, Paris 102, 110, 143
Luvian (Luwian, Hittite) 29, 30, 52, 167, 169, 170, 173, 290

Malay 57
Marcus, Joyce 294, 295
markedness 37
    marked categories of 35
    unmarked categories of 35
Martin, Simon 14

Marxism 7
Maya 40, 80, 84, 88, 289, 290, 292, 293, 295, 299, 302, 306, 315, 334
    adzes 306
    altars 302
    architecture 302, 303
        façades 300, 303
        Preclassic 303
    calendar 301
    chronology 306, 308
        Classic period 280, 302
        Early Classic 299, 306, 308
        Late Classic 299
        Late Preclassic 301, 352
        Long Count 278
        Middle Preclassic 301
        Preclassic 306
        proto-Classic 308
    cities 304
    civilization 351
    Classic 286, 287, 291, 299, 300, 303, 305, 308
    decipherment of 299, 304, 308
    deities 303, 304, 308
        heads of 303, 304
        lists of 304
    Early Classic cache vessels 303, 306
    "house" metaphors for pots 303
    iconography 301
    kings 303
    labels 306
    labor organization 303
    language 275, 300, 301, 305, 306
        Ch'olan 305
        Ch'olti' 33
        derivation 305
        ergative pronouns 300, 306
        inflection 305
        instrumentals 305
        prefixes 305
        pronouns 302, 306
        suffixes 302, 305
        syntax 308
        vowels 305
        Yukatek 275
    Lowlands 300, 301, 302
    metallurgy 71
    periods of script development 302–308
        Period IA 302
        Period IB 302, 303, 305, 306
        Period II 302, 303, 306

Maya (cont.)
  petroglyphs 300
  place-notation 300
  region 277
  scholarship of 282, 299
  scribes 200, 300
  use of Olmec heirlooms 303
  writing (glyphs) 3, 7, 10, 11, 12, 30, 31, 32, 33, 34, 36, 38, 42, 44, 48, 51, 52, 54, 63, 71, 72, 80, 87, 90, 92, 164, 172, 274, 275, 280, 282, 287, 290, 293, 294, 298, 299, 301, 302, 303, 304, 305, 306, 308, 351
    acrophony in 306
    as incantatory cues 304
    Classic-period 32, 90, 92, 283
    royal courts 99
  codification 306, 308
  de-semantization 305
  Diker Bowl 306
  Dumbarton Oaks Pectoral 303, 306
  early 298–308
  extension principle 11
  Hauberg "Stela" 306
  head variants 303
  highland 306
  "Hombre de Tikal" 303
  iconic origin of 305
  morphosyllables 305
  "name tags" in 304
  nominal 302, 303
  on palm leaves 300
  on wooden objects 300
  Peabody Museum Statuette 306, *307*
  piedmont 306
  Preclassic 300
  "Primary Standard Sequence" 304
  rebus 299, 304, 305
  reinterpretation principle 11
  replacement meaning 305
  "retroactive conceit" 299
  sampling problems of 299
  semantic replacement 305
  signary 280, 299
  syllabification principle 11
  synchronic views of 351
  "synoptic fallacy" 299
  syntactic opacity of 304
Mayanists 185
McDowell, Andrea 244
Mecquenem, Roland de 103, 120

memory 189, 350
merchants 224
Meriggi, Piero 103, 141, 143, 144
  list of 104, 141
Meritneith 188
Mesoamerica 3, 4, 6, 9, 10, 12–14, 47, 53, 80, 88, 92, 94, 152, 174, 177, 207, 235, 274, 275, 276, 277, 278, 280, 281, 282, 283, 284, 286, 287, 288, 290, 291, 292, 293, 298, 301, 308, 309
  calendar of 349
  chronology of 279
    Early Formative 279
    Middle Formative 279, 284, 288, 290
    Middle Preclassic 284, 287
    Late Preclassic 291, 292, 309
  Formative centers in 293
  highland 48
  iconography in 301
  onomastics of 349
  Postclassic 276
  Precolumbian 288–293
  rulers in 290
  sacred calendar of 292
  seals and cylinders in 286, 287, 292
  writing of 71, 72, 80, 227, 244, 245, 246, 247, 349
    "closed" 275, 276, 277, 278, 279, 288–308
    Oaxacan 279
    of names 290, 292, 301
    Olmec origin of *285*, 284–293, 298, 308
    onset of punctuated narrative 300
    ontological properties of 291
    "open" 275, 276, 277, 278, 279, 286, 296
    relation to names and bodies 288
    Southeastern 279
Mesoamericanists 44
Mesopotamia 40, 48, 71, 72, 73, 74, 78, 80, 87, 88, 89, 93, 94, 95, 96, 100, 101, 104, 112, 117, 118, 119, 122, 124, 127, 140, 141, 143, 150, 152, 154, 171, 172, 174, 175, 176, 177, 180, 182, 186, 188, 190, 199, 207, 220, 221, 222, 223, 224, 225, 226, 231, 232, 233, 234, 235, 236, 239, 244, 245, 254, 255, 259, 351, 352
  administrative centers in 117
  animal products in 122
  "archaic" language in 188
  beveled bowls in 115, 117, 141, 147
  chronology of 95

Early Dynastic I–II 142, 143
Early Dynastic III 101
Jemdet Nasr 143
Uruk III 100, 124, 140, 143
Uruk IV 100, 101, 124, 139, 140, 143
dual gender system in 112, 146
  animate 112, 146
  non-animate 112, 146
  non-animate objects 112
economies of 122
envelopes in 122
exercise tablets of 222
genres of literature in 221
grain in *81*, 122, 147
historians of 119
history of 119
ideographs of 119
laborers of 112
letters in 223, 224, 225
lexical lists of 101
linguistic environment of 248
list of professions in *79*, 186
personal names of 112
proto-cuneiform in *86*, 254, 260
ration distribution 147
schoolboys in 221
schools in 222
scribes of 253, 254
seals of 119, 120, 122, 123, 141, 142
slave laborers of 112
stamps in 119
writing in 150, 152, 154, 171, 172, 174, 175, 176, 177, 180, 182, 186, 188, 190, 191, 216, 230, 259
  lists 220, 222, 243
Mesopotamianists 227
metonymy 84
metrology 78
Metropolitan Museum of Art, New York 168, 170
Mexican pictography 279, 315, 317, 335
  organized by event 335
  organized by time 335
Mexican pictorial codices 44, 315, 342
  as almanacs 335, 336, 337, 338, 339, *339*, 340, *340*, *341*, 342, *343*, *344*, 346
  as biographies 317
  as cosmogonies 317
  as divinatory books 335, 337, 340
  as genealogies 317
  as map-based histories 335
  as maps 317
  as tribute lists 276, 317
  for taxation purposes 317
  painted 315
Mexico 40, 47, 48
  Spanish conquest of 40
Michalowski, Piotr 95, 97, 188, 239, 244
Michel, Rudolph 148
Midant-Reynes, Béatrix 187
Middle East 42, 56, 64, 65
  Iron Age of 56
  Late Bronze Age of 56
  merchants of 60
  Middle Bronze Age of 56
Mirador Basin 9, 352
Mixe-Zoquean languages 283
Mixtec 276, 289, 315
  writing 8, 94, 335
mnemonics 40, 63
molecules 324, 325, *325*, 327
Mongolian phonography 59
monogeneticism 10, 11
monograph 294
monosyllables 177, 178
Monte Albán, Mexico 276, *277*, 294, 295, *295*
  Lápida de Bazán from 296
  SP-1 from 296
Moore, Oliver 237, 242
Morgan, Jacques de 102, 120
morphemes 27, 33, 41, 44, 45, 50, 51, 52, 53, 59, 63, 91
  under-representation of 32–34
morphophones 45
Mosul, Iraq 94
Musée Cernuschi, Paris *206*
Museum of Archaeology and Ethnology, University of São Paolo 143
Museum of Far Eastern Antiquities, Stockholm 241
music 16

names (appellatives) 315, 317
Naqada, Egypt 166
Naxi (pictography) 10, 245
Near East *73*, 95, 100, 119, 151, 176, 190, 220, 225, 226, 228, 236
  token systems of *75*, 236
  writing of 102, 216, 224
Neo-Assyrian 53

neoevolutionism 39
Nile river 72
Nimrud (Kalkhu), Iraq 88
Nineveh, Iraq 73
Nippur, Iraq 94
Nissen, Hans 95, 97, 101, 119, 141, 142, 143, 144, 186, 239, 243, 244, 245
Noble, David 6
Noleby, Sweden 270
North American natives 55
    Cherokee syllabary of 55, 58
Norway 58
Norwegian Archaeological Review 68
notations 314, 320
    algebraic 319, *319*, 320, 332
    chemical 37, 324–329, 336
    dance 37, 314, 320, *321*, *322*, 333
        Feuillet system *322*
    for technical instruction and safety 330–332
    logic 314, 319, 323–324, 336
    mathematical 37, 314, 319–320, 333, 334
    music 37, 314, 319, 320, *321*, 332, 333, 334
    of molecular formula 324, *325*, 334
    of physics 319–320
    scientific 314, 319, 333, 336
    statistical 314, 319, 335
    systems of 101
nouns 53, 91
    proper 38
Nubian A-Group 187
numbers 46, 63, 78, 81, 154, 157, 159, 187, 333
    systems of 100, 101, 104, 105, 106, 107, 108, 110, 113, 117, 118, 122, 123, 126, 127, 139, 141, 145, 146, 148
Nylan, Michael 237

Oaxaca, Mexico 276, 292
    Valley of 277, 293, 294, 295
Odenstedt, Bengt 270
Ogam 10, 14, 286, 287, 301
Old Norse 270
Old World 259
Olmec 10, 94, 283, 284, 286, 287, 288, 290, 291, 293, 301
    artistic conventions 283
    as "mother civilization" 283
    deity impersonation 289
    "heartland" 293

iconography 48, 284, *285*, 296, 308
    "birth" *285*, 286, 287
    "clouds" *285*, 286, 287
    "wind" 286, 287, 301
lapidary work 303
mannequins 288
pars pro toto principle 284
pectorals 291
portraiture 288
sculptures 292
supposed "writing" among 293
onomastics 349
onomatopoeia 19, 37
orality 350
oral traditions 40, 65
origins
    anachronistic fallacy in studies of 12
    as invention 80, 92, 95, 161, 162, 170
    bureaucratic 72–80
    diffusionism in studies of 71, 95
    episodes of 10–12
    ethnographic 13
    history of 3
    iconic 284, 352
    monogeneticism 10, 11
    nonlinguistic 151
    primary 151, 351
    process of 3
    revelatory 13
    secondary 3, 139, 300
    sophisticated 10
    stimulus diffusion as explanation for 95, 176, 190, 191, 198, 199, 200, 202, 207, 213, 214, 216, 217, 220, 222, 223, 224, 225, 226–227, 229, 230, 235, 236, 240, 241, 242
    synoptic fallacy in studies of 11
    unsophisticated 10
orthography 28, 29, 36, 91, 163
Otomanguean language family 293
Ottoman Turkish 57
Owen, Charles 334
Oxtotitlan, Guerrero, Mexico 289
Ozbaki, Iran 143

painting 16
palaeographers 236
Palestine 161
Pāṇini 189
papyrus 243

Parkinson, Richard 185, 186
Pashto 57
pedagogy 6, 220, 221, 222
   for royal children 239
   in administrative units 221
      for creation of clerks 221
      for creation of overseers 221
      for needs of bureaucracies 221
   in palaces 221, 239
   in private homes 221
Peirce, Charles 18, 19, 28, 36, 37, 349
perception *17*, *18*, 19, 20, 35
   auditory 16, 19, *19*, 22, *22*, 35
   visual 16, 17, 18, 19, *19*, 20, 21, 25, 27, 34, 35, 313, 314, 317, 318
Persia 102, *103*, 117, 119, 121, 122, 124, 126, 128, 140, 141, 147
   archaic 112, 147
   people of 112
   settlements in 119, 121
   western 119
Persian Gulf 94
Peru 40, 99
   people of 44
Petén, Guatemala 302, *302*
Petrie, Flinders 188
Pettersson, John 95, 96, 98, 189
philology 181, 265
Phoenician 56, 57
   consonantary 57
phonemes 20, 28, 35, 41, 150, 158, 165, 176, 262, 266, 267
phonemicization 65
phoneticism 16, 34, 89, 93
phoneticization 51
phonography 31, 34, 36, 38, 41, 44, 45, 52, 54–61, 63, 64, 65, 66, 67
phonology 27, 31, 35
physics, discoveries in 319
pictographs 16, 23, 25, 26, 27, 28, 29, 36, 38, 40, 44, 84, 88, 89, 92, 97, 276, 314, 332, 333, 334
   as history 335
   as holistic presentation 318
   Mexican 80, 93, 94
place names 284, *285*, 286, 294, 295, 315, 317
Plains Indian 47
   year lists 46
Poetic Edda 270

Poland 271
polities 166
   regional 166, 188
polyphony 22, 24, 27
polysyllables 177, 178
Pope, Clayne 14
Porada, Edith 143
Postclassic Mexico 8
Postgate, Nicholas 227, 244, 245, 246, 247
pragmatics 9
"primitive" societies 43
principles 315
   of exclusion 315
   of inclusion 315
   of proximity 315
   of sequence 315
processed grain 115, 117
propaganda 300, 308
proteins 325
proto-cuneiform 47, 52, 76, 77, 80, 84, 85, *86*, 90, 97, 100, 101, 102, 104, 107, 108, 110, 111, 113, 117, 118, 119, 120, 122, 124, 127, 139, 140, 142, 144, 145, 146, 147, 148, 216, 243, 246, 254, 260
   absence of decimal system in 145
   administrative texts 108, 141
   bisexagesimal system 113
   fractions 117
   numerical notations 106, 107, 108, 117, 122, *127*, 145
   personal names 142
   pictographs 147
   rebus 142
   relation to proto-Elamite *125*, *130*
   scribes 101
   sexagesimal system 112
proto-Elamite 3, 12, 52, 96, 100, 103, *103*, 104, 105, 106, 107, 108, 110, 113, 117, 118, 121, 122, 124, 126, 127, 128, 129, 130, *138*, 139, 140, 141, 142, 143, 144, 145, 146, 147, 148, 246, 349, 350, 351, 352
   accounting formats 124
   administration 113, 119, 140
   administrative texts in 104, *105*, *107*, 119, 122, 127
   arable land 119
   as example of secondary script origin 139
   bureaucracy 140
   cities of 126

proto-Elamite (*cont.*)
  colophons 144
  commodities 110
    breads 115, 117
    cracked barley 115, 117
    flour 115, 117
    malt 115, 117, 141, 147
  craftsman 108
  description of 104–119
  entries 144
  expressions of hierarchy in 105
  fields 118
  filing of 148
  grain 117, 118, 147
    sowing of 118
  grain capacity systems 113, *115*, 115–119, 124, 144, 145, 146, 147, 148
    barley rations 113
    cereal products 113, 115, 117, 146, 147
  grain distributions 118
  graphotactical analysis of 129, *138*, 144
  headings in 104, 144
  high-status humans 108, 110, 145
  Hurrian elements in 141
  ideographic signs 105, 106, 108, 113, 117, 122, 123, *125*, 126, 139, 140, 145
    animal husbandry offices 105
    animals 105, 124
    beer (?) 148
    cattle 110
    dairy products 122, 127, 148
    foreman 146
    goats 122
    high-status humans 145
    institutions 105
    objects 105
    persons 105, 124, 142
    sheep 122
    textiles 122
  inchoate standardization of 126, 140
  labor units 105, *126*
  language of 105, 106, 127, 128, 138, 139
  Late Uruk loan 122–127
  linearization 117
  liquid capacity system of 127
  literacy 104
  logographs 144
  low-prestige objects 112
  Meriggi list of 104, 141
  metrology 127, 140

  monthly rations 117
  non-metrological contexts 113
  number words 127
  numerical notations in 100, 101, 104, 105, 106, 107, *107*, 108, 110, 113, 117, 118, 122, 123, 126, 127, 139, 141, 145, 146, 148
    bisexigesimal 108, 111, *114*, 113–115, 117, 124, 146
    decimal 108, *111*, 110–113, 124, 127, 129, 130, 147
    sexagesimal *109*, 108–110, 112, 113, 115, 119, 129, 145, 146, 148
    surface area 108
  numero-ideographs *76*, 128, *129*, *130*, 140
  orientation of 104, *123*, 141
  people 127, 140
  personal names 138, 143, 144
  pictography 148
  plow animals 118
  precursors of *121*, 119–122
    period of clay envelopes 122
    period of early numerical tablets 122
    period of early tokens 122
    period of late numerical tablets 122
    period of numero-ideographic tablets *76*, 122
  proper nouns 138
  ration products 146
    cheese 146
    fish 146
  research 145
  school exercises in 143
  scribes 107, 139, 140
  semantics of 124, 144
  sign clusters in 139
  sign variants of 103, 126, 139
  slave labor 124
  stylus on texts of 104, 122, 126, 148
    made of wood or reed 148
  surface measures in 118, *118*, 145, 147
  syllables in 127, 140, 143
  syntax of 104, 106, 124, 127, 144
  tablets 103, 104, 108, 110, 112, 113, 120, 121, 122, 123, 124, 126, 141, 143, 146
    rotation of *123*, 124
  text genres of 144
  transliterations 127
  vessels 110, 127
  worker categories 117

workers 118, *126*, 130, 147
    dependent 117
    male dependent 146
"Protosinaitic" 178
proto-writing 11
    grammaticalization of 12
    phonic opacity in 12, 224
    sampling problems with 12
    under-grammaticalization in 12
punctuated equilibrium 6
punctuation 28, 29, 37
Pyrgi tablets 10

Qiu Xigui 232, 242, 245, 246, 247

radiocarbon dating 154, 188
Reade, J. 98
reading 54, 333
    order as indicated by direction of "heads" 291, 292
rebus 16, 22, 23–24, 27, 47, 48, 49, 88, 89, 98, 142, 165, 177, 178, 179, 181, 188, 231, 232, 246, 247, 251, 299, 304, 305, 349
recitation literacy 6, 8
representational systems 8
    figural 315, 331
    iconic 22
Reynolds, Noel 14
Río Azul, Guatemala 302
Río Pesquero, Veracruz, Mexico 288
    masks from 286, 292, 293
Ritner, Robert 98
road signs 331
Robertson, John 4, 13, 14, 16, 268, 349, 350, 353
Rome, Italy 13
    armies of 266
    empire of 266
    soldiers of 266
    writing of 279
Rongorongo script 13
Rosetta Stone 10
Rotman, Brian 315, 319, 333
Rubio, Gonzalo 98, 149, 188
runes 13, 35, 58, 67, 262–263, 264, 265, 266, 267, 268, 269, 270, 271, 272, 273, 299, 349
    alphabetic origin of 265–266
    communication with 269

    functions of 268–271
    graphemes 266, 267, 272, 273
    inventor of 266–268
    letters 262
    magical uses of 269, 270, 272
    Mediterranean origin of 264
    North Italic origin of 265
    of Germanic tribes 262, 265
    on bracteates 271
    on combs *264*, 268
    on spearheads 264, 268, 272
    on weapons 268, 272
    on women's brooches 268, *269*, 272
    on wooden boxes 268
    origins of 262–273
    place of invention 263–264
    proto-runic stage of 271
    Roman influence on 266
    time of invention 264
runestones 270
runologists 264, 265

Sais, Egypt *174*
Sampson, Geoffrey 20, 30, 35, 38, 48
San Bartolo, Guatemala 352
San Diego, Guatemala 300, 306
San José Mogote, Oaxaca, Mexico 292, 293
    Monument 3 from 292, 293
San Lorenzo, Veracruz, Mexico 288, 292, 293
    colossal heads at 288, *289*
    Palangana phase at 292
Sanxingdui, Sichuan, China 224
Saussure, Ferdinand de 83, 84
Scandinavia 262, 264, 270, 271, 299
Scania (Skåne), Sweden 263
Scheil, Vincent 143
Schenkel, Wolfgang 179
Schleswig, Germany 263
Schmandt-Besserat, Denise 95, 100, 119, 120, 121, *121*, 127, 151
Schøyen collection 147
sciences 314, 319, 333, 336
Scott, James 9
scribes 24, 47, 51, 66, 85
script community 235, 286, 299, 306, 351
seals 73, 84
    cylinder 73, *74*, 95
    stamp 74
Selz, Gebhard 95, 96

semasiography 38, 40, 42, 43, 44, 46–49, 50, 55, 61, 62, 63, 313–346
  complex 59
  non-verbal visualizations in 314
semasiologographs 47, 48, 52, 63
semiotics 314
Semitic
  language 52, 56, 57, 177, 178, 186, 188
  West 56
  writing 30, 34, 38, 178
Senner, Wayne 3
Sequoyah 10, 55
Sethe, Kurt 64
sex 84
Shaanxi, China 240
Shandong province, China 50
Shang 49, 50, 215, 242, 250, 253, 254, 260
  administration 223, 224, 228, 234
  Ancestor Bing among 243
  Ancestor Geng among 243
  ancestors 198, 200, 206, 210, 211, 213, 214, 217, 223, 224, 234
    dedications to 206, 211, 241
  Anyang period of 191, 193, 202, 206, 211, 213, 215, 216, 220, 223, 224, 241, 242
  beer 210, 225
  Bi Qi 190
  Bi Wu 223
  bronze 207, 208, 210, 211, 212, 213, 215, 216, 217, 218, 220, 224, 227, 228, 240, 241, 242
    casters 200, 202, 241
    foundries 223, 224, 225
    hoards 242
    pre-Anyang 234, 246
    weapons 240
  calligraphers 202, 206, 207, 211, 228
  campaigns 223
    Renfang 223
  casting inscriptions 200, 223, 224, 242
  ce 243
  chime-stones 242, 243
  civilization 207, 223, 226, 241
  clerks 225
  court 223, 224, 225, 226, 234
    ceremonies at 213
    officials at 209, 210
  courtiers 239

diviners 196, 197, 199, 206, 213, 223, 226, 230, 234, 235, 237, 239, 242
  Dui-group of 238
dynasty 191, 224, 237, 240, 250, 258, 259
emblems 208
enemy chiefs 214
family crest 208
Father Ding among 208, 211
Father Gui among 206, 209, 211, 213, 242, 243
Father Jia among 198, 243
Father Xin among 243
Father Yi among 241
feasts 206, 241
fief 210
funerals 211
Gongfang (an enemy) against 197, 198, 224
high officials 200
kings 196, 199, 200, 208, 210, 211, 213, 214, 224, 235, 237, 238, 239, 240, 241
  art of 199, 200
  as overlords 214
  consorts of 214
  gifts from 213, 215
  hunts of 213, 223
  literate 200
  trophies of 213, 214
kinship 198, 241
Lady Hao among 192, 193, 196, 197, 198, 199, 200, 202, 211, 212, 215, 238
  childbearing of 196, 197, 198
  ge (blade) of 214, *215*, 224
  jade collection 215, 242
  name of 200, 202, 240
  tomb of 200, *201*, 202, *203*, 204, 206, *207*, 212, *215*, 242
literacy 200, 211, 212, 213, 221, 239, 244
Lufang X among 215
luxury goods 224
Marquis of Zheng among 204
metals trade 224
monograms 200, 202, 204, 206, 212, 242
monopolies 224
Mother Xin among 206
nobility 200, 211, 212
offices 210
oracles 191, 193, 197, 237
pit deposits 199
pottery marks 243
pre-Anyang sites 236

Prince Yu among 202
pyro-scapulomancy 250, 259
Que (a diviner) among 193, 197, 234, 239
rank 202, 208, 210
  of marquis 202
record-keeping 200, 244
Renfang (an enemy) against 214
sacrifice 214, 223, 234, 243
scribes 191–200, 201, 204, 206, 209, 211, 213, 214, 215, 218, 219, 220, 221, 223, 224, 225, 228, 231, 232, 235, 236, 240, 241, 242, 243, 245
  names of 209
spirits 199, 250
state formation 236
tablets 243
titles 204, 208
tombs 192, *201*, 202, *203*, *207*, *215*, *219*, 239, 240, 242, 243
tribes 253, 254, 255
Tufang (an enemy) against 197, 202, 224
vessels 206, 211, 213, 239, 240, 241, 242, 245, 246
Wei (a name) among 206
writing (Anyang, oracle bone inscriptions, Wu Ding) 3, 4, 7, 10, 20, 24, 26, 34, 37, 50, 78, 84, 88, 89, 92, 96, 98, 172, 177, 178, 181, 182, 190, *192*, *193*, 194, *195*, 198, *201*, 202, 204, *204*, 206, 207, 208, 211, 215, 217, 218, 222, 223, 225, 227, 228, 229, 230, 235, 236, 237, 240, 242, 243, 245, 247, 250, 251, 254, 255, 256, 257, 258, 305, 350, 352
  account of deliveries 214
  aesthetics of 219
  Anyang corpus 191, 196, 243
  as documents 206
  as mnemonic system 225, 231, 234, 240
  as phonetic representation 230, 232, 246
  as record of connected discourse 225, 230, 232
  as record of language 230
  as symbols 251
  audience for 199, 200
  biased sample of 217–222
  brushes used in 215, 216, 219
  brush writing *193*, 199, 201, 202, 211, 215, *215*, 216, *217*, 218, 219, *219*, 220, 232
  carver of 197, 199, 201, 244
  carving process 199
  clan emblems 78, 211, 213, *229*, 227–230, 233, 234, 239, 241
  compound characters in 231
  dates on 241
  determinatives 210
  divination (oracle) texts *192*, *193*, *195*, 191–200, 201, 204, 206, 209, 211, 213, 214, 215, 218, 219, 220, 221, 223, 224, 225, 228, 231, 232, 235, 236, 240, 241, 242, 243, 245
  divination process 191, 193, 196, 197, 198, 199, 200, 214, 217, 225, 230, 234, 235, 238, 239
  divinatory function of 78, 79, 250, 255
  draftsmanship 199, 211
  for display 199, 200, 225, 234, 235, 236, 239
  functions of 222–226
  graphs (graphemes) 215, 216, 227, 228, 229, 241, 242, 245, 246, 247, 250, 251, 252, 253, 254, 255, 256, 257, 258, 260
  handwriting of 240
  iconicity of 202, 227, 240, 243, 246
  inventors of 233, 235, 248
  numeration 198, 235
  of names 199, 201, 202, 211, 215, 216, 218, 219, 220, 232
  of nouns 231
  of verbs 231
  on axes 204, *205*, 214, 215, 241
  on bone 50, 213, 214, 215, 218, 220, 240
  on bovine scapulas 191, 193, 196, 214, 224, 238
  on bronze vessels 50, 78, 187, 190, 191, 198, *201*, *203*, *205*, *206*, *207*, *208*, *209*, *210*, *212*, 200–213, 215, 216, 218, 223, 235, 236, 241, 246
  on jade *215*, 214–216, 217, 243
  on oracle bones 78, 79, 96, 151, 187, 190, 191, 196, 197, 199, 200, 201, 236, 237, 239, 244, 250, 255, 351
  on perishable surfaces 222
  on pottery 216, 217, *217*, *218*
  on shell 50, 213, 214, 217, 218, 226, 235, 236, 239, 240
  on stone 214–216, 243

Shang (*cont.*)
    on turtle shells (plastrons) 78, 79, 192, *192*, 193, *193*, 194, *195*, 196, 197, 199, 200, 214, 237, 239, 250, 255
    on wood or bamboo slips (*ce*) 216, 217, 218, *219*, 230
    origins of 226–236
    orthographic variation in 198, 238
    pictographs in 231, 232
    pictorial elements in 227
    pigments of 199, 214
    pre-Wu Ding history of 227, 228
    prognostication 196
    rebus in 231, 232, 246, 247
    reform of 202
    relation to writing tool 243
    scholars of 214, 237, 240
    Shima's concordance of 231
    stimulus diffusion 190, 191, 198, 199, 200, 202, 207, 213, 214, 216, 217, 220, 222, 223, 224, 225, 226–227, 229, 230, 235, 236, 240, 241, 242
    sudden origins of 230–233
    supposed pre-Anyang 190, 226
    texts 83
    Wu Ding among 191, 192, *192*, 193, *193*, 194, *195*, 197, 198, 199, 200, 202, 206, 214, 224, 226, 230, 232, 233, 234, 235, 236, 238, 239, 240, 244, 246, 247
        court of 223, 224, 225, 226, 234
        divinations of *192*, 240
        diviners of 221
    Xie ritual 242
    Yu among 240
    Zai Feng among 213
    Zhi Guo 197, 198, 222, 224, 238
    Zhizi (a scribe) among 209, 210, 211, 212, 213, 216, 242
Shanxi Zhouyuan, China 260
Sharer, Robert 309
Shima Kunio 247
Sialk, Iran 126
Sichuan, China 244
signified 251, 290, 291
signifier 251, 290, 291
sign types *62*, 185, 305
    allography of 280
    alphabet as 16, 36, 37, 94, 262, 264, 265, 266
    cataloguing of 350
    complements as 305
    determinatives (classifiers) as 24–25, 49, 91, 98, 210
        semantic 220
    ideographs (ideograms) as 16, 25, 26, 27, 28, 36, 37, 38, 90, 98
    indexical 25
    phonograms as 15, 251
    pictographs as 16, 23, 25, 26, 27, 28, 29, 36, 38, 84, 88, 89, 92, 97, 120, 251, 253, 260, 261
    logographs (logograms) as 6, 11, 16, 23, 26, 27, 28, 29, 30, 34, 36, 37, 38, 90, 91, 98, 262, 335, 349
    logophonetic 90, 92, 96, 98
    logosyllabic 49, 51, 52, 55, 96, 98
    morphosyllables as 33
    phonetic complements as 49, 50
    rebus as 16, 22, 23–24, 27, 88, 89, 98, 165, 177, 178, 179, 181, 188, 299, 304, 305, 349
    semantic classifiers as 51
    semiotic features of 185
    spoken 20, 21, *21*, 22, 23, *23*, 24, 25, 27, *27*, *29*, 34–35, 36
    syllables as 20, 25, 27, 28, 29, 33, 37, 97, 98, 150, 299, 305, 306
    taxograms as 49, 53
    written 20, 22, 25, *29*, 34–35, 36
Sinai, Egypt 10
Sinologists 185
skin 286, 287
Slavic languages (Belarusian, Bulgarian, Macedonian, Russian, Serbian, Ukrainian) 58, 66
south Asian scripts 60
southeast Asian scripts 60, 66
South Korea 59, 65
Soviet Union 58
    non-Slavic languages of 58
    Republics of 59
Spain 55
spearheads 264, 268, 272
speech 45
    as spoken word 36
    relation to writing 20–21
spelling 29, 54
    amorphophonemic 31, 33, 36, 37
    as heterography 28, 29, 31–34, 36
    as orthography 28, 29, 36
St. John's College, Oxford 345

states 153, 162, 171
  unitary 166
Stearns, Stephen 98
Steinke, Kyle 237
Steinkeller, Piotr 142, 188
stela 286, 287
Stoklund, Marie 271
Stravinski, Igor *321*
  Dumbarton Oaks Concerto *321*
Structure B-XIII, Uaxactun 308
  mural text in 308
Stuart, David 8, 239, 299, 309
stylus 31, 38, 85, 98, *127*
Sürenhagen, Dietrich 148
Suleiman, Antoine 148
Sumer 42
Sumerian 47, 48, 49, 52, 63, 64, 97, 164, 177, 178, 181, 188
  bookkeeping 82, 97, 220, 224, 225, 232, 234, 235, 236, 246
  cuneiform 23, 24, 38, 42, 48, 49, 50, 52, 53, 54, 61, 71, 80, *85*, 90, 91, 92, 95, 96, 98, 101, 142, 146, 149, 188
  grammar 118, 146
  language 23, 80, 82, 89, 90, 92, 97, 98, 233
    grammatical affixes 248
    nouns 248
    pronouns 146
    verbs 248
  Listenliteratur 101
  literature 221
  loan-words from early Semitic 149
  loan-words from Indo-European 149
  logographs 52
  number words 146
  numerical systems 146
  onomastics 101
  relation to non-Sumerian names 149, 248
  sign *zíz* 115, 117
  sila 147
  substrate lexemes in 149
  syllables 50
  ugula 146
Sumerologists 101
Sumerology 101
Sundance seminar 4–5, 13–15, 97, 185, 236, 273, 351

Surinam 55
  Ndjuka creole language of 55
Susa, Iran *73*, 74, *75*, *76*, 96, 100, 102, 110, 117, 119, 120, 121, 122, 124, 126, 128, 139, 141, 143, 147
  French excavations of 102
  levels of 143
  plain of 103, 141, 143
  proto-Elamite period at 143
  relative chronology of 124
  stratigraphy of 121, 122, 124, 143
  texts at 143
sutras 181
Swadesh, Morris 282
Sweden 58, 263
  language of 36
syllabary (syllabic writing) 16, 30, 36, 37, 40, 41, 42, 43, 46, 49, 50, 51, 52, 53, 54, 55, 58, 59, 60, 61, 64, 65
  Cherokee 55, 58
  CV 51
  Cypriot 55
  Mayan 30, *30*, *31*
syllables 41, 51, 54, 55
  monosyllables 51
syllabograms 48, 49, 53
symbol 18, 19, 25, 26, 28, 34, 36, 38, 284, 315, 331, 349
synecdoche 84
synonyms 22, 23–24, 25
synoptic fallacy 11
syntax 81, 82, 286, 287, 292, 315
Syria 73, 74, 99, 119, 122, 140, 188

tables 329, 330, *331*, 333, 336, 337, 340–342, 346
tablets *75*, 77, 103, 104, 108, 110, 112, 113, 120, 121, 122, 141, 143, 146, 151, 175
  archaic 80, 96, 98
  Uruk IV *77*, 154
Tajikistan 59
Takashima, Ken'ichi 237
Tall-i Malyan 143
tattoos 286, 287, 292
Taube, Karl 292, 309
taxograms 49, 53
Taylor, Isaac 40
teachers 244
technology 39, 67
  efficiency of 67

Tehran Museum, Tehran 143
Teotihuacan, Basin of Mexico, Mexico 277, 278, *278*, 300, 308
   emblematic writing 277
Tepe Yahya, Iran 143
   excavations at 148
   proto-Elamite presence at 148
thinking 333
Thompson, J. Eric S. 71
Thote, Alain 241
Tibetan-Burman languages 53
Tigris 94
Tikal dynasty 302, *302*, 303
Tinney, Stephen 244
Tlatilco, Basin of Mexico, Mexico 288
tokens 40, 73, 74, *75*, 77, 83, 84, 95, 100, 101, 119, *119*, 120, 121, 122, 126, 140, 175
   complex *119*, 126
Toynbee, Arnold 11
tribute 47
Trigger, Bruce 4, 39, 80, 83, 95, 352
Tsien Tzuen-hsuin 243
Turkish 66
typewriter 332

Ugarit, Syria 56
Ugaritic 176
U-j tomb 11, *155*, 156
Umma, Iraq 100, 102, 110, 117, 119, 120, 121, 122, 124, 126, 128, 139, 141, 143, 147
Umm al-Aqirib 124
Unger, Marshall 66
uniliterals 54, 56
universals 93, 94
Uqair, Iraq *81*
Ur, Iraq 80, 82, *82*, 142, 147
Urartian 53
Urcid Serrano, Javier 294
Urton, Gary 13, 14, 93, 97, 99, 351
Uruk, Iraq 72, 73, 74, 75, *75*, 76, *76*, *81*, 84, 86, 93, 95, 97, 102, 119, *119*, 120, 121, 122, 124, 126, *127*, *128*, 142, 146, 147, 151, 171, 220, 244
   adjusted chronology of 142, 148
   Expansion *73*, 74, 95, 119, 140
   German excavators of 102, 121
   Late Uruk at 72, 74, *103*, 119, 121, 122, 141, 147, 151, 175, 188
      scribes 112
   phase III at 76, 81, 85, 86, 184

   phase IV at 76, 85, 86, 122, 146, 164, 172, 176, 177, 184, 188
      tablets 120, 126
   phase V at 148
   radiocarbon dating of 142, 148
   Red Temple at 122
   scribes 139
   sexagesimal notations at 146
   sign list 101, 107, 143
   stratigraphy of 126
   tradition 140
Uto-Aztecan languages 283
Uyghur 59
   Aramaic writing of 59

Vachek, Josef 83
Vaiman, Aizik 147
Vallat, François 146
van Ess, Margarete 142
van Stone, Mark 14
verbs 53
Venn, John 323
Venn circles 323, 330, 334
Veracruz, Mexico 276, 297
   Early Classic period 297
verbs 53
   auxiliary 53
   medio-passive 33
   transitive 33
Vimose, Denmark 263, *264*
vowels 41, 42, 44, 45, 50, 54, 56, 57, 59, 60, 61, 63, 65
   complex 32
   disharmonic 32, 34
   silent 32
   synharmonic 32, 34

Wadi Qena, Egypt 166
Wallace, Rex 273
Wanderwörter 149
Wang Haicheng 237, 239, 243
warriors 268
Watson, James 328, *329*, 329–330
Webster, David 14
Welch, Jack 14
West Africa 40, 55
Westenholz, Joan 97
western Asia 52, 54, 65, 95, *102*
Western culture 333
Western technology 319
Wheeler, Mortimer 275

Whitmore, Simon 15
Whittaker, Gordon 98, 141
Wilcke, Claus 97, 239
Wilkinson, Endymion 243
Williams, Bruce 187
Williams, Henrik 14, 262, 263
Williams, Ronald 239, 244
Wolf, Eric 275
  view of "peasants" 275
words 40, 41, 57, 65, 96, 150, 290, 333
  dividers of 59, 60
  spoken 36
writing 39, 42, 44, 65, 67, 220, 224, 290, 308, 333
  alphabetic 6, 314, 332, 333, 334
  alternative systems 313–346
  as fetish 350
  as information retrieval 333
  as information storage 83, 151, 318, 333
  as means of decontextualization 83
  as means of marking ownership 228, 235
  biological analogies of 7, 279, 353
  Brahmi 60
  "closed" 164, 275, 276, 277, 278, 279, 288–308
  cognitive effects of 6
  consonantal 178
  creators of 351
  cursive 266
  Darwinian metaphors of 279
  definitions of 43–46
  east Asian 172
  "ethnogenetic" 352
  extinction of 14
  fossil metaphors of 280–282
  "full" 351
  function of 19, 20, 35
  gradualistic models of 5
  hieroglyphic 8
  iconic 290
  Indian 60
  invention of 161, 162, 170
  Kharoshthi 60
  Lamarckian metaphors of 279
  linearity of 286, 287, 292
  logoconsonantal 50, 52
  materiality of 350
  mechanistic models of 349
  non-phonic definitions of 313–315
    non-verbal 313
  permitting correct reading of religious texts 57
  semasiographic 313, 314, 317, 318
  Phoenician 56, 57, 64, 65
  phonemic 56, 60
  phonic 319, 332, 351
  presentist models of 4, 5
  relation to speech 20–21, 80–84
  Siniform 53
  statist views of 8–10, 300, 352
  syllabic 179
  Tangut 53
  technological metaphors of 6, 7
  teleological misconception of 233, 248
  Tukic Orkhon 59
  unievolutionary models of 5
  universals of 93, 94
  utilitarian models of 5
  value judgments of 314
  Yi 53

Xochicalco, Morelos, Mexico 277
Xoxoctolan Tomb 9 294
Xu, Jay 244
Xu Shen 220, 243
  dictionary of 220, 243

Yangzi region, China 224, 244
Yiddish 57
Yoffee, Norman 9
Yucatan peninsula 301

Zapotec 294, 295
  calendar 294
  calendar names 294, 295
  conquest slabs 293, 295
  "Danzantes" 276, *277*, 295, *295*
  highland 293
  language 292, 293, 294, 296
  morphemes 294
  mummy bundles 293
  syntax 294, 295
  writing 7, 274, 280, 293–296, 298, 300
    as brief labels 296
    as complex texts 296
Zealand, Denmark 271
Zhengzhou, China 246
Zimansky, Paul 95
zodiac 346

Printed in Germany
by Amazon Distribution
GmbH, Leipzig